Y0-ECR-096

ESSAYS ON FIELDING'S
Miscellanies

ESSAYS ON FIELDING'S
Miscellanies

A COMMENTARY ON VOLUME ONE

BY

HENRY KNIGHT MILLER

PRINCETON, NEW JERSEY

PRINCETON UNIVERSITY PRESS

1961

120165

Copyright © 1961 by Princeton University Press
ALL RIGHTS RESERVED
LC Card: 61-7410

✧

Publication of this book has been aided
by the Research Fund of Princeton University, and
by the Ford Foundation program to support publication,
through university presses, of work in the
humanities and social sciences.

Printed in the United States of America by
Princeton University Press, Princeton, New Jersey

*TO MY TWO JESSIES
AND MY TWO BERTITAS*

PREFACE

A LITTLE more than a year after the appearance of *Joseph Andrews*, Fielding published by subscription a three-volume set of *Miscellanies, by Henry Fielding Esq*; (April 1743). The second and third volumes of this collection offered two plays and two works of prose fiction, *A Journey from This World to the Next* and *The Life of Mr. Jonathan Wild the Great*. The first volume, which alone is the concern of the present study, was truly "miscellaneous," including most of his short poems, several important formal essays, a translation from the Greek, and a group of satirical sketches and Lucianic dialogues.

The first volume of the *Miscellanies* is almost a microcosm of Henry Fielding's intellectual world, offering explicit commentary on most of his major themes and attacking most of his abiding antipathies. The reader seeking to assess the full richness of Fielding's novels may find here a peculiarly useful guide to his thought and his habits of composition; for the varied contents of this volume epitomize the literary activity of his early years and in many respects anticipate the work to come. The dramatic movement of the novels, confronting idea with idea in comic action, has sometimes misled those seeking from particular aspects of this interplay to derive Fielding's own values and commitments. Again, the novels so transmute their materials that it is no easy matter to assess their debt to earlier traditions. The first volume of the *Miscellanies* presents more directly some of the multitude of literary and intellectual traditions that touched Fielding the novelist. It offers what one may call a prolegomenon to the novels—and to criticism of the novels—that really deserves more scrupulous attention than it has received.

The length of this study perhaps requires apology. If the reader interested in Fielding and his time finds the work of service I need say no more. But I may explain what I

PREFACE

have sought to do beyond summarizing the individual pieces and placing them in the broader frame of Fielding's thought and in the context of the literary and intellectual traditions upon which he drew. The first volume of the *Miscellanies* has seemed to me to offer a particularly fruitful point of departure for thinking about Fielding: and I have therefore enlarged upon the given material to consider in some detail its significance in his total view of man and society. The poem *Of Good-Nature*, for instance, does not say the last word about this conception in Fielding's thought: but it raises certain crucial questions that force the reader (or commentator) into some attempt to explain the total conception. So also with such topics as "true greatness" and "liberty." In addition to these titular themes, some other relevant ideas have been explored: namely, "good breeding" under the *Essay of Conversation*, "hypocrisy" and Fielding's image of human nature under the *Essay on the Knowledge of the Characters of Men*, and his attitude toward Stoicism under the *Remedy of Affliction*.

I have attempted, further, in connection with each major grouping of the materials, to deal with some narrower aspect of his work that did not seem to me adequately to have been investigated. The essay on the *Poems* speculates upon the relationship between Fielding's apprentice work in verse and the style of his prose; the comment upon the *Essays* analyzes Fielding's formal prose style; that upon the *Satires*, the rhetorical and parodic techniques employed in two formal satires. The remarks upon *Translation* are primarily concerned with the question of Fielding's knowledge of Greek; and the essay upon the *Lucianic sketches* is simply an analysis of the fellowship in tone and style between Lucian and Fielding.

I should perhaps set forth some of my assumptions. To be brief, I assume in the first place that comedy is among the most profound of literary activities. This would scarcely require enunciation did not a strong current in modern criticism derive from the fashionable institution of the Marchioness of Chaves (at which solemn house in *Gil Blas*, it will be remembered, comedy was treated as a weak effort of the brain, whereas the "most microscopical work in the serious style . . . was trumpeted to the skies as the most illustrious effort of a learned and poetical age"). As "it not unfrequently fell out that the public reversed the decrees of this chancery for genius," so also the student of the comic in our own time may hope to reverse the decrees of the Solemn School and insist upon the human need for and the aesthetic depth of comedy.

A particular difficulty that arises in this endeavor, however, stems from the double duty that is required of the word "serious." One cannot avoid the ambiguity (at least I have not been able to), but one can be conscious of it. In a sense, "serious" is all that we have to place opposite the word "comic"; and we mean by it simply the nonemployment of devices of humor and irony. But a very, well, *serious* confusion has thus been spawned, because we also use the term to mean those things about which we are morally (or aesthetically) in earnest, the things that "matter." This is the confusion that lies at the heart of objections to the serious discussion of comedy or of a comic author: the assumption that, somehow, to take comedy seriously is to falsify it. Doubtless the heavy elaboration of obvious jokes represents an extreme condition of what the serious treatment of comedy can fall into: but for any person not totally unresponsive to the comic muse, comedy is highly deserving of inclusion among those things that *matter*, and it is demonstrably among the things that many great artists have been morally and aesthetically in earnest about. Fielding, we may be sure, was most vitally serious about his artistic and moral aims and we may seriously discuss them. He was only occasionally dull, it is true: if his analyst must be more often so, it is only in part, I fear, because the modes of creation and of analysis differ.

PREFACE

My second obvious assumption, and one that I have not attempted in this book to "prove," is that Fielding holds a high place among the world's major literary figures, that he occupies (with, say, Dickens and Joyce) a comparable place in English literature to that which Aristophanes and Lucian hold in the Greek, Cervantes in Spanish, and Rabelais in French literature. Each of these masters of the comic remains *sui generis*: the greatness of each lies not in the tradition that he inaugurated (later dramatic comedy, for example, owes relatively little to the characteristic structure and techniques of Aristophanes), but in his own unique masterpieces. Hence I can quite agree with those modern scholars who have argued that our contemporary novel does not descend in a direct line from Fielding (though for the modern comic novel, as Mr. Kingsley Amis assures us, Fielding is still a major inspiration) without believing, as some of them seem to, that Fielding's magnitude as a writer is thereby diminished. This would surely be to allow too great an importance to the teleological view that our modern novel is what the world has been aiming at all along. I should prefer to take the indubitably fascinating and various modern novel in its place and honor greatness wherever I find it.

Fielding's reputation (among critics if not the reading public) did, I think, suffer for a time from the combined effect of being taken for granted by the readers who loved him and asked no questions, and of being neglected by those who sought—with entire legitimacy, let me add—to make of the novel something more plastic, more responsive to the pressures of the modern age. That he is being seen, however, with a fresh eye in our own time is attested by the appreciation of critics so broadly different as the late Mr. Middleton Murry and Professor Empson, as well as by the attention of scholars so eminent as Professor R. S. Crane and Professor George Sherburn. Recent detailed studies by responsible younger critics like Martin C. Battestin and

PREFACE

Wolfgang Iser seem to me further to indicate that a significant reappraisal of the terms of Fielding's greatness, of his unique contribution to the literature of England, is now underway. The aim of the following essays is to contribute in some modest degree to this reexamination through the detailed scrutiny of an important but little-studied group of Fielding's lesser works. It is my cheerful hope that they will lend some clearer illumination to his aims as a writer and highlight some of the literary and intellectual traditions upon which he sharpened his mind and genius.

Acknowledgment is made to the following for permission to quote from copyrighted material: The Clarendon Press, for *The Literary Works of Matthew Prior*, ed. H. Bunker Wright and Monroe K. Spears (Oxford, 2v., 1959); the Harvard University Press, for *Lucian*, transl. by A. M. Harmon (Loeb Classical Library), vols. i-v (Cambridge, Mass., 1913-1936); the Oxford University Press, for *The Poetical Works of John Gay*, ed. G. C. Faber (London, 1926); the Yale University Press, for *The Twickenham Edition of the Poems of Alexander Pope*, ed. John Butt: Vol. iii, i, *An Essay on Man*, ed. Maynard Mack (New Haven, Conn., 1950), and Vol. iii, ii, *Epistles to Several Persons*, ed. F. W. Bateson (New Haven, Conn., 1951). Part One of Chapter IV incorporates material from my article upon "The Paradoxical Encomium," which appeared in *Modern Philology* (copyright, the University of Chicago Press, 1956); Part Two of Chapter IV, in slightly different form, originally appeared in *Studies in Philology*. They are here employed with the kind permission of those journals.

To name all the friends who have helped and encouraged me during the years in which I have been engaged upon this study would be a pleasant task, but would extend my Preface beyond reason. I must express my warm thanks to the library staffs of Princeton, Yale, and Harvard universities, and to the Folger Shakespeare Library, the Library of Congress, the New York Public Library, the library of the University

PREFACE

of London, and the British Museum. Miss Miriam Brokaw and Miss Judy Walton of the Princeton University Press have been most helpful and considerate in their attention to my manuscript.

I am indebted to Princeton University for the award of the John E. Annan Bicentennial Preceptorship, which gave me the opportunity to read in England and to bring this work to completion.

I am deeply grateful to Professor George Sherburn and Professor James Thorpe for their generous and searching criticism of the manuscript. To Professor Louis A. Landa, whose suggestions originally led me into this study and whose patience and wisdom have sustained me throughout its development, I owe a debt that only friendship can justify or repay.

I could not conclude without here recording, in justice and in love, the part that my wife has played in this work. Helpmeet, secretary, research staff, and cheering section, she has touched every page of the book, and continues stoutly to insist that she has enjoyed the entire labor as thoroughly as I.

H. K. M.

Princeton University
November 1, 1960

CONTENTS

PREFACE	vii
A NOTE ON ABBREVIATIONS AND TEXTS	xiv
CHAPTER I. CIRCUMSTANCES OF PUBLICATION	3
CHAPTER II. POETRY	29
1. The Verse Essays	42
(1) Of True Greatness	42
(2) Of Good-Nature	54
(3) Liberty	88
(4) To a Friend on the Choice of a Wife	103
(5) To John Hayes, Esq;	113
2. The Light Verse	118
CHAPTER III. ESSAYS	143
1. An Essay on Conversation	164
2. An Essay on the Knowledge of the Characters of Men	189
3. Of the Remedy of Affliction for the Loss of Our Friends	228
CHAPTER IV. SATIRES	272
1. An Essay on Nothing	291
2. Some Papers Proper to be Read before the Royal Society	315
CHAPTER V. TRANSLATION	337
The First Olynthiac of Demosthenes	344

CONTENTS

CHAPTER VI. LUCIANIC SKETCHES   365

  1. A Dialogue between Alexander the
     Great and Diogenes the Cynic   386

  2. An Interlude between Jupiter, Juno,
     Apollo, and Mercury   409

CHAPTER VII. SOME CONCLUDING
  OBSERVATIONS   420

INDEX   429

A NOTE ON ABBREVIATIONS AND TEXTS

I have used the "Henley" edition of Fielding's *Works* (which, for all its faults, is the most inclusive yet issued) except, of course, for those materials not therein reprinted and for the items to be found in the *Miscellanies*. The reader should perhaps be reminded that the first edition of *Jonathan Wild*, printed in the *Miscellanies*, has an extra chapter in the Second Book and another in the Fourth Book that will change the chapter numbering from that of Henley and most modern editions. The edition of the Everyman *Spectator* that I have used is the edition of 1945, not that of 1907.

Cross. Wilbur L. Cross, *The History of Henry Fielding* (3v., New Haven and London, 1918).

Dudden. F. Homes Dudden, *Henry Fielding, His Life, Works and Times* (2v., Oxford, 1952).

Henley. *The Complete Works of Henry Fielding, Esq. With an Essay on the Life, Genius and Achievement of the Author*, by William Ernest Henley, LL.D. (16v., London, 1903).

Jensen. Henry Fielding, *The Covent-Garden Journal. By Sir Alexander Drawcansir Knt. Censor of Great Britain*, edited by Gerard E. Jensen (2v., New Haven and London, 1915).

Misc. Henry Fielding, *Miscellanies, by Henry Fielding Esq; in Three Volumes* (3v., London, 1743).

CGJ   Covent-Garden Journal
JA   Joseph Andrews
JW   Jonathan Wild
TJ   Tom Jones

The titles of learned journals are abbreviated according to standard practice. The place of publication of all works cited is London, unless otherwise indicated.

ESSAYS ON FIELDING'S

Miscellanies

CHAPTER I.

CIRCUMSTANCES OF PUBLICATION

And now, my good-natured Reader, recommending my Works to your Candour, I bid you heartily farewell; and take this with you, that you may never be interrupted in the reading these Miscellanies, with that Degree of Heartach which hath often discomposed me in the writing them.—PREFACE

THE first reference that we find to Fielding's *Miscellanies* is a note in the ledger of Henry Woodfall, the London printer who had handled the first edition of *Joseph Andrews* (and soon would print the second).[1] On 3 June 1742, Woodfall entered in his ledger that he had printed "700 proposals for Mr. Fielding, paper print."[2] Two days later, the *Daily Post* advertised the proposals (see page 4). The apology for delay and the reference to "his last Receipts" make it clear that although this is the first public notice we have of the subscription, it must have been underway for some time. Apparently the *Miscellanies* had been projected before the winter of 1741-1742, hence well before *Joseph Andrews* was sent to the printer's in February of 1742.

There is more evidence than the allusion here to "a Train of melancholy Accidents" to suggest that these were indeed difficult times for Fielding, now settled with his

[1] There were two Henry Woodfalls, father and son. Woodfall the elder, a friend of Pope, had an establishment without Temple Bar after 1724; he seems to have died about 1747. His son was a printer in Paternoster Row and other locations from about 1737 to 1764. Extracts from the ledgers of both men were published in *Notes and Queries* in a series of articles by "P. T. P.": 1st Ser., XI (1855), 377-78, 418-20; XII (1855), 197, 217-19. It is clear from these excerpts that Woodfall the elder was the printer of *Joseph Andrews*.

[2] P. T. P., "Woodfall's Ledger, 1734-1747," N&Q, 1st Ser., XI (1855), 419.

> *This Day are publish'd,*
> Proposals *for* printing *by* Subscription,
> MISCELLANIES in Three VOLUMES Octavo.
> By HENRY FIELDING, *Esq;*
> The first Volume will contain all his Works in Verse, and some short Essays in Prose.
> The second Volume will contain, a Journey from this World to the next.
> The third Volume will contain, the History of that truly renowned Person Jonathan Wyld, Esq; in which not only his Character, but that of divers other great Personages of his Time, will be set in a just and true Light.
> The Price to Subscribers is One Guinea; and Two Guineas for the Royal Paper. One Half of which is to be paid at Subscribing, the other on the Delivery of the Book in Sheets. The Subscribers Names will be printed.
> Note, The Publication of these Volumes hath been hitherto retarded by the Author's Indisposition last Winter, and a Train of melancholy Accidents scarce to be parallell'd; but he takes this Opportunity to assure his Subscribers, that he will most certainly deliver them within the Time mentioned in his last Receipts, viz. by the 25th of December next.
> Subscriptions are taken in by Mr. A. Millar, Bookseller, opposite St. Clement's Church in the Strand.
> As the Books will very shortly go to the Press, Mr. Fielding begs the Favour of those who intend to subscribe to do it immediately.[3]

[3] *Daily Post*, No. 7098, 5 June 1742; cf. Cross, I, 380-81.

little family in Spring Garden, near Charing Cross. Things had quite obviously gone from bad to worse since the Licensing Act ended his dramatic career in 1737. For, although he had been called to the bar in June 1740, the practice of law did not afford him enough remuneration to maintain his household. Arthur Murphy tells us, in his usual vague way, that Fielding's pursuit of the law was hampered by want of means and by attacks of the gout;[4] and Dr. Dudden says (1, 245) that "his name does not appear in connexion with any important case" between 1740 and 1748. In November of 1740, Fielding surrendered (possibly because he could not maintain them) the chambers in Pump Court which had been granted him for life by the Benchers of the Middle Temple.[5] In 1742, one Joseph King instituted suit to force payment of a note that Fielding had given him for £197 in March 1741.[6] Moreover, the variety of miscellaneous writing in which he indulged from 1740 to 1743 gives the impression that Fielding was casting about almost frantically for some lucrative possibility, whether in "literature" or in mere "hackney-writing."

For example, in 1740, though he was contributing regularly to the *Champion*, and, as a novice man-of-law, attending Westminster Hall during term time and travelling the Western circuit in hopeful search for briefs, he never-

[4] "An Essay on the Life and Genius of Henry Fielding, Esq;" in *The Works of Henry Fielding, Esq.* (4v., 1762), 1, 28.

[5] The granting of the chambers may, however, have been a mere formality in the first place (see B. M. Jones, *Henry Fielding, Novelist and Magistrate* [1933], pp. 71-72 and Dudden, 1, 243). Normally, I believe, only bachelors occupied these chambers.

[6] Cross, 1, 376. At the same time (Trinity Term, 1742), Fielding apparently prosecuted a "judgment for debt" against one Randolph Seagrim (a relative of Black George?), though since the roll containing this case seems to be lost, we cannot say what the amount of the judgment was (cf. Cross, 1, 376n.). It may have been at this point that Ralph Allen came to Fielding's rescue with the £200 that Samuel Derrick mentioned in later years (Cross, 1, 376-77); but the praise of Allen's generosity in *Joseph Andrews* would suggest that Fielding had enjoyed his patronage well before this date.

theless managed to take some part in a translation of Gustaf Adlerfeld's *Military History of Charles XII*.[7] In 1741, while engaged in writing *Joseph Andrews* and at least some of the material in the *Miscellanies* (one item, the poem *Of True Greatness* addressed to Dodington, was published in January), Fielding found time to write for the *Champion*, until mid-year at least, to dash off his satirical attack on Richardson, *Shamela*, and to turn out a number of commentaries on the current political situation: the mock-pedantic *Vernoniad*, *The Crisis: A Sermon*, and (late in the year), *The Opposition, A Vision*. Then for a time his political pen was silent. In the preface to the *Miscellanies* he defended himself against the charges that in the winter of 1741-1742 "two opposite Parties thought fit to cast on me, *viz*. the one of writing in the *Champion*, (tho' I had not then writ in it for upwards of half a Year) the other, of writing in the *Gazetteer*, in which I never had the Honour of inserting a single Word"; and he concluded: "To defend myself therefore as well as I can from all past, and to enter a Caveat against all future Censure of this Kind; I once more solemnly declare, that since the End of *June* 1741, I have not, besides *Joseph Andrews*, published one Word, except *The Opposition, a Vision. A Defence of the Dutchess of Marlborough's Book. Miss Lucy in Town*, (in which I had a very small Share.)"[8]

[7] See John E. Wells, "Henry Fielding and the History of Charles XII," *JEGP*, XI (1912), 603-13.
[8] *Misc.*, I, xxxvi-xxxvii, misnumbered xxvi-xxvii. The minutes of a meeting (1 March 1742) of the partners in the *Champion* say that Fielding had withdrawn as a writer "for above Twelve Months past"; the last meeting that he had actually attended was on 29 June 1741 (G. M. Godden, *Henry Fielding: A Memoir* [1910], pp. 138-39 and 115-16). John E. Wells observed that the *Champion* in June 1740 "is written in such a manner as to indicate that its author meant it as a sort of gathering up, perhaps as a farewell" ("The 'Champion' and Some Unclaimed Essays by Henry Fielding," *Englische Studien*, XLVI [1913], 363). As Fielding was admitted to the bar 20 June 1740, this is a likely supposition; but Wells is surely correct in further assuming that Fielding continued to make random contributions to the periodical until sometime in the summer of 1741.

CIRCUMSTANCES OF PUBLICATION

Miss Godden is doubtless correct in suggesting that Fielding "may by now have found that politics afforded, in those days, but scanty support to an honourable pen."[9] Certainly the portrait of himself and Ralph as starved asses in *The Opposition* would indicate that his pamphleteering against Walpole had not proved very lucrative. But it is equally likely that his vacation from political writing was simply the result of a thoroughgoing disillusionment with the "Patriots" who, as the hour of their triumph approached, began more to resemble hungry place-seekers than patriotic statesmen. A recent study of Fielding's activity in this period has argued with great cogency that he had indeed broken with the Opposition sometime in 1741, and that his pamphlet upon them represented a definite alignment with the Walpole forces.[10] Be this as it may, the conflict between Walpole and the Opposition, which had provided the focus of Fielding's early political activity, came to an effectual end in February 1742, with Walpole's retirement and elevation to the peerage.

In this same month, *Joseph Andrews* was published, launching Fielding on a new career. It scarcely satisfied his immediate needs, however: the £183/11s. that he received for the rights to this novel fell short of the amount that he owed to Joseph King. Hence his ardent defense of the Duchess of Marlborough in April was probably a bid for patronage, rather than a purely chivalrous gesture (as Cross would have it).[11] In May he took part in his first dramatic activity since the passage of the Licensing Act, with the "very small Share" in the production of *Miss Lucy in Town* (for which he had, small share or no, already sold the copyright in April, receiving £10/10s.). And he hopefully set out

[9] Godden, p. 120.
[10] Martin C. Battestin, "Fielding's Changing Politics and *Joseph Andrews*," PQ, xxxix (1960), 39-55.
[11] Cross, 1, 360-62. Miss Godden finds (I think correctly) an expression of Fielding's disappointed hopes in the laconic obituary notice in the *True Patriot* some years later: "A Man supposed to be a Pensioner of the late Duchess of Marlborough. . . . He is supposed to have been Poor" (cited Godden, p. 138).

with William Young to translate all of the plays of Aristophanes. Their first effort, *Plutus, The God of Riches,* apparently did not succeed, for we hear no more of the enterprise. It is in this context, then, that the announcement of 5 June appears: "Proposals *for* printing *by* Subscription, MISCELLANIES in Three VOLUMES Octavo. *By* HENRY FIELDING, *Esq;*"—and we can see it as another in a series of Fielding's attempts (themselves of the most miscellaneous nature) to augment a bare legal income through the resources of his indefatigable pen.

Two more items (besides the earlier poem addressed to Dodington) eventually to appear in the *Miscellanies* were first published separately: the satire on the Royal Society and a five-act play, *The Wedding Day*, both published in February 1743. In extenuating the faults of the latter work, Fielding incidentally provided us with a vivid sketch of the pressures under which the *Miscellanies* were composed: he resurrected the play from his papers, as a last-minute replacement for another that he had written especially at Garrick's request but that had proved unsatisfactory:

"I accordingly sat down with a Resolution to work Night and Day, during the short Time allowed me, which was about a Week, in altering and correcting this Production of my more juvenile Years; when unfortunately, the extreme Danger of Life into which a Person, very dear to me, was reduced, rendered me incapable of executing my Task.

"To this Accident alone, I have the Vanity to apprehend, the Play owes most of the glaring Faults with which it appeared. . . .

"Perhaps it may be asked me, Why then did I suffer a Piece, which I myself knew was imperfect, to appear? I answer honestly and freely, that Reputation was not my Inducement; and that I hoped, faulty as it was, it might answer a much more solid, and in my unhappy Situation, a much more urgent Motive. If it will give my Enemies any

Pleasure to know that they totally frustrated my Views, I will be kinder to them, and give them a Satisfaction which they denied me: for tho' it was acted six Nights, I received not 50 *l.* from the House for it"—(*Misc.*, I, xii-xv).

The person very dear to him was, of course, his wife Charlotte, who did not survive another winter. Fielding wrote from the heart when he later declared in *Amelia* that "the kindness of a faithful and beloved wife" is a blessing "which, though it compensates most of the evils of life, rather serves to aggravate the misfortune of distressed circumstances, from the consideration of the share which she is to bear in them" (IV, viii; Henley, VI, 215-16). Besides the straitened circumstances of their life in London, Charlotte had shared with Fielding illness, vilification, and grief. In June 1741, his father had died; and in March 1742, his first-born child, Charlotte, had died just short of her sixth birthday. One of the essays that Fielding wrote for the *Miscellanies*, "Of the Remedy of Affliction for the Loss of Our Friends," surely derives from this troubled period; and its elegiac note conveys some sense of the trials of spirit that he had faced and mastered. That he should have been able to bring together (and compose much of) the material of the *Miscellanies* in these disheartening circumstances is nothing short of incredible. Fielding himself seems to have regarded his powers of recuperation and concentration with reasonable pride, as is suggested by his words near the conclusion of the preface:

"It remains that I make some Apology for the Delay in publishing these Volumes, the real Reason of which was, the dangerous Illness of one from whom I draw all the solid Comfort of my Life, during the greatest Part of this Winter [1742-1743]. This, as it is most sacredly true, so will it, I doubt not, sufficiently excuse the Delay to all who know me.

"Indeed when I look a Year or two backwards, and survey the Accidents which have befallen me, and the Distresses I have waded through whilst I have been engaged in these Works, I could almost challenge some Philosophy to myself, for having been able to finish them as I have; and however imperfectly that may be, I am convinced the Reader, was he acquainted with the whole, would want very little Good-Nature to extinguish his Disdain at any Faults he meets with.

"But this hath dropt from me unawares: for I intend not to entertain my Reader with my private History: nor am I fond enough of Tragedy, to make myself the Hero of one"—(*Misc.*, I, xxxii-xxxiii, latter misnumbered xxxi).

2

Aurélien Digeon has described Fielding's *Miscellanies* as "une liquidation de son passée littéraire";[12] and this is true both in the sense that these volumes sum up his career to that point and also that he doubtless filled them out with whatever material he had at hand. Most of the short poems, for example, were clearly youthful work. Nevertheless, I believe that many of the pieces in the collection were written especially for it. Fielding's observation upon the "Year or two backwards . . . whilst I have been engaged in these Works"; the many allusions that can be dated about 1741-1743 in the individual pieces themselves; and the fact that although he specifically identified most of the poetry and his two dramatic productions as early work, none of the other pieces was so characterized—all point to the supposition that much if not the greater part of the *Miscellanies* was composed in the years immediately preceding its publication. Some of the pieces may well have been reworkings of earlier material, but it is perhaps a futile exercise to attempt to separate these refurbished items from those originally composed between 1741 and 1743.

One thing, at any rate, is certain: Fielding's personal difficulties and his other commitments led to several post-

[12] *Les romans de Fielding* (Paris, 1923), p. 118.

CIRCUMSTANCES OF PUBLICATION

ponements of the original publication date. On 18 November 1742, about a month before the date for which the *Miscellanies* had been promised, Fielding repeated the announcement of 5 June in the *Daily Post*, substituting for the final paragraphs this appeal:

> Whereas the Number of Copies to to be printed is to be determin'd by the Number of Subscribers, Mr. Fielding will be oblig'd to all those who have subscrib'd to those Miscellanies, or who intend him that Favour, if they will please to send their Names and first Payment (if not already made) to Mr. Millar, Bookseller, opposite to Katharine-Street in the Strand, before the 5th of December next.[13]

December came and went without further word, however. On 12 February 1743 the *Daily Post* carried the following notice:

> On Monday the 28th Instant will be deliver'd to the Subscribers,
>
> By A. MILLAR, Bookseller, opposite Katherine-Street in the Strand,
>
> MISCELLANIES. In Three Volumes, Octavo.
>
> By HENRY FIELDING, Esq;
>
> Those who are pleased to subscribe to these Miscellanies, and have not yet sent in their Names, are desir'd to do it before the 22d Instant, on which Day the Subscription will be closed. And all such as have disposed of any Receipts, and have not yet sent in the Names of the Subscribers, are requested to do it within the above-mention'd Time.[14]

[13] *Daily Post*, No. 7240, 18 November 1742.
[14] *Ibid.*, No. 7314. The notice was repeated on 14 February in the *Daily Post* and also in the *Daily Advertiser* of that date.

11

Despite this promise, however, the volumes were not ready on 28 February. In the latter part of March, the *St. James's Evening Post* again advertised the *Miscellanies* as forthcoming, this time on 7 April, and the *General Evening Post* for 5 to 7 April also advertised that delivery to subscribers would be made on that date.[15] And this time they were correct. On 7 April the *Daily Post* announced:

> This Day will be deliver'd to the Subscribers, MISCELLANIES in three Volumes, 8vo.
>
> By HENRY FIELDING, Esq;
>
> . . . .
> Printed for the Author, and to be had of A. Millar, opposite to Katherine-Street in the Strand.[16]

Andrew Millar, the bookseller who published all of Fielding's novels and much of his other work, acted merely as distributor for the subscription edition, the proceeds of which (after printing costs) went entirely to Fielding. The printing of the three volumes was divided by Millar among three different houses—a not unusual practice. Thus an entry in the ledger of William Strahan (who handled a number of Fielding's other works for Millar) describes the printing of Volume I: "April 2 [1743]. For printing the first Volume of Fielding's Miscellanies 26½ Sheets Pica 8vo N°. 1000 Coarse and 250 fine @ £1:2:6 p Sheet   [£] 29/16/—"[17]

---

[15] Cf. John E. Wells, "Fielding's 'Miscellanies,'" *MLR*, XIII (1918), 481-82. One cause of the further delay may have been Fielding's revision of *Joseph Andrews* for the elaborate third edition, which was published on 24 March (*Daily Post*, No. 7346, of that date).

[16] *Daily Post*, No. 7358, 7 April 1743. The *London Daily Post and General Advertiser*, No. 2640, 7 April 1743, also advertised the *Miscellanies* as "published, And ready to be delivered to the Subscribers." This notice did not appear in the *Daily Advertiser* until 8 April.

[17] British Museum Add. MS. 48800, p. 38 verso. This entry was previously cited by J. Paul De Castro ("The Printing of Fielding's Works," *The Library*, 4th Ser., I [1921], 250); he erred in recording the number of copies printed on "fine" paper as "200." The printing was charged to Andrew Millar, not to Fielding, which suggests that Millar financed

CIRCUMSTANCES OF PUBLICATION

The paper-stock ledger of another printer often associated with Millar, William Bowyer (the younger), contains a series of entries recording delivery of copies to the publisher under the heading:

Jonathan Wild for Mr. Millar		Coarse	Fine
1743	27 sh.	1000	250[28]

This, then, is obviously Volume III. The printer of Volume II cannot be so easily identified. The most likely possibility would be Henry Woodfall the elder, who had printed Fielding's proposals, as well as the first two editions of *Joseph Andrews*; but the excerpts from his ledger reprinted in the nineteenth century, though recording these items, make no mention of the *Miscellanies* in 1743.[19] Nevertheless, I venture to assign Volume II tentatively to Woodfall on the basis of the printer's devices that appear in it. Since this is largely unexplored territory in eighteenth-century bibliographical studies (with a few brilliant exceptions, such as Professor Sale's study of Richardson),[20] I speak in a smaller voice than I otherwise should; but the appearance of printer's ornaments found in Volume II in other works known to have been printed by Woodfall is reasonably convincing evidence that he is our missing printer.[21]

---

the project until the final receipts were in. He settled with Strahan for the printing of the volume on 11 May 1744 (MS., p. 39).

[18] Bodleian Library MS. Don. b. 4., fol. 112 recto. This entry was kindly transcribed for me by Professor D. W. Robertson, Jr.

[19] The transcriber, "P. T. P.," might well have overlooked an entry recording the *Miscellanies*, for he did not understand the significance of the entry previously cited: "The '700 proposals' I must leave to the interpretation of the better informed" (*N&Q*, 1st Ser., XI [1855], 419).

[20] William M. Sale, Jr., *Samuel Richardson: Master Printer* (Ithaca, N.Y., 1950).

[21] Thus: (1) the device on the title page of Fielding's second volume seems to be the same as that in the *Works of Mr. [James] Thomson* (2v., 1738), II, 56 (sig. E₄v), printed by Woodfall.
(2) The device of Fielding's II, 253, had appeared in Volume II of Thomson's *Works* (no pag., sig. C₄), in Samuel Johnson of Cheshire's *Vision of Heaven* (1738), p. 41, in William Hatchett's *Chinese Orphan* (1741), pp. 14 and 44, and in William Collins' *Persian Eclogues* (1742), p. 10.
(3) Fielding's tailpiece (II, 420) is found in Johnson's *Vision*, pp. 37

CIRCUMSTANCES OF PUBLICATION

Later in the month of April 1743, a "second edition" was variously proclaimed,[22] as in this notice in the *Daily Advertiser* on 27 April:

> *This Day is publish'd,*
> *(Price bound 15 s.)*
> The SECOND EDITION of
> MISCELLANIES, in three Volumes,
> Octavo.
>
> By HENRY FIELDING, Esq;
>
> . . . .
> Printed for A. Millar, opposite Katherine-Street in the Strand. Such Gentlemen and Ladies as were Subscribers for these Miscellanies, are desir'd to send for their Books to the said A. Millar's.

Despite the advertisements, however, and the brave inscription on the new title page of Volume I ("The SECOND EDITION"), these volumes represented merely the remaining unsold copies of the first impression, with the subscriber's list removed and new title pages substituted.[23] Their sale to the general public must have been slow, for Millar was still advertising them in the *True Patriot* of 18 February 1746 and after, as Cross noted (I, 381), and indeed as late as October and November 1748, in the *Jacobite's Journal* (nos. 44, 46, 48, and 49). There was a

---

and 63, in Hatchett's *Chinese Orphan*, p. 28, in *Persian Eclogues*, pp. 9, 19, and 24, and as the tailpiece of the first edition of *Joseph Andrews* (2v., 1742), II, 310. Several of these devices are poorly inked or printed, but the figure is identifiable. The possibility that another printer could have imitated Woodfall's ornaments must be kept in mind.

[22] The *Daily Post* of 23 April and the *General Evening Post* of 21-23 April advertised the "second edition" as forthcoming "next week"; publication was noted in the *General Evening Post* of 23-26 April and in the *Daily Post* of 2 May.

[23] Wells (MLR, XIII, 482) said that he possessed "two copies of this Second Edition. One copy contains the list [of subscribers]; the other omits it." I have not come across any copies that retain the subscription list.

Dublin reprint by John Smith of the *Miscellanies*, in two volumes, in 1743.

3

The "LIST OF SUBSCREBERS [sic]" in the original edition came to a total of 427 individual subscribers and 556 sets, 214 of which were on royal paper. At two guineas for the royal and one guinea for the regular paper, this represented (on the cheerful supposition that everyone paid according to promise) a comfortable gross of 770 guineas for Fielding, the largest sum—even after he had reimbursed Millar's printers—that he gained from the publication of any of his works except *Amelia*. The *Miscellanies* created no great literary splash; but the three volumes were definitely a financial success, and the preface makes clear that this satisfied Fielding's most "urgent Motive" in publishing them. The idea of subscription publication was, of course, nothing new in Fielding's time: the practice had been employed throughout the seventeenth century by authors and booksellers in the fields of music, divinity, law, and the sciences (not to mention the travel books of John Taylor, the Water Poet) before the elder Tonson published *Paradise Lost* and Dryden's *Virgil* through subscription and made it a standard practice for literature as well. By 1741, Fielding had before him as a spur the phenomenally successful subscriptions of Prior, Rowe, Pope, and Gay, as well as other modestly fortunate examples.[24] Moreover, he could at this time count upon a reputation for wit and ingenuity if not for "literary" genius (his name had not appeared on the title page of *Joseph Andrews* until the third edition of March 1743); and it must have struck him as an entirely happy idea, particularly in his financial straits, to engage in a labor whose return was pledged beforehand.

[24] Cf. Mr. Wilson's brief history of the practice of subscription: "Thus Prior, Rowe, Pope, and some other men of genius, received large sums for their labors from the public. This seemed so easy a method of getting money that many of the lowest scribblers of the times ventured to publish their works in the same way . . ." &c. (JA, III, iii; Henley, I, 244).

The enterprise might not have proved such a resounding economic success, however, had not his fellows in the legal profession (some of whom, apparently, had also contributed to the *Champion*)[25] given it their whole-hearted support. In his preface Fielding gratefully observed, "I cannot . . . forbear mentioning my Sense of the Friendship shewn me by a Profession of which I am a late and unworthy Member, and from whose Assistance I derive more than half the Names which appear to this Subscription" (*Misc.*, I, xxxii). Analyzed even superficially, the list of subscribers shows how very large a role the Inns of Court play in it: seventy-five names are specifically attached to their respective Inns ("William Abney, Esq; of the Inner Temple," "Mr. Adamson of Lincolns-Inn," and so on); and to this one would have to add the names of at least seventy-five more who had at one time or another been members of the Inns.

A full-scale analysis (à la Namier) of the subscribers would doubtless provide some interesting hints concerning the range and character of Fielding's social acquaintance at this day, but unfortunately one cannot by any means assume that he personally knew everyone whose name appears. As he said in the preface, in thanking "those Friends who have with uncommon Pains forwarded this Subscription": "I believe I owe not a tenth Part to my own Interest" (*Misc.*, I, xxxi). This is sufficient to discourage any detailed attempt to picture his immediate circle from the list of subscribers. Yet, a great many of the names fall naturally into groupings—professional, geographical, political, and the like—which, when analyzed, do not surprise us but do pleasantly support our presuppositions with fact.

For instance, we should expect to find a strong representation from the anti-Walpole "Patriots" with whom Fielding had been so closely associated in the previous decade;

[25] Cf. the letter in the *Champion*, 8 April 1740, signed "Morpheus" and dated from the "Inner-Temple," and the letter from "Somnus" of Gray's Inn, 13 May 1740 (coll. ed. [2v., 1741], II, 80-86 and 205-11). The addresses may, of course, be fictitious.

and of course we do. Heading the list was His Royal Highness, the Prince of Wales, with "Fifteen Setts"—on royal paper naturally. In this group also were most of Fielding's patrons: the Duke of Bedford, the Duke of Argyll, the Duke of Roxburghe (styled Marquess of Bowmont in the thirties), the Earl of Chesterfield, Lord Cobham, Lord Barrington, George Lyttelton, Bubb Dodington, and Lord Talbot, to whom Fielding and Young dedicated their translation of the *Plutus* in 1742.[26] Also represented were such anti-Walpole peers as the Duke of Queensberry, the recently "converted" Duke of Newcastle, the new peer William Pulteney, Earl of Bath, the "architect Earl" of Burlington, and his cousin the Earl of Orrery, later Swift's biographer. In the Commons, there were Lord Thomas Gage, Lord Arthur Doneraile, and Lord John Perceval whom Fielding or a close imitator of his style (cf. Cross, II, 93-95 and III, 339) severely attacked in the pamphlet of a decade later, *A Genuine Copy of the Tryal of J[ohn] P[erceva]l, Esq; &c. Commonly Call'd, E[arl] of E[gmont]* (1749).

Among the fifty or so other M. P.'s that the subscription list could boast were Sir Francis Dashwood of later Hell-Fire Club fame, less notorious baronets like Sir Edmund Thomas, Sir James Dashwood, Sir Cordell Firebrace, Sir Robert Long, and Sir Erasmus Philipps, and various busy politicians like Henry Furnese, Thomas Bootle (Chancellor to the Prince of Wales), and that rising young man, William Pitt. Not all M. P.'s but of some political importance were such affluent country gentlemen as Peter Bathurst of Clarendon Park, Wiltshire (at whose home Fielding "had lived for victuals," according to Horace Wal-

---

[26] Cross (I, 382) is mistaken in listing the Duke of Richmond as a subscriber. Strangely enough, although Fielding's poem *Of Good-Nature* is dedicated to him, his name does not appear in the list. However that of his duchess does. She was linked with the Countess of Shaftesbury in a compliment to beauty in the same poem (*Misc.*, I, 19).

pole's malicious anecdote);[27] Edward Bayntun-Rolt of Spye Park, Wiltshire; Norreys Bertie of Weston-on-the-Green, Oxford; Anthony Henley of the Grange in Hampshire, good-humored son of the Queen Anne wit of the same name (another of whose sons, Robert Henley, later Earl of Northington, was also a subscriber to the *Miscellanies*); Norborne Berkeley of Stoke Gifford, Gloucester (who was, with Lord Barrington, one of the Earl of Halifax's inner circle); William Strode of Punsborne, Hertfordshire; and George Vandeput of Twickenham, who is remembered for his vast expense in later contesting the Westminster election of 1749.

It is impossible to determine whether Fielding knew all these gentlemen personally; but they surely knew one another, and Fielding's subscriptions probably came through such acquaintance or in such a chain as that suggested by the interrelationship of the Harris-Knatchbull-Wyndham families. It is well known that James Harris of Salisbury, the author of *Hermes*, was intimate with Fielding and his family; he was a subscriber and so also were his mother-in-law Lady Elizabeth Harris (sister of the third Earl of Shaftesbury) and his brother Thomas.[28] Thomas had married Catharine Knatchbull, daughter of Sir Edward Knatchbull, Bart., of Mersham-Hatch in Kent; and although Sir Edward (having died in 1730) was not himself a subscriber to the *Miscellanies*, a son-in-law, a son, and a brother-in-law of his were—for he had married Alice Wyndham, sister of Thomas, Lord Wyndham of Finglass (a subscriber), and his third son Edward Knatchbull was also a subscriber. It is even possible (to expand the circle further) that the John Clark and John Clark, Jr. whose names appear in the sub-

[27] *The Yale Edition of Horace Walpole's Correspondence* (New Haven, Conn., 1937, in progress), Vol. IX (*Correspondence with George Montagu*, Vol. I, ed. W. S. Lewis and Ralph S. Brown, Jr., 1941), p. 84.

[28] There was also a London bookseller named Thomas Harris, and I cannot prove that it was not he or some other personage of the name who subscribed: but James Harris' brother seems the most likely candidate: the "Esq;" connotes a gentleman.

CIRCUMSTANCES OF PUBLICATION

scription list were the father and brother of James Harris' wife Elizabeth; but with so common a name it is difficult to be certain. This kind of circle of interrelationships does suggest, however, the way in which Fielding came by his subscriptions.[29]

An even more famous illustration can be found in the "Cobham cousinhood," the family group of Richard Temple, Viscount Cobham, of Stowe. He and his wife Lady Anne were subscribers. His sister Christian had married Sir Thomas Lyttelton, and their son George was Fielding's friend and patron. A second sister Hester had married Richard Grenville, and their sons Richard and George were prominent among the "Boy Patriots"; hence if the "George Greenville, Esq; of the Inner Temple" who subscribed to the *Miscellanies* is George Grenville, as seems quite probable, we have another link (as well as a name memorable to young students of American history, who are taught to associate this gentleman with the Stamp Act and tyranny).[30] In any case, *his* sister Hester later married William Pitt, who was assuredly a subscriber. And finally, a third sister of Cobham, Penelope, married Moses Berenger; and their son Richard Berenger, a poet of modest pretensions and a most elegant gentleman, was also a subscriber to Fielding's work.[31]

[29] This Wiltshire group may also remind us that some three dozen or more of the subscribers were associated with that county. They included Arthur Collier, the Salisbury metaphysician, father of Jane and Margaret Collier; and Dr. John Barker and the surgeon Mr. Edward Goldwyre (see J. Paul De Castro, "A Forgotten Salisbury Surgeon," *TLS*, 13 January 1927, p. 28, and comment by Arthur E. Du Bois, *TLS*, 19 March 1931, p. 234, with reply by De Castro, *TLS*, 26 March 1931, p. 252). The seats of the Earl of Pembroke, Lord Thomas Wyndham, Lord Windsor (who magnanimously subscribed to ten copies on royal paper), Peter Bathurst, Edward Bayntun-Rolt, and Sir Robert Long were all in Wiltshire.

[30] Likewise, the "James Greenville, Esq; of Lincolns-Inn," who subscribed to the *Miscellanies* is probably James Grenville, one of the less famous brothers of George and Richard. The latter seems not to have subscribed, unless he is the "―― Greenville, Esq;" who took one copy on royal paper.

[31] Another family well represented in the subscription list was that

19

If Fielding drew the majority of his subscriptions from such strongly Whig groups as this, he also found a number of Tories who had no great love for Walpole. They ranged from those of true Jacobite sympathies like Lord Gower, Sir John Hynde Cotton and Sir Watkin Williams-Wynn to Tories like the Duke of Beaufort, the Earl of Cardigan, Lord Leigh, Lord Craven, the unfortunate Lord Deerhurst (who died the next year at 23), and Henry Bathurst, whose famous father Allen, Lord Bathurst, that indefatigable patron of letters, is strangely missing from Fielding's list.

The most surprising thing, however, in terms of political alignments, is the dozen or so names that appear of men who were associated with Walpole's government or very closely with Walpole himself. Unless one accepts Martin Battestin's argument (cited above) that Fielding had joined the Walpole camp in 1741, this group of names seems difficult to explain. We might dismiss Walpole's own subscription ("The Right Hon. the Earl of Orford") to ten sets on royal paper as a gesture, like the earlier gesture of Bolingbroke in giving Booth fifty guineas for his portrayal of Addison's Cato. But how does one account for the name of the Duke of Devonshire, one of Walpole's most loyal supporters, or the Duke of St. Albans, or Earl Cholmondeley (Walpole's brother-in-law), the Earl of Pembroke, Lord Cornwallis, or General Churchill? Battestin's argument apart, there are several possible explanations for particular names in the list. Thus the garrulous old General Churchill (natural son of Marlborough's brother) was close to Walpole through his marriage with Anna Maria, Sir Robert's natural daughter; but he was also a brother-in-arms of Fielding's father. Edmund Fielding, Charles Churchill, and the Earl of Pembroke had in fact all been

---

of the Stanhopes, with three branches: (1) William, first Earl of Harrington; (2) Philip, second Earl Stanhope; and (3) Philip, fourth Earl of Chesterfield, as well as his brothers, Sir William and the Hon. John Stanhope.

CIRCUMSTANCES OF PUBLICATION

created major-generals on the same date in 1735:[32] it seems colorable that this old association accounts for the latter two names, mere political differences being overlooked. It is even more probable that this kind of explanation may account for the presence of such further associates of Walpole as the young Duke of Marlborough (who deserted the Opposition in 1738, to the old Duchess' horror), Lord De La Warr, Henry Fox, Sir Charles Hanbury Williams, and the Earl of Harrington (although the latter was never very cordial with Walpole in any case): the explanation here, of course, being that they were all Old Etonians—though not all schoolmates nor even necessarily acquaintances of Fielding. Hanbury Williams alone could have garnered most of the subscriptions in this group, for despite his loyalty to Walpole he is numbered among Fielding's most generous and constant friends.

Pitt also, Lord Talbot, George Grenville, and Sir Francis Dashwood, among those we have previously mentioned, were of the *amicitiae Etonienses*. Altogether Etonians account for about twenty-five subscriptions, including those of the Duke of Rutland and Fielding's distant cousin the Duke of Kingston, the Earls of Halifax, Rockingham, Westmorland, and Radnor, Earl Fitzwilliam, Lord Lymington, Lord Romney, Lord Montfort, whom he praised in *Of Good-Nature* (*Misc.*, I, 19), and such commoners as the learned Andrew Ducarel (who, quite incidentally, followed Fielding's example and married his maid-servant in 1749) and his brother James Coltee Ducarel.

Mention of the Duke of Kingston, who was Lady Mary Wortley Montagu's nephew, may remind us that other of Fielding's nearer relatives also could have offered entry into their circles. Thus his noble kinsman, William, fifth Earl of Denbigh, probably opened doors for him. It certainly seems likely, for instance, that the Marchioness of

[32] John Chamberlayne, *Magnae Britanniae Notitia: or, the Present State of Great Britain* (1737 ed.), Pt. II, p. 97.

Blandford is on the subscription list because she was sister to Denbigh's countess.[33] Less aristocratic but probably even more helpful would have been Henry Gould, son of Fielding's maternal uncle. Gould, a subscriber, had become a barrister of the Middle Temple in 1734 (he became a bencher in the year of Fielding's death, 1754); and, besides smoothing the way for his cousin in his legal studies, he may have been responsible for some of the older barristers on Fielding's list.

The legal profession, as we have seen, accounted for a sizeable proportion of the subscribers. Names of interest include John Cay, whose *Abridgement of the Publick Statutes* (2 v., 1739) was in Fielding's library; William and Robert Salkeld, sons of the William Salkeld whose *Reports of Cases Adjudg'd in the Court of King's Bench* (2 v., 1717-1718) was also among Fielding's law books; Wentworth Odiarn, Sergeant-at-Arms to the House of Commons; the distinguished Matthew Skinner, His Majesty's Prime Sergeant-at-Law, who appeared for the Crown against the Jacobite rebels in 1746; Thomas Garrard, who had earlier succeeded Skinner in his place as one of the four common pleaders of the City of London; the Hon. John Sherrard (a son of the Earl of Harborough), who in 1745 proposed the regiment of volunteers that was raised by the gentlemen of the law to fight against the rebels; and the Hon. Heneage Legge, a son of the Earl of Dartmouth, and later the justice who tried the case of the famous parricide, Mary Blandy, at the Oxford assizes in 1752.

Perhaps closer to Fielding were men like Richard Willoughby, whom Cross (II, 174) is surely correct in identifying as the "Justice Willoughby, of Noyle, a very worthy good gentleman," alluded to in *Tom Jones* (VIII, xi; Henley, IV, 122); Robert Henley; William Wright and William

---

[33] A striking example of pure coincidence is to be found in the case of another relative, Lady Evelyn Pierrepont (who died in 1727): she was aunt to one subscriber, the Duke of Kingston, wife to another, Lord Gower, and mother to a third, Gertrude, Duchess of Bedford.

CIRCUMSTANCES OF PUBLICATION

Wynne, later neighbors of Fielding when he resided in Old Boswell Court (cf. Cross, II, 11); and Robert Ketelbey, a Sergeant-at-Law known to history primarily, it would seem, for his magnificent full-bottomed wig. Some of the younger men of law enjoyed distinguished careers in other fields: Andrew Mitchell, for instance, was Under-Secretary of State for Scotland, 1741-1747 (under the fourth Marquis of Tweeddale, also a subscriber), and later the British envoy to Frederick the Great; Owen Salusbury Brereton became a well-known antiquary and was vice-president of the Society of Arts for thirty years; and James Dawkins was to become intimately associated with the discovery of the famous ruins of Palmyra and Balbek.

Other professions were less generously represented. The sprinkling of clergymen is notable only for two of the Prince of Wales's chaplains, Philip Sone and John Hoadly, the latter also chancellor of the diocese of Winchester and (not coincidentally) son of the Bishop of Winchester. The "Dr. Hoadley" who subscribed to the *Miscellanies* is surely not the Bishop, as Cross (I, 382) believed, but his other son, Benjamin, physician to the royal household. The brothers Hoadly were literary amateurs and apparently quite close to Fielding. Linked with Dr. Hoadly in a line of Fielding's Juvenal (*Misc.*, I, 105) was Dr. William Wasey, physician of St. George's Hospital and later president of the Royal College of Physicians. Fielding numbered several other important medical men among his friends: John Ranby, Sergeant-Surgeon to the King, was a subscriber and remained a friend; Fielding alluded to him in *Tom Jones* and *Amelia*. Dr. Edward Harrington was also mentioned in *Tom Jones*, and so (probably) was Dr. Thomas Brewster, the "Glory of his Art," as Fielding called him in the *Miscellanies* (see below, poem "TO MISS H—AND at *Bath*" and the *Essay on Conversation*). Finally, if the Dr. Wilmot who appears on the list is Edward (later Sir Edward) Wilmot, we have another of the King's medical men, for he was Physician-in-Ordinary both to George II and George III, and attended Frederick, Prince of Wales, in his last illness.[34]

The only representative of the Navy who subscribed was Admiral Edward Vernon, whom Fielding had celebrated in the *Vernoniad*; and of the Army, we have already mentioned General Churchill and the Earl of Pembroke. The doughty old Earl of Westmorland and Lord Lymington, both of whom had fought under Marlborough at Oudenarde, might be included here. The only other persons of interest in this group are the brothers Fairfax—Robert, a Major in the First Troop of Life Guards, and Thomas, the elder, Baron Fairfax of Cameron. Thomas had held a commission in the Blues and had been intimate with Addison and Steele; but in the 1740's he retired to his estates in Virginia. Here he enters American legend through his encouragement of the young George Washington, to whom he gave the task of surveying his property in the Shenandoah Valley.

That Fielding had not been forgotten by his old friends of the theatre is well attested by the illustrious names from that circle; but that he was still not seriously regarded as a "literary" figure may be inferred from the dearth of distinguished names in literature. The theatrical subscriptions (and indeed all others) were topped by the magnanimous order for twenty sets by Charles Fleetwood, manager of Drury Lane. David Garrick, Peg Woffington, and Fielding's favorite actress, Kitty Clive, were subscribers, as well as the lesser lights, Robert Hippisley and James Lacy—if the "Mr. Lacy" of the subscription list is this actor who took part in several of Fielding's plays and later succeeded Fleetwood as manager of Drury Lane. In literature the major names are those of Edward Young and Richard Savage—

[34] Most of these medical men were fellows of the Royal Society, as were over a dozen of Fielding's subscribers, including the Duke of Leeds, the Earl of Radnor, Earl Stanhope, Lord De La Warr, and Lord Gage. One wonders what they thought of the satire in *Some Papers Proper to be Read before the Royal Society*.

but even these are questionable, for the Edward Young of the list is not designated as "the Rev." and there were other men of the name in London (the "William Whitehead, Esq; of Grays-Inn" in the subscription list is definitely not the contemporary poet of that name); and Richard Savage had left London in 1739 and was, indeed, confined in Bristol prison when the *Miscellanies* appeared. Other than this, one finds only David Mallett, Benjamin Martyn,[35] Thomas Cooke, and a "Mr. Carey," who might be the author of "Sally in our Alley." Add the Hoadlys, Lyttelton, Hanbury Williams, and a few amateurs (like Richard Berenger) and scribbling peers, and the list is nearly complete.

It is not impressive. We know that Aaron Hill got a copy of the *Miscellanies* through Richardson,[36] and that Pope ordered copies for himself and for Fielding's self-effacing new patron, Ralph Allen—probably through Richardson's brother-in-law, the Bath bookseller James Leake, whose name is on the subscription list for twelve sets. But neither Hill nor Pope was inclined to grace Fielding's list with his name, although they had not hesitated to put themselves down a decade or so earlier for the ineffable Joseph Mitchell's *Poems on Several Occasions* (1729), along with Arbuthnot, Congreve, Richardson, Steele, and Swift, and a host of luminaries. It would appear that the publication of the *Miscellanies* was not greeted as a literary event: the majority of subscribers seem rather to represent political or professional or merely personal connections. Fielding was

[35] Mallett's appearance is probably a matter of political affiliation: he was in the train of the Prince of Wales. And Martyn was a kind of general factotum to the fourth Earl of Shaftesbury. The subscription process at work can, incidentally, be seen in Martyn's letter to Thomas Birch concerning the *Lives and Characters of Illustrious Persons of Great Britain* (Vol. I, 1743): "Lord and Lady Shaftesbury are desirous of subscribing to your Work, I should therefore be oblig'd to you if you could let me know the Terms, and would give me an Opportunity (the first time you come this way) of paying it for them" (Brit. Mus., Birch MS. 4313, p. 134; dated 17 January 1742/3).

[36] See Alan D. McKillop, *Samuel Richardson: Printer and Novelist* (Chapel Hill, N.C., 1936), p. 77.

thought of at this time as a dramatic wit and political sharpshooter; but probably few of his subscribers really believed that they were furthering the career of a literary genius when they put down their friendly guineas.[37]

4

The same impression is conveyed by the very quiet reception that the Miscellanies received when they were published. Even *Jonathan Wild*, the most important of the three volumes, seems not to have excited any general comment at the time. Perhaps Walpole's fall a year before (even though his administration was still being critically anatomized) made it seem out-of-date as political commentary—and no one was prepared to see it as a significant contribution to the world's literature. The principal notice taken of it was in the subsequent attacks upon Fielding by such noisy enemies as the periodical, *Old England*.[38] Richard Cumberland was genteelly disturbed in later years when he recalled that Dodington had read *Jonathan Wild* aloud before ladies at Eastbury.[39]

---

[37] The names of a few other subscribers of interest may be mentioned: Jonathan Tyers, the amiable proprietor of Vauxhall whom Fielding celebrated in *Amelia* (IX, ix; Henley, VII, 167-68); Thomas Winnington, whose memory he later defended in *A Proper Answer to a Late Scurrilous Libel* (1747); the eccentric baronet Sir Henry Hoo Keate; and the equally eccentric William Holles, Lord Vane, husband of Smollett's notorious patroness; Robert Dodsley, the well-known bookseller; Abraham and Isaac Elton of the family that perennially supplied Bristol with mayors and aldermen; the Hon. John Spencer, a "frollicker" like his brother the young Duke of Marlborough; and the Hon. George Berkeley, an M. P. and sometime Master of St. Katherine's by the Tower, who married George II's mistress, Lady Suffolk.

[38] See Frederic T. Blanchard, *Fielding the Novelist* (New Haven, 1926), pp. 22 and 32-34. Cross (II, 2) suggested that an anecdote in the *Annual Register* of 1762, referring to proposals Fielding was once supposed to have made for a new law-book, arose from a confused memory of the *Miscellanies*. B. M. Jones took issue with this interpretation, however, and cited some jesting allusions from *Old England* that apparently refer to Fielding's projected law-book (*Henry Fielding* [1933], pp. 93-96).

[39] *Memoirs of Richard Cumberland, Written by Himself*, ed. Henry Flanders (Philadelphia, 1856), p. 101.

CIRCUMSTANCES OF PUBLICATION

The relative public indifference is shown in the fact that the "second" edition of the *Miscellanies* offered to readers at large had a very slow sale; and the Dublin publisher apparently had no call for an edition after the first. Again, comment in the private letters and diaries of the period is almost totally lacking or, when existent, perfunctory—on the order of Pope's remark to Allen in a letter of 12 April 1743: "Fielding has sent the Books you subscribd for to the Hand I employd in conveying the 20 ll. to him. In one Chapter of the Second vol. he has payd you a pretty Compliment upon your House."[40] And allusions in later years are usually such casual things as Goldsmith's observation that Fielding had said "that he never knew a person with a steady glavering smile, but he found him a rogue" (apparently based upon a passage in the *Essay on the Knowledge of the Characters of Men*),[41] or William Creech's remark that Fielding was one of the "best writers on the subject of politeness," which one may take as an allusion to the *Essay on Conversation*.[42] The author of *The History of Jack Connor* (1752) used some lines from the poem "Of Good-Nature," as a chapter-heading in his work;[43] and the first poem to Walpole in the *Miscellanies* was reprinted in a somewhat different form in Dodsley's *Collection of Poems in Six Volumes* of 1758. Gibbon's appreciation of Fielding as the "great master" whose *Journey from This World to*

---

[40] *Correspondence of Alexander Pope*, ed. George Sherburn (5v., Oxford, 1956), IV, 452.
[41] *The Works of Oliver Goldsmith*, ed. J. W. M. Gibbs (Bohn Library, 5v., 1884-86), V, 202. Fielding's actual words were: "That glavering sneering Smile, of which the greater Part of Mankind are extremely fond, conceiving it to be the Sign of Good-Nature; whereas this is generally a Compound of Malice and Fraud, and as surely indicates a bad Heart, as a galloping Pulse doth a Fever" (*Misc.*, I, 189).
[42] "According to the best writers on the subject of politeness (among whom I reckon Fielding, Swift, and Lord Chesterfield), 'he is the most polite man who makes his company easy and happy in his presence'" (*Edinburgh Fugitive Pieces, with Letters . . . by the Late William Creech* [Edinburgh and London, 1815], p. 150). Cf. Blanchard, p. 211.
[43] [William Chaigneau?], *The History of Jack Connor* (Dublin, 1752), I, 27, epigraph to Chapter IV.

the Next "may be considered as the history of human nature" led Lord Chedworth (in a letter of 1788) to wonder that he himself had been "so stupid as never to read" this work until he came across Gibbon's allusion.[44] But it is certain that neither the *Miscellanies* as a whole nor any of the individual pieces aroused anything like the amount of contemporary comment or discussion that attended *Joseph Andrews, Tom Jones*, and *Amelia*. This is not surprising, of course; but the actual paucity of reference to one of Fielding's most laborious and copious enterprises is disappointing.

All of the prose works in the *Miscellanies*, except the *Essay on Nothing*, were reprinted in the first collected edition of Fielding's *Works* in 1762. The omitted essay, which was reprinted by Isaac Reed in Volume IV of his *Repository* in 1783 (along with *Some Papers Proper to be Read before the Royal Society*), was first included in the collected works in 1806. But it was not until the edition of J. P. Browne in 1871-1872 that the whole of the *Miscellanies*, including the poems, was finally reprinted in a "complete" edition of the *Works*.

[44] Cited by Blanchard, p. 237. Gibbon's allusion, often mistakenly credited to *Tom Jones*, is in *The Decline and Fall of the Roman Empire*, ed. J. B. Bury (7v., 1897), III, 363, n. 13.

CHAPTER II. POETRY

Accept the Muse whom Truth inspires to sing, Who soars, tho' weakly, on an honest Wing.—*Liberty*

FIELDING is by no means a great poet, as he himself was quite ready to admit. A "correspondent" in the *Covent-Garden Journal* (No. 58, 8 August 1752) submitted his translation of Tibullus to Sir Alexander Drawcansir with the observation: "THO' your own Genius, I think, turns not much to Poetry, I do not suppose you are an Enemy to the Musical Inhabitants of Parnassus . . ." (Jensen, II, 74-75). In the preface to the *Miscellanies*, Fielding sounded a modest and extenuating note:

"The Poetical Pieces which compose the First Part of the First Volume, were most of them written when I was very young, and are indeed Productions of the Heart rather than of the Head. If the Good-natured Reader thinks them tolerable, it will answer my warmest Hopes. This Branch of Writing is what I very little pretend to, and will appear to have been very little my Pursuit, since I think (one or two Poems excepted) I have here presented my Reader with all I could remember, or procure Copies of"—(*Miscellanies*, I, ii).

Some of his light verse shows a flair for epigram and a satirical bite; but his longer poems display most of the defects common to those who attempted Popeian couplets without the rhythmical genius of a Pope. Yet, if Fielding cannot put ten good lines together without flaw, he offers a respectable number of satisfactory (or even striking) individual lines. And, though one must wince at the appearance of occasional candidates for the *Peri Bathous* (in nature, Fielding says, "Each [beast] freely dares his Appetite to treat, / Nor fears the Steed to neigh, the Flock to bleat"),[1] the poems are nevertheless worth a thoughtful perusal. The verse essays in particular repay the reader's attention with a concentrated and explicit rendering of themes that were to maintain a prominent place in Fielding's narratives.

One finds, in surveying Fielding's poetic output, that so far as the shorter poems are concerned (theatrical work apart), he was as good as his word in claiming to have presented here the bulk of them: inclusiveness indeed is the only reasonable excuse for the appearance of a few of his trifles. Not much of his short verse besides that included in this collection has come to light. A poem entitled "Plain Truth," on one of the reigning beauties of Bath, was included in Dodsley's *Collection* of 1758; a song on *The Beggar's Opera* attributed to Fielding was rediscovered in 1943; and attention has been called to "A DIALOGUE between a BEAU'S HEAD and his HEELS . . . By Mr. FIELDING," which appeared in the sixth volume of Watts's *Musical Miscellany* (6v., 1729-1731), and which could possibly be Timothy Fielding's rather than Henry's. In addition, there are a few poems in the *Champion* and the *Covent-Garden Journal* which Fielding may well have written himself.[2]

---

[1] *Misc.*, I, 21. The rhyming in some of the lyrics more befits an eager lover than a conscientious poet: Venus, in a poem "TO CELIA," sees Celia's "Bosom heave," because she "heard a distant Sound of Thieve" (*Misc.*, I, 57). One thinks of the scribblers in *The Author's Farce*: "DASH. . . . End rhymes very well with wind. BLOTPAGE. It will do well enough for the middle of a poem" (Henley, VIII, 217).

[2] Dodsley, V, 302-05 (the poem is reprinted in Henley, XII, 345-47); on the song, see Howard P. Vincent, "Early Poems by Henry Fielding," *N&Q*, CLXXXIV (1943), 159-60; the dialogue was also noted by Vincent and by Helen S. Hughes, "A Dialogue—Possibly by Henry Fielding," *PQ*, I (1922), 49-55. The suspicion that verses cited without attribution in Fielding's journals are often of his own composing is bolstered by the example of the lines in the *Champion*, 27 November 1739 (Henley, XV, 80), which are by him and reappear in his poem, *Of Good-Nature*. See also the *Covent-Garden Journal*, Nos. 28, 50, and 58 (Jensen, I, 298-300; II, 35-38; and II, 74-77). There are, in addition, such pieces as the song in *Joseph Andrews*, II, xii (Henley, I, 176-78) and the extemporary poem on Parson Adams made by the poet at the "roasting" squire's (*JA*, III, vii; Henley, I, 278).

POETRY

The most notable omissions from this collection of his poetry are the long poem (his first published work, so far as we know), The Masquerade, of 1728;[3] the mock-heroic Vernoniad of 1741; the three light-hearted poems attributed to him in the Dublin edition of The Important Triflers in 1749; various prologues and epilogues; and numerous songs from his plays. The songs, in particular, represent some of Fielding's best work in verse; and though he apparently was not concerned to collect them, they should be taken into account in any estimate of his poetic powers. At least two of them, "The Dusky Night Rides Down the Sky," and "The Roast Beef of Old England,"[4] are worthy of inclusion in any anthology of eighteenth-century poetry. They seem to spring directly from the heart of England, as the best of the old ballads do, and they are free of that more formal poetic manner Fielding usually assumed when he applied himself to verse.

The thirty-seven poems included in the Miscellanies display a surprising range of types, despite the fact that with one exception they are all couched in heroic or tetrameter couplets.[5] We are offered several verse essays and verse epistles, numerous epigrams and mock epitaphs, a rebus, two songs, a parody, a short translation, a burlesque imitation, and a number of light pieces in a romantic or satiric vein. Though perhaps no poet himself, Fielding shows a lively awareness of what other poets of his day were doing!

The models that Fielding set himself were apparently Pope (as one would expect) and Young, in the heroic couplet, and Butler and Prior in the octosyllabic line. This

---

[3] Cf. L. P. Goggin, "Fielding's The Masquerade," PQ, XXXVI (1957), 475-87.
[4] On the unresolved claim of Richard Leveridge to this latter song, of which there are several different versions, see Cross, I, 109-10, and Dudden, I, 94, n. 4.
[5] Eighteen of the poems are in heroic couplets, fourteen in octosyllabics, four in anapestic tetrameter, and one (a song) has the form 868688 (ababcc).

was the usual pattern for young versifiers of the time. An anonymous poet of 1729 complained of the octosyllabic tradition:

> As some will strain at Simily,
> First work it fine, and then apply,
> Add BUTLER's Rhymes, to PRIOR's Thoughts,
> And chuse to mimick others Faults:
> By Head and Shoulders, bring in a Stick,
> To shew their Knack at HUDIBRASTICK.
>
> ("To HENRY POWNEY, *Esq;*" in *Miscellaneous Poems*, ed. James Ralph [1729], pp. 174-75)

Hints and echoes from Gay and Swift may enter into Fielding's verse from time to time; but (though the Latin poets ever lurk in the background) this very nearly completes the range of significant influence that one can observe. No interest is shown in Miltonic or Spenserian imitations, in the pastoral or topographical poetry of his contemporaries, or in the lyric graces of Waller, Cowley, and Denham. Fielding owned the works of these latter influential poets and occasionally quoted them; but his own amorous lyrics strive for the good-humored ease of Prior, if anyone, not the liquid smoothness of the seventeenth-century group. The truth of the matter is that Fielding seldom displayed any very extensive enthusiasm for earlier English poetry. He was able to quote appropriately from Suckling ("and him of all the sweetest"—*Amelia*, VI, i) or Waller or Donne, as the occasion demanded; but he called upon the Restoration playwrights more frequently than the poets—and he manifestly preferred to quote Horace or Juvenal or Virgil to any of the English poets except Shakespeare. Doubts concerning the acuteness of his (English) poetic ear are unfortunately bolstered by noticing that when Fielding did cite something that pleased him, it frequently turned out to be—like the lines from Boyse's *Deity* in *Tom Jones* (VII, i)—a work of small poetic merit. It would appear that what interested Fielding was primarily the matter, the particular ideas expressed, rather than the manner; and the same emphasis can be seen in his own verse.

2

On the other hand, it must be said that Fielding had obviously studied in some detail the techniques that enabled Pope to combine ease and dignity in the movement of the verse essay. If this ultimate mastery was beyond his skill, he nevertheless learned to impart a variety to his couplets and an energy to his phrasing that rescue the verse essays of the *Miscellanies* from the droning banality of most of the Popeian epigoni. Brief pedestrian analysis of a random passage from one of the essays may serve to illustrate this point:

> While a mean Crowd of Sycophants attend,   1
> And fawn and flatter, creep and cringe and bend;   2
> The Fav'rite blesses his superior State,   3
> Rises o'er all, and hails Himself the Great.   4
> Vain Man! can such as these to Greatness raise?   5
> Can Honour come from Dirt? from Baseness, Praise?   6
> Then *India*'s Gem on *Scotland*'s Coast shall shine,   7
> And the *Peruvian* Ore enrich the *Cornish* Mine.   8
> (*Miscellanies*, I, 3-4)

The iambic rhythm is firmly established; but Fielding gains variety by a sprinkling of anapests ("superior State," "*India*'s Gem," and "*Peruvian* Ore");[6] by substitution of trochees in the initial foot (lines 1 and 4), or even (in line 8) by beginning with an anacrusis of two unstressed

---

[6] These apparent anapests may have been pronounced as iambics by synaeresis. Cf. Paul Fussell, Jr., *Theory of Prosody in Eighteenth-Century England* (New London, Conn., 1954), pp. 68-80.

syllables—though he may have intended this line as an Alexandrine. The position of the caesura, it will be noted, is varied in almost every line. The contrast and antithesis natural to the heroic couplet are turned to his thematic purpose—the contrast between false and true greatness—by such pairings as "Honour . . . Dirt" and "Baseness, Praise"; and the antithesis between the ideal and the pretended is reinforced by the mocking tone of the whole verse paragraph.

It is scarcely necessary to call attention to the devices borrowed from Pope (for though some of them are also in Dryden, there is little doubt that Pope was Fielding's model): the favorite scheme of a string of characterizing verbs connected by "and"; or the manner of imparting a forward movement to the verse through triads of predicates ("blesses . . . Rises . . . and hails"); the exclamatory apostrophe and rhetorical question; and the succession of questions resolved by an antithesis or a paradoxical statement. More specific echoes of Pope's very phrasing occur through all the verse essays.[7] Effects like these do not come by accident. They show clearly that Fielding in his younger days had set himself seriously to learn the art of writing verse—and, like most other literary youths, had chosen the reigning poets as his models.

This energetic interest in style, in the art of framing and disciplining his expression, Fielding of course carried over to his prose labors; and it is pleasant to speculate upon (though quite impossible to prove) the extent to which his apprenticeship in verse contributed to the bold assur-

---

[7] See, for example, the echoes of Pope's "Atticus" lines in the concluding stanza of the poem *Of True Greatness*, or the parallel with Pope's *Epilogue to the Satires* (Dialogue I, ll. 159-60) in Fielding's lines:
> . . . this *Gothick* Leaden Age . . .
> When Nonsense is a Term for the Sublime,
> And not to be an Ideot is a Crime (*Misc.*, I, 10).

Though, of course, Dryden also has: "a Clime / Where Vice triumphs, and Vertue is a Crime" (*Eleonora*, ll. 363-64; *Poems of John Dryden*, ed. James Kinsley [4v., Oxford, 1958], II, 594).

ance he achieved in prose. None of the varied tones of his poetry, from the rather hortatory verse essays to the cheerfully nonsensical lyrics, actually approached the perfectly controlled and well-mannered jocularity of his novels and humorous essays. Yet it must be remembered that much of the verse is youthful stuff and one should look not merely for parallels but for adumbrations. The light verse seems most immediately pertinent in this regard, for it displays something of that sportiveness and fine irreverence for pomposity that awaits us in the later comic works; but the verse essays, however stilted they may be (and they *are* stilted), probably have a greater significance for the development of Fielding's style. The easy fooling and burlesque came naturally to him; the light verse called for no effort. But it is obvious—even painfully obvious—that he had to struggle with the heroic couplet; and it is out of struggle that a controlled style emerges.

Anything that can be offered on this subject necessarily rests upon uncertainties. For example, if the verse essays are, as they seem to be, the work of the *Champion* years and after, then their relevance as discipline would seem questionable. Fielding was already turning out a mature and polished prose by that time. Nevertheless, the verse essays themselves testify to an earlier apprenticeship; it seems impossible to me that Fielding could have written poetry as technically competent, if uninspired, as this without a respectable amount of practice. And it is of the significance of this (unprovable but assumed) apprenticeship that I would hazard some remarks.

The heroic couplet is without doubt the most difficult English meter in which to write *well*; if Fielding never achieved a sense of ease and command in it, there is always the consolation that the poets who have can be numbered on the fingers of one hand. But assuredly it is excellent discipline—and the discipline alone, one would suppose, must have been fruitful. It could have helped to heighten a style that displayed an early tendency to veer toward the carefree "lowness" of Tom Brown and his compeers. Moreover, it could scarcely have failed to concentrate Fielding's attention upon niceties of diction—what has been called the "tact" of style. Fielding could not, in most of his verse, ascend to Pope's art of "endowing . . . common words with a power to surprise us";[8] but one may believe that the focus placed upon each individual word by the precise frame of the couplet (and the consequent necessity of rigorously selecting those words) made its own contribution to his supreme mastery in prose of that same power of surprising his reader with the complex overtones of common words.[9]

Whether Fielding's interest in rhetoric or in poetry came first we cannot say; but as the classical and Renaissance wedding of rhetoric and poetic had not yet quite come to unholy divorce, the point is perhaps merely academic. Certainly the poems display an inclusive acquaintance with the tropes and figures that gave a proper poetic pleasure to his contemporaries. Fielding could ring inventive metaphorical changes on the "character" of A Critic, portraying him in terms of a conquering general, a beau on the Grand Tour, a gardener, an insect, and a drone. And his individual metaphors were embellished through the devices of repetition, inversion, parallel, antithesis, and chiasmus that typically marked the rhetoric of the heroic couplet:

> Thro' Books some travel, as thro' Nations some,
> Proud of their Voyage, yet bring nothing home.
> Criticks thro' Books, as Beaus thro' Countries
>   stray,
> Certain to bring their Blemishes away.

. . . .

[8] Tillotson, *Pope and Human Nature* (Oxford, 1958), p. 168.
[9] One aspect of this question has been pleasantly treated by Sheridan Baker, in "Henry Fielding and the Cliché," *Criticism*, I (1959), 354-61.

POETRY

> Others, with friendly Eye run Authors o'er,
> Not to find Faults, but Beauties to restore;
> Nor scruple (such their Bounty) to afford
> Folios of Dulness to preserve a Word. . . .
>
> (1, 8)

Another example may indicate that Fielding had learned the Augustan trick of rising to an *epiphonema* (or forceful close) that on finer inspection proves to be an anticlimax:

> For now the Savage Host, o'erthrown and slain,
> New Titles, by new Methods, Kings obtain.
> To Priests and Lawyers soon their Arts apply'd,
> The People these, and those the Gods bely'd.
> The Gods, unheard, to Pow'r Successors name,
> And silent Crowds their Rights divine proclaim.
> Hence all the Evils which Mankind have known,
> The Priest's dark Mystery, the Tyrant's Throne;
> Hence Lords, and Ministers, and such sad Things;
> And hence the strange Divinity of Kings.
>
> (1, 23)

Again, the single verb with double subject and object of the fourth line and the paradox of the sixth are representative poetical-rhetorical devices, as is the *anaphora* of "Hence . . . Hence . . . ," with which he builds up to his anticlimactic climax. One more example, before we indulge in some generalizations, may serve to illustrate in its opening lines the Augustan fondness for *sententiae*, as well as Fielding's further use of some of the previously noted devices. It will be observed that this particular aphorism is given vigor through the combined forces of antithesis, paradox, *polyptoton* ("prone . . . proner"), *asyndeton* ("To cheat, deceive, conceal . . .") and inversion:

> Women by Nature form'd too prone to Ill,
> By Education are made proner still,

To cheat, deceive, conceal each genuine Thought,
By Mothers, and by Mistresses are taught.
The Face and Shape are first the Mother's Care;
The Dancing-Master next improves the Air.
To these Perfections add a Voice most sweet;
The skill'd Musician makes the Nymph compleat.
Thus with a Person well equipp'd, her Mind
Left, as when first created, rude and blind.
She's sent to make her Conquests on Mankind.

(I, 34)

It is possible, I think, without resorting to a documentary catalogue of devices, to maintain that a number of the particular techniques that Fielding employed in these poems also served him in his prose. We shall have occasion to remark, when we come to the prose of the essays in the *Miscellanies*, that he found the series of rhetorical questions, as well as the other very numerous devices of repetition and emphasis still useful in his essays and in his novels. The inversion of his poetry he could also (more rarely) use for particular effects in his prose—and even the alliteration in moments of heightened expression. And so on. All this is not to suggest that Fielding learned to use such elementary devices only through the writing of poetry. The point is, rather, that there exists a surprising family resemblance between the poetry and the prose despite Fielding's general ineptness in one and his greatness in the other. And this is not without interest.

The rhetoric of the heroic couplet as it is found from Jonson through Pope shares many of the characteristics of what has been called the "curt" form of Senecan prose. Most striking, perhaps, as Professor Williamson has pointed out, is their common dependence upon a group of rhetorical devices that Puttenham included under the denomination "Figures sententious"—namely, *epiphonema, sententia, antimetabole, antitheton,* and (much less in the often asymmetrical "curt" Senecan prose than in the symmetrical couplet) *parison*.[10] This cultivation of sententiousness, of epigrammatic point, of antithesis and witty inversion (*antimetabole* became the favored "turn" of Restoration poetics) had the effect in both prose and verse of tightening up the syntax and of producing a style that, as M. W. Croll has remarked, "is always tending toward the aphorism, or *pensée*, as its ideal form."[11]

Even at its most formal, Fielding's prose is obviously much more rhythmical and "loose" than the "curt" Senecan style, and his normal preference was for the hypotactic (subordinating) period, not the paratactic. I shall argue in the commentary upon the essays of the *Miscellanies* that his formal prose is a modification of the late-seventeenth-century "loose" Senecan style, which itself represented a modification of the "curt" form. Thus, although several steps removed from that style, his prose displays a certain lingering fondness for the "figures sententious," as well as for the rhetorical devices associated with the heroic couplet; and to this degree, it is allied to "the rhetoric of neo-classical wit" discussed by Williamson.

In this context of "neo-classical wit," the "family resemblance" between Fielding's verse and prose makes the gulf between them less unbridgeable. Hence the concentration in one upon techniques might well have had a salutary effect upon the other. But just as Fielding's heroic couplets are less compressed, much "freer" both in structure and diction than Pope's (Fielding's tendency was less toward what the period admired as "strength"[12] than toward the expansion of an idea), so, too, his prose displays a like

[10] George Williamson, "The Rhetorical Pattern of Neo-Classical Wit," *MP*, xxxiii (1935), 55-81; and *The Senecan Amble* (1951).
[11] Croll, "The Baroque Style in Prose," *Studies in English Philology, A Miscellany in Honor of Frederick Klaeber*, ed. Kemp Malone and Martin B. Ruud (Minneapolis, 1929), p. 435.
[12] See the brief but illuminating discussion of this conception in Donald Davie, *Articulate Energy: An Enquiry into the Syntax of English Poetry* (1955), pp. 56-64.

relationship to the "curt" Senecan prose whose shaping rhetoric was so much like that of the couplet. One can see, then, in both Fielding's verse and his prose, a development that moves away from the rhetoric of neo-classical wit at the same time that it conserves and exploits for its own purposes some of the characteristic features of that rhetoric. The happy blend of easy humor and formal dignity that this development brought to Fielding's prose may not be paralleled by an equal triumph in his verse, but both represent a kindred technical evolution from a kindred tradition. This, of course, is not unrelated to developments in the broader stream of eighteenth-century literature: the loosening of Pope's line was to be ultimately fatal for the couplet, but the new experiments in prose were to prove the greatest triumph of the century.

3

The points of *difference* between the poetry and the prose are too many and surely too apparent to summon critical commentary. One thing that stands out (negatively), however, is the comparative absence in his poetry of that most characteristic feature of Fielding's prose style, the parenthesis. Whether a simple parenthetical addition or reservation or whether a fully expanded commentary (as in the "rehearsal" plays and, frequently, in the novels), the parenthesis was accountable for much of Fielding's most delightful wit and humor—as well as for much of the complexity of judgment and response demanded from his reader. The verse essays, carrying few of those brilliant asides, subversive footnotes, or pleasant "undercuttings" of sententiousness, tend to set the preacher who always dwelt within the humorist in somewhat too bare a light. The verse essays have little of that secondary level of assesssment, that tentativeness of judgment (because, with some exceptions, Fielding could laugh at even his best-loved personal prejudices), in a word, that broadly ironic vision,

POETRY

which marked Fielding the novelist. And it is this fact, as much as the lack of a finished skill in versifying, that makes Fielding's poetry—even that of a later date—seem relatively immature and callow when set against his prose. The best productions in a poetic way in the *Miscellanies* are the brief jocose epistles and the burlesque or "realistic" items found among the collection of light verse. The love poems are more interesting for personal than for literary reasons; and the rhymed jests and epigrams are, of course, mere bagatelles. Much of this work strikes one as almost extemporaneous, as indeed several of the poems are declared to be; and to most of it we may apply Fielding's own observation (*Amelia*, VIII, viii; Henley, VII, 99) on a couplet of Vanbrugh's: "the sentiment is better than the poetry."

The patent shortcomings of his poetry admitted (as the author at the bail-house says to Booth, "Rhymes are difficult things; they are stubborn things, sir"), one may still argue that with a writer of Fielding's stature, even his comparative failures have their mite to contribute. I have no intention of seeking to rehabilitate Fielding's reputation as a poet; but I would insist that his verse invites heedful scrutiny. Many of these pieces display in embryo the wit and humor which were to inform the novels of his maturity. They testify to the variety of interests, literary and intellectual, that Fielding entertained at this period; and they point quite plainly the path that he would take, for the burlesque, the comic, chime rings pleasantly through this collection. They testify, further, to the energy with which Fielding set himself to school to learn the rhetorical and poetic techniques that would impart vigor and grace to the expression of his fundamental convictions. Finally, some of the poems give us personal and amusing insights into the character of the young Harry Fielding—insights that few of his other writings offer us— and this lends them an appeal well beyond anything they might legitimately demand on critical grounds.

POETRY

1. THE VERSE ESSAYS

The poems that smell most of the lamp are the five verse essays, which treat in turn five subjects very near to Fielding's heart—true greatness, good-nature, liberty, marriage, and the inconsistency of human nature. One need not dwell upon the importance of these themes to him. I shall wish to dwell, however (particularly with respect to "good-nature" and "liberty"), upon their complex significance for him and their relevance to his conception of the good society. For the common focus of these various abstract ideas is, after all, precisely that: the problem of the *civitas bona*. Like his classical mentors from Plato to Plutarch, like the great humorists and satirists he constantly invoked, and like the Christian humanists in whose tradition he stood, Fielding was passionately concerned with the human qualities and ideals that made for the realization of a just and virtuous society—and (necessarily) with the human flaws and follies that threatened it. This larger question offers a true center not only for the *Miscellanies*, but for Fielding's varied aims as a comic moralist. It provides a consistent pattern and intention for his portraits of social parasites and moral degenerates in the early "manners" comedies, his critical equation of vanity and hypocrisy with the "true ridiculous," his fictional dissection of the vices peculiar to selfishness and malice, and his unceasing attack on all forms of behavior contrary to man's moral nature—which to Fielding meant inevitably his *social* nature as well.

(1) "OF TRUE GREATNESS. An EPISTLE to The RIGHT HONOURABLE GEORGE DODINGTON, Esq;"

The *locus classicus* for Fielding's treatment of the theme of greatness is obviously *Jonathan Wild*, with its sustained ironic commentary on the "Great Man." But his most straightforward distinctions between true and sham greatness are contained in the preface to the *Miscellanies* and in this poem.[13]

> 'Tis strange, while all to Greatness Homage pay,
> So few should know the Goddess they obey.
> That Men should think a thousand Things the same,
> And give contending Images one Name.
>
> (*Misc.*, I, 3)

The poetic statement goes right to the heart of the matter in these opening lines: namely, the unhappy fact that society at large consistently fails to distinguish true greatness from sham pretensions, and thus lends the support of public admiration and approval, the *aura popularis*, to mere opportunists, demagogues, and rogues.[14] The dilemma is all too obviously one that we have not outgrown: each age has had to puzzle out its own analysis of this elementary but crucial human weakness that has plagued social philosophers from Plato to our own scientists of societal planning.

The problem is attacked in Fielding's poem through a sardonic review of the various claimants to "greatness"— the court favorite, the ascetic hermit, the conqueror, the learned pedant ("How pleas'd he smiles o'er Heaps of conquer'd Books"), the critic:

[13] *Of True Greatness*, along with *Some Papers Proper to be Read before the Royal Society* (q.v.) and *The Wedding Day*, had seen previous publication. The poem appeared in January 1741 (see Cross, III, 302-03), with a preface—not included in the *Miscellanies*—that defended Bubb Dodington against the attacks of Walpole's scribblers. The preface announced that the poem "was writ several Years ago, and comes forth now with a very few Additions or Alterations . . ." (p. 3).

[14] This fundamental contrast between true greatness and false—or, as it is often expressed, the *modern* conception of greatness—appears in its most characteristic form in an essay letter by Richard Steele, written some time during the first decade of the century ("Greatness Among the Moderns," a manuscript letter, first printed in *Tracts and Pamphlets by Richard Steele*, ed. Rae Blanchard [Baltimore, 1944], pp. 618-25). See J. R. Moore, "Steele's Unassigned Tract against the Earl of Oxford," *PQ*, XXVIII (1949), 413-18.

POETRY

> Great is the Man, who with unwearied Toil
> Spies a Weed springing in the richest Soil.
> If *Dryden's* Page with one bad Line be blest,
> 'Tis great to shew it, as to write the rest.
>
> (*Misc.*, I, 8)

An interesting indication of the improved stature of the once-scorned merchant in England near mid-century is given in the lines following (which express Fielding's normal attitude toward the worthy trader):

> Awake, ye useless Drones, and scorn to thrive
> On the Sweets gather'd by the lab'ring Hive.
> Behold, the Merchant give to Thousands Food,
> His Loss his own, his Gain the Publick Good.
> Her various Bounties Nature still confines,
> Here gilds her Sands, there silvers o'er her Mines:
> The Merchant's Bounty Nature's hath outdone,
> He gives to all, what she confines to one.
> And is he then not Great? Sir *B.* denies
> True Greatness to the Creature whom he buys;
> Blush the Wretch wounded, conscious of his
>   Guile.
> B[ar]nard and H[eath]cote at such Satyr smile.
>
> (*Misc.*, I, 8-9)

The necessities of his theme lead Fielding to say, "But if a Merchant lives, who meanly deigns / To sacrifice his Country to his Gains," that such a (presumably untypical) wretch is ranked "with the meanest Throng."

The review continues, with commendable objectivity, by subjecting the claim of the poet to analysis:

> Thus the great tatter'd Bard, as thro' the Streets
> He cautious treads, least any Bailiff meets.
> . . . .
> . . . with Want and with Contempt opprest,
> Shunn'd, hated, mock'd, at once Men's Scorn and
>   Jest,

44

POETRY

Perhaps, from wholesome Air itself confin'd,
Who hopes to drive out Greatness from his Mind?
(Misc., I, 10)

And Fielding suggests, rather coyly, "Some Greatness in myself, perhaps I view; / Not that I write, but that I write to you." Then, after an assertion that his satire assuredly is not aimed at good poets, he turns to his last subject, one that he could attack with unfeigned enthusiasm: the beau. The most vigorous lines of the poem, with almost a Popeian ring, are devoted to this miserable creature:

> The lowest Beau that skips about a Court,
> The Lady's Play-thing, and the Footman's Sport;
> Whose Head adorn'd with Bag or Tail of Pig,
> Serves very well to bear about his Wig;
> Himself the Sign-Post of his Taylor's Trade,
> That shews abroad, how well his Cloaths are made;
> This little, empty, silly, trifling Toy,
> Can from Ambition feel a Kind of Joy;
> Can swell, and even aim at looking wise,
> And walking Merit from *its* Chair despise.
(Misc., I, 11-12)

What wonder then, Fielding inquires, that "all Men find a Corner to be Great," that every little squire with a few underlings can suppose himself to possess the qualities of greatness? But the claim of each of the types reviewed is patently spurious; for, in Fielding's view, none of these *soi-disant* "great men" makes any significant contribution to humanity, none represents that full realization of man's potential capacities as a social being, wherein true greatness lies.

> To no Profession, Party, Place confin'd,
> True Greatness lives but in the noble Mind;
> Him constant through each various Scene attends,
> Fierce to his Foes, and faithful to his Friends.
(Misc., I, 13)

So he is able to pay tribute to his hero, Marlborough (I, 7), and to those of his contemporaries—Hoadly, Argyll, Sir William Lee, and Carteret, Chesterfield, and Lyttelton —who were representative, as he saw it, of this "True Greatness" in the religious, military, judiciary, and political spheres (I, 13). In a concluding stanza he describes his ideal:

> Lives there a Man, by Nature form'd to please,
> To think with Dignity, express with Ease;
> Upright in Principle, in Council strong,
> Prone not to change, nor obstinate too long:
> . . . .
> To whose blest Lot superior Portions fall,
> To most of Fortune, and of Taste to all,
> Aw'd not by Fear, by Prejudice not sway'd,
> By Fashion led not, nor by Whim betray'd,
> By Candour only bias'd, who shall dare
> To view and judge and speak Men as they are.
> In him, (if such there be) is Greatness shewn. . . .
>   (*Misc.*, I, 13-14)[15]

This, then, is the *"true Sublime* in Human Nature" to which Fielding refers in the preface to the *Miscellanies* (I, xxviii). In that crucial discussion he maintains that *three* kinds of character are involved in the concept of greatness. The opposition of goodness and greatness in the structure of Fielding's moral hierarchy has often been remarked: this simple dichotomy is complicated, however, by the further distinction between true and false greatness, a *tertium quid* made explicit in the preface and in this poem, and implicit, I believe, in all of Fielding's work. As that greatness devoid of goodness represents the false sublime

---

[15] One cannot deny that the concluding line is somewhat anticlimactic: "In him, (if such there be) is Greatness shewn, / Nor can he be to *Dodington* unknown." Fielding's extravagant compliments to Dodington ("one of the greatest men this country ever produced"—*Amelia*, XI, ii; Henley, VII, 251) always come as something of a shock.

in human nature, so the great-and-good is the true sublime. Mere goodness alone, on the other hand, is meritable and warrants our love, but it seldom has the "parts" or genius to attain true greatness, which is, among other things, "the Union of a good Heart with a good Head" (*Misc.*, I, xxviii-xxix and p. 145).

Goodness alone may be seen in the character of Heartfree in *Jonathan Wild;* and his simple-minded honesty has sometimes been taken as representing Fielding's ideal for human nature. In one sense, perhaps, this is true: Heartfree's goodness represents the *root* quality necessary to the social (or, one might say, the Christian) man. It is the quality absolutely lacking in the false sublime of Jonathan Wild himself, of the politicians in the early farces, and most of the noble lords scattered through Fielding's plays and novels. But mere uninformed and unarmed goodness possesses a dangerously negative character. Although Heartfree is "by no Means a Fool" (*JW*, II, ii; *Misc.*, III, 109), the kind of trusting simplicity he represents is precisely the quality that permits hypocritical and designing villains like Wild to exist and thrive.[16] The lesson that most of Fielding's good-natured characters—Mr. Boncour, Heartfree, Joseph Andrews, Tom Jones, Booth—must learn, in one way or another, is that goodness alone, unsupported by social intelligence or prudence or the higher moral imperative of religion, is not enough in the world as it is. A major portion of the material in the *Miscellanies* is concerned with the serious attempt to educate men of good will in the additional qualities that must be added to goodness if it is to be a truly valid and useful social force—and these qualities lie on the line leading to true greatness.

The combination of good-and-great appears, if at all in Fielding's novels, in Squire Allworthy and Dr. Harrison;

[16] This point has also been made by Allan Wendt in "The Moral Allegory of *Jonathan Wild*," ELH, XXIV (1957), 306-20.

POETRY

but perhaps nowhere in his fiction does Fielding really try to embody through a single character this idea in its highest form: the benevolent and wise statesman of the order depicted in the lines that close our poem.[17] This may be due to nothing more than a simple disinclination on Fielding's part to treat of statesmanship fictionally; or, as I rather suspect, it may be that Fielding was himself more keenly interested in the earthier human qualities of the average "good" man (which offered such varied grist for his comic mill) than in the somewhat awesome dignity of the "true sublime."[18] In his dramatized moral scheme, the latter functioned rather as an implicit ideal balance of qualities that few men in common life needed fully developed, but that all good men could use as a source of moral inspiration and model of worldly sapience: "This is indeed a glorious

[17] See also the discussion of the qualities of a good statesman in the *True Patriot*, No. 8 (24 December 1745). Fielding's ideal statesman may be compared with the portrait sketched by "Walpole's poet," Joseph Mitchell, some years earlier:

> True *Greatness* most superior Worth displays,
> When with false *Lustre* we compare its *Rays*.
>
> . . . .
>
> The Man, whose Vertues shew his noble Blood,
> Can risque his Fortune for his Country's Good;
> Abhors all selfish, mean and private Ends;
> Relieves the Needy, and obliges Friends;
> Ne'er from the golden Rules of Order swerves;
> Nor fears the Stings of Envy, nor deserves;
> Who ev'ry Thing at its just Value rates;
> Nor courts blind Fortune's bounteous Gifts, nor Hates;
> And, 'midst the Charms of Nature, and of Art,
> Is modest still, and humble in his Heart:
> 'Tis *He*, that best deserves our chosen Lays—
> A Man, so great, 'tis impious not to Praise.
>   ("To the Right Honourable CHARLES, Earl of Lauderdale, &c." in Mitchell's *Poems on Several Occasions* [2v., 1729], I, 265-66)

Such pictures as this or Hildebrand Jacob's in "The Patriot" (*Works* [1735], pp. 10-11) show that there was nothing novel in Fielding's portrait. The "truly great" statesman was essentially Aristotle's magnanimous man and Cicero's *vir honestus* with benevolist trimmings.

[18] A more subtle examination of this question may be found in the opening pages of an essay by William B. Coley, "The Background of Fielding's Laughter," *ELH*, XXVI (1959), 229-52.

48

Object, on which we can never gaze with too much Praise and Admiration" (*Misc.*, I, xxviii).

If ordinary men need models of rectitude and true greatness, however, they can also well use cautionary examples of the false semblances of greatness and goodness that abound in a less-than-perfect world. The utter antithesis of true greatness is the false "hero-statesman," the darling of the *mobile vulgus*, who cheats the people into believing he is their champion and has their interests at heart, in order to feed his own monstrous egoism and his private ambitions. This vicious breed represents the epitome of the false sublime, and it is this "Bombast Greatness" that Fielding concerned himself to expose in *Jonathan Wild*, and toward which throughout his career he maintained the most relentless and bitter indignation. A "Composition of Cruelty, Lust, Avarice, Rapine, Insolence, Hypocrisy, Fraud and Treachery [almost the definitive pantheon of Fielding's antipathies!] . . . glossed over with Wealth and a Title, [has] been treated with the highest Respect and Veneration," he says scornfully in the preface to the *Miscellanies* (I, xxi). But "greatness" of this kind consists "in bringing all Manner of Mischief on Mankind" (*JW*, I, i; *Misc.*, III, 4). It grinds up all considerations of human integrity and the welfare of mankind in the maw of its hungry lust for personal aggrandizement. The components of this "greatness," as exemplified in Jonathan Wild, are overriding ambition, sneaking ingenuity, dishonesty, and the "pantheon" cited above, combined with an utter lack of humility and good-nature. Most characteristic, however, is its *insatiability*. "For this restless amiable Disposition, this noble Avidity which encreases with Feeding, is the first Principle or constituent Quality of these our GREAT MEN . . ." (*JW*, I, xiv; *Misc.*, III, 85). Modern sociologists and criminologists have of late been making much of the "discovery" that the truly criminal personality invariably displays an egoism that cannot brook frustration and that cannot enter imaginatively into the feelings of other persons. This would scarcely have come as a surprise to Henry Fielding.

The "Bombast Greatness" of *Jonathan Wild* is, like the "True Sublime" of the poem under consideration, almost *sui generis* in Fielding's work. In his other novels and plays—and in the body of the poem "Of True Greatness"—he set himself to rip the mask of social and moral respectability from the numerous *minor* claimants to the titles of goodness and greatness. These manifested a less dramatic but a more omnipresent problem. The question that Fielding asked again and again was: how is it possible that the public can tolerate such impostors, much less—God save the mark!—admire and respect and emulate them? Unwilling to believe that human nature is so degraded as actually to sanction and exalt greatness of this cast, he came in the course of his career to two fundamental conclusions: first, that men do not in general know their own true interests, and therefore require education in social values;[19] secondly, that good men are essentially gullible, and easily fall victim to the false pretensions of "Great Men." Like Parson Adams, as they never have an intention to deceive, so they never suspect such a design in others.[20] Part of the task of the socially responsible writer, then, was to place spurious

[19] Cf. the *True Patriot*, No. 6 (10 December 1745): "NOtwithstanding the universal Desire of Happiness which Nature hath implanted in the Mind of every Man, such are the Mistakes both in Opinion and Practice, and so far are the Actions of the Generality of Mankind from having any visible Tendency towards their real Good, that one is sometimes tempted to predicate of the human Species, that Man is an Animal which industriously seeks his own Misery."

[20] As Queen Common-Sense says in *Pasquin* (Act v; Henley, xi, 220): "Could Common-sense bear universal sway, / No fool could ever possibly be great." But the lamentable failure in common sense is dramatized by such ridiculous actions as that of the "Debtors" of Newgate (that is, the voting public) who take violent sides in the Wild-Johnson opposition, though they are "the destined Plunder of both Parties" (*JW*, iv, iii; *Misc.*, iii, 305). Fielding's point is underlined by the "very grave Man" who points out to them that they will continue to be dupes until they reform their own manners and set up adequate political ideals.

greatness in such a light that honest men could clearly see it in its actual meanness and egoism. The other part of the task was to contribute to the understanding of a true and valid social ideal, an understanding of true greatness. To these ends (among others, of course) Fielding dedicated not only many of his serious poems and essays but also the persuasive force of his comic pen.

2

Some further significant comments on the theme of greatness are to be found in the preface to the *Miscellanies*. One of these is Fielding's exasperated outburst: "Nothing seems to me more preposterous than that, while the Way to true Honour lies so open and plain, Men should seek false by such perverse and rugged Paths: that while it is so easy and safe, and truly honourable, to be good, Men should wade through Difficulty and Danger, and real Infamy, to be *Great*, or, to use a synonimous Word, *Villains*"—(*Misc.*, I, xxii-xxiii). This perverse ambition in some men seems genuinely to have been inexplicable to Fielding. He dramatized the same idea in the *Journey from This World to the Next* (chap. v), where he portrayed two roads leading back to the earth from the other world: one road was beset with briars and bogs, whereas the second wound through verdant meadows, bright with flowers. The traveller saw to his astonishment great crowds of "new-born" souls attacking the dangers of the bad road and only a few solitary spirits moving down the sweet path of the other—these being, as someone explained to him, the roads to greatness and goodness respectively.[21]

[21] The two roads are, of course, an ancient allegorical emblem. A contemporary, the anonymous author of a parody of Bunyan called *The Statesman's Progress, or a Pilgrimage to Greatness* (1741), had pictured Badman abandoning the difficult road that Truth was leading him to "Greatness-Hill," and gaining it more quickly by way of "Vice-Road" (pp. 7-13; cited by W. R. Irwin, *The Making of Jonathan Wild* [New York, 1941], pp. 46-47). Some fifty years earlier, one G. B. (George

POETRY

Fielding never ceased to marvel that men should choose this danger, difficulty, and disgrace, in preference to the rewards of honor and decency. Even the life of a beggar, he insisted, was more desirable than that existence which found itself tortured by the relentless goad of Ambition (cf. the *Journey from This World to the Next*, chap. xix; *Misc.*, II, 160). Throughout *Jonathan Wild* this point is labored: "What can be imagined more miserable than a *Prig* [in this context, a "Great Man"]? How dangerous are his Acquisitions! how unsafe, how unquiet his Possessions! Why then should any Man wish to be a *Prig*, or where is his GREATNESS?" (II, IV; *Misc.*, III, 125). Wild is forced so consistently to be on his guard and in a state of apprehension "that his Condition, to any other than the glorious Eye of Ambition, might seem rather deplorable, than the Object of Envy or Desire" (III, xiv; *Misc.*, III, 275). The Ordinary of Newgate rings a final change on this theme, when in one of the few straightforward speeches given to him, he compares the pains of Hell with the joys of Heaven, and demands: "Who then would, for the pitiful Consideration of the Riches and Pleasures of this World, forfeit such inestimable Happiness! ... Or who would run the Venture of such Misery, which, but to think on, shocks the human Understanding! Who, in his Senses, then would prefer the latter to the former?" (IV, xiv; *Misc.*, III, 388). Fielding's own conclusion is that "when we reflect on the Labours and Pains, the Cares, Disquietudes, and Dangers which at-

---

Burghope?) had put the case against this pursuit of "greatness" in eloquent terms: "And for the desire of being great I would fain know where's the Pleasure of forcing a Man's Way through the Briars and Thorns, the Dark Methods of Secret Plots, and the Labyrinths of Infernal Combinations? When by many dangerous Steps he is arriv'd at the unsteady Seat of Greatness, and has put on the (*Incendialis Toga*, the) poisonous Robe of Jealousies and Fears; When he is hated by some, and feared by others, and made a common Curse by most; Is this that which you call a state of Happiness?" (*Autarchy: or, The Art of Self-Government* [1691], pp. 77-78). Cf. the famous passage in Lucretius, concluding, "o miseras hominum mentes, o pectora caeca!" (*De rerum natura* II.7-14; also V.1120-35).

52

tend their Road to GREATNESS, we may say with the Divine, *that a Man may go to Heaven with half the Pains which it costs him to purchase Hell . . ."* (IV, xvi; *Misc.*, III, 420). And as an important corollary to this view, Fielding says in his preface: "Tho' it is, I believe, impossible to give Vice a true Relish of Honour and Glory, or tho' we give it Riches and Power, to give it the Enjoyment of them, yet it contaminates the Food it can't taste, and sullies the Robe which neither fits nor becomes it, 'till Virtue disdains them both" (*Misc.*, I, xxx-xxxi). The first part of his statement represents a conviction that Fielding held to in everything he wrote: that evil in the final analysis could not, by its inherent nature, enjoy or truly savor the things it staked its all to gain. This was the ultimate irony—and the tragic comedy—of greatness.

Although the specific target in Fielding's most pointed attacks on greatness was obviously Sir Robert Walpole, there are, as we have seen, broader implications to his critique than the merely political. W. R. Irwin has pointed out that "the basic idea of greatness—the quality which 'consists in bringing all Manner of Mischief on Mankind'—was a moral commonplace during the first half of the eighteenth century."[22] Irwin has documented copiously this attack of the eighteenth-century moralists on greatness and great men—whether statesmen, courtiers, conquerors, or tyrants—as the symbols of an insatiable lust for power and wealth, which ignored the tenets of both philosophic and religious morality.[23] The larger moral opposition appears, for ex-

[22] *Op.cit.*, p. 55.
[23] The conventional attitude of the pulpit toward "greatness" was clearly expressed by one of Fielding's favorite divines, Isaac Barrow: "Great men should not take themselves for another sort of creatures, or another race of men than their poor neighbours; that the world is theirs, and all things are for them; that they may do what they please; that they are exempted from laws, which oblige others; for in moral and spiritual accounts they are upon a level with others. They are but fellow-subjects and fellow-servants with others; all accountable to the same Master" (Sermon LVII, "No Respect of Persons with God," in the *Theological Works of Isaac Barrow, D.D.*, ed. Alexander Napier [9v., Cambridge,

ample, in John Rooke's dedication to George II of his translation of Arrian (1729); Rooke "emphasizes the contrast between Alexander's 'mistaken Greatness' and George's 'real Goodness.' "[24] A similar and doubtless more valid contrast furnishes the dominant dramatic emphasis of Fielding's *Jonathan Wild*, with its juxtaposition of Wild's "mistaken Greatness" and Heartfree's "real Goodness." The poem, *Of True Greatness*, in picturing a greatness beyond moral censure, a nobility which is as good as it is great, adds another dimension to the basic contrast.

If *Of True Greatness* illuminates the opposition of genuine versus sham, the poem next to be considered, *Of Good-Nature*, serves to complete the levels of contrast. As we have already noted, Fielding's comic imagination was more taken by the dramatic conflict of false greatness with artless good-nature than by that of the two kinds of greatness, and it is the former which is made the focus of most of his writings on the subject. But the particular importance of this poem is that it presents us with a necessary constituent in the *implicit* structure of Fielding's moral view of man—the opposition of true and false greatness—a constituent that was seldom so clearly delineated elsewhere in his work.

(2) "OF GOOD-NATURE. To his GRACE the DUKE of RICHMOND."

"Good-Nature" is (to borrow a word from philology) a holophrastic term for Fielding, the compend of an attitude.

1859], IV, 269). Fielding echoes Barrow's criticism in *Amelia*, x, ix (Henley, VII, 236). One may observe that in the *Covent-Garden Journal*, long after the personal application to Walpole of the term "Great Man" had become stale (in 1754, the revised *Jonathan Wild* eliminated many of the details and characterizing phrases linking Wild to Walpole, though the general identification was preserved), Fielding defined the term in his "Modern Glossary": "GREAT. Applied to a Thing, signifies Bigness; when to a Man, often Littleness, or Meanness" (No. 4; Jensen, I, 156). Fielding's lifelong attack on false greatness had larger aims than the displacement of Walpole, who simply served as a convenient and representative symbol of the more general evil.

[24] Cf. Irwin, p. 121, n. 34.

He defined it variously in various places—sometimes it seems to be a passion, at other times a faculty of moral judgment, or even a moral abstraction, like "virtue"—but it remained for him the core of a complex of ideas having to do with moral man. The poem that he dedicated to Richmond, taken in conjunction with a significant essay in the *Champion*, offers some useful insights into the associations that "Good-Nature" had for Fielding in his early career.[25]

He begins his poem with the rhetorical question: "WHAT is Good-nature?"

> Is it a foolish Weakness in the Breast,
> As some who know, or have it not, contest?
> Or is it rather not the mighty whole
> Full Composition of a virtuous Soul?
> Is it not Virtue's Self? A Flow'r so fine,
> It only grows in Soils almost divine.
> (*Misc.*, I, 15)

Indeed, he continues, although some virtues can exist side by side with vices in the same person's character, good-nature cannot:

> Good-nature, like the delicatest Seeds,
> Or dies itself, or else extirpates Weeds.
> (*Misc.*, I, 15)

[25] In the sixth issue of the *Champion* (27 November 1739), Fielding quoted four lines from a poem "not yet communicated to the public":
> Nor in the tiger's cave, nor lion's den,
> Dwells our malignity. For selfish men,
> The gift of fame like that of money deem;
> And think they lose, whene'er they give esteem.
> (Henley, xv, 80)

As John E. Wells noted ("Fielding's Signatures in 'The Champion,' and the Date of His 'Of Good-Nature,'" *MLR*, VII [1912], 97-98), these lines, in a slightly different form, occur in the *Miscellanies* in the poem, *Of Good-Nature*. Thus it is certain that at least some of the poem had been written before November 1739, and also that before including it in the collection of 1743, Fielding had reworked it, as he seems to have done with much of his material. A compliment to Henry Bromley, first Baron Montfort (the "Mountford" of *Misc.*, I, 19) presumably can be dated after his elevation to the peerage in May 1741.

POETRY

This assertion, that good-nature drives out vice or itself disappears, is somewhat enthusiastic;[26] but Fielding may have genuinely believed, at this point in his career, that such a sweeping statement had real psychological validity, and the ancient Stoic paradox that virtue and vice could not exist together provided a traditional sanction for it. He certainly continued to believe that the truly good-natured man should be incapable of an intentionally mean or vicious act.

The poem goes on to warn that no virtue is so easily feigned as this one; and that frequently we mistake for good-nature those actions which have their source in other passions: friendship, love (or even lust), pride, or fear. (In the essay *On the Knowledge of the Characters of Men*, he added that "Good-Humour," too, is often mistaken for "Good-Nature," although the former "is nothing more than the Triumph of the Mind, when reflecting on its own Happiness, and that perhaps from having compared it with the inferior Happiness of others") (*Misc.*, I, 190). What, then, is the *true* mark of good-nature?

What by this Name, then, shall be understood?
What? but the glorious Lust of doing Good?
The Heart that finds it Happiness to please,
Can feel another's Pain, and taste his Ease.
The Cheek that with another's Joy can glow,
Turn pale, and sicken with another's Woe;
Free from Contempt and Envy, he who deems
Justly of Life's two opposite Extremes.

[26] The admirers of good-nature customarily waxed more than eloquent in its praise: two early celebrants (of a multitude), Benjamin Whichcote and Samuel Parker the Younger could cry, as enthusiastically as Fielding, "*They* that maintain the Principle of *good Nature*, are the Representatives of God in the World" (Whichcote, Sermon VI in *Select Sermons of Dr Whichcot* [1698], p. 218), or "Malice and Envy lose all their Force, and blush at their own Deformity, when Good Nature encounters 'em. This is that bright *Astræa*, which as she cannot abide, but in an Heavenly Soul; so makes a golden Age, a *Millennial* State, as it were, where'er she comes" (Parker, "OF GOOD NATURE," Letter x in *Sylva* [1701], pp. 214-15).

56

POETRY

Who to make all and each Man truly blest,
Doth all he can, and wishes all the rest?
(*Misc.*, I, 16)

This "glorious Lust of doing Good," arising from a sympathetic identification with others' woes, remained a primary element in Fielding's conception of good-nature. The first part was common to the whole benevolist tradition, but the second—sympathetic identification, or what we tend today inaccurately to call "empathy"—is, though not original with Fielding, an interesting anticipation of Adam Smith's moral theories basing sympathy upon the ability of the imagination to form a picture and thereby enter into another's woes or joy.[27] Fielding's great effort in his imaginative works was to set a speaking picture before his readers' eyes that would compel such a sympathetic identification. Often the novels invited in dramatic terms what Fielding asked directly of his readers in the *Enquiry into the Causes of the Late Increase of Robbers*: "Let the good-natured man, who hath any understanding, place this picture before his eyes, and then see what figure in it will be the object of his compassion." (Henley, XIII, 112).

Fielding now turns in his poem to a celebration of Richmond[28] as the exemplar of good-nature ("Happy the Man with Passions blest like you, / Who to be ill, his Nature must subdue"), and, in effect, narrows his subject down to

[27] *The Theory of Moral Sentiments* (1759), Part I, Section i. Ernest Tuveson has remarked the significance of Locke's "yoking of the image to thought" and placing "the pivot of intellectual action in the imagination," in its impact on Shaftesbury and Addison ("The Importance of Shaftesbury," *ELH*, XX [1953], 278-79, and n. 22). Fielding—or Adam Smith, for that matter—could have drawn upon all three of these popular ethical writers for his own sense of the efficacy of the image in creating emotional identification.

[28] Fielding's celebration of Richmond's generosity seemingly proved inefficacious for, as we have seen, the Duke's name does not appear in the subscription list of the *Miscellanies*. *The Miser* had been dedicated to Richmond in 1733; but after 1735 the Duke had become a strong supporter of Walpole. This does not necessarily mean that he had ceased to patronize Fielding, however; there may be some other explanation for his missing name.

an identification of good-nature with the virtue of pecuniary charity. In the preliminary lines:

> High on Life's Summit rais'd, you little know
> The Ills which blacken all the Vales below;
> Where Industry toils for Support in vain,
> And Virtue to Distress still joins Disdain.
> Swelt'ring with Wealth, where Men unmov'd can hear
> The Orphans sigh, and see the Widow's Tear:
> Where griping Av'rice slights the Debtor's Pray'r,
> And Wretches wanting Bread deprives of Air.
>
> (*Misc.*, I, 17)

After these vigorous lines, his theme leads Fielding into a primitivistic strain:

> So full the Stream of Nature's Bounty flows,
> Man feels no Ill, but what to Man he owes.
> The Earth abundant furnishes a Store,
> To sate the Rich, and satisfy the Poor.
>
> . . . .
>
> See how the lowing Herd, and bleating Flock,
> Promiscuous graze the Valley, or the Rock;
> Each tastes his Share of Nature's gen'ral Good,
> Nor strives from others to with-hold their Food.
> But say, O Man! wou'd it not strange appear
> To see some Beast (perhaps the meanest there)
> To his Repast the sweetest Pastures chuse,
> And ev'n the sourest to the rest refuse.
>
> (*Misc.*, I, 17-18)[29]

A diatribe against the uncharitable ("And dost thou, common Son of Nature, dare / From thy own Brother to withhold his Share?") is quite fitting in this context; but Fielding then leaps without transition into an attack upon the

---

[29] Cf. the letter of "Misargurus" in *CGJ*, No. 35: "Where there are no Rich, there will of Consequence be found no Poor: For Providence hath in a wonderful Manner provided in every Country, a plentiful Subsistence for all its Inhabitants; and where none abound, none can want" (Jensen, I, 339-40).

POETRY

censorious, those who refuse another "the cheap Gift of Fame":

> Dwells there a base Malignity in Men,
> That 'scapes the Tiger's Cave, or Lion's Den?
> Does our Fear dread, or does our Envy hate
> To see another happy, good, or great?
> Or does the Gift of Fame, like Money, seem?
> Think we, we lose, whene'er we give Esteem?
> (*Misc.*, I, 18-19)[30]

These are the lines (revised) that Fielding had earlier published in the *Champion* (see above, n. 25); and one wonders whether the poem in its original form might not have dealt more at large with such antitypes of good-nature as envy and censoriousness and less with the virtue of opening one's pockets to worthy men in need. The transition at this point is certainly abrupt. The concluding lines of the poem follow well enough upon this section, however, consisting of a series of compliments to patrons and patronesses which illustrate the related theme that good-nature does not make invidious comparisons:

> Oh! great Humanity, whose Beams benign,
> Like the Sun's Rays, on just and unjust shine;
> Who turning the Perspective friendly still,
> Doth magnify all Good, and lessen Ill;
> Whose Eye, while small Perfections it commends,
> Not to what's better, but what's worse attends....
> (*Misc.*, I, 19)

That is, good-nature does not dismiss minor beauties by calling attention to the transcendent Countess of Shaftesbury or Duchess of Richmond; it does not lessen average "Sense and Goodness" by contrasting Montfort's fame.

[30] On Fielding's attitude toward censoriousness and "a base Malignity in Men," see below, *Essay on the Knowledge of the Characters of Men.*

Where much is Right, some Blemishes afford,
Nor look for Ch[esterfiel]d in ev'ry Lord.

(*Misc.*, I, 19)

2

If far from satisfactory as a poem, *Of Good-Nature* is interesting for its assertions about the virtue most often associated with Fielding. A number of these assertions had been set forth in a prose essay of 27 March 1740 in the *Champion*. "Good-nature," Fielding there said, "is a delight in the happiness of mankind, and a concern at their misery, with a desire, as much as possible, to procure the former, and avert the latter; and this, *with a constant regard to desert*";[31] and he continued, "as good-nature *requires a distinguishing faculty*, which is another word for judgment, and is perhaps the sole boundary between wisdom and folly; it is impossible for a fool, who hath no distinguishing faculty, to be good-natured" (Henley, xv, 258; italics mine). The italicized phrases should be particularly noted, because the emphasis on judgment in Fielding's conception of good-nature has been sometimes ignored, despite his frequent insistence upon it.[32] It is in part this emphasis that distinguishes Fielding's "good-nature" from the indiscriminate sentimentalism that flourished later in the century.

Having called attention to the distinction, however, one must also admit that Fielding himself did not always abide by the standard that good-nature involves good judgment

[31] Cicero's *beneficentia* or *liberalitas* is a somewhat sterner concept than Fielding's "good-nature" or "charity"; but the *De officiis* (I. xiv. 42) stresses, as Fielding does, the fact that beneficence should be proportioned to the merit of the recipient (*ut pro dignitate cuique tribuatur*), for only this is justice. Eighteenth-century divines frequently made the same point in speaking of charity.

[32] Cf., for example, the *Champion*, 16 February 1740 (Henley, xv, 203-07); the *True Patriot*, No. 8, 24 December 1745; the "Proceedings at the Court of Criticism" in the *Jacobite's Journal*, Nos. 31-32, 2 and 9 July 1748; *Tom Jones*, IV, vi (Henley, III, 164); the *Enquiry into the Causes of the Late Increase of Robbers* (Henley, XIII, 110); and *CGJ*, No. 44 (Jensen, II, 9-13).

as well as tenderness of heart. All the examples of and allusions to good-nature in Fielding's works could perhaps be arranged on a scale or continuum of values, with a conception such as the foregoing at one end and (alas!) a rather cloying faith in the "self-approving joy" of benevolent actions at the other. Such a scale, indeed, would run roughly parallel to the line between true greatness (the union of a good heart with a good head) and mere goodness that has previously been posited. The upper end remains the ideal, but Fielding often slides off (if one may so phrase it) into a less qualified admiration for simple goodness or the overflowing heart.

The truth is, that although Fielding was likely to emphasize good judgment when defining "good-nature" or in discussing the proper allocation of charity, he had an overriding faith in "natural" feelings. For all his honest (and meaningful, let us not forget) bows to reason and judgment, he clearly could not feel that they *alone* were completely dependable assurances of benevolent conduct. As he put it in *Amelia*, discussing the possibility of a friendship not based upon tenderness: "Such friendship is never to be absolutely depended on; for whenever the favorite passion interposes with it, it is sure to subside and vanish into air. Whereas the man whose tender disposition really feels the miseries of another will endeavor to relieve them for his own sake; and in such a mind friendship will often get the superiority over every other passion" (VIII, v; Henley, VII, 90).

The frequent emphasis on judgment rather than feeling, however, arose in part from Fielding's concern to obviate the charge that good-nature was a mere passive sentiment, "a foolish Weakness in the Breast, / As some who know, or have it not, contest." In the *Champion* he insisted that "good-nature is not that weakness which, without distinction, affects both the virtuous and the base, and equally laments the punishment of villainy, with the disappointment of merit; for as this admirable quality respects the whole, so it must give up the particular, to the good of the general.

"It is not that cowardice which prevents us from repelling or resenting an injury; for it doth not divest us of humanity, and like charity, though it doth not end, may at least begin at home"—(27 March 1740; Henley, xv, 258).

Good-nature does not exclude just punishment of crime, nor (we may particularly note) is it inconsistent with satire of vice and folly; indeed, by itself, it does not even forbid avenging an injury.

This argument that good-nature was a strength, not a weakness, suffered somewhat, however, when it came into conflict with Fielding's outraged conviction that the good-hearted man was invariably taken advantage of by a designing world. The theme appears over and over again, in statement and in dramatized form in his work. It was the impetus for his labor on such essays as *On the Knowledge of the Characters of Men*, in which he hoped to arm good-natured readers against this imposition. He had declared in the *Champion*: "Lastly, that as good-nature is a delight in the happiness of mankind, every good-natured man will do his utmost to contribute to the happiness of each individual; and consequently that every man who is not a villain, if he loves not the good-natured man, is guilty of ingratitude" (*ibid.*, p. 259). But he was so concerned to expose villainy and ingratitude toward the good-natured man, to dramatize it in its darkest terms, that he frequently made his good man appear (like Mr. Boncour of *The Good-Natured Man* or Heartfree in *Jonathan Wild*) something of a simpleton. Parson Adams, indeed, is rescued from this fate by his extraordinary vigor; but he too is in some ways an artistic projection of Fielding's continued obsession with the idea that the open-hearted man is the natural prey of hypocritical villains ("Bless us!" says Adams, "how good-nature is used in this world!") (*JA*, II, xvi; Henley, I, 201).[33]

He came in time, I believe, to feel the moral inadequacy of this theme (and thus Dr. Harrison does not share the simplicity of Heartfree and Boncour, or even Adams); but he never altogether gave it up—Amelia's bitter comment to her children springs from the same pessimistic conception: "He [Booth] is the best man in the world, and therefore they hate him . . ." (IV, iii; Henley, VI, 190). Good-nature was to Fielding the primary social virtue, and he felt that those who failed to appreciate its value were, in a very real sense, undermining society. But his concern to expose and denigrate these "villains" and his equal concern to insist on the strength and judgment of good-nature sometimes got in the way of each other.

3

Good-nature was for Fielding an "out-going" force. He defined virtue in *Tom Jones* (xv, i; Henley, v, 141) as "a certain relative quality, which is always busying itself without-doors, and seems as much interested in pursuing the good of others as its own" (here too, incidentally, he insists that it meets with ingratitude). Good-nature, "the mighty whole / Full Composition of a virtuous Soul," is just such an active temper, concerned with good works as well as benevolent feelings. It is the characteristic of the individual "Who to make all and each Man truly blest, / Doth all he can, and wishes all the rest." Hence for Fielding the

[33] Robert South's like feeling would doubtless have reinforced Fielding's views on the subject; in a sermon from which Fielding elsewhere drew several quotations, South had asked: "[Is a man] unhappy and calamitous in his friendships? Why, in this also, it is because he built upon the air, and trod upon a quicksand, and took that for kindness and sincerity, which was only malice and design, seeking an opportunity to ruin him effectually, and to overturn him in all his interests by the sure but fatal handle of his own good nature and credulity" ("The fatal Imposture and Force of Words," *Sermons Preached upon Several Occasions* [7v., Oxford, 1823], II, 134).

virtues of charity and good-nature often become one and the same. Good-nature is "the glorious Lust of doing Good" —charity (in *CGJ* No. 29; Jensen I, 308) is "the Delight . . . in doing Good." Parson Adams' definition of charity is "a generous disposition to relieve the distressed." And Peter Pounce's reply to Adams makes clear (by inversion) Fielding's insistence upon the active nature of charity: " 'There is something in that definition,' answered Peter, 'which I like well enough; it is, as you say, a disposition, and does not so much consist in the act as in the disposition to do it' " (*JA*, III, xiii; Henley, I, 310). Moreover, just as Fielding had emphasized the element of judgment in good-nature, so too he was always concerned to decry a weak and indiscriminate charity and, as we have already seen, to exalt that prudent benevolence which carefully distinguished the objects of its bounty.

When he was *defining* good-nature (or charity) he tended to argue that it had no selfish interests, that it was primarily concerned with "the good of the whole." But when he sought to persuade his readers that they should be good-natured, that is, when he was seeking a *motive* to virtuous action, he often fell back upon a more immediately appealing argument, namely, self-interest. In the dedication to *Tom Jones* he said: "Besides displaying that beauty of virtue which may attract the admiration of mankind, I have attempted to engage a stronger motive to human action in her favour, by convincing men, that their true interest directs them to a pursuit of her" (Henley, III, 12). He had argued much earlier, in the *Champion*, that even the selfish man could not fail to discover incentives to good-nature, "for as it is more easily and safely satisfied than ambition, revenge, or any of those pernicious passions, so are its joys more exquisite, and less interrupted" (27 March 1740; Henley, xv, 260). With a like argument he had proved in another essay that "virtue and interest are not . . . as repugnant as fire and water" (24 January 1740; Henley, xv, 165-69). Good-nature, then, definitely did not exclude self-interest; indeed, the element of judgment in it required that a man have some sensible concern with self, for "to pursue that which is most capable of giving him Happiness, is indeed the Interest of every Man . . ." (*CGJ* No. 44; Jensen II, 9). Like Cicero in *De inventione* (II. lii. 157-58), Fielding could argue as though there were a third ground beyond or between *honestas* and *utilitas*: good-nature was not only a good in itself, to be recommended by its intrinsic merit, but it was also useful—some profit or advantage could be derived from it. Since Fielding was usually seeking to motivate as well as define or admire, this approach became customary to him when recommending a virtue to the attention of his readers. Its most characteristic form in Fielding's works, however, is found in the repeated assertion that good-nature or any other virtue brings a man personal satisfaction and pleasure, not that it will necessarily advance his worldly interests—though, as Parson Adams argues in his letter to the *True Patriot*, 17 December 1745, "It is laying up a much surer and much greater reward for itself" (Henley, xiv, 28).

Good-nature is obviously the most inclusive of all virtues for Fielding. It is a *social* virtue, for it looks to the end of the whole and promotes the well-being of all men. In a lesser sense of "social," it is the very quality of mind most essential to good breeding (*Misc.*, I, 126-27). It is a *moral* virtue, for it makes a man better in himself, extirpating the weeds (as he phrased it in his poem) of vice and ill-nature. Finally, it is a *religious* or spiritual virtue, to be identified with charity ("a virtue not confined to munificence or giving alms, but that brotherly love and friendly disposition of mind which is everywhere taught in Scripture") (*Champion*, 5 April 1740; Henley, xv, 269); and charity "comprehends almost the whole particular duty of a Christian" (*ibid.*, p. 272). Fielding cited nothing from Shaftesbury with more pleasure than the assertion that God was "the best-natured being in the universe" (*Champion*, 27 March 1740; Henley, xv, 260);[34] and his own conclusion was: "The more therefore we cultivate the sweet disposition in our minds, the nearer we draw to divine perfection...."

4

It is not difficult, of course, to place Fielding's conception of good-nature in the general tradition of the benevolist view of man, the "Genealogy of the 'Man of Feeling.' " The stress throughout his writings on the value of works over doctrine; the emphasis upon the positive value of the passions; the insistence that benevolence is "natural" to man and that he lives most in conformity with his nature in displaying it; and the "egoistic hedonism" of a "self-approving Joy"—all these characteristics of his moral creed are clearly in the latitudinarian-benevolist line.[35] Fielding, it is well known, had read and admired the works of such men

[34] Shaftesbury's statement, as one might expect, is actually phrased in a much more skeptical vein. Asking whether there is *"a Mind which has relation to the Whole,"* he concludes: "For if unhappily there be *no Mind*, we may comfort our selves, however, that Nature has *no Malice*: If there be really *a* Mind, we may rest satisfy'd, that it is *the best-natur'd one in the World*" (*Letter concerning Enthusiasm* [1708], in *Characteristicks* [3rd ed., 3 v., 1723], I, 40). Earlier in the same work, he had asserted "that nothing beside ill Humour can give us dreadful or ill Thoughts of a Supreme Manager. Nothing can persuade us of Sullenness or Sourness in such a Being, beside the actual fore-feeling of somewhat of this kind within our-selves . . ." (*ibid.*, p. 23). This was an argument Fielding often used to his own purpose.

[35] The designated characteristics are drawn, of course, from R. S. Crane's classic article, "Suggestions toward a Genealogy of the 'Man of Feeling,' " *ELH*, I (1934), 205-30. See also James A. Work, "Henry Fielding, Christian Censor," in *The Age of Johnson: Essays Presented to Chauncey Brewster Tinker* (New Haven, 1949), pp. 139-48; and the excellent survey of Fielding's relationship to the latitudinarians in Martin C. Battestin, *The Moral Basis of Fielding's Art: A Study of Joseph Andrews* (Middletown, Connecticut, 1959). Stuart M. Tave, *The Amiable Humorist: A Study in the Comic Theory and Criticism of the Eighteenth and Early Nineteenth Centuries* (Chicago, 1960) came to my attention too late to figure in my conclusions; but his examination of the idea of "good-nature" is relevant here.

as Tillotson, Barrow, Burnet, and Hoadly; yet it is perhaps to the point to observe that by the middle of the eighteenth century, the ideas described above had become widely disseminated (a young man could become conscious of them as modern youths assimilate Freud without ever reading him), and the influence of Shaftesbury and Hutcheson had given them new emphases; so that it is scarcely possible to trace all the component elements of Fielding's conception to specific sources. One should observe, incidentally, that the benevolist view of man was by no means confined to the schools of moral sense and feeling. Confirmed rationalists like Clarke and the physico-theologians also preached that universal benevolence was required by natural law and the order of things. Even non-juring clergymen like Jeremy Collier insisted that man is "both obliged and naturally inclinable to universal Benevolence. . . ."[36]

Finally, although the reigning benevolist philosophy unquestionably had its influence upon Fielding's view of life, the source for much of his own specific moralizing on good-nature, as on other subjects, is to be found in the ethic writings of the classical philosophers, many of whose pages were quite susceptible of a benevolist interpretation. "Indeed," said Fielding, "the ancients seem to have looked on what we call good-nature as a quality almost inseparable from nature itself" (*Champion*, 27 March 1740; Henley, xv, 256). Hence one often finds him setting forth some primary tenet of the benevolists, with an attribution not to the perhaps expected latitudinarians or Shaftesbury, but to Cicero or Aristotle. The Ciceronian *humanitas*, indeed, bears more than a casual resemblance to Fielding's "good-nature" in its less emotive phases.[37] The classical moralists

[36] *Essays upon Several Moral Subjects* (5th ed., 1703), Part I, p. 7.

[37] In arguing that the Greeks and Romans had answerable conceptions and terms for "good-nature," Fielding asked, in the *Champion* article cited in the text, "Or what idea do we conceive from *comitas, benignitas, benevolentia, humanitas*, &c.?" (Henley, xv, 256). If it were really possible to break down into its component elements and contributing sources Fielding's complex idea of good-nature, one might suggest that the sterner

were, obviously, a fundamental source for most of the benevolist writers; but some modern scholarship has tended to overlook the fact that Fielding, in shaping his own ethic, could fatten his moral muse on the rich common of the ancients quite as freely as his latitudinarian and philosophical predecessors in the century.

Despite the many elements shared with these predecessors, Fielding's "good-nature" may be differentiated from their values in certain definite ways. The basic distinction between his concept and the benevolism of Clarke and the physico-theologians is that they believed themselves to be erecting an objective, universal moral system:[38] this was not at all Fielding's purpose, and, though he often cited (or echoed) particular passages from Clarke's theology with approval,[39] he could not believe that rationalist theorizing as such led to virtuous action. The philosopher Square in *Tom Jones* is sufficient evidence of that. Moreover, most of the rationalist divines were moral rigorists (that is, insistent that virtue was defined by choice on principle, not natural tendency),[40] and Fielding was well aware that such

---

"intellectual" element derives from his classic inspiration, the "emotive" element from the latitudinarians; but I fear that the matter is not so simple as all this.

[38] See A. R. Humphreys, " 'The Eternal Fitness of Things': An Aspect of Eighteenth-Century Thought," *MLR*, XLII (1947), 188-98.

[39] Cf. A. R. Towers, "Fielding and Dr. Samuel Clarke," *MLN*, LXX (1955), 257-60.

[40] An interesting member of the school of Cudworth and Clarke who is not mentioned in Humphreys' informative survey, John Balguy, vicar of Northallerton in Yorkshire, phrased the case for moral rigorism and against sentimental benevolence very clearly, concluding: "But surely there is a manifest and wide Difference between a *rational Determination*, and a *mere Impulse* of Nature. It is only *Reason*, or the Appearance of Reason, that can *justify* the *Choice* of a moral Agent; who is no further *Praise-worthy*, than as he acts in Conformity thereto. . . . In short, I cannot have any other Idea of *moral Merit*, than *conforming*, or endeavouring to conform, *our Actions to the Reasons of Things*" (*The Foundation of Moral Goodness*, 4th ed., in *A Collection of Tracts Moral and Theological* [1734], pp. 94-95). Obviously enough this is in diametrical opposition to Fielding's way of thinking on the subject of moral goodness—it might almost be the philosopher Square speaking! Joseph Addison had, however, made much the same point in *Spectator* No. 177, where

a position was antithetical to his own. In the *Enquiry into the Causes of the Late Increase of Robbers* (1751), he praised the natural energies of "a tender-hearted and compassionate disposition," and declared that "those who, because they are natural, have denied them the name of virtues seem not, I think, to be aware of the direct and impious tendency of a doctrine that denies all merit to a mind which is naturally, I may say necessarily, good" (Henley, XIII, 109).[41]

Fielding agrees (strictly) in almost no important regard with the approach of Hutcheson, whose ethics of feeling is very nearly as rigorous and rationalistic as the scheme of Clarke and his followers. The relationship to Lord Shaftesbury, however, is more complex. Sir John Hawkins' attack on Fielding ("the inventor of that cant-phrase, goodness of heart") in 1787 linked him with Shaftesbury: "His morality, in respect that it resolves virtue into good affections, in contradiction to moral obligation and a sense of duty, is that of lord Shaftesbury vulgarised...."[42] Hawkins is correct in setting them both in opposition to the moral rigorists; but however close their relationship might have seemed to the casual reading public, there was a mean-

---

he dealt with good-nature as a "Moral Virtue"—in contradistinction to good-nature as "one of the Blessings of a happy Constitution" (No. 169). The distinction was one that Fielding ordinarily did not wish to make.

[41] Cf. the letter of "Axylus" in the *Covent-Garden Journal*: "Morose and austere Men may, if they please, preach up Mortification and Self-Denial, may insinuate that a Man cannot be good and happy at the same Time, and may deny all Merit to all Actions which are not done in Contradiction to Nature; but I say, with Dr. Barrow, *Let us improve and advance our Nature to the utmost Perfection of which it is capable,* I mean by doing all the Good we can; and surely that Nature which seems to partake of the divine Goodness in this World, is the most likely to partake of the divine Happiness in the next. To speak a solemn Truth, such Natures alone are capable of such Beatitude" (*CGJ*, No. 29; Jensen, I, 309). This was not a purely benevolist conception. Aristotle, although insisting that an act of virtue must be deliberately and knowingly chosen, had also said that "the act must spring from a fixed and permanent disposition of character" (*Nicomachean Ethics* II. iv. 3; 1105a; translated by H. Rackham [Loeb Library, 1934], p. 85).

[42] *The Life of Samuel Johnson, LL.D.* (1787), p. 215.

ingful gulf between Fielding and Shaftesbury. Fielding's ethical construct, like the great Earl's, is an amalgam of Platonic-Aristotelian-Stoic principles, low-church Christian doctrine, and empirical observation of human psychology. But if he could find much to approve in Shaftesbury, that "noble author whom we have so often quoted, and shall quote" (as he said in the *Champion*, 27 March 1740; Henley, xv, 260), there were nonetheless crucial differences in their leading assumptions. When Fielding defined good-nature, in his *Essay on the Knowledge of the Characters of Men*, as independent of "any abstract Contemplation on the Beauty of Virtue," he may not have had Shaftesbury particularly in mind, but he was drawing a line between them nevertheless.[43] The most significant difference, however, lies in the opposed attitudes of the two men toward the place of the Christian religion in the scheme of human ethics. Fielding could be severely critical of re-

[43] The whole quotation is of interest: "Good-Nature is that benevolent and amiable Temper of Mind which disposes us to feel the Misfortunes, and enjoy the Happiness of others; and consequently pushes us on to promote the latter, and prevent the former; and that without any abstract Contemplation on the Beauty of Virtue, and without the Allurements or Terrors of Religion" (*Misc.*, I, 190).

At first sight, the concluding phrase might well seem to place Fielding *with* Shaftesbury in arguing that the benevolent impulse, to be genuine, must be independent of religious rewards and punishments. In view of Fielding's iterated attachment to the latter concept (see next note), it is more likely that his intended stress is simply upon the "naturalness" of good-nature. This is assuredly the stress in a like comment by the quite orthodox Thomas Herring (who was successively Bishop of Bangor, Archbishop of York, and Archbishop of Canterbury); in a sermon published in 1739, Herring had said: "It is the Property of Mercy to pity the Infirmities of other Men; to put on, as the Scriptures express it, Bowels of Mercy, to cultivate a Tenderness and Humanity of Temper, a quick and ready Feeling of each others Wants and Pains; by which I would not be understood to mean, a soft and unmanly Weakness, Passion without the Power and Constancy of Reason, but a generous Sympathy and Affection, steadily and wisely pitying and considering the unhappy Circumstances of other Men. And this is what indeed we are naturally carried to *without the Discipline of Reason, or the Precepts of Religion* [italics mine].—There is something in the Human Constitution that naturally melts at Human Misfortunes; and it is well for the World that it is so . . ." (*A Sermon Preached before the Right Honourable the Lord-Mayor . . . By Thomas Lord Bishop of Bangor* [1739], pp. 5-6).

ligious principles that led to self-righteousness or what he considered unsocial behavior, but he never doubted that the Christian religion as he understood it was the ultimate basis of moral behavior; and here, of course, he and Shaftesbury part company. Fielding, for example, was just as strenuous in asserting the necessity of after-life rewards and punishments to any moral scheme as Shaftesbury was in insisting upon their irrelevance.[44] They agreed that man had a natural sense of right and wrong antecedent to religious belief; but Shaftesbury went on to argue that this moral sense was therefore *independent of* religion, whereas for Fielding the original notions had been implanted by God (cf. Allworthy's statement, *TJ*, II, ii; Henley, III, 67-68) and were thus to be *identified with* religious imperatives. As he said in the same passage of the *Enquiry* previously quoted: "The natural energies of this temper [a tender-hearted and compassionate disposition, which inclines men to pity and feel the misfortune of others] are indeed the very virtues principally inculcated in our excellent religion . . ." (Henley, XIII, 109). For Fielding, good-nature (or, in effect, virtue, benevolence, charity) and

[44] In attacking the "political philosophers" (presumably Hobbes, Mandeville, and the Deists) in the *Champion*, Fielding declared that "these philosophers have carried on their war against virtue two ways. They have first, as much as in them lay, endeavoured to ridicule and extirpate all our expectations of any future reward in another life; and secondly, they have represented it as directly incompatible with our happiness and advancement in this" (22 January 1740; Henley, xv, 163). Shaftesbury might be glanced at here; and there are various other statements on the validity of the concept of rewards and punishments that run precisely counter to the noble philosopher's—for example, "Can the heart of man be warmed with a more ecstatic imagination, than that the most excellent attribute of the great Creator of the universe is concerned in rewarding him?" (*Ibid.*, 4 March 1740; Henley, xv, 230). From first to last, Fielding chose, like Dr. Harrison, "rather to rely on its [religion's] rewards and punishments than on that native beauty of virtue which some of the ancient philosophers thought proper to recommend to their disciples" (*Amelia*, XII, v; Henley, VII, 313); for, although in a certain sense he could agree that Virtue is its own reward (cf. *CGJ*, No. 29; Jensen, I, 308), he could never agree with Shaftesbury (or even with Bishop Hoadly) that a morality based upon the conception of rewards and punishments in after-life was weak or spurious.

religion were complementary moral forces, together constituting the very "bands of civil society" (*TJ*, III, iv; Henley, III, 117); and of the two, religion went beyond good-nature, both in giving promise of a life to come and in inspiring a more sublime morality than could any mere human passion.[45] Though Fielding, as we shall see, often seemed in practice to exalt "moral" virtues over strictly "religious" ones, his ultimate and considered judgments always returned to Christianity as the basis of the moral life. This fact alone would differentiate his "good-nature" from Shaftesbury's "moral sense," although the two conceptions have other elements—for example, innateness, in the sense of seeds that require cultivation—that are very much alike.

There can be, of course, no doubt that Fielding very early in his career had read Shaftesbury closely and been much impressed by him both as a stylist and a thinker. In Shaftesbury, besides an elegant restatement of many classic truths, he could find weapons against the ethical egoism of Hobbes and Mandeville, a mannerly defense of the use of ridicule (about which Fielding later had second thoughts),[46] a sympathetic acceptance of the ancient theory

---

[45] As early as 1740 (in an argument obviously aimed at the Deists), Fielding had made a point of the greater compass of Christianity: "That as good-nature, which is the chief if not only quality in the mind of man in the least tending that way, doth not forbid the avenging of an injury, Christianity hath taught us something beyond what the religion of nature and philosophy could arrive at; and consequently, that it is not as old as the creation, nor is revelation useless with regard to morality, if it had taught us no more than this excellent doctrine, which, if generally followed, would make mankind much happier, as well as better than they are" (*Champion*, 27 March 1740; Henley, xv, 258; cf. also 5 April 1740; Henley, xv, 270). However, a good many years later, in *Amelia*, Fielding (through Dr. Harrison) had the following to say about abstaining from the pleasure of revenge: "And this is an abstinence to which wisdom alone, *without any divine command*, hath been often found adequate, with instances of which the Greek and Latin authors everywhere abound" (IX, viii; Henley, VII, 165; italics mine).

[46] In his last years, in the *Fragment of a Comment on Lord Bolingbroke's Essays*, Fielding observed that Shaftesbury had been censured for suggesting that ridicule was a good light in which to view truth, and

of man's mixed nature that Fielding found so congenial, an appealing emphasis upon taste and breeding, and—whatever their particular differences—a serious concern for moral values and for the betterment of human character. The many echoes of Shaftesbury in Fielding's work and his frequently expressed admiration for the noble philosopher make it clear that Fielding owed him a great debt—but, in the end, it must still be admitted that if he was a Shaftesburian, he wore his rue with a difference.

Thus far, Fielding's conception of good-nature can be seen to be perfectly compatible with the moral values of any typical low-church Anglican divine of his day. Like many of them, also, he encountered a fundamental difficulty in reconciling the orthodox doctrine of man's depravity with his wish to believe in man's essential goodness (see the discussion below, *On the Knowledge of the Characters of Men*). This ambiguity, insofar as it is related to the question of good-nature, manifests itself in the contradictory statements Fielding made about the prevalence of naturally good hearts. If I may digress for a moment, the contradiction is worth noting.

A letter from "Philander" in the *True Patriot* (No. 25; 15-22 April 1746) set forth what one may call the orthodox benevolist view:

"Man is universally allowed to have been created a Social Animal, and intended for a Life of Society; we find therefore that he has implanted in his Nature several Passions

---

he commented: "Perhaps there may be some justice in this censure, as truth may by such a trial be subjected to misrepresentation, and become a more easy prey to the malice of its enemies; a flagrant instance of which we have in the case of Socrates" (Henley, xvi, 317). He had in mind, of course, Aristophanes' ridicule, which he had subjected to severe comment in the *Covent-Garden Journal* No. 10; significantly enough, Shaftesbury had used the same example to draw precisely the opposite conclusion, namely, that Socrates had been damaged not at all by the ridicule of the comic dramatist (*Letter concerning Enthusiasm*, Sect. iii, in *Characteristicks* [3rd ed., 3v., 1723], 1, 31).

and Affections, which tend to prompt him to the Practice of Benevolence, and the Exercise of the other Social Virtues. . . ."

In the "optimistic" atmosphere of *Tom Jones*, we find Fielding confidently declaring, "There is in some (I believe *in many*) human breasts a kind and benevolent disposition which is gratified by contributing to the happiness of others" (vi, i; Henley, iii, 272; italics mine) and, "To say the truth, want of compassion is not to be numbered among our general faults . . ." (xvii, v; Henley, v, 267), and so on. But in *Amelia* we come across numerous bitter reflections of the following nature:

"Here, reader, give me leave to stop a minute, to lament that so few are to be found of this benign disposition; that, while wantonness, vanity, avarice, and ambition are every day rioting and triumphing in the follies and weakness, the ruin and desolation of mankind, scarce one man in a thousand is capable of tasting the happiness of others"— (iv, iv; Henley, vi, 194-95).

So also, Dr. Harrison is described as having "a tenderness of heart which is rarely found among men; for which I know no other reason than that true goodness is rarely found among them . . ." (ix, iv; Henley, vii, 142).[47] This latter, more skeptical attitude is the one to be found in the early poem, *Of Good-Nature*, which, as we have seen, declared that it was "A Flow'r so fine, / It only grows in Soils almost divine," and, further along, asked:

> Who wonders that Good-nature *in so few*,
> Can Anger, Lust, or Avarice subdue?
> When the cheap Gift of Fame our Tongues deny,
> And risque our own, to poison with a Lie.
> (*Misc.*, i, 18; italics mine)

[47] The difference in mood between *Tom Jones* and *Amelia* is, of course, not really this simple; there is "pessimism" in the former, and in the latter, such "optimistic" statements as Dr. Harrison's, that the nature of man "abounds with benevolence, charity, and pity," however obscured by bad education and customs (ix, v; Henley, vii, 145).

Both the confident and the skeptical views on the prevalence of good-nature in the world are perhaps equally typical of Fielding in different moods; but the skeptical, emphasized by the poem under consideration, has been frequently overlooked. In part, the inconsistency in his views can be explained only by admitting that in some moods he was willing to believe that good-nature was widely diffused and in other moods he was not—it is as simple as that, and it represents an almost universal inconsistency of the inconsistent human animal. One can, however, make a further distinction. When he attempted to formalize or define his intuitions about good-nature, Fielding often fell back upon the theoretical bases of that benevolism which saw man in the abstract as, not naturally good, but naturally *inclined to* goodness; this theory asserted the general prevalence of the beneficent impulses (even when corrupted by bad customs). But an artist's rationalizations and formal opinions are not always of a piece with his artistic vision. In the novels and many of his essays, Fielding projected his own experience of men; and that experience told him that good-nature and benevolence were rare enough in the world—he could scarcely have admired Lucian and Swift so much had he not felt this. Hence, even in the "optimistic" atmosphere of *Joseph Andrews* and *Tom Jones*, the fools and villains outnumber the good-natured by a sizeable margin; in *Jonathan Wild*, the *Journey from This World to the Next*, and *Amelia*, the proportion is overwhelming.

Of course I am not saying that Fielding was essentially a pessimist who was really writing tragedies. Although one need not have an optimistic view of human nature to write comedy, I am sure that Fielding was an optimist. He was not ordinarily, however, a sentimental, and never a simple-minded, optimist; and the complexity of his hard-won belief in basic human decency can be measured by the leavening mixture of practical pessimism that informs it. Arguing in the *Essay on the Knowledge of the Characters of Men* that mere laughter is no certain sign of good-nature, he said soberly: "For admitting, that laughing at the Vices and Follies of Mankind is entirely innocent, (which is more perhaps than we ought to admit) yet surely their Miseries and Misfortunes are no Subjects of Mirth: And with these, *Quis non vicus abundat?* the World is so full of them, that scarce a Day passes without inclining a truly good-natured Man rather to Tears than Merriment" (*Misc.*, I, 191). Fielding was very much interested in theories (optimistic and pessimistic) about human nature; but ultimately his judgment was that of Aristotle: "Such arguments then carry some degree of conviction; but it is by the practical experience of life and conduct that the truth is really tested, since it is there that the final decision lies. We must therefore examine the conclusions we have advanced by bringing them to the test of the facts of life."[48]

Whereas the postulates of sentimental benevolism can lead—and have led—to a rather puerile and shallow optimism, Fielding avoided such an obvious pitfall in his dramatizations of the human scene by depending more upon the evidence gleaned from his own broad and deeply felt experience, than upon theoretical moral structures. His, of course, *is* the comic rather than tragic vision; and to the comic vision evil must appear ultimately impotent. It should not, however, appear nonexistent; Fielding does not blink the *fact* of evil in the world, and it is this in large measure that sets him apart from more naive followers of the ethics of feeling while it brings him closer to the Christian vision of the low-church latitudinarian clergy.

Both Fielding and the latitudinarian tradition strongly emphasized the social utility of religion and the individual's moral conduct rather than a complex theology. And Fielding's emphasis upon the good life as against a slavish following of doctrine can be found in almost all Augustan

---

[48] *Nicomachean Ethics* xx. viii. 12; 1179a (Loeb Library, p. 627).

POETRY

clerical writings except those of some high-flying Tories.[49] The most significant difference between Fielding and the latitudinarians is, obviously, that Fielding was not writing sermons but comic moral drama—hence one hears less from him than from the divines about such religious virtues as faith, obedience, and patience.[50] Likewise, one finds a much more genial tolerance of such sins as fornication, drunkenness, and other weaknesses of the flesh than the clergy were accustomed to display. The emphasis on good-nature as the essential moral virtue is much greater in Fielding than in even the latitudinarians, simply because it is not surrounded with equal insistences that grace is essential as a ground for human goodness, that salvation is only through Christ, or like crucial doctrines of the church. If, as Robert

---

[49] This emphasis was to be found in the late seventeenth century, not only in the sermons of the major latitudinarians, but in the tracts of many minor moralists, such as G. B. (George Burghope?) in his *Autarchy*, and John Hartcliffe in *A Treatise of Moral and Intellectual Virtues*, both 1691. G. B. averred that the man who controls his passions, maintains a pure heart, and practices charity, "this Man (notwithstanding some Errours in his Judgment, and Heterodoxes in Opinion) can be no other but a Son of God, and an Heir of Heaven" (p. 41). Hartcliffe explained in his dedication, "I have not troubled your Lordship with the fine and nice Speculations in Divinity, because they have done our Religion much Dis-service, by raising a multitude of Questions, which neither advance true Piety, nor good Manners . . ." (sig. A4ᵛ).

[50] A sermon by Robert South begins: "IF we would give one general account of all the duties that are incumbent upon a Christian, we shall find them reducible to these three, *faith, obedience,* and *patience*; and the vital principle that animates and runs through them all is *submission*" (*Sermons Preached upon Several Occasions* [7v., Oxford, 1823], VI, 486). Though a high-churchman who had little regard for "our modern, orthodox, and more authentick Pelagians," South was one of Fielding's favorite writers, particularly in his early career; but it is doubtful that Fielding would have subscribed very enthusiastically to the argument of this sermon (cf. below, p. 252). On the other hand, it would have won the assent without question of most of the latitudinarian clergy—who, themselves, were fond of emphasizing this or that particular virtue by such a formula ("That *Repentance* and *Faith* are the sum and substance of the gospel"; "The necessity of *supernatural grace* in order to a Christian life"; "Of the necessity of *Good Works*"; and so on). One of the differences between Fielding and the latitudinarian clergy, then, is that themes which they emphasized only in particular sermons Fielding emphasized in all of his work, whereas many of the themes that they stressed received little or no attention from him.

South said, "The Truths of Christ crucified are the Christian's *Philosophy*, and a good Life is the Christian's *Logick*,"[51] then Fielding's novels dealt almost entirely with the "Logick." He certainly thought of himself as a "defender of the faith" and clearly believed that liberal clergymen like Hoadly were staunch allies, and there can be no doubt that from first to last his writings show him to have been a "conservative, consistent, and orthodox" low-church Anglican; but from his first three novels alone, a religious reader could very well fail to derive such a truth. And it was upon the evidence of the novels that Fielding's contemporaries largely judged his moral and religious orthodoxy.

The *Gentleman's Magazine*, for example, in March 1750, reprinted approvingly "A *literary Article from* Paris" which, in reviewing *Tom Jones,* said of Fielding's dedicatory claim that the book contained "nothing prejudicial to the cause of religion and virtue":

"We must here suppose that, by *virtue*, M. *Fielding* would not have us understand a rigorous observation of all the precepts in the christian system of morality, but only the practice of the principal offices of justice and humanity; otherwise the loose manners of his heroe might give occasion to upbraid the author with neglecting to fulfil exactly the first of his promises . . ."—(p. 117).

In 1752, the very literary Miss Mulso wrote to ask Miss Carter if she did not find a tendency in Fielding's works "to soften the deformity of vice, by placing characters in an amiable light, that are destitute of every virtue except good nature?"[52] In a collection called *Admonitions from the Dead, in Epistles to the Living*, which enjoyed two editions in the year of Fielding's death, a fictional (and

---

[51] "A SERMON Preached upon JOHN vii. 17," in *Twelve Sermons Preached upon Several Occasions* (6th ed., 6v., 1727), I, 251; repr. in *Sermons* (Oxford, 1823), I, 171.

[52] Cited by Frederic T. Blanchard, *Fielding the Novelist* (New Haven, 1926), p. 96.

POETRY

highly moral) letter "*From* JOSEPH ADDISON *to the Author of* TOM JONES. *On the Qualifications of modern Writers, and the Art of Writing*" scolded Fielding in these terms:

"It has grieved me to see so much Power to do good as you have possess'd, employ'd to so little Purpose as you have employ'd it. . . . [In your writings] when there appears any thing that has the Face of Morality, it seems to have fallen in your Way by Chance, rather than to have been an original Part of the Design. . . . As I would have you put to a more proper Use those Things which you possess, so I would wish you to avoid making Pretences to such as you have not. . . . If God and Religion are in your Heart, you are so much the better, and the happier Man; but unless they are in your Practice also, they have no Business to be upon your Tongue."[53]

The many like observations in the thirty years following were capped by Sir John Hawkins' famous diatribe, already referred to, which declared that *Tom Jones* was "a book seemingly intended to sap the foundation of that morality which it is the duty of parents and all public instructors to inculcate in the minds of young people, by teaching that virtue upon principle is imposture, that generous qualities alone constitute true worth, and that a young man may love and be loved, and at the same time associate with the loosest women."[54]

One is tempted to dismiss Hawkins (whom Frederick Lawrence called "the veritable Pecksniff of the age")[55] as simply an ill-tempered old man; but we must in all fairness observe that he represented a point of view which many of his contemporaries shared and which, indeed, must be said to possess a respectable philosophic validity. There is most certainly a rigorous conception of moral duty implicit in Christianity, and insofar as Fielding ex-

[53] Pp. 216-17, 219-20.
[54] *The Life of Samuel Johnson, LL.D.*, pp. 214-15.
[55] *The Life of Henry Fielding* (1855), p. 356.

POETRY

cused "mere" sins of the flesh and—more to the point—exalted the virtues of goodness of heart over both the virtues of positive observance of Christian duties (and rituals) and negative abstention from sin, he was emphasizing a fundamentally social criterion at the expense of those criteria which distinguish a religion from a simple set of moral values.

Even the latitudinarian, low-church Whig clergy—who in some degree also emphasized "social" as distinct from "religious" criteria and in whom Fielding could find parallels for most of his moral positions—even they balanced the picture by giving requisite attention in their sermons to the theological elements that Fielding naturally tended to scant in his fiction and, relatively speaking, even in his essays.[56] My point, of course, is not that Fielding *should* have turned his novels and all of his essays into sermons, but simply that he did not; and therefore not only his techniques but his emphases necessarily differed from those

[56] When Fielding's admired Bishop Tillotson preaches upon the text, "The fruits of the SPIRIT, the same with moral virtues," and discusses goodness, righteousness, and truth, one feels comfortably in Fielding's moral atmosphere (goodness, says Tillotson, "is not a zeal for indifferent things," like ritual and ceremony). Suddenly, though, one finds oneself in an area that was natural ground to Tillotson, and that Fielding himself might well have accepted to the last detail—but which simply does not appear (to the last detail) in his narratives:

"I do not say that these virtues [goodness, righteousness, and truth] are all religion, and all that is necessary to make a man a complete christian, and a good man. For there must be knowledge to direct us in our duty; there must be faith or a hearty assent to the revelation of the gospel, (especially concerning the forgiveness of our sins, and of our justification and acceptance with GOD, for the sake of the meritorious sufferings of our blessed SAVIOUR,) to be the root and principle of all religious actions; there must be piety and devotion towards GOD, and the constant practice and exercise of religious duties in publick and private, such as prayer, hearing and reading the word of GOD, frequent and reverent receiving of the holy sacrament, which are the best and most effectual means in the world to make men good, because they are appointed by GOD, and attended with his blessing to that end; I say, there must be all these, because they are the principles and means of religion, which are always supposed as necessary to that which is the end [that is, the perfection of the fruits of the Spirit]" (Sermon CCII, in *The Works of the Most Reverend Dr. John Tillotson* [12v., 1757], x, 387).

of the latitudinarians. This may seem obvious; but our recent scholarly concern to place Fielding in that religious camp by selecting quotations from the sermons that harmonize with quotations from Fielding's works (a practice of which I am as guilty as any) has perhaps tended to obscure the fact that the surrounding contexts of each are far from the same. Now that the old nullifidian image of Fielding has been satisfactorily destroyed, our concern may perhaps come to lie in rescuing him from canonization. Ernest Tuveson has pertinently observed of the latitudinarian clergy:

"It would be a fatal mistake to assume that the Christian and other worldly elements in the thinking of these preachers were mere vestigial remains, so to speak, hanging on to a new, secular, optimistic opinion about human nature. However great their 'latitude' . . . they were never really out of touch with the great traditional belief that men are destined to recover, by supernatural aid, from a disastrous cosmic fall into a transcendental state."[57]

This reminder may help us to see that although Fielding's own secular Pelagianism made the latitudinarian clergy his natural allies, his emphasis was not—as theirs of necessity was—*primarily* upon otherworldliness and salvation and *secondarily* upon human psychology and social amelioration. Important as his Christian philosophy was to him, Fielding's emphasis nevertheless lay the other way around. He would have been a poorer comic author, had it not.

5

The great moral generosity and tolerance of "natural" masculine flaws that Fielding displayed in most of his works depend, I believe, upon an exaltation of "mere" good-nature to a higher moral position than any Christian clergyman, high- or low-church, could *consistently* have afforded it.

[57] "The Importance of Shaftesbury," *ELH*, xx (1953), 271.

Fielding's conception (his "ideal" or "dream" conception, one might say) of otherworldly judgment is perhaps not inaccurately rendered in the judgments of Minos, in chapter vii of the *Journey from This World to the Next*. The traveller—whom Fielding more than once, though perhaps unconsciously, identifies with himself—stands before Minos to be judged. He says:

"THE Judge then address'd himself to me, who little expected to pass this fiery Trial. I confess'd I had indulged myself very freely with Wine and Women in my Youth, but had never done an Injury to any Man living, nor avoided an Opportunity of doing good; that I pretended to very little Virtue more than general Philanthropy, and private Friendship.—I was proceeding, when *Minos* bid me enter the Gate, and not indulge myself with trumpeting forth my Virtues"—(*Misc.*, II, 62).

Another claimant for a place in Elysium, who declares that he has constantly frequented his church, observed the fast-days, and ceaselessly censured vice in others as well as being himself free from "Whoring, Drinking, Gluttony, or any other Excess," is turned away: "He said, he had disinherited his Son for getting a Bastard.—Have you so, said *Minos*, then pray return into the other World and beget another; for such an unnatural Rascal shall never pass this Gate" (*Misc.*, II, 53-54). We have in these contrasted personalities a dramatization of Fielding's claim in the *Champion* of 27 March 1740 that good-nature is "that amiable quality, which, like the sun, gilds over all our other virtues. . . . Whereas all other virtues without some tincture of this, may be well called *splendida peccata*" (Henley, xv, 259-60). In effect, as the poem *Of Good-Nature* insists, it is "Virtue's Self."

Mrs. Miller's defence of Jones to Allworthy, it will be remembered, is that his faults "are all the faults of wildness and of youth; faults which he may, nay, which I am certain he will, relinquish, and, *if he should not*, they are *vastly overbalanced* by one of the most humane, tender, honest hearts that ever man was blessed with" (*TJ*, xvii, ii; Henley, v, 251; italics mine). Square, after his conversion to Christianity, exculpates Jones in the same terms (xviii, iv; Henley, v, 308). Obviously enough, the sins of the senses are morally outweighed by a good heart; whereas, like the rigorist turned away from Elysium by Minos, Thwackum, for all his religiosity, is presumably doomed. Fielding never casts any doubts upon the sincerity of Thwackum's theology; he is portrayed, moreover, as an excellent scholar, and one may "add to this the strict severity of his life and manners, an unimpeached honesty, and a most devout attachment to religion." But Allworthy "knew him to be proud and ill-natured; he also knew that his divinity itself was tinctured with his temper . . ." (*TJ*, xviii, iv; Henley, v, 310). Yes, it is as clear that Thwackum would be turned away from Elysium as it is that Old Laroon, the good-natured, roistering ancient of Fielding's early play, *The Old Debauchees*, would be welcomed there: "I have no sins to reflect on but those of an honest fellow. If I have loved a whore at five-and-twenty, and a bottle at forty, why I have done as much good as I could in my generation; and that, I hope, will make amends" (Scene xiv; Henley, ix, 321).

I am not concerned to quarrel with Fielding's morality; it served him admirably for most of his life and produced two of the world's comic masterpieces—and that, perhaps, is sufficient to "vastly overbalance" the faults that a professional moralist could surely find in his ethical scheme. However, I think that Fielding's own attitude toward "good-nature" became more complicated in his later years; and this is worth comment.

Fielding did not cease to look upon good-nature as the most important secular virtue (see, for example, *Covent-Garden Journal* No. 16) and doubtless he would at any time have maintained that an ethic based upon the good heart was superior to any scheme of rigorous or merely theoretical morality. But it does appear that he came to suffer substantial doubts about the complete sufficiency of the good heart as an ultimate moral guide and ethical imperative. The date of such a shift in viewpoint cannot, of course, be precisely set; but the doubts are most obviously dramatized in *Amelia*, and I should suppose that it was in the period after 1748 (and after the greater part of *Tom Jones* had been written), when Fielding became a magistrate, that he began seriously to reexamine his ideas on the subject (as he also reexamined his conceptions of what the novel should be and do). It is in this period that his various pamphlets on the social evils of robbery and poverty appear; and the sordid and disheartening parade of human wickedness and degradation that passed in review before him at Bow Street each day could scarcely have failed to influence his practical moral conceptions (cf. below, p. 212). There are various indications of a sterner assessment of moral deviation and a more profound awareness of the need for some ethical imperative transcending mere good-nature: "the passions of the man are to give way to the principles of the magistrate."[58]

[58] *Enquiry into the Causes of the Late Increase of Robbers*, sect. x; Henley, XIII, 119. Since I shall frequently argue in these essays that there was some modification in Fielding's attitudes in his later years, it may be well at this point to make clear that I do not believe any essential change in his fundamental principles took place after he mounted the bench. But I do believe that his conceptions matured, that he explored new ramifications of beliefs that he had held from the earliest days of his career, and that in some cases (as with the overriding power of "good-nature" discussed above), there was a shift in emphasis. It is true that much of the evidence for such "changes" derives from his legal or sociological pamphlets, written in these years. This is precisely my point: forced to examine the empirical workings of some of his principles, Fielding found modifications necessary. Many of the indications of the greater rigor in moral judgments arise from this contrast of Fielding the novelist with Fielding the magistrate. Drunkenness is a case in point:
In *Tom Jones*: "To say the truth, in a court of justice drunkenness must not be an excuse, yet in a court of conscience it is greatly so; and therefore Aristotle, who commends the laws of Pittacus, by which drunken

Thus in *Amelia*, although good-nature as such is still treated with commendation and is still contrasted with hypocrisy and malice, there are clear indications that it no longer possesses that overriding power assigned to it in the poem of the *Miscellanies*, the power to drive out all other vices. Nor does it any longer "vastly overbalance" the faults of passion, as it had in *Tom Jones*. Colonel James is frequently described by Fielding (not merely by the deluded Booth) as "one of the best-natured men in the world," but his good-nature cannot balance morally his ruling passion of libertinism (cf. IV, v; Henley, VI, 199-200). The snobbish Mrs. James is "at the bottom a very good-natured woman" (VIII, ix; Henley, VII, 105). When Booth, after his skirmish with Colonel Bath, characterizes him as "a man of great honor and good-nature," Amelia cries, "Tell me not . . . of such good-nature and honor as would sacrifice a friend and a whole family to a ridiculous whim" (v, vi; Henley, VI, 253). Shortly after, the noble lord who seeks to seduce

---

men received double punishment for their crimes, allows there is more of policy than justice in that law" (v, x; Henley, III, 258);

In the *Enquiry*: "I do not know a more excellent institution than that of Pittacus, mentioned by Aristotle in his Politics; by which a blow given by a drunken man was more severely punished than if it had been given by one that was sober" (sect. ii; Henley, XIII, 29).

Or one might compare Partridge's fulminations against Jones for his mercy to the highwayman (*TJ*, XII, xiv; Henley, v, 29-30) with Fielding's very similar warnings to the public in the aforementioned pamphlet; or the landlady's ungenerous complaints against beggars and the poor (*TJ*, IX, iv; Henley, IV, 174) with Fielding's later recommendations (not so brutal, it is true, but equally rigorous) in the *Proposal for Making an Effectual Provision for the Poor*. Less patent, but equally interesting, is the increasing tendency to associate gravity and sobriety with the Ciceronian *gravitas* (as he had, to be sure, with Adams and Allworthy), rather than with, say, Jonathan Wild's maxim for greatness: "To maintain a constant Gravity in his Countenance and Behaviour . . ." (IV, xvi; *Misc.*, III, 412). Shaftesbury had been quoted approvingly in the *Essay on the Knowledge of the Characters of Men*, "Gravity is of the Essence of Imposture" (*Misc.*, I, 188; from *A Letter concerning Enthusiasm*, sect. ii, in *Characteristicks* [3rd ed., 3v., 1723], I, 11); and the weight of Fielding's early comments on gravity tends to associate it with hypocrisy; whereas the weight (though not all) of later comment tends to associate it with social respectability and solidity. And so on.

Amelia comes with "his usual good-nature" to inform Booth of hopes for preferment (Henley, VI, 257). One might think the denomination here purely ironic; but even Mrs. Ellison, the lord's bawd, is described by Mrs. Bennet as "not void of generosity or good-nature" (VII, viii; Henley, VII, 51). Clearly, "good-nature" in these instances does not carry any automatic stamp of approval by Fielding, as it most often had in his earlier work. The word appears with increasing frequency in a skeptical or ironic context.

In the novel, Booth himself is brought to the ultimate awareness that good-nature offers no guarantee for moral behavior. Jones had learned a different lesson: that in order not to be misjudged by society—and to avoid embarrassing difficulties—good-nature must be directed by prudence. Allworthy, it is true, counseled him to add both prudence and religion to his good-nature (*TJ*, v, vii; Henley, III, 243), but the dramatic action of the book illustrates primarily the necessity of the former. Booth, on the other hand, is represented as morally incorrigible until Dr. Barrow's sermons bring him to the right path. It is clear from the dramatic action of *Amelia* that mere good-nature must be fortified by religious conviction to make it a morally valuable quality.[59] One might guess that the worthy Dr. Harrison found Esprit's *La fausseté des vertus humaines* "one of the best [books], indeed, that I ever read" (IX, viii; Henley, VII, 162) precisely because the Frenchman proved by a

---

[59] Booth's "conversion" is less an artistic device than a moral one. It is doubtless true that Fielding was seeking to avoid the artistic error he found in contemporary plays—in which the hero is a notorious rogue for four acts and a "very worthy" gentleman in the last, for no other reason than that "the play is drawing to a conclusion" (*TJ*, VIII, i; Henley, IV, 65)—and that he was trying to provide a sufficient and reasonable dramatic motivation for Booth's reform. But to emphasize this, it seems to me, is to miss the real point: namely, that Fielding is dramatizing here his mature conviction that religious belief is essential to the good life—indeed, more than this, the very *sine qua non*. Mere good-nature, even fortified by natural prudence, was no longer enough: a moral imperative transcending the moral feelings of the individual was ultimately necessary.

POETRY

series of paradoxes that none of the human virtues, including prudence and good-nature, were really true virtues *except* in a Christian frame.[60]

What one might call Fielding's "normal" ethical position, however, would see religion and good-nature as complementary moral forces. Religion was assuredly the ultimate imperative for moral behavior; but without a shaping good-nature it could become mere empty ritual and theory. In a world where to Fielding the prime necessity was that men should get along with one another in mutual charity, and where each should take it upon himself to make the difficult pilgrimage of life as pleasant and rewarding for his fellows as possible, the "good heart" remained for him the most reliable and efficacious human bond in society. This ideal of an effective goodness (good-nature and religion joined, as in Parson Adams and Dr. Harrison) was Fielding's answer to that darling of the vulgar, the great man. "Benevolence, Honour, Honesty, and Charity, make a good Man; . . . Parts, Courage, are the efficient Qualities of a Great Man" (*Misc.*, I, xxvi); but if we are restricted, as by the very nature of things we usually are, to only one cluster of qualities, the choice should most surely lie not with a self-seeking greatness, but with goodness and good-nature. If Fielding sermonizes in his comedy, it is to preach that the world can be the pleasant and harmonious dwelling-place it should ideally be and the Christian vision can be most perfectly realized only when men have learned to act toward one another with compassion, openness, and love—good-nature in its best and broadest sense. This is not an extraordinarily "original"— and surely not a recondite—idea, and worshippers of the original and the recondite have hinted that Fielding was perhaps a bit simple-minded in propounding it. The truth

[60] A copy of *La fausseté des vertus humaines* by Jacques Esprit (2v., Paris, 1677-1678), in the Amsterdam edition of 1710, was in Fielding's library.

is that most of the great writers in the Christian tradition have propounded it in one form or another, for it is one of the root-ideas of Western civilization. Fielding's distinction is to have embodied that idea in characters and situations of imperishable humor and dramatic force.

(3) "LIBERTY. TO GEORGE LYTTLETON, *Esq*;"

This panegyric on liberty, addressed to Fielding's friend and patron Lyttelton, was clearly intended as a contribution to the "patriot" opposition to Walpole in the 1730's.[61] In it Fielding traces, in the popular manner of the progress poem, the "historic" rise of the concept of society and liberty—a favorite exercise of the time. Lyttelton himself had indulged in a reconstruction of the rise of society that is very close to Fielding's.[62] According to the fable—which owes as much to the fifth book of Lucretius (esp. ll. 925-1168) as it does to Sidney, Locke, and company—men were originally created free, in the state of nature ("Where

---

[61] Charles Hanbury Williams satirically portrayed Lyttelton in 1740 as recalling, like Lee's Alexander:

> When I, great Liberty, thy standard bore,
> And Walpole pale sat trembling on the floor;
> When all th' applauding patriot band allow'd
> That I myself appear'd their leading god. . . .
> ("A Political Eclogue," in *The Works of the Right Honourable Sir Chas. Hanbury Williams* [3v., 1822], I, 65.)

[62] Cf. *Letters from a Persian in England* (1735), Letters x-xxi, in *The Works of George Lord Lyttelton* (1774), pp. 122-40. Lyttelton's purpose was, by continuing Montesquieu's history of the "Troglodites" (*Lettres Persanes*, Letters xi-xiv) "to shew . . . by what steps, and through what changes, the original good of society is overturned, and mankind become wickeder and more miserable in a state of government, than they were when left in a state of nature" (p. 122). So Fielding cries:

> But Men, it seems, to Laws of Compact yield;
> While Nature only governs in the Field.
> Curse on all Laws which Liberty subdue,
> And make the Many wretched for the Few.
> (*Misc.*, I, 21)

Both Lyttelton and Fielding could sound like primitivists when the Age of Walpole was in question: to read these lines as an adumbration of, say, the nineteenth-century Reform Bills is completely to misconceive them.

POETRY

Nature dictates, see how Freedom reigns"), but were subdued by the stronger among them and made slaves. In the course of time, however, a "nobler Sort" appeared, who though strong were not tyrannical:

> With warm Humanity their Bosoms glow'd,
> They felt to Nature their great Strength they ow'd.
> (*Misc.*, I, 22)

These guardians broke the tyrant power and set the people free:

> O'er abject Slaves they scorn'd inglorious Sway,
> But taught the grateful freed Man to obey;
> And thus by giving Liberty, enjoy'd
> What the first hop'd from Liberty destroy'd.
> (*Misc.*, I, 22)

Thus, through a "Compact," government was established, the people giving up power in order to enjoy freedom under law.

> The People Pow'r, to keep their Freedom, gave,
> And he who had it was the only Slave.
> (*Misc.*, I, 22)[63]

But the inevitable corruption of this equitable scheme ensued. Kings arose, and with them Priests (and Lawyers!), "belying" not only the people but their gods.

> Hence all the Evils which Mankind have known,
> The Priest's dark Mystery, the Tyrant's Throne;
> Hence Lords, and Ministers, and such sad Things;
> And hence the strange Divinity of Kings.
> (*Misc.*, I, 23)

[63] Cf. the chief magistrate of the wild country in which Mrs. Heartfree suffers her shipwreck: "His Office is of such Care and Trouble, that nothing but that restless Love of Power, so predominant in the Mind of Man, could make it the Object of Desire; for he is indeed the only Slave of all the Natives of this Country" (*JW*, IV, xii; *Misc.*, III, 376). Fielding usually conceived of the Good King as the "slave" of his people —cf. the Gypsy chief in *Tom Jones* (XII, xii) or the King-to-be of the *Journey from This World to the Next* (chap. v).

His vague historic fable concluded, Fielding moves into the long apostrophe to liberty that makes up a third of the poem.

> Thro' thee, the Lawrel crown'd the Victor's Brow,
> Who serv'd before his Country at the Plough:
> Thro' thee (what most must to thy Praise appear)
> Proud Senates scorn'd not to seek Virtue there.
> . . . .
> [Thou] Hast shewn the Peasant Glory, and call'd forth
> Wealth from the barren Sand, and Heroes from the North;
> The southern Skies, without thee, to no End
> In the cool Breeze, or genial Show'rs descend:
> Possess'd of thee, the *Vandal*, and the *Hun*,
> Enjoy their Frost, nor mourn the distant Sun.
> (*Misc.*, I, 23-24)

After these customary associations of liberty with classical republicanism and with Gothic peoples of the north, the apostrophe to Liberty is continued (also in traditional vein) with the argument that since Greece and Rome no longer shelter freedom, its natural home is Britain. The familiar roll call of Agincourt and Crécy, of Edward III and Henry V, is sounded; but Fielding gives largest space to the deeds of his personal hero, the Duke of Marlborough. And he concludes his panegyric with a higher eloquence than he usually mustered in poetry:

> O! teach us to withstand, as they withstood,
> Nor lose the Purchase of our Father's Blood.
> Ne'er blush that Sun that saw in *Blenheim*'s Plain
> Streams of our Blood, and Mountains of our Slain;
> . . . .
> Ne'er blush that Sun to see a *British* Slave.
> (*Misc.*, I, 24-25)

POETRY

Like James Thomson's *Liberty* (1735-1736), and a spate of poems and plays in the 1730's, Fielding's poem was inspired by immediate political motives; but this "Liberty literature" belongs also to a broad tradition of English social and political development, and, more narrowly, to the so-called "Whig tradition" that grew out of the Glorious Revolution of 1688. These traditions have been subjected to exhaustive analysis by recent scholarship and need not be examined here.[64] It is, of course, true that the English populace of the eighteenth century prided itself upon a greater degree of "liberty" than it actually possessed (as, even later, Goldsmith's imprisoned debtor in the *Citizen of the World*, Letter IV, amusingly illustrates). Nevertheless, the Glorious Revolution had truly been a death-blow to the theory of divine right. Seen in retrospect, it represents a major step in the creation of a climate receptive to the social and political reforms which were to come in the next two centuries. There is a certain accuracy to the remark of Thomas Gordon that "as popular Discontents and Clamour are seldom known in Arbitrary Governments, the Frequency of them in *England* is the greatest Instance of our Freedom we can give...."[65] The English tradition, when compared with that of most countries on the continent, offered a source of legitimate pride to every Englishman; and Addison, touring Italy in 1701, could count on an echo in the hearts of all his compatriots when he declared:

> We envy not the warmer clime...
> 'Tis liberty that crowns Britannia's isle,

[64] See Alan D. McKillop, *The Background of Thomson's Liberty* (Houston, Texas, 1951); Zera S. Fink, *The Classical Republicans* (Evanston, Ill., 1945); and Samuel Kliger, *The Goths in England* (Cambridge, Mass., 1952). On the history of contract theory, see J. W. Gough, *The Social Contract* (2nd ed., Oxford, 1957).
[65] "*Of* PATRIOTISM," *The Humourist* (2v., 1720-1725), II, 202.

And makes her barren rocks and her bleak mountains smile.[66]

This concept of traditional British liberty was appealed to as a sanction for such disparate enterprises as war with Spain, protest against the excise tax, anti-Catholic propaganda, or justification of particular political and economic policies; and, clearly, it was often exploited for sheer political opportunism.[67] Just as the Whigs had taken "liberty" for their shibboleth after the Revolution, so in the 1730's the "patriot" opposition to Walpole made it the watchword of their own vigorous campaign.[68] Professor McKillop has observed the ease with which the transition from something like Addison's generalized celebration of Liberty (cited above) to the specific attack on Walpole could be made:

"The Briton on the grand tour viewed the monuments of history and art with frequent reference to British freedom. But such themes might be used to point a contrast

[66] "Letter from Italy to the Right Hon. Charles Lord Halifax, in the Year MDCCI," *The Works of Joseph Addison*, ed. G. W. Greene (6v., 1887), I, 167.

[67] See C. A. Moore, "Whig Panegyric Verse, 1700-1760: A Phase of Sentimentalism," *PMLA*, XLI (1926), 362-401, reprinted in *Backgrounds of English Literature, 1700-1760* (Minneapolis, 1953), pp. 104-44; and Clement Ramsland, "Britons Never Will Be Slaves: A Study in Whig Political Propaganda in the British Theatre, 1700-1742," *Quarterly Journal of Speech*, XXVIII (1942), 393-99. Bonamy Dobrée has indicated that the ardor for liberty was only one of many guises under which the insurgent patriotism of the time appeared in poetry ("The Theme of Patriotism in the Poetry of the Early Eighteenth Century," *Proceedings of the British Academy*, XXXV [1949], 49-65).

[68] Thus an anonymous attack on Walpole in 1741 declares: "Give us none of your Cant about *Allegiance, Oaths, Compacts,* and *Terms of Submission*: These Things will not go down now-a-days; LIBERTY, Sir, LIBERTY, I say, in its widest Extent, is what we want, and will have, cost what it will" (*A Seasonable Admonition to a Great Man* [1741], pp. 21-22). As McKillop points out, the apologists for Walpole answered with a Whiggish argument of their own, concentrating upon the gains in English liberty since 1688, and tending to belittle the Opposition's emphasis on primordial liberty and the undermining of liberty by corruption (*The Background of Thomson's Liberty*, p. 87).

not only between continental tyranny and British freedom, but between true constitutional government in Britain and the political degeneration that came from jobbery and corruption. This pattern of ideas was taken up by the opponents of Walpole."[69]

Thus the Opposition pamphleteers argued *ad nauseam* that Walpole's corruption and bribery appealed to man's baser instincts and instituted a general weakening of moral fibre, thereby creating in the nation a climate in which liberty could not survive. Walpole was seen as responsible, both in an oblique and in a direct sense, for the "decay of liberty": obliquely, in that he contributed to the degeneration of national virtue upon which liberty depended,[70] and directly, in his highhanded efforts to maintain power and silence criticism. This was the dual theme that the Opposition writers exploited with every weapon in their literary arsenal for over a decade (the *Craftsman* declared, "THERE are some Subjects, which cannot be handled too often; especially That of LIBERTY . . .").[71] It was this note that Fielding was primarily concerned to sound in his poem to Lyttelton:

> But thou, great Liberty, keep *Britain* free,
> Nor let Men use us as we use the Bee.
> Let not base Drones upon our Honey thrive,
> And suffocate the Maker in his Hive.
>
> (*Misc.*, I, 25)[72]

---

[69] "Ethics and Political History in Thomson's *Liberty*," in *Pope and His Contemporaries: Essays Presented to George Sherburn*, ed. J. L. Clifford and L. A. Landa (Oxford, 1949), p. 218.

[70] Cf. Thomson, *Liberty*, Part v, ll. 93-98.

[71] No. 183, 3 January 1730; coll. ed. (14v., 1731-1737), VI, 1.

[72] For the conventional enough image of the drones, cf. Thomson, *Liberty*, Part IV, ll. 850-53. Fielding used the same image again in *Amelia* (IV, viii; Henley, VI, 217-18), when he argued that the public could afford to support soldiers in a better fashion.

POETRY

2

Though somewhat general, Fielding's observations in this period upon the theme of liberty have an interest that goes beyond mere political controversy: for his personal attitude toward the idea of liberty was rather complex and underwent a gradual and natural progression in the direction of greater conservatism as he grew older and took on more public responsibility.[73]

There can be no doubt that in the thirties he was completely sincere in the belief, implicit in the poem to Lyttelton, that Walpole's policies were sapping the moral strength of the nation and threatening English liberty. In the "Dedication to the Public" of his *Historical Register* in 1737 he said:

"I hope too it will be remarked, that the politicians are represented as a set of blundering blockheads rather deserving pity than abhorrence, whereas the others [that is, the "patriots" of Act III] are represented as a set of cunning, self-interested fellows, who for a little paltry bribe would give up the liberties and properties of their country. Here is the danger, here is the rock on which our constitution must, if ever it does, split. The liberties of a people have been subdued by the conquest of valour and force, and have been betrayed by the subtle and dexterous arts of refined policy, but these are rare instances; for geniuses of this kind are not the growth of every age, whereas, if a

[73] Archibald B. Shepperson ("Fielding on Liberty and Democracy," in *English Studies in Honor of James Southall Wilson* [Charlottesville, Va., 1951], pp. 265-75) has capably surveyed some of the leading themes in Fielding's writings on liberty; but I feel that in his eagerness to stress the "democratic" elements in Fielding's work, Professor Shepperson tends to read into statements calling for an eighteenth-century context a twentieth-century conception of their intent and meaning. My own examination of the evidence may well overstress the "anti-democratic" element in Fielding, for I have been concerned to bring forward some of the important statements of his own views on the subject that have often been overlooked in modern studies of his political principles (though not in George Sherburn's shrewd appraisal, "Fielding's Social Outlook," *PQ*, xxxv [1956], 1-23).

general corruption be once introduced, and those who should be the guardians and bulwarks of our liberty, once find, or think they find, an interest in giving it up, no great capacity will be required to destroy it . . ."—(Henley, XI, 235-36).

In *Jonathan Wild*, he ironically remarked the ingratitude of governments toward the glory of great men: "And this from a foolish Zeal for a certain ridiculous imaginary Thing called Liberty, to which GREAT MEN are observed to have a great Animosity" (IV, ii; *Misc.*, III, 295); and when Wild and Johnson misled the inhabitants of Newgate with their charges and countercharges, Fielding placed his own solemn convictions in the mouth of the "grave Man" who arose to tell the debtors that nothing less than a total change of political mores would actually preserve their "liberty":

"To preserve, therefore, the Liberty of *Newgate* [that is, of England, in this context], is to change the Manners of *Newgate*. . . . Let us consider ourselves all as Members of one Community, to the public Good of which we are to sacrifice our private Views; not to give up the Interest of the whole for the least Pleasure or Profit which shall accrue to our selves. Liberty is consistent with no Degree of Honesty inferiour to this . . ."—(IV, iii; *Misc.*, III, 307-8).

The poem to Lyttelton expressed, to be sure, only one aspect of Fielding's views on liberty, and that an occasional one dictated by the contemporary political situation. But the lengthy discussion of government some years later, inspired by the discipline of the gypsy band in *Tom Jones* (XII, xii), shows clearly that whatever Fielding may have thought of government in the abstract, or of Walpole in particular, he continued to believe in the practical advantages of that limited monarchy founded on the honest virtue of both governor and governed, which he had celebrated in *Liberty*. As he saw it, this was the only satisfactory *mean*, protecting the citizens of a state from the ambition of unlimited monarchs and the license of uncontrolled democracy.

Fielding would never, of course, any more than any other normal political thinker of his time, have taken the possibility of a truly democratic government seriously. He saw such a state as "inconsistent with all government, and which befits only that which is sometimes called the state of nature, but may more properly be called a state of barbarism and wildness."[74] He had little faith in the political astuteness of the masses, and in his later years his estimate of the "lower sort of people" was clearly in terms of a group to be told what to do. From the start, he had been keenly aware that the populace had no real sense of the meaning of that "liberty" they clamored for; moreover, he saw that their emotionalism and ignorance made them mere pawns in the hands of dangerous demagogues. Thus Sir Harry and the country party in *Pasquin*, though representative of the anti-Walpole sentiment Fielding himself was stressing, are depicted as shouting senselessly on all occasions the popular slogan of the Opposition, "Liberty and property, and no excise!" In the Newgate campaign of *Jonathan Wild*, referred to above, the debtors or populace, who "were the destined Plunder of both Parties," are pictured as taking enthusiastic and unthinking sides in the campaign. In the second (1754) edition, this phrase was added to the description: "And the poor Debtors re-echoed *the Liberties of Newgate*, which in the Cant Language signifies *Plunder*, as loudly as the Thieves themselves" (IV, iii; 2nd ed., p. 194).

It is in the productions of his last years that Fielding's distrust of—even contempt for—the mob appears most strongly. He pictures in a humorous way in *Amelia* the unthinking automatism of the lower classes: "Booth desired the bailiff to give him his opinion of liberty. Upon

---

[74] *A Proposal for Making an Effectual Provision for the Poor* (1753); Henley, XIII, 138.

which he hesitated a moment, and then cried out, 'Oh, 'tis a fine thing, 'tis a very fine thing, and the constitution of England'" (VIII, ii; Henley, VII, 70). But in the *Covent-Garden Journal* and the *Voyage to Lisbon* the matter was treated more seriously. The severe attack on the "*profanum vulgus*" in *Covent-Garden Journal* No. 49 offers as one of the reasons for the frightening elevation of the mob "the mistaken Idea which some particular Persons have always entertained of the Word Liberty";[75] and in a later paper he further explains this as a notion of "Exemption from all Restraint of municipal Laws" and "of those Rules of Behaviour which are expressed in the general Term of good Breeding."[76]

The *Voyage to Lisbon* contains some of Fielding's bitterest animadversions on the rapacity and bestiality of the lower classes. After suffering the tauntings of the watermen as he is carried helplessly aboard ship in the Thames, Fielding reflects:

"It may be said, that this barbarous custom is peculiar to the English, and of them only to the lowest degree; that it is an excrescence of an uncontroul'd licentiousness mistaken for liberty, and never shews itself in men who are polish'd and refin'd, in such manner as human nature requires, to produce that perfection of which it is susceptible, and to purge away that malevolence of disposition, of which, at our birth, we partake in common with the savage creation"—(Henley, XVI, 201).

---

[75] Jensen, II, 35. The attack on this rising "fourth Estate" is prefaced by Horace's "Odi profanum vulgus," as *CGJ* No. 47 is by a tag from Silius Italicus (*Punica*, IX, 636; also used for the *Champion*, 1 March 1740): "Heu plebes scelerata!"—translated as "O ye wicked Rascallions!"

[76] *CGJ*, No. 55; Jensen, II, 59-60. In No. 58, a letter from "A true Englishman" describes the Westminster Elections: A cobbler delivers a harangue which "consisted of frequent Repetitions of the Words Liberty and true Englishman, but to what Purpose they were introduced, I must confess myself at a Loss to determine; so far I observed, that they conveyed to his Hearers a great Idea of the Dignity and Independency of the Speaker" (*ibid.*, p. 78). The writer adds of the mob as a whole, "Nor can I help observing that Liberty was in all their Mouths, and served like Lillaburlero, as a kind of Burthen to close the End of every Speech" (p. 79).

This usage of "liberty" may seem to be a different thing altogether from the concept of *political* liberty, but that the two were clearly associated in Fielding's mind is shown by a later comment in the *Voyage*, which may serve as his final and well-considered judgment on the subject:

"The whole mischief which infects this part of our economy [that is, in the case "between the mob and their betters"], arises from the vague and uncertain use of a word called Liberty, of which, as scarce any two men with whom I have ever conversed, seem to have one and the same idea, I am inclined to doubt whether there be any simple universal notion represented by this word. . . .

"By liberty, however, I apprehend, is commonly understood the power of doing what we please: not absolutely; for then it would be inconsistent with law, by whose controul the liberty of the freest people, except only the Hottentots and wild Indians, must always be restrained.

"But, indeed, however largely we extend, or however moderately we confine the sense of the word, no politician will, I presume, contend that it is to pervade in an equal degree, and be with the same extent enjoyed by every member of society; no such polity having been ever found, unless among those vile people just before commemorated"— (Henley, XVI, 239).

We may see, comparing this statement with the earlier poetical celebration of an abstract freedom, that Dr. Johnson's remark on "that indistinct and headstrong ardour for liberty which a man of genius always catches when he enters the world, and always suffers to cool as he passes forward"[77] is, in a sense, applicable to Fielding. Yet it is probably true that the element of change is not so great as might appear; for the idea of liberty was customarily considered by Fielding, as by his contemporaries, on two planes: first, the liberty of the responsible middle- and

[77] "Lyttelton," *Lives of the English Poets*, ed. G. B. Hill (3v., Oxford, 1905), III, 446.

upper-class citizen, which he defended from first to last; and second, that "Licence they mean when they cry libertie" (cf. Milton, Sonnet XII), which was attributed to the lower classes, the irresponsible mob, and which he consistently mocked and consistently detested. He defined his generalized concept of liberty in the *Charge Delivered to the Grand Jury* in 1749: "What other idea can we have of liberty than that it is the enjoyment of our lives, our persons, and our properties in security; to be free masters of ourselves and our possessions, as far as the known laws of our country will admit; to be liable to no punishment, no confinement, no loss, but what those laws subject us to! Is there any man ignorant enough to deny that this is a description of a free people?" —(Henley, XIII, 209).

It is well to remember, however, that the key word here is not "freedom," but "law," or better, "freedom under the law." Order was the first great desideratum of society, and any freedom that threatened order was, in Fielding's view, evil and subversive. What I have described as a stratified concept—that is, one degree of liberty for the aristocratic, the substantial, and the responsible citizens, and another for the great body of laboring (or nonlaboring) poor—was regarded as eminently consistent with the proper order and constitution of society. Hence Fielding saw no contradiction between the definition of liberty presented in his charge to the jury and his insistence upon the necessity of forcing the poor to work—at wages fixed by their employers—or his projected laws to prevent the poor from wandering about without restriction.[78] In the *Proposal for*

---

[78] See *An Enquiry into the Causes of the Late Increase of Robbers* (Henley, XIII, 7-127), *passim*. Irvin Ehrenpreis, in making the same point about Swift's view of liberty, observes, "As Walton had said, '*Laws are not made for private men to dispute, but to Obey*' [*Life of Hooker*]. Only with this understanding did either Swift or Burke claim that liberty was every man's birthright" ("Swift on Liberty," *JHI*, XIII [1952], 131-46). This is assuredly true of Fielding as well. The preface to the *Enquiry* declares, "In plain truth, the principal design of this whole work is to

Making an Effectual Provision for the Poor, he was frankly incredulous that anyone could suppose such a project to be contrary to the tradition of English liberty:

"I should scarce apprehend, though I am told I may, that some persons should represent the restraint here laid on the lower people as derogatory from their liberty. Such notions are indeed of the enthusiastical kind, and are inconsistent with all order and all government. They are the natural parents of that licentiousness which it is one main intent of this whole plan to cure—which is necessarily productive of most of the evils of which the public complains; of that licentiousness, in a word, which among the many mischiefs introduced by it into every society where it prevails, is sure at last to end in the destruction of liberty itself"—(Henley, XIII, 181).

Fielding has often been praised by modern writers for his democratic tendencies. This is not altogether an error: Fielding was a "democrat," insofar as he believed that "we are by Nature all equal. We bring with us the same Perfections and Imperfections (I speak generally) both of Body and Mind, into the World. And again, as we were equal in the Womb, so we are equal in the Grave."[79] But

---

rouse the civil power from its present lethargic state. A design, which alike opposes *those wild notions of liberty that are inconsistent with all government*, and those pernicious schemes of government which are destructive of true liberty. However contrary indeed these principles may seem to each other, they have both the same common interest; or, rather, the former are the wretched tools of the latter; for anarchy is almost sure to end in some kind of tyranny" (Henley, XIII, 17; italics mine).

[79] *CGJ*, No. 43 (30 May 1752; Jensen, II, 6-7). The quotation is from a letter undoubtedly written by Fielding, purporting to be from one "Paul Traffick," a representative of the merchant class. Although Fielding puts some of his own views in Mr. Traffick's mouth, one must be cautious in quoting such material as evidence of Fielding's own convictions. Mr. Traffick, for example, might well be supposed to believe that "in some Countries perhaps these Marks [of virtue and genius] have been mere chimerical; but among every trading People, as I take it, Money is that which stamps a Value on the Possessor, and places a Man at the Head of his Countrymen" (p. 7); but this could scarcely be quoted as a straightforward statement of Fielding's own sentiments!

equality in the sight of God, and even in the eyes of the law, does not argue equality of ability and intelligence, nor is it, Fielding assuredly believed, an argument for social or political equality. He is properly known for his broad human sympathies and his ability to recognize honesty and decency (as well as to censure folly and selfishness) in whatever garb they might be clothed. In *Tom Jones* he had defined "mob" as "persons without virtue or sense, in all stations; and many of the highest rank are often meant by it" (I, ix; Henley, III, 46).[80] But this should not blind us to the fact that Fielding time and time again asserted the necessity for recognizing and respecting social and political hierarchy, and always concluded, with Goldsmith, that "just experience tells, in every soil, / That those who think must govern those that toil."[81] Fielding could

[80] Cf. Seneca, *De vita beata* II. 2: "Vulgum autem tam chlamydatos quam coronatos voco."
[81] "The Traveller," ll. 371-72; *Works*, ed. J. W. M. Gibbs (5v., 1884-1886), II, 17. The attempt to reconcile—and justify—the fact of equality in the eyes of God with the inequality of men in a hierarchical society is persistently made in the sermons of the time (cf. Louis A. Landa, "Jonathan Swift and Charity," *JEGP*, XLIV [1945], 337-50). It is true that Fielding, a lover of good men in whatever station, and certainly no admirer of the mores of the *beau monde*, frequently offers such arguments as Booth returns to Miss Matthews when she finds Atkinson's behavior astonishing "in so low a fellow." He replies that greatness of mind may be found in one rank as well as another: "Love, benevolence, or what you will please to call it, may be the reigning passion in a beggar as well as in a prince; and wherever it is, its energies will be the same" (*Amelia*, III, vii; Henley, VI, 139). But it must be observed that such views are always associated with that worthy type of the lower-class citizen, like honest Sergeant Atkinson, who knows his place and shows proper respect for his (literal) "betters." Fielding had little sympathy with pretensions above their station in the lower classes (cf. the "Robinhoodians" in *CGJ*, No. 8); he distrusted their capacity, as a class, to understand the responsibilities of suffrage (see, for example, *CGJ*, No. 58, cited in part above, and the *Jacobite's Journal*, No. 45, 8 October 1748); and after his appointment as a magistrate had introduced him more intimately to the lawlessness and impudence of "the Dregs of the People" (*CGJ*, No. 9; Jensen, I, 188), his earlier tolerance gave way to an increasing disgust with their laziness and insolence as a class (cf. *CGJ*, Nos. 9, 47, 49, etc., for animadversions on "the Mob"; and see, among other passages, the *Voyage to Lisbon*, Henley, XVI, 239-42).

Of his making a footman the hero of *Joseph Andrews*, which has often

believe that mere ceremony constitutes "the only external Difference between Man and Man" (*Misc.*, I, 131-32), but he was industrious to insist that this was precisely what gave ceremony its importance—it maintained the structure of society, the social fabric (cf. the *Essay on Conversation*).

Ideally, those who by birth or natural talent occupied high rank in society and the nation's government should turn the benefits and privileges they (rightly) enjoyed to the use of that society and that nation. Fielding bitterly attacked those who ignored or failed to live up to this ideal; but he expressed no wish to change the structure of society itself. He was concerned to correct the abuses precisely *because* they threatened the continued existence of this order of society and government. Thus when he strikes out against the aristocracy or polite society, it is because they (at large or as individuals) are failing to recognize their responsibilities, the real sense of *noblesse oblige*. When he contrasts the virtues of the lower classes—and most of his good Samaritans are from their ranks—with the vices of the upper, it is neither because he is a leveller nor a republican: the contrast is in part a device intended to shame the natural leaders of society into an awareness of their neglected duties, of their failures both in the realm of social conduct and of political affairs.[82]

---

been cited as an example of his democratic sympathies, it should be noted (not in refutation, but as a corrective) that the parodic element of the work demanded a hero from the lower class as a parallel to Pamela's low origins. Fielding had no love for footmen as a group, the Footmen's Riot at Drury Lane in 1737 having been partly responsible for the failure of *Eurydice* (cf. his satirical picture of the footman-critic in *The Wedding Day*, III, viii; Henley, XII, 109-10).

[82] Fielding argued that such vices as excessive luxury and gaming were "rather a moral than a political evil" among the upper classes (*Enquiry*, Henley, XIII, 21); but that when extended to the lower classes, they threatened the very life of the state (*Enquiry*, *passim*, and *Proposal for . . . The Poor*, *passim*). Though he feared the corruption of the "useful part of mankind" by the example of "persons of fashion and fortune," he could use some very Mandevillian arguments to justify the luxuries of the latter (for example, Henley, XIII, 14, 28, 138).

Liberty to Fielding, as to Jonathan Swift and Samuel Johnson,[83] was a grant to the educated and responsible members of society, and it carried with it the obligations of intelligent use, restraint, and the recognition of an inherent scale of subordination. This is that "virtuous liberty" which Addison's *Cato* (II, i) celebrated, and it is this concept which underlies Fielding's general social construct as well as the more specifically political ideas expressed in the poem, *Liberty*, of the *Miscellanies*.

(4) "TO A FRIEND ON THE CHOICE of a WIFE."

Wilbur L. Cross (I, 384) takes this poem to have been a compliment to Lyttelton on his marriage in the summer of 1742; but there is no convincing internal evidence to that effect.[84] Indeed, the verses are clearly addressed to someone seeking to choose a wife, not to someone just married. It seems wiser, lacking other evidence, to consider the poetic advice as addressed to a purely hypothetical friend, providing its author with the opportunity to expatiate upon one of his favorite subjects: marriage.

The opening lines of the poem comment knowledgeably enough upon the difficulty of giving advice to friends ("Men frequent wish another's Judgment known, / Not to destroy, but to confirm their own"); but, as men will, Fielding proceeds to give the advice anyway. He observes that al-

[83] See Edward A. Bloom, "Johnson on a Free Press: A Study in Liberty and Subordination," *ELH*, XVI (1949), 251-71.

[84] Lyttelton's marriage to Lucy Fortescue, a reigning beauty of Devonshire, took place in June 1742. It is true that some of Fielding's lines could apply well enough to Lyttelton: "Happy *Alexis*, sprung from such a Race, / Whose Blood would no Nobility disgrace" (*Misc.*, I, 32). Lyttelton's father was only a baronet, but he came from a good and ancient family; and Fielding had paid Lyttelton something of the same kind of compliment in his poem, *Liberty*: "Brave, tho' no Soldier; without Titles, great" (*Misc.*, I, 20). Nevertheless, the tone (and the "advice" itself) of the poem would seem somewhat impertinent, I believe, addressed to a man who was patron as well as friend—and the bulk of the poem can scarcely be described as a celebration of the marital state!

though marriage was ordained by Heaven for our good, the modern confusion about what is "good" leads to choices based on mere beauty or fortune or great family:

> Who to himself, now in his Courtship, says,
> I chuse a Partner of my future Days;
> Her Face, or Pocket seen, her Mind they trust;
> They wed to lay the Fiends of Avarice or Lust.
> (*Misc.*, I, 27-28)

This "profanation of a most holy ceremony" (cf. *Tom Jones*, I, xii; Henley, III, 58) is contrasted with a nobler ideal:

> But thou, whose honest Thoughts the Choice intend
> Of a Companion, and a softer Friend;
> A tender Heart, which while thy Soul it shares,
> Augments thy Joys, and lessens all thy Cares.
> One, who by thee while tenderly carest,
> Shall steal that God-like Transport to thy Breast,
> The Joy to find you make another blest.
> Thee in thy Choice let other Maxims move,
> They wed for baser Passions; thou for Love.
> (*Misc.*, I, 28)

The eloquence of these lines—and this is one of Fielding's most eloquent poems—suggests the lurking image of his most well beloved Charlotte. But the felicity of his own marriage was unlikely to blind such a practical and observant spectator of the current matrimonial lotteries to the woes arising from a choice less wise or less fortunate than his own. Hence the bulk of the poem is taken up with a delineation of the miseries attendant upon those who have married, not so much in haste as for altogether the wrong reasons—espoused reigning beauties, wits, fools, heiresses, titled ladies, coquettes, or prudes—and repented at their unhappy leisure. The portraits of these assorted shrews enjoy, of course, the benefit of ancient tradition; but they are sketched with knowing perceptiveness:

> Beauties think Heav'n they in themselves bestow,
> All we return is Gratitude too low.
> (*Misc.*, I, 29)

And "To praise a Wit enough, is harder still." On the other hand, if one's choice should light upon some frivolous coquette whose very puerilities are charming—beware!

> Tho' now, perhaps, those childish Airs you prize,
> Lovers and Husbands see with diff'rent Eyes.
> (*Misc.*, I, 30)

Those, again, who promise themselves the profit of a fortune or connection with a fine name discover too late that in the package as well are the taunts, upbraidings, and scorn of wives highly conscious of their deserts.[85]

A digression, excoriating the education in matrimonial ideals that women commonly receive, touches upon one of Fielding's particular *bêtes noires*:

> Women by Nature form'd too prone to Ill,
> By Education are made proner still,
> To cheat, deceive, conceal each genuine Thought,
> By Mothers, and by Mistresses are taught.
> (*Misc.*, I, 34)

Fielding's chapter in *Joseph Andrews,* entitled "PHILOSOPHICAL REFLECTIONS, THE LIKE NOT TO BE FOUND IN ANY LIGHT FRENCH ROMANCE" (IV, vii) had begun with a descant on the theme of women's education: viz., that they are con-

---

[85] All of these types find their dramatic portraits or appropriate commentary elsewhere in Fielding's works; but apparently he considered most insufferable those women who compared their husband's families unfavorably with their own. Speaking of the switch that Black George kept to maintain peace in his house, Fielding says that this is a medicine proper only for the vulgar, "unless in one single instance, viz., where superiority of birth breaks out; in which case, we should not think it very improperly applied by any husband whatever . . ." (*Tom Jones*, IV, ix; Henley, III, 178-79).

POETRY

tinually instructed in deceit until they become habitually deceitful. So in *Tom Jones* (xiv, i), speaking in his own proper person, Fielding later declared: "Our present women have been taught by their mothers to fix their thoughts only on ambition and vanity, and to despise the pleasures of love as unworthy their regard; and being afterwards, by the care of such mothers, married without having husbands, they seem pretty well confirmed in the justness of those sentiments...."[86]

But at the end of his poem, he eschews the pose of Juvenalian misogyny (for, as Fielding said elsewhere, "I am much more inclined to Panegyric on that amiable Sex, which I have always thought treated with a very unjust Severity by ours...");[87] and we return to that happier image, which had been adumbrated in the opening sketch, of his own paragon:

> May she then prove, who shall thy Lot befall,
> Beauteous to thee, agreeable to all.
> Nor Wit, nor Learning proudly may she boast;
> No low-bred Girl, nor gay fantastic Toast:
> Her tender Soul, Good-nature must adorn,
> And Vice and Meanness be alone her Scorn.
> Fond of thy Person, may her Bosom glow
> With Passions thou hast taught her first to know.
> A warm Partaker of the genial Bed,
> Thither by Fondness, not by Lewdness led.
> Superior Judgment may she own thy Lot;
> Humbly advise, but contradict thee not.
> Thine to all other Company prefer;

---

[86] Henley, v, 95. The same theme in almost the same words is elaborated upon by Job Vinegar in the *Champion* (4 September 1740; and cf. 5 August 1740). See *The Voyages of Mr. Job Vinegar, from The Champion* (1740), ed. S. J. Sackett (Augustan Reprint Society No. 67; Los Angeles, Calif., 1958), pp. 31 and 15-17.
[87] Preface to the *Miscellanies* (i, iii).

POETRY

May all thy Troubles find Relief from her.
If Fortune gives thee such a Wife to meet,
Earth cannot make thy Blessing more complete.

(*Misc.*, I, 35)

2

Fielding's poem has affinities with a number of popular (and familiar) traditions involving the role of women in a masculine society. It resembles, first of all, that *Sixth Satire* of Juvenal which he had himself "modernized" in his youth (see below), and which Dryden a half-century earlier had characterized as "a Common-place, from whence all the Moderns have notoriously stollen their sharpest Raileries [against the fair Sex]."[88] Fielding's plan is roughly the same as Juvenal's: the author counsels his friend, who is contemplating marriage, to consider the behavior of modern women and to review in his mind the convincing arguments against a thoughtless marriage. He then proceeds to enumerate the various types of women who make the wedded state a familiar Hell. The principal difference between Juvenal's diatribe and Fielding's is that the former all too plainly treasured no reserve image of a Charlotte Cradock in his mind.

One need not scan the ancient and abiding tradition of antifeminist literature to establish that Fielding's poem belongs in that line. A less vituperative but perhaps a more trying tradition to the ladies found copious representation, through poems, prose treatises, and sermons in the eighteenth century (as before): the genre that one might call "Advice to Women." Included in its scope are disquisitions on manners, education, morals and, most important

[88] Argument to "The Sixth Satyr of Juvenal" in *Poems of John Dryden*, ed. James Kinsley (4v., Oxford, 1958), II, 694. Cf. also *The English Theophrastus* (a collection attrib. to Abel Boyer, 1702): "*What Lady, nay, what* Eloping *Lady, has not been entertain'd with the Sixth Satyr of* Juvenal?" (Preface, A4-A4v).

of all, marriage; it comprises such well-known commentaries as Halifax's *Advice to a Daughter* (1688); Swift's *Letter to a Very Young Lady on Her Marriage*, in the Motte *Miscellanies*, Vol. II (1727); and the *Advice to a Lady* of George Lyttelton. Courtesy books like *The Young Ladies Conduct . . . and Advice to Young Wives* (1722) by John Essex, the dancing master, or that amalgam of seventeenth-century snippets, the popular *Ladies Library*, published by Steele in 1714, anticipated the flood of wholesome advice that was to be incorporated in such tomes as the century wore on.[89] Handbooks on the relative duties carefully inculcated the submission of wives to their husbands, and numberless sermons were preached on the text: "Ye Wives, be in subjection to your own Husbands. . . ."[90] The poetic fascicule of the total somewhat wearying book may be represented by Edward Young's Satires V-VI, "On WOMEN," in *Love of Fame* (1728), and Pope's *Epistle to a Lady: Of the Characters of Women* (1735). Some of these various works are nominally addressed to a man, as Fielding's poem is, but their ultimate goal is the feminine ear: the "advice" that Fielding offers is as much for nubile young ladies as it is for his bachelor friend.

The ladies and their defenders occasionally struck back, with broadsides like *The Lady's Advocate, or An Apology for Matrimony* (1741) or such tracts as *The Woman's Advocate, or The Baudy Batchelor out in His Own Calculation, Being the Genuine Answer . . . to the Batchelor's Estimate* (1729). The latter, incidentally, was in reply to

[89] See Katherine Hornbeak, "Richardson's *Familiar Letters* and the Domestic Conduct Books," *Smith College Studies in Modern Languages*, XIX, ii (1938), 1-29; A. R. Humphreys, "The 'Rights of Woman' in the Age of Reason," *MLR*, XLI (1946), 256-69; and Joachim Heinrich, *Die Frauenfrage bei Steele und Addison* (Leipzig, 1930). Ian Watt has some interesting remarks on the condition of women and the marriage relationship in the eighteenth century, in *The Rise of the Novel* (Berkeley & Los Angeles, 1957), pp. 135-73. Ruth Kelso, *Doctrine for the Lady of the Renaissance* (Urbana, Ill., 1956) is also relevant.

[90] I Peter 3:1; cf. also the advice of Ephesians 5:22-24, another favorite text. See Hornbeak, pp. 10-15.

POETRY

a famous pamphlet that Fielding several times spoke of disparagingly, *The Batchelor's Estimate of the Expences of a Married Life. In a Letter to a Friend* (1725).[91] This work, along with a later companion, *None but Fools Marry; or a Vindication of the Batchelor's Estimate* (1730), precipitated a paper war that Fielding alluded to in 1740 and that was still of enough popular interest in 1748 to warrant reprinting of the pamphlets.[92] Though the feminists may not have been defeated by direct attacks like these, one feels that they must surely have been worn down by such ponderous tomes as Thomas Salmon's *Critical Essay concerning Marriage* (1724), the *Present State of Matrimony; or the Real Causes of Conjugal Infidelity and Unhappy Marriages* by "Philogamus" (1739), and that copious handbook, the anonymous *Art of Governing a Wife; with Rules for Batchelors* (1747), which cried: "There are two things most prejudicial to the Female Sex; too much Tongue, and too little Patience: hence it follows, that she who is silent will be respected by all Men, and she who is submissive will live happily with her Husband. O how miserable is the Man that marries a high-spirited Woman!"[93]

3

The ridicule of marriage so popular on the Restoration stage—which never, of course, really represented the attitude of more than a small coterie—might be summed up in the couplet dubiously attributed to Rochester: *"Marriage!*

[91] Cf. the *Champion*, 1 January 1740 (Henley, xv, 130), and the *Journey from This World to the Next*, chap. iii (*Misc.*, II, 31).
[92] The *Champion*, loc.cit. The pamphlets were reprinted as appendices to an allegory called *Cupid and Hymen: A Voyage to the Isles of Love and Matrimony*; see Frederick T. Wood, "Henry Carey and an XVIII Century Satire on Matrimony," *N&Q*, CLXV (1933), 363-68.
[93] *Art of Governing a Wife* (1747), p. 16. Fielding's conclusions do not differ greatly from those of this anonymous author; nor, for that matter, do either of them offer much that had not been covered by Sir Thomas Overbury a century earlier, in his famous poetic essay, *A Wife* (1614), which was still being reprinted in the eighteenth century.

'Tis but a Licens'd way to Sin, / A Noose to Catch Religious Woodcocks in."[94] Fielding's own *beau-monde* characters often speak in this conventional vein; but there is nothing of this attitude in his poem, for all of its warnings against the wrong choice of a mate. Like many of his contemporaries, he approached the subject with much more seriousness than the court wits and their Augustan followers might suggest was characteristic of the age.

The concern, indeed, that Fielding displayed throughout his works with the whole question of marriage and of ideal conjugal behavior has been well documented by a modern student of *Amelia*, who calls particular attention to the fact that Fielding's poem on the choice of a wife "contains two passages that form an excellent summary of the wifely ideal embodied in Amelia."[95] The ironic description in *Jonathan Wild* of Mrs. Heartfree's "mean-spirited, poor, domestic, low-bred" conduct as a loving wife accords very well with Fielding's basic marital ideal. Mr. Wilson's wife in *Joseph Andrews* is pictured in much the same terms. That gentleman praises his wife's intelligence, but is quick to add that "he would not be apprehended to insinuate that [she] had an understanding above the care of her family; on the contrary, says he, my Harriet, I assure you, is a notable housewife, and the housekeepers of few gentlemen understand cookery or confectionery better . . ." (*JA*, III, iv; Henley, I, 257). The position assigned to a proper wife in the conjugal hierarchy is, moreover, clear enough from Allworthy's praise of Sophia:

". . . Her good nature, her charitable disposition, her modesty, are too well known to need any panegyric. . . . I never heard anything of pertness, or what is called repartee, out of her mouth. . . . Indeed, she always showed the highest deference to the understandings of men; a quality

[94] "A Satyr Against Marriage," in the *Collected Works of John Wilmot, Earl of Rochester*, ed. John Hayward (1926), p. 94.
[95] A. R. Towers, "*Amelia* and the State of Matrimony," *RES*, new ser., V (1954), 148.

POETRY

absolutely essential to the making a good wife"—(*TJ*, XVII, iii; Henley, v, 255-56). Feminists may bristle, but it is probable that Fielding was more "enlightened" in his views toward women than the average man of the day who needed no documentation in works like *Man Superior to Woman; or, A Vindication of Man's Natural Right of Sovereign Authority over the Woman* (anon.; published by Thomas Cooper in 1739) to assure him of his hierarchical advantage. Squire Western was not alone in believing that "women should come in with the first dish, and go out after the first glass" (*TJ*, VII, iv; Henley, III, 345). The *Advice to a Lady* of Fielding's friend Lyttelton, for example, abounds in such sentiments as these:

> The *houshold sceptre* if he bids you bear,
> Make it your pride his *servant* to appear:
> Endearing thus the common acts of life,
> The *mistress* still shall charm him in the *wife*. . . .

Lady Mary Wortley Montagu was not far from the truth when she epitomized Lyttelton's *Advice* in one witty couplet:

> Be plain in dress, and sober in your diet;
> In short, my deary, kiss me! and be quiet.[96]

If Fielding shared the predominant view that woman was the inferior partner in marriage, he was at least ever insistent upon one thing above all others: marriage must be based on love.[97] Allworthy expressed this conviction in full:

[96] *The Works of George Lord Lyttelton* (1774), p. 614 (the poem was originally published in 1733); "A SUMMARY OF LORD LYTTELTON'S ADVICE TO A LADY," *The Letters and Works of Lady Mary Wortley Montagu*, ed. Lord Wharncliffe (3rd ed. rev. by W. Moy Thomas, 2v., 1861), II, 494.
[97] Friedrich Antal, relating this conception to middle-class ideals, has pointed out that moral tracts like Defoe's *Use and Abuse of the Marriage Bed* (1727) also insisted that one should not marry without love. Hogarth had planned a cycle on the "Happy Marriage" based on love as a contrast to his "Marriage à la Mode" (the same contrast, of course, expressed in

"I have always thought love the only foundation of happiness in a married state, as it can only produce that high and tender friendship which should always be the cement of this union; and, in my opinion, all those marriages which are contracted from other motives are greatly criminal; they are a profanation of a most holy ceremony, and generally end in disquiet and misery: for surely we may call it a profanation to convert this most sacred institution into a wicked sacrifice to lust or avarice: and what better can be said of those matches to which men are induced merely by the consideration of a beautiful person or a great fortune?"—(*TJ*, I, xii; Henley, III, 58).

In contrast, the one idea upon which the positive Squire Western and his learned sister are agreed is that marriage for love is all romantic nonsense. Toward this perversion of his ideal Fielding felt so strongly that on occasion he was not content merely to represent it as comic. When, for example, Mrs. Western seizes happily on the prospect of catching Lord Fellamar for Sophia, he comments: "Now this was the affair which Mrs. Western was preparing to introduce to Sophia by some prefatory discourse on the folly of love, and on the the wisdom of legal prostitution for hire . . ." (*TJ*, XVI, viii; Henley, v, 237). It was in precisely these terms that he regarded the great majority of the unions in high-life, and his cynic's definition of marriage in the "Modern Glossary" of the *Covent-Garden Journal* was only the summation of many previous statements to the same effect:

"MARRIAGE. A Kind of Traffic carried on between the two Sexes, in which both are constantly endeavouring to cheat each other, and both are commonly Losers in the End"— (*CGJ*, No. 4; Jensen, I, 156).

His early comedies of manners abound in portraits of this kind of marriage, nor are they lacking in the novels.

Fielding's poem). See Antal, "The Moral Purpose of Hogarth's Art," *Journal of the Warburg and Courtauld Institutes*, xv (1952), 169-97.

POETRY

But the ultimate thing to remember is, that if Fielding could grow sternly acid on the subject of this "legal prostitution for hire," he could also portray in the most tender language, as the poem *On the Choice of a Wife* well illustrates, the profound joy of a marriage radiant with honest love. Few sweeter tributes to a woman have been offered than that which he paid to Charlotte Fielding in drawing his beautiful portrait of Amelia. And though one may feel that she is on occasion almost too good for this world, her warm comfort to the disheartened Booth can ring false only to a confirmed misogynist:

"Make yourself easy therefore, my dear love; for you have a wife who will think herself happy with you, and endeavor to make you so, in any situation. Fear nothing, Billy; industry will always provide us a wholesome meal, and I will take care that neatness and cheerfulness shall make it a pleasant one"—(IV, iii; Henley, VI, 185).

Here, as Fielding well understood, was what Horace meant when he said: "Felices ter et amplius, / Quos irrupta tenet Copula...."[98]

(5) "TO *JOHN HAYES*, Esq;"

Fielding's short poem (of some fifty lines) to John Hayes[99] pursues the theme that Pope had explored in the

[98] The epigraph on the title page of *Amelia*: "Thrice happy and more are these held by an unbreakable union" (*Carm.* I. xiii. 17-18). Fielding also included on the title page an epigraph from Simonides to the effect that "a man can be possessed of nothing better than a virtuous woman, nor more terrible than a bad one."

[99] The John Hayes to whom this poem is addressed is presumably the man described in the subscription list of the *Miscellanies* as "John Hayes, Esq; of the Middle Temple" (I, sig. A₇ᵛ). There were at least two men of this name associated with the Middle Temple in Fielding's time: One, John Hayes of Dublin, was admitted 9 September 1730, but there is no record of his having been called to the bar (*Register of Admissions to the Honourable Society of the Middle Temple*, ed. H. A. C. Sturgess [3v., 1949], I, 309). He was probably about the same age as Fielding (who, it will be remembered, began his study of the law at a later age than the norm); and he may well be the John Hayes who was placed in the Exchequer office by Sir Robert Walpole sometime in the late thirties (see

113

Epistle to Cobham and in the second epistle of the *Essay on Man*: namely, the contradictions displayed in any man's individual nature and the strange inconsistency of human actions. Thus Fielding says that only those who know little of humankind (like "Codrus," who confines "all his Knowledge, and his Art, / To this, that each Man is corrupt at Heart") (*Misc.*, I, 36) will be surprised to see

>   . . . one Man at several Times appear,
> Now gay, now grave, now candid, now severe;
> Now save his Friends, now leave 'em in the Lurch;
> Now rant in Brothels, and now cant in Church.
>   (I, 36)

The rhythm of Pope's similar lines to Cobham permits little doubt as to Fielding's technical model for the sentiment:

> See the same man, in vigour, in the gout;
> Alone, in company; in place, or out;
> Early at Bus'ness, and at Hazard late;
> Mad at a Fox-chace, wise at a Debate;
> Drunk at a Borough, civil at a Ball;
> Friendly at Hackney, faithless at Whitehall.[100]

the notice of his death in 1792, at the age of 84, in the *Gentleman's Magazine*, November 1792, p. 1059).

The more likely candidate for Fielding's wise friend is the (presumably) older man, John Hayes of Wolverhampton, Staffordshire, who was admitted to the Middle Temple 13 February 1722/3 and called to the bar 8 May 1730 (*Register*, I, 292). He is almost certainly the John Hayes of Staffordshire who was admitted to Corpus Christi, Cambridge, in 1723 and matriculated in the Lent term, 1724 (*Alumni Cantabrigienses*, ed. John and J. A. Venn, Part I [4v., 1922-27], II, 339). As an Englishman, an older man with some university training, and one whose continued connection with the law can be established, he seems in every respect the logical choice of the two.

[100] Ll. 130-35 (*Epistles to Several Persons*, ed. F. W. Bateson [Twickenham ed., Vol. III, ii, 1951], p. 24). See also ll. 41-86 (*ed. cit.*, pp. 18-20). As Professor Mack says, the second epistle of the *Essay on Man* deals more at large with "the fundamental antithesis, in all the traditional psychologies, between regulatory and appetitive elements in man's nature . . . usually connected in one way or another with the doctrine of his two souls, rational and sensitive," and one aspect of which is the problem of man's changeful

Fielding did not have to go to Pope for the ideas expressed in this poem, however; they were part of his intellectual equipment almost from the time that he started to write. It was the strange mixture of warring passions in the human bosom that made man precisely the unpredictable and the humorous (with a pun intended) being that he was—fit object for the comic writer's pen. And it was the mixture of virtues and vices in any man's nature that made the pronouncement of moral judgments upon him such a delicate affair (one of Fielding's favorite themes, of course):

> Yet farther with the Muse pursue the Theme,
> And see how various Men at once will seem;
> How Passions blended on each other fix,
> How Vice with Virtues, Faults with Graces mix;
> How Passions opposite, as sour to sweet,
> Shall in one Bosom at one Moment meet.
> With various Luck for Victory contend,
> And now shall carry, and now lose their End.
> The rotten Beau, while smelt along the Room,
> Divides your Nose 'twixt Stenches and Perfume:
> So Vice and Virtue lay such equal Claim,
> Your Judgment knows not when to praise or blame.
>
> (1, 36-37)

If, says Fielding, the motives for human actions could be found always in a single source, then even "Codrus" would be an adequate judge of human psychology. But God, "the Great Artist," has joined differing passions in man's composition in the same way (poetically speaking) that Titian blends his colors and "variegates his clouded Sky"; and thus nature has created in man an eternal puzzle. Pope expressed this contemporary psychological skepticism (if it may be called that) in its extremist form in the *Epistle to Cobham*:

---

character (cf. *Essay on Man*, ed. Maynard Mack [Twickenham ed., Vol. III, i, 1950], p. 62n.).

POETRY

> Judge we by Nature? Habit can efface,
> Int'rest o'ercome, or Policy take place:
> By Actions? those Uncertainty divides:
> By Passions? these Dissimulation hides:
> Opinions? they still take a wider range:
> Find, if you can, in what you cannot change.[101]

As Pope suggests, and as Fielding goes on to say, the confusion introduced by nature is compounded by men themselves, who struggle to appear other than they really are, seek by "art" to dissimulate their true "nature," and thus show forth in completely variant lights, depending on the part they are acting at the moment. In this language of the stage, Fielding concludes:

> Thus while the Courtier acts the Patriot's Part,
> This guides his Face and Tongue, and that his Heart.
> Abroad the Patriot shines with artful Mien,
> The naked Courtier glares behind the Scene.
> What Wonder then to Morrow if he grow
> A Courtier good, who is a Patriot now.
>
> (I, 37-38)[102]

The sources of this conception of human nature are too various to cite. In this poem Fielding himself chooses to

[101] Ll. 168-73 (Bateson ed., p. 28).
[102] One is tempted to apply these lines not only to Fielding's general disillusionment with the "patriot" Opposition to Walpole, but more specifically to the notorious defection of Pulteney in the summer of 1742. William Pulteney, it will be remembered, had been the tireless leader of the Opposition through the 1730's; but after Walpole's fall, he had "turned courtier" and been created Earl of Bath by George II in July, 1742. Although Bath was a subscriber to the *Miscellanies*, Cross (I, 412-13) thought, with reason, that a famous passage in the 1743 edition of *Jonathan Wild* (II, xii) had reference to him: "DEBAUCHING a Member of the House of Commons from his Principles, and creating him a Peeer [sic], is not much better than making a Woman a Whore, and afterwards marrying her" (*Misc.*, III, 178). So far as the lines in the poem to Hayes are concerned, however, I suppose one must remember that the theme is of general application and that Fielding had made the same point long before William Pulteney ever hankered for a peerage.

mention only Horace, declaring that Hayes (with his superior knowledge of the heart) "Canst with thy *Horace* see the human Elves / Not differ more from others than themselves" (1, 36).[103] Like Montaigne, La Rochefoucauld, Pascal, and many another student of human nature, Fielding found these contradictions irresistibly fascinating, a constant source of vexation and amusement. And if the conception itself was a commonplace, Fielding could make use of it (as of other commonplaces) ironically to throw a fresh and humorous light upon experience and character. Thus, to confine ourselves to a single instance, he affected surprise at Mrs. Western's changeful humor in *Tom Jones*: she had once very kindly refused to prosecute a highwayman who robbed her (and called her a "handsome b - - - -"); her animus, however against Mrs. Honour, who had dared to call her ugly, was unrelenting ("But now, so uncertain are our tempers, and so much do we at different times differ from ourselves, she would hear of no mitigation") (*TJ*, VII, ix; Henley, IV, 15).

Pope had suggested in the *Epistle to Cobham* and the *Essay on Man* that the best way out of this psychological maze was to "Search then the Ruling Passion . . . ," which remains at least relatively constant amidst the flux and turmoil of man's nature. Fielding's concern in the little poem to Hayes was merely to point out and describe the fact of man's mixed and inconsistent nature, not to offer a handle by which one could hope to seize upon any constant element. That such a handle was most urgently needed, particularly by honest and undesigning men, was, however, one of his abiding beliefs; and in the *Miscellanies* he dealt with that problem more at large (as I shall hope to

[103] Fielding may have had particularly in mind the lines:
. . . quid, mea cum pugnat sententia secum,
quod petiit spernit, repetit quod nuper omisit,
aestuat et vitae disconvenit ordine toto. . . .
(*Epist.* 1. i. 97-99)

do) when he came to the *Essay on the Knowledge of the Characters of Men.*

2. THE LIGHT VERSE

The most pleasant feature of the numerous short poems that follow the verse essays in the *Miscellanies* is the series of brief glimpses that they offer of Fielding as a romantic young man—dancing at the Salisbury assemblies, wooing Charlotte Cradock (in verse more notable for its sentiment than its execution), commenting with youthful arrogance upon London, and so on. Perhaps more significantly, these poems show Fielding trying his hand at a good many of the currently fashionable types and meters of light verse with that zest for experimentation that led him into such a variety of literary avenues.

Not all of the poetic trifles here can be dated, but they seem mostly to have been composed in the period 1728 to 1733, that is, in Fielding's early twenties. One fairly long poem, the burlesque of Juvenal's *Sixth Satire,* was quite possibly sketched out as early as 1725 or 1726. Since this is the most considerable item in the collection, outside of the verse essays, I shall reserve discussion of it; the other light verse will be treated in loosely chronological order.

Two amorous complaints, presumably antedating his acquaintance with Miss Cradock, belong to the year 1728. The first, "TO *EUTHALIA.* Written in the Year 1728," seems to have London (or Salisbury?) as its setting, and could very well belong to the period of Fielding's early appearances in print (*The Masquerade* and *Love in Several Masques*), before he went off to Leyden in March. Phrased in stiff, conventional terms, it presents the young lover, "Alexis," "Burning with Love, tormented with Despair," unable to drive Euthalia's image from his mind:

> In *Lock's* or *Newton's* Page her Learning glows;
> *Dryden* the Sweetness of her Numbers shews;

POETRY

> In all their various Excellence I find
> The various Beauties of her perfect Mind.
>
> (*Misc.*, I, 71)

Neither books, wine, nor other women serve; for, repairing to "Sappho" and "Rosalinda," he finds,

> In vain to them my restless Thoughts would run;
> Like fairest Stars, they show the absent Sun.
>
> (*Misc.*, I, 71)

The other complaint was most probably sketched out in the fall, while Fielding was on vacation from the University of Leyden and staying for a time in Hampshire: "A DESCRIPTION OF U[pton] G[rey], (alias *New Hog's Norton*) in *Com. Hants*. Written to a young Lady in the Year 1728."[104] This lugubrious composition amusingly contrasts the pleasant retreat of Rosalinda (who apparently displaced Euthalia, after all!) with the shabby and un-Horatian rusticity of his own lodgings. His vivid portrait of the run-down farmhouse with its neglected garden and "Hay-Stacks, Faggot Piles, and Bottle-Ricks," and its unromantic surroundings, where "For purling Streams, we've Puddles fill'd with Rains," indicates that Fielding's delight in painting "low" scenes came to him naturally and early:

[104] The "Hog's Norton" alluded to in the title was a village in Oxfordshire, Hock Norton, proverbial from Elizabethan days for boorishness and the organ music of its pigs. Upton Grey, a village in northeast Hampshire, on the northern edge of the Hampshire Downs, was described in a document of 1725 as Fielding's usual abode (see J. Paul De Castro, "Fielding and Lyme Regis," *TLS*, 4 June 1931, p. 447). Cross (I, 71) conjectured that "perhaps he was on a visit at Hoddington House overlooking the village, the seat of the Sclaters, then an ordinary farmhouse." If Cross, in this ambiguous passage, supposes that the manor house belonged to the Sclaters in the eighteenth century, he is in error: according to a standard authority, it was then the property of one John Limbrey, whose family held it until it passed to the Sclaters in 1800 (cf. *The Victoria History of the Counties of England: Hampshire and the Isle of Wight*, ed. William Page, et al. [6v., 1900-14], III, 384). Further, although the house was used as a farmhouse for some time, it was "an Elizabethan structure with a finely carved oak staircase and panelled rooms" (*ibid.*, p. 383). This does not sound much like the combined house-and-shed that Fielding is describing. The notion that he was at Hoddington House would seem to have little to recommend it.

I've thought (so strong with me Burlesque prevails,)
This Place design'd to ridicule *Versailles*;
Or meant, like that, Art's utmost Pow'r to shew,
That tells how high it reaches, this how low.
(*Misc.*, i, 40)

A playful set of verses, probably of this general period, "Written *Extempore*, on a Half-penny, which a young Lady gave a Beggar, and the Author redeem'd for Half a Crown," displays that delicacy of touch which is somehow always a bit surprising to find in the hearty, masculine work of Fielding, but which the idea of a charming woman seemed naturally to evoke in him:

> DEAR little, pretty, fav'rite Ore,
> That once encreas'd *Gloriana*'s Store;
> That lay within her Bosom blest,
> Gods might have envy'd thee thy Nest.
> I've read, imperial *Jove* of old,
> For Love transform'd himself to Gold:
> And why, for a more lovely Lass,
> May he not now have lurk'd in Brass?
> (*Misc.*, i, 45)[105]

The sentiment may remind us of Joseph Andrews' "little piece of broken gold, which had a ribbon tied to it" and was the remembrance of his beloved Fanny (i, xiv; Henley, i, 76).

The animated triplet, "To the MASTER of the *SALISBURY* ASSEMBLY; Occasioned by a Dispute, whether the Company should have fresh Candles," introduces another inamorata:

[105] There is more to the poem, but Fielding seldom knew when to leave well enough alone in his poetry: the rest is less felicitously handled. Cross (i, 257) noticed that these verses, in an earlier sixteen-line version, had been printed in the *Champion*, 27 May 1740 (not reprinted in the collected edition of 1741), as "writ some years ago by one of the family of the Vinegars, on a half-penny; which a young lady gave to a beggar, and the author purchased at the price of half a crown." The poem was reworked and expanded to twenty-eight lines for the *Miscellanies*.

POETRY

Take your Candles away, let your Musick be mute,
My Dancing, however, you shall not dispute;
Jenny's Eyes shall find Light, and I'll find a Flute.
(*Misc.*, 1, 64)

Just when the Rosalindas, Euthalias, Glorianas, and Jennies were eclipsed in the brighter light from the eyes of Charlotte Cradock we do not know. But a pretty (untitled) fable "writ when the Author was very young," gives us our first glimpse of her, for it belongs to that brief period when he adored both of the graceful Cradock sisters alike. Internal evidence would place the piece sometime in or after 1729.[106] Beginning, "The Queen of Beauty, t'other Day . . . ," the fable involves Venus' choice of the fairest nymphs of the earth to serve as vice-regents of her empire. The conclusion, announced by Jove, is that the "C[rado]cks, to whose celestial Dower / I gave all Beauties in my Power," should "bear an equal Sway" (*Misc.*, 1, 68). The progress of the narrative is interrupted by a hodge-podge of allusions and brief digressions. There are passing tributes to Lady Mary Wortley Montagu ("Like Wit from sparkling W[or]tley's Tongue"), Pope, and Young; an attack on the bribery of voters, later to become so central a theme for Fielding; and an encomium upon Britain, "The Queen of Beauty's favour'd Isle." Some further allusions bearing more directly upon the fable were omitted in publication, as Fielding explains in a characteristic little note (really worth more, one is tempted to say, than the whole of the verse):

"The middle Part of this Poem (which was writ when the Author was very young) was filled with the Names of several young Ladies, who might perhaps be uneasy at see-

---

[106] One allusion in the poem ("So Borough Towns, Election brought on, / E'er yet Corruption Bill was thought on . . .") presumably refers to the act of 1729 (2 Geo. II, c. 24), a bill for the more effectual preventing of bribery and corruption at Parliamentary elections, which is something of an early landmark in the history of parliamentary reform (see Edward Porritt, *The Unreformed House of Commons* [2v., Cambridge, 1903], 1, 9; and Sir William Holdsworth, *A History of English Law* [1903, in progress], x, 573-74).

POETRY

ing themselves in Print, that Part therefore is left out; the rather, as some Freedoms, tho' gentle ones, were taken with little Foibles in the amiable Sex, who to affront in Print, is, we conceive, mean in any Man, and scandalous in a Gentleman"—(*Misc.*, I, 67, n.).

In 1730 comes the first of the "Celia" poems, most of which clearly refer to Charlotte, who now stood alone in his affections. The "ADVICE TO THE NYMPHS of *New S[aru]m*. Written in the Year 1730" argues, in high-flown and somewhat stilted diction, that contending Salisbury nymphs should recognize the hopelessness of striving to outshine the "victorious *Celia*":

> And if your Glass be false, if blind your Eyes,
> Believe and own what all Mankind aver,
> And pay with them the Tribute due to her.
>
> (*Misc.*, I, 56)

At least one of the "Celia" poems, "THE QUESTION," may not be intended specifically for Charlotte. In it, Celia, in Strephon's arms, begs him to speak of his love, but his soul "in Bliss dissolv'd away," leaves him dumb. However:

> The Charmer pitying my Distress,
> Gave me the tenderest Caress,
> And sighing cry'd, You need not tell;
> Oh! *Strephon*, Oh! I feel how well.
>
> (*Misc.*, I, 48)

It may be mere naiveté to suppose that even in an age of considerable license, such an effusion as this would not have been directed by a young lover to a specific lady; but I find it difficult to believe that Celia here is anything more than the conventional poetic charmer. Like "Chloe," "Celia" served many an amorous young rhymer; and I see no more reason to believe that Charlotte Cradock is Celia in this poem than that she is the Chloe of Joseph Andrews' song (*JA*, II, xii), who blushingly tells Strephon he "ne'er

POETRY

was so pressing before." On the other hand, the Lilliputian poem addressed to Charlotte (see below) is suggestive enough in its implications, though it is scarcely so blunt as this one. More imaginative, too, is the epigram that begins "WHEN *JOVE* with fair *Alcmena* lay," which draws upon the legend of Jupiter's visit to that lady—the issue of which conjunction was, of course, Hercules—and the god's forbidding the sun to rise, that he might spend several uninterrupted nights in Alcmena's arms. Fielding declares that had he the power of Jove, and were he possessed of Celia's charms, "Sun, thou should'st never rise again" (*Misc.*, I, 47).[107]

In any case, a series of six lyrics in the *Miscellanies* assuredly is addressed to Charlotte; and these poems include some of Fielding's most Prioresque graces. The first bears the lengthy ascription, "TO *CELIA*. Occasioned by her apprehending her House would be broke open, and having an old Fellow to guard it, who sat up all Night, with a Gun without any Ammunition. CUPID call'd to Account." The title tells us all we know about this amusing circumstance in Salisbury, so we cannot be certain of the source of Celia's apprehensions; but Fielding turned the private joke to account with a rather charming fable in tetrameter couplets. Venus, seeing Celia, her "lov'd Citadel of Beauty," left unguarded, "With none but *Sancho* upon Duty,"—and he with an empty gun!—calls Cupid angrily to her and demands to know why he has neglected his guardianship. The little god whimpers that he was hiding safely in one of Celia's dimples, when "Thence, by a Sigh I dispossest, / Was blown to *Harry Fielding*'s Breast," and could not find a way out. However, he chortles, he was not idle:

---

[107] Prior's "The Wedding Night" treats of the same legendary subject, and the resemblance of the first lines might indicate that Fielding had this poem in mind when he began his own. Prior's opening couplet reads: "WHEN *Jove* lay blest in his *Alcmæna*'s Charms, / Three Nights in one he prest her in his Arms . . ." (*The Literary Works of Matthew Prior*, ed. H. B. Wright and M. K. Spears [2v., Oxford, 1959], I, 213).

123

> But did Mamma know there what Work
> I've made, how acted like a Turk;
> What Pains, what Torments he endures,
> Which no Physician ever cures,
> She would forgive. . . .
>
> *(Misc.,* I, 58)

The goddess smiles and, chucking the wicked boy under the chin, bids him return and take more care.

The next, a fantasy "To the SAME. On her wishing to have a LILLIPUTIAN, to play with," interestingly reflects the widespread popular appeal of Swift's little people.[108] Fielding's answer to Celia's impulsive wish is that he would gladly "Be five Foot shorter than I am" to please her. He sports with the notion of hiding in her gown or riding on her shoulder; but when he begins to visualize himself standing guard on her pillow at night and watching her in bed,

> While I survey, what to declare
> Nor Fancy can, nor Words must dare,
> Here would begin my former Pain,
> And wish to be myself again.
>
> *(Misc.,* I, 60)

This may remind us of Ovid's "felix . . . anule" (*Amores* II. xv). The following poems in the series represent three popular poetic exercises: "SIMILES. To the SAME" illustrates the vast admiration of the Augustans for detached similes; "THE PRICE. To the SAME" is a conventional epigram; and "Her CHRISTIAN NAME. To the SAME. A Rebus" is one of those riddling poems that the *Gentleman's Magazine* delighted in so thoroughly.

---

[108] Fielding had commented upon the rage for the Lilliputians in his first produced play, *Love in Several Masques* (1728). In Act III, sc. x, the foppish Lord Formal says: "Her ladyship is indebted to my instructions; for 'tis well known, before I had the honour of her acquaintance, she has publicly spoke against that divine collection of polite learning written by Mr. Gulliver: but now, the very moment it is named, she breaks out into the prettiest exclamation, and cries, O the dear, sweet, pretty, little creatures! Oh, gemini! would I had been born a Lilliputian!" (Henley, VIII, 55).

POETRY

The final two "Celia" poems are interesting for their allusions to the current London scene. The first, "To the SAME; Having blamed Mr. GAY for his Severity on her Sex," probably (though not necessarily) refers to *The Beggar's Opera*. The second is more copious and deserves quotation. Entitled "TO CELIA [I Hate the Town, and all its Ways]," it most probably dates from 1730, Fielding's first full-time season with the London stage.[109] Encompassing almost every aspect of contemporary London life (rather lightly, to be sure), the opening diatribe in rollicking octosyllabics is intended as a contrast to the final reversal in which Fielding declares that he loves nought the town has to offer but his Celia:

I Hate the Town, and all its Ways;
Ridotto's, Opera's, and Plays;
The Ball, the Ring, the Mall, the Court;
Wherever the Beau-Monde resort;
Where Beauties lie in Ambush for Folks,
Earl *Straffords*, and the Duke of *Norfolks*;
All Coffee-Houses, and their Praters;
All Courts of Justice, and Debaters;
All Taverns, and the Sots within 'em;
All Bubbles, and the Rogues that skin 'em.
I hate all Critics; may they burn all,
From *Bentley* to the *Grub-street Journal*.
All Bards, as *Dennis* hates a Pun:
Those who have Wit, and who have none.
All Nobles, of whatever Station;
And all the Parsons in the Nation.

[109] The terminal dates would be 8 January 1730 (the first issue of the *Grub-Street Journal*) and 3 January 1731 (the death of Anthony Boheme, Lincoln's-Inn Fields actor: *Gentleman's Magazine*, January 1731, p. 33). The references to Booth and Dennis would be more apt at this time also, for though they died in 1733 and 1734 respectively, each suffered a mental decline in his last years and in that period would scarcely be a fit object for Fielding's humorous diatribe. Booth, with Cibber, had rejected Fielding's *Don Quixote in England* for Drury Lane, probably some time in 1728 or 1729, which may help to explain his inclusion here.

All Quacks and Doctors read in Physick,
Who kill or cure a Man that is sick.
All Authors that were ever heard on,
From *Bavius* up to *Tommy Gordon*;
Tradesmen with Cringes ever stealing,
And Merchants, whatsoe'er they deal in.
I hate the Blades professing Slaughter,
More than the Devil Holy Water.
I hate all Scholars, Beaus, and Squires;
Pimps, Puppies, Parasites, and Liars.
All Courtiers, with their Looks so smooth;
And Players, from *Boheme* to *Booth*.
I hate the World, cram'd all together,
From Beggars, up the Lord knows whither. . . .

(*Misc.*, I, 49-50)

The affinities of this outburst are not so much with the Hudibrastic tradition, which its eccentric rhymes make it resemble, as with that voluminous body of verse and prose one might call "satires on the town," taking in the many imitations of Juvenal's *Third Satire*; the "town eclogues" of Gay and Pope and Lady Mary Wortley Montagu; Gay's *Trivia* and its imitators; and such "journeys" about town as Ned Ward's *London Spy*.[110] Because of its brevity, Fielding's poem suffers from comparison with most of these: the very life of this kind of survey lies in its detail and its genre portraits. He was later to treat in prose—an instrument much more suited to his hand—and at greater length, many of the subjects sketchily anticipated here. The misanthropic pose is something of a conventional one, particularly for young writers, and Fielding's wholesale condemnation of everything from coffee-houses to courts, and clergy to players, is obviously not representative of his mature convictions. Yet it is most certainly true, as

[110] See W. H. Irving, *John Gay's London, Illustrated from the Poetry of the Time* (Cambridge, Mass., 1928), for a survey of such "satires on the town."

George Sherburn has said, that "Fielding drops his high spirits whenever he writes about London."¹¹¹ From first to last, he saw the town as subtly degenerative, as offering a milieu that pandered to men's vices and failed to call up their better instincts. Thus Lady Booby finds that Joey begins to "show some spirit"—that is, becomes more like a coxcomb—after he has been in London for a time: "She plainly saw the effects which the town air hath on the soberest constitutions" (*JA*, I, iv; Henley, I, 35). And Lady Bellaston laments to Lord Fellamar, of Sophia, "Alas! my lord . . . consider the country—the bane of all young women is the country. There they learn a set of romantic notions of love, and I know not what folly, which this town and good company can scarce eradicate in a whole winter" (*TJ*, xv, ii; Henley, v, 146). Although the mass indictment of trades and professions in the poem cannot be considered seriously, the attitude toward the town is of a piece with Fielding's usual feelings about London and is an interesting if somewhat extreme expression of his anti-urban prejudices.

Probably the best known of Fielding's poems in the *Miscellanies* is another "town" poem, the jesting epistle "TO THE RIGHT HONOURABLE Sir ROBERT WALPOLE, (Now Earl of ORFORD) Written in the YEAR 1730."¹¹² With mock seriousness Fielding the "Bard," looking down from his little garret upon the Prime Minister's lodgings in Ar-

---

¹¹¹ "Fielding's *Amelia*: an Interpretation," *ELH*, III (1936), 4, n. 3. A poem much like Fielding's is Thomas Gilbert's "*A View of the Town, a Satire. In an Epistle to a Friend in the Country*" (in *Poems on Several Occasions* [1747]; originally published alone in 1735). It condemns everything from clerics to sodomites in a wild sweep that again displays more youthful attitudinizing than *saeva indignatio*.

¹¹² It has not, I think, been noticed that this epistle to Walpole was first printed (in a shorter, somewhat mangled version) in the *Gentleman's Magazine*, December 1738, p. 653, where it is titled "*To Sir R. W-----LE*" and is signed "F------G." This inferior version is the one reprinted (with a few variants) in the 1758 edition of Dodsley's *Collection* (v, 117-18). It was probably sent to the *Gentleman's Magazine* by someone who wished to embarrass Fielding.

127

lington Street,[113] proposes to demonstrate that he, the threadbare poet, is actually a greater man than the one who rides at the helm of state, "Our Nation's Envy, and its Pride." This superior "greatness" he proves by examining all the minister's claims and overreaching them: for example, philosophers tell us that great men are frequently wretched; on this score, "Forbid it, Gods, that you should try / What 'tis to be so great as I." Great families, again, are known to dine the latest; but can they compare with him, who never dines at all? The poet not only looks down upon Arlington Street from a superior height (in the garret), but his "levees" are three times as frequent as the Minister's—indeed his door is quiet only on Sundays (that is, when he is free from dunners). The ingenious epistle was written, of course, before Fielding aligned himself definitely with the anti-Walpole patriots, and he may not be altogether speaking in jest when he says:

> If with my Greatness you're offended,
> The Fault is easily amended.
> For I'll come down, with wond'rous Ease,
> Into whatever Place you please.
> . . . .
> What fittest for?—you know, I'm sure,
> I'm fittest for a—*Sinecure.*
>
> (*Misc.*, I, 43)

Another epistle, "To the same. *Anno* 1731," expands the levee joke of the 1730 verses, comparing the poet's "mighty Levée" of menacing creditors to Walpole's attendance, and

[113] John E. Wells ("Fielding's First Poem to Walpole and His Garret in 1730," *MLN*, XXIX [1914], 29-30) decided from the allusion that Fielding probably lived on Piccadilly near Arlington Street at the time this poem was written; but of course it is quite possible that Fielding is merely taking the character—and lodgings—of a Grub Street poet for the purposes of the jest. Cross (I, 76) says flatly: "Probably the only garret from which he ever saw Walpole's mansion in Arlington Street was an upper window of his father's house in or near Piccadilly." Though it is a likely supposition, I know of no real evidence that Fielding ever lived at his father's house in London.

POETRY

begging the use of his imposing porter to deny entrance to the dunners. The opening lines could well portray Fielding's actual experience:

> GREAT Sir, as on each Levée Day
> I still attend you—still you say
> I'm busy now, To-morrow come;
> To-morrow, Sir, you're not at Home.
> (*Misc.*, I, 44)

The numerous portrayals of levees in Fielding's plays and fiction are authentic in detail. And he presents them with a bitterness which adds color to the supposition that he had himself often cooled his heels in great men's antechambers—along with most of the writers of his time.

One other poem of the early 1730's, "J[OH]N W[AT]TS at a PLAY," springs directly from his London (theatrical) experience. Watts, who printed about half of Fielding's plays, as well as those of many other contemporary dramatists,[114] was naturally interested in the success or failure of any new performance; and Fielding gives us to understand that Watts and other booksellers haunted the theatres in the hope of winning the rights to successful plays. In *Eurydice Hissed*, the playwright Pillage is shown before the performance of his new farce besieged by booksellers who want to publish it; but in describing the failure of the play soon after, Fielding has a gentleman observe:

> And John Watts,
> Who was this morning eager for the copy,
> Slunk hasty from the pit, and shook his head.
> (Henley, XI, 307)

[114] John Nichols declared that "the fame of Mr. John Watts for excellently good printing will endure as long as any public library shall exist . . ." (*Literary Anecdotes* [qv., 1812-1815], I, 292). In Fielding's *Pasquin*, Trapwit, upon finding that his epilogue to "The Election" had not enough *double-entendres* to satisfy the actresses, "went to Mr. Watts's, and borrowed all his plays; went home, read over all the epilogues, and crammed it as full as possible; and now, forsooth, it has too many in it" (Henley, XI, 200).

POETRY

In the poem of the *Miscellanies,* Watts is shown at the same kind of performance:

> WHILE Hisses, Groans, and Cat-calls thro' the Pit,
> Deplore the hapless Poet's want of Wit:
> J[oh]n W[at]ts, from Silence bursting in a Rage,
> Cry'd, *Men are mad who write in such an Age.*
> Not so, reply'd his Friend, a sneering Blade,
> *The Poet's only dull, the Printer's mad.*
>
> (*Misc.,* I, 49)

With the exception of one poem of later date (that to Miss Husband, below), the rest of the light verse is given over to epigrams, epitaphs, songs, and what one can only call schoolboy exercises. The epigrams are not distinguished, but they sting some of the follies that continued to exercise Fielding's wit in later years. For example, the complaisance shown by the ladies of the polite world to beaus and fops always annoyed him beyond measure. One of his epigrams, "ON A LADY, Coquetting with a very silly Fellow," presents this commentary:

> CORINNA's Judgment do not less admire,
> That she for *Oulus* shews a gen'rous Fire;
> *Lucretia* toying thus had been a Fool,
> But wiser *Helen* might have us'd the Tool.
> Since *Oulus* for one Use alone is fit,
> With Charity judge of *Corinna's* Wit.
>
> (*Misc.,* I, 51)

And he varies one of Prior's well-known epigrams, to offer another judgment on the fop:

> WHILE Men shun *Oulus* as a Fool;
> *Dames* prize him as a Beau;
> What Judgment form we by this Rule?
> Why this it seems to shew.

> Those apprehend the Beau's a Fool,
> These think the Fool's a Beau.
> (Misc., I, 51)[115]

Still another couplet on the same theme led W. L. Cross (I, 174) to toy with the idea that Fielding might have had Catherine Cradock, his sister-in-law, in mind when he wrote:

> THAT *Kate* weds a Fool what Wonder can be,
> Her Husband has married a Fool great as she.
> (Misc., I, 63)

Nothing is known of Catherine Cradock after 1735, when her mother's will cut her off with one shilling, so Cross's guess cannot be substantiated; I should suppose that Fielding was merely directing his wit at the fashionable "fine lady" whose ideas on marriage he satirized often and at length. One of his epigrams carries this pertinent observation:

> MISS *Molly* lays down as a positive Rule,
> That no one should marry for Love, but a Fool:
> *Exceptions* to Rules even *Lilly* allows;
> *Moll* has sure an *Example* at Home in her Spouse.
> (Misc., I, 63)

The last epigrams in the collection (some of the "Celia" poems are also epigrams) are directed at another of Fielding's butts, the miser. One, called "THE CAT and FIDDLE. TO THE Favourite CAT of a Fiddling MISER," proceeds:

> THRICE happy Cat, if in thy A—— House,
> Thou luckily shouldst find a half-starv'd Mouse.

---

[115] Prior's epigram (*Literary Works*, ed. Wright and Spears, I, 454) reads:
> YES, every Poet is a Fool:
>   By Demonstration NED can show it:
> Happy, cou'd NED's inverted Rule
>   Prove every Fool to be a Poet.

Though the subject is different, the relationship is obvious.

The Mice, that only for his Musick stay,
Are Proofs that *Orpheus* did not better play.

Thou too, if Danger could alarm thy Fears,
Hast to this *Orpheus* strangely ty'd thy Ears:
For oh! the fatal Time will come, when he,
Prudent, will make his Fiddle-strings of thee.
(*Misc.*, I, 64-65)

The final epigram is a couplet "On one who invited many Gentlemen to a small Dinner":

PETER (says *Pope*) won't poison with his Meat;
'Tis true, for *Peter* gives you nought to eat.
(*Misc.*, I, 52)[116]

The couplet's wit is less interesting than the suggestion of Fielding's early and consistent animus against its obvious subject, Peter Walter, the notorious usurer and miser. Among other things, Walter served as the model for Peter Pounce in *Joseph Andrews* and shared the satirical thrust in Fielding's piece on the Royal Society. But then he was a favorite target of the Augustan wits, and drew the fire of Pope and Swift and Fielding's friend, Sir Charles Hanbury Williams, as well as many others.

If the composition of epigrams was an extraordinarily congenial exercise to Augustan wits, the writing of epitaphs was only slightly less so. Many of the epitaphs of the time were satiric (much to Dr. Johnson's distress), and many even carried a sting in the final line reminiscent of the pointed epigram. Both of Fielding's are of this sort.[117]

[116] The allusion in Fielding's epigram is to Pope's lines in his *First Satire of the Second Book of Horace Imitated* (ll. 85-90). The theme of the inadequate (or ostentatious) dinner is an ancient one; cf. L. R. Shero, "The *Cena* in Roman Satire," *Classical Philology*, XVIII (1923), 126-43.

[117] There is a mock epitaph "upon *a very passionate Man* and *a great Snorer*" in *CGJ* No. 13 (Jensen, I, 218) that Fielding may also have written. Captain Blifil's epitaph in *Tom Jones*, II, ix (Henley, III, 104) gives us Fielding's tongue-in-cheek impression of the kind of conventional

POETRY

The first celebrates that favorite legend of eighteenth-century poets, the callous neglect of genius shown in the case of Samuel Butler, who had died in 1680 supposedly alone and forgotten. It is at least true that he was not honored with burial in Westminster Abbey, and it was not until 1721 that a monument was set up to his memory in the Abbey by the well-known London printer, John Barber. Fielding's "EPITAPH ON *BUTLER's* MONUMENT" reads:

> WHAT tho' alive neglected and undone,
> O let thy Spirit triumph in this Stone.
> No greater Honour could Men pay thy Parts,
> For when they give a Stone, they give their Hearts.
>
> (*Misc.*, I, 51)[118]

The other example of mortuary humor is written upon the burial of an obvious hypocrite, which accounts well enough for the malice of its satirical twist. It is titled "ANOTHER [Epitaph]. On a wicked Fellow, who was a great BLUNDERER":

> INTERR'D by Blunder in this sacred Place,
> Lies *William*'s wicked Heart, and smiling Face.
> Full Forty Years on Earth he blunder'd on,
> And now the L—d knows whither he is gone.
> But if to Heav'n he stole, let no Man wonder,
> For if to Hell he'd gone, he'd made no Blunder.
>
> (*Misc.*, I, 52)

---

sentiments that Samuel Johnson recommended in "An ESSAY on EPITAPHS" (*Gentleman's Magazine*, December 1740, pp. 593-96).

[118] Samuel Wesley's poem "ON The setting up Mr. BUTLER'S Monument in WESTMINSTER-ABBEY" (*Poems on Several Occasions. By Samuel Wesley, A. M.* [1736], p. 62), like Fielding's, plays with the idea of the stone—as a substitute for bread. Fielding, incidentally, did his bit to contribute to the legend of Butler's starvation: see the *Champion*, 27 November 1739 (Henley, xv, 78), *Eurydice Hissed* (Henley, xi, 302), and *Tom Jones*, IV, viii (Henley, III, 170-71). The Romantics were not the only writers to enjoy a certain titillating self-pity in the spectacle of neglected genius.

Two songs were included in the *Miscellanies'* stock of poems. One is designated as having been originally intended for a play, and it is likely that both of them were. The first, a four-stanza lyric called "THE BEGGAR. A SONG," is in the conventional idiom of Petrarcan frustration: the lover begs the charity of his mistress' favors. Do not act the miser's part, he cries:

> What, parted with, gives Heav'n to me;
> Kept, is but Pain and Grief to thee.
> (*Misc.*, I, 47)

And so on. Fielding has nothing to contribute that might bring the (by then) hackneyed and tiresome banalities of the convention to life. But in his other lyric, "A SAILOR'S SONG. Design'd for the STAGE,"[119] he achieves a rollicking rhythm that almost sings itself. The first stanza will give the movement of this vigorous chanty:

> COME, let's aboard, my jolly Blades,
>   That love a merry Life;
> To lazy Souls leave home-bred Trades,
>   To Husbands home-bred Strife;
> Through *Europe* we will gayly roam,
> And leave our Wives and Cares at Home.
>   *With a Fa la,* &c.
> (*Misc.*, I, 53)

Though not distinguished poetry, this could be a very fine song; and the same may be said of most of the songs scattered through Fielding's plays. He had little poetic genius,

[119] None of Fielding's known plays has any sailor characters (unless Charon's man in *The Author's Farce* is called a sailor!); but on 3 May 1737 a ballad-opera was played at the Little Theatre in the Haymarket—then under Fielding's management—which was titled *The Sailor's Opera: or, an Example of Justice to Present and Future Times* (see Emmett L. Avery, "Fielding's Last Season with the Haymarket Theatre," *MP*, XXXVI [1939], 289). Nothing is known of this piece, but the demon of speculation whispers that it could conceivably have been the work for which Fielding's song was intended.

POETRY

but he did own a strong rhythmic sense. Set to music, his compositions must have had a happy vitality that is not always apparent on the printed page.

The academic exercises that round out this collection may be quickly disposed of. One is merely the translation of "A SIMILE, FROM *SILIUS ITALICUS*" (*Misc.*, I, 70), such as could be done by any Eton schoolboy; the other indicates Fielding's bent for travesty and burlesque. Called "A PARODY, FROM THE FIRST ÆNEID," it could equally well date from Eton days, though an allusion to Holland suggests a date in or after Fielding's attendance at Leyden. The "parody" displays quite clearly his relish for the contrast between orotund Latin rhetoric and its antithesis, either in burlesque or—as here—in blunt, unsavory realism.

DIXIT; et avertens Roseâ Cervice refulsit,
Ambrosiæque Comæ divinum Vertice Odorem
Spiravere: Pedes vestis defluxit ad imos,
Et vera Incessu patuit Dea. ─────────

SHE said; and turning shew'd her wrinkled Neck,
In Scales and Colour like a Roach's Back.
Forth from her greasy Locks such Odours flow,
As those who've smelt *Dutch* Coffee-Houses, know.
To her Mid-Leg her Petticoat was rear'd,
And the true Slattern in her Dress appear'd.
(*Misc.*, I, 69)[120]

This kind of poetic jesting is in the tradition of Scarron, or—since Scarron's *Virgile Travesty en vers burlesques* was

[120] The Virgil is from Book I, ll. 402-5. The most interesting thing about the poem is that one finds its opening lines at the end of an unfinished poem by Lady Mary Wortley Montagu (*Letters and Works*, ed. Lord Wharncliffe, 3rd ed. rev. by W. Moy Thomas [2v., 1861], II, 468-70). It is impossible to say who borrowed from whom, but the duplication offers another bit of evidence that Fielding and Lady Mary took a literary interest in each other. See my note, "Fielding and Lady Mary Wortley Montagu: A Parallel," *N&Q*, CCIII (1958), 442-43.

135

not really well-known in England, except by reputation—of Charles Cotton. Cotton's *Scarronides*, a travesty of Book I (and later, Book IV) of the *Aeneid*, enjoyed an enormous popularity from the time of its publication in 1664. By 1725, when the second edition of Cotton's collected poems appeared, the *Scarronides* had reached its eleventh edition. Here is Cotton's rendering of the same lines Fielding handled:

> With that she turn'd to go away,
> And did her freckl'd Neck display;
> By which, and by a certain Whiff,
> Came from her Arm-pits, or her Cliff,
> And a fine Hobble in her Pace,
> Æneas knew his Mother's Grace....[121]

Obviously Fielding has not copied Cotton's images or his meter; but the tone is the same. Fielding's lines are fully as antiheroic (or anticlassical) as Cotton's, but although equally vulgar, they do somewhat avoid the salaciousness that marked the latter's travesties.

Fielding presumably meant to conclude the poetic assemblage in the *Miscellanies* with his burlesque of Juvenal, but at the last minute he threw in one more poem that he had written just a few months before publication. More than likely it was included to fill up the final blank verso page that resulted from facing off the Latin and English in his Juvenal. Entitled "TO MISS H——AND at *Bath*. Written *Extempore* in the Pump-Room, 1742," it is a graceful tribute to (probably) Miss Jane Husband, a beautiful young invalid who had come to seek the healing powers of the famous waters:

> SOON shall these bounteous Springs thy Wish bestow,

---

[121] *The Genuine Poetical Works of Charles Cotton, Esq*; (2nd ed., 1725), p. 32. For the background tradition, see Sturgis E. Leavitt, "Paul Scarron and English Travesty," *SP*, XVI (1919), 108-20.

POETRY

Soon in each Feature sprightly Health shall glow;
Thy Eyes regain their Fire, thy Limbs their Grace,
And Roses join the Lillies in thy Face.
But say, sweet Maid, what Waters can remove
The Pangs of cold Despair, of hopeless Love?
The deadly Star which lights th' autumnal Skies
Shines not so bright, so fatal as those Eyes.
The Pains which from their Influence we endure,
Not *Brewster*, Glory of his Art, can cure.

(*Misc.*, I, 114)

If the identification of this young lady with Jane Husband is correct, then the conclusion was a happy one: she did recover her health, and soon after (December 1743) married Fielding's friend, Robert Henley, later Earl of Northington and Lord Chancellor.[122]

2

The final poem with which we have to deal, the burlesque of Juvenal's famous satire on women, was (in its original form) probably Fielding's earliest extant work. "My Modernization of Part of the sixth Satire of *Juvenal*, will, I hope, give no Offence to that Half of our Species,

[122] "Miss H——AND" was first identified as Miss Husband by J. Paul De Castro, "Fieldingiana," N&Q, 12th Ser., I (1916), 483-84. Cross (I, 377-79) gave further details. The poem was reprinted some years later in the Reverend Samuel Rogers' *Poems on Various Occasions* (2v., Bath, 1782), I, 291, as "By the late Henry Fielding, Esq.," with the mistaken claim that it was "not printed in any edition of Fielding's Works." (See "H. K. St. J. S.," "Poem by Fielding," N&Q, 10th Ser., v [1906], 446, and J. P. De Castro's note, cited above.) In Rogers' collection, the poem was entitled "AN EXTEMPORE . . . TO MISS H——LAND." This might cast doubt upon the identification of the lady addressed in the poem, as Jane Husband; but since nothing is known of the authority of Rogers' manuscript, and in view of his obvious ignorance of the history of earlier publication, it seems safer to accept De Castro's plausible case for Miss Husband. Nevertheless, one ought at least to note that Rogers might reasonably have come by an authentic copy of the poem: his circle of acquaintance at Bath included, for instance, the son of Fielding's friend, Dr. Edward Harrington (see Jerom Murch, *Biographical Sketches of Bath Celebrities* [1893], pp. 143-51).

for whom I have the greatest Respect and Tenderness. It was originally sketched out before I was Twenty, and was all the Revenge taken by an injured Lover"—(*Misc.*, I, iii).

The date of composition, then, would be sometime before 1727; and Cross (I, 50-52) took the poem to be Fielding's comment on his tragi-comic affair with Sarah Andrew, the youthful heiress of Lyme Regis, in the autumn of 1725.[123] But, since Cross also suggested that Fielding's love-stricken attempt to abduct that young lady was made with her entire consent, he would appear to be arguing against his own assertion; for if the design was foiled by Miss Andrew's guardians, there was no reason for Fielding to revenge himself with a satire against the fair sex. No real evidence exists, one way or the other; but if Miss Andrew were to be taken as the efficient cause of this poem, one would have to suppose that she in some way contributed to the miscarriage of Fielding's amorous plan. Whatever the original date of the poem, however, it was obviously touched up for publication, since several of the numerous allusions scattered through it are of a considerably later date—for example, the reference to *Pamela* (*Misc.*, I, 91) and the footnote on "our [Fielding's and William Young's] Notes on the *Plutus* of *Aristophanes*" (I, 77, n.), which work had been published in May 1742.

The "modernization" of the first three hundred lines of Juvenal's satire[124] is couched in hudibrastic couplets; but, unlike the burlesque passage from Virgil, it is not in the Cottonian mode of travesty. In point of fact, Fielding's burlesque is far less vulgar than Dryden's paraphrase.[125]

[123] On Sarah Andrew, see also J. P. De Castro, "Fielding and Lyme Regis," *TLS*, 4 June 1931, p. 447.
[124] There are some 660 lines in the original. Fielding broke off (with good reason) at line 300, explaining: "We shall here close our Translation of this Satire: for as the Remainder is in many Places too obscene for chaste Ears; so, to the Honour of the *English* Ladies, the *Latin* is by no Means applicable to them, nor indeed capable of being modernized" (*Misc.*, I, 113, n.).
[125] Dryden is, of course, generally credited with the translations of

POETRY

He follows his original rather closely (in ideas, not in tone), expanding or contracting particular passages according to the demands of rhyme and the opportunities for contemporary allusion. The final effect is that the virulence of Juvenal is metamorphosed into a kind of amiable commentary on the theme of female vice and foible. The Latin and the English are given on facing pages, according to common custom in imitations of the classics; and Fielding has added long pedantic notes (in Latin) to the original, and humorous asides and explanations to his own version. A brief citation may serve to illustrate some of the foregoing remarks:

>   . . . necte coronam
> Postibus, & densos per limina tende corymbos.
> Unus Iberinæ vir sufficit? ocyùs illud
> Extorquebis, ut hæc oculo contenta sit uno.
> Magna tamen fama est cujusdam rure paterno
> Viventis: vivat Gabijs, ut vixit in agro;
> Vivat Fidenis, & agello cedo paterno.
> Quis tamen affirmat nil actum in montibus, aut in
> Speluncis? adeò senuerunt Jupiter & Mars?
>   [ll. 51-59]

> But come, your Equipage make ready,
> And dress your House out for my Lady.
> Will one Man *Iberine* supply?
> Sooner content her with one Eye.
>   But hold; there runs a common Story
> Of a chaste Country Virgin's Glory.

Satires I, III, VI, X, and XVI, in the collaborative edition of 1693, *The Satires of Decimus Junius Juvenalis. Translated into English Verse. By Mr. Dryden, and Several Other Eminent Hands.* Some possible echoes of Dryden's version in Fielding's rendition lend faint support to the natural assumption that he was familiar with the earlier work; but the influence of Samuel Butler's style is more pervasive than Dryden's. Fielding's octosyllabic couplets, varying from an even tetrameter to mere doggerel, his frequent double rhymes and wrenched accents, and the inflated (and bathetic) figures of speech, are very much in the *Hudibras* mode.

> At *Bath* and *Tunbridge* let her be;
> If there she's chaste, I will agree.
> And will the Country yield no Slanders?
> Is all our Army gone to *Flanders*?
>   (*Misc.*, I, 80-83)

Fielding's note on his own last line reads: "As the Patron of these Gentlemen is mentioned in the Original, we thought his Votaries might be pleased with being inserted in the Imitation" (*Misc.*, I, 83, n.).

One would guess that all the critical apparatus represents a later adjunct to the original poem—possibly devised as an homeopathic relief at the same time that Fielding and Young were engaged in the serious business of compiling footnotes for their *Plutus*. And perhaps it is the extensive reworking to which the poem has been subjected that accounts for its primary failure: namely, the inconsistency of tone. Sometimes the original is vulgarized and sometimes it is refined; at points the translation is quite purely *literatim* and then again it will be rendered in a literal way but colloquially or flippantly. Thus the familiar "Rara avis in terris, nigroque simillima cygno" is given as:

> She's a rare Bird! find her who can,
> And much resembling a black Swan.
>   (*Misc.*, I, 97)

Clearly, nothing is gained here: this is neither good burlesque nor even good translation. When Fielding is adapting the original allusions to modern circumstances, however, he achieves some happier parallels:

> Ast aliæ, quoties aulæa recondita cessant,
> Et vacuo clausoque sonant fora sola theatro,
> Atque à plebeijs longè Megalesia; tristes
> Personam, thyrsumque tenent, & subligar Accî
>   [ll. 67-70].

is thus expanded to:

> But others, when the House is shut up,
> Nor Play-Bills, *by Desire,* are put up;
> When Players cease, and Lawyer rises
> To harangue Jury at Assizes;
> When Drolls at *Barthol'mew* begin,
> A Feast Day after that of *Trin'.*
> Others, I say, themselves turn Players,
> With *Clive* and *Woffington's* gay Airs;
> Paint their fair Faces out like Witches,
> And cram their Thighs in *Fle[et]w[oo]d's* Breeches.
>
> (*Misc.,* 1, 82-85)

The best parts of the poem give, as this does, a high sense of intimacy with the current London scene and a thumping rhythm that sorts perfectly with the burlesque intent.

On the other hand, in the concluding lines of Fielding's fragment, drawn from Juvenal's attack upon the luxury and the mania for foreign ways that he felt were sapping Rome's moral strength, there is a sharp change in tone. The subject is too close to Fielding's own heart for burlesque treatment and we are given instead a straightforward diatribe (with an almost Skeltonic ring) against similar evils in England:

> Now from Security we feel
> More Ills than threaten'd us from Steel;
> Severer Luxury abounds,
> Avenging *France* of all her Wounds.
> When our old *British* Plainness left us,
> Of ev'ry Virtue it bereft us:
> And we've imported from all Climes,
> All sorts of Wickedness and Crimes:
> *French* Finery, *Italian* Meats,
> With *German* Drunkenness, *Dutch* Cheats.
> Money's the Source of all our Woes;
> Money! whence Luxury o'erflows,

POETRY

And in a Torrent, like the *Nile*,
Bears off the Virtues of this Isle.

(*Misc.*, I, 113)

This is rather good invective—and it is quite consonant with Fielding's later posture on the subject—but it assuredly does not accord with the flippant air of the rest. It is clear throughout that once he had departed from the ruling tone of the original, he could not achieve a tonal unity for his own rendition.

But one must not be too severe upon a simple *jeu d'esprit*. The piece offers some good individual lines and some delightfully bustling impressions of London activities. And, significantly enough, it emphasizes once again the direction in which Fielding's native talent led him from the beginning: toward a juxtaposition of authentic moral indignation with an irresistible impulse laughingly to subject the world and its affairs to burlesque commentary. Out of this amalgam would develop a mature tone of benevolent irony and good-humored detachment, still paradoxically united to a most personal and passionate concern for the human creature, that would be—then as now—unique in the world of prose fiction.

CHAPTER III. ESSAYS

> I have now secured myself from the imitation of those who are utterly incapable of any degree of reflection, and whose learning is not equal to an essay.—*Tom Jones*, IX, i

THE three serious essays included in the *Miscellanies* are members of that class which has been denominated "essays of purpose"; that is, they aim quite frankly to instruct and reform rather than to amuse. *Amoto quaeramus seria ludo.* Thus in one regard they are of a piece with such later tracts as the *Enquiry into the Causes of the Late Increase of Robbers* and *A Proposal for Making an Effectual Provision for the Poor*, wherein Fielding set himself to call attention to and amend the most glaring social evils of his day. The integrity and the essential consistency of Fielding's moral aims are manifest in these three essays, which show him earnestly anatomizing a group of crucial problems that had drawn his attention very early in his writing career and were to remain for him throughout his life the objects of a most lively and profound concern.

The first, the *Essay on Conversation*, takes us into the world of eighteenth-century social talk and manners. Obviously enough, this is the stage for many of Fielding's fictional activities, but we need not move very far into his inquiry to see that more is involved than a societal milieu. The ostensible design of the essay is to draw up a "courtesy book" in little, an enchiridion of good breeding that will seek to maintain in happy balance the *forms* of politeness, which make social intercourse graceful and orderly, and the *spirit* of honorable complaisance, which makes it reciprocally pleasing. This is the center: but there are concentric rings of implication, for the social values that Fielding here endorses have (for him) a more inclusive significance. They are not mere rules for talk and visits; they involve his whole conception of the relationships of the good man to other men in the very actions most central to the full realization of his basic nature. For man is the *animal sociale,* and the complex of social relationships in which he exists is not merely *a* world—it is *the* world. Fielding's *social* values, then, are closely and meaningfully interwoven with his primary *moral* values; and the implications of the essay are accordingly enlarged.

The *Essay on the Knowledge of the Characters of Men* is again concerned with social man, but now in "psychological" terms and in a more sombre key. I have previously argued that from Fielding's examination of "Bombast Greatness" and its shocking success in the world arose a dual conviction: namely, that people at large do not recognize their own proper interests, and that good men are by their very nature easy victims of deceit and hypocrisy. This essay consequently is an attempt to achieve the corrective end that the plays and novels effected through a vigorous humor and through character in action—to rip the mask from the face of pretense by exposing the real motives behind human actions and by educating the "undesigning part of mankind" in the characteristic subterfuges and disguises of evil and malicious men. There needs no ghost come from the grave to tell us that Fielding abhorred hypocrisy. But the terms of his assessment of the human psyche in this guide to double-dealing carry beyond the immediate end of the work and lead us into some of the ambages (and ambiguities) of Fielding's conception of human nature.

Human society, human nature, and finally, the human soul. The last essay, *Of the Remedy of Affliction for the Loss of Our Friends,* sounds an elegiac note that may seem somewhat untypical of our greatest comic novelist. I think it can be said with more than casual validity, however, that the mood and tone of the *consolatio* are as truly expressive of the total man as that high-spirited joy in life which he

ESSAYS

communicated to his comic masterpieces. Fielding obviously loved the good things of this world; but he was too percipient and too intimately acquainted with grief and deprivation to indulge in an uncritical philosophic optimism. The *Remedy* attests that he could see man's existence as an affair at once serious and brief, and that he did not believe one could escape either the afflictions or the end of life by pretending that neither existed. The philosophic atmosphere of the Stoic-Christian tradition evoked in this essay is, despite its soberness, the very air that is breathed in his comic world. In the sources of the *consolatio* one finds the sources also of Fielding's basic moral and religious convictions.

2

Stylistically, the essays show a high degree of competence. It is true that Fielding's happiest powers as an essayist lay in the brief periodical sketch or the kind of short introductory chapter found in *Joseph Andrews* and *Tom Jones*, but he displayed in the *Miscellanies* an ability to organize a larger and, of course, more literal-minded discourse, and to maintain a pleasant assurance and easy manner throughout. If there is little season here (or, one might remark, in certain sections of *Amelia*) of that vivifying wit and humor which more typically grace his work, there is a moral earnestness, a forceful sense of purpose, that has its own particular charm.

The history and development of the English essay have been many times sketched, and we need not tread that ground again;[1] but it is interesting to speculate upon the structural models that Fielding might have chosen for these efforts. They obviously required a longer form than that to which the *Champion* had accustomed him. There were adequate contemporary exemplars of the brief periodical

[1] An excellent bibliography and a better introduction to the subject than most longer studies have offered is to be found in the exemplary text, *Century Readings in the English Essay*, ed., Louis Wann (N.Y., 1939).

ESSAYS

essay, most notably, the *Tatler* and *Spectator* papers; but in the longer essay, the immediate models—Clarendon, Halifax, Temple, Dryden, St. Évremond, Shaftesbury, Bolingbroke—displayed (like Montaigne) a rambling tendency, a discursiveness, that Fielding clearly did not wish to follow. The concept of the essay as an "imperfect offer" or trial flight persisted well into the eighteenth century; but this was not to Fielding's purpose in the present compositions. He looked for a more solid logical structure, the kind of disciplined movement from point to point that could be found in, say, the philosophic essays of Hobbes or Locke. I should suppose, finally, that he turned to the structural pattern of the classic oration, as it had been modified by the sermons of the Restoration and early eighteenth century.

The classical model Fielding would have known intimately from school exercises and personal readings. The essay as such was not a classical genre, of course; and the analogues that one might find in a Cicero or Seneca or Plutarch often leaned more toward a discursive than a logical structure.[2] But, just as an Elizabethan writer (following a French model) could declare that the formal letter was "nothing else but an Oration written,"[3] so, later, could the author of a formal discourse organize his argument after the same model of the classic oration. This pattern was firm but flexible; and it offered an appropriate rhetoric for many particular occasions.[4] The classical rhetors,

[2] See R. M. Gummere, "The English Essay and Some of Its Ancient Prototypes," *Classical Weekly*, xiv (1921), 154-60. The influence of the classical moralists upon later essayists (including Fielding) is, to be sure, pervasive in style and subject matter: but I do not think that his *structure* derives from their models.

[3] William Fulwood, *The Enimie of Idlenesse* (1568), f1 recto; cited by Katherine G. Hornbeak, *The Complete Letter Writer in English, 1568-1800* (*Smith College Stud. in Mod. Lang.*, xv, iii-iv; Northampton, Mass., 1934), p. 8.

[4] I have drawn my translations throughout this section from the Loeb Classical Library: Aristotle: *Rhetoric*, transl. John H. Freese (1926); Cicero: *De oratore* (and *De partitione oratoria*), transl. E. W. Sutton and H. Rackham (2v., 1942); Quintilian: *Institutio oratoria*, transl. H. E.

ESSAYS

following Aristotle, normally divided the oration into three *genera*: the deliberative, forensic (judicial), and epideictic (demonstrative), developed to satisfy the general requirements of oratory for the assembly, the courts, and the public platform respectively. Aristotle categorized the *ends* of the three kinds of oratory as follows: the expedient or harmful, involving exhortation or dissuasion (deliberative), the just or unjust, involving accusation or defense (forensic), and the honorable or shameful, involving praise or blame (epideictic), and he recommended particular topics and procedures for each. In practice, however (and in later rhetorics), there was much admixture. The Latin rhetorics of the Empire were most largely concerned with forensic oratory, and its characteristics often served as a standard for the other types as well. The divisions of the model oration, as set forth by the *Rhetorica ad Herennium* (III. ix-x) and (with various modifications) most other rhetorics, normally included the following: *exordium, narratio, divisio, confirmatio* (and *refutatio*), and, finally, *peroratio*.

One need not assign Fielding's essays strictly to particular *genera*; but the essays on conversation and on the character of men are essentially deliberative, taking the expedient and the harmful as their area of discussion and employing exhortation and dissuasion as their techniques. The latter essay is concerned with justice as well, and resembles, in its analysis of motivations to evil, Aristotle's discussion under forensic rhetoric. The essay on consolation is in an ancient tradition that came under the classification of the epideictic.

More immediately useful perhaps is the structural paradigm that the oration presented: The *exordium* was an opening intended to win attention or sympathy, to arouse interest. Thus, in the *Essay on Conversation*, Fielding does not plunge directly into his central thesis, but begins, "MAN is generally represented as an Animal formed for and delight-

---

Butler (4v., 1921-22). I must acknowledge a substantial debt to Wilbur S. Howell, *Logic and Rhetoric in England, 1500-1700* (Princeton, 1956).

ing in Society..." (*Misc.*, I, 117). This generalized opening makes use of a commonplace that could be calculated to win the immediate attention of the eighteenth-century reader. It leads into a section that might be considered part of the *exordium* or that might be said to serve as a *narratio*. The latter was a statement of the facts, a brief (and often slanted) account of the circumstances from which the general argument arose or an exposition of that which was to be proved; it was calculated to make the audience regard the following matter in the same light as the speaker. Fielding in this section establishes the intimate connection of society with conversation, and makes a preliminary *divisio* ("Conversation is of three Sorts. Men are said to converse with God, with themselves, and with one another"—*Misc.*, I, 120). Narrowing his subject to the latter topic, he then proceeds to the *divisio* proper, which involves a definition ("The Art of pleasing or doing Good to one another is therefore the Art of Conversation"—*Misc.*, I, 123) as well as a partition (conduct is to be considered in actions and in words—*Misc.*, I, 125). The *confirmatio* or essay proper (the "proof," *probatio*) follows, and is carefully ranged into arguments, with illustration, comparison, repetition, digression, and other devices of amplification. The *refutatio* (*confutatio*), or answer to contrary positions, is introduced as required (common practice in nonjudicial classic orations); and the whole is concluded with a *peroratio* (*conclusio*) in which Fielding sums up the design by stressing the fundamental distinction between good-breeding and ill-breeding which lies at the heart of his argument.

The other two essays (or, indeed, many of Fielding's periodical essays) can be analyzed in much the same fashion and found to follow the same kind of structure.[5] The

---

[5] The (limited) relevance of this kind of rhetorical analysis to the essay has been remarked by Donald C. Bryant, " 'A Peece of a Logician': The Critical Essayist as Rhetorician," in *The Rhetorical Idiom. Essays in Rhetoric, Oratory, Language, and Drama Presented to Herbert August Wichelns* (Ithaca, N.Y., 1958), pp. 293-314.

ESSAYS

divisions are not always precise, for the classical delimitation had never been intended to impose an unvarying rigidity upon the discourse. Cicero, for example, in his little treatise, *De partitione oratoria* (IX. 27-33), omitted the *divisio* and classified *confirmatio* and *reprehensio* (refutation) together. Other rhetors made their own changes. The value of all such structures is simply to suggest a method of procedure: that is, attention is won, the apology for the treatise is made, and the subject is announced, proved, and brought to a conclusion. The precise ordering, as the *Ad Herennium* had said (III. ix. 16-17), was to be left to the skill of the orator in adapting his material to particular circumstances.

Now the Elizabethan sermon, as well as the Elizabethan formal letter, had tended to follow this same traditional structure; but in the seventeenth century the widespread revaluation of rhetorical conventions following upon the Ramistic reforms had opened up new possibilities of organization for the sermon. The *Rhetoricae Ecclesiasticae* of Bartholomew Keckermann, for example, offered a structure which began directly with the text to be preached upon, divided the subject, explicated the passage, and then amplified and applied it. As W. Fraser Mitchell says, "This is not simply the old parts of the Greek oration renamed":[6] the new structure led to a greater concentration upon the text and a lesser concern for the flourish and display that had previously marked the *exordia* and *peroratione* of the sermon.

The significance of this (very briefly described) development for Henry Fielding lies in the fact that his essays reveal an obvious debt to the Restoration sermon. The classical *partes* are still, I believe, to be discerned; but Fielding's *exordia* and *peroratione* are brief, he tends to follow the *explicatio verborum* of sermon usage (as in his etymology and categorization of "conversation"), and his

[6] *English Pulpit Oratory from Andrewes to Tillotson: A Study of Its Literary Aspects* (1932), p. 95. My brief discussion of this subject is largely based upon Mitchell.

149

main argument (*confirmatio*) is marked by the kinds of division (for example, into first, second, and third points) and the kinds of transitional and summarizing phrases that marked the sermon.[7] Indeed, these phrases ("We will begin then . . . ," "Let us now consider . . . ," "Having thus briefly considered . . . ," or "I have now done with my first head. . . . I shall in the next place . . .") sometimes appear almost obtrusive. They seem more proper to the spoken than the written discourse. Yet seen in context, they clarify the progress of Fielding's argument and give the whole a sense of firm integration which permits animated illustration and digression without the loss of orderly forward movement.

3

So much for structure. To turn to the style of the essays—a question with many more ramifications—we might characterize it, I think without impertinence, in the terms of Johnson's familiar description of Addison's "middle style": "pure without scrupulosity, and exact without apparent elaboration; always equable, and always easy, without glowing words or pointed sentences. [He] never deviates from his track to snatch a grace; he seeks no ambitious ornaments, and tries no hazardous innovations. His page is always luminous, but never blazes in unexpected splendour."[8] Fielding had undoubtedly given his days and nights to the volumes of Addison, and Johnson's phrases would accurately enough describe the basic style of the essays. Yet

---

[7] In his (I believe it to be his) imitation of a sermon published in April 1741, to attack the administration from the highest possible moral plane (*The Crisis: A Sermon, on Revel.* xiv.9,10,11 . . . *By a Lover of His Country*), Fielding followed this pattern precisely. It might be incidentally noted that the particular formula of *hypophora* (anticipating and answering an objection) that Fielding employs more than once in the essays, namely, to put the objection and follow with the phrase, "To which I answer" (*Misc.*, i, 200; cf. also p. 206), is a notable mannerism of Robert South, perhaps Fielding's favorite divine in the early years of his career.

[8] *Lives of the English Poets*, ed. G. B. Hill (3v., Oxford, 1905), ii, 149.

ESSAYS

there is an irregular fervor in Fielding's essays that one does not often find in Addison. For the most part, it is true, Fielding's tone is one of good-mannered modesty (although at times this apparent modesty conceals the rhetorical gambit known as *synchoresis*), accented by numerous concessive clauses and qualifying phrases ("I believe," "I apprehend," "I hope");[9] but when he comes to describe the insolence of prideful men in conversation, or the hypocrisy of "a sour, morose, ill-natured, censorious Sanctity," or when he seeks to convey the ecstatic hope of immortality, he finds an answering style. The obvious advantage of his basically even-tempered tone is that departures from it, for the purpose of emphasis or emotional appeal, are so much the more striking. A style that is all climaxes cannot make an effective climax when it will.

The diction is almost unfailingly simple and precise. Occasionally Fielding introduces, for a particular end, a touch of school-boy slang ("Dabs"—I, 173) or a vulgarism ("Kicks in the B - - - ch"—I, 194); and, at the other end of the scale, when he rises to denounce or arouse there is a corresponding elevation of diction. But taken as a whole, these essays are good examples of the middle style (or more accurately, the "elegant middle" style), a sparseness of imagery going hand-in-hand with the calculated simplicity of diction. When images are used, it is normally for emphasis rather than embellishment and they tend to be homely: for example, the description of the insolent as "those strutting Animals, who sometimes stalk in Assemblies" or the nourishment of Deceit "when it hath sucked in the Instruction of Politicians" (*Misc.*, I, 128, 183). On the other hand,

[9] It should be observed that, although Fielding's use of numerous formulae of polite deprecation in the essays of the *Miscellanies* is normally serious, only a slight twist is necessary to turn any one of them into irony. The use of such phrases as the following (drawn from these essays), is, indeed, one of the distinctive features of his ironic manner: "I would not be understood to," "as I have before hinted," "I will [not] venture to affirm," "that almost obliges us to," "give me leave," "I am more apt to," or "we may reasonably conclude."

151

ESSAYS

if Fielding in these essays, like Addison in his, sought for *simplicitas*, it was for a Ciceronian *simplicitas*. Not that he (or Addison, for that matter) really emulated Cicero's amazing rhythmical techniques; but that the language, though plain, is "copious"—that is to say, it displays a calculated redundancy and multiplication of members. The *copia verborum* serves its Ciceronian function of contributing both to the rhythm and to the structure of Fielding's periods.

Unlike Addison—who obviously devoted much attention to his cadences and, according to the investigations of Jan Lannering, "consciously strove after the flowing effect of *velox*,"[10] the long cadence of the medieval *cursus*—Fielding was not so enamored of the falling close. Although there are a number of perfect *cursus*, short and long, in his clausal and sentence endings, one rather suspects that they came without being called (as Crassus puts it, in Cicero's dialogue).[11] Frequently, in fact, he chooses with presumable deliberation to close a sentence on a pair of clashing accents, when a mere reversal of words would have provided a falling close—for example, "wanton Abortions, or extravagant Births" (I, 122); "between English Farmers and Dutch Boors" (I, 131); "some other Motive than Generosity or Good-will" (I, 202). Thus Fielding's endings are more frequently masculine than feminine; and, although this characteristic excludes him from the company of the "numerous style" that such contemporary theorists of harmony as James Geddes and John Mason liked to extol, it is none-

[10] *Studies in the Prose Style of Joseph Addison* (Upsala, 1951), p. 134. In the discussion that follows I have profited immeasurably from the painstaking investigations of Dr. Lannering and from W. K. Wimsatt's *Prose Style of Samuel Johnson* (New Haven, 1941). I have also drawn upon George Williamson's *The Senecan Amble* (1951), and upon the various pioneering articles of Morris W. Croll, particularly, "The Baroque Style in Prose," in *Studies in English Philology, a Miscellany in Honor of Frederick Klaeber* (Minneapolis, 1929), pp. 427-56.

[11] *De oratore* III. xlix. 191: "Neque vos paean aut herous ille conturbet: ipsi occurrent orationi, ipsi inquam, se offerent et respondebunt non vocati."

152

theless more typical of the native English rhythm—which, even under the influence of Latin prose, never *quite* learned to be comfortable with the *cursus*.

Perhaps most immediately striking in the style of the essays is the structure of Fielding's sentences (which to discuss properly will demand, I fear, some jargon). The sentences are sufficiently varied in length to escape tedium; but in the longer sentences that carry most of the emphasis, the norm is a hypotactic period, that is, one with heavy dependence upon subordinating conjunctions. Only occasionally does Fielding make use of the suspended period (the so-called "periodic sentence"), but in his introductory, closing, and emphatic paragraphs, the sentences are typically lengthened by subordinate (and coordinate) members and marked by a notable balance and parallelism. Even the shorter "working" sentences that carry the bulk of the argument often become surprisingly complex in structure. The citation of a paragraph in his "heightened" vein (from *On the Knowledge of the Characters of Men*) may help to illustrate some of the basic elements of Fielding's style in these essays, since the devices used here for emphasis reappear characteristically, if less obviously, throughout. I have arranged the constituent thought units (a rough equivalent of the *cola*) in separate lines and italicized the words which call attention to parallel constructions, coordination, and subordination:

> I have been somewhat diffusive in the censorious Branch of this Character,
> *as* it is a very pernicious one;
> *and* (according to what I have observed) little known *and* attended to.
> I shall not describe all its other Qualities.
> Indeed there is no Species of Mischief *which* it doth not produce.

> *For,* not to mention the private Villanies it daily transacts,
>> most of the great Evils which have affected Society, Wars, Murders, *and* Massacres, have owed their Original to this abominable Vice;
>>> *which* is the Destroyer of the Innocent, *and* Protector of the Guilty;
>>>> *which hath* introduced all manner of Evil into the World,
>>>>> *and hath* almost expelled every Grain of Good out of it.
>>>>>> *Doth it not attempt to* cheat Men into the Pursuit of Sorrow *and* Misery, *under the* Appearance of Virtue,
>>>>>>> *and* to frighten them from Mirth *and* Pleasure, *under the* Colour of Vice, or, if you please, Sin?
>>>>>>>> *Doth it not attempt to* gild over that poisonous Potion, made up of Malevolence, Austerity, *and* such cursed Ingredients,
>>>>>>>>> *while* it embitters the delightful Draught of innocent Pleasure with the nauseous Relish of Fear *and* Shame.
>>>>>>>>>> (*Misc.*, I, 212-13)

The variety of sentence length in the essays is here demonstrated in little. Fielding begins his paragraph with a sentence of average length, followed by two brief staccato sentences. The long period that comes next is loosely linked to the preceding sentence by the weak conjunction "For." This period is extended by two relative "which"-clauses, one of which is itself extended by a double predicate ("which hath . . . and hath . . ."). The paragraph is then concluded with the *anaphora* of "Doth it not attempt" in two coordinate and symmetrical (but not perfectly isocolic) sentences.

ESSAYS

This is a style that makes use of the subordination and duplication of elements found in "Ciceronian" prose, but that makes no attempt to cultivate the cumulative effect of the suspended period which is so typical of that style. Fielding's thought here moves by linear addition rather than flowing to a suspended climax. On the other hand, there is a definite order, a premeditated rhythmic effect, that distinguishes it from "loose" or "natural" prose without a committed syntax. Neither truly periodic nor truly loose, then, Fielding's formal style resembles to that extent what George Williamson (*pace* Shaftesbury) has called "the Senecan amble," a hybrid mode that may be described as the "loose period," combining features of both extremes. Much of the prose of Dryden, Halifax, and even of the more Ciceronian Sir William Temple displays the characteristics of this "loose" Senecan mode (as distinguished from the "curt" Senecan style that was more popular before the Restoration); and Fielding's prose has very real affinities with theirs. It seems to me, however, to have even closer affinities with the further development of this "loose period" by two great stylists, Archbishop Tillotson and Joseph Addison.

The loose Senecan mode tended in appearance to be quite casual. Even Temple fell into the practice of employing a sequence of main clauses that had no syntactic links between subjects or predicates—a loose device that Lannering declares to have been "so typical of the English essay from the Restoration down to Queen Anne that it may well be said to be the chief criterion of the prose style of the age."[12] Lannering credits Addison with having been

[12] Lannering, pp. 117-18. The characteristic thing about this movement, he says, is "that what is in fact incidental matter is made to appear as a main statement through the absence of a subordinating conjunction" (p. 117). Since these are fairly abstract observations, it may be well to illustrate with one of Lannering's examples, namely, that from Temple's *Essay upon the Ancient and Modern Learning*: "If our wit and eloquence, our knowledge or inventions would deserve it; yet our languages would not: there is no hopes of their lasting long, nor of any thing in them;

155

the first important writer of the time to eschew this loose, nonparallel sequence and to develop, while keeping many features of the "Senecan amble," a non-Senecan *copia*—an artistic use of the superfluous words and phrases for their rhythmic rather than their "thought" function—and devices of parallelism and redundancy that distributed, rather than concentrated, the main emphasis. (The double effect was a prose that was easier to understand, but that was flowing and pleasantly rhythmical.) Addison surely brought this style to perfection; but it seems to me that he had been anticipated in these effects by several of the famous Restoration preachers—most notably, as I have suggested, John Tillotson, whom Addison, along with many others in his age, is reported to have taken as "a standard of English writing."[13]

John Mason, stealing a march on Dr. Johnson, said of Addison: "In a Word, the best way to acquire a chaste, expressive, and numerous Stile, is to read and copy him."[14] I believe Fielding did; but I also believe that if he had not read Tillotson when a boy (as the surgeon in *Joseph Andrews* had—*JA*, I, xvi), he had nonetheless read him very early in his career and gained from him, as from Addison, a

---

they change every hundred years so as to be hardly known for the same, or any thing of the former styles to be endured by the latter; so as they can no more last like the ancients, than excellent carvings in wood, like those in marbles or brass."

[13] Peter Smithers, *The Life of Joseph Addison* (Oxford, 1954), p. 423. On Tillotson, see Louis G. Locke, *Tillotson: A Study in Seventeenth-Century Literature* (*Anglistica*, Vol. IV; Copenhagen, 1954), esp. chap. III, "The Style of Tillotson." This somewhat general chapter needs to be supplemented, however, by an analysis of Tillotson's sermons in the light of Lannering's more technical survey of Addison's devices of structure and rhythm. I have not mentioned the sermons of Isaac Barrow, because I am not sure that Fielding read him in early career, and because I agree with Mitchell, that "greater man and greater preacher than Tillotson as Barrow was, the fact must be faced that his style, although splendidly adapted for the oration or formal speech, could never have become a model for prose" (*English Pulpit Oratory*, p. 401). The same, incidentally, might be said of Bolingbroke's sounding prose.

[14] *An Essay on the Power and Harmony of Prosaic Numbers* (2nd ed. 1761; orig. ed. 1749), p. 50.

sense of the easy formal style. In the language of the turf (not inappropriately used, I trust, for the era that saw the Byerly Turk, the Darley Arabian, and the Godolphin Arabian arrive in England), one might describe the sample of Fielding's essay style cited above as "Formal, by Addison out of Tillotson, by the Senecan Amble." This perhaps fails to do justice to another important figure who clearly influenced Fielding's style, as he influenced his early thought—the witty high-churchman, Robert South. But South's influence may be said to lie less on the formal side than on the expressive and animating side—with Swift and Steele, with Lucian and the translations of Lucian, with the Englishings of *Don Quixote* (where pleonasm is an instrument of ironic exaggeration), and with the multitude of other lively classical, foreign, and native elements that were distilled and metamorphosed in the alembic of Fielding's great humorous imagination.

On the formal side, we may remark some of the more obvious qualities of the "copiousness" of Addison (and Tillotson): a clausal parallelism in which the thought, rather than moving directly forward, advances by a series of repetitions and variations; the use of pleonastic word-pairs which do not concentrate but distribute the major emphasis; and the duplication of predicates and of predicate elements. In the illustrative paragraph above, the intent of individual clauses is (clearly) less to advance the total argument of the essay than to expatiate upon one aspect of it (here, "censoriousness"), to illuminate this aspect, as it were, from various angles, and to support the appeal to the emotions with a rhythmic ground-bass. The repetition and parallelism serve not only a rhythmic function but distribute the emphasis, making for a less sententious but more easily comprehended scheme of thought. Such pleonastic pairs as "Sorrow and Misery," "Mirth and Pleasure," again have primarily a rhythmical and distributive function; and the same may be said for the triplets, "Malevolence, Austerity, and such cursed Ingredients," and "Wars, Murders, and Massacres" (the alliteration that Fielding in emotional passages often falls into is quite un-Addisonian and equally untypical of Tillotson). The duplication of predicate, which we have already remarked, and of the predicative element (as in "Destroyer of the Innocent, and Protector of the Guilty") are distinctive marks of the Tillotson-Addison *copia*; and they serve, once again, the same rhythmic and distributive function for Fielding. It is true, however, that some of his parallels of longer elements have both a rhythmic and a "thought" function: for example, the sentence which contains the aforementioned pleonastic pairs is balanced within itself and is further balanced against the sentence that follows; but it also makes a very definite point. The function of the following sentence, however, is again primarily rhythmic and distributive of the emphasis—it is a redundant variation of its twin.

These stylistic devices are to be found, as I have said, in less striking form throughout the straightforward sections of the essays; and they are employed much in the manner of our sample in the *exordia* and *peroratione* (where, according to classical precept, the appeals of *ethos* and *pathos* were most appropriate) and at other points of heightened argument. I would note particularly that since they are the elements that invite attention, they give to the style of the essays its characteristic flavor; this may serve as my apology for dwelling perhaps to the point of weariness upon them. I should like to cite two further examples, one to illustrate Fielding's paratactic manner and one to illustrate the looser and more rambling form of his hypotactic period.

The paratactic structure is that most typical of the "curt" Senecan style, a series of clauses linked together not by logical subordination, but by a coordination that omits connectives. The normal function of this structure in Fielding's work is to present an idea and then to characterize it by repetition and variation; for example: "But indeed

ESSAYS

there are few whose Vanity is so foul a Feeder, to digest Flattery, if undisguised: It must impose on us, in order to allure us: Before we can relish it, we must call it by some other Name; such as, a just Esteem of, and Respect for our real Worth; a Debt due to our Merit, and not a Present to our Pride" (*Misc.*, 1, 202). Even better (but longer) examples, the "character" of pride in the *Essay on Conversation* (*Misc.*, 1, 147) or of hypocrisy in the *Essay on the Knowledge of the Characters of Men* (*Misc.*, 1, 209), remind us that this paratactic manner is precisely that of the seventeenth-century character writers, and that Fielding's normal use of it is in such Theophrastan portraits.[15]

More significant is the "rambling" form of the hypotactic period that looks back to the distinctive manner of Halifax, the elegant Temple, and ultimately to the late Montaigne. It is this structure (combined with rather frequent inversions and a cavalier use of anacoluthon) that accounts for the engaging sense of the "old fashioned" one often has in reading Fielding, that makes him seem less "modern," for example, than Addison.[16] To illustrate, we may choose a typical passage from the *Essay on Conversation*. Although some of the pleonasm of the illustration we cited earlier is still present, the end of the present structure is less a matter of rhythm and distribution of the emphasis than it is of extending and developing the *thought* by qualification and addition (I have italicized the subordinating elements):

"Conversation is of three Sorts. Men are said to converse with God, with themselves, and with one another. The two first of these have been so liberally and excellently spoken to by others, *that* I shall, at present, pass them by, and confine myself, in this Essay, to the third only: *Since* it seems to me

[15] So also with Addison: see Lannering, p. 105.
[16] The oft-noted characteristic of Fielding's style, his habitual use of "thee-thou" and "hath-doth" (as well as an occasional "whilst"), also looks back to the seventeenth-century essayists and divines. Fielding's favorite locution, "to say [the] truth," is anticipated in many places, including Cotton's translation of Montaigne and Tom Brown's translations from Lucian.

amazing, *that* this grand Business of our Lives, the Foundation of every Thing, either useful or pleasant, should have been so slightly treated of; *that while* there is scarce a Profession or Handicraft in Life, however mean and contemptible, *which* is not abundantly furnished with proper Rules to the attaining its Perfection, Men should be left almost totally in the Dark, and without the least Light to direct, or any Guide to conduct them in the proper exerting of those Talents, *which* are the noblest Privilege of human Nature, and productive of all rational Happiness; and *the rather as* this Power is by no means self-instructed, and in the Possession of the artless and ignorant, is of so mean Use, *that* it raises them very little above those Animals who are void of it" (*Misc.*, I, 120-21).

A few other determinants of Fielding's style in these essays may well be mentioned, since they remain relatively constant characteristics from the early years of his career to the latest. He is fond of sequences (particularly triplets) of adjectives, substantives, or even phrases and clauses. The sequence of rhetorical questions he tends to reserve for points of highest emphasis. His most noteworthy coordinate constructions are the correlative "as . . . so . . ." and the adversative "though . . . yet . . . ," both used so often that the characteristic balance of Fielding's formal prose might almost be attributed to them alone. Also typical, but employed less frequently (one might almost say relentlessly), is the coordinate explanatory formula, "as . . . and as . . . I shall. . . ." Again, no reader of Fielding can have overlooked his strong inclination to the parenthesis. It ranges from the habitual "I conceive" or "I apprehend," to such a mélange as this: "I shall therefore recommend one more certain Rule, and which, I believe, if duly attended to, would, in a great measure, extirpate all Fallacy out of the World; or must at least so effectually disappoint its Purposes, that it would soon be worth no Man's while to assume it, and the Character of Knave and Fool would be more apparently (what they are at present in Reality) allied, or united" (*Misc.*, I, 219-20). Finally, as this illustration may also indicate, Fielding habitually—indeed, almost compulsively—extended his periods with a final qualification or negation, or an additional instance. The phrases typically introducing such an extension are "or," "nor," "or even," "the rather," "especially," "and that," "much less," and—that old favorite of both the seventeenth and eighteenth centuries—"nay."[17]

Perhaps enough has been said to make clear to any reader of Fielding's novels that his essay style is rather more involved and formal than his narrative style.[18] A simple comparison of the introductory chapters in *Tom Jones* with the

[17] It may be worth observing that Fielding scrupulously avoids splitting the infinitive and (usually) avoids ending a sentence with a preposition. Addison, on the other hand, frequently concluded with a preposition to achieve a falling close.

[18] It should be further noted that among the non-narrative essays themselves there are conspicuous differences in style. The exhortation to the citizens of London in the *Champion* of 18 December 1739, "written with so elegant and proper a spirit" (Henley, xv, 107), shows that Fielding conceived the "elegant" or heightened middle style ("I am warm, gentlemen," says the exhortation) to be precisely that which we have analyzed above in our first illustration. All the devices discussed there appear in emphatic form in the *Champion* paper. Less elevated subjects, on the other hand, receive a treatment that more closely resembles that of the essays' straightforward portions, a style appropriate to simple instruction that we might designate as the Plain Style (the equivalent of Cicero's *subtilis* or *tenuis*). Some parallelism and balance, pleonastic word-pairs, sequences and multiplication of elements, can also be found in such sections; but they are not given the prominence that they receive in the "elegant" style. *Elegance* does not here (or normally, in the time) imply the Grand Style (Cicero's *gravis* or *vehemens*), but a more elaborate version of the Middle Style (Cicero's *medius*). That Fielding obviously conceived of a higher (that is, more copiously figured) style than the "elegant" is indicated by the very different devices employed in the "sublime" chapter of *Tom Jones* (IV, ii) and by such remarks as that in the dedication to A *Proposal for Making an Effectual Provision for the Poor*—where, addressing Henry Pelham, he employed an extended metaphor of the statesman as captain of a ship, and concluded: "There is perhaps, sir, something above the style of prose in this allusion, but there is nothing in it beyond that of truth. To return, however, to the plainest style . . ." (Henley, XIII, 133). What he actually returns to (as befitting a dedication) is the elegant Middle Style, and what immediately follows is a balanced triplet of predicates ("will remove . . . will complete . . . will heap . . .").

same novel's narrative chapters (or, better, of the formal essays in the *Champion* with such papers as those of 27-29 December 1739, presenting the narrative vision of the Palace of Wealth) will reveal the degree to which the contemporary speech of every day entered not only into his dialogue but into the very texture of his narrative prose. I should insist, however, that despite the greater ease and informality of his narrative style, it is *fundamentally* the prose of the essays, employing the same structures and the characteristic devices and turns of phrase that we have been examining.[19] In large measure it is this *formal* basis of his

[19] I cannot here carry these observations on style over to the novels; but a mere random sampling of the early pages of *Joseph Andrews* may indicate the significance for his humorous narrative of some of the structures and devices that we have discussed: Notice, for example, how the long sentence beginning, "Joey was now preferred . . ." (I, ii; Henley, 1, 29) moves forward through a series of subordinating elements from Lady Booby's notice of Joseph to Parson Adams' catechizing of him. Fielding's paratactic manner appears (typically) in the set description of Joseph (I, viii; Henley, 1, 48). The innuendo that is a central characteristic of his humor frequently depends upon his habit of parenthesis. The support afforded it by sequences (as of predicates) may be indicated by the following passages concerning Lady Booby and Joseph in London (all italics in these citations are mine): "She would now walk out with him into Hyde Park in a morning, and when tired, *which happened almost every minute*, would lean on his arm, and converse with him in great familiarity. Whenever she stepped out of her coach, she would take him by the hand, and sometimes, *for fear of stumbling*, press it very hard; she *admitted* him to deliver messages at her bedside in a morning, *leered* at him at table, *and indulged* him in all those innocent freedoms which women of figure may permit without the least sully of their virtue" (I, iv; Henley, 1, 35).

Fielding's habit of extending the final member of his periods by a phrasal or clausal addition, which we have cited as a typical feature of his formal style, also serves here to give us some of his most delicious afterthoughts: as, the familiar one on Adams' twenty-three pounds a year, "*which, however,* he could not make any great figure with, because he lived in a dear country, *and* was a little incumbered with a wife and six children" (I, iii; Henley, 1, 30); or the fillip given to this simile: "As a person who is struck through the heart with a thunderbolt looks extremely surprised, *nay*, and perhaps is so too . . ." (I, viii; Henley, 1, 49). The formula of deprecation appears frequently: for example, of Mrs. Slipslop's little gifts to Joseph, Fielding says: "Joseph, however, had not returned the least gratitude to all these favors, not even so much as a kiss; *though I would not insinuate* she was so easily to be satisfied; for

162

easy and humorous narrative style that lends to Fielding's novels their characteristic dignity and air of detachment— qualities that he and Cervantes, alone perhaps among the great comic writers, share.

The primary requisite of a good essay style was perspicuity, the lucid presentation of the material.[20] Fielding was too dedicated a student of the art of style not to experiment with all the devices that could prove possibly useful;[21] but his first concern was always clarity. He was entirely capable of stylistic niceties (witness the onomatopoeia of "gives his fat Entertainer a Sweat, and makes him run the Hazard of breaking his Wind up his own Mounts"—*Misc.*, I, 138); and he consciously sought in these essays to achieve a more notably rhythmic and formally eloquent prose than was his normal wont: yet, his *matter* in the last analysis came before his *manner*. From his argument he would not deviate to snatch a grace.

If the essays of the *Miscellanies* display a pellucid firmness of argument, however, it must be once again confessed that they lack the charm and wit of his short introductory chapters in *Tom Jones* and of his best periodical essays.

---

surely then he would have been highly blamable" (I, vi; Henley, I, 40-41). And even such constructions as the coordinate "though . . . yet . . ." (I, iv; Henley, I, 35) and the favorite "as . . . so . . ." are turned to humorous purpose, the latter indeed offering the formal basis of the mock-epic simile: "As when a hungry tigress . . . so did Mrs. Slipslop . . ." (I, vi; Henley, I, 42).

[20] With reference to the essay style, Fielding surely agreed with the verdict of the ancients, as rendered by Quintilian: "Nobis prima sit virtus perspicuitas" (*Institutio oratoria*, VIII. ii. 22).

[21] I have passed over (for want of space to do the matter justice) Fielding's copious use of the standard rhetorical tropes and *figurae verborum et sententiarum* in these essays. Something of this is discussed below in connection with his satires. Perhaps I should caution the reader that my discussion of Fielding's formal style does not claim that any of the features mentioned are *unique* with Fielding: many of them were shared by his contemporaries. Cf. the parallels in the style of Fielding and James Ralph noted by William B. Coley (although I cannot agree with all of his generalizations about their individual styles): "The Authorship of *An Address to the Electors of Great Britain*," *PQ*, XXXVI (1957), 488-95.

The free conversational style employed in those delightful disquisitions brings one very close to the man; and the reader who seeks this same *rapprochement* in the essays of the *Miscellanies* is likely to find himself repelled by them. But if they give less of the man, they give perhaps more of his naked ideas; and they illuminate a side of Fielding that was never quite absent from his work—the side that saw life as a highly serious (not *solemn*) affair, a difficult pilgrimage, in which fallible man could well use the support offered by fully realized social relationships, by the advice which would help him to see through hypocritical and designing pretensions, and by the consolations for affliction to be found in the wisdom of antiquity and in the unique Christian hope of redemption and immortality. The influence of "the dramatist" in Fielding has often been remarked; but the influence of "the essayist" was equally strong, and these earnest statements of his social and philosophical ideals provide an illuminating direct commentary upon the values dramatized in his comedies and his novels.

1. "AN ESSAY ON CONVERSATION"

Several allusions of relatively late date in the *Essay on Conversation* would suggest either that Fielding completed it sometime in 1742 or that he gave it a final reworking in that period. Early in the essay, he cites a statement made by "my Friend, the Author of *An Enquiry into Happiness*," observing in a footnote, "The Treatise here mentioned is not yet public" (*Misc.*, I, 122 and n.). This friend was the philosopher, James Harris (1709-1780) of Salisbury, and the work described was published in his *Three Treatises* (1744), as "Concerning Happiness, A Dialogue." Harris' *Works* were edited in 1801 by his son, the Earl of Malmesbury, and on the title page of the reprint of this treatise on happiness, the editor noted below the title: "*Finished*

Dec. 15, A. D. 1741."[22] Since Harris' paper would appear to have been completed though not published before the allusion in Fielding's essay, that allusion can be dated as sometime later than the middle of December, 1741.

Further on in the essay, Fielding alludes to a citation from Persius by "the late ingenious Translator of that obscure Author" (*Misc.*, I, 174). The "ingenious Translator" was Dr. Thomas Brewster, who published anonymously in 1741-1742 a five-part translation of the six *Satires* of Persius. Fielding's quotation is from the *First Satire*, which appeared in 1741.[23] J. Paul De Castro, who identified Brewster as the figure referred to by Fielding, took "late" to mean that Brewster had recently died.[24] The doctor had been born in 1705, but there is no record known of his death. In the poem, "TO Miss H ----- AND at *Bath*. Written . . . 1742," in the *Miscellanies* (see above, p. 136), Fielding declares that the pains which the fair Miss Husband's eyes engender "Not *Brewster*, Glory of his Art, can cure" (*Misc.*, I, 114). Here then we have evidence that Brewster was alive at whatever period—probably in the fall—of 1742 that this poem was extemporized. Thus, if Brewster died before the *Miscellanies* were published, the allusion in the *Essay on Conversation* would belong to late 1742 or early 1743.

The possibility must be considered, however, that by "late," Fielding was referring to Brewster's labors on Persius (that is, he meant the *recent* translator), not to his demise. In *Tom Jones*, Square's letter to Allworthy from Bath says: "Dr. Harrington and Dr. Brewster have informed me that

[22] *The Works of James Harris, Esq.* (2v., 1801), I, 61. See J. Paul De Castro, N&Q, 12th Ser., II (1916), 441.

[23] Brewster had published A *Translation of the Second Satyr of Persius* as early as 1733; but the First Satire was not published until 1741. Fielding quotes ll. 258-63 of this translation (*The Satires of Persius, Translated into English Verse . . . Satire the First* [1741], p. 24). The accuracy of the quotation makes it likely that Fielding had Brewster's work immediately before him.

[24] N&Q, 12th Ser., II (1916), 441-42.

there is no hopes of my recovery" (xviii, iv; Henley, v, 306). If, as seems likely, this is another reference to Fielding's friend, Thomas Brewster, it would appear logical to conclude that he was alive about 1749 when Fielding paid him the compliment of an allusion.[25] If so, the reference in the *Essay* can still be said to date after the publication of Brewster's translation of the *First Satire* of Persius in February 1741, but no closer dating based upon the supposed death of the doctor can be inferred.[26]

2

The *Essay on Conversation* treats of "conversation" in the broadest sense of the term: "the action of consorting or having dealings with others; living together; commerce, intercourse, society, intimacy" (*N. E. D.*). It is only slightly confusing to find that Fielding uses this broad application interchangeably—and ambiguously—with the ordinary sense of the word; for in a society which held social discourse to be, as Swift had said, "the greatest, the most lasting, and the most innocent, as well as useful Pleasure of Life," it is scarcely surprising that the idea of conversation as social talk should be inseparably linked with the whole notion of social intercourse.[27] Hence what Fielding really offers

---

[25] The fact that Brewster was, like Harris, a subscriber to the *Miscellanies* is of no help in this matter, since subscriptions were clearly being solicited long before June 1742, when the first proposals were printed, and he need not have been alive when the volumes were published (Lady Betty Harris, for example, whose name appears in the subscription list, had died in January 1743). The second edition of Brewster's translation, published in 1751, added two sentences to the advertisement of the 1741 edition. These might have been written by the bookseller, but they are so phrased as to suggest that Brewster himself had penned them.

[26] The suggestion has frequently been made that the *Essay on Conversation* was written in 1737 (for example, CBEL, II, 121; CHEL [1914 ed.], x, 26; John E. Mason, *Gentlefolk in the Making* [Philadelphia, 1935], p. 274). I have shown elsewhere that this dating arises from confusion with a poem of 1737 that had the same title. See "Benjamin Stillingfleet's *Essay on Conversation*, 1737, and Henry Fielding," PQ, xxxiii (1954), 427-28.

[27] "Hints towards an Essay on Conversation," *Prose Works of Jonathan Swift*, ed. Herbert Davis (14v., Oxford, 1939, in progress) IV, 94. Swift

ESSAYS

in this essay on "conversation" is a kind of courtesy-book in little, an amiable guide to manners in everyday relations with others.

He begins at the beginning, with the familiar Aristotelian premise that man is a social animal and, as such, naturally inclined to the pleasures of conversation (defined at this point as "that reciprocal Interchange of Ideas, by which Truth is examined, Things are, in a manner, *turned round*, and sifted, and all our Knowledge communicated to each other"—*Misc.*, I, 119). Given this natural inclination, then, all that is necessary is that the social individual should understand the *means*, or the art, of conversation. This art, Fielding tells us, can be summed up as "The Art of pleasing or doing Good to one another" (I, 123).

The best term to designate a facility in this art is "Good Breeding"; but regrettably, he says, the word has been corrupted by the unfortunate habit of applying it to external gloss rather than to good character. Authentic good breeding can be recognized in two ways: by its expression (unsurprisingly) in actions and in words. Conduct in both, Fielding avers, "may be reduced to that concise, comprehensive Rule in Scripture; *Do unto all Men as you would they should do unto you*" (I, 125).[28] But curiously enough, men do not always seem capable of rightly judging either their own happiness or what will contribute to that of others; hence, some further and more explicit rules and precautions are requisite, the more so as "even Good-

---

defined good manners as "the Art of making those people easy with whom we converse" ("On Good-Manners and Good-Breeding," *ibid.*, p. 213). Sir William Temple, in his "Heads Designed for an Essay on Conversation" (*Works* [4v., 1814], III, 541-48), had naturally shaded over from his designated subject into a discussion of good breeding and sociable qualities. Locke's definition of good manners is very much like Swift's; and he adds that "*Good-Breeding* . . . has no other use nor end, but to make People easie and satisfied in their conversation with us" (*Some Thoughts Concerning Education* [1693], p. 169).

[28] In the *Covent-Garden Journal*, No. 55, Fielding cites the Golden Rule once again as the "summary" of all the rules of good breeding (Jensen, II, 63).

Nature itself, the very Habit of Mind most essential to furnish us with true Good Breeding . . . sometimes shoots us beyond the Mark" (I, 126-27).

The main body of the essay, then, is concerned with the rules that Fielding offers, first under "our *Actions*," and next under "our *Words*."[29] The former heading is broken down, for purposes of dramatic illustration, into a discussion of behavior in a visit to a country home and behavior in public assembly. Before coming to this, however, Fielding has two important general precepts to offer: first, sedulously avoid hurting or giving offense through disrespect, insolence, or haughtiness, for "Contempt is a murtherous Weapon" (I, 128), and the man who exhibits it to pamper his own vanity assuredly cannot be called well-bred. This is recognizably a sore point with Fielding; he brings it up several times again in this essay, and his other works furnish abundant commentary upon the theme.[30] The second major precept: pay the respect due to others. "My Lord *Shaftsbury* hath a pretty Observation," says Fielding, "that the Beggar, in addressing to a Coach with, my Lord, is sure not to offend, even though there be no Lord there; but, on the contrary, should plain Sir fly in the Face of a

---

[29] This is a conventional *divisio*; cf. *The Whole Art of Converse* by "D.A. Gent." (1683), pp. 3-4: "A Civil Conversation may be taken either as related to our Actions, or to our Discourse; in the first sence 'tis a certain accurateness and decency in all our Actions . . .[and secondly] related . . . to their Discourse . . . 'tis a certain exactness in all our words and expressions, in order to gain, conserve, or encrease the esteem and friendship of those we Converse with. . . ."

[30] Cf., for example, the essay on "Roasting" in the *Champion*, 13 March 1740; Fielding says there: "Contempt is, I believe, of all things the most uneasily to be endured by the generality of men" (Henley, xv, 242). In *Tom Jones*, he speaks of Captain Blifil, whose deference to Bridget Allworthy's opinions disappeared after their marriage, when he "began to treat the opinions of his wife with that haughtiness and insolence which none but those who deserve some contempt themselves can bestow, and those only who deserve no contempt can bear" (II, vii; Henley, III, 93). A whole paper of the *Covent-Garden Journal* (No. 61) was devoted to contempt, which Fielding there declared to be "a Mixture of Pride and Ill-Nature"; "the most contemptible," he said, "are generally the most contemptuous" (Jensen II, 89).

ESSAYS

Nobleman, what must be the Consequence?" (I, 130).[31] "Meer Ceremonies" may be only form, not substance, but they are "imposed by the Laws of Custom," and are essential to Good Breeding. The "Business of the whole is no more than to convey to others an Idea of your Esteem of them . . ." (I, 131).

Moving into the area of illustration, Fielding, in his hypothetical visit to the country, sets forth some rules and cautions, first for the host (for example, after the ladies have retired from the dinner table, he is to see that there is sufficient circulation of the bottle, but not "besotting, and ostentatious Contention for Pre-eminence in their Cups" —I, 136),[32] and then for the visitor ("Never refuse any Thing offered you out of Civility, unless in Preference of a Lady . . . for nothing is more truly Good Breeding, than to avoid being troublesome"—I, 138). Following the example of many of the "courtesy-books," slight character sketches are presented to dramatize the infractions of these rules. We are given Sophronus, a host who is as miserly with his liquor as Peter Walter with his shillings; the overzealous Desmophylax, "who never suffers any one to depart from his House without entitling him to an Action of false Imprisonment"; and such guests as Hyperphylus, whose ceremonious departure, with "bowes and kisses, and squeezes by the Hand," makes one think he is leaving for the East Indies (I, 136-39).

The lesson to be learned in every case is complaisance, or, once again, "the Art of pleasing, or contributing as

[31] Fielding was so pleased with this observation from Shaftesbury's *Letter concerning Enthusiasm* (*Characteristicks*, 3rd ed. [3v., 1723], I, 35-36) that he repeated it in the *Journey from This World to the Next*, chap. xix (*Misc.*, II, 155-56).

[32] One feels a sense of very personal grievance in Fielding's restrained comment: "The Order in helping your Guests is to be regulated by that of placing them: but here I must with great Submission recommend to the Lady at the upper End of the Table, to distribute her Favours as equally, and as impartially as she can. I have sometimes seen a large Dish of Fish extend no farther than to the fifth Person, and a Haunch of Venison lose all its Fat before half the Table had tasted it" (*Misc.*, I, 134).

much as possible to the Ease and Happiness of those with whom you converse," that is, those with whom you share a social situation (I, 125). But, leaving his country visit, Fielding turns to some rules for behavior in "public Assembly," dealing in turn with behavior to superiors, to equals, and to inferiors.[33] With the first, he says, the principal consideration is to avoid either an abject servility or "an impudent and encroaching Freedom" (I, 140). The ideal lies in "that golden Mean, which declares a Man ready to acquiesce in allowing the Respect due to a Title by the Laws and Customs of his Country, but impatient of any Insult, and disdaining to purchase the Intimacy with, and Favour of a Superior, at the Expence of Conscience or Honour" (I, 140-41). Equals are defined as those "not raised above each other by Title, Birth, Rank in Profession, Age, or actual Obligation" (I, 142). Once again, the ruling motif is complaisance. Fielding presents examples of those who sullenly refuse to give over their own pleasures in order to contribute to the happiness of others, and contrasts this brutish behavior with that of Charistus, "the Benevolence of whose Mind scarce permits him to indulge his own Will, unless by Accident. Though neither his Age nor Understanding incline him to dance, nor will admit his receiving any Pleasure from it, yet would he caper a whole Evening, rather than a fine young Lady should lose an Opportunity of displaying her Charms by the several genteel and amiable Attitudes which this Exercise affords the skilful of that Sex" (I, 143-44).

This contrast recalls to Fielding's mind the aforementioned "murtherous Weapon" wielded by those who "make

[33] This, again, is a division of the topic observed by almost all eighteenth-century writers on the art of conversation. It is, of course, to be expected in an age where hierarchy was a very real and present fact of social life. Swift, commenting on the art of good manners, observed: "One principal point of this art is to suit our behaviour to the three several degrees of men; our superiors, our equals, and those below us" ("On Good-Manners and Good-Breeding," *Prose Works*, ed. Davis, IV, 213).

no Scruple of satisfying their own Pride and Vanity, at the Expence of the most cruel Mortification of others" (1, 144); and he cannot resist hallooing after them. There is no behavior, he insists (as did a multitude of contemporary clergymen and moralists), "more contemptible, nor, in a civil Sense, more detestable than this." The character of these odious individuals is compounded of pride, folly, arrogance, insolence, and ill-nature, the last-named being its very crux, for "A Good-natured Man may indeed (provided he is a Fool) be proud, but arrogant and insolent he cannot be . . ." unless he is an *absolute* fool, and totally ignorant of human nature (1, 148). So overwhelmed with indignation is Fielding at this social monster that he cannot tear himself away from the character without several more trenchant observations, placing it "in so ridiculous a Light, that a Man must hereafter be possessed of a very considerable Portion, either of Folly or Impudence, to assume it" (1, 149). Those who have the weakest presumptions to superiority, he declares, commonly exhibit the greatest insolence ("It visits Ale-Houses and Gin-Shops, and whistles in the empty Heads of Fidlers, Mountebanks, and Dancing-Masters"); their very caution to preserve "superiority" indicates a sufficient self-doubt of its real existence. And with vehement finality Fielding drives home the severest indictment he can conceive: "This Contempt of others is the truest Symptom of a base and a bad Heart" (1, 151).

This villain of society satisfactorily crushed, Fielding glances at a few "inferior Criminals in Society," including the obstreperous, who will do anything to be noticed and, at the other extreme, the utterly bashful, who cannot even observe the amenities. He ends the division on actions by recommending as a desirable general rule, condescension (in a pleasant sense) to inferiors, for, he observes thoughtfully, we are prone to "set too high an Esteem on the Things [that is, our own qualities and perfections] themselves, and consider them as constituting a more essential Difference between us than they really do" (I, 154). Before leaving entirely the subject of men's actions, however, Fielding stops to take a final fling at "those two Disgracers of the human Species, common called a Beau, and a fine Lady" (I, 155), creatures he never grew weary of ridiculing.

In his second large subdivision, he proposes to consider conversation proper, or good breeding expressed in words; and he advances some rules by which the well-bred man "may, in his Discourse as well as Actions, contribute to the Happiness and Well-being of Society" (I, 157). Equality of understanding would of course be the ideal basis for conversation; but since society is not ranked on this basis, and all degrees of comprehension meet in average intercourse ("a visible but unavoidable Imperfection in Society itself"), the well-bred man will try to bring conversation to as near a common level as he can, by adapting himself to the interests and intelligence of his auditors (I, 158).

Some of the most notable sins against good breeding that occur to Fielding at this point are: conversing in the jargon of a particular profession (to the mystification of non-adepts); discussing private affairs in company; monopolizing the talk; and arguing too vociferously. Appended to this is a listing of topics that should be avoided in well-bred conversation—among them, slander, blasphemy, irreverence, and indecency. Even if no ladies are present, obscene jests are not "rational Mirth"; and he adds soberly, "For my own Part, I cannot conceive how the Idea of Jest or Pleasantry came ever to be annexed to one of our highest and most serious Pleasures" (I, 170).

Inevitably the subject of raillery arises, and here he has more detailed comment to offer. Reiterating that "the End of Conversation [is] the Happiness of Mankind, and the chief Means to procure their Delight and Pleasure"

(1, 173), and that therefore nothing conduces to that end which makes men uneasy or dissatisfied with themselves, Fielding warns that raillery is dangerous except when managed with great skill—"to which I may apply the Fable of the Lap-Dog and the Ass: for while in some Hands it diverts and delights us with its Dexterity and Gentleness; in others, it paws, dawbs, offends, and hurts" (1, 172). This kind of banter has its best chance for succeeding when the person rallied may join in the mirth,[34] as, for example, when men are ridiculed for vices and faults from which they are universally known to be free (1, 177). And Fielding is able to slip in some adroit compliments of his own at this point, citing as permissible the ridicule of Chesterfield's dullness or Argyll's cowardice, implying, of course, that no one could take such ridicule seriously; "and thus *Lyt[telto]n*," he says, "may be censured for whatever Vice or Folly you please to impute to him" (1, 177-78).

This said, the essay is then concluded with two fundamental observations:

"First, That every Person who indulges his Ill-nature or Vanity, at the Expence of others; and in introducing Uneasiness, Vexation, and Confusion into Society, however exalted or high-titled he may be, is thoroughly ill-bred.

"Secondly, That whoever, from the Goodness of his Disposition or Understanding, endeavours to his utmost to cultivate the Good-humour and Happiness of others, and to contribute to the Ease and Comfort of all his Acquaintance, however low in Rank Fortune may have placed him, or however clumsy he may be in his Figure or Demeanour, hath, in the truest Sense of the Word, a Claim to Good-Breeding"—(1, 178).

[34] Cf. Fielding's apology in the preface to *Joseph Andrews*, where, in solemnly protesting that he had "no intention to vilify or asperse any one," he declared that any character taken directly from life had been sufficiently disguised to make identification impossible—"and if it ever happens otherwise, it is only where the failure characterized is so minute that it is a foible only which the party himself may laugh at as well as any other" (Henley, 1, 24).

ESSAYS

3

On a subject of this nature, we should not expect to find Fielding offering precepts of surprising originality. Most of his recommendations or "rules" had appeared a multitude of times before, in one form or another, in the large body of courtesy-book literature of the seventeenth and eighteenth centuries.[35] His treatment of well-bred behavior on the part of host and guest differs from the norm, perhaps, in its simplicity and direct common sense; for the Italian tradition of formal elegance was still fairly strong in books of etiquette—the anonymous *Art of Conversation* (1738), for example, was largely the reworking of an earlier translation of Stefano Guazzo's *La civil conversatione* (Brescia, 1574)[36]—and such popular works as Obadiah

[35] See John E. Mason, *Gentlefolk in the Making* (Philadelphia, 1935); Gertrude E. Noyes, *Bibliography of Courtesy and Conduct Books in Seventeenth-Century England* (New Haven, 1937); Joyce Hemlow, "Fanny Burney and the Courtesy Books," *PMLA*, LXV (1950), 732-61; and Herbert Davis, "The Conversation of the Augustans," in *The Seventeenth Century: Studies . . . by Richard Foster Jones and Others Writing in His Honor* [Stanford, 1951], pp. 181-97).

Detailed advice on the proper way to conduct one's conversation is found not only in the courtesy books and specific conversation books, but in numerous sermons (for example, Tillotson's "Of sincerity towards God and man," Sermon LV in *The Works* [12v., 1757], IV, 343-68), fiction, satirical tracts (for example, O. Sedgewick's *Universal Masquerade: or, The World Turn'd Inside-Out*, 2v., 1743), such moral tracts as Timothy Nourse's *Discourse upon the Nature and Faculties of Man* (1686), or John Hartcliffe's *Treatise of Moral and Intellectual Virtues* (1691), and even in volumes of philosophy. The ancients were frequently called upon, of course; as Anthony Blackwall said, "The best *Classics* lay down very valuable Rules for the Management of *Conversation*, for graceful and proper *Address* to those Persons with whom we converse" (*An Introduction to the Classics* [4th ed., 1728], p. 76). Horace, Cicero, and Plutarch were obvious favorites; and even in George Stanhope's translation of *Epictetus His Morals, with Simplicius His Comment* (1694), a group of the later precepts are headed: "Rules for Conversation" (see "Table" at the end of the volume, a$_2$^{v}). Among the educational letters of Samuel Richardson's formulary is one offering "General Rules for agreeable Conversation in a young Man" (Letter VIII, *Letters Written to and for Particular Friends, on the Most Important Occasions* [1741], pp. 16-18).

[36] See John L. Lievsay, "Notes on *The Art of Conversation* (1738)," *Italica*, XVII (1940), 58-63. Lievsay calls the work "an unabashed piratical paraphrase" of George Pettie's translation (Books I-III, 1581) of Guazzo.

174

ESSAYS

Walker's *Of Education* (1672; many later editions) showed a great concern for detailed rules in visiting and entertaining. Walker, following his Italian models, makes much of such egregious social errors as dipping one's fingers in the sauce or making noises in eating; and, at the other extreme, he elaborates a highly artificial code of ceremonies in making visits.[37] Not all the courtesy-writers were content to accept this formality in manners. An author quoted in *The English Theophrastus*, for example, protested that formal civility and ceremonies represented "a kind of Tyranny"; and Ozell's translation of Ortigue's famous *Art de plaire dans la conversation* called for "a just medium" between overmuch ceremony and mere negligence.[38] But,

[37] Walker's book had reached a sixth edition by 1699. In the later eighteenth century Sterne knew it well enough to pilfer materials for *Tristram Shandy* from it (see John M. Turnbull, "The Prototype of Walter Shandy's *Tristra-pædia*," RES, II [1926], 212-15). With reference to the Italianate tradition, it is only fair to note that one of the most popular Italian guides, Giovanni della Casa's *Galateo* (first translated into English in 1576), continually insists that the real foundation of good manners is the wish to please, and that the desirable norm is to follow common usage or custom with Reason. But even Della Casa's precept proves superior to his practice (see the *Galateo of Manners & Behaviours*, with an introduction by J. E. Spingarn [Boston, 1914], passim).

[38] *The English Theophrastus* (1702), p. 106; John Ozell (transl.) *The Art of Pleasing in Conversation* (2v., 1736), I, 63. One of the most lively early protests was made by Timothy Nourse in 1686: "Ceremonies are to be avoided in Private and Familiar Society. Some little Forms of Complement are useful, to Usher in Converse, but whatsoever is Studied or Pointed, looks Pedantick, and would be as Comical and Ridiculous as to see a Man with a *Spanish* Tread, with a Paste-board Collar, and starcht Whiskers, to make his Entry, and after a profound Reverence, to Invite the Company to a Collation" (*Discourse upon the Nature and Faculties of Man* [1686], p. 320). Congreve, arguing against affectation in social intercourse, had said in one of his poems:

> All Rules of Pleasing in this one unite,
> Affect not any thing in Nature's Spight . . .
> None are, for being what they are, in Fault,
> But for not being what they wou'd be thought.
> ("OF PLEASING; AN EPISTLE To Sir RICHARD TEMPLE," in *Works* [5th ed., 3v., 1730], III, 334)

Fielding obviously approved of this sentiment; he quoted the last couplet in the preface to *Joseph Andrews* (Henley, I, 23).

despite such deprecation of mechanical formality, these writers, too, included much of the trifling kind of detail found in Walker.

Fielding's observations stem from an ideal of general complaisance and good-nature rather than from any extensive artificial code of conduct. He was more concerned with "civility" than with "ceremony"—to use the distinction often made in the eighteenth-century courtesy books[39] —and his intention was to establish a broad frame of reference, a general well-bred attitude which could serve to make social intercourse more rewarding rather than merely more refined. Fielding's stress was always upon the contribution the well-bred man could make to society. He would have agreed completely with Richard Fiddes's dictum: "A good Man, then, will make it the great End of his Conversation to promote, as much as in him lies, the Good and Advantage of all Men."[40]

That he was fully conscious, however, of the importance attached to ceremony by the reigning society and that he did not altogether condemn it himself is indicated by the previously cited observation that ceremonies "being imposed by the Laws of Custom, become essential to Good Breeding." Most of the visits and conversations in his novels begin and end with "the proper ceremonials"—Fielding might sometimes grow bored with them, but he was too much of a gentleman to omit them. Those who would portray him as an eighteenth-century social iconoclast might further ponder the fact that when he cites the Golden Rule he carefully qualifies it by observing that commentators on the passage have rightly added, "IF THEY WERE IN YOUR SITUATION AND CIRCUMSTANCES, AND YOU IN THEIRS," which he explains is necessary in ethics and "useful in this our Art, *where the Degree of the Person is always*

---

[39] See George C. Brauer, Jr., "Good Breeding in the Eighteenth Century," *University of Texas Studies in English*, XXXII (1953), 25-44, esp. 27-30.

[40] *Fifty Two Practical Discourses on Several Subjects* (1720), p. 403.

ESSAYS

to be considered" (I, 126; italics mine).[41] In further emphasizing the importance of recognizing a just hierarchy and precedence of title, Fielding concludes, "The Truth is, we live in a World of common Men, and not of Philosophers; . . . we are therefore to adapt our Behaviour to the Opinion of the Generality of Mankind, and not to that of a few odd Fellows" (I, 130-31).[42] What does arouse his ire, however, is the elevated air assumed by some possessors of "Titular Excellence" who treat inferiors "with a Disdain even beyond what the Eastern Monarchs shew to their Slaves." This, he says, "is considering the Difference not in the Individual, but in the very Species; a Height of Insolence impious in a Christian Society, and most absurd and ridiculous in a trading Nation" (I, 157).

The art of conversation in its restricted sense, as well as in the sense of manners, had been the subject of frequent discussion for many years. Explorations of this desirable skill drew freely from such standard courtesy books as those of Castiglione, Giovanni della Casa, Courtin, Guazzo, Ortigue, and—Fielding's favorite—Bellegarde.[43] Every im-

[41] Daniel Waterland, preaching a sermon "before the Sons of the Clergy" observed that "the office of *exhorting* . . . may indeed be exercised toward *equals* or *superiors*: only then it requires a different manner, a more cautious treatment, and a more ceremonious address" (*Works* [11v., Oxford, 1823-28], VIII, 419).

[42] So Ozell, following his French text: "However, we must follow this custom [of effusive greetings], instead of attempting to change it. . . . When all the world falls into a fault, no body can be blam'd; and how extravagant soever a mode may be, a man would yet be still more extravagant, if he refused to comply with it. Shall he alone offer to withstand the general consent of his country?" (*Art of Pleasing*, I, 55). So also Bellegarde, *Reflexions upon Ridicule* (English translation, 1706-1707): "And yet there are some Formalists who think themselves neglected, if you don't pay them certain Devoirs they demand. You must content them; the great Rule being to humour the Taste of those we are obliged to live with" (5th ed., 2v., 1739; I, 263).

[43] These French and Italian works, in turn, often were mere *pasticci* of such classic authorities on manners as Aristotle, Theophrastus, Plutarch, Cicero, and Horace. The latter was, of course, a special favorite in the eighteenth century; his two epistles on the proper behavior to a patron (*Epist*. I. xvii-xviii) were particularly quoted and imitated.

177

ESSAYS

aginable aspect of the subject was treated in generous detail by comprehensive handbooks like *The Art of Complaisance or the Means to Oblige in Conversation* by "S. C." (1673; in part a reworking of the *Traité de la cour* of Eustache du Refuge); *The Whole Art of Converse* by "D. A. Gent." (1683); *The Conversation of Gentlemen Considered* (1738); or the pithy little *Essay on Polite Behaviour: wherein the Nature of Complaisance and True Gentility is Consider'd and Recommended. Address'd to the Gentry* (1740). The first-named treatise has, for example, not only a chapter "Of the Conversation of the Court," but even one "Of the Conversation of the Inns of Court"; and *The Whole Art of Converse* categorizes rules for "the familiar Conversation," "the Learned Conversation," and "the Interess'd Conversation" (which latter deals with "our own, or our Neighbours Concerns"), and dwells at length on various kinds of specific incivility in converse.

Most of these conversation books touched upon the same errors and gaucheries with which Fielding concerns himself. Thus the like cautions against slander, blasphemy, indecency, and raillery in discourse are found in that popular compilation, *The Gentleman's Library, Containing Rules for Conduct in All Parts of Life* (1715), and in Col. Forrester's *Polite Philosopher* (1734). The aforementioned *Conversation of Gentlemen Considered* includes the same warnings against jesting about religion, being of censorious humor, or boring the company with one's own interests, that we find in Fielding, and characteristically sets up as its ideal the man who is "inviolably true to the great Rule of Civility, *never to make any one in the Company uneasy.*"[44] This primary law of complaisance—"the Soul of

[44] P. 28. The author (John Constable?) offers a happy anecdote (p. 5) on the subject of obstreperous claims for attention: "A Gentleman assured me, that when he was at *Rome* viewing the *Vatican* in Company of an Embassador, a *French* Gentleman struck into a *Minuet*, with a very easy Air. Being told however, that the Step was unseasonable, he answered, *Il faut faire quelque chose pour se distinguer.*"

Civil Society," as Bellegarde called it[45]—is insisted upon by almost everyone in the early eighteenth century who writes on conversation at all: Locke, Temple, Steele, Addison, Swift, Shaftesbury, Chesterfield, the horde of minor writers, and Fielding himself. It accounts for the concern these commentators on the art of conversation display with the question of raillery. Swift, for example, thought raillery was "the finest Part of Conversation," but he meant only in the sense of an apparent reproach which by a turn of wit ended in a compliment; and he, like the others, warned of the dangers it offered when handled clumsily.[46] As Steele put it: "To railly well, it is absolutely necessary that Kindness must run thro' all you say."[47]

The distinction of Fielding's *Essay on Conversation* lies not in its originality, but in the characteristic verve, good humor, and moral earnestness with which he treats the commonplaces of the tradition. A further distinction between Fielding's essay and the popular courtesy manuals lies in the fact that almost without exception the latter displayed an obvious utilitarian concern. "Civility is a strong Political Magick," says an author quoted in *The English Theophrastus* (p. 104); and the ruling motif in these works —as in our own self-help manuals—was that the arts of conversation and civility were an open sesame to success and position in the world. This is a consideration that Fielding scarcely notices: he writes as one primarily mindful of the sheer pleasure and the strengthening of social ties that

---

[45] *Reflexions upon Ridicule*, 5th ed., II, 131.
[46] "Hints towards an Essay on Conversation," *Prose Works*, ed. Davis, IV, 91. *The Art of Complaisance* had argued in like terms that "nothing so much animates discourse [as raillery], provided it be honest and pleasant, and it ought to be so far from being banished from conversation, that we may say 'tis that alone which seasons discourse, and preserves it from growing faint and languishing . . ." (p. 58). Shaftesbury defended raillery— and his theory of the test of truth by ridicule—at length in *Sensus Communis; an Essay on the Freedom of Wit and Humour* (1709), but he, too, warned that "none can understand the Speculation, beside those who have the Practice" (*Characteristicks* [3rd ed., 3v., 1723], I, 65).
[47] *Spectator*, No. 422 (Everyman ed., III, 310).

good conversation and good manners can guarantee. What Herbert Davis says of Swift is equally true of Fielding: "He is not concerned with conversation as one of the arts of the courtier or as an accomplishment for ladies and gentlemen who wish to enter polite society, but as a human privilege common to all civilized societies." Mr. Davis has, moreover, observed that Fielding's view in the *Essay on Conversation* was somewhat broader than that of Swift and the early Augustans. He is concerned not only with the "sublimer Pleasures" found in conversation among "Men of exalted Genius and extensive Knowledge," but with the possibilities for social pleasure that conversation, properly understood, offers to every literate man. As Davis says, "He does not challenge the Augustan ideal; like them he regards it as the chief art of human life, but he is more aware that it is also necessary to the happiness of the subordinate levels of society."[48]

4

Fielding chose to deal with his subject for the most part in a straightforward and nonsatiric fashion. He felt seriously, with his age, that the whole question of social relationships was one of the most significant and engrossing with which a writer could deal; and he could soberly declare that the talents of conversation in its broader sense are "the noblest Privilege of human Nature, and productive of all rational Happiness" (*Misc.*, I, 121).[49]

[48] "The Conversation of the Augustans," pp. 183 and 194.
[49] Fielding many times echoed Sir William Temple's observation, "No man willingly lives without some conversation . . ." (*Works* [4v., 1814], III, 541). One feels keenly the frustration which shadows those entries in the *Journal of a Voyage to Lisbon* where he records his loneliness (for example, Henley, XVI, 217 and 252); and it will be remembered that upon arrival in Lisbon, one of the first things Fielding did was to direct a letter to his brother John, asking that he send along some "conversible Man to be my companion in an Evening, with as much of the Qualifications of Learning, Sense, and Good humour as yᵒ can find, who will drink a moderate Glass in an Evening or will at least sit with me till one when I do" (quoted by Cross, III, 56). No man ever savored the pleasures of human companionship and conversation with more relish than Henry Fielding.

ESSAYS

Thus in this "essay of purpose" he set himself to present a reasoned picture of the abuses current in the social scene as he saw it, with a persuasive commentary that would establish, by contrast, his own ideal. But certain specific abuses called for stronger medicine. It will be recalled that in the case of the arrogant, who satisfy their own vanity through the mortification of others, Fielding purposed to make them appear so ridiculous that only extreme folly or impudence would dare to assume the stance. Not surprisingly, the essay comes to life most vividly when the sins against good breeding are dramatized and ridiculed in his brief "characters." Though necessarily slight, these characters bring his abstract points into focus and give human movement to the catalogue of errors. Lyperus, for example, who tumbles over benches and tea-tables to pick up a dropped fan or glove, and proves a nuisance in his "impertinent Civility" (*Misc.*, 1, 153-54), is for all times and social groups a familiar figure. As has often been observed, Fielding believed that satiric portraits of social abuse were likely to have greater moral impact than examples of good actions (for which reason the Spartans exposed drunken men to the view of their children);[50] hence the "social criminals" outnumber the paragons depicted in the essay. We are given an occasional portrait of the ideal, however, for purposes of contrast: Sophronus personifies the learned man who thoughtfully suits his conversation to his audience, rather than comporting himself like the ill-bred Cenodoxus who "talks of the Classics

[50] *CGJ*, No. 21; Jensen, 1, 258. Fielding continued: "*Examples may perhaps have more Advantage over Precepts, in teaching us to avoid what is odious, than in impelling us to pursue what is amiable.*" Cf. also the *Champion*, 10 June 1740: "I shall venture . . . to assert that we are much better and easier taught by the examples of what we are to shun, than by those which would instruct us what to pursue" (Henley, xv, 330). The tradition of "characters" upon which Fielding drew in this and other essays had always tended to emphasize social vices rather than virtues; this was also true of the great exemplar, Theophrastus.

181

ESSAYS

before the Ladies; and of *Greek* Criticisms among fine Gentlemen" (*Misc.*, I, 160).[51]

The brief "characters" sketched in here are expanded and given dramatic force in Fielding's novels.[52] The old wit in the stage coach in *Joseph Andrews* (I, xii), who takes delight in salacious jesting; Parson Trulliber, who snatches the cup of ale from Adams' hands because he "caal'd vurst" (*JA*, II, xiv; Henley, I, 189-90); the "roasting" squire who practices his unsocial humor on Parson Adams (*JA*, III, vii); Beau Didapper and Lady Booby, in their "polite" visit to Adams' home (IV, ix)—all are examples of the "social criminals" described in the *Essay on Conversation*. The graphic depiction of such "disgracers of the human species" is continued in *Tom Jones* and *Amelia*, the latter in particular presenting them in something of the sober tone of the *Essay*: for example, Mrs. James, "who considered form and show as essential ingredients of human happiness, and imagined all friendship to consist in ceremony, courtesies, messages, and visits" (IV, vi; Henley, VI, 209; and cf. also *Amelia*, V, iv); the vicious "sparks" at Vauxhall, whose brutal jesting destroys the company's happiness (IX, ix); and the arrogant young clergyman who disputes uncivilly with Dr. Harrison (IX, x). Swearers and slanderers, ill-bred guests and ceremonious bores, the abjectly

---

[51] One is reminded of the plaintive protest of Samuel Parker (the Younger), in detailing his own list of minor criminals in conversation: "Add to these your *Critical Insects*, your Anatomizers of Words, and Menders of Propositions. A Man cannot utter a familiar Sentence, but an Inquisition of *Jackanapes* immediately sets upon't" ("OF CONVERSATION," in *Sylva. Familiar Letters upon Occasional Subjects* [1701], p. 79).

[52] The copious illustrations that could also be drawn from the plays indicate well enough that the subject possessed Fielding's mind from the beginning. Charles W. Nichols has presented evidence that his satire on the insipidity of current social conversation was drawn from the life ("Social Satire in Fielding's *Pasquin* and *The Historical Register*" *PQ*, III [1924], 309-17; and cf. Swift's *Compleat Collection of Genteel and Ingenious Conversation*, published in 1738). Thomas Gordon found the most necessary elements in "the Art of Modern Conversation" to be a diamond ring on the finger and ruffles of Brussels lace (*The Humourist* [2v., 1720-1725], I, 100-04).

182

ESSAYS

servile, and those who, like the "vile pettifogger" at the Bell Inn, usurp a freedom with their betters (*TJ*, VIII, viii; Henley, IV, 93-94)—all the violators of those fundamental precepts of social decency set forth in the *Essay* appear again and again in the novels. And the old lieutenant in *Tom Jones* (VII, xii) lectures the vicious ensign in much the same tone as that of the *Essay*: "But prithee, Northerton, leave off that foolish as well as wicked custom of swearing; for you are deceived, I promise you, if you think there is wit or politeness in it. I wish, too, you would take my advice, and desist from abusing the clergy. Scandalous names, and reflections, cast on any body of men must be always unjustifiable, but especially so when thrown on so sacred a function; for to abuse the body is to abuse the function itself . . ." (Henley, IV, 33).[53] Even the good fall now and then into inconsiderate habits—for Parson Adams when he sits down to punch with Barnabas and two others enters "into a discourse on small tithes, which continued a full hour, without the doctor or exciseman's having one opportunity to offer a word" (*JA*, I, xvi; Henley, I, 89).

There is no need to dwell on the superior force of the dramatizations in Fielding's novels to the somewhat labored precepts of the *Essay*. The contrast of Sophia's goodness to her inferiors with the vulgar Mrs. Honour's great air of condescension (*TJ*, x, iii-iv) speaks volumes. When Jones is visiting Mrs. Fitzpatrick and Lady Bellaston in London, Fielding describes the arrival of the great Irish lord, who immediately engrossed the whole attention of the ladies: "And as he took no more notice of Jones than if no such person had been present, unless by now and then staring at him, the ladies followed his example" (*TJ*, XIII, iv—"WHICH CONSISTS OF VISITING"—Henley, V, 46). Here the animadversions upon contempt and ill-breeding in the *Essay on Conversa-*

[53] So also Dr. Harrison, who surely expressed Fielding's own sentiment: "No man is fonder of true wit and humor than myself, but to profane sacred things with jest and scoffing is a sure sign of a weak and wicked mind" (*Amelia*, x, iv; Henley, VII, 204).

183

tion are illuminated with dramatic force and immediacy by one brilliant sentence.

The *Essay* does provide, however, a formal statement that increases one's appreciation of the character-sketches in the novels. The social villains he describes in so many guises are not merely "human nature illustrated": as the *Essay* makes clear, they represent for Fielding the utter negation of the bases upon which social discourse, "the noblest Privilege of human Nature," rests. His animus against these characters, some of whom seem relatively harmless in themselves, might appear excessive if one did not remember that Fielding saw each of them in his own way as poisoning the very springs of society.

5

Since good breeding is, in a sense, the real subject of our story, something further should be said on what it meant to Fielding. We have already shown the natural tendency of the eighteenth century to associate the ideas of conversation and of good breeding. Fielding's own definition of the latter might be summed up as "the Art of pleasing." In the preface to the *Miscellanies* he asserted that the whole purpose of his *Essay on Conversation* was to show that "true Good-Breeding consists in contributing, with our utmost Power, to the Satisfaction and Happiness of all about us" (*Misc.*, I, iv). The earnest essays in the *Covent-Garden Journal* (Nos. 55 and 56) on the same subject really add very little to this fundamental statement.[54]

Almost without exception, the courtesy writers and popular moralists of the century agreed with this definition. The ideal of the true gentleman (in the handbooks, at

---

[54] With these may also be compared the equation between "GD BRDING" (in the language of the Ptfghsiumgski) and Lying, in the *Champion*, 19 August 1740; see *The Voyages of Mr. Job Vinegar, from The Champion* (1740), ed. S. J. Sackett (Augustan Reprint Society, No. 67; Los Angeles, 1958), pp. 23-26.

least) was no longer epitomized in the Renaissance conception of a highly mannered and broadly talented courtly figure obsessed with "honor," but in the man who possessed to the highest degree the social virtues of complaisance and affability.[55] One comes to suspect, it is true, that this "new" gentleman did not make his way without some resistance: the moralists, Fielding included, note with sadness (or irritation) that the concept of good breeding in the polite world stubbornly refuses to square with their own definition. But with equal stubbornness they continue to insist that *true* good breeding is the art of pleasing or rendering oneself agreeable to others. Thus the highly influential Locke had said that a child need not be taught much of "Punctilio's, or Niceties of Breeding," for real courtesy was the result not of minute observances of ceremony but of "that general Good-will and Regard for all People, which makes any one have a care not to shew, in his Carriage, any contempt, disrespect, or neglect of them." Sir William Temple had centered "Good breeding in doing nothing one thinks will either hurt or displease [others]."[56] Steele and Addison made the same point numerous times, as did Swift and Shaftesbury; and the eighteenth-century courtesy books maintained with great consistency and unanimity that the true gentleman made an art of affability, complaisance, and easiness of temper.

Good breeding, then, was a social virtue in a social world, and Fielding's conception of this virtue is of a piece with his exaltation of good-nature (roughly speaking, his "Good Breeding" amounts to "Good-Nature polished and refined"), his definition of true greatness (see above), and his whole-hearted acceptance of the view that man is naturally and fundamentally a social animal. With this in mind,

[55] See George Brauer, *op.cit.*, and W. Lee Ustick, "Changing Ideals of Aristocratic Character and Conduct in Seventeenth-Century England," *MP*, xxx (1932), 147-66.
[56] Locke, *Some Thoughts concerning Education* (1693), pp. 68 and 168; Temple, "Heads Designed for an Essay on Conversation," *Works*, III, 547.

we can better appreciate both his undisguised contempt for the values of those members of the *haut monde* who estimated good breeding in terms of a jealous concern for personal honor or the ability to make a leg gracefully,[57] and his equal distaste for the values of the pushing mercantile classes, whose own utilitarian criteria were reflected in those vulgar courtesy books written particularly for them. The benevolent carriage of the good man in Fielding's novels finds its antithesis both in the absurd posture of the man of honor and in the petty pretensions of the innkeepers and their ilk.

Socrates, Fielding says, "though I believe he was very little instructed" by dancing-masters or periwig-makers, is a true example of good breeding (*Misc.*, I, 124). The beau and the fine lady, on the other hand, are worthless insects who contribute nothing to the society which they imagine themselves so gracefully to adorn. Nevertheless, for Fielding—and for many of the courtesy books—the truly well-bred man could only be formed in the "best" company, which alone offered the models of politeness and grace necessary to his social education. As Bellegarde said, "Nothing forms the Mind like the Use of the World; this gives it that Tincture of Politeness which is only obtain'd by the frequent Sight of polite Persons, and copying from their Plan."[58] Edward Young, like Fielding, gave equal weight to both elements, the "natural" and the "artificial":

> Good-breeding is the blossom of good sense;
> The last result of an accomplisht mind,
> With outward grace, the *body's virtue*, join'd.[59]

[57] Lord Formal, the fop of *Love in Several Masques*, protests: "But, really, I have been at some pains to inculcate principles of good-breeding, and laid down some rules concerning distance, submission, ceremonies, laughing, sighing, ogling, visits, affronts, respect, pride, love" (III, vi; Henley, VIII, 49).
[58] *Reflexions upon Ridicule*, 5th ed., I, 281.
[59] Satire v, *Love of Fame, the Universal Passion* (2nd ed., 1728), p. 112.

ESSAYS

What Fielding satirized in the Lord Formals was their singleminded concentration upon the mere *forms* of politeness and their ignoring of the human values of good-nature, sincerity, and complaisance—the "body's virtue" without which "outward grace" was merely a mockery. His view was, once again, very much like that of Locke. Although insisting in *Some Thoughts concerning Education* on the primacy of good-nature and virtue in polite conduct and decrying excessive emphasis on ceremony, Locke made quite an equal point of "that decency and gracefulness of Looks, Voice, Words, Motions, Gestures, and of all the whole outward Demeanour, which pleases in Company, and makes those easie and delighted, whom we converse with" (p. 168). And this social grace, Locke, like Fielding after him, derived from education and from being "bred in good Company," which "does more than all Precepts, Rules and Instructions" to form the well-bred gentleman (pp. 69 and 71).

Hence Fielding's satirical attacks on the affectations and studied graces of high society must not be taken to mean that he despised the forms of politeness per se. He never underestimated the value of true polish. In *Tom Jones* he pointed out the necessity of frequenting the best circles to come by examples of "refinement, elegance, and a liberality of spirit; *which last quality I myself have scarce ever seen in men of low birth and education*" (IX, i; Henley, IV, 159; italics mine). Tom himself, who is described as having "a certain air of natural gentility," finds that it is necessary to *acquire* the additional gloss which marks true good breeding. When (in XIII, iv) Mrs. Fitzpatrick dismisses him from the company, asking him to leave his address, Fielding explains: "Jones had natural, but not artificial, good-breeding. Instead, therefore, of communicating the secret of his lodgings to a servant, he acquainted the lady herself with it particularly, and soon after very ceremoniously withdrew" (Henley, V, 46-47). Clearly, he makes himself ridiculous and the company uncomfortable by his lack of schooling in the necessary *artificies* of social conduct. Fielding does not condemn artificial good breeding; rather, he accepts it as necessary to that "refinement, elegance, and . . . liberality of spirit" that make conversation delightful. In the *Covent-Garden Journal*, a good-natured Somersetshire landlord's awkward politeness is spoken of as "a Sort of good Breeding undrest" (No. 33; Jensen, I, 327); the "dress" could come only from education and good company.

Though no great lover of the French nation, Fielding more than once praised them for their pleasant manners. Decrying the lack of good breeding to be found among Englishmen, he hypothesized that part of the difficulty "seems to me to arise from the great Number of People, who are daily raised by Trade to the Rank of Gentry, without having had any Education at all . . ." (*Covent-Garden Journal*, No. 56; Jensen, II, 68), which is to say those people who had not enjoyed the benefits of instruction and example in "that decency and gracefulness" which Locke saw as essential to a polite society. Mr. Wilson, in *Joseph Andrews*, characterizes "the lower class of the gentry, and the higher of the mercantile world" as "in reality, the worst-bred part of mankind" (III, iii; Henley, I, 246). In retrospect, some of Fielding's own values may appear on the "bourgeois" side. But in a social sense, there is no doubt that his sympathies lay nearer to the values of the aristocratic world —despite his attacks on its excesses—than to the middle-class norms with which he has so often been associated in modern estimates. It will be remembered that, in *Joseph Andrews* (II, v), when the coach prepares to leave the inn where Joseph has been recuperating from the attack upon him, the young lady who is an earl's granddaughter begs compassionately that he be included among its passengers; but Mrs. Grave-airs, whose father had risen from postilion to great man's steward, is genteelly horrified at the sug-

ESSAYS

gestion of riding with a footman. It was the affected, the ill-natured, the useless, the *unsocial* (in its deepest sense) that Fielding despised, regardless of class. True good breeding was the necessary and fundamental counter to these qualities that were destructive of all decent social intercourse.

The *Essay on Conversation* is perhaps Fielding's most downright exposition of the social values that underlay his personal philosophy of life. Once again the centrality of the idea of "good-nature" is manifest; but here it is considered in its necessary social context, shaped by the imperatives of custom and accepted hierarchy. His concept of ideal social intercourse was clearly not revolutionary; it was in accord with the views of most thinking men of his age. Steering between the Scylla of frivolous ceremony and the Charybdis of uncultured boorishness, he followed the path marked out by common sense, tradition, and a high sense of the need for tolerance and decency and grace in the relations of man with man.

2. "AN ESSAY ON THE KNOWLEDGE OF THE Characters of Men."

The *Essay on the Knowledge of the Characters of Men* contains little or no evidence of the date of composition. Reference to a phrase from one of Pope's letters must date after 1735.[60] There are a number of parallels to observations

---

[60] Fielding's allusion reads: "It is well said in one of Mr. *Pope's* Letters; 'How shall a Man love five Millions, who could never love a single Person?'" (*Misc.*, I, 223). In the 1735 edition of Pope's letters printed for J. Smith (Griffith, *Bibliography*, No. 408), the passage appears in a letter of 20 August [1716], to Lady Mary Wortley Montagu, thus: "For (as a Friend of mine says) how is it possible for that Man to love twenty thousand People, who never loved one?" (p. 124). The same wording appears in the "authorized" edition of 1737 (p. 95), and according to Sherburn continues in all editions through 1742. The MS. reading, which Sherburn uses, says, "To love a hundred thousand men" (*Correspondence of Alexander Pope* [5v., Oxford, 1956], I, 357). Fielding's "five Millions" is probably his interpolation for his own purposes. He did somewhat the same thing with a scriptural quotation in the *True Patriot*, No. 2 (12 November 1745): "It is certain that no Man can love his Country, who

189

made in the *Champion* in 1739-1740,[61] which might suggest this period as the time of original composition; but in truth such evidence is not decisive, for Fielding often repeated allusions or phrases almost word-for-word in publications that were a decade apart.[62] Some of the *Essay* is not too well thought out and suggests rather hurried composition of the sort Fielding was engaged in during 1741-1742, when the greater part of the material in the *Miscellanies* was probably written. Writing under pressure was scarcely confined to that period in his life; but the *Essay* does not appear to me to have been very thoughtfully revised for publication, which would indicate either that it was an old piece

---

doth not love a single Person in it. . . . If such a Person as is above described, should presume to affect this Character, let us answer him in the sacred Words of Scripture: *If thou lovest not thy Brother whom thou hast seen, how canst thou love seven Millions whom thou hast not seen?*" The "sacred Words" (I John 4:20) read, "For he that loveth not his brother whom he hath seen, how can he love God whom he hath not seen?" The sentiment, at any rate, was a favorite with Fielding; he expressed it again in still another form in *CGJ* No. 44 (Jensen, II, 12).

[61] For example: (1) The quotation from Rochester, "Man differs more from Man" &c. (*Misc.*, I, 182; cf. *Champion*, 15 December 1739; the line is quoted again in the *Jacobite's Journal*, No. 42, 17 September 1748); (2) the quotation from Dr. South on detraction, followed by a quotation from Martial (*Misc.*, I, 211-12; the same quotation from South is used in the *Champion*, 6 March 1740, and the same quotation from Martial appears as the motto of this paper); (3) the allusion to naked virtue's beauty (*Misc.*, I, 217) is also found in the *Champion*, 24 January 1740; and the words, "[Virtue] is conscious of her innate Worth" (*Misc.*, I, 218) are repeated almost exactly and in a like context in the *Champion*, 4 March 1740; (4) the issues of the *Champion* for 11 and 15 December 1739, and 22 January 1740, among others, are particularly concerned with the question of human nature (and hypocrisy), and display other close parallels with the ideas of the *Essay on the Knowledge of the Characters of Men*. Fielding must, in any case, have been drawing upon the same sections of his commonplace book!

[62] A good example of this repetition (many could be cited) occurs in the essay under discussion. Fielding says, "There is a Countenance . . . which hath been called a Letter of Recommendation" (*Misc.*, I, 189). The same observation is repeated by the Man of the Hill in *Tom Jones* (VIII, x; Henley, IV, 112) and by Dr. Harrison in *Amelia* (IX, v; Henley, VII, 144). Another example is Fielding's oft-repeated quotation from Dr. South on revenge (see Allan Wendt, "Fielding and South's 'Luscious Morsel': A Last Word," *N&Q*, CCII [1957], 256-57, and Arthur Sherbo, "Fielding and Dr. South: A Post Mortem," *ibid.*, pp. 378-79).

ESSAYS

thrown in at the last moment or a new one hastily composed specifically for the *Miscellanies*. The centrality of its theme to the whole collection recommends the latter supposition to me.[63]

2

The *Essay* is, in effect, a handbook on hypocrisy, springing avowedly from Fielding's indignation at the fact that so many men have devoted themselves to inventing systems by which the cunning and unscrupulous might impose upon the rest of the world, but so few have endeavored to arm the innocent and undesigning against imposition (*Misc.*, I, 181). A motto for the essay might well be taken from *Tom Jones*, where Fielding declares that "simplicity, when set on its guard, is often a match for cunning" (VII, vi; Henley, III, 352).[64]

The essay opens with some general reflections on human nature, which lead into the premise that an inclination to evil inherent in some men, when nurtured by modern education "in the *Art of thriving*" (an anonymous tract with this title actually was published in the seventeenth century!) or the "*Art of Politics*," results in the exaltation of individual

[63] An allusion to insincere patriots (see below, p. 198) might indicate that the *Essay* was penned after Fielding's break with the Opposition in 1741 (see Martin C. Battestin, "Fielding's Changing Politics and *Joseph Andrews*," PQ, XXXIX [1960], 39-55). Battestin believes that this break could have occurred as early as February 1741 (p. 47, n. 10); my belief that Fielding was the author of *The Crisis: A Sermon* (April 1741) forces me to suppose a date around mid-summer—a date which would still be consonant with Battestin's main argument. The allusion cannot, in any case, be taken as certain evidence: Fielding has allusions to false patriots as early as his theatrical days.

[64] Fielding said in *Jonathan Wild*, "There is one Misfortune which attends all great Men and their Schemes, viz. That in order to carry them into Execution, they are obliged in proposing their Purpose to their Tools, to discover themselves to be of that Disposition, in which certain little Writers have advised Mankind to place no Confidence . . ." (III, v; *Misc.*, III, 219-20). And he made the point a number of times that "the honest part of mankind would be much too hard for the knavish, if they could bring themselves to incur the guilt, or thought it worth their while to take the trouble" (*TJ*, VII, ix; Henley, IV, 17; cf. *Amelia*, VIII, ix; Henley, VII, 109-10).

191

self-interest above all else. This is the very reverse "of that Doctrine of the Stoics; by which Men were taught to consider themselves as Fellow-Citizens of the World, and to labour jointly for the common Good, without any private Distinction of their own" (I, 183). The service of self requires that others' interests should be subordinated; this in turn requires the use of deceit to make others sacrifice their natural interests by persuading them that their particular good is designed. Thus the world becomes "a vast Masquerade" (I, 184-85).[65] In the midst of this chaos and deceit, then, Fielding proposes to offer some rules whereby one may recognize "the pernicious Designs of that detestable Fiend, Hypocrisy" (I, 186). Though not new, he admits, they may be useful to the inexperienced, for "that open Disposition, which is the surest Indication of an honest and upright Heart," leaves one, unfortunately, all the more vulnerable to craft and deceit.[66]

The first section of the essay is concerned with the uses of physiognomy. Fielding begins by defending "an Art on which so wise a Man as *Aristotle* hath thought proper to compose a Treatise" (I, 187), and he repeats the ancient notion that "the Passions of Men do commonly imprint sufficient Marks on the Countenance" (I, 188); but he concludes with some doubts as to the ultimate efficacy of

[65] As L. P. Goggin has observed ("Fielding's *The Masquerade*," *PQ*, xxxvi [1957], 479-80), the allusion here is one of a series by Fielding in which masks and masquerades stand as basic symbols for hypocrisy.

[66] Cf. the discussion of this point in connection with "good-nature," above (pp. 62ff.). Like Fielding, Edward Young was highly conscious of a moral atmosphere "Where generous hearts the greatest hazard run, / And he who trusts a *brother* is undone" (Satire II, *Love of Fame* [2nd ed., 1728], p. 35). The dilemma which this naturally posed is frankly stated in a quotation included in *The English Theophrastus* (1702) to the effect that it is base to suspect everyone, but bad to be imposed upon by hypocrisy, "So that the Character of a Wise Man lies at Stake upon matter of Judgment one way, and of a Good-natur'd Man the other . . ." (p. 108). Fielding was no more able than any other moralist has been to resolve this crux; but the only possible way out, as he saw it, lay in a better knowledge on the part of good-natured men of the motives of human action.

his guide.[67] In point of fact, the illustrations that he cites (I, 186-95) give small assurance to the reader that physiognomy is a reliable "art," for he argues that austerity of countenance is no real index to wisdom, but rather a symptom of pride, ill-nature, and cunning; that the "glavering sneering Smile" of apparent good-humor is really compounded of malice and fraud;[68] and, finally, that a fierce aspect denotes, not courage, but a bully (I, 195).

At this point it does seem to occur to him that his examples might be taken to contradict the earlier assertion on the value of physiognomy, and he declares (somewhat lamely) that the marks of the ruling passions are really there, but "the Generality of Mankind mistake the Affec-

[67] The ancient and abiding art of physiognomy was still popular in the eighteenth century. An act of parliament in 1743 reaffirmed the punishment for its abuse as a method of divination, and its value was still being disputed by medical men late in the century (cf. R. D. Loewenberg, "The Significance of the Obvious," *Bulletin of the History of Medicine*, x [1941], 666-79). It had taken on definite pseudo-scientific overtones, however, and was roundly satirized in the *Scriblerus Papers* (ed. Charles Kerby-Miller [New Haven, 1950]; see esp. pp. 102, 131, 168, and notes). Thus Fielding's wavering attitude (which is duplicated in Addison's paper on physiognomy in the *Spectator*, No. 86) is easily explicable. The early essay on the knowledge of human nature, in the *Champion*, 11 December 1739, had confined its discussion to words and actions: "As to the doctrine of physiognomy, it being somewhat unfortunate in these latter ages, I shall say nothing of it" (Henley, xv, 94; cf. also 4 March 1740; Henley, xv, 227-30). Parson Adams defends the art against his host at the inn, who sneers: "Symptoms in his countenance, quotha! I would look there, perhaps, to see whether a man had the smallpox, but for nothing else" (*JA*, II, xvii; Henley, I, 208); and though various incidents in the novels reflect Fielding's doubt on the subject, his final opinion, as expressed in the *Journal of a Voyage to Lisbon* (Henley, xvi, 236), echoes the same confidence with which the essay on the characters of men began. On the interesting relationship of Fielding's observations to Hogarth's "Characters and Caricaturas" (1743) and the significance of both for later controversy in Germany over the art of physiognomy, see Friedrich Antal, "The Moral Purpose of Hogarth's Art," *Journal of the Warburg and Courtauld Institutes*, xv (1952), 191 and n.

[68] In attacking empty laughter, Fielding hastily introduces some qualifications, concluding: "Lastly; I do by no means hint at the various Laughs, Titters, Tehes, &c. of the Fair Sex, with whom indeed this Essay hath not any thing to do; the Knowledge of the Characters of Women being foreign to my intended Purpose; as it is in Fact a Science, to which I make not the least Pretension" (*Misc.*, I, 194-95).

tation for the Reality" and overlook the true symptoms for the more apparent ones. He attempts to contrast these *affected* signs with the genuine indices of character: for example, "that sprightly and penetrating Look" of true Understanding, or "that cheerful composed Serenity" of real good-nature; but once again he seems to feel the dubious value of such loose characterizations. Hence, after qualifying them out of existence (for example, the rules are not without exceptions, and "they are of no Use but to an Observer of much Penetration," and even then a subtle hypocrisy sometimes escapes the highest discernment—I, 196-97),[69] he decides to move on to "a more infallible Guide": namely, the *Actions* of men.

"Actions are their own best Expositors," Fielding says, citing scriptural authority (Matt. 7:20): *"By their Fruits you shall know them"* (I, 197).[70] This time he anticipates the obvious protest that the knowledge thus gained comes too late—after the injury is already done—by declaring that he is seeking armor "not against Force, but Deceit," that is, against those "who can injure us only by obtaining our

[69] One of Jonathan Wild's maxims for greatness, in fact, was "THAT Virtues, like precious Stones, were easily counterfeited; that Counterfeits in both Cases adorned the Wearer equally, and that very few had Knowledge or Discernment sufficient to distinguish the counterfeit Jewel from the real" (*JW*, IV, xvi; *Misc.*, III, 413). His final maxim was "THAT the Heart was the proper Seat of Hatred, and the Countenance of Affection and Friendship" (*ibid.*).

[70] He had reached the same conclusion in the *Champion* article on human nature: "The only ways by which we can come at any knowledge of what passes in the minds of others, are their words and actions; the latter of which, hath by the wiser part of mankind been chiefly depended on, as the surer and more infallible guide" (Henley, xv, 94). So Locke had said: "I have always thought the actions of men the best interpreters of their thoughts" (*Essay concerning Human Understanding*, I, ii. 3; ed. A. C. Fraser [2v., Oxford, 1894], I, 66-67); and so also many others— including this strongly worded statement by Samuel Clarke, in a sermon on "How to judge of Moral Actions": "By the *Actions* of a man's Life, by the whole *Course and Tenour* of his Behaviour in the World, and by *no other distinction* whatsoever, can be ascertained the *True Character* of any *Person*, and the *Real Goodness* or *Badness* of his *Principles* . . ." (*Sermons on Several Subjects* [7th ed., 11v., 1749], III, 82).

good Opinion" (1, 200).[71] Thus he is concerned to expose the arts by which deceit ingratiates itself. The most common mistakes in judgment, in this connection, stem from taking men's words as against their actions, or from coloring their actions by the accepted public character of the actors rather than judging from the visible tendency of the acts themselves (1, 198-200). More specifically, Fielding warns that there are certain hypocritical characters who should be received with particular caution, namely: the flatterer, for "no one uses [flattery], without some Design on the Person flattered" (1, 201-02); the "professor," who "on a slight or no Acquaintance, embraces, hugs, kisses, and vows the greatest Esteem for your Person, Parts, and Virtues" (1, 203);[72] the promiser, who makes vows he either cannot or does not intend to carry out (1, 204-05); the inquisitive man, of whom Fielding warns, "Men no more desire another's Secrets, to conceal them, than they would another's Purse, for the Pleasure only of carrying it" (1, 205); the inescapable slanderer (1, 206); and, finally, the "saint," whose sanctity "flows from the Lips, and shines in the Countenance," but in truth serves only to cover a vile and rotten interior (1, 206).

This last character leads Fielding into a detailed and energetic dissection of the vice he never tired of castigating, censoriousness. Of the "saint" he says that "a sour, morose, ill-natured, censorious Sanctity, never is, nor can be sincere,"

[71] Nevertheless, as Fielding himself said later: "It is a more useful capacity to be able to foretell the actions of men, in any circumstance, from their characters, than to judge of their characters from their actions" (*TJ*, III, i; Henley, III, 106-07). Predictability *before* an action was performed was the real desideratum, and this is what physiognomy and other eighteenth-century character-reading devices claimed to offer. Fielding still felt, in *Tom Jones*, that it was possible, saying of the two capacities above, "The former, I own, requires the greater penetration; but may be accomplished by true sagacity with no less certainty than the latter" (*ibid.*, p. 107). There are no rules for true sagacity, however.

[72] Fielding concludes: "FORGIVE THE ACTS OF YOUR ENEMIES hath been thought the highest Maxim of Morality; FEAR THE PROFESSIONS OF YOUR FRIENDS, is perhaps the wisest" (*Misc.*, I, 204).

but is rather the true mark of hypocrisy—"Is a Readiness to despise, to hate, and to condemn, the Temper of a Christian?" (I, 207).[73] Since this character is so detestable and bends its attacks against the best and worthiest men, Fielding determines to "take some Pains in the ripping it up," exposing to public view (as Samuel Butler had done with Hudibras, the very type of the religious hypocrite) both its "inside" and its "outside." After copious quotation of scriptural diatribes against hypocrisy (with a lavish use of italics and full capitals to carry the strong emphasis his emotion dictated), Fielding insists that the hypocrite is censorious of any merit not based on rigid observance of external forms in Scripture. He cites Burkitt's commentary on the scriptures as support: *"This is indeed the Bane of all Religion and true Piety, to prefer Rituals and human Institutions before divine Commands, and the Practice of Natural Religion.* THUS TO DO IS A CERTAIN SIGN OF GROSS HYPOCRISY" (I, 217).[74] Moreover, this character hates most the really good men, for he envies them their surety of Heaven. Fearing exposure, he is suspicious of everyone; and further, "As the Business of such a Man's Life is to procure Praise, by acquiring and maintaining an undeserved Character," he seeks by detraction to destroy the reputation of truly virtuous men (I, 207-13).

Fielding justifies the space he has devoted to censoriousness by declaring that "it is a very pernicious [vice]; and (according to what I have observed) little known and attended to" (I, 212). Besides being responsible for "private Villanies," he insists heatedly—and somewhat expansively— it is the source of "most of the great Evils which have af-

[73] Shaftesbury's *Letter concerning Enthusiasm* had brilliantly stigmatized the religious hypocrite and the "snappish Spirit" in religion, and a multitude of sermons and tracts did likewise; the association of the two is compendiously suggested by an entry in the Index to Volume II of Bellegarde's *Reflexions upon Ridicule* (5th ed., 2v., 1739): "Hypocrites. See Religion."

[74] Cf. William Burkitt, *Expository Notes, with Practical Observations, on the New Testament* (3rd ed., 1707), sig. I₃v, commentary on Matt. 23:23-24.

fected Society, Wars, Murders, and Massacres . . . the Destroyer of the Innocent, and Protector of the Guilty; which hath introduced all manner of Evil into the World, and hath almost expelled every Grain of Good out of it" (I, 212-13). Moving now to the "outside" of this pernicious character, Fielding suggests he can be detected, first, in his "sanctified" appearance; second, in the placing of all virtue and religion in the observation of *"Austerities and Severities"*; third, in "all Ostentation of Virtue, Goodness, or Piety"; and, finally, in that readiness to censure the faults of others which Fielding calls "sanctified Slander" (I, 213-19).

Concluding with this his discussion of men's actions, Fielding observes regretfully that so long as even good men allow themselves to be blinded by vanity and self-love, and while hypocrisy knows how to adapt to this weakness of human nature, "It will be difficult for honest and undesigning Men to escape the Snares of Cunning and Imposition" (I, 219). He gives, therefore, one further rule: to observe with particular care the *actions toward others* of men proposed to our trust, especially their actions toward those to whom they are allied in some way,[75] for "Nothing indeed can be more unjustifiable to our Prudence, than an Opinion that the Man whom we see act the Part of a Villain to others, should on some minute Change of Person, Time, Place, or other Circumstance, behave like an honest and just Man to ourselves" (I, 221-22).

In a third division of the essay, the foregoing observations are extended into public life. The point is made that just as a man's behavior to those close to him is an augury of his honest conduct toward a stranger, so is the "worthy Discharge of the social Offices of a private Station, the strongest

[75] Dr. Harrison makes this point in *Amelia*. As Booth tells it, "The doctor was so kind to say he had inquired into my character, and had found that I had been a dutiful son and an affectionate brother. Relations, said he, in which whoever discharges his duty well, gives us a well-grounded hope that he will behave as properly in all the rest" (II, vii; Henley, VI, 96).

Security which a Man can give of an upright Demeanour in any public Trust . . . ," for no man can have general philanthropy who has no private affection. This might be aimed at Walpole, but it is more likely that Fielding had the leaders of the ungrateful "patriot" Opposition in mind, for he concludes that the bad relation or friend, "in a Word, the bad Man in private can never be a sincere Patriot" (1, 223).

After a short digression on patriotism—which Fielding takes to be a passion not native to human nature, but which must be introduced by education or else based on "Philanthropy, or universal Benevolence" (1, 226)—the essay is concluded with a brief recapitulation of the methods of frustrating the cunning and designs of hypocrisy, noting once again that the first method—by the marks of the countenance—is "liable to some Incertainty" (1, 226). "But however useless this Treatise may be to instruct," Fielding says in closing, "I hope it will be at least effectual to alarm my Reader; and sure no honest undesigning Man can ever be too much on his Guard against the Hypocrite, or too industrious to expose and expel him out of Society" (1, 227).

The *Essay on the Knowledge of the Characters of Men* is, although less logically coherent, much more personal and incisive in tone than the *Essay on Conversation*, because Fielding is here descanting on a subject that always roused him to the highest pitch of indignation. Although it is once again an "essay of purpose," an essentially didactic piece of work, the author does not consistently maintain the didactic essayist's normal attitude of lofty objectivity: when he comes to the hypocritical "saint," the pose is dropped and Fielding speaks to us in his proper person. The cumulative force of his iterated charges and the severe and strenuous sincerity of the attack combine to make this "ripping up" one of Fielding's most impassioned indictments of the pharisaical character—"this malignant cursed Disposition, which is the Disgrace of Human Nature, and the Bane of Society" (1, 213). It would be difficult to better the simple scorn of his question: "Can he who passes Sentence on the Souls of Men with more Delight and Triumph than the Devil can execute it, have the Impudence to pretend himself a Disciple of one who died for the Sins of Mankind" (1, 207).

3

The literary and moral history of the hypocrite as a figure of anathema would call for a good-sized volume in itself. The man who would seem that which he is not and who seeks to impose upon others under a false cloak of virtue has been from the beginnings of recorded literature the object of dissection and vilification by countless satirists and moralists. The imagination of the literary artist has given us the Malvolios and Tartuffes; but Scripture, too, portrayed the type (as Fielding's copious citations let us know), and the history of homiletics abounds with moral and theological pronouncements on his character.

Thus Fielding's indictment of the hypocrite is in a tradition as old as literature itself. His attempts to warn good-hearted men of the monstrous designs of their hypocritical fellows had been anticipated in plays, poems, sermons, character-books and courtesy-books, in periodicals and pamphlets. He could well say, "Neither will the Reader, I hope, be offended, if he should here find no Observations entirely new to him" (1, 186). But the very persistence of the character justified the persistence of the warnings; analogically, Fielding says (offering, incidentally, a theme for all humane studies): "Nothing can be plainer, or more known, than the general Rules of Morality, and yet thousands of Men are thought well employed in reviving our Remembrance, and enforcing our Practice of them" (1, 186). And since Fielding is one of those whose own portraits of the hypocrite have transcended mere vilification or mere moral condemnation, it may be worth considering what explicit views he offers in a practical and pragmatic study of the hypocrite in action.[76]

The essay reveals two basic types of hypocrisy: first, there is the kind that practises deceit in order to lead others to sacrifice their interests, the kind that persuades the innocent that their own good is designed. This is, says Fielding, "the very Essence of that excellent Art, called *The Art of Politics*" (I, 184). Second, there is the type of hypocrisy that Fielding designates here as "Censoriousness," proceeding from envy and ill-nature.

The first kind is personified most eminently by Jonathan Wild, who sums up in his own character most of the arts of deceit examined in the *Essay*:

"WITH such infinite Address, did this truly GREAT MAN know to play with the Passions of Men, and to set them at Variance with each other, and to work his own Purposes out of those Jealousies and Apprehensions, which he was wonderfully ready at creating, by Means of those great Arts, which the Vulgar call Treachery, Dissembling, Promising, Lying, Falshood, &c. but which are by GREAT MEN summed up in the collective Name of Policy, or Politicks, or rather *Pollitricks*; an Art of which, as it is the highest Excellence of Human Nature, so perhaps, was our GREAT MAN the most eminent Master"—(II, v; *Misc.*, III, 138).

Individual images of the flatterer, the "professor" of esteem, the promiser, and the inquisitive friend (the first kind of hypocrites warned against in the *Essay*) are scattered in great variety throughout Fielding's plays, essays, and novels. Flattery greases the wheels of state and society throughout Julian's account in the *Journey from This World to the Next*, but he finds that those who have most reduced flattery to a science are the beggars: for "No Profession requires a deeper Insight into human Nature, than

[76] The *locus classicus* for Fielding's use of the terms Hypocrisy, Affectation, and Deceit is, of course, the preface to *Joseph Andrews*. Fielding makes there, however, some distinctions which he did not always himself observe.

ESSAYS

the Beggar's. Their Knowledge of the Passions of Men is so extensive, that I have often thought, it would be of no little service to a Politician to have his Education among them" (chap. xix; *Misc.*, II, 154-55). Most of Fielding's oily villains are good flatterers, but perhaps only Blifil is shrewd or politic enough to flatter his victims (Square and Thwackum) behind their backs by praising them to another who repeats the compliments—and "to say the truth, there is no kind of flattery so irresistible as this, at second hand" (*TJ*, III, v; Henley, III, 124). Few are those able to resist the pleasant balm; even the sagacious Dr. Harrison seems to soak up the praise with which the wily old flatterer in *Amelia* (IX, x) inundates him, a speaking instance of Fielding's belief that no one was immune.[77] He was not, of course, alone in trying to alert society to the deceit beneath the pretty words: warnings against flattery fill the conduct-books and sermons of the time (Robert South, indeed, preached three consecutive long sermons on the text, "A man that flattereth his neighbour, spreadeth a net for his feet").[78] But no contemporary offered more striking and dramatic illustrations of the vice in action than Fielding.

Examples of the other hypocritical wheedlers will readily suggest themselves to every reader. The most memorable picture of a false promiser is the gentleman with the smiling countenance in *Joseph Andrews* who offers Adams a living, suggests that the travellers use his horses, and so on—and then sends word the next day that he has gone on a long journey (II, xvi-xvii). Joseph is the least surprised because his experience as a footman has taught him that "it is a maxim among the gentlemen of our cloth that those masters who promise the most perform the least" (Henley, I, 203).

[77] As Bellegarde said, "The Profession of a Flatterer is base and scandalous, but it seems to be a necessary Profession, since every Body wants Flattery" (*Reflexions upon Ridicule* [5th ed., 2v., 1739], I, 182).
[78] *Sermons Preached upon Several Occasions* (7v., Oxford, 1823), Vol. V, Sermons VII-IX.

201

ESSAYS

As Fielding said in *Amelia*, "This art of promising is the economy of a great man's pride, a sort of good husbandry in conferring favors . . ." (v, iii; Henley, vi, 240).

Although there are many inquisitive and prying hypocrites in Fielding's pages, one of the most egregious and troublesome is, curiously enough, not detestable at all—the self-serving and strangely lovable Partridge in *Tom Jones*. The commentary on this kind of character in the *Essay*, however, puts Partridge in something of a new light (and perhaps explains why when the rewards of virtue were distributed in the last chapter of *Tom Jones*, Partridge came off poorly—unless the possibility of being saddled with Molly Seagrim is looked upon as a *reward!*) because for all his great good humor, he bears out perfectly Fielding's warning: "The Man who is inquisitive into the Secrets of your Affairs, with which he hath no Concern, is another Object of your Caution" (*Misc.*, I, 205).

The second basic type of hypocrisy, comprehending the slanderer and the "saint," requires little further remark. More than once Fielding insisted (seriously, one must suppose) that slander was as vicious a crime as murder and deserved a like punishment;[79] he reserved his lowest comparisons for the mean creature guilty of it—"Vice hath not, I believe, a more abject slave; society produces not a more odious vermin; nor can the devil receive a guest more worthy of him, nor possibly more welcome to him, than a slanderer" (*TJ*, XI, i; Henley, IV, 243). But it was the "saintly" censurer, the type that we know as "holier-than-thou," that drove Fielding to the highest pitch of fury.[80] To a man of his broad tolerance and honest good-

---

[79] See, for example, the *Champion*, 6 March 1740 (Henley, xv, 230-35) and the *Covent-Garden Journal*, No. 14 (Jensen, I, 219-24).

[80] A few divines, including Isaac Barrow, argued that it was wise to countenance some hypocrisies to a degree: "For it is no great harm that any man should enjoy undeserved commendation, or that a counterfeit worth should find a dissembled respect . . . but it may do mischief to blemish an appearance of virtue; it may be a wrong thereto to deface its very image; the very disclosing hypocrisy doth inflict a wound on goodness,

nature, no character could have been more hateful and disgusting than that of the austere ascetic—and nothing more bitter than such a man's censoriousness. We may repeat two sentences that we have previously analyzed: "Doth it not [he cries] attempt to cheat Men into the Pursuit of Sorrow and Misery, under the Appearance of Virtue, and to frighten them from Mirth and Pleasure, under the Colour of Vice, or, if you please, SIN? Doth it not attempt to gild over that poisonous Potion, made up of Malevolence, Austerity, and such cursed Ingredients, while it embitters the delightful Draught of innocent Pleasure with the nauseous Relish of Fear and Shame"—(*Misc.*, I, 213).

Fielding delighted to display this character in its most blatant and self-revealing terms. For example, of his incarnation as a monk in the *Journey from This World to the Next* (chap. xiv), Julian declares: "As I was of a sour morose Temper, and hated nothing more than the Symptoms of Happiness appearing in any Countenance, I represented all kinds of Diversion and Amusement as the most horrid Sins. I inveighed against Chearfulness as Levity, and encouraged nothing but Gravity, or, to confess the Truth to you, Hypocrisy"—(*Misc.*, II, 107).

So also, in an early play, *The Temple Beau*, Lady Lucy Pedant bares the character of the prudish Lady Gravely: "The virtue in your mouth no more proceeds from the purity of your heart, than the colour in your cheeks does from the purity of your blood . . . , your ardency to improve the world is too often rank envy . . . , you rail at the diver-

---

and exposeth it to scandal . . ." (*Theological Works of Isaac Barrow*, ed. Alexander Napier [9v., Cambridge, 1859], II, 162, 163). This doubtless has its truth; but Barrow's advice found no echo in Fielding's other favorite preachers, Tillotson, Clarke, and South, all of whom preached repeated sermons against the religious hypocrite; and Fielding's own conclusion was precisely opposite to Barrow's: "It is better that one real Saint should suffer a little unjust Suspicion, than that Ninety Nine Villains should impose on the World, and be enabled to perpetrate their Villainies under this Mask" (*Misc.*, I, 207).

sions of the town, for several reasons: but the love of goodness has nothing to do with any"—(I, i; Henley, VIII, 105-06).

Almost all of Fielding's meanest hypocrites have a strong tincture of this vice, this malicious pleasure in censuring others under the guise of a superior virtue: Parson Trulliber, Peter Pounce, Blifil, Thwackum, Amelia's sister, all come readily to mind. Normally he exposed them by displaying dramatically the gulf between their virtuous pronouncements and their ugly actions; but often he could not resist the temptation to add an extra fillip by throwing in a word of his own. In *Jonathan Wild*, for example, the reception by that hypocritical prude, Laetitia, of news of her sister's dishonor should really speak for itself, since the reader is well aware of her own moral laxity:

"She fell into the utmost Fury at the Relation, reviled her Sister in the bitterest Terms, and vowed she would never see nor speak to her more. Then burst into Tears, and lamented over her Father, that such a Dishonour should ever happen to him and herself. At length she fell severely on her Husband, for the light Treatment which he gave this fatal Accident. . . . She concluded with desiring her Father to make an Example of the Slut, and turn her out of Doors . . ."—(III, xiii; *Misc.*, III, 272-73).

Fielding could not let it go at this. He felt too strongly about the nasty Laetitia and her school—and he allowed his feelings to lead him into an artistic blemish, a gratuitous comment that is not only superfluous, but lets the mask of irony slip: "So violent, and indeed so outragious [he says] was this chaste Lady's Love of Virtue, that she could not forgive a single Slip (indeed the only one *Theodosia* had ever made) in her own Sister, in a Sister who loved her, and to whom she owed a thousand Obligations"—(*Misc.*, III, 273).

More often he let his hypocrites expose themselves. Nevertheless, although Fielding was quite capable of high subtlety in portraying the little, inadvertent hypocrisies and vanities common even to the best of men, when he sketched the portrait of that contemptible deceit and hypocrisy which springs from a warped soul and a design upon others, he did so with his broadest, most spacious strokes. He wanted no one to be doubly deceived: his purpose was to lay bare in its most unmistakable terms the rotten foundation that underlay the cant and pose of a "virtue" which lay in the mouth and not in the heart.

In the preface to the *Miscellanies*, Fielding said that his set purpose in the *Essay on the Knowledge of the Characters of Men* was to expose a "great Evil, namely, Hypocrisy; the Bane of all Virtue, Morality, and Goodness"; for, as he continued, "I believe a little Reflection will convince us, that most Mischiefs (especially those which fall on the worthiest Part of Mankind) owe their Original to this detestable Vice" (*Misc.*, I, iv-v). He never wavered in this belief.

4

Although its primary concern is hypocrisy, Fielding's essay belongs generically to the tradition of the moral treatise on human nature, a tradition which includes at one end of the philosophical scale the work of the great English empiricists and, at the other, a multitude of discourses by minor moralists and divines seeking to establish the natural and moral bases of human action.

The grounds of a more "scientific" psychology than the long-lived Aristotelian-scholastic had, of course, been set forth in the seventeenth century by such philosophers as Hobbes, Descartes, and Malebranche; and Locke's treatise led to a spate of popular studies on human nature. Any number of amateur theorists discoursed confidently of the springs of human action, drawing eclectically from other contemporary works and from Christian, Aristotelian, Platonic, Stoic, or Epicurean sources, usually to find and establish sanction for a particular set of preconceived moral values. The underlying concern was normally an attempt to relate moral judgments to specifically human values, to a morality whose implicit measure was man; and this tendency is seen at work even in the religious philosophers and moralists, particularly those who leaned toward the neo-Pelagian, benevolist, or sentimental view. The earnest search for moral sanctions necessarily resulted, then, in a plethora of studies on human nature. The characteristic work of such philosophic writers as Shaftesbury, Hutcheson, and Mandeville, among others, is a part of this great examination—indeed, most of the major figures of the period touch it at one point or another, for if there was one moral emphasis upon which they could all agree, it was that the proper study of mankind is man.

Fielding's study is, after all, only an essay, not a formal treatise. And despite the somewhat grandiose title, his specific concern is, as we have seen, really hypocrisy, not human nature in the large. Yet, though not the usual extensive analysis of human "psychology," the *Essay* includes a number of suggestive statements about the nature of man; and the conclusions reflect certain basic assumptions about man that it seems proper to explore further. The scrutiny of a few of the problems that Fielding wrestled with, as he shaped for himself a generalized idea of human nature, may also serve to throw into relief that often ignored darker side of his thought which (paradoxically, perhaps) gave to the comic, optimistic world of his imaginative creations its peculiar depth and validity.

It is somewhat startling, for instance, to find Fielding beginning his discourse with the reflection, "I Have often thought it a melancholy Instance of the great Depravity of Human Nature . . ." (*Misc.*, I, 181)—for we should not normally be inclined to place Fielding in the theological camp that stressed man's depravity. And indeed this statement is shortly qualified by a disclaimer (such as Fielding

ESSAYS

frequently made after some hearty generalization) that he intends no inclusive statements about man's disposition in general; for "*Man differs more from Man, than Man from Beast,*"[81] and we are able to see, he says, even in men of the same climate, religion, and education, sufficient variety to dissuade us from unqualified generalizations about the human species. This sounds more like the Fielding that we normally think of. Yet, it is interesting to speculate upon his use of the term "depravity." In the essay, *Of the Remedy of Affliction*, he observed that one who seeks to prescribe consolation "should consider the human Mind (as is often the Case of the Body) in too weak and depraved a Situation to be restored to firm Vigour and Sanity . . ." (*Misc.*, I, 300). On the very next page, he declared that the calm demeanor of Stilpo when he lost his children was "owing to meer Insensibility; to a Depravity of the Heart, not Goodness of the Understanding" (I, 301). In the *Essay on Conversation* (to cite only one more example), he insisted that a cruel pride which enjoys the mortification of others "proceeds from the Depravity of both [the Heart and Head], and almost certainly from the Badness of the latter" (I, 145). This is enough, perhaps, to suggest that Fielding is using the term in its nontheological sense; and yet, although "pravity" and "depravation" were at that date the commoner theological terms, "depravity" may have had nevertheless something of a theological ring to it, with attendant implications for psychology.[82]

[81] Quoted from Rochester's "Satyr against Mankind," l. 224 (*Poems by John Wilmot, Earl of Rochester*, ed. Vivian de Sola Pinto [1953], p. 124; this is the concluding line of the so-called "addition" to the shorter form of the poem). The quotation is ultimately from Plutarch (*Bruta animalia ratione uti*, 992e; in the Loeb Library *Moralia*, xii, 531), and is repeated by Montaigne, Book I, chap. xlii, "Of the Inequality Which Is Between Us" (*Essays*, ed. W. C. Hazlitt [4v., 1902], II, 51).

[82] See *N. E. D.*, s. v. "Depravity": according to this authority, the term came into common use to designate "the innate corruption of human nature due to original sin" only after Jonathan Edwards' *Great Christian Doctrine of Original Sin Defended* (1758). The more normal sense before that was apparently, like some of Fielding's uses, merely a rendering of

The Anglican church continued to hold officially to the dogma of the depravity of man (as Article IX of the XXXIX Articles sufficiently indicates). But reaction against Hobbes and against the "Puritan" emphasis had led to a softening of that doctrine, observable, for instance, in Isaac Barrow's sermon on "Motives and Arguments to Charity," where he prefaced an attack on the position of Hobbes by asking:

"We may appeal to the conscience of each man, if he doth not feel dissatisfaction in that fierceness or frowardness of temper, which produceth uncharitableness; if he have not a complacence in that sweet and calm disposition of soul, whence charity doth issue; if he do not condemn himself for the one, and approve himself in the other practice.

"This is the common judgment of men; and therefore, in common language, this practice is styled humanity, as best sorting with our nature, and becoming it; and the principle whence it springeth is called good-nature: and the contrary practice is styled inhumanity, as thwarting our natural inclinations, or divesting us of manhood; and its source likewise is termed ill-nature, or a corruption of our nature."[83]

Barrow and the other latitudinarians tended to place the blame for malicious and evil dispositions upon neglect of good education and good customs rather than upon innate depravity, though none of them failed to insist that God's grace was of first importance to the awakening of goodness in man. Cognizance was normally taken of the Fall; but

---

the classical "depravatio," perversion: for example, the opening of the *Remedy* follows closely the opening of Book III of the *Tusculan Disputations*, which includes the phrase "quos celeriter malis moribus opinionibusque depravati . . ." [which, under the corrupting influence of bad habits and beliefs] (III. i. 2; Loeb Library, trans. J. E. King, pp. 224-26). This may even have suggested Fielding's use of "too weak and depraved" cited above.

[83] *Theological Works*, ed. Napier, II, 373.

ESSAYS

as even a country vicar could protest in 1694: "To assert Humane Nature in general, as the great patroness of all Vice and Villany, because 'tis now faln from its original perfection, and adulterated with some vicious mixtures, is just as if we should say, that there is no Gold in the mass of Ore, because mixt with greater quantity of Dross or Sand."[84]

Fielding is, of course, in this latitudinarian and benevolist tradition; and, like others of the tradition, he maintains in uneasy balance a consciousness of the still orthodox dogma of the Fall and man's depravity, and a personal desire to refute such contemners of human nature as Hobbes and Mandeville.[85] This may help to account for the cautious phrasing of an essay in the *Champion*:

"THOSE authors who have set human nature in a very vile and detestable light, *however right or wrong such their sentiments may be* [italics mine] ... have often succeeded in establishing an infamous character to themselves. ... [and, later in the essay] ... though I am unwilling to look on human nature as a mere sink of iniquity, I am far from insinuating that it is a state of perfection. ... [and, following the citation of a letter from a professed hypocrite] ... though the certain existence of such sort of persons, as my correspondent, may justify us in some degree of suspicion and caution in our dealing with mankind; yet should it by no means incline us to their opinions, who have represented human nature as utterly bad and depraved ..."
—(11 December 1739; Henley, xv, 94-96).

This is, one may at least suggest, rather ambiguous for the brightly cheerful optimist about human nature who

[84] James Lowde, *A Discourse concerning the Nature of Man* (1694), sig. A₄v.
[85] See the analysis of this dilemma, as it appeared in the work of Steele and his contemporaries, in Rae Blanchard's introduction to her edition of *The Christian Hero* (1932). Fielding's attitude toward Hobbes and Mandeville is ambiguous. He felt very strongly the *psychological* validity of their skeptical analysis of man's nature: but he believed that *morally* man was capable of rising about that "nature," and that their skepticism was morally paralyzing.

ESSAYS

appears in some critical assessments of Fielding! In another quite curious essay, he seems almost to agree seriously with Swift's ironic conclusion that the sublime and refined point of felicity is the possession of being well deceived:

"Was human nature really as depraved, and totally bad as [a set of political philosophers] represent it, surely the discovery is of the same kind with his, who with great pains persuaded his friend that a wife, who had agreeably deceived him, and with whom he lived extremely happy, was false to him. . . . An evil which admits of no remedy, a wise man would surely wish to remain in ignorance of" —(*Champion*, 22 January 1740; Henley, xv, 162).

This would seem to admit the possibility of natural depravity, but to insist that it is better—wiser—for a man not to believe it. Fielding did not usually employ this shuffling kind of argument in matters upon which he held really firm convictions.

On the other hand (and of course it is time for the other hand), Fielding would, we can be certain, have agreed with William Melmoth, commenting upon the malice shown toward virtue: "Nothing, perhaps, stings a generous mind more sensibly in wrongs of this sort, than to consider them as evidences of a general malignity in human nature."[86] It was not only stinging to the mind, it was frankly dangerous to follow such thoughts. As Allworthy argued in *Tom Jones*, "Nothing less than a persuasion of universal depravity can lock up the charity of a good man; and this persuasion must lead them, I think, either into atheism or enthusiasm; but surely it is unfair to argue such universal depravity from a few vicious individuals . . ." (II, v; Henley, III, 84). Jones himself answered the misanthropy of the Man of the Hill with a straightforward (and frequently quoted) declaration against uni-

[86] *Letters of Sir Thomas Fitzosborne* (7th ed., 1769), p. 352.

versal or innate depravity as a dogma (VIII, xv; Henley, IV, 152). And that he was clearly reflecting Fielding's own mind is shown by the anticipation of his argument in the preface to the *Miscellanies*, where Fielding in speaking of Jonathan Wild declared:

"I solemnly protest, I do by no means intend in the Character of my Hero to represent Human Nature in general. Such Insinuations must be attended with very dreadful Conclusions; nor do I see any other Tendency they can naturally have, but to encourage and soothe Men in their Villainies, and to make every well-disposed Man disclaim his own Species, and curse the Hour of his Birth into such a Society. For my Part, I understand those Writers who describe Human Nature in this depraved Character, as speaking only of such Persons as *Wild* and his Gang; and I think it may be justly inferred, that they do not find in their own Bosoms any Deviation from the general Rule" —(*Misc.*, I, xix-xx).

But for all this, the *conception* remained in Fielding's own mind. The theoretical arguments about the good or evil tendencies of human nature set forth by divines and philosophers provided a set of polar opposites between which he tended to vacillate. Drawing illustrations from his own experience, he argued now at one end of the scale, now at another. This may perhaps be indicated by contrasting two speeches put in the mouth of his "mentor character," Dr. Harrison:

"As the malicious disposition of mankind is too well known, and the cruel pleasure which they take in destroying the reputations of others, the use we are to make of this knowledge is to afford no handle to reproach . . ."— (*Amelia*, III, i; Henley, VI, 109).

"The nature of man is far from being in itself evil; it abounds with benevolence, charity, and pity, coveting praise and honor, and shunning shame and disgrace . . . [and Harrison goes on to explain, like Barrow, that the

ESSAYS

real difficulty is due to bad education and bad customs which debauch the original good]"—(IX, v; Henley, VII, 145).

Of course, these two postures might be reconciled without affronting logic, since the "malicious disposition of mankind" is not declared to be innate; nevertheless, they face in different directions.[87] It would be too much to describe Fielding's state of mind through one of Hazlitt's aphorisms: "I believe in the theoretical benevolence, and practical malignity of man"[88] (sometimes, indeed, the terms were reversed for him!)—but in the works of his later years, Fielding perhaps tended to give greater weight to the practical malignity of man, even though his *wish* was still not to believe it a general characteristic of human nature.

Like "Axylus," his good correspondent of the *Covent-Garden Journal*, Fielding could have said for and of himself: "I cannot bear those Pictures which represent human Nature in a wretched, or in an odious Light; but cherish every Thing which fills my Mind with Ideas of the Wisdom, the Goodness, the Mirth, and the Happiness of Mankind." But this pleasant "possession of being well deceived" is contrasted, by "Axylus" with the grim reality of Fielding's actual position: "How can your neighbouring Justice bear the Sight of all those Wretches who are brought before him [?]" (*CGJ*, No. 16; Jensen, I, 234-36).[89]

---

[87] Marking the extremes of the two directions, of course, are the redoubtable Thwackum, who "maintained that the human mind, since the fall, was nothing but a sink of iniquity, till purified and redeemed by grace" and the philosophic Square, who "held human nature to be the perfection of all virtue, and that vice was a deviation from our nature" (*TJ*, III, iii; Henley, III, 114). We do not need Fielding's remark, quoted above from the *Champion*, to understand that he was "unwilling" to accept the one view and "far from insinuating" the other; that is clear enough. But what has been less clear, perhaps, is the extent to which at various times he nevertheless felt the pull of each conviction in a less extreme form.

[88] "Aphorisms on Man," *Collected Works of William Hazlitt*, ed. A. R. Waller and A. Glover (13v., 1902-1906), XII, 222.

[89] As William Melmoth—whose temper is in many ways extraordinarily like Fielding's—remarked, "It is difficult indeed to preserve the mind from

ESSAYS

Though Fielding remained unwilling to impute to human nature in general any conclusions drawn from the depravity of individual men,[90] the undeniable fact of the latter was increasingly forced upon him in such ugly terms that he could no longer even treat it humorously. "In serious and sorrowful truth," he said in *A Clear State of the Case of Elizabeth Canning* (1753), "doth not history, as well as our own experience, afford us too great reasons to suspect, that there is in some minds a sensation directly opposite to that of benevolence, and which delights and feeds itself with acts of cruelty and inhumanity?" (Henley, XIII, 230). In the *Covent-Garden Journal* he could find even "in the worthiest human Minds" some "small innate Seeds of Malignity" (No. 16; Jensen, I, 232); and in his last work, the *Journal of a Voyage to Lisbon*, for all its brave good humor, there are signs of a profound pessimism about human nature. In a reflection that I cited on the subject of liberty, Fielding finds the "gauntlope" of jeering watermen on the Thames "a lively picture of that cruelty and inhumanity, in the nature of men, which I have often contemplated with concern; and which leads the mind into a train of very uncomfortable and melancholy thoughts" (Henley, XVI, 200-01). And as he meditates on the spectacle, he is led to observe that this kind of barbarous behavior "never shews itself in men who are polish'd and refin'd, in such manner as human nature requires, to produce that perfection of which it is susceptible, and to

---

falling into a general contempt of our race, whilst one is conversant with the worst part of it." (*Letters of Sir Thomas Fitzosborne*, p. 341).

[90] The phrasing, in terms of volition rather than conviction, is Fielding's own in the *Journal of a Voyage to Lisbon*. Having described with shock and sorrow the advantage taken of mariners' distress by the people who live along the shore, he concluded, "Now, *as I am unwilling* that some conclusions, which may be, I am aware, too justly drawn from these observations, should be imputed to human nature in general, *I have endeavoured* to account for them in a way more consistent with the goodness and dignity of that nature . . ." (Henley, XVI, 220; italics mine).

purge away *that malevolence of disposition, of which, at our birth, we partake in common with the savage creation*" (Henley, XVI, 201; italics mine). Here—as in *Covent-Garden Journal* No. 55, where he described good-breeding in terms of "the Art of rooting out all those Seeds of Humour [in a bad sense] which Nature had originally implanted in our Minds" (Jensen, II, 60)—human "malevolence" rather than natural goodness would really appear to be considered as the innate quality; and education, rather than corrupting original good, would be seen as the only force capable of modifying an original evil in man.

Even with such apparently unambiguous declarations, however, it is necessary to take account of the context. When Fielding contemplated some particularly shocking example of man's inhumanity to man, he was often moved to declare a belief in something very much like innate or universal depravity (though almost never with *theological* implication); but the truth is that a benevolent deed would just as likely call forth from him an enthusiastic assertion of the natural tendency to good in man when uncorrupted by evil customs. If one can trace in Fielding, as he grows older, an inclination to give greater and more somber weight to the elements of evil in man, this is *not* to say that he moved from an easy optimism to a despondent pessimism.[91] He maintained through all of his life a dynamic awareness of the possibilities both for good and evil in the soul of man, and he set forth these possibilities as a thoughtful (and emotional) artist, not as a systematic philosopher or theologian.

[91] One can point to various early statements that follow the tenor of Mr. Wilson's observation in *Joseph Andrews*, "There is a malignity in the nature of man which, when not weeded out, or at least covered by a good education and politeness, delights in making another uneasy or dissatisfied with himself" (III, iii; Henley, I, 246). Indeed, the poem *Of Good-Nature* in the *Miscellanies* had asked: "Dwells there a base Malignity in Men . . . ?" (I, 18). My argument is merely that such comments multiply in number and deepen in intensity in Fielding's later years.

5

Consistently unwilling to believe that *all* men are, in any theological sense, naturally evil, and certainly unable to believe that *all* men are naturally good, Fielding sought (unsystematically) various ways to propound a theory of human nature that would sort with the psychology of the day and prove amenable to the purposes of the moralist as well. Clearly, it is necessary that any man who sets himself up as a reformer should believe in the individual's capacity to ameliorate, to change, his own character—if the moralist lost his faith in this possibility, he could no longer well believe in the efficacy of his own urgings. But he needs also (if one may put it this way) a theory that will explain why a considerable part of humanity ignores those urgings. This dual set of desiderata finds satisfaction in Fielding's basic conception of the human being as having, individually, almost an innate propensity to goodness or to viciousness that his subsequent education and circumstances intensify or ameliorate. Thus the possibility of reform exists; but some evil natures can never be moved by it.

Fielding's own statement upon this question in the *Essay on the Knowledge of the Characters of Men* is significant enough to quote in full:

"Those who predicate of Man in general, that he is an Animal of this or that Disposition, seem to me not sufficiently to have studied Human Nature; for that immense Variety of Characters so apparent in Men even of the same Climate, Religion, and Education . . . could hardly exist, *unless the Distinction had some original Foundation in Nature itself.* Nor is it perhaps a less proper Predicament of the Genius of a Tree, that it will flourish so many Years, loves such a Soil, bears such a Fruit, &c. than of Man in general, that he is good, bad, fierce, tame, honest, or cunning.

"This original Difference will, I think, alone account for that very early and strong Inclination to Good or Evil, which distinguishes different Dispositions in Children, in their first Infancy; in the most un-informed Savages, who can be thought to have altered their Nature by no Rules, nor artfully acquired Habits; and lastly, in Persons who from the same Education, &c. might be thought to have directed Nature the same Way; yet, among all these, there subsists, as I have before hinted, so manifest and extreme a Difference of Inclination or Character, that almost obliges us, I think, to acknowledge some *unacquired original Distinction,* in the Nature or Soul of one Man, from that of another"—(*Misc.*, I, 182-83; italics mine).

Jones and Blifil are the most obvious paired dramatization of this statement, but one might argue that they have different fathers. A better example can be found in Amelia and her sister Betty, who share the same parents, education, and environment, but nevertheless display from their early years an essential propensity to good and evil nature respectively, which can only be attributed to that "unacquired Distinction" posited here. Fielding more than once argued like Joseph Andrews:

"I remember when I was in the stable, if a young horse was vicious in his nature, no correction would make him otherwise; I take it to be equally the same among men: if a boy be of a mischievous, wicked inclination, no school, though ever so private, will ever make him good: on the contrary, if he be of a righteous temper, you may trust him to London, or wherever else you please—he will be in no danger of being corrupted"—(III, v; Henley, I, 262).

In the *Journey from This World to the Next* (chap. vi), the voyager beyond the veil sees the spirits who are about to enter bodies and be "born" on earth imbibe a "Pathetic Potion" and a "Nousphoric Decoction." The latter is "an Extract from the Faculties of the Mind," which presumably determines the intellect of the individual to be born.

ESSAYS

The former is a mixture of all the Passions, in varying proportions—indeed, says Fielding, in the hurry of making it up, one or another ingredient is sometimes completely omitted (*Misc.*, II, 48-49). Fable though this may be, it expresses fairly accurately, I think, Fielding's normal abstract view of the human composition, complete with the essential ingredients of each individual character at birth. Thus man —conceived in terms of contemporary psychology—is a compound of certain definite passions and intellect, with the proportions fixed in embryo, so to speak.

Significantly enough, the faculty of the will is passed over in this fable. This could be explained by supposing that Fielding thought of the will as a faculty not present at birth but developed through habit and education—as he most likely did. But I think a more consequential explanation is that he was not here concerned with man's educability, but rather with his abstract "basic" nature. In this latter frame of reference, Fielding was more likely to think in static terms. On the other hand, when he was working in the frame of exhortation to reform, the will naturally assumed considerable importance for him. For, although Fielding, like Booth in *Amelia*, tended to place greater emphasis upon the passions than the will as the determinant of action, he did not make Booth's mistake of forgetting that the latter faculty existed. From the *Champion* to the *Covent-Garden Journal* he asserted, whenever the context called for it, his fundamental belief that it was "greatly within [Man's] Power . . . to imitate the most benevolent and virtuous, or the most wicked and base of all Beings" (*CGJ*, No. 16; Jensen, I, 233).

When in an early essay he cited Shaftesbury's description of God as "the best-natured being in the universe," and suggested that we drew nearer to divine perfection by cultivating "the sweet disposition in our minds," he concluded: "All his other attributes throw us immediately out of sight, but this virtue *lies in will,* and not at all in power" (*Champion,* 27 March 1740; Henley, xv, 260; italics mine—"power" used here, of course, in a different sense from that above). *Jonathan Wild,* in the revised edition, ended with the assertion (not ironic) that "it is in the Power of every Man to be perfectly Honest" (2nd ed., 1754, p. 263); and in *Amelia* Fielding assured his "worthy reader" that innocence "is always within thy own power" (viii, iii; Henley, vii, 78). Again, like Shaftesbury, Fielding believed that conquest of self, harmony in the individual soul, came from an "exact balance of the passions" that would "preserve order and regularity in the mind" (*Champion,* 2 February 1740; Henley, xv, 179). The reason dictated this conclusion, but it lay in the power of the active will to make the decision to carry out "that glorious precept *vince teipsum*" (*ibid.,* p. 178).

Obviously enough, a belief in the freedom of the will was essential to Fielding's belief in man's educability. And though he occasionally admitted (like Joseph Andrews) to some skepticism about the force of education to sway original tendencies, he normally insisted (like Parson Adams) upon its power—even to declaring, as we have seen, that artificial "passions," such as patriotism, could be introduced by art and thus join the natural passions that make up the human complex (see above, p. 198). The force of his pronouncements upon an original, given nature was, moreover, often qualified by his use of the term "seeds" to express it, suggesting the possibility of cultivation and growth, either favorably or unfavorably. For instance, after having maintained (not altogether humorously, the context considered) that impudence is "the Gift of Nature," that a man must be *born* with it, he continued in a typical vein: "Tho' Nature however must give the Seeds, Art may cultivate them. To improve or depress their Growth is greatly within the Power of Education" (*CGJ,* No. 48;

ESSAYS

Jensen, II, 27).[92] In the *Covent-Garden Journal* he assigned to early habits (hence early education) a large role in shaping the mature individual:

"Habit hath been often called a second Nature, the former may indeed be said to govern and direct the latter. I am much deceived, (and so was Mr. Lock too) if from our earliest Habits we do not in a great Measure derive those Dispositions, which are commonly called our Nature, and which afterwards constitute our Characters"—(*CGJ*, No. 66; Jensen, II, 110).[93]

Thus one line of emphasis in Fielding is upon man's free will, his educability, his power to change himself or win a conquest over his passions. Running quite counter to this belief, however, is a strain that one might almost call deterministic, a conception of man's character as directed by "some unacquired original Distinction" found in the soul at birth. Lying between these two contrary assumptions was a third which leaned, if anything, toward the deterministic (and which must somewhat qualify Fielding's faith in education): namely, the belief that a character formed by *early* education and habits was incapable of further modification, but remained immutably what it had been created

[92] Cf. (as analogue, not source) Cicero's "Sunt enim ingeniis nostris *semina innata virtutum* . . . &c." (*Tusculan Disputations* III. i. 2; italics mine). The whole passage is interesting: "The seeds of virtue are inborn in our dispositions and, if they were allowed to ripen, nature's own hand would lead us on to happiness of life; as things are, however, as soon as we come into the light of day and have been acknowledged, we at once find ourselves in a world of iniquity amid a medley of wrong beliefs, so that it seems as if we drank in deception with our nurse's milk . . ." (Loeb Library, p. 227).

[93] This was a commonplace of contemporary psychology that even a high-churchman like Daniel Waterland could repeat: "Perhaps a great deal of what we are used to call *natural temper*, is little more than that particular frame of heart which was first infused in our education" ("Religious Education of Children . . . A Sermon," in *Works* [11v., Oxford, 1823-1828], VIII, 477). Though Locke gave it new currency (as Fielding's comment suggests), the idea is ultimately Platonic in origin (for example, *Laws* 653). It is also stressed by Aristotle in the *Nicomachean Ethics*.

219

ESSAYS

by its rearing.[94] When Fielding speaks of man's "nature," it is not always clear whether he means "original nature" or this "second nature"; but he very often conceived of it as unyielding and unalterable. Thus, in the essay under consideration, he had argued as the better part of prudence that "I think we may with Justice suspect, at least so far as to deny him our Confidence, that a Man whom we once knew to be a Villain, remains a Villain still" (*Misc.*, I, 222). And he had slight hope of converting such "Bad Minds," to use his own favorite phrase. No amount of benevolence, Fielding said in *Jonathan Wild*, could eradicate from "bad and Great Minds" the opinion that those they had injured would seek retaliation (III, iv; *Misc.*, III, 214); neither "history nor fable," he declared in *Tom Jones*, "have ever yet ventured to record an instance of any one who, by force of argument and reason, hath triumphed over habitual avarice" (XIV, viii; Henley, v, 134). And so on. The character of Robinson in *Amelia* is a dramatization of Fielding's belief, not so much in innate evil (for Robinson "had naturally a good disposition" before he was led into the paths of vice), but in the incapability of corrupted minds to reform. This character, moved by the miseries of Booth and his family, brings evidence against Amelia's evil sister and restores Amelia to her inheritance. But in the last chapter Fielding offers him no forgiveness:

"The witness for some time seemed to reform his life, and received a small pension from Booth; after which he returned to vicious courses, took a purse on the highway,

[94] Fielding could have found ample justification for this conviction, of course, in earlier moralists. Aristotle, for example, says that although the choice of good or evil is voluntary and within man's power, a continued course of vice may make reform impossible: "When you have thrown a stone, you cannot afterwards bring it back again, but nevertheless you are responsible for having taken up the stone and flung it, for the origin of the act was within you. Similarly the unjust and profligate might at the outset have avoided becoming so, and therefore they are so voluntarily, although when they have become unjust and profligate it is no longer open to them not to be so" (*Nic. Ethics* III. v. 14; 1114a; Loeb Library, transl. H. Rackham, p. 149).

was detected and taken, and followed the last steps of his old master [to the gallows]. So apt are men whose manners have been once thoroughly corrupted, to return, from any dawn of an amendment into the dark paths of vice."— (XII, ix; Henley, VII, 339-40).

This tendency to find mature human nature relatively fixed and incapable of growth or change was given support by rhetorical and literary as well as psychological principles. The Aristotelian-Horatian dictum of self-consistency or "decorum" of character in literature had, of course, been firmly established by a host of later commentators and critics,[95] and its influence was still operative in the eighteenth century. Fielding capped a discussion of this *literary* principle ("what the dramatic critics call conservation of character") in *Tom Jones* by moving to a *psychological* conclusion: "I will venture to say that for a man to act in direct contradiction to the dictates of his nature is, if not impossible, as improbable and as miraculous as anything which can well be conceived" (VIII, i; Henley, IV, 65). Here, one's "nature" is obviously thought of as a permanent and unchangeable fact. So also Fielding's habit of dividing "Mankind" into definite categories—in the *Essay*, for example: "the artful and cunning Part of Mankind" or "the crafty and designing Part of Mankind," as opposed to "the more open[,] honest

[95] See John S. Coolidge, "Fielding and 'Conservation of Character,'" *MP*, LVII (1960), 245-59; and Marvin T. Herrick, *Comic Theory in the Sixteenth Century* (Urbana, Ill., 1950), pp. 130 ff. and esp. p. 149. The insistence upon "character development" in fiction is, of course, a notion of very recent vintage; for most of the history of fiction, consistency ("decorum") has been a more important desideratum. There is a measure of "development" in Tom Jones, but Fielding's nearest approach to this fashion of our times comes perhaps with Booth in *Amelia*. As I have previously argued, however (p. 86, n. 59), it is my belief that his major concern in presenting Booth's "conversion" was not literary (in a narrow sense), but moral. He was seeking, I think, to assure his readers—and, given his doubts about the re-educability of a once-corrupted mind, perhaps himself—that Booth's reformation would be permanent, that a true *change* had been effected. This assurance, it would seem, could only be offered in terms of religion, of an outside force that introduced a new determinant in the man's very nature.

and considering Part of Mankind"—shows a tendency to consider men in general as possessing static or fixed natures. It is this habit of mind, I think, that lay behind his flirtation with physiognomy; for that "science" presupposed a basic and unchanging nature behind the appearance or the mask:

"But however cunning the Disguise be which a Masquerader wears: however foreign to his Age, Degree, or Circumstance, yet if closely attended to, he very rarely escapes the Discovery of an accurate Observer; for Nature, which unwillingly submits to the Imposture, is ever endeavouring to peep forth and shew herself; nor can the Cardinal, the Friar, or the Judge, long conceal the Sot, the Gamester, or the Rake"—(Misc., I, 185).

Or, as he had said in the poem, "TO JOHN HAYES, Esq;"—"Men what they are not struggle to appear, / And Nature strives to shew them as they are . . ." (Misc., I, 37).

These opposed emphases in Fielding's thought—upon free will or educability when urging positive reform, and upon the stable or immutable when generalizing about man's original or habitual nature—were really not reconcilable, and they led him into some uneasy moments. An interesting analogy is presented by a discussion of taste in the *Covent-Garden Journal,* which I should like to quote. It seems to me that if one substitutes "goodness" for "taste" in this rather tortuous argument, a real insight is gained into the dilemma that faced Fielding as a practical moralist. He begins with a generalization, such as we have previously seen him make about good-nature, that "as for the Bulk of Mankind, they are clearly void of any Degree of Taste"; then, as the full implications of this pronouncement strike him, he qualifies it in a manner that has obvious corollary implications in the moral sphere:

"From what I have said, it may perhaps be thought to appear, that true Taste is the real Gift of Nature only; and if so, some may ask, *To what Purpose have I endeavoured*

ESSAYS

to show Men that they are without a Blessing, which it is impossible for them to attain? [italics mine]

"Now, tho' it is certain that to the highest Consummation of Taste, as well as of every other Excellence, Nature must lend much Assistance; yet great is the Power of Art almost of itself, or at best with only slender Aids from Nature; and to say the Truth, there are very few who have not in their Minds some small Seeds of Taste. *All Men* (says Cicero) *have a sort of tacit Sense of what is right or wrong in Arts and Sciences, even without the help of Arts.* This surely it is in the Power of Art very greatly to improve. That most Men therefore proceed no farther than as I have above declared, is owing either to the want of any, or (which is perhaps yet worse) to an improper Education"—(*CGJ*, No. 10; Jensen, I, 196-97).

Fielding was not unaware, I think, that his emotional commitment to the belief, "once a villain, always a villain," conflicted with his hope that human nature could be brought to "that perfection of which it is susceptible" (*Voyage to Lisbon*, Henley, XVI, 201). He sought at times to evade the conflict by setting forth, like Shaftesbury, a theory of the mixed nature of man that he had learned from experience as well as from history and biography.[96] Hence we find the reiterated assertion that we should "not too hastily nor in the Gross . . . bestow either our Praise or Censure: Since we shall often find such a Mixture of Good and Evil in the same Character, that it may require a very accurate Judgment and elaborate Inquiry to determine

[96] Parson Adams reproaches the gentleman-hunter in *Joseph Andrews* (II, ix), for declaring that he would hang all cowards: "Adams answered, 'That would be too severe; that men did not make themselves; and if fear had too much ascendance in the mind, the man was rather to be pitied than abhorred; that reason and time might teach him to subdue it.' He said, 'A man might be a coward at one time, and brave at another. Homer,' says he, 'who so well understood and copied nature, hath taught us this lesson; for Paris fights and Hector runs away'." (Henley, I, 157). Hence Fielding's objections (in theory) to the drawing of perfectly good or completely evil characters (see *Jonathan Wild*, IV, iv, *Misc.*, III, 315; *Tom Jones*, VII, i, Henley, III, 334-35; and X, i, Henley, IV, 195).

ESSAYS

which Side the Ballance turns..." (JW, I, i; Misc., III, 2-3). This was the burden of his poem to John Hayes in the *Miscellanies*,[97] and it was an argument Fielding often employed in asking for a more tolerant judgment of his fellow men. It did not, however, satisfactorily resolve his dilemma as a practising moralist.

In effect, Fielding escaped the dilemma by narrowing the sphere of his moral exhortations. As we have seen, his "theory" admitted the possibility of reform in natures not totally corrupted, but saw some men as possessed by ineradicable evil. The latter, therefore, he realistically dismissed from consideration (as had some of the Stoic philosophers, incidentally), and set himself rather to carry out a two-fold program of trying to bring essentially uncorrupted men to an awareness (a *felt* and imaginatively *pictured* awareness) of their own follies and vices, and concurrently of schooling them in the traps set by the evil and designing part of mankind. In the *Champion*, for example, after a strong reprehension of malice and slander, he declared:

"But, as *it would be absurd to represent the baseness of an action, with a view of dissuading such corrupted minds from its pursuits*; I shall therefore address myself only to those who, from less criminal principles, assist these persons

[97] There, it will be remembered, he employed the idea of man's mixture of passions to confute "Codrus,"

> Who nothing knows of Humankind, but Ill:
> Confining all his Knowledge, and his Art,
> To this, that each Man is corrupt at Heart.
> (*Misc.*, I, 36)

Rather, Fielding says,

> ... see how various Men at once will seem;
> How Passions blended on each other fix,
> How Vice with Virtues, Faults with Graces mix;
> How Passions opposite, as sour to sweet,
> Shall in one Bosom at one Moment meet.
> (*Misc.*, I, 36-37)

It should be noted that such statements as these do not at all imply that man is capable of growth or change in *essential* character, but only that any man *as he is* represents a complex of passions rather than a simple unity.

ESSAYS

in spreading their calumnies, and, being moved perhaps by a little envy or spleen, or wantonness, content themselves that they were not the original authors of the slander, which they use their utmost diligence in promoting. *To such, as they are not totally abandoned, though very far from being innocent, it may not be improper to represent this vice in its natural, odious colours,* and of which the reporter is guilty, though not in so detestable a degree as the first inventor"—(6 March 1740; Henley, xv, 232-33; italics mine).

As he expressed it a decade later in the Preface to *Tom Jones*: "Lastly, I have endeavoured strongly to inculcate, that virtue and innocence can scarce ever be injured but by indiscretion; and that it is this alone which often betrays them into the snares that deceit and villainy spread for them. A moral which I have the more industriously laboured, as the teaching it is, of all others, the likeliest to be attended with success; since, I believe, *it is much easier to make good men wise, than to make bad men good*"—(Henley, III, 12; italics mine).[98]

In his direct exhortations Fielding followed the usual practice of eighteenth-century moralists, urging upon his readers, who would mostly believe with him that the passions were the springs of human action, the necessity of (1) acting habitually from the dictates of their *good* passions (for example, benevolence), and (2) moderating and harmonizing the complex of passions in the human soul by a shaping reason and will. But he characteristically had more faith in example than in precept, and what he set himself particularly to do was to seize his readers' imaginations by dramatic pictures of good and evil in action. David Hume, in his *Enquiry*, began by distinguishing two ways of treating moral philosophy: one which would "consider man in the light of a reasonable rather than an active being, and

[98] Cf. Swift: "The Preaching of Divines helps to preserve well-inclined Men in the Course of Virtue; but seldom or never reclaims the Vicious" ("Thoughts on Various Subjects," *Prose Works*, ed. Herbert Davis, IV, 246).

endeavour to form his understanding more than cultivate his manners," and another which "considers man chiefly as born for action; and as influenced in his measures by taste and sentiment." Fielding, for all of his honest respect for human reason, assuredly belonged as an artist to the latter group—which Hume further described as follows:

"As virtue, of all objects, is allowed to be the most valuable, this species of philosophers paint her in the most amiable colours; borrowing all helps from poetry and eloquence, and treating their subject in an easy and obvious manner, and such as is best fitted to please the imagination, and engage the affections. They select the most striking observations and instances from common life; place opposite characters in a proper contrast; and alluring us into the paths of virtue by the views of glory and happiness, direct our steps in these paths by the soundest precepts and most illustrious examples. They make us *feel* the difference between vice and virtue; they excite and regulate our sentiments; and so they can but bend our hearts to the love of probity and true honour, they think, that they have fully attained the end of all their labours."[99]

To make men *feel* the difference between vice and virtue was precisely Fielding's end. He believed that if, in Lockean terms, he could "annex the ideas of fear and shame to every idea of evil" (cf. *Amelia*, IV, iii; Henley, VI, 191),[100] if he could enlist his readers' imaginations by "painting"—for imagination and pictures always go together in Fielding's mind—the scenes that would raise tender or indignant "ideas," he would be able to achieve his purpose of winning men of good will to the side of virtue and decency.[101] Good-

[99] An *Enquiry concerning the Human Understanding*, ed. L. A. Selby-Bigge (Oxford, 1894), pp. 5-6.
[100] Thus in dealing wtih the problem of executions, in Section xi of the *Enquiry into the Causes of the Late Increase of Robbers*, he conceived the main end to be "to unite the ideas of death and shame" (Henley, XIII, 123).
[101] See above, p. 57 and n. 27; and Tom Jones's appeal to Nightingale (XIV, vii), in which he proceeds "in the liveliest manner to paint the

natured men sometimes were guilty of thoughtless follies or crimes—as, for example, joining in the cruel sport of "roasting." "These," says Fielding, "did they consider the nature and consequence of their pursuing this amusement, would, I believe, soon condemn it" (*Champion*, 13 March 1740; Henley, xv, 242). It was in this faith that if the imagination of good men could be stimulated to see things "in their true and proper light," they would naturally follow the reasonable and humane path, that Fielding carried on the first half of his two-fold moral program.

The second purpose—to set simplicity on its guard and make it a match for cunning—was, of course, a primary theme of the *Miscellanies* and of Fielding's work in general. His desire was to inculcate "some degree of suspicion and caution in our dealing with mankind" (*Champion*, 11 December 1739; Henley, xv, 96), so that the good-natured man might be on equal terms with the designing villains who, in Fielding's favorite image, were like great pikes seeking to fatten themselves on unsuspecting gudgeons. It is this desire to even the scales that accounts for Fielding's continual insistence upon the virtue of Prudence, despite the curious fact that most of the people actually described as "prudent" in his novels are hypocrites or knaves.[102]

---

tragical story" of poor Nancy. His argument is crowded with such phrases as, "Set the alternative fairly before your eyes . . . On the one side, see . . . Paint to your imagination the circumstances . . . View the poor, helpless orphan infant; and when your mind hath dwelt a moment only on such ideas . . ." (Henley, v, 121-26). This is, of course, the *enargeia* encompassed by rhetorical techniques variously termed *descriptio*, *diatyposis*, or *hypotyposis*. (On *enargeia* see, besides Longinus, Quintilian, *Inst. orat.* vi. ii. 26-36.) Fielding praised Edward Moore's *Foundling* in the *Jacobite's Journal* No. 16 (19 March 1748), for carrying out a like endeavor: "The Redemption from Evil, by the conscious Shame which results from having a base Action set before him in its true and genuine Deformity, shews great Knowledge of Human Nature in the Author. . . ."

[102] Though I have foregone a long excursus on the matter, it is perhaps worth pointing out that Fielding's conception of prudence, like that of good-nature, could be placed on a scale or continuum of values, one end of which would represent the Aristotelian φρόνησις, or rational sense of the good and advantageous for humankind in general, whereas

ESSAYS

The *Essay on the Knowledge of the Characters of Men* illustrates very graphically Fielding's hope that if honest men could be schooled in seeing beyond the masks worn by those who would prey on them, if they could learn to recognize the real passion—of ambition, or of greed, or of spurious sanctity—which was the spring of the hypocrite's actions, they could then set up their defenses accordingly. Fielding did not believe that the knowledge of men could be reduced to a positive science; all he hoped to do in this essay was to provide some of the more obvious indices by which an inherent hypocrisy and tendency to evil could be discerned. Unfortunately, any such hope rested perforce upon a belief in somewhat elementary and more or less static psychological principles of human nature. The *Essay*, though it embodies some of Fielding's major convictions, is rather less acute in its perceptions than his novels, for in them he turned from a theory of descriptive psychology to the dramatization of the human comedy and based his portraits of men more largely upon his own superb intuitions and upon empirical observation drawn from the vast authentic Doomsday-book of nature. *Alter praecepta virtutis dat, alter exemplar.*[103]

3. "OF THE REMEDY OF AFFLICTION For the LOSS of our FRIENDS"

The best evidence of a *terminus a quo* for the composition of the *Remedy* lies in a passage that has frequently been quoted by biographers of Fielding. He says, near the end of the essay:

"I remember the most excellent of Women, and tenderest of Mothers, when, after a painful and dangerous Deliv-

---

the lower end would represent something very close to that calculating sense of personal advantage which Aristotle also considers (*Nic. Ethics* VI. viii. 3-4; 1141b-1142a) and which we normally think of today when we hear the word.

[103] "The one gives the precepts of virtue, the other its exemplification" (Seneca, *Epist. mor.* xcv. 66).

ESSAYS

ery, she was told she had a Daughter, answering; *Good God! have I produced a Creature who is to undergo what I have suffered!* Some Years afterwards, I heard the same Woman, on the Death of that very Child, then one of the loveliest Creatures ever seen, comforting herself with reflecting, that *her Child could never know what it was to feel such a Loss as she then lamented"—(Misc.,* I, 319).

This passage refers, of course, to the birth and death of Fielding's daughter, Charlotte, who was buried at St. Martin's in the Fields on 9 March 1742.[104] Earlier in the essay, Fielding had declared that he was undertaking to present his reader with the best remedies for the alleviation of grief that he was capable of furnishing, "many of which have this uncommon Recommendation, that I have tried them upon myself with some Success" (*Misc.*, I, 302). That this refers to his own grief at his daughter's death seems beyond question.

From this organic evidence, then, the essay would appear to have been written in the period between March 1742 and April 1743, when the *Miscellanies* were published.

2

Fielding opens his essay[105] with a citation from Book III of the *Tusculan Disputations*: "IT would be a strange Consideration (saith *Cicero*) that while so many excellent Remedies have been discovered for the several Diseases of the human Body, the Mind should be left without any Assistance to alleviate and repel the Disorders which befal it" (*Misc.*, I, 297). Cicero and other sages had recommended the remedy of philosophy and of that detached

---

[104] The child had been born in April 1736 (Cross, I, 177, 351).

[105] I have drawn my translations throughout this section from the following volumes in the Loeb Classical Library: Cicero: *Epistulae ad familiares*, transl. W. Glynn Williams (3v., 1927-29); *Tusculan Disputations*, transl. J. E. King (1927). Seneca: *Ad Lucilium epistulae morales*, transl. Richard M. Gummere (3v., 1917-25); *Moral Essays*, transl. John W. Basore (3v., 1928-35); Plutarch: *Moralia* (Vol. II [1928], transl. Frank C. Babbitt) (14v., in progress).

229

attitude which could "look on Poverty, Pain, Disgrace, and Death, as Things indifferent" (1, 299). The fallacy, however, in this admirable philosophic stance, says Fielding, is that in truth it is but to have a sound mental constitution: the great authorities are saying "no more, than that Health is a Remedy against Disease" (1, 299). The masters themselves could not be said always to have honored their precepts by their examples and in succeeding years they have found few perfect disciples. Ordinary mortals suffering from affliction have need of "a mental Physician" who will consider the human mind "in too weak and depraved a Situation to be restored to firm Vigour and Sanity, and should propose rather to palliate and lessen its Disorders, than absolutely to cure them." Specifically, then, Fielding proposes to suggest remedies for one type of "disease" to which the mind is unhappily subjected, namely "*Affliction for the Death of our Friends* . . . a Malady to which the best and worthiest of Men are chiefly liable" (1, 300). One of the most agonizing trials that life can offer, such affliction may be effectually overcome only by reason and time; but, says Fielding, even though in a humane disposition the calamity cannot be soon or totally removed, it is worth seeking a means to lessen it.[106]

Fielding argues first that, even before the affliction occurs, we should prepare ourselves for it; while still enjoying our friends, we should reflect upon the certainty of

[106] Perhaps the most effective way to indicate the highly traditional nature of Fielding's topics of consolation is to offer a running parallel with some of the famous classic *consolatione* and with a good contemporary specimen of the genre, the latitudinarian Simon Patrick's "A Consolatory Discourse To prevent *Immoderate Grief* FOR THE DEATH OF OUR FRIENDS," included in *The Hearts Ease. Or, A Remedy against All Troubles* (my citations from the 7th ed., 1699; the original ed. of *The Hearts Ease* was 1660). Fielding's *exordium* draws heavily upon the opening section of Book III of the *Tusculan Disputations*, even to the argument he directs against the "sages" (on this cf. also *Tusc. Disp.* III. xxxii. 77, Cicero's criticism of Cleanthes). In his consolatory letter to Titius (*Epistulae ad familiares* v. xvi), Cicero, like Fielding, offers only "some such measure of consolation as might mitigate, if it could not succeed in remedying, your sorrow" (v. xvi. 1).

230

our ultimately losing them. For "one of the first Ingredients of a *wise* Man [is], that nothing befals him entirely unforeseen, and unexpected"; this is "the principal Means of taking his Happiness or Misery out of the Hands of Fortune" (1, 303). By considering beforehand that any human relationship is necessarily brief and subject to accident, we may prepare ourselves in some measure to accept the inevitable. "Had not the wise Man frequently meditated on these Subjects, he would not have cooly answered the Person who acquainted him with the Death of his Son—I KNEW *I had begot a Mortal*";[107] whereas the grief of some men might lead one to suppose "that something uncommon, and beyond the general Fate of Men, had happened to them" (1, 305). Further, he says, just as the loss of a blessing teaches us its true value, so these reflections should add a relish to the present possession of our friends—"Shall we not, in a Word, return to their Conversation, after such Reflections, with the same Eagerness and Extasy, with which we receive those we love into our Arms, when we first wake from a Dream which hath terrified us with their Deaths?" (1, 306).[108]

[107] This famous *exemplum*, the hero of which is usually said to be the philosopher Anaxagoras, is a favorite in the *consolatione*. See Cicero, *Tusc. Disp.* III. xiv. 30; Seneca, *De consolatione ad Polybium* XI. 2; Plutarch, *Consolatio ad Apollonium* 118d-e; and Patrick, *op.cit.*, p. 107. It is curious, however, that Fielding should have been able to cite this story with approval when a mere four pages earlier he had fulminated against "the calm Demeanor" of Stilpo, the Cynic philosopher, on a like occasion, declaring that "this sudden unruffled Composure is owing to meer Insensibility; to a Depravity of the Heart, not Goodness of the Understanding" (1, 301). Seneca approved heartily of Stilpo's firm behavior (see *Epist. mor.* IX. 18-19); and, according to W. L. Ustick, Stilpo was "frequently cited by sixteenth- and seventeenth-century writers on conduct" as the extreme example of "Stoic" indifference ("Changing Ideals of Aristocratic Character and Conduct in Seventeenth-Century England," *MP*, xxx [1932], 149, n. 3).

[108] Patrick advises reminding our friends that we and they are mortal: "Doth it make our love the less? Doth it make us avoid their presence? No, therefore we are so greedy of our friends society, because we know not how long we may enjoy them" (p. 108). Seneca says gnomically, "He robs present ills of their power who has perceived their coming beforehand" (*De consolatione ad Marciam* IX. 5). Cicero urges the "prae-

He now goes on to present some suggestions for rational conduct once the catastrophe has actually befallen. "And here I address myself to common Men, and who partake of the more amiable Weaknesses of Human Nature; not to those elevated Souls whom the Consummation of Virtue and Philosophy hath raised to a divine Pitch of Excellence, and placed beyond the Reach of human Calamity . . ." (1, 306-07). Tears and lamentations, he insists, are not marks of effeminacy, but "Symptoms of a laudable Tenderness"; nevertheless, he warns, we are not to abandon ourselves to this emotion, natural though it be. With the passage of time, the violence of first passions may be expected to subside, and then Reason is to be called to our assistance (1, 307-08).[109] Unwillingness to heed the voice of reason arises from "a foolish Opinion, that Friendship requires an exorbitant Affliction of us," a sacrifice to the

---

meditatio futurorum malorum" (*Tusc. Disp.* III. xiv. 29) and the consolation "that all that has happened is natural to human life" (III. xxiii. 57). Cf. also Plutarch, *Consolatio ad Apollonium* 112d. The "consolatio pervulgata" that we are all mortal is offered by Cicero (*Ad fam.* v. xvi. 2) and, again, by Plutarch (*Ad Apoll.* 103-04).

[109] Patrick explains that he is not setting out to extirpate grief "by taking you off from all love and friendship. . . . Neither do I intend to write like a Stoick, and stupifie all your passions, so that you should not mourn at all, for that is an impossible thing, if we have any love" (p. 89). He warns against an *intemperate* grief, however, as unreasonable, unnatural, and unchristian (pp. 250-51). Plutarch also insists that grief is natural and attacks the Stoic *ataraxia* as "impossible and unprofitable" (*Ad Apoll.* 102c). In point of fact, however, the most famous Stoic *consolatione* say the same thing: "But never will I demand of you that you should not grieve at all. And I well know that some men are to be found whose wisdom is harsh rather than brave, who deny that the wise man will ever grieve. But these, it seems to me, can never have fallen upon this sort of mishap. . . . Reason will have accomplished enough if only she removes from grief whatever is excessive and superfluous; it is not for anyone to hope or to desire that she should suffer us to feel no sorrow at all" (Seneca, *De consolatione ad Polybium* XVIII. 5-6); or, "We are not sprung from rock, but our souls have a strain of tenderness and sensitiveness of a kind to be shaken by distress as by a storm" (Cicero, *Tusc. Disp.* III. vi. 12). Seneca's wise maxim, "lacrimandum est, non plorandum"—we may weep, but we must not wail (*Epistulae morales ad Lucilium* LXIII. 1)—was, in fact, cited with approval by Patrick (p. 90).

ESSAYS

manes of the departed, so to speak; or, from the curious satisfaction that we ourselves feel in this indulgence which serves as a kind of temporary release for pent-up emotions.[110] This present relief ultimately results in an increase of the distemper (I, 308-09).[111]

Advising that one should avoid circumstances which may revive memories of the deceased, Fielding declares: "Such is the Perverseness of our Natures, we are constantly endeavouring, at every Opportunity, to recal to our Remembrance the Words, Looks, Gestures, and other Particularities of a Friend," or are carrying about tokens of the dead. This is to fail in lending assistance to time, "the truest and best Physician on these Occasions" (I, 310). Again, he permits himself to doubt the efficacy of "Diversions of the lightest Kind," music, dancing, and the like, for the nature of the former in particular is "to soothe or inflame, not to alter our Passions." Rather than as a cure, he suggests in a witty inversion that they should be used as a test: "For when they can be pursued with any good Effect, our Affliction is, I apprehend, very little grievous or dangerous" (I, 311).[112]

[110] Booth tells Miss Matthews that "those know little of real love or grief who do not know how much we deceive ourselves when we pretend to aim at the cure of either. It is with these, as it is with some distempers of the body; nothing is in the least agreeable to us but what serves to heighten the disease" (*Amelia*, II, iii; Henley, VI, 78).

[111] Cicero declared, "But when . . . we entertain also the idea that it is an obligation, that it is right, that it is a matter of duty to be distressed at what has happened, then, and not before, the disturbing effect of deep distress ensues. In consequence of this idea come the different odious forms of mourning . . ." (*Tusc. Disp.* III. xxvi. 61-62). Seneca is even more severe: "We seek the proofs of our bereavement in our tears, and do not give way to sorrow, but merely parade it. . . . There is an element of self-seeking even in our sorrow" (*Epist. mor.* LXIII. 2).

[112] The first notion seems to be Fielding's own personal conviction; it is not among the normal *topoi* of the classic *consolatio*. The second may have been partly inspired by Cicero's mocking attack upon the Epicurean ideas of consolation (*Tusc. Disp.* III. xv. 32ff.). The *Spectator*, in like vein, recommended "Books of Morality, which indeed are of great use to fortifie and strengthen the Mind against the Impressions of Sorrow," rather than St. Évremond's suggestion of reading *Don Quixote* and other mirthful works (No. 163, Everyman ed., I, 491-93). Against

233

ESSAYS

The two greatest instruments for the relief of such perturbations of the spirit (my elegancy: Fielding says "mental Disorder") are philosophy and religion. From the former "Fountain"—and it will be noted that he has here introduced a new and unnecessary *divisio*, since the foregoing arguments have proceeded from the same fountain—he draws the following considerations: first, "the Injustice of our Complaint," since we are, after all, but "Tenants at Will to Fortune, and as we have advanced no Consideration on our Side, can have no Right to accuse her Caprice in determining our Estate" (I, 312); and the reminder is made that the "Condition of our Tenure" must be fulfilled sooner or later, and we should be grateful for whatever time it lasts (I, 313).[113]

"I shall not go into the hackneyed Common-place of the numberless Avenues to Death," Fielding continues, "a Road almost as much beaten by Writers, as those Avenues to Death are by Mankind"; nevertheless, it is certain that all of us must die, must travel one or another of those avenues in good time (I, 313-14). Our lamentations, he says, are indeed not for the death itself of our friend, but

---

this background we may consider Lady Booby at the death of her husband, "who, departing this life, left his disconsolate lady confined to her house as closely as if she herself had been attacked by some violent disease. During the first six days the poor lady admitted none but Mrs. Slipslop, and three female friends, who made a party at cards . . ." (JA, I, v; Henley, I, 36).

[113] Patrick demands, "Did he [God] ever promise you how long you should have it [your mortal friend]? may he not call for his own when he thinks good?" (p. 102); and, repeating the argument later that the person was only a loan, he advises: "Think then of the time past, and rejoyce that thou didst find so sweet a friend" (p. 184). Seneca, in his *De consolatione ad Marciam* (x. 1-4), points out that all our fortuitous possessions "are not our own but borrowed trappings; not one of them is given to us outright. . . . The use and the enjoyment are ours, but the dispenser of the gift determines the length of our tenure." Plutarch, after citing Euripides on the same theme—"We keep and care for that which is the gods' "—says, "We ought not, therefore, to bear it with bad grace if the gods make demand upon us for what they have loaned us for a short time" (*Ad Apoll.* 116a-b). So also Cicero on the term of Nature's loan (*Tusc. Disp.* I. xxxix. 93).

ESSAYS

for the *time* of his dying: "We desire not a Pardon, we desire a Reprieve only. A Reprieve, for how long? *Sine Die*" (I, 314). But no matter how long extended, the time looked back on must always seem as a short span. And even if it should be in some way extended, "shall we not, in Imitation of a Child who desires its Mamma to stay five Minutes, and it will take the Potion, be still as unwilling as ever?" (I, 315).[114]

One of the useful functions of philosophy is that it shows us "the Folly of immoderate Affliction." If tears served to wash our friend back, says Fielding, "I would commend him who out-did the fabled *Niobe* in weeping"; but since no such hope exists, "the Part of a wise Man [is] to bring himself to be content in a Situation which no Wit or Wisdom, Labour or Art, Trouble or Pain, can alter" (I, 315-16).[115] Indeed, Fielding says, "let us seriously ex-

[114] For the "numberless Avenues," Patrick may suffice: he observes with grim satisfaction that wind, lightning, fire, smoke, the dust of the earth, water, our meat and drink, "our own passions, our Joy, our Sorrow, and a thousand other things can bring us to our Graves" (p. 100); later, more effectively, he quotes Erasmus' *mot*: "*There is one way of coming into the World, but a wonderful variety of going out*" (p. 114). In denying that there was any such thing as an "untimely" death, the classical moralists frequently drew an analogy between man's brief existence and that of the ephemera, or some like insect. "What lifetime in fact is long, or what is there long at all for a human being?" asks Cicero (*Tusc. Disp.* I. xxxix. 94); and Seneca tells a mourner who complains that his son perished "too soon and before his time," "suppose he had survived—grant him the very longest life a man can have—how many years are there after all? Born as we are for the briefest space, and destined soon to yield place to another coming into his lease of time, we view our life as a sojourn at an inn" (*Ad Marc.* xxi. 1). Cf. also Plutarch, *Ad Apoll.* 113c-e.

[115] Analogues on immoderate grief have already been considered; but the image of tears was equally conventional. So Patrick: "If you can bring them back again with your tears, if there be any hopes that with the noise you make they should revive to comfort you; then you have leave to weep as much as you please" (p. 101). Seneca advises Marcia: "If tears can vanquish fate, let us marshal tears. . . . But if no wailing can recall the dead, if no distress can alter a destiny that is immutable and fixed for all eternity, and if death holds fast whatever it has once carried off, then let grief, which is futile, cease" (*Ad Marc.* vi. 1-2). And Plutarch cites some vigorous lines from the comic dramatist, Philemon, to the same effect (*Ad Apoll.* 105f).

ESSAYS

amine our Hearts, whether it is for the Sake of our Friends, or ourselves, that we grieve"—and he finds himself ready to agree with La Rochefoucauld[116] "that *the Lamentation expressed for the Loss of our dearest Friends, is often, in Reality, for ourselves; that we are concerned at being less happy, less easy, and of less Consequence than we were before; and thus the Dead enjoy the Honour of those Tears which are truly shed on Account of the Living*: concluding, —that *in these Afflictions Men impose on themselves*" (I, 316).[117]

If the mourner grieves for himself, Fielding says, "I shall leave the Patient to seek his Remedy elsewhere; having first recommended to him, an Assembly, a Ball, an Opera, a Play, an Amour, or, if he please, all of them, which will very speedily produce his Cure" (I, 316). But if "our Sorrow arises from that pure and disinterested Affection which many Minds are so far from being capable of entertaining, that they can have no Idea of it," in a word, if our fears are sincerely on our friend's account, it may be worth considering "the Nature and Degree of this Misfortune which hath happened to him"; for if it can be shown that death is not the "dreadful Calamity" we suppose, then "the very Foundation of our Grief will be removed, and it must, of necessary Consequence, immediately cease" (I, 317).[118]

[116] Cf. La Rochefoucauld, *Maximes & Réflexions Diverses*, ed. Henry A. Grubbs (Princeton, 1929), pp. 55-56 (Maxim No. 233), and also "Maximes Suprimées," p. 119 (No. 619).

[117] This is one of the commonest topics of the *consolatio*, and is sometimes presented very bluntly. Patrick says that the first question to ask yourself is *"For whose sake dost thou weep?* For the sake of him that's dead, or for thy own?" (p. 174). Seneca advises Polybius, "It will also serve as a great relief, if you will often question yourself thus: 'Am I grieving on my own account, or on account of him who has departed? If on my own account, this parade of affection is idle . . .'" (*Ad Polyb.* IX. 1). He poses the same question to Marcia (*Ad Marc.* XII. 1). So also Cicero to Titius (*Ad fam.* v. xvi. 4), and Plutarch to Apollonius, the latter less directly: "But do those who mourn for the untimely dead, mourn on their own account or on account of the departed?" (*Ad Apoll.* 111e).

[118] One marvels at the miraculous "suddenty" (as the Scots have it)

ESSAYS

Arguing next "that Death is not that King of Terrors, as he is represented to be" (I, 318), Fielding cites Thales, Socrates, Solomon, and Cicero (*De senectute*) as eminent authorities who have assured us that there is a balance of evil over real happiness in life. He concludes, "If therefore Life be no general Good, Death is no general Evil" (I, 318).[119] But even "if we will be hardy enough to fly in the Face of these and numberless other such Authorities," Fielding says, and maintain the worth of Life's pleasures, still we cannot claim them as "lasting, certain, or the Portion of many among us"; whereas no one denies the presence of certain and widespread evil in life. Just as we could not "insure the Possession of [pleasures] to our Friend" nor secure him from evils, so his death makes it as likely that he escaped many of the latter as that he was cut off from the former (I, 319). It is at this point that Fielding introduces the story of his wife's grief at giving birth to one who must undergo a like suffering—and her consolation at the girl's death, "that *her Child could never know what it was to feel such a Loss as she then lamented*" (I, 319). In reality, he adds, she was right in both responses; for however youth, instinct, high spirits, or folly may blind us, "the

---

with which the *consolateurs* expected their logic to operate. Patrick says, "Let me then propose these Questions to be answered, some of which will discover that there is no cause of sad lamentations when our friends dye. And if there be no cause that the fountain of tears should run, that is cause enough to stop it up" (p. 174). And Cicero declares that when the mourner realizes that his grief is not an act of duty, "By the removal of what is wholly an act of will, the distress of mourning which we have spoken of will at once be done away with . . ." (*Tusc. Disp.* III. xxxiv. 83; the "at once" is perhaps only implicit in the original).

[119] The arguments against the fear of death (such as the First Book of the *Tusculan Disputations* is given over to) take in a larger area than the *consolatio*, as do the complementary arguments that life is a dreadful misery. Plutarch caps a series of citations on this latter point (*Ad Apoll.* 115) with the observation, "One might cite thousands and thousands of examples under this same head, but there is no need to be prolix." This may serve as a timely reproof: I shall let Seneca's phrase represent the whole theme: "Mors dolorum omnium exsolutio est et finis"—death is a release from all our suffering (*Ad Marc.* XIX. 5).

Day of Death is (to most People at least) a Day of more Happiness than that of our Birth, as it puts an End to all those Evils which the other gave a Beginning to" (I, 320).[120] If death, then, is no evil, he concludes, "there is certainly no Reason why we should lament its having happened to our Friend . . ." (I, 320). For any one who might remain unconvinced, either by his own observation or by Plato, Cicero, or Montaigne,[121] "that Death is not an Evil worthy our Lamentation," he offers what may seem a dubious consolation—"Let such a Man comfort himself, that the Evil which his Friend hath suffered, he shall himself shortly have his Share in" (I, 320).[122]

The essay is brought to a close with one of Fielding's most eloquent and explicit statements of religious faith. Religion, he observes, goes much further than human philosophy can on such an occasion, "and gives us a most delightful Assurance, that our Friend is not barely no Loser, but a Gainer by his Dissolution; that those Virtues and good Qualities which were the Objects of our Affection on

[120] Servius Sulpicius consoled Cicero on the loss of his daughter Tullia by pointing out that she, at least, would not have to watch the impending downfall of the Republic (*Ad fam.* IV. v. 3-5), and Cicero consoled Titius with the same observation (*Ad fam.* v. xvi. 3). In like fashion, Plutarch reflected that if Priam had died before the sack of Troy he would have been happier, and drew the moral: "Since you have, then, so very many examples regarding the matter, bear in mind the fact that death relieves not a few persons from great and grievous ills which, if they had lived on, they would surely have experienced" (*Ad Apoll.* 113f-114c).
[121] Fielding presumably refers to Book I, chap. xix, in Montaigne, "That to Philosophize is to Learn to Die"; but that he had consulted the immediately preceding chapter as well ("That We Are Not to Judge of Our Hour Till After Death") is suggested by the coincidence that both Montaigne and Fielding allude to an *exemplum* of Croesus and Solon, and cite in the immediate context the same illustrative lines from Ovid.
[122] We may conclude our parallels with Seneca's words to Marcia: "What tortures us . . . is an opinion, and every evil is only as great as we have reckoned it to be. In our own hands we have the remedy. Let us consider that the dead are merely absent, and let us deceive ourselves [that is, by pretending this]; we have sent them on their way—nay, we have sent them ahead and shall soon follow" (*Ad Marc.* XIX. 1).

Earth, are now become the Foundation of his Happiness and Reward in a better World" (1, 321).

"Lastly [he concludes]; It gives a Hope, the sweetest, most endearing, and ravishing, which can enter into a Mind capable of, and inflamed with, Friendship. The Hope of again meeting the beloved Person, of renewing and cementing the dear Union in Bliss everlasting. This is a Rapture which leaves the warmest Imagination at a Distance. *Who can conceive* (says *Sherlock*, in his Discourse on Death) *the melting Caresses of two Souls in Paradice?*[123] What are all the Trash and Trifles, the Bubbles, Bawbles and Gewgaws of this Life, to such a Meeting? This is a Hope which no Reasoning shall ever argue me out of, nor Millions of such Worlds as this should purchase: nor can any Man shew me its absolute Impossibility, 'till he can demonstrate that it is not in the Power of the Almighty to bestow it on me"—(1, 321-22).

3

Fielding's essay on consolation is, as I have tried to indicate, in a very ancient and continuing tradition.[124] All the major schools of classical philosophy had sought to come to terms, in one way or another, with the greatest insoluble human problem—the fact of death—and most of

[123] Fielding is, as usual, quoting from memory. The passage in Sherlock reads: "Our imperfect Conceptions of God in this World, cannot help us to guess what the Joys of Heaven are; we know not how the sight of God, how the thoughts of him, will peirce our Souls, with what extasies and raptures we shall sing the Song of the Lamb, with what melting affections perfect Souls shall embrace, what glories and wonders we shall there see and know . . ." (William Sherlock, *Practical Discourse concerning Death* [1689], pp. 85-86).

[124] I have attempted to place Fielding's essay only in the specific tradition of consolation for death, rather than in the broader tradition of consolation in general (cf. Cicero, *Tusc. Disp.* III. xxxiv). A book like the seventeenth-century *Art of Patience under All Afflictions* (1684), for example, offers comfort "In time of Sickness," under "Affliction of Conscience," on "Loss of Reputation," in case "Of publick Calamities," exile, poverty, blindness, sterility—and even in the event "Of Gray-Hairs."

ESSAYS

them were concerned with the solace of the living for the losses death occasioned them. Seneca (*Ep. mor.* xcv. 65) tells us that Posidonius, the head of the Stoic school at Rhodes (and Cicero's mentor), considered the problem of consolation as a part of moral philosophy; and it was often so treated. The *consolatio* (παραμυθία) was the third topic of the ancient *epitaphios*, the public oration celebrating and memorializing those fallen in battle; it was closely related to the funeral oration, one of the most important forms of epideictic oratory.[125]

The arguments and recommendations in such famous works as Cicero's *Tusculan Disputations* (I and III) and *Epistulae ad familiares* (IV, v; v, xvi); Seneca's *De consolatione ad Marciam, Ad Polybium, Ad Helviam matrem* (on exile, not death) and *Epistulae morales ad Lucilium* (LXIII, XCVIII, and the severe XCIX); and Plutarch's (attributed) *Consolatio ad Apollonium,* among others, were adopted by the patristic writers, particularly Ambrose, Jerome, and Paulinus,

---

[125] The foremost study of the literature of consolation in classic times is that of Carolus [Charles] Buresch, "Consolationum a Graecis Romanisque Scriptorum Historia Critica," in *Leipziger Studien zur classischen Philologie,* IX (1886), 1-164. The influence of the classical *consolatio* upon the early Fathers has been exhaustively analyzed by Charles Favez in *La consolation latine chrétienne* (Paris, 1937), a work to which I am deeply indebted in this study. Further materials concerning the tradition may be found in Constant Martha, "Les consolations dans l'antiquité," in *Études morales sur l'antiquité* (Paris, 1883), pp. 135-89; Sister Mary Evaristus [Moran], *The Consolations of Death in Ancient Greek Literature* (Washington, D.C. [1917?]), and Sister Mary E. Fern, *The Latin Consolatio as a Literary Type* (St. Louis, 1941). Benjamin Boyce has contributed an interesting study of the *consolatio* in the Renaissance, particularly as it appears in the formularies of Erasmus and Angel Day: "The Stoic *Consolatio* and Shakespeare," *PMLA,* LXIV (1949), 771-80. One must suppose that the traditional materials could have come to Fielding through such sources also; and, as Boyce points out, "The consolatory arguments of Cicero, Seneca, and Plutarch were reiterated not only in their several works but also as *sententiae* in popular Renaissance collections of *flores* and in other Renaissance books" (p. 774). For the relationship of the *consolatio* to epideictic oratory, see Theodore C. Burgess, "Epideictic Literature," in *University of Chicago Studies in Classical Philology,* III (1902), 89-261, esp. pp. 156ff. For a larger consideration of the epideictic mode and its significance for Fielding, see below, the *Essay on Nothing.*

ESSAYS

and thus entered from the earliest times into the structure of Christian consolatory literature. But unlike the dominant note in the pagan *consolatio*—that, although we can have no power over exterior conditions, the power of a reasonable man over his own will gives him effectual means to counter the mental ravages of the death of loved ones— the Christian emphasis fell upon the certain hope of immortality and the bliss of the other world which should make the death of those we love a cause for rejoicing rather than sorrow. These contrary emphases persist in Fielding's essay, in the distinction that he makes between the consolatory power of philosophy and the greater efficacy of religion.[126] The distinction may be seen again, briefly stated, in *Tom Jones*; here, after describing Allworthy's sincere grief at the death of Captain Blifil, Fielding says:

"Again, what reader doth not know that philosophy and religion in time moderated, and at last extinguished, this grief? The former of these teaching the folly and vanity of it, and the latter correcting it as unlawful, and at the same time assuaging it by raising future hopes and assurances which enable a strong and religious mind to take leave of a friend on his death-bed with little less indifference than if he was preparing for a long journey; and, indeed, with little less hope of seeing him again"—(III, i; Henley, III, 105-06).

The themes employed in the "philosophical" portion of the *Remedy of Affliction* are largely drawn, as we have

[126] The *divisio* is, of course, a commonplace: "Do but consider, my dear Friend, the many comfortable Arguments, which both Religion and Philosophy suggest to you, on this Occasion . . ." ("To Mr. H." ["A consolatory Letter to a Friend"], in *The Works of Mr. Henry Needler* [2nd ed., 1728], p. 83); "But besides the Considerations of Wisdom and Morality, which ought to set Bounds to extravagant Sorrows, we are to go higher, and call in Sentiments of Religion to our Assistance" (Letter XXVII, "Against immoderate Grief for the Death of Friends," in *A Collection of Miscellany Letters, Selected out of Mist's Weekly Journal* [3v., 1722-1727], III, 133). As Goldsmith's vicar says: "Thus philosophy is weak: but religion comforts in a higher strain" (*The Vicar of Wakefield*, chap. XXIX).

seen, from the commonplaces of classic consolatory literature. Perhaps the most often used, to review them briefly, are (1) the *praemeditatio futurorum malorum,* which prepares one to accept the inevitable event; (2) that "consolatio pervulgata" which Cicero recommended, of recalling the brevity of human life; and (3) the related dwelling upon the fact of human mortality—death is common to all: men must die and others must grieve—"Non tibi hoc soli" [you are not the only one]; (4) the insistence that a public display of grief is not a duty expected of the mourner; (5) the injustice of supposing that one has an eternal right to loved objects, rather than understanding that they are after all but a loan, "mutua accepimus," as Seneca says —a loan which must be surrendered on call (this argument, repeated by Ambrose and Jerome,[127] found its most famous statement in the *De consolatione* of Boethius); (6) the folly of tears and the unnaturalness of excessive despair; (7) the self-interrogation: "Utrumne meo nomine doleo an eius qui decessit?" [Am I grieving on my own account, or on account of him who has departed?];[128] (8) the overall misery of life and the liberation of death: "Mors dolorum omnium exsolutio est"; (9) the theme of *opportunitas mortis*: death has obviated all the ills, trivial and great, that might have plagued the dead one had he lived.

In one point, at least, Fielding clearly differs from both classic and patristic tradition. (10) Seneca and others had agreed that the mourner should console himself with frequent reflections on the happy moments that he had passed in the company of his friend (rather than being guilty of— as it was later termed—*recordationem timere,* the dread of recollection). The Christian Fathers, Paulinus, Jerome, and Ambrose, also agreed with this view.[129] But Fielding insists quite strenuously that it is sheer madness: "What is all this less than being Self-Tormentors, and playing with Afflic-

---

[127] Favez, pp. 65, 70; Seneca, *Ad Marc.* x. 2.
[128] Seneca, *Ad Polyb.* ix. 1.
[129] Favez, pp. 71-73.

tion?" Rather, he says, one should "avoid all Circumstances which may revive the Memory of the Deceased, whom it is now his Business to forget as fast, and as much as possible" (*Misc.*, I, 310). One might suppose that Henry Fielding had tried the classical precept in practice and found that his own heart could not bear the memories that touched it.

Finally, (11) the classic philosophers, and most particularly the Stoics, invariably emphasized the sovereign remedy of time (the medicine "tarda . . . sed tamen magna," as Cicero put it).[130] They also insisted, however—as Fielding observes (*Misc.*, I, 297-301)—that the period of grief could be much curtailed or even, for the truly wise, made unnecessary through the greater power of the human reason and will. This argument, that a natural and spontaneous grief can be overcome by a determined and schooled will, is perhaps the fundamental contribution of the classic moralists to the tradition of the *consolatio*.

Like most of the other philosophical themes, the insistence that the man of sound mind should anticipate the slow workings of time became an integral part of the consolatory sermons and writings of the Christian church. As the example of Simon Patrick has indicated, this ancient tradition then maintained a remarkable consistency for many centuries. With respect to the last-mentioned theme, Patrick, in his usual vigorous manner, declared that religion and reason "will not let us expect that time should take away this sickness from us. That is the Remedy of vulgar Spirits. . . . It is the part of a wise man to outstrip time and get before it: To prevent a grief that is a growing, and strangle it in the very birth" (p. 180). Isaac Barrow, among many other divines, phrased it more equably in one of his sermons on affliction:

"Time certainly will cure us; but it is better that we should owe that benefit to reason, and let it presently comfort us: it is better, by rational consideration, to work con-

[130] *Tusc. Disp.* III. xvi. 35.

ESSAYS

tent in ourselves, using the brevity and frailty of our life as an argument to sustain us in our adversity. . . ."[131]

Not only were the classic themes deeply ingrained in Christian philosophy from its earliest history, but the seventeenth- and eighteenth-century divines often returned directly to pagan sources as authority for their consolatory arguments; and the presence of Seneca or Plutarch side-by-side with Scripture or the Fathers (on consolation as on many other topics) is, of course, a normal thing in their sermons. It is instructive to find Thomas Emlyn, the Irish nonconformist, quoting Cicero to convey the exalted joys of an afterlife: "*O! præclarum Diem!* &c. . . . *Oh! glorious Day indeed, when I shall come to that Assembly of Divine Spirits!*" Emlyn goes on, however, as many other preachers conscientiously did, to apply the a fortiori argument: "If a *Pagan* could, with so lofty a Rapture, think and speak of *that* blessed Day . . . (when yet his Expectation was only supported by probable *Conjecture*) how much more should it elevate the Heart of an assured *Christian*. . . ."[132]

Thus it is not the citation of classic examples nor the use of classic topics that sets Fielding's essay apart from the orthodox Christian treatises on consolation. The striking difference lies in the appeals that Fielding does *not* employ. Such representative Christian consolatory works as Thomas Burroughs' *Soveraign Remedy for All Kindes of Grief* (1657), Patrick's *The Hearts Ease* (1660), Richard Allestree's (?) *Art of Patience under All Afflictions* (1684), Thomas Emlyn's *Funeral Consolations* (1703), George Stanhope's *Christianity the Only True Comfort*

[131] *Theological Works*, ed. Napier, III, 75.
[132] *Funeral Consolations . . . Being the First Sermon Preached by the Author after the Death of his Wife* [1703] (4th ed., 1750), p. 30. So too Dr. Harrison, in his consolatory letter to the Booths on their afflictions, cites the *Tusculan Disputations* and follows a fortiori: "With how much greater confidence may a good Christian despise, and even deride, all temporary and short transitory evils!" (*Amelia*, III, x; Henley, VI, 155-56). The concluding passages of Cicero's *De senectute* which inspired Emyln bear, to my mind, a striking resemblance to the conclusion of Fielding's own essay.

244

ESSAYS

for Troubled Minds (1706), or the funeral sermons preached by all ranks and persuasions of clergymen—Barrow, Tillotson, Clarke, Fiddes, Doddridge, Secker—almost invariably agree in stressing the following fundamental points: that affliction is from God and that it is presumptuous to question his providence; that patient submission under God's correction is therefore the Christian's duty;[133] that Christ should be taken as the exemplar of right conduct under affliction; and that the loss of friends or relatives is balanced by the continuing presence of the Deity:

"The death of friends doth, it may be, oppress thee with sorrow. But canst thou lose thy best friend? canst thou lose the presence, the conversation, the protection, the advice, the succour of God?"[134]

Other themes are more or less emphasized, according to the persuasion of the speaker: Burroughs' "soverain remedy" against grief, for example, is to remain dumb under God's hand, to pray and search your heart for the sin that

[133] Burroughs says: "There is no way to frame the soul to a patient submission . . . under affliction, but this Consideration, 'Tis God that doth it" (*A Soveraign Remedy* [1657], p. 15). Samuel Clarke carried this a step further; the argument of his sermon on "The End of GOD's afflicting Men" is that "none of the Afflictions which befal Mankind, are the Effects either of blind Chance or of fatal Necessity; but that they are all under the direction of infinite Wisdom and Goodness governing the World, and *in the general* intended by Providence some way or other for our advantage . . ." (*Sermons on Several Subjects* [11v., 7th ed., 1749], VI, 173). The more impatient divines waxed sarcastic; thus Simon Patrick demanded, that if it is God's will that we should suffer affliction, "Let us then cease our complaints, unless we would have him to let us govern the World" (*Hearts Ease*, 7th ed., p. 190). So, too, the dissenter, Doddridge: "Shall the most High God learn of us how to govern the World, and be instructed by our Wisdom when to remove his Creatures from one State of Being to another?" (*Sermons and Religious Tracts of the Late Reverend Philip Doddridge* [3v., 1761], I, 77). This is not exclusively a Christian theme: "For we have come into this world, not to make laws for its governance, but to obey the commandments of the gods who preside over the universe, and the decrees of Fate or Providence" (Plutarch, *Ad Apoll.* 111e).

[134] Isaac Barrow, sermon "Of Contentment," *Theological Works*, ed. Napier, III, 51. It is somewhat disconcerting to find Seneca offering Polybius the same consolation—because of the continued presence of Claudius Caesar! (*Ad Polyb.* VII. 1ff.)

245

called forth your chastisement; and the author of the *Art of Patience* suggests that rather than mourning, the afflicted one should prepare his own soul for death.[135]

Fielding uses none of these various arguments. He makes no such efforts to rationalize the loss of friends as part of the divine plan. He concerns himself not with the theological "why?" but with the practical relief or alleviation of the affliction itself. To this end, he employs only two consolations usually taken as peculiar to Christianity.[136] These are, as we have seen, the assurance that death is the loved one's gain, and—most intoxicating—the certainty of meeting him again, for "He is but gone Home a little before thee. . . ."[137] These two hopes, needless to say, are stressed in all the Christian consolatory writings, and call

[135] Burroughs, p. 9; *Art of Patience*, p. 103. Many of the orthodox consolations appear in Edward Young's *Night Thoughts*, wherein Young, of course, continually argues the necessity of thinking upon Death:

> Why are Friends ravisht from us? 'tis to bind,
> By soft Affection's Tyes, on human Hearts,
> The Thought of Death. . . .
> (*The Complaint. Or, Night Thoughts* [1742-1745], "Night the Fifth," p. 26)

[136] The possibility of an existence after death, and even the suggestion that the dead found a greater and happier life than that of this earth, were fairly common in classical literature (for example, the ecstatic description of a meeting in Elysium in Seneca, *Ad Marc.* xxv. 1-3, or Cicero's *De senectute*). Nevertheless, Christian writers from the beginning stressed the uncertainty and inadequacy of the pagan conception; and the hope of eternal life was taken to be a peculiarly Christian concept (see Favez, pp. 127-29, 152-67). The Christian writers of Fielding's time and before are fond of citing I Thessalonians 4:13 ("Sorrow not, even as others which have no hope"), in contrasting the pagan with the Christian consolation.

[137] *The Art of Patience*, p. 101. Cf. *Tom Jones* (I, ii): Allworthy, whose beloved young wife had died some years ago, "sometimes said he looked on himself as still married, and considered his wife as only gone a little before him, a journey which he should most certainly, sooner or later, take after her . . ." (Henley, III, 21). The conception that "my friend is not gone, but gone before. . . . He hath taken a journey into a far Country, and there I may go to see him" (Patrick, p. 182) was not only a popular Christian image, but also a favorite with Seneca: "He whom you count as passed away has simply posted on ahead" (*Ep. mor.* xcix. 7; cf. also LXIII. 16, *Ad Marc.* XIX. 1, and *Ad Polyb.* IX. 9).

forth, as with Fielding, the authors' most ecstatic passages: Emlyn, describing the joys of the heavenly inhabitants, cries: "Look up, *Christians*, and see if these be Objects of Lamentation";[138] and Sherlock's famous picture of two souls meeting in Paradise, cited by Fielding, is typical of the raptures with which the divines dwelt upon the happy assurance of meeting the loved ones again in heaven. Finally, the structural logic of Fielding's *Remedy of Affliction* follows the reiterated theme of the sermons, that a failure to mourn at all is mere insensibility: rather "Let us sorrow like Men . . . but let us not, in the mean Time, forget that we are Christians."[139]

In Fielding's time, as before, consolatory sermons, poems, essays, and epistles[140] often tended to merge with a more inclusive argumentation against the fear of death.[141]

[138] *Funeral Consolations*, p. 27.
[139] Doddridge, *Sermons*, I, 96. So Patrick, "Not to be sensible of evils, is not to be men; not to bear them patiently, is not to be Christians" (p. 90)—Patrick cites Seneca to enforce this point.
[140] Letters addressed to particular mourners, or what the ancients called *solacia*, as distinguished from *praecepta* or abstract precepts (see Favez, pp. 62-73), repeated much the same consolatory arguments as the latter, drawn from the general stock. Thus Sir William Temple's famous letter to the Countess of Essex upon the loss of her daughter argues, *inter alia*, that God's gifts are in His power to bestow and take away, and declares that if weeping served, it would be commendable, but as it is futile so is it foolish if too long continued ("To the Countess of Essex; Upon Her Grief Occasioned by the Loss of Her Only Daughter," *Works* [4v., 1814], III, 519-30). The irrepressible Tom Brown, who had done straightforward translations of the familiar epistles from Sulpicius to Cicero and from Cicero to Titius (see *The Works of Mr. Thomas Brown* [9th ed., 4v., 1760], I, 266-72), mimicked the genre with "A Consolatory Letter to my Lady ———— *upon the Death of her Husband*," which contained such arguments as this: "'Tis true, Madam, you have lost a husband, and what of that? Have not thousands done so before you? But then consider, that this death makes room for a new election" (I, 196). More conventional are the *solacia* of John Norris of Bemerton ("The Extract of a Letter written upon the occasion of the Death of a Friend," in *A Collection of Miscellanies* [9th ed., 1730], pp. 361-66) and John Toland ("A CONSOLATORY LETTER To the honorable Sir ROBERT CLAYTON, Kt.," in his *Miscellaneous Works* [2v., 1747], II, 318-24), as well as the samples offered in Samuel Richardson's formulary, *Letters Written to and for Particular Friends* (1741), nos. CLXXI-CLXXIII.
[141] The enormous literature of the *meditatio mortis* in the late seven-

ESSAYS

Thus William Sherlock's *Practical Discourse concerning Death* contains consolatory thoughts, many of which echo again the classical precepts. But Sherlock was principally concerned with preparing the Christian to look to his own death, to see it as a part of God's providence and as a certain argument for the transitory nature of this world. The famous pulpit orators, like Tillotson and South, offered numerous sermons against the fear of death; and there was a flood of books and pamphlets in the period on the subject of Christian remedies against the terrors of death, one of the most popular of which was Charles Drelincourt's *The Christian's Defence against the Fears of Death* (transl. 1675).[142] These, in turn, impinged upon the tradition of the *Ars moriendi*, or as Caxton had phrased it, the "Arte & Crafte to Knowe Well to Dye"; and such literary traditions as that of the elegy or the "graveyard poem" are clearly affined with the never-dying interest in the subject of death. Reflection upon death, said Joseph Addison, "ought to be the daily Entertainment of every reasonable Creature."[143]

---

teenth and early eighteenth century has been briefly surveyed by C. A. Moore, "John Dunton: Pietist and Impostor," *SP*, XXII (1925), 467-99; repr. in *Backgrounds of English Literature. 1700-1760* (Minneapolis, 1953), pp. 145-78. Discussing the career of one of the leading publishers of this material, Moore examines the general tradition: "Personal predilection and public demand united," he says, "to make treatises upon death the most prolific field of [Dunton's] literary enterprise" (*Backgrounds*, p. 151).

[142] The *Practical Discourse concerning Death* (1689) by Prior's "wond'rous good Man" reached a twenty-seventh edition by 1751; it was a requisite volume for every pious library—even that of Addison's Leonora (*Spectator* No. 37). Drelincourt's work was second only to Sherlock's in popularity within the genre. Translated from the French in 1675, it reached a seventeenth edition by 1751 (see C. A. Moore, *Backgrounds*, p. 177).

[143] See Sister Mary C. O'Connor, *The Art of Dying Well: The Development of the Ars Moriendi* (N.Y., 1942), which gives further testimony to the abundance and popularity of the literature of Death in the seventeenth century. On the literary traditions, see Amy L. Reed, *The Background of Gray's Elegy* (N.Y., 1924), esp. pp. 34-47, and J. W. Draper, *The Funeral Elegy and the Rise of English Romanticism* (N.Y., 1929). Addison's observation is from the *Spectator*, No. 289 (Everyman ed., II, 362).

ESSAYS

4

Few, perhaps, of Fielding's writings sprang so directly from his personal experience as this work. Like his honored Cicero, he sought to alleviate a terrible grief by setting out precepts of consolation for others, "ut ipse [se] per litteras consolarer."[144] Something of the anguish Fielding himself must have suffered on the death of his daughter is surely present in his comment upon the ravage the good heart undergoes at the loss of loved ones:

"It is tearing the Heart, the Soul from the Body; not by a momentary Operation, like that by which the most cruel Tormentors of the Body soon destroy the Subject of their Cruelty; but by a continued, tedious, though violent Agitation: the Soul having this double unfortunate Superiority to the Body; that its Agonies, as they are more exquisite, so they are more lasting"—(*Misc.*, I, 301-02).

One recalls the violent fit of despair into which the soldier falls in the *Journey from This World to the Next* (chap. xxi), when his sweetheart dies; here Fielding says: "THE Loss of one we tenderly love, as it is one of the most bitter and biting Evils which attends human Life, so it wants the Lenitive which palliates and softens every other Calamity; I mean that great Reliever, Hope" (*Misc.*, II, 183). These reflections seem almost prophetic; for the year after the *Miscellanies* were published, Fielding's beautiful and beloved wife died, and Murphy tells us that her death "brought on such a vehemence of grief, that his friends began to think him in danger of losing his reason." However, "when the first emotions of his sorrow were abated, philosophy administered her aid; his resolution returned, and he began again to struggle with his fortune."[145]

The *Spectator* had observed that "enquiries after Happiness, and Rules for attaining it, are not so necessary and

[144] Cf. *Ad Atticum* XII. xiv.
[145] "An Essay on the Life and Genius of Henry Fielding, Esq;" in *The Works of Henry Fielding*, ed. Arthur Murphy (4v., 1762), I, 38.

249

useful to Mankind as the Arts of Consolation, and supporting one's self under Affliction."[146] Fielding seems often to have felt the same: even the characters of the novels are likely at opportune times to break into the "story" with extended easement for the troubled soul. Heartfree in prison moralizes upon the instability of fortune and the hopes of immortality, with topics drawn directly from the traditions of the *consolatio* (*JW*, III, ii); Adams addresses a consolatory sermon to Joseph upon the supposed loss of Fanny (*JA*, III, xi); Allworthy on his presumed deathbed comforts the blubbering Blifil with precepts from the same general stock (*TJ*, v, vii); and the clergyman father of Mrs. Bennet, as she tells the story in *Amelia* (VII, ii), exhorts her and her sister to patience and submission after their mother's death, with another typical sermon of consolation. Such "digressions" win small critical approval today; but Fielding clearly did not consider them to be excrescences. The familiar arguments, echoed in every eighteenth-century pulpit, would have provided for his readers that element of recognition which constituted a significant part of their pleasure in literature; and, more organically, they would have contributed to the texture of inclusive "realism" that Fielding notably achieved. The modern reader may not take the same pleasure in this "didactic" aspect of eighteenth-century life that he does in more rollicking features; but it is nonetheless "real" for all that. Moreover, it is in part through such passages as these that one becomes aware of an elegiac undertone in Fielding's work, an honest (and pervasive) sense of the *lacrimae rerum*, that adds immeasurably to the depth and complexity of his comic world.

Of less pertinence for the literary critic, but of no less importance for Fielding, such consolatory argument could have practical ends. If, as Murphy tells us, Fielding himself "could quietly read *Cicero de Consolatione*" under the

[146] No. 163; Everyman ed., I, 491.

pressure of affliction, he may well have hoped that his own contributions might bring some ease to another's labored spirit in like circumstances.[147] The head-title to Parson Adams' little *consolatio* (*JA*, III, xi; Henley, I, 298) is only partly in jest: "CONTAINING THE EXHORTATIONS OF PARSON ADAMS TO HIS FRIEND IN AFFLICTION; CALCULATED FOR THE INSTRUCTION AND IMPROVEMENT OF THE READER."

The fact that Fielding chose to employ only two specifically Christian consolations in the *Remedy* is interesting; but such negative evidence tells little about his own convictions. The commonplace arguments that he omits in the essay are precisely those which Adams stresses in the sermon to Joseph: namely, that no accident happens to us without divine permission, "and that it is the duty of a man, much more of a Christian, to submit"; the fact that "that which at first threatens us with evil may in the end produce our good," by satisfying the anger of heaven for our sins; and "the folly and absurdity of our complaints; for whom do we resist, or against whom do we complain, but a power from whose shafts no armor can guard us, no speed can fly?—a power which leaves us no hope but in submission" (III, xi; Henley, I, 298-300). Yet, one may be moved to ask if Fielding's reaction to these conventional exhortations might not have been the same as Joseph's: "O sir! . . . all this is very true, and very fine, and I could hear you all day if I was not so grieved at heart as now I am."

I shall shortly argue that there are certain useful conclusions which can be drawn from this scene and from Fielding's attitude toward the tradition of the *consolatio* in general; but for the present it may serve to suggest that Fielding was conscious of an element of insensibility in that tradition—pagan and Christian—which simply did not

[147] Murphy, I, 48. Parson Adams was enough of a classical scholar to know that this work which passed as Cicero's lost treatise was spurious (*JA*, III, xi; Henley, I, 301).

square with the natural response, as he saw it, of a good man under circumstances of loss. He did not deny that the ideal set forth in the typical Christian sermons we have cited was both just and useful; but there is no doubt that the element of *hope* offered by Christianity appealed much more strongly to him than the orthodox demand for *submission*.

In any event, *Of the Remedy of Affliction* offers no evidence of skepticism or lack of faith on Fielding's part; for the strongest emphasis in his essay indubitably rests upon the final declaration of the Christian belief in a life after death—and a place where souls torn asunder in this world will join once again in eternal bliss. From the *Champion* (for example, 22 January 1740; Henley, xv, 163) to the *Covent-Garden Journal* (for example, No. 69; Jensen, II, 130), Fielding repeatedly and forcefully asseverated his abiding faith in the Christian promise of immortality. This was one of his most fervent convictions, and one, as he says, in which he could not be shaken. It was this conviction which was to comfort Allworthy—the figure here of Fielding himself—for the loss of that young wife he had loved so well (*TJ*, I, ii; Henley, III, 21); it was this which struck the repentant and converted Square as "a much stronger support to a good mind than all the consolations that are drawn from the necessity of nature, the emptiness or satiety of our enjoyments here, or any other topic of those declamations which are sometimes capable of arming our minds with a stubborn patience in bearing the thoughts of death, but never of raising them to a real contempt of it, and much less of making us think it is a real good" (*TJ*, xviii, iv; Henley, v, 306); and it was this conviction that Fielding expressed so emotionally in the *Journey from This World to the Next* (chap. viii), when he described the traveller entering Elysium:

"I presently met a little Daughter, whom I had lost several Years before. Good Gods! what Words can describe the Raptures, the melting passionate Tenderness, with which we kiss'd each other, continuing in our Embrace, with the most extatic Joy, a Space, which if Time had been measured here as on Earth, could not be less than half a Year"—(*Misc.*, II, 63).

Only the confirmed skeptic could question the ardent sincerity of this passage and the hope that it reflects.

5

Bishop Tillotson, preaching on "The excellency of the Christian religion," had, like Fielding himself in many other places than the *Remedy*, insisted upon the superior efficacy of religious consolation over the "philosophical" (which normally implied the pagan philosophy):

"The Christian religion furnisheth us with the best motives and considerations to patience and contentedness under the evils and afflictions of this life. This was one great design of philosophy . . . [but] All the wise sayings and advices which philosophers could muster up to this purpose have proved ineffectual to the common people and the generality of mankind. . . ."[148]

Though Fielding had a like sense of this inadequacy of "philosophy" in terms of everyday human experience, he also believed that its ethical heroism was valuable and inspiring. Just as he could doubt the healing value of Christian counsels to "submit," and yet honor the Chris-

[148] *Works of the Most Reverend Dr. John Tillotson* (12v., 1757), I, 142-43. See Square's confession above, and the contrast drawn by the Man of the Hill in *Tom Jones*: "True it is, that philosophy makes us wiser, but Christianity makes us better men. Philosophy elevates and steels the mind, Christianity softens and sweetens it. The former makes us the objects of human admiration, the latter of Divine love. That insures us a temporal, but this an eternal happiness" (VIII, xiii; Henley, IV, 136). Thus, although Heartfree, soliloquizing in prison, meditates wisely and at length on the proper office of Reason under affliction, his real eloquence is reserved—as was Fielding's in the *Remedy*—for that hope of a future state, the prospect of which "must be allowed the loveliest which can entertain the Eye of Man"; and it is in this hope that his most solid comfort resides (*JW*, III, ii; *Misc.*, III, 202).

tian moral ideal, so too, though doubting the infallible power of philosophy to overcome man's "natural" passions, he could find in the classical moralists—most notably, Plato, Aristotle, Cicero, Seneca, and Plutarch—an image of the wise man and the good life which made philosophy for him second only to the Christian religion as a force of moral control and inspiration.

I do not think Fielding's attitude has always been well understood, particularly when the term "Stoicism" has entered into discussions of his philosophy. I should like to enlarge, therefore, upon this much mishandled question, trusting that a degree of complication may ultimately serve a larger clarification.[149] First of all, then: the "Stoics."

We may begin with the caveat that few of those who alluded confidently to "Stoicism" in this period (as in many other periods) had a very clear idea of the distinction between historic Stoic doctrine and what contemporaneously *passed for* Stoic doctrine. And, except in histories of philosophy, very few writers made any attempt to distinguish the early Stoics from those of the Roman era. Hence the picture of the "Stoic" remained somewhat fuzzy about the edges—always a useful characteristic for a term that is used to arouse an emotional rather than a rational response. Fielding himself would seem to have had in his mind two

[149] The reaction against Dr. Maria Joesten's misguided (though not valueless) attempt to prove that Stoicism was the "eigentlich belebenden Atem" of Fielding's work (*Die Philosophie Fieldings* [Leipzig, 1932]) has perhaps been as excessive as her own argument. The most vigorous polemic has come from Wolfgang Iser who, in his quite valuable study, *Die Weltanschauung Henry Fieldings* (Tübingen, 1952), relentlessly tramples underfoot the Joesten thesis (pp. 295-303). But Dr. Iser allows his own preconceptions equally to dull his ear and on this theme uncharacteristically misreads his evidence—for example, when Fielding, in the most palpable and explicit terms, contrasts the virtue of the ancient Stoic conception of human nature with that of the degraded modern "political philosophers" (*Champion*, 22 January 1740; Henley, xv, 161-62), Iser's comment is: "Dieses Zitat zeigt deutlich Fieldings Wendung gegen den stoischen Volkommenheitskult, gegen den schon die Gestaltung seines ganzen Werkes spricht, sowie gegen alles Extreme und Übermenschliche" (p. 299, n. 25). Iser's own portrait of the Stoic echoes the benevolist caricature: it will not do for Fielding's total picture.

ESSAYS

quite different images associated with the word "Stoic." One of these would have been influenced by the numerous diatribes directed against Stoic "apathy," "indifference," and "pride," in the sermons and benevolist tracts and lay writings that reflected the prevailing "anti-stoicism" of his age:

> In lazy Apathy let Stoics boast
> Their Virtue fix'd; 'tis fix'd as in a frost,
> Contracted all, retiring to the breast;
> But strength of mind is Exercise, not Rest....[150]

Citations enough may be found to show that Fielding had imbibed this "anti-stoic" attitude. He repeated the stock phrases uncritically: Colonel James, he says in *Amelia*, had a mind "formed of those firm materials of which nature formerly hammered out the Stoic, and upon which the sorrows of no man living could make an impression" (VIII, v; Henley, VII, 90); in the *Proposal for Making an Effectual Provision for the Poor*, the phrase, "I do not affect an absolute or stoical indifference on this occasion" (Henley, XIII, 193), came easily from him; and in *Tom Jones*, after citing from Addison's *Cato* to describe Allworthy's calmness under stress, he added: "In reality, he could say this with ten times more reason and confidence than Cato, or any other proud fellow among the ancient or modern heroes . . ." (v, vii; Henley, III, 239-40). This echo (perhaps) of Steele's argument in *The Christian Hero* points to the basic source of Fielding's "anti-stoic" bias: namely,

[105] Pope, *Essay on Man*, Ep. II, ll. 101-04; ed. Maynard Mack (Twickenham ed., Vol. III, i [1950]), p. 67. On the unsystematic (and uncritical) current of "anti-stoicism," see Henry W. Sams, "Anti-Stoicism in Seventeenth- and Early Eighteenth-Century England," *SP*, XLI (1944), 65-78; R. S. Crane, "Suggestions toward a Genealogy of the 'Man of Feeling,'" *ELH*, I (1934), 205-30, esp. pp. 214-19; T. O. Wedel, "On the Philosophical Background of *Gulliver's Travels*," *SP*, XXIII (1926), 434-50; W. Lee Ustick, "Changing Ideals of Aristocratic Character and Conduct in Seventeenth-Century England," *MP*, XXX (1932), 147-66; and Rae Blanchard's edition of Steele's *Christian Hero* (1932).

255

ESSAYS

the contrast (indeed, threat) that Stoic rationalism and its high ideal offered to the pretensions of Christian philosophy and particularly to the school of benevolism. The whole question was complicated, however, by the very intimate relationship between Stoicism and Christianity in their historical development. With the early Christian borrowings from the Stoic moralists and the later Christian overlay given to the classical philosophy by the neo-Stoics of the sixteenth and seventeenth centuries,[151] the two, *as ethical doctrines*, had come to share a great many conceptions and ideals. But if Guillaume du Vair had been able to argue that a fair examination of the Stoics would bear this out and further show that *"they haue been and will be a reproch vnto vs Christians,"*[152] the English clergy (and laity) of the Restoration and eighteenth century were less generous: the rival philosophy had become too useful as a stick with which to beat Christianity rather than shame Christians into their duty. Hence "Stoicism" as a philosophy was contemned at every opportunity. And yet, strangely enough, Seneca and Epictetus and Marcus Aurelius continued to be quoted from the pulpit as familiarly (and almost as often) as St. Paul and St. Jerome. Taken abstractly, as "Stoicks," they were to be reprehended; taken individually, as moralists, they were too rich a source of wisdom to ignore.

The same paradox appears in Fielding; but more than this, he clearly possessed another image of the Stoics quite different from the negative caricature provided by the

[151] See, in addition to the items in n. 150, Jason L. Saunders, *Justus Lipsius: The Philosophy of Renaissance Stoicism* (N.Y., 1955); Lipsius, *Two Bookes Of Constancie*, ed. Rudolf Kirk and C. M. Hall (New Brunswick, N.J., 1939); Guillaume du Vair, *The Moral Philosophie of the Stoicks*, ed. Rudolf Kirk (New Brunswick, 1951); Joseph Hall, *Heaven vpon Earth and Characters of Vertues and Vices*, ed. Rudolf Kirk (New Brunswick, 1948); and Audrey Chew, "Joseph Hall and Neo-Stoicism," *PMLA*, LXV (1950), 1130-45.

[152] "To the French Reader," in *The Moral Philosophie of the Stoicks*, transl. Thomas James (1598); ed. Kirk (1951), p. 50.

benevolists. He declared, for example, that the modern "*Art of thriving*" was "the very Reverse of that Doctrine of the Stoics; by which Men were taught to consider themselves as Fellow-Citizens of the World, and to labour jointly for the common Good . . ." (*Misc.*, I, 183). After alluding elsewhere to "that ancient tenet of the Stoic school, that virtue is the greatest good," he continued: "It was the aim and earnest endeavour of the Stoics, and other sects of the ancient writers, to raise and elevate human nature to the highest pitch of goodness and virtue. . . . [They] had before them the pattern of divine perfection, the imitation of which they assiduously preached up to their disciples and followers, the whole course of their labours visibly tending to bring mankind as near as possible to the excellence of the Deity" (*Champion*, 22 January 1740; Henley, xv, 161-62). Precisely the same sentiment, with an epigraph from Cicero, is expressed twelve years later in the *Covent-Garden Journal* for 16 May 1752 (No. 39; Jensen, I, 354). This celebration of the Stoic ideal is commensurate with the admiration that Fielding normally expressed for the writings of individual Stoic philosophers such as Seneca and Marcus Aurelius and the great eclectic moralist that Fielding habitually linked with them (as I shall), Cicero. To draw from a multitude of references, he called Aurelius "that Glory of human Nature"; argued that "great Matter of Comfort and Utility"—not to mention delight—could be found in the pages of Seneca; and, in his very last work of philosophic concern, warmly alluded to "that idea of perfect goodness, of which Tully hath given us a pattern" in the *De officiis*.[153]

What are we to make of this apparent contradiction? In part, we may admit it as one of those contradictions incident to any active mind—and particularly to the creative mind, which has a habit of seizing what is useful to

[153] Aurelius, *CGJ*, No. 52, Jensen, II, 49; Seneca, *CGJ*, No. 10, Jensen, I, 195; Cicero, "A Fragment of a Comment on Lord Bolingbroke's Essays," Henley, XVI, 322.

it at a given moment. In part, it is simply that Fielding found some things in the Stoic creed of which he approved and other things of which he disapproved. He could, for example, sympathize fully with the benevolist attack upon Seneca's *De clementia* (which argued that feeling or sympathy should not enter into charity); but his obvious admiration for Seneca is nonetheless incontestable. And, if we were more largely to concern ourselves with the historical aspect of the question, we might suppose that Fielding's understanding of philosophy was considerable enough to distinguish between the body of doctrine (and legends) connected with Zeno and the Old Stoa and the modified form of that moral doctrine contained in the late Stoic philosophers, Seneca, Epictetus, and Marcus Aurelius. One might hope that Fielding would not have confused, as the general public usually did, the inhuman creed of indifference found in the Cynics (Zeno's teachers) with that of the later Stoics; but his failure to identify Stilpo, whom he attacks in the *Remedy*, as a Cynic rather than a Stoic, leaves this questionable. Seneca, correctly or not, had distinguished between the Stoics and the Cynics: "Our ideal wise man feels his troubles, but overcomes them; their wise man does not even feel them."[154] This kind of distinction would have represented to Fielding as well as to Seneca the essential difference between wisdom and mere inhumanity. Having said in the *Remedy* (with Seneca and Cicero) that not to grieve for the loss of a loved one was inhuman, Fielding added (as they did) that wisdom, "our Shield against all Calamity," must nevertheless be called upon as soon as possible. "The Mind of a wise Man may be ruffled and disordered, but cannot be subdued: in the former it differs

[154] *Ep. mor.* IX. 3: "Hoc inter nos et illos interest: noster sapiens vincit quidem incommodum omne, sed sentit; illorum ne sentit quidem." Cicero, who was sometimes critical of the early Stoics (as was Seneca, for that matter), rejected the Cynic philosophy out of hand—"Cynicorum vero ratio tota est eicienda" (*De officiis* I. xli. 148).

from the Perfection of the Deity; in the latter, from the abject Condition of a Fool" (*Misc.*, I, 307).

The phrasing here is almost precisely echoed in Fielding's description of the Christian sage, Allworthy (*TJ*, VI, iii; Henley, III, 282-83); and, recalling the earlier declaration that the Stoic philosophy visibly tended "to bring mankind as near as possible to the excellence of the Deity," we may infer a close association in Fielding's mind between the ideals he found most laudable in Stoicism and in Christianity. The same implicit association can be found in another passage (sometimes cited as evidence of his "*anti*-stoicism"), which describes a set of self-centered "heathen" philosophers who "are so taken up, in contemplating themselves, that the Virtues or Vices, the Happiness or Misery of the rest of Mankind scarce ever employ their Thoughts" (*CGJ*, No. 29; Jensen, I, 306). He declared that "in the sublimer Schools of the Christian Dispensation" such men would be called severely to account "for converting solely to their own Use, what was entrusted only to their Care for *the general Good*" (Jensen, I, 307; italics mine).

In the contrast between Christianity and philosophy, Fielding always exalted the former. But to cite this passage as anti-Stoic is to suppose that whenever he describes an inhuman or selfish rigidity of character he necessarily has the Stoics in mind. Apart from the fact that this argument chases its tail, it will not answer to the purpose in this case; for Fielding quoted Cicero just ten issues later in the *Covent-Garden Journal* (see above, p. 257) to make the same point enforced here, and more than once (as we have seen) he linked the philosophic conception of "the general Good" properly with the Stoics. Hence the Christian judgment upon these selfish philosophers would, if anything, be equated with the Stoic judgment upon them.

Should this particular argument appear to smack of sophistry, I am willing enough to abandon it, for my case does not depend upon it. The argument truly seems colorable to me, assuming Fielding's consistency in the use of the phrase, "general Good": but of that consistency I must admit something less than absolute assurance. My concern, however, is to establish the fact that Fielding had two quite different attitudes toward "Stoicism," and that one of these (the most weighty, I think) manifested itself explicitly and implicitly as approval. Not only did he approve of their conception of the good man as a citizen of the world, responsible for all his fellows, and not only did he call upon the Stoic *sapiens* for his portrait of the Wise Man (as the *Remedy* sufficiently indicates), but he could also, despite the popular image, find in many passages of the great Stoic moralists authority for his own creed of warm humanity. Fielding would surely recall that Seneca on more than one occasion insisted that "the first thing which philosophy undertakes to give is fellow-feeling with all men; in other words, sympathy and sociability."[155] Although he could occasionally slip into the benevolist cant, as in his description of Colonel James, there is no question but that his ideal conception of the *vita beata* had more than a little in common with the good life presented by the Stoic moralists. In fact, when he confronted the "barking critics" in *Tom Jones* (VI, iii) with a digression concerning "true wisdom," he did not stray very far from the conception of that quality to be found in the *Vita beata* of Seneca.[156]

[155] *Ep. mor.* v. 4: "Hoc primum philosophia promittit, sensum communem, humanitatem et congregationem."

[156] Fielding: "True wisdom, then, notwithstanding all which Mr. Hogarth's poor poet may have writ against riches, and in spite of all which any rich well-fed divine may have preached against pleasure, consists not in the contempt of either of these. A man may have as much wisdom in the possession of an affluent fortune as any beggar in the streets. . . . To say truth, the wisest man is the likeliest to possess all wor[l]dly blessings in an eminent degree; for as that moderation which wisdom prescribes is the surest way to useful wealth, so can it alone qualify us to taste many pleasures. The wise man gratifies every appetite and every passion, while the fool sacrifices all the rest to pall and satiate one.

"It may be objected that very wise men have been notoriously avaricious. I answer, Not wise in that instance. It may likewise be said, That the

ESSAYS

On the other hand, once we admit Fielding's very real admiration for the later Stoics, we can go on to make some uninvidious qualifications. In the *Remedy of Affliction*, after citing Cicero and Seneca as representative of "those wise and illustrious Antients" who prescribed philosophy and virtue to overcome the disorders of the troubled human mind, Fielding said, "Now that this Supreme Philosophy, this Habit of Virtue, which strengthened the Mind of a *Socrates*, or a *Brutus*, is really superior to every Evil which can attack us, I make no doubt . . ." (*Misc.*, I, 298). As I have been arguing, this seems to me to represent an honest conviction that Fielding held to from first to last: that true wisdom (like true greatness) was *possible* and that it served as a noble inspiration to all. There is more to the matter, however, than this. The assertion that I have just cited concludes: "But in Truth, this is to have a sound, not a sickly Constitution"; and, although he goes on to honor the soul that is "*Totus teres atque rotundus*" (*Misc.*, I, 299),[157] his ultimate point is that the majority of the

---

wisest men have been in their youth immoderately fond of pleasure. I answer, They were not wise then" &c. (*TJ*, VI, iii; Henley, III, 284).

Seneca: "For indeed the wise man does not deem himself undeserving of any of the gifts of Fortune. He does not love riches, but he would rather have them; he does not admit them to his heart, but to his house, and he does not reject the riches he has, but he keeps them and wishes them to supply ampler material for exercising his virtue. . . ."

Or again: "You embrace pleasure, I enchain her; you enjoy pleasure, I use it. . . . But I do not call him a wise man who is dominated by anything, still less by pleasure" &c. (*De vita beata* XXI. 4 and X. 3–XI. 1; in *Moral Essays* [Loeb Library], II, 155, 125).

My purpose here is neither to establish a "source" nor to suggest that Fielding would have uncritically accepted every argument in the *Vita beata*, but simply to draw attention to a few of the many convictions that Fielding would have *known* he shared in common with a Stoic philosopher like Seneca, despite the vulgar image of the Stoic as a self-denying, unfeeling recluse. Can anyone suppose that Fielding would have rejected this: "A man thus grounded must, whether he wills or not, necessarily be attended by constant cheerfulness and a joy that is deep and issues from deep within, since he finds delight in his own resources, and desires no joys greater than his inner joys" (*De vita beata* IV. 4; Loeb, II, 111)?

[157] Horace, *Sat.* II. vii. 86. The Man of the Hill cited the same passage, in arguing that "philosophy and religion may be called the exercises of the

human race are men of a lesser order, not "elevated Souls" but "common Men . . . who partake of the more amiable Weaknesses of Human Nature" (*Misc.*, I, 306-07). This being true, his own function as a moralist, as a "mental physician," was to care for those souls that had real need of help.

In discussing a like problem, the conquest of self ("that glorious precept *vince teipsum*"), in the *Champion*, Fielding echoed the phrasing of the *Remedy*: "I have been often surprised, that among all the divines and philosophers, who have declaimed on this subject, few or none have laid down any good rules for the attaining so desirable a conquest. The former have ascribed all to grace, and the latter to that consummate virtue of the Stoics, which was able to do all things. They have both trumpeted out much on this head, and sufficiently demonstrated the great glory of our self-conquest. But, by their leave, this is acting little unlike to a physician who should sing forth the praises of health, when he should prescribe men the method of attaining it . . ." (2 February 1740; Henley, xv, 178). The phrasing not only parallels that of the *Remedy*, but also anticipates the individual shibboleths of Thwackum and Square;[158] and this echo well considered may lead us to the following conclusion: that whereas Fielding held in the greatest

---

mind, and when this is disordered they are as wholesome as exercise can be to a distempered body" (*TJ*, viii, xiii; Henley, iv, 137).

[158] Square as the fallible "Stoic" is displayed (among other places) in Fielding's description of his "consolatio" to Jones upon his broken arm: "Such accidents as a broken bone were below the consideration of *a wise man*. That it was abundantly sufficient, to reconcile the mind to any of these mischances, to reflect that they are liable to befall the wisest of mankind, and are undoubtedly for *the good of the whole* . . . with more of the like sentences, extracted out of the second book of Tully's Tusculan questions [which deals with enduring pain], and from the great Lord Shaftesbury. In pronouncing these he was one day so eager that he unfortunately bit his tongue, and in such a manner that it not only put an end to his discourse, but created much emotion in him, and caused him to mutter an oath or two . . ." (*TJ*, v, ii; Henley, iii, 211-12; italics mine). This makes fun of cant and pretension: but to take it as ridicule of Cicero's *Tusculan Disputations* would be absurd.

veneration the noble ideals of both Christianity and Stoicism, he could nonetheless see in *both* disciplines the possibilities of a self-lacerating denial of life and of a vicious rigidity (*corruptio optimi pessima*). Perhaps even more significant, he could sometimes see in both an ideal so far beyond ordinary human achieving as to be in many practical difficulties or afflictions almost irrelevant—though only almost.

A like disparity or conflict suggests itself in an area that Fielding would intimately have known, the law. For the eternal confrontation of law and equity posed precisely the same problem: the law must deal with the ideal, the letter; equity concerns itself with the spirit and the intention. As Aristotle said, in discussing the oratory of the law, "It is equitable to pardon human weaknesses, and to look . . . not to the letter of the law but to the intention of the legislator; not to the action itself, but to the moral purpose. . . ."[159] From the invented *controversiae* of the schools to the firsthand experience at courts and assizes, Fielding would have been made conscious of this conflict and of the valid arguments that could be adduced for both sides. And if his heart, we may suppose, leaned always toward equity, his mind and his training could not let him ignore the necessity of a firm, traditional and ideal law. So, too, in the broader frame of ethical and rational behavior, he held in awful regard the stern dictates of religion and philosophy; but his heart went out to the fallibility of mankind. His greatest problem, then, as a practical moralist, was to maintain and guard authentic ideals of moral and spiritual conduct while he strove to bring them down to dwell in clubs and assemblies, at teatables and in coffee-houses. His serious essays and his comic creations alike had such an end in view. And, as with the ideals of greatness and goodness, the end of his philosophical examinations was to celebrate the true ideal, to expose

[159] *Rhetoric* I. xiii. 17; 1374*b* (transl. John H. Freese [Loeb Library, 1926], p. 147).

and mock the false, and to lead good men, *so far as in them lay*, toward the achievement of the true.

6

This may seem obvious enough; but the achievement of that laudable moral end is complicated in Fielding's work by a number of factors. We may confine ourselves to two of these. First, there is Fielding's continuing comic appreciation of the ludicrous in things, for example, of the disparity between profession and conduct, even in the case of good men and laudable ideals. This sense of the ridiculous took him well out of the paths of the conventional moralist. Second, there is the omnipresent *duality* in Fielding's thought (which, incidentally, makes every attempt to categorize him in any set of unilateral terms, to make him the uncritical follower of any given school or way of life, necessarily a falsification), a duality that made the moral simplicity he honestly sought very difficult to achieve.

There are examples in plenty of the first factor. Perhaps Fielding's most often used comic technique is this of following an inflated (or simply elevated) declaration of principle with an ignominious failure or retreat in action. Frequently, as with the man of courage in *Joseph Andrews* (II, ix), who "DESCANTS ON BRAVERY AND HEROIC VIRTUE, TILL AN UNLUCKY ACCIDENT PUTS AN END TO THE DISCOURSE" (Henley, I, 156), Fielding is merely "showing up" the propounder of a view which not only tickles his sense of the ridiculous, but for which he has little sympathy. More complex, however, is the famous scene (*JA*, IV, viii) in which Parson Adams, immediately after having lectured to Joseph on patience in adversity, is confronted with the apparent fact of his son's death and drops his Christian stoicism to grieve like any human being. An interesting (though imperfect) parallel to this scene is to be found in the failure of the classical consolations, which the sponging-house philosopher in *Amelia* (VIII, x) so competently rehearses, to protect him against the simple disappointment of missing an expected dinner with his family. In neither of these two cases are the excellent precepts themselves being mocked. The comedy lies, rather, in the universal incongruity between principle (even of the noblest order) and practice. *Video meliora proboque, deteriora sequor.* The fact remains a continuing anomaly of human behavior; but it has never served as, nor does Fielding see it as, a valid argument against the inherent worth of elevated moral principles themselves. Even if one were to argue that the inefficacy of high moral principles in given cases constituted a serious flaw in them, Fielding's counterargument would unquestionably be that which he adduced in discussing weaknesses in those we love: "The finest composition of human nature, as well as the finest china, may have a flaw in it; and this, I am afraid, in either case is equally incurable; though, nevertheless, the pattern may remain of the highest value" (*TJ*, II, vii; Henley, III, 96).

Obviously, in the two scenes I have cited above, the "philosopher" is a weaker character than Adams (and the comedy of his reversal thereby the less interesting);[160] but the philosophy that he outlines is essentially the same (in brief compass) that sustained Heartfree and Allworthy in time of affliction—and essentially the same that Fielding presented to his readers in the essay, *Of the Remedy of Affliction*.[161] Booth's reply to the little philosopher, therefore, seems to me to have often been taken too simply:

[160] It is likely that Fielding introduced his comment upon Adams' strong Christian stoicism ("For he was a great enemy to the passions, and preached nothing more than the conquest of them by reason and grace"—*JA*, IV, viii; Henley, I, 351) at this point simply to heighten still further the contrast between ideal principle and human practice.

[161] The sponging-house philosopher says: "By philosophy, I do not mean the bare knowledge of right and wrong, but an energy, a habit, as Aristotle calls it; and this I do firmly believe, with him and with the Stoics, is superior to all the attacks of fortune" (*Amelia*, VIII, x; Henley, VII, 114). Fielding's own serious words are: "And when *Seneca* tells us, that *Virtue* is sufficient to subdue all our Passions, he means no other (as he explains it in many Parts of his Works) than *that exalted divine Philos-*

ESSAYS

"You have expressed yourself extremely well," cries Booth; "and I entirely agree with the justice of your sentiments; but, however true all this may be in theory, I still doubt its efficacy in practice. And the cause of the difference between these two is this; that we reason from our heads, but act from our hearts. . . . Nothing can differ more widely than wise men and fools in their estimation of things; but, as both act from their uppermost passion, they both often act alike"— (*Amelia*, VIII, x; Henley, VII, 113). This is particularly interesting in connection with the present essay; for Booth's "answer" to the philosopher might almost represent Fielding's criticism of his own *Remedy* in the *Miscellanies*. He places in Booth's mouth, for example, that famous reply of Solon to those who were consoling him with the customary *topos* of life's brevity: "Is not [Booth demands] this very shortness itself one of their afflictions?" (Henley, VII, 113-14).[162] Nevertheless, to suppose that Booth has here *refuted* the philosopher and given us Fielding's own considered view would, to my way of thinking, be a disastrous error. This is to reduce the dialectic of Fielding's debate to an obvious unilateral declaration—which all too many critics of this complex man have been entirely willing to do—and thereby to miss not only the drama of ideas involved but the directions in which they point for the story itself. Because each of these men has presented an argument *with its own peculiar validity*, and each of the arguments remains to be tested in practice, not only once but a number of times before the narrative comes to a close.

To move to the second "complicating" factor: I have suggested before that I think there are fundamental duali-

---

ophy, which consisted not in vain Pomp, or useless Curiosity, nor even in the Search of more profitable Knowledge, but in acquiring solid lasting Habits of Virtue, and ingrafting them into our Character"; and, as we have seen, Fielding goes on to say that his own conviction is that "this Habit of Virtue . . . is really superior to every Evil which can attack us" (*Misc.*, I, 298).

[162] Cf. Diogenes Laertius, *De vitis . . . clarorum philosophorum* I. 63.

ties in Fielding's thought. Where these take the form of good-evil (for example, true greatness as opposed to false), they are simple enough to deal with; but when they take the form of one good contrasted with another (true greatness and goodness), the analysis becomes more difficult; and when they take the form of opposed aspects of the same good (as I have tried to illustrate in my discussion of good-nature), the complexity of the conception forbids any simple analysis in terms of a single obvious value. The problem of consolation dealt with in the *Remedy*, ushers into a stark light several of the dualities (a word I am not pleased with, but they are more than mere "inconsistencies") that marked Fielding's mode of thinking about and responding to human experience.

To make this clearer, there may perhaps be no great harm in the use of a few oversimplified terms to express the "poles" of his thought, so long as it is clearly understood that he did not finally commit himself unreservedly to any of the individual poles. Thus, to appreciate the stresses and the overtones involved in a pair of given scenes that I should like to quote, we might designate a particular "set" of values in terms of the following polarities: philosophy-human nature (or perhaps more specifically, stoic-benevolist), reason-passions, "masculine"-"feminine," and so on. Fielding's insistence upon the virtues of *both* elements in each dichotomy, *and* the complex of particular empirical values that can be associated with each abstraction, give to the two following scenes (one from an early work of fiction, the other from a late autobiographical account) precisely that broad human reference which has been more often noted than analyzed in Fielding's work, and which accounts for the fact that some have placed him among the "intellectual" and others among the "emotional" ranks of our great novelists:

"THE Day was now come when poor *Heartfree* was to suffer an ignominious Death. *Friendly* had, in the strongest

Manner, confirmed his Assurance of fulfilling his Promise, of becoming a Father to one of his Children, and a Husband to the other. This gave him inexpressible Comfort, and he had, the Evening before, taken his last Leave of the little Wretches, with a Tenderness which drew a Tear from one of the Keepers, joined to a Magnanimity which would have pleased a *Stoic*"—(*JW*, IV, v; *Misc.*, III, 316).

"Wednesday, June 26, 1754. On this day, the most melancholy sun I had ever beheld arose, and found me awake at my house at Fordhook. By the light of this sun, I was, in my own opinion, last to behold and take leave of some of those creatures on whom I doated with a motherlike fondness, guided by nature and passion, and uncured and unhardened by all the doctrine of that philosophical school where I had learnt to bear pains and to despise death.

"In this situation, as I could not conquer nature, I submitted entirely to her, and she made as great fool of me as she had ever done of any woman whatsoever: under pretence of giving me leave to enjoy, she drew me in to suffer the company of my little ones, during eight hours; and I doubt not whether, in that time, I did not undergo more than in all my distemper.

"At twelve precisely my coach was at the door, which was no sooner told me than I kiss'd my children round, and went into it with some little resolution"—(*Journal of a Voyage to Lisbon*; Henley, XVI, 199).

Nothing could be simpler than the diction and the dramatic action of these two parting scenes. Their complexity (seen here only in little, of course) lies in the fact that nothing which pertains to the basic nature of man is glossed over or denied. The "stoic" element, which can respond to the exemplary pattern of the wise man and seek to emulate it; the "rational" assessment of the situation (which Heartfree had previously made more thoroughly in a colloquy with himself, III, ii); the manly firmness of behavior—

ESSAYS

all of these "masculine" qualities in human nature which Fielding consistently honored in his fiction and his essays are here displayed in the characters of his protagonists. But there is an antipodal set of qualities to which an equal weight is given: the "nature" which says to a rational consolation, "O sir! . . . all this is very true, and very fine, and I could hear you all day if I was not so grieved at heart as now I am"; the involuntary and unruly "passions" that can drive man to terrible excess but that also serve crucially to define his humanity—in a word, we are shown the constellation of qualities that Fielding (and the eighteenth century) tended to denominate as "feminine," the irrational, softer, more amiable and, indeed, in some ways more fundamental aspects of man's mixed nature.

The recognition that man has within himself unresolved dualities is not in itself so remarkable. It is Fielding's dramatic and comic exploitation of this source of incongruities in human behavior that is remarkable. But I have thought it nevertheless worth stressing that a great part of Fielding's strength comes from his ability to entertain and give full weight to *both* the major opposites in the elemental dichotomies of man's nature; for perhaps an unnecessary amount of ink has been spilled in trying to prove, by selected examples, that he belonged to the passional or the rational camp or was enlisted under some other banner of particularities. Intimately and personally engaged on the great comic battleground of human nature he was: but he also sat on a high seat above it, a benignant umpire, and afforded each side its due.[163]

Fielding believed that high ideals—pagan or Christian—could serve to inspire and invigorate imperfect men. But he also feared lest the delineation of unattainable ideals or models of perfection should leave ordinary mortals in de-

[163] This, I take it, is something along the lines of what Mr. Empson means by Fielding's "habitual double irony" ("Tom Jones," *Kenyon Review*, xx [1958], 217-49).

spair;[164] and his comic gifts were often turned not to belittlement but to the purpose of *reassurance*, by demonstrating to ordinary fallible human beings the equal and natural fallibility of even the most noble ideals and men when confronted with the fact, not the theory, of human experience.[165] So also, in his serious essays, such as those of the *Miscellanies*, he was solicitous to appeal to the best in men, to present ideals of conduct, but he was further concerned to address himself "to common Men, and who partake of the more amiable Weaknesses of Human Nature," and to keep his adjurations within the bounds of human competence.

The essay *Of the Remedy of Affliction*, in which he sought to bring solace to the wounded souls of ordinary men, is part of a long and living tradition. The topics of the classic *consolatio* were by Fielding's time an almost indistinguishable part of the texture of orthodox Christian consolation; and although he chose to emphasize them in terms of pure "philosophy," as distinct from the unique Christian contribution, there can be little doubt that his own strongest emphasis lay upon that ultimate—and most personal—hope of a life after death and the prospect of renewed joy with those whom death had taken. The three major sources of Fielding's ripe and humane wisdom are drawn upon and displayed in this essay: the classical tradition, the

---

[164] Here was, of course, one of his objections to inserting characters of "angelic perfection" into a work of art: the honest reader might very well "be both concerned and ashamed to see a pattern of excellence in his nature, which he may reasonably despair of ever arriving at" (*TJ*, x, i; Henley, iv, 195).

[165] Thus: "Philosophers are composed of flesh and blood as well as other human creatures; and however sublimated and refined the theory of these may be, a little practical frailty is as incident to them as to other mortals. . . . They know very well how to subdue all appetites and passions, and to despise both pain and pleasure; and this knowledge affords much delightful contemplation, and is easily acquired; but the practice would be vexatious and troublesome; and, therefore, the same wisdom which teaches them to know this teaches them to avoid carrying it into execution" (*TJ*, v, v; Henley, iii, 226-27).

ESSAYS

Christian faith, and the rich personal experience of the world's delights and hurts that kept his work always rooted in realities of the human heart and mind. The *Remedy*, though scarcely a "comic" work, presents in little the fundamental pattern of the Christian *comoedia* (as Dante understood it), that is, the progress from darkness to light, from a desperate grief to consolation and assured hope. This is truly the abstract pattern of all Fielding's great comic novels; and the deeper sense that we gain from the *Remedy* of a pervasive elegiac undertone in his work can bring us not only to a fuller awareness of the *chiaroscuro* in his literary and moral world, but also—one may hope, in an age that often seems wilfully determined not to comprehend the meaningfulness of comedy—to a higher understanding of the fundamental human need for community and reassurance that great comedy satisfies in its social-moral realism and in its concurrent shaping of experience nearer to the heart's desire.[166] Fielding's comic world would be neither so vital nor so satisfying were his sense of the tears in things—the sad realities of human existence—not so complete. In this lies the dark complement to his laughing sensibility: in this, the starting-point of his elemental, profound, and triumphant comic progress.

[166] Northrop Frye says bluntly: "Happy endings do not impress us as true, but as desirable, and they are brought about by manipulation. The watcher of death and tragedy has nothing to do but sit and wait for the inevitable end; but something gets born at the end of comedy, and the watcher of birth is a member of a busy society" (*Anatomy of Criticism* [Princeton, 1957], p. 170).

CHAPTER IV. SATIRES

> Why, sir, my design is to ridicule the vicious and foolish customs of the age. ... I hope to expose the reigning follies in such a manner, that men shall laugh themselves out of them before they feel that they are touched.—Medley, in Fielding's *Historical Register*

CROSS grouped the *Essay on Nothing* and *Some Papers Proper to Be Read before the Royal Society* with the *Dialogue between Alexander and Diogenes* as "experiments in those brief Menippean satires such as Lucian sometimes composed" (I, 394). Actually the form and content of the two former pieces owe comparatively little to Lucian (except insofar as the Syrian satirist's influence may be considered pervasive in Fielding's work);[1] and it has seemed more "furthersome" to comment upon these two works apart from those that I see as "Lucianic." The distinction, however, remains somewhat arbitrary.

Both of the works under present scrutiny are "formal" satires in the sense that they have a definite structure and that satire is their primary end, not merely (as in the novels) one among many incidental means. Satire has no structure peculiar to itself, of course, and must borrow: the *Essay on Nothing* is a mock encomium and derives its ordering from the rhetorical formulae proper to the panegyric; the satire on the Royal Society is a parody and derives its form from the work parodied, a scientific report. In both satires the borrowed frame itself contributes to the total effect, inviting the pleasure of recognition and complicating that pleasure by humorous and ingenious distortion. Both dis-

---

[1] It is true that Lucian had written several mock encomia (notably, *Laus muscae* and *Parasitus*), to which genre the *Essay on Nothing* belongs; but Fielding clearly drew upon this tradition at a later stage of its development: the form of his encomium does not resemble Lucian's.

play, in little, Fielding's mastery of "that delightful mingling of scholarly niceness with the salty idiom of the common man which is the hallmark of most great satire."[2] And in both works Fielding turned the immediate satiric level to account in constructing a second level of response: that is to say, the rhetorical paradoxes arising from the praise of Nothing and the incongruities of his straight-faced scientific account of the "chrysipus" or English guinea (in place of the polyp described in the original report), effects which could be enjoyed for their own sakes, were employed functionally to deride such larger follies as a starched pride in titles or a mean and grasping avarice.

It is in great part this consistent ability to turn his immediate material to a broader purpose, to strike out parallels of peculiar exactness and applicability and to invent ever new and ingenious variations upon his single theme, which gives Fielding title to be called a master satirist. It is this same power that we admire in (the true master) Swift, whose *Tale of a Tub*, for instance, seems so perfectly adapted to his satirical ends that one is almost tricked into believing it a piece of luck that the artist should have "stumbled upon" something so inherently suitable.

At one time or another in his literary career, Fielding turned his hand to very nearly every kind of satire and every satirical tone that tradition made available or that invention could discover. The first (known) work that he published was a satiric poem, *The Masquerade*; and in a poetic vein he experimented, as we have seen, with epigrams and mock epitaphs, with parody, travesty, and burlesque, with the satiric epistle and satiric allegory (the *Vernoniad*), and with the Popeian verse essay that mingled satire and direct statement. The only kind of current poetic satire that he apparently did not feel to be within his range was

---

[2] David Worcester, *The Art of Satire* (Cambridge, Mass., 1940), p. 50; Mr. Worcester is speaking of Erasmus and Rabelais, but I think he would agree that the remark is equally applicable to Fielding.

the Horatian imitation. In the drama he made use of the witty satire of the Restoration comedy of manners and the satiric humours of the Jonson-Shadwell line. He wrote numerous farces and burlesques that ranged from satiric allegory (as in the *Grub-Street Opera*) and travesty (as in the blank-verse *Covent-Garden Tragedy*), to splendid mock-heroic (most notably, of course, the *Tragedy of Tragedies*). And he developed the rehearsal technique into a form peculiarly his own that one may call simply dramatic satire—a form so devastatingly effective that it led directly to the Licensing Act.

In his journals, besides employing such *personae* as Captain Hercules Vinegar for satiric effect, he made use of epistles, puffs, burlesque criticism, diatribes, dream-visions, mock encomia, essays, mock scholarship and burlesque history, dialogue, the comment of an ingénu, the censorial court, and a host of other forms and devices to convey his satirical commentary. In miscellaneous prose, one can point to dream-vision (*The Opposition*), parody and mock encomium, satiric dialogue, Lucianic journeys, and the kind of dogged satirical tracking of an original (cf. Fielding's unfinished *Comment on Lord Bolingbroke's Essays*) that he could find a model for in, say, Marvell's *Rehearsal Transprosed*. Clearly enough, satire was no casual or peripheral concern of Fielding's writing life.

Thoroughly steeped in satirical method—having experimented with all its devices and tones, from slashing invective to highly subtle ironic innuendo—Fielding could bring to his serious and vastly sympathetic examination of the human scene the techniques and the sure command of a variety of styles that would give his more inclusive comic vision its unique overtones. The borderline between satire and comedy is shifting and nebulous: strict definition is perhaps a futile exercise. But if it is argued that one end of satire is surely to expose in order to destroy or reform, and that the answerable end of comedy is to expose in order to reconcile—that is, to reconcile man to his own essential humanity with all its diversiform incongruities—then one difference between Fielding's pure satires and his larger comic works can be readily seen. For comedy makes use of the legionary satiric devices only to subserve a higher function: that of bringing man into some accommodation with the paradoxes of the inescapable human situation. The definition of the ridiculous in Fielding's preface to *Joseph Andrews* has reference in fact to his limited satirical vision only, and it is illustrated in such figures as Slipslop and Peter Pounce; but the famous scene in Book IV, Chapter viii—where Parson Adams lectures Joseph on patience under affliction and then is confronted with the (false) news that his son is drowned—is comic, in the sense of which I speak. It presents the universal human paradox that rational systems fade before the exigencies of real human experience: for, we can plead the traditional consolations all we wish, but when confronted with the actual fact of personal loss, we must be humanly overwhelmed with grief. It is this vision, invested with all the *possibilities* of the tragic, that gives much of Fielding's comedy its profound force and its great humanity.

The assurance necessary to the comic world, that possible tragedy will never issue in true catastrophe (in effect, the artistic projection of faith in a providential moral order), is partly achieved by the use of familiar conventions of character and plot; but it is more effectively and more subtly achieved through tone and mood.[3] The sense of assurance that the reader enjoys in the comic works of Fielding is due in no small degree to the controls of his personal commentary, a style that answers every demand for nuance that he can make of it, and his absolute mastery of an extraordinary range of satiric devices. A mere catalogue of

---

[3] See R. S. Crane's masterful analysis, "The Plot of *Tom Jones*," *Journal of General Education*, IV (1950), 112-30; repr. in *Critics and Criticism*, ed. R. S. Crane (Chicago, 1952), pp. 616-47.

the latter would require several pages, and illustration would take a book.

Although Fielding's satires qua satires are sometimes shaped by a narrative structure, their most characteristic feature is the set of ingenious variations upon a given theme and the turning of these variations to a functional satiric use. The technique of the *Tragedy of Tragedies* and *Shamela*, taken in conjunction with *Some Papers Proper to Be Read before the Royal Society*, may draw attention to the strong element of parody in Fielding's most successful satires. We have seen in one of his poems that Fielding early recognized his bent for the "burlesque": after painting a vividly "low" picture of Upton Grey, he declared: "I've thought (so strong with me Burlesque prevails,) / This Place design'd to ridicule *Versailles*" (*Misc.*, 1, 40). His innate and pervasive sense of the ludicrous in things—in books as well as manners—seemed to find a natural outlet in the twin arts of burlesque and parody.[4] Thus the *Tragedy of Tragedies* bundled together all the clichés of heroic drama for half a century past and wove them together in a new creation, an original amalgam one might call it, which was not only magnificent burlesque but could stand on its own as a work of art. Less successful as an independent work is the *Covent-Garden Tragedy*, but in its very funny vulgarizing of Ambrose Philips' *Distrest Mother*[5] it employed a technique used again in *Tumble-Down Dick*, in *Shamela*, and in the satire on the Royal Society: namely,

---

[4] Worcester has some very thoughtful and just remarks upon the consistently underrated art of burlesque: "Burlesque . . . first moves us to the purposeless laughter of pure comedy by its ludicrous plot or frame. This explains the mechanics whereby most of the greatest satires convey an air of geniality and warm humanity"; and, again, "Of all the types of satire—here classified as invective, burlesque, and irony—burlesque offers the greatest freedom to the artist and exacts the most from him in terms of creative invention" (*The Art of Satire*, pp. 46 and 49).

[5] Fielding doubtless shared the impatience of a later reader who observed that for Philips to bestow upon the tragic drama of Andromache his title of *The Distrest Mother* was equivalent to denominating the epic tragedy of Prometheus, "The Man with the Liver Ailment."

the close and detailed adaptation of its model with adroit and inventive modifications that remove the work to an entirely new plane.[6] Normally, the effect is reductive, but in every case it is to expose the weaknesses or absurdities or falseness of its exemplar; and in every case a new fable or situation is created which is amusing in its own right. One may point out in passing that this parodic or burlesque element is central to *Jonathan Wild*, specifically in its parallels with rogue-biography and travel literature, and generally in the mock-encomiastic nature of the whole. Its appearance in the early chapters of *Joseph Andrews* is too well known to require comment; and it plays a lesser but occasionally significant part in *Tom Jones* and *Amelia*.

2

Turning now to the two satirical essays of the *Miscellanies*, we may examine them narrowly, with an eye for some of the devices that Fielding could typically exploit in formal satire. The parody of the *Philosophical Transactions* of the Royal Society clearly offered a more restricted imaginative range than the *Essay on Nothing*. Parody asks that one stay very close to the original, and this not only limits the range of the material but also of the arguments that can be "invented" and brought to bear upon it. Moreover, the pleasure that one finds in happy parallels between the original and the copy, though it may be exquisite when the original is well known and fresh to recollection, diminishes with time and distance. Fielding obviated this danger, in part, by citing extracts from the specific work that he parodied, *Some Papers Lately Read before the Royal Society, concerning the Fresh-Water Polypus*; but it nevertheless remains true that the parodic element in his piece,

[6] See Winfield H. Rogers, "Fielding's Early Esthetic and Technique," *SP*, xl (1943), 529-51; Charles B. Woods, "Fielding and the Authorship of *Shamela*," *PQ*, xxv (1946), 248-72; and Charles W. Nichols, "Fielding's *Tumble-Down Dick*," *MLN*, xxxviii (1923), 410-16.

SATIRES

Some Papers Proper to Be Read before the Royal Society, concerning the Terrestrial Chrysipus . . . or Guinea, is an academic joke that one enjoys in retrospect rather than with a compelling immediacy. In any case, the heart of the jest lay in a step-by-step parallel with the Society's solemn paper describing a "polypus" (or polyp, a fresh-water invertebrate). Hence Fielding's account (which substitutes a "chrysipus" or English guinea for the "polypus") follows the order of topics proper to a biological report, pausing to have its fun with each: a description of the "chrysipus" (with diagram), its size and species, general habitat, attempt at classification, account of its motion and its methods of generation, a long section on experiments with it, and a conclusion concerned with its longevity and local habitat. To this Fielding added an uncustomary account of the creature's virtues.

As the original paper had been the publication of a continental naturalist's report by a member of the Royal Society, so Fielding invents a *persona*, one "Heer Rottenscrach," who offers to the public the materials of a continental naturalist, "Petrus Gualterus"—and who inserts admiring editorial comments or diffident qualifications of his own from time to time. Worth noting here is the resemblance to the "rehearsal" technique of many of Fielding's plays; for a secondary level of comment upon another (primary) level was a procedure that seemed to hold particular charms for Fielding. His alert mind seized upon analogies, contradictions, ironies, and contrasts in the primary material (whether a simple report, as here, or a human action, as in the rehearsal plays and the novels), and he was irresistibly moved to comment upon them. In *Tom Jones* this multi-leveled mode would be employed to establish a personal relationship with the reader that is unique in literature.

The straight-faced sincerity and the uncritical naiveté of the *persona* who presents the paper to the Royal Society are reminiscent of Swift's Modest Proposer. That Fielding handles this kind of figure with considerably less ironic skill than Swift is suggestive of the difference in their talents. For Swift is at his best with the pure figure of *prosopopoeia* who provides the locus for a set of abstractions that then can be employed, directly or by contrast, to satirize the world of things-as-they-are. Fielding is never quite comfortable with this figure alone. In effect, *he* seeks to become the *persona*, and only when he has a dramatic action to comment upon is he entirely in his element. It cannot be said that Fielding had no interest in abstractions, and it can scarcely be said that Swift abhorred concretions: but I think it is true that Swift used his human figures as rhetorical devices to move into an analysis of the most meaningful abstract truths about man, whereas for Fielding the abstract (*and* the rhetorical) served as devices to illuminate another level of the intimately felt and directly observed dramatic human comedy.

The style of this paper reminds us once again of the stylistic variety that Fielding could command. He is not at all concerned here with the devices we remarked in the serious essays of the *Miscellanies* (and that reappear in the *Essay on Nothing*): one finds no striving after rhythm or cadence, no (or few) pleonastic pairs and no artful redundance, little parallelism or balance. The *copia verborum* has been replaced by a close, naked, natural way of speaking. That this striving after scientific precision struck Fielding as merely the substitution of an academic redundance for an artful redundance is perhaps indicated in his punctilious description of the Chrysipus: "This Animal or Vegetable is of a rotund, orbicular, or round Form, as represented in the Figure annexed. In which A. denotes the Ruffle. B. the Hand. G. [*sic*] the Thumb of that Hand. D. the Finger. E. the Part of that Finger to which the CHRYSIPUS sticks . . ." (*Misc.*, I, 260), and so on. Again, Fielding was no more able than Swift to appreciate the spirit of a scientific caution in the face of uncertainties: "I have not [Rottenscrach says], after the minutest Observation, been able to settle with any degree of Certainty, whether this be really an Animal or a Vegetable, or whether it be not strictly neither, or rather both" (*Misc.*, I, 261). The paper is dotted with pretentious Greek terms and coinages, and Fielding even allows the learned Rottenscrach a literary gesture—the quotation of some most profoundly relevant lines from Virgil—to make a scientific point. But on the whole, the diction and the syntax throughout attest the virtuoso of the Royal Society; the ornament of discourse is severely curtailed.

If the learned reporter will have nought to do with rhetoric, however, his creator is not so scrupulous. Fielding characterizes his cautious scientist through the use of a pervasive litotes ("whence I have been almost inclined to conclude . . . ," "which I think is not yet settled by the Learned to be *absolutely* . . ."), although he amusingly "undercuts" this exemplary reserve by permitting the pride of discovery to carry his reporter into hyperbole (the Chrysipus differs from or surpasses "all other Animals or Vegetables whatever") (*Misc.*, I, 264, 275). The multi-leveled irony is the result of a series of rhetorical juxtapositions and antitheses between the Polypus and the Chrysipus, or, in a more complex way, between Rottenscrach and his original (the "publisher") and between Gualterus and *his* original (the continental "experimenter").

Finally, although little use is made of the "colors" of rhetoric, the total situation or "action" is built (as is so often the case in Fielding) upon the elaboration of a single rhetorical device or concept. In the *Papers Proper to be Read before the Royal Society*, that rhetorical concept is the flaw known as *periergia* (or, as Quintilian calls it, "supervacua . . . operositas"),[7] that is, excessive care or

---

[7] *Institutio oratoria* VIII. iii. 55. My subsequent quotations from Quintilian are drawn from the translation in the Loeb Library by H. E. Butler

fussiness in building up a point of little importance. This flaw can be seen in many specific instances in the report; but, in effect, the whole report *itself* is just such an instance —an "overlabor," to use Puttenham's term[8]—on a subject that to the humanistic eye offered little excuse for such operose and minutely detailed investigation.

3

The devices employed in the *Essay on Nothing* offer much more copious (indeed, overwhelming) evidence of the part that Fielding's intimacy with all aspects of rhetoric played in his satire. The "essay" is actually a mock encomium, a kind of burlesque or parody (again) of the serious encomium, which was the most important species of epideictic, or demonstrative, rhetoric. Now, Aristotle (*Rhetoric*, 1368a) had said that, as *examples* were most suitable for deliberative orations and *enthymemes* for forensic, so *amplification* was most suitable for epideictic speakers. By "amplication" (*auxesis*) Aristotle seems to have meant simply aggrandizement or intensification; but by the time the term (*amplificatio*) came to Quintilian, it carried with it a complete panoply of devices for expansion —and of these, as we shall see, Fielding made good use. Again, although amplification was the most useful device to the epideictic orator, he also found it necessary to employ proofs; and proofs ultimately reduced to examples (and maxims) and enthymemes. Hence Aristotle's long discussion of these latter devices (1393a-1403b) actually was almost as useful for epideictic oratory as for the other branches.

The structure of the mock encomium may be most readily discussed when we come to the summary of Fielding's *Essay*

(4v., 1921-1922). Quotations from Aristotle's *Rhetoric* employ the translation in the Loeb Library by J. H. Freese (1926).
[8] *The Arte of English Poesie by George Puttenham*, ed. Gladys D. Willcock and Alice Walker (Cambridge, 1936), p. 258.

on Nothing. At this point it may serve to say that he not only creates a primary frame, the panegyric upon (and amplification of) his subject, but also a secondary level in which the inversions that are inherent in every statement about Nothing are applied to those contemporary values that Fielding found most lacking in true substance. The *persona* or mock panegyrist here has no features that need distinguish him from Fielding himself; but, whatever name we give to him, he occasionally creates a third level of response by dropping the ironic pose and speaking out directly. This same device also enabled him in certain cases to add an extra twist of the knife to his ironic commentary. We may illustrate both of these points by a citation from Fielding's argument that Nothing can be felt: "Nay, I have heard it asserted (*and with a Colour of Truth*) of several Persons, that they can feel nothing but a Cudgel. Notwithstanding which, some have felt the Motions of the Spirit; and others have felt very bitterly the Misfortunes of their Friends, *without endeavouring to relieve them.* Now these seem two plain Instances, that Nothing is an Object of this Sense" (*Misc.*, I, 239; italics mine).

The twenty or so devices that Quintilian (VIII. iv) suggested for amplification of a discourse can be reduced to six major heads, each of which could be copiously illustrated from Fielding's mock encomium: (1) the use of emotive or charged words. This, of course, Fielding uses throughout, speaking of "the great and noble Subject of this Essay" (I, 231), "such is the Awe with which this Nothing inspires Mankind" (I, 232), and so on.

(2) *Incrementum,* or building up to a climax (of which Quintilian remarked that it is "most impressive when it lends grandeur even to comparative insignificance"). Fielding employed this device in his catalogue of the kinds of Nothing (I, 243) and, more impressively, in equating Ambition with Nothing: "Nor is this the End of private Ambition only. What is become of that proud Mistress of

SATIRES

the World,—the *Caput triumphati Orbis?* that *Rome*, of which her own Flatterers so liberally prophesied the Immortality, In what hath all her Glory ended? surely in Nothing" (1, 248-49). Another form of *incrementum*, not attained by gradation, is "to make a thing so great as to be incapable of augmentation." This Fielding achieved in discussing the worship of empty titles: "The most astonishing Instance of this Respect, so frequently paid to Nothing, is when it is paid (if I may so express myself) to Something less than Nothing; when the Person who receives it is not only void of the Quality for which he is respected, but is in Reality notoriously guilty of Vices directly opposite to the Virtues, whose Applause he receives. This is, indeed, the highest Degree of Nothing, or, (if I may be allowed the Word) the *Nothingest* of all Nothings" (1, 246-47).

(3) Comparison or parallel to make something appear even greater (in Fielding, more egregious) by contrast. In the *Essay*: "For Instance; when a Bladder is full of Wind, it is full of Something; but when that is let out, we aptly say, there is Nothing in it"; likewise, "The same may be as justly asserted of a Man as of a Bladder. However well he may be bedawbed with Lace, or with Title, yet if he have not Something in him, we may predicate the same of him as of an empty Bladder" (1, 237).

(4) *Ratiocinatio*, by which Quintilian seems to mean a use of analogy, subsequent events, antecedent circumstances, or allusion, to create an augmentation by inference. So when Fielding says, "Certain it is, that except a hardy Wit in the Reign of *Charles* II. none ever hath dared to write on this Subject" (1, 232), the inference is that the subject is too great for ordinary mortals. Or again, when he says, "One of the wisest Men in the World declared, he knew nothing" (1, 240), the inference is that Nothing was of sufficient magnitude to draw the attention of a Socrates.

(5) Accumulation (*congeries*) of words and sentences identical in meaning (which, as Quintilian observes, is re-

lated to the second head, *incrementum*). Thus Fielding can say: "Ambition, the greatest, highest, noblest, finest, most heroic and godlike of all Passions, what doth it end in?—Nothing" (1, 248); or, of the Miser: "May we not therefore, nay, must we not confess, that he aims at Nothing? especially if he be himself unable to tell us what is the End of all this Bustle and Hurry, this watching and toiling, this Self-Denial, and Self-Constraint!" (1, 249).

(6) Quintilian postpones a consideration of *hyperbole* for his account of Tropes, but admits that it is often regarded as a species of amplification. This is related to the use of words under the first head, and is pervasive in Fielding's essay; but we may perhaps cite his claim for Nothing, that "it possesses the greatest and noblest Place on this Earth, *viz.* the human Brain" (1, 236).

This rather mechanical set of parallels between Quintilian's theory of the amplification proper to an epideictic discourse and Fielding's practice in a formal satire may not only indicate that Fielding well knew what he was about when he worked in a traditional rhetorical mode, but may also suggest the source (in rhetoric, not merely in Quintilian) of many of his most characteristic devices of irony and humor in the plays and novels. The very large investigation that this suggests must be left to another time and place. For the present, if I may venture another set of parallels between theory and practice, I should like to offer a few notes on Fielding's acquaintance with the Aristotelian modes of proof.

In the *Rhetoric* (1355b), Aristotle had categorized proofs as *inartificial* and *artificial*. The first included such aids as laws and documents and witnesses, which encompassed the testimony of ancient writers—and ancient witnesses, he said, were more trustworthy because they were incapable of being corrupted (1376a)! Fielding makes only slight use of the inartificial proof, calling upon the testimony of historians, for example, to establish the antiquity of Nothing. Artificial proofs, however, were of great importance to his case. Aristotle had reduced these, as we have previously observed, to examples (under which head he also considered maxims) and enthymemes. We need not pause over Fielding's use of examples, historical and invented: some have already been cited in the previous discussion. He also employs anecdote (1, 239, 241) and quotation (for example, "a strong Instance" from Horace; 1, 238). His use of maxim ranges from the homely ("How commonly do we hear, that such a Thing smells or tastes of Nothing?"—1, 239) to the philosophic ("That every thing is resolvable, and will be resolved into its first Principles, will be, I believe, readily acknowledged by all Philosophers"—1, 248). Aristotle had also suggested (1395a) that maxims might be used to counter other popular sayings. Fielding uses this technique to oppose certain common notions fatal to his own argument: "THERE is nothing falser than that old Proverb . . . *Ex Nihilo nihil Fit* . . . Whereas in Fact, from Nothing proceeds every Thing. And this is a Truth confessed by the Philosophers of all Sects . . ." (1, 233).

As the *Example* was to rhetoric what the induction was to dialectic: so, Aristotle said, the *Enthymeme* was to rhetoric what the syllogism was to dialectic. The enthymeme was, in effect, a truncated syllogism, omitting either the major or the minor premise. Moreover, it often drew its major premise not from a universal truth but a merely contingent one, that is, from general opinion or the like. A good part of Fielding's argument is made up of enthymemes; for example, proving that Nothing is the object of the senses:

"For First; Nothing may be seen, as is plain from the Relation of Persons who have recovered from high Fevers; and perhaps may be suspected from some (at least) of those who have seen Apparitions, both on Earth, and in the Clouds. . . . Admitting then that there are two Sights, viz. a first and second Sight, according to the firm Belief of some, Nothing must be allowed to have a very large

Share of the first; and as to the second, it hath it all entirely to itself"—(1, 238).

The first is an example; the second is an enthymeme, having this structure: major premise (omitted): apparitions are Nothing; minor premise: second sight can see apparitions; conclusion: second sight can see Nothing. A slightly more complex illustration is found when Fielding touches upon "a too vulgar Error among Persons unacquainted with the Mystery of Writing, who imagine it impossible that a Man should sit down to write without any Meaning at all; whereas . . . it may be incontestably proved, *ab Effectu*, that Nothing is commoner among the Moderns" (1, 242). The form of the enthymeme here is something like this: major premise (omitted): to write about Nothing creates an effect of no meaning; minor premise: modern writers commonly create an effect of no meaning; conclusion: modern writers commonly write about Nothing.

It can be seen that Fielding stretches the "contingent" element in his enthymemes to the breaking point; but if a degree of stretching was permitted to the authentic encomium (Aristotle had said, "We must . . . assume, for the purpose of praise or blame, that qualities which closely resemble the real qualities are identical with them; for instance, that the cautious man is cold and designing, the simpleton good-natured, and the emotionless gentle"—1367*a*), then surely the mock encomium enjoyed a correspondingly greater liberty! As a matter of fact, Fielding was able to find in Aristotle's discussion an even more "illegitimate" source of argumentation. For, having considered at some length the topics from which enthymemes might be derived, Aristotle concluded by warning against a handful of fallacious or merely apparent enthymemes (1401*a*-1402*a*). And these Fielding found directly to his purpose.

The first of them, for example, consisted "in ending with a conclusion syllogistically expressed, although there has been no syllogistic process." This is precisely the form of some of Fielding's high-handed argumentation: "ANother Falsehood which we must detect in the Pursuit of this Essay, is an Assertion, *That no one can have an Idea of* NOTHING: But Men who thus confidently deny us this Idea, either grossly deceive themselves, or would impose a downright Cheat on the World: for so far from having none, I believe there are few who have not many Ideas of it . . ." (1, 235). Aristotle's fourth fallacy was "that of constructing or destroying by exaggeration"; Fielding's construction by exaggeration takes the place of true argument throughout. Again, there is the eighth fallacy, that of "taking what is not the cause for the cause" (*post hoc ergo propter hoc* is a special case of this fallacy); this kind of argument is involved in Fielding's proof that Nothing is the origin of all things (1, 233-34). In Fielding's attempt to define Nothing, there is perhaps an echo of the phrasing of Aristotle's tenth fallacy. This complicated error arises "as the result of considering a thing first absolutely, and then not absolutely, but only in a particular case. For instance, in Dialectic, it is argued that that which is not *is*, for that which is not *is* that which is not; also, that the unknown can be known, for it can be known of the unknown that it is unknown" (1402*a*). Compare Fielding's argument: "Farther; as Nothing is not Something, so every thing which is not Something, is Nothing; and wherever Something is not, Nothing is: a very large Allowance in its Favour, as must appear to Persons well skilled in human Affairs" (1, 237).

The most significant of Aristotle's fallacious enthymemes for Fielding's purposes, however, was the second, "homonymy," meaning not merely a like sound but an equivocation: "For instance, if one were to say that the mouse [μῦς] is an important animal, since from it is derived the most honoured of all religious festivals, namely, the mysteries [μυστήρια]" (1401*a*). This may serve, as *periergia* did for the satire on the Royal Society, to symbolize the procedure of the entire encomium; for it is in the fallacious and farfetched equivocations on the term "Nothing" that the whole work is obviously constituted. The test of a mock encomium was, after all, not truth but ingenuity.

4

We have seen that parodic and rhetorical devices and arguments play a major role in shaping the structure, carrying out the purposes, and defining the character of the two formal satires. The discussion of these satires, however, has necessarily confined itself for the most part to questions of diction, tone, and style: the larger satire of the plays and novels could draw upon a multitude of different and more flexible techniques having to do with plot and action, with the delineation of character and setting, with dialogue and conflict, and other elements that are of little consequence in the *Essay on Nothing* and *Some Papers Proper to be Read before the Royal Society*. Some of these elements will fall within our purview when we come to discuss Fielding's Lucianic satires; but his inclusive mastery of techniques and tones can barely be hinted at in any consideration of these minor works. I should hope only to suggest here a few of the elements that contributed to the ultimate shaping and ordering of Fielding's satiric perspective. That rhetoric was a determinant of considerable significance may be further indicated, however, by its obvious contribution to each of the following heads (under which, I think, most of Fielding's enormous variety of satirical techniques could be ranged): irony (devices of indirection); distortion (devices of exaggeration and diminution); inversion (devices of shifting perspective); ambiguity; juxtaposition (including devices of incongruity); commentary; exemplum and trope

SATIRES

(taking in narrative and symbolic devices, and devices of personification); imitation (devices of analogy and parody); and mechanism (devices of formal theorizing). To this list might be added the overlapping set of rhetorical figures of thought and diction, many of which would fall under the cited heads.

Most of the techniques that these heads suggest could be classified as disjunctive. That is, irony, inversion, shifts in perspective, ambiguity, incongruity and the like, all *disjoin* the reader from the comfortable world of normal expectation, force him into re-examination, drive him into unfamiliar territory. On the side of the conjunctive, linking the reader of any satire *with* the familiar and expected, is normally a group of shared assumptions that permit the satirist (and more particularly, the ironist) to work. These assumptions set out the field upon which he is to play and provide the rules of the game. To this conjunctive condition he may add such controls as he is master of: the control of narrative, of parody, of particular genre, and so on, to maintain (as one end) an obligatory nexus with his reader of the familiar or expected, that in turn makes possible his abruptions of or departures from that world.

It seems to me that the most important *control* that Fielding developed to mediate between the disjunctive and the conjunctive facets of his satire was the mastery of direct commentary. Not only does this commentary, as I have argued before, contribute to the distinctive quality of Fielding's humor, of his comic world: it also serves to make of his satire an instrument that can uniquely combine impersonality and detachment (the disjunctive) *with* a warm involvement and most personal attachment (the conjunctive), in a manner that is not possible to, say, the devastating irony of Swift, at one end of the scale, or the emotional commitment to his satire of a Dickens, at the other.[9] The

[9] To carry the matter further, most satire involves an emphasis upon one pole of each of the following representative dichotomies, at the ex-

shaping of this subtle and flexible instrument of commentary was not entirely a matter of rhetoric, as it was not entirely a matter of any one thing—Fielding's dramatic or journalistic or poetic experience, or his training in the law, or his direct experience of the worlds of high and low society. All contributed; but I should claim for the determinants of rhetoric and parody a high place in modeling the command of diction and tone that make Fielding's personal commentary the astonishing and delightful artistic achievement that it is.

This then, I believe, is the larger significance of the two works before us. Taken in themselves, of course, they are minor enough; though even in themselves alone they well illustrate Fielding's talent for finding apt contrivances (the task of *inventio*) to carry the ridicule of current folly; his skillful reworking of material to his own satiric ends (the task of *dispositio*); and the lambent wit and humor (the task of *elocutio*) that play through all of his endeavors in formal satire.

If the *Essay on Nothing* is a trifle, a leap into the ridiculous, it is a learned trifle and one with a very ancient tradition behind it; and Fielding turns his jest to broader account by encompassing organically within its formal structure a pungent satirical broadside against the emptiness of contemporary social ideals. Much of the humor of *Some Papers Proper to be Read before the Royal Society* is lost to us now, not only because it is a *pièce d'occasion,* but because our normal assumptions about scientific research have undergone a considerable modification. That a virtuoso should spend many hours cutting up polyps seemed much

pense of the other pole. I think that it could be argued, and copiously illustrated, that Fielding's commentary serves as a mediating device between the disjunct poles of such basic dichotomies in satirical method as Abstraction-Concentration; Type-Individual; Affectation-Deformity; Superiority-Sympathy; Probability-Improbability; Predictability-Unpredictability; Consistency-Inconsistency; Economy-Amplification; Understatement-Emphasis; Openness-Deception; Seriousness-Play. And so on.

more ridiculous to Fielding's day than it does to our own; today, indeed, the position of the scientist and the satirist appear to have been reversed, and the last good laugh may belong to the former. In any case, one can still relish the cleverness and the dexterity with which the parody of a learned naturalist's report to the Society is handled; and the metamorphosis of the naturalist (as we shall see) into a usurer, and of the polypus (as we have seen) into the chrysipus or guinea, is a stroke of pure liberated fancy. Satire on avarice, at least, is still in fashion; and it has not often been presented in a more exquisitely ridiculous guise than in the report of the learned Petrus Gualterus upon the Terrestrial Chrysipus. In a word, Fielding's two satires are admittedly mere jokes: but they are good jokes, and the laughter they excite is thoughtful laughter.

1. "AN ESSAY ON NOTHING"

A passing allusion to "The inimitable Author of a Preface to the Posthumous Eclogues of a late ingenious young Gentleman" (*Misc.*, I, 242) in the second section of the *Essay on Nothing* can be dated rather precisely. The work referred to has long since been identified as the *Love Elegies. By Mr. H - - - - nd. Written in the Year 1732. With a Preface by the E. of C - - - - - - - - d*, printed for G. Hawkins in 1743. The author was James Hammond, an adherent of the opposition to Walpole; he died in June 1742.[10] The "inimitable Author" of the preface was Hammond's—and Fielding's—friend and patron, the Earl of Chesterfield.

The *Love Elegies*, though dated 1743, were apparently published as early as November 1742, since they are listed by the *London Magazine* of that date: "Love Elegies. Printed for G. *Hawkins*, price 1 *s*" (p. 572). Hence Fielding's allusion to the work must have been made only a few

[10] See J. Paul De Castro, "Fieldingiana," *N&Q*, 12th Ser., II (1916), 443. The quoted title page is that of the octavo edition: there was also a folio edition in 1743, titled simply *Love Elegies. Written in the Year 1732.*

months before the publication of the *Miscellanies* in April. It is always possible, of course, that the allusion was merely inserted at that time into a previously written text, so I am not inclined to see it as certain evidence for the date of composition of the *Essay on Nothing*.

2

The *Essay on Nothing*, as we have previously observed, is in the form of an epideictic oration, or "show-piece," with an introduction (*exordium*) and an argument (*confirmatio*) divided into three parts: "*Of the Antiquity of* NOTHING"; "*Of the Nature of* NOTHING"; and "*Of the Dignity of* NOTHING; *and an Endeavour to prove, that it is the End as well as Beginning of all Things.*" Now, Cicero and Quintilian had agreed that the "status" of any case turned on three fundamental questions: *an sit?, quid sit?,* and *quale sit?*—whether a thing is, what it is, and of what moral quality or value it is.[11] Following (implicitly) this essential outline, Fielding's concern is to show that Nothing exists, to define it, and to assert its qualities. And since his "essay" is actually a panegyric, he draws his arguments from three of the traditional *topoi* (or "places") for the praise of Things—*antiquitas, utilitas,* and *dignitas*.

In "The INTRODUCTION" or *exordium*, Fielding expresses his surprise that "while such trifling Matters employ the masterly Pens of the present Age, the great and noble Subject of this Essay should have passed totally neglected," especially as it is one most excellently adapted to "the Genius of many of those Writers who have unsuccessfully applied themselves to Politics, Religion, &c. . . ." (*Misc.*, I, 231). "Perhaps," he continues, "their Unwillingness to handle what is of such Importance, may not improperly be ascribed to their Modesty; though they may not be remark-

---

[11] Cicero, *Orator* XIV. 45, and *De oratore* II. xxiv. 104; Quintilian, *Inst. orat.* III. vi. 44 and 80. Of an *act* one would inquire: was it done, what was done, and what was the moral nature of it?

ably addicted to this Vice on every Occasion. Indeed I have heard it predicated of some, whose Assurance in treating other Subjects hath been sufficiently notable, that they have blushed at this" (1, 232). With characteristic good humor (and in a facetious inversion of the so-called "ethical appeal" based on the personal character of the speaker), he turns the joke upon himself, announcing that he hopes his own attempt "will not be imputed to me as an Act of Immodesty; since I am convinced there are many Persons in this Kingdom, who are persuaded of my Fitness for what I have undertaken" (1, 232-33).

Omitting the *Narratio* or statement of the facts (which was frequently done in epideictic orations), Fielding then proceeds "without any more Excuse or Preface," to his *Confirmatio* or proof. His first task is the dual one of proving that Nothing exists and of celebrating its antiquity. Hence he begins with the cosmological tenet that in the beginning was Nothing. On this all the philosophers agree, Fielding says (employing a tongue-in-cheek argument from authority), their controversy being only "whether Something made the World out of Nothing, or Nothing out of Something" (1, 233). Either will serve the present purpose, for "whether Nothing was the *Artifex* or *Materies* only," it is still the origination of all things. Its antiquity may be further observed "from its being so visible in the Accounts we have of the Beginning of every Nation," observable in the first pages—and sometimes entire books—of all "general Historians." It is, moreover, the entire study of the Antiquary, "and is commonly at last discovered by him with infinite Labour and Pains" (1, 234).

Having established to his satisfaction the antiquity of Nothing, and answered the question, *an sit?*, Fielding goes on, in Section II, to the nature of Nothing (*quid sit?*). He indignantly refutes the false assertion, "*That no one can have an Idea of* NOTHING," with the syllogistic argument that everyone certainly has "an Idea of immaterial Substance"—and *that* is Nothing.[12] Not entirely satisfied with this easy triumph, he breaks in to declare (and, incidentally, to offer an audacious thumbnail sketch of the entire essay): "But here we are artfully deceived by the Use of Words"!— "For were we to ask another what Idea he had of immaterial Matter, or unsubstantial Substance, the Absurdity of affirming it to be Something, would shock him, and he would immediately reply, it was *Nothing*" (I, 235-36). The tangle that faces him in carrying this argument any further is rather formidable; so Fielding simply puts a brave face on the matter and blusters his way through (employing the rhetorical prolepsis known as *rejectio* or dismissal of anticipated objections): "Some Persons perhaps will say then, we have no Idea of it: but as I can support the contrary by such undoubted Authority, I shall, instead of trying to confute such idle Opinions, proceed to shew, First, what Nothing is; Secondly, I shall disclose the various Kinds of Nothing; and lastly, shall prove its great Dignity, and that

[12] Fielding adds a note (*Misc.*, I, 235) to make clear that he is not arguing against "the Doctrine of Immateriality" or the theological idea of immaterial essence, but of immaterial *substance*, which is, he says, a pure contradiction in terms. The background of the controversy over this concept is presented very succinctly by Charles Kerby-Miller in his edition of *Memoirs of . . . Martinus Scriblerus* (New Haven, 1950), pp. 280-85ff. Hobbes had attacked the notion in strong terms, and several Boyle lecturers had argued for it with equal vehemence, claiming that the soul or spirit of man was an immaterial substance (see John Hunt, *Religious Thought in England* [3v., 1870-1873] III, 99-101). In the first decade of the eighteenth century, Samuel Clarke, Anthony Collins, and Henry Dodwell became involved in a vituperative controversy on the subject, and it was this intricate theological argument that was ridiculed in the Scriblerus papers. To Fielding, as to the Scriblerians, such abstruse speculations were detrimental to the cause of true religion, and he had an innate distaste for them. Parson Williams in *Shamela* labels himself such a speculator— as well as a hypocrite: "As he went along [Shamela says], he began to discourse very learnedly, and told me the Flesh and the Spirit were too [sic] distinct Matters, which had not the least relation to each other. That all immaterial Substances (those were his very Words) such as Love, Desire, and so forth, were guided by the Spirit: But fine Houses, large Estates, Coaches, and dainty Entertainments were the Product of the Flesh" (*Shamela*, repr. Augustan Reprint Soc., Publ. No. 57 [Los Angeles, 1956], p. 47).

it is the End of every thing" (I, 236). This is also, somewhat belatedly, the formal *divisio* of his discourse.

Proceeding to the task of definition (he is still on the question, *quid sit?*), Fielding admits that "it is extremely hard to define Nothing in positive Terms, I shall therefore do it in Negative. Nothing then is not Something." And, although we cannot get at the true essence of Nothing any more than we can of Matter, we may "in Imitation of the Experimental Philosophers, examine some of its Properties or Accidents" (I, 237); and this he sets out to do, proving by a series of exempla, maxims, and analogies that Nothing can be seen, heard, tasted, smelled, and even felt ("Nay, I have heard a Surgeon declare, while he was cutting off a Patient's Leg, that *he was sure he felt nothing*"—I, 239).[13] And of course all this is additional evidence of "the infinite Advantages which Nothing hath over Something: for while the latter is confined to one Sense, or two perhaps at the most, Nothing is the Object of them all" (I, 237). (This touches upon the question *quale sit?* and also contributes to the *topos* of utility.) Again, Nothing can be the object of the passions or of the understanding. Sometimes, it is true, the latter may be puzzling, "for where a Book, or Chapter, or Paragraph, hath seemed to the Reader to contain Nothing, his Modesty hath sometimes persuaded him, that the true Meaning of the Author hath escaped him, instead of concluding, as in Reality the Fact was, that the Author, in the said Book, &c. did truly, and *bonâ Fide*, mean Nothing" (I, 241).

Section II is concluded with a finely discriminatory list of the varieties of Nothing (an example of Quintilian's *incrementum*). Some imagine, Fielding says, that these differ in name only; but this is absurd, "especially as these

---

[13] One is reminded of the surgeon in *Tom Jones* who stretched and examined Jones's broken arm until the young man grimaced in pain, "which the surgeon observing, greatly wondered at, crying, 'What is the matter, sir? I am sure it is impossible I should hurt you'" (IV, xiv; Henley, III, 199).

different Kinds of Nothing occur frequently in the best Authors." The "kinds," then, are: "Nothing *per se* Nothing; Nothing at all; Nothing in the least; Nothing in Nature; Nothing in the World; Nothing in the whole World; Nothing in the whole universal World. And perhaps many others, of which we say—Nothing" (1, 243).

The final and longest section of the treatise satisfies the third question, *quale sit?*, and expands the third *topos*, after *antiquitas* and *utilitas*, namely *dignitas*. "NOTHING," Fielding begins importantly, "contains so much Dignity as NOTHING." Indeed, if one should ask "an infamous worthless Nobleman (if any such be) in what his Dignity consists," such a titled person would ultimately be forced, "in the Face of downright positive Proof," to admit that "his Dignity arises from Nothing, and in Reality is Nothing." Yet, Fielding concludes triumphantly, "that this Dignity really exists; that it glares in the Eyes of Men, and produces much Good to the Person who wears it, is, I believe, incontestable" (1, 244-45).

Up to this point Fielding has been, one might say, merely enjoying the rhetorical game, flaunting his ingenuity. Here, however, his irony has for the first time flushed real game, an object of true social concern; and in the rest of the essay the satirical thrust becomes sharper as well as more particularized. It is not surprising, Fielding says, that men fail to be ashamed of paying or receiving this respect for Nothing, since the great importance of Nothing has been clearly demonstrated; but it is indeed curious and "more worthy Reprehension" that one who quite obviously has Nothing in him should pretend to Something, and even be supported by others less likely to be deceived: "Now whence can this proceed, but from their being ashamed of Nothing? A Modesty very peculiar to this Age." (A delightful ambiguity there!) Even though the man of discernment may be forced through necessity or corruption to "comply with the vulgar Worship and Adulation," he will nevertheless know in his own mind to what this respect is paid: "namely, to *Nothing*" (1, 246).

Continuing to play upon the satiric possibilities inherent in this respect paid to Nothing, Fielding builds to the "most astonishing Instance" of the phenomenon. This "is when it is paid (if I may so express myself) to Something less than Nothing; when the Person who receives it is not only void of the Quality for which he is respected, but is in Reality notoriously guilty of Vices directly opposite to the Virtues, whose Applause he receives." This, he says, in the passage we have cited to illustrate the highest kind of *incrementum*, an augmentation that permits of no increase, "This is, indeed, the highest Degree of Nothing, or, (if I may be allowed the Word) the *Nothingest* of all Nothings" (1, 246-47).

From this climax the essay tapers off in its satirical energy with the "proof" by maxims, exempla, and enthymemes, that "Nothing is the End as well as Beginning of all Things." Having already demonstrated the latter, he calls upon an *argumentum ad hominem* to establish the former: "As I am writing to a Nation of Christians, I have no need to be prolix on this Head; since every one of my Readers, by his Faith, acknowledges that the World is to have an End, *i.e.* is to come to Nothing" (1, 248). Again, consider the world's "two greatest and noblest Pursuits," Ambition and Avarice. "What did *Alexander, Cæsar*, and all the rest of that heroic Band, who have plundered, and massacred so many Millions, obtain by all their Care, Labour, Pain, Fatigue, and Danger?—Could they speak for themselves, must they not own, that the End of all their Pursuit was Nothing?" (1, 248). And "What is the End of Avarice? Not Power, or Pleasure, as some think, for the Miser will part with a Shilling for neither: not Ease or Happiness; for the more he attains of what he desires, the more uneasy and miserable he is. . . . May we not therefore, nay, must we not confess, that he aims at Nothing?" (1, 249).

Fielding declines to tire his reader further by demonstrating that Nothing is the end of all the other pursuits "of the busy Part of Mankind." He therefore concludes his "essay" with a *peroratio* "which aptly enough suggests itself from what hath been said." The conclusion (I, 251) is that it surely "becomes a wise Man to regard Nothing with the utmost Awe and Adoration; to pursue it with all his Parts and Pains; and to sacrifice to it his Ease, his Innocence, and his present Happiness." And he closes emphatically with a long suspended period: "The Virtuous, Wise, and Learned may then be unconcerned at all the Changes of Ministeries and of Government; since they may be well satisfied, that while Ministers of State are Rogues themselves, and have inferior Knavish Tools to bribe and reward; true Virtue, Wisdom, Learning, Wit, and Integrity, will most certainly bring their Possessors—NOTHING."

3

Rochester's famous poem, *Upon Nothing,* may possibly have influenced Fielding's choice of subject; he alludes to "a hardy Wit in the Reign of *Charles* II" as his predecessor. But other than this, the connection with Rochester's poem is slight, and only a few obvious parallels between the two satires can be marked.[14] Moreover, the theme was scarcely new with Rochester. Jesters and moralists had been ringing the changes upon "nothing" for several hundred years. Dr. Johnson, who called *Upon Nothing* "the strongest effort of [Rochester's] Muse," cited as its exemplar a Latin poem called *Nihil* by Joannes Passerati, the sixteenth-century

---

[14] For example, Rochester also begins with the cosmological primacy of Nothing:

> NOTHING! thou Elder Brother ev'n to Shade,
> That hadst a Being e're the World was made . . .
> (*Poems,* ed. V. de Sola Pinto [1953], p. 77)

And some of Rochester's modern instances of Nothing, such as "the great Man's Gratitude to his best Friend," are in the same vein as that exploited by Fielding.

SATIRES

French critic and poet.[15] Passerati's poem itself was by no means the earliest attempt to play upon the word (William of Poitiers, we are told, had written a poem on Nothing in the twelfth century),[16] but the inversions of Passerati's *Nihil* are typical of all that followed:

> *Ecce autem, partes dum sese versat in omnes*
> *Invênit mea Musa Nihil. ne despice munus:*
> *Nam Nihil est gemmis, Nihil est pretiosius auro.*
> . . . .
> *Sed tempus finem argutis imponere nugis,*
> *Ne tibi, si multâ laudem mea carmina chartâ*
> *De Nihilo, Nihilli pariant fastidia versus.*[17]

Other continental humanists treated the theme in Latin or vernacular verses;[18] and in England, Edward Daunce composed a highly moral tract which he called *The Prayse of Nothing* (1585), and which he turned to the good purpose of attacking mankind's dedication to mere *temporalia*. A ballad of the early seventeenth century with the same

[15] *Lives of the English Poets*, ed. G. B. Hill (3v., Oxford, 1905), I, 224 and 227-28.
[16] See Swift's *Tale of a Tub*, ed. A. C. Guthkelch and D. N. Smith (2nd ed., Oxford, 1958), p. 208, n. 1. Paul Lehmann has noted several medieval parodic sermons on *Nihil*, which apparently grew out of the scholastic concern with the question of creation "ex nihilo" (*Die Parodie im Mittelalter* [Munich, 1922], pp. 244-45).
[17] "NIHIL. IOANNIS PASSERATII *Lusus ad V. Cl.* ERRICVM MEMMIVM," in *Argumentorum ludicrorum* (1623) [Part II], pp. 107, 109.
[18] The *Argumentorum ludicrorum* has a poem, shortly following Passerati's, by Theodore Marcilius called "DE NEMINE" (pp. 113-18). Passerati's Italian contemporary, Francesco Beccuti (Il Coppetta) wrote a comparable set of reflections, "Capitolo nel quale si lodano le Noncovelle," which has as good a claim as Passerati's to have given Rochester some hints (repr. in *Rime di Francesco Beccuti Perugino, detto Il Coppetta* [Venice, 1751], pp. 164-68). See also V. de Sola Pinto, "Rochester and Salvator Rosa," *English Miscellany* [Rome], VII (1956), 19-24 (Rosa mentions certain "versi del Niente" in a letter to Ricciardi of 1662). Adolf Hauffen, in his copious study of the paradoxical encomium in German literature, says, after citing Ulrich Von Hutten's *Nemo* (1518), "In ähnlicher Weise werden Aliquid, Nihil, Nullus, Omnia u.a. gepriesen," but he gives no specific titles ("Zur Litteratur der ironischen Enkomien," *Vierteljahrschrift für Litteraturgeschichte*, VI [1893], 167-68).

title, "the Praise of Nothing," followed Daunce's moral lead, arguing that although "Nothing's regarded more then gold," usurers would ultimately be called to account:

> When Nothing from the grave can call
> Such mizers, who their soules inthrall
> To gripe and hoord the devill and all;
> but better they had Nothing.[19]

Other seventeenth-century investigations of Nothing include Sir William Cornwallis' "*Prayse of* Nothing" (a loose verse-paraphrase of Passerati), and a doggerel burlesque of such enterprises by one S. S. in 1653, "In the praise of Nothing," which begins, "How do they err (beshrew their Bums) / That say of nothing, nothing comes?"[20] Another verse "Praise of Nothing" was included in Nicholas Billingsley's ΚΟΣΜΟΒΡΕΦΙΑ, *or the Infancy of the World* (1658); *Merry Drollery Complete . . . The First Part* (1691) has an anti-Puritan ballad, "A Song of Nothing," which repeats the theme that all comes from Nothing and shall end in Nothing and which declares:

> If any man tax me with weakness of wit
> And say that on Nothing, I nothing have writ,
> I shall answer *ex nihilo nihil fit*.[21]

In the eighteenth century Rochester was usually referred to as the exemplar. John Dunton included his poem (along with that of Cornwallis) in his *Athenian Sport: or, Two Thousand Paradoxes Merrily Argued* (1707); Pope wrote a youthful imitation of it; the *Spectator* referred to it ("his admirable Poem upon that barren Subject");[22] and

---

[19] *A Book of Roxburghe Ballads*, ed. J. P. Collier (1847), p. 150.
[20] Cornwallis, *Essayes or rather, Encomions* (1616), sigs. E₃v-E₄v. The burlesque is in *Paradoxes or Encomions . . . by* S. S. (1653), pp. 6-7.
[21] Ed. J. W. Ebsworth (Boston, Lincolnshire, 1875), p. 68.
[22] *Athenian Sport*, pp. 354-57; Pope, "On SILENCE" (*Minor Poems*, ed. Norman Ault and John Butt [Twickenham ed., Vol. VI, 1954], pp. 17-19); *Spectator*, No. 305 (Everyman ed., II, 417).

SATIRES

later writers often began, as Fielding does, by alluding to Rochester. The theme seized the attention of a great number of minor wits, and the popular press joined with a will in the celebration of Nothing. Contemporary periodicals offer a galaxy of such things as "A Ballad *on* Nothing," queries and riddling poems on the subject, a *"humourous Letter"* by a writer who *"professes to treat upon* Nothing," and so on. A work called "The Elogy of Nothing. Dedicated to *no Body"* (probably a translation of Coquelet's *Éloge de rien dédié à personne*, Paris, 1730) was published by T. Cooper in 1742.[23] In the years after Fielding's essay, Francis Coventry included "A *Dissertation upon* Nothing" in his *History of Pompey the Little* (1751);[24] an imitator of Sterne wrote a "Meditation" on the subject in 1760;[25] and the jest finally died with such things as Hugo Arnot's *Essay on Nothing: A Discourse Delivered in a Society*, in 1776—though Robert Burns gave it one last

[23] For the ballad, see the London Magazine (April 1737), p. 218. The Athenian Oracle offered several questions and answers on Nothing (3rd ed., 4v., 1728; I, 537-38, II, 441-43), as did its imitator, The British Apollo (3rd ed., 3v., 1726; I, 89). Riddles on Nothing appeared in the Gentleman's Magazine in September 1737 (p. 567) and September 1740 (p. 462), inspiring a host of replies. The *"humourous Letter"* was reprinted in the same journal (September 1737, pp. 559-61) from the Weekly Miscellany No. 247; as usual it cited Rochester's example: "A famous Peer and Wit, you know, wrote a Poem on *Nothing*; and I know Hands, in which a Parcel of *Nothings* would make a finer Appearance than other Peoples *Somethings"* (p. 560). The *Elogy*, "With a Preface. By T. TRIPLER, Esq. of the Middle Temple," was noticed in the Daily Advertiser for 7 July 1742.

[24] Coventry's dissertation is the prefatory chapter to Book II of *Pompey the Little* (pp. 125-33). He had taken this practice of prefatory chapters from Fielding; but he displayed no awareness of the *Essay on Nothing*, saying: "I DO not recollect any Writer before myself, excepting the great Lord Rochester, who has professedly treated this abstruse, learned and comprehensive Subject" (p. 127). This may be merely a formula, what we might call the *topos* of It-is-curious-that-no-one-has-written-on-this. Fielding opens his own essay in the same manner, and there is a multitude of other examples.

[25] *Yorick's Meditations upon Various Interesting and Important Subjects. viz. Upon Nothing. Upon Something. Upon the Thing [&c.]* . . . (1760), pp. 1-4.

SATIRES

fling in his "Extempore to Gavin Hamilton: Stanzas on Naething."[26]

Fielding himself played with the idea in various ways: for instance, his satirical attack in the *Covent-Garden Journal* upon the lower-class debating group, the Robin-Hood Society, pictured them earnestly considering the question, "Whether infinite Power could make the World out of Nothing?" Their recorder declared, "It was well argued, that Nothing can be made out of Nothing, for, *ex nihil O Nothing is fit*" (*CGJ*, No. 8; Jensen, I, 184-85). This last paper, incidentally, may have been the inspiration for a burlesque letter in Bonnell Thornton's *Drury-Lane Journal*, entitled, "METAPHYSICAL DISQUISITION on NOTHINGISM."[27] All in all, Swift's comment at the conclusion of *A Tale of a Tub* (1704) can be said to have retained its point for a good many years: "I am now trying an Experiment very frequent among Modern Authors; which is, to write upon Nothing. . . ."[28]

4

The *Essay on Nothing* belongs, however, as we have already observed, to a rhetorical tradition long antedating Rochester or the other celebrants of Nothing: namely, that of the paradoxical encomium.[29] The encomium itself, as treated by all the classical rhetors, was an oration in the epideictic mode, which eulogized a person, place, or thing, according to a fairly consistent form and employing a conventional set of relevant *topoi* or arguments. But very early in the development of formal rhetoric, the game arose of composing such encomia upon unworthy, un-

[26] *Poetry of Robert Burns*, ed. W. E. Henley and T. F. Henderson (4v., Edinburgh, 1896-1897), II, 93-95.
[27] *Have at You All: or, The Drury-Lane Journal* (coll. ed., 1752), pp. 52-53. Cf. Jensen, II, 171.
[28] *A Tale of a Tub*, ed. cit., p. 208.
[29] I have treated this subject at greater length in "The Paradoxical Encomium, with Special Reference to Its Vogue in England, 1600-1800," *MP*, LIII (1956), 145-78.

SATIRES

expected, or trifling subjects.[30] The most famous of the early rhetoricians, Gorgias and Isocrates, themselves wrote paradoxical encomia; Lysias, Polycrates, and Alcidamas are said to have written encomia on such themes as mice, pebbles, pots, and bumblebees; and even the drama reflected this interest, burlesque or playful laudations appearing, for instance, in a number of the plays of Aristophanes. Fronto sent a praise of smoke and dust to Marcus Aurelius; and later such eminent men of learning as Dion Chrysostom (Dio of Prusa) and Synesius of Cyrene sported with the form, praising the gnat, the parrot, and hair— or baldness.

Probably the most influential mock encomium for later generations was the *Laus muscae* (Μυίας ἐγκώμιον), or praise of a fly, written by Lucian in the second century. It was cited as an exemplar by numerous writers in Latin and English during the Renaissance and after, though its loose structure was improved upon. The *Tragopodagra*, a burlesque tragedy on the gout, was often taken as Lucian's in the Renaissance and also inspired a number of paradoxical encomia.[31] For if this species of jesting rhetoric had declined in the middle ages, it returned in a great burst of wit and learning in the sixteenth century. Rabelais' famous praise of debt and debtors (Book III, chaps. iii-iv) is only one of a host of such mock encomia in the vernacular;[32] but the form was also a favorite with the mighti-

[30] See Theodore C. Burgess, "Epideictic Literature," in *University of Chicago Studies in Classical Philology*, III (1902), 89-261; Arthur S. Pease, "Things without Honor," *Classical Philology*, XXI (1926), 27-42; and Eugène Talbot, *De ludicris apud veteres laudationibus* (Paris, 1850).
[31] The subject is dealt with in some detail by Craig R. Thompson, "Lucian and Lucianism in the English Renaissance" (unpublished Ph.D. dissertation, Princeton, 1937), pp. 64-84, *et passim*. Aspects of the Renaissance interest in the paradoxical encomium have been treated by R. B. McKerrow in his edition of Thomas Nashe (5v., 1904-1910), IV, 389-95 and 438-39; and by Alexander H. Sackton, "The Paradoxical Encomium in Elizabethan Drama," *University of Texas Studies in English*, XXVIII (1949), 83-104.
[32] See C. A. Mayer, "Rabelais' Satirical Eulogy: The Praise of Borrowing," in *François Rabelais: ouvrage publié pour le quatrième centenaire*

est of Latin scholars, men like Daniel Heinsius and Melanchthon and Justus Lipsius. One incredible collection, the *Amphitheatrum sapientiae socraticae joco-seriae* of Caspar Dornavius (Hanover, 1619) offered over half a thousand Latin mock encomia, drawn from ancient and contemporary authors alike and ranged under suitable heads. But of course the most famous—and the best—of the Latin paradoxical encomia was the *Moriae encomium* of Desiderius Erasmus, published in 1509. Translated into English by Thomas Chaloner in 1549, the *Praise of Folly* gave an enormous impetus to the writing of such *jeux d'esprit* and provided an eminent exemplar that subsequent encomiasts of the trivial and paradoxical could cite as authority for their own productions—as the Renaissance scholars themselves had cited Isocrates and Lucian. In England the enthusiasm for this rhetorical game did not die until the enthusiasm for rhetoric itself waned in the nineteenth century. In the years between, a host of writers, great and small, exhausted their ingenuity in the praise of the unpraiseworthy.

The popularity of this curious genre had perhaps been best explained at its birth, by Isocrates (who claimed, himself, to detest the form): the Sophists, he said, "have the effrontery to write that the life of beggars and exiles is more enviable than that of the rest of mankind, and

---

de sa mort 1553-1953 (Geneva and Lille, 1953), pp. 147-55. Rabelais also has a panegyric on the codpiece (*la braguette*) in Book III, chap. viii, and on "Messere Gaster," the source of all inventions, in Book IV, chap. lvii. For other French examples of the paradoxical encomium, see C. A. Mayer, "L'honnête homme: Molière and Philibert de Vienne's 'Philosophe de court,'" MLR, XLVI (1951), 196-217; for German examples, Adolf Hauffen's "Zur Litteratur der ironischen Enkomien," previously cited, and his "Die Trinklitteratur in Deutschland bis zum Ausgang des sechzehnten Jahrhunderts," *Vierteljahrschrift für Litteraturgeschichte*, II (1889), 481-516; in Italy the popularity of the genre may be illustrated by a collection of sixteenth-century poems, *Delle rime piacevoli del Berni, Casa, Mavro, Varchi, Dolce, et d'altri auttori* (3v., Venice, 1603), which contains several dozen encomia by important poets and humanist scholars, lauding the plague, the chamber pot, the ass, spittle, lying, the nose, and other like subjects.

they use this as a proof that, if they can speak ably on ignoble subjects, it follows that in dealing with subjects of real worth they would easily find abundance of arguments." So also he says at another point: "no one who has chosen to praise bumble-bees and salt and kindred topics has ever been at a loss for words"; and he continues: "while on famous subjects one rarely finds thoughts which no one has previously uttered, yet on trifling and insignificant topics whatever the speaker may chance to say is entirely original."[33]

The hope that ingenuity would be taken for oratorical genius doubtless *was* an impetus to bravura pieces of perverse encomium; but the opportunity that was offered of testing one's powers of original invention provided the real rationale for the genre throughout its history. Thomas Nashe phrased this argument colorfully in 1599: "Euery man can say Bee to a Battledore, and write in prayse of Vertue and the seuen Liberall Sciences, thresh corne out of the full sheaues and fetch water out of the Thames; but out of drie stubble to make an after haruest, and a plentifull croppe without sowing, and wring iuice out of a flint, thats *Pierce a Gods name*, and the right tricke of a workman."[34]

The paradoxical encomium (like the encomium itself) could range in length from a page to a book. The more formal specimens of the genre continued to follow the structural pattern of the classical epideictic oration, and to draw upon the topics that the major rhetors had suggested as proper for their subject. The topics for praise of the gods and of men and cities were fairly well established; but the praise of mere things was less fully treated. A

[33] *Encomium on Helen* 8-13; *Isocrates*, transl. George Norlin and Larue Van Hook (Loeb Library, 3v., 1928-1945), III, 65-67.
[34] *Nashes Lenten Stuffe . . . the Praise of the Red Herring* (1599) in the *Works*, ed. R. B. McKerrow, III, 151-52. A line from Lucretius ("Juvat integros accedere Fontes / Atque haurire") that Fielding used as the epigraph for the *Covent-Garden Journal*, No. 55, was translated as: "It is pleasant to handle / An untouched Subject" (Jensen, II, 59).

formula grew up, however, by practice as much as by precept, of proving the antiquity, the nobility or beauty (*honestas*), the dignity, the utility, and the easiness or difficulty (*facilis* or *difficilis*) of the thing being praised. Henry Fielding's awareness of this traditional set of topics is shown in one of his essays in the *Champion*, which propounds in a short set discourse "the antiquity, the dignity, and the efficacy" of the *argumentum baculinum* or "knockdown argument" (5 January 1740; Henley, xv, 138-41).

At the beginning of the same paper he also put his finger on what was probably the greatest single guarantee of continuity in the tradition, in alluding to "the sophistical schools of the universities, where men are taught to defend the whimsical systems of philosophers, but not their own persons or purses" (Henley, xv, 138). The training in rhetoric that all scholars of the time received invariably included training in the encomium; and this meant not only that there would be men to write, but also an audience to appreciate, parodies and inversions of its formal rules. Again, the frequent public declamations, especially during the Acts or Commencement (at Oxford and Cambridge, respectively), and the tradition through 1713 of a satiric address by Oxford's *terrae filius* provided both models and a tone for mock declamation. Tom Brown has "*An* Oration *in Praise of* Drunkenness" which he claims was "*Design'd to be spoken at* Oxford *in the Time of the Act*"; and one would suppose that he was not alone in being moved to satirize the university *declamatio*.[35]

[35] See *The Works of Mr. Thomas Brown, Serious and Comical, in Prose and Verse* (9th ed., 4v., 1760), I, 31-38. He also has "A Declamation . . . in Praise of Poverty," a contrary declamation lauding Wealth, and "A Comical Panegyrick on . . . a Louse," the latter being his completion of a poem by one Mr. Willis of Oxford (I, 87-105, 83-87, and 128-29, respectively). On the university declamations, particularly at Oxford, see Christopher Wordsworth, *Social Life at the English Universities in the Eighteenth Century* (Cambridge, 1874), pp. 283-307. Fielding would doubtless have heard like declamations at Leyden which had a strong tradition of rhetorical disputation (see G. D. J. Schotel, *De academie te Leiden* [Haarlem, 1875], p. 332, *et passim*).

SATIRES

On the other hand, the literary tradition by itself possessed a continuing vigor. When Addison apologized for his essay on nonsense in the *Whig Examiner*, he cited the obvious exemplar: "This short panegyric upon nonsense . . . may appear as extravagant to an ordinary reader, as Erasmus's Encomium of Folly." And Swift, in his loose mock encomium of Bishop Fleetwood, mocked the Bishop's repeated use of the word "such," by exclaiming: "O! the irresistible Charm of the Word *Such*! Well, since *Erasmus* wrote a Treatise in Praise of Folly; and my Lord *Rochester* an excellent Poem upon *Nothing*, I am resolved to employ the *Spectator*, or some of his Fraternity, (Dealers in Words) to write an Encomium upon SUCH."[36] Following the lead of Erasmus on Folly, sixteenth- and seventeenth-century writers had praised madness, the ass, red herring, woman's inconstancy, discord, beggars, bawds, thieves, jails, folly and knavery, and even—the grunting of a hog. Sir William Cornwallis, one of the earliest English essayists, had written panegyrics on sadness, Julian the Apostate, debt, "the *French Pockes*," and, as we have seen, on Nothing. And a multitude of the happy pot-valiant had echoed John Taylor's panegyric, *Ale Ale-Vated into the Ale-Titude* (1651), or followed the bumping doggerel of "The contented Prisoner his praise of Sack" in *Choyce Drollery* (1656), which roared:

> 'Tis Sack makes our faces
> Like Comets to shine,
> And gives beauty beyond
> The Complexion mask,
> *Diogenes* fell so
> In love with this Wine,
> That when 'twas all out,
> He dwelt in the Cask.[37]

---

[36] Addison, *Whig Examiner*, No. 4 (5 October 1710), in *Works*, ed. G. W. Greene (6v., 1887), II, 608; Swift, *A Letter of Thanks from My Lord W[harton] to the Lord Bᵖ of S. Asaph* (1712), in the *Prose Works*, ed. Herbert Davis (14v., Oxford, 1939, in progress), VI, 153.

[37] Ed. J. W. Ebsworth (Boston, Lincolnshire, 1876), pp. 93-96.

The early seventeenth century saw the apogee of paradox, both for its own sake and as a method of argumentation; and a number of popular paradoxes were, in effect, paradoxical encomia. But the renewed interest in playful burlesque and satire ushered in by the Restoration provided an even more receptive milieu for the mock-heroic and the rhetorical *jeu d'esprit*. The eighteenth century was, bating only the Latin Renaissance, the high-water mark of the tradition of learned playfulness.

The technique of ironic praise is, of course, one of the most useful tools of the satirist; and the influence of the paradoxical encomium bulks large in many of the best eighteenth-century satires. The *Dunciad*, for instance, is (particularly in Book 1) an elaborate praise of Dulness, as Dryden's *Mac Flecknoe* had been; Book IV of *Gulliver's Travels* may prove, if recent arguments denying the ideal character of the Houyhnhnms are correct (though I fear they are not), to owe something to the ironic encomium—and the *Tale of a Tub* assuredly does. For although the "Digression in Praise of Digressions" is the nearest thing the *Tale* offers to a formal mock encomium, the spirit and technique of paradoxical praise are employed throughout: the advertisement of "Treatises wrote by the same Author" prefixed to the *Tale* includes "A Panegyrical Essay upon the Number THREE"; the preface speaks of "this little Panegyrick" on the Moderns; the "Digression concerning Criticks" is a mock encomium upon "the TRUE CRITICK"; and the later sections include the Æolists' encomium upon Wind as the primordial force and the praise of Madness.[38] Fielding's own *Jonathan Wild* is, of course, from beginning

[38] John M. Bullitt has observed that "in A *Tale of a Tub* Swift first displayed his remarkable talent as a mock eulogist. Indeed, the whole tale is ironically organized as a panegyric upon the moderns, written by a modern and for the moderns" (*Jonathan Swift and the Anatomy of Satire* [Cambridge, Mass., 1953], p. 51). The anonymous abstract of the *History of Martin*, attached to the *Tale* in 1720, proposed to write "A Digression on the nature usefulness & necessity of Wars & Quarels" (Guthkelch-Smith ed., p. 305), and the outline promised panegyrics on war, famine, and pestilence, as well as a "Panegyrick on Mankind."

to end, a sustained ironic praise of villainous greatness. Defoe's *Hymn to the Pillory* and parts of Mandeville's *Fable of the Bees* bear a close affinity to the paradoxical encomium; and, although the multitude of mock-heroic narratives and georgics on trifling subjects belong (technically) to another genre, they represent an aspect of the same impulse that inspired the flood of mock encomia.[39]

A number of the Restoration and eighteenth-century paradoxical encomia are loose in form and rather cavalier in their treatment of the customary *topoi*. William Wycherley, who had a particular fondness for the genre—writing poetic praises of poverty, quibbling, old age, prisons, laziness, ignorance, dulness, cowardice, impudence, and avarice—seldom bothered to organize his arguments in terms of any set topics. His poems are often personal satires (for example, "The PRAISE of AVARICE. To Sir JOHN CUTLER," which is a pointed attack on that gentleman) or occasional pieces ("*In Praise of a* PRISON, *call'd by its* Prisoners *their* College; *and written there*"), and their affinity is rather with the popular seventeenth-century miscellanies than with the formal encomium itself.[40] There are many of these loose occasional pieces in the eighteenth century also. Besides such personal mock praises as that of Sir Richard Blackmore (1706), Gay's of Thomas Snow (1721), or Pope's of George II (1737), one finds Addison's encomium on nonsense in political journals, an *Essay in Praise of Knavery* (1723), Carey's famous panegyric on

[39] As the preface to one of the many imitations of John Philips' *Splendid Shilling* (1701) argued, "It must be own'd, that to raise Flowers and Fruits on a barren Soil, requires a masterly Skill: Every Poet is not equal to such an ardous [sic] Task.... Imagination and Invention are the Soul of Poetry; and scanty Subjects are the best Touchstones of Genius and Inspiration" (*The Shoe-Heel: A Rhapsody. By Mr.* [*Joseph*] *Mitchell* [1727], "THE BOOKSELLER TO THE READERS," pp. iv-vi). John Dunton stated the matter more bluntly: "To write upon barren Subjects, is to try what Ingenuity will do, when put hard to it" (*Athenian Sport* [1707], p. 5).
[40] See *The Complete Works of William Wycherley*, ed. Montague Summers (4v., 1924), Vols. III and IV, *passim*.

Ambrose Philip's versification (1725), a mock praise of freethinkers (1733), several inverted gibes at Sir Robert Walpole, and a host of other such commentaries on current fashions or follies: the anonymous *Doctor Anthony's Poem in Praise of the Pox* (1725?), the *Essay on Gibing* (Dublin, 1725), *Geneva: A Poem* (1729), and later, Sheridan's *Ridotto of Bath, a Panegyrick* (Bath, 1771) and *Ode to the Genius of Scandal* (1781).[41] Fielding's own "sarcastical panegyric" to Vanity, in *Joseph Andrews* (I, xv) is in this informal tradition.[42]

However, not a few of the mock panegyrists in the eighteenth century displayed an obvious familiarity with the conventional *topoi* for the praise of things. Their very titles often indicate this awareness: for example, *A Learned Dissertation on Dumpling; Its Dignity, Antiquity, and Excellence* (1726); "*A Dissertation on the Dignity, Benefit and Beauty of* UGLINESS" (ca. 1751); *An Essay on the Antiquity, Dignity, and Advantages of Living in a Garret* (1751), and so on. Thomas Gordon wrote a discourse in *The Humourist*, "*Of* PRATING," which displays all the

---

[41] Anon., *A Panegyrick Epistle . . . to S. R[ichard] B[lackmore]* (1706); John Gay, *A Panegyrical Epistle to Mr. Thomas Snow* (1721); Pope, *The First Epistle of the Second Book of Horace, Imitated* (1737); Henry Carey, *Namby-Pamby. A Panegyrick on the New Versification* (1725); Anon., "The Modern Goliah; or, The Heroe of Heroes. A Panegyric, humbly address'd to the venerable and worthy set of Free-thinkers," in the *Grub-Street Journal*, No. 196 (27 September 1733); on Walpole, Paul Whitehead, *The State Dunces* (1733), in which the Goddess Dulness pronounces an encomium upon Walpole, and Anon., *A Panegyric on a Court* (1739), in which Walpole is "lauded" under the name of "Sylla"; *Robin's Panegyrick; or, The Norfolk Miscellany* (2v., 1729-31) is a collection of attacks on Walpole, but it includes no mock "panegyricks." Sterne, Gray, and Cowper are among the more famous writers who made an incidental use of the mock panegyric in the later part of the century. A number of paradoxical encomia are included (though not so labeled) in the poems discussed by Richmond P. Bond in his standard work, *English Burlesque Poetry, 1700-1750* (Cambridge, Mass., 1932).

[42] So also is the letter to the *Champion* from "H. BOTTLE" of Norwich, in praise of drinking (20 May 1740; coll. ed. [2v., 1741], II, 236-40). This issue, not reprinted in Henley, is surely by Fielding. The praise of Silence by "MUM BUDGET" in *Common Sense*, 13 May 1738 (coll. ed. [2v., 1738-1739], II, 86-91), though probably not by Fielding, is very much in his vein of pleasantry.

SATIRES

formal characteristics of the genre, pointing out his subject's antiquity and authority, its pleasures, advantages, and uses; and a poem addressed to Swift by Joseph Mitchell, "ET CÆTERA. A PANEGYRICK," traces the birth and importance of and the debt writers owe to that most indispensable "Et Cætera."[43]

Quite clearly, then, Fielding's *Essay on Nothing*, with its paradoxical praise of the antiquity, the dignity, and the value to mankind of Nothing, is not an isolated phenomenon. It belongs to a tradition that itself could boast the antiquity and the dignity of a history spanning two millennia, a tradition that died only when a new class dictating new literary principles turned its back upon the great rhetorical heritage of the classical past and pronounced its epitaph: "The age of Rhetoric, like that of Chivalry, has passed amongst forgotten things."[44] Normally no more than a piece of learned jesting, the paradoxical encomium (like many another such bagatelle) rose above itself in the hands of an Erasmus or a Swift to become a satirical weapon of the first order. Its inherently ironic nature and its scope and flexibility endeared it to the great masters of irony—Aristophanes, Lucian, Erasmus, Rabelais, Swift, and Henry Fielding—and, though necessarily a minor genre, it is assuredly dignified by the stature of those who have used it. It appealed to, and perhaps in its own small way helped

---

[43] The *Dissertation on Dumpling* was published anonymously in 1726 and later included in Volume I of that great catchall, *The Miscellaneous Works of the Late Dr. Arbuthnot* (2nd ed., 2v., Glasgow, 1751); it was attributed to Henry Carey by Frederick T. Wood ("An Eighteenth-Century Original for Lamb?" *RES*, v [1929], 442-47). The dissertation on ugliness first appeared in Christopher Smart's periodical, *The Midwife* (coll. ed. [3v., 1751?-53], I, 241-45), and was reprinted in *The Nonpareil* (1757), a selection from that periodical. The anonymous essay on a Garret, published in December 1750, with a title page date of 1751, may be compared with Dr. Johnson's praise of garrets in the *Rambler*, No. 117 (30 April 1751). Gordon, *The Humourist: Being Essays upon Several Subjects* (2v., 1720-1725), II, 75-82. Mitchell, *Poems on Several Occasions* (2v., 1729), II, 314-21; Mitchell also has a mock encomium on Indolence (I, 55-66).

[44] *Collected Writings of Thomas DeQuincey*, ed. David Masson (14v., Edinburgh, 1889-1890), X, 97.

to create, flexible minds. By placing in a new context persons or objects traditionally seen in a contrary light, it established ironic tensions that evoked not only laughter, but thoughtful laughter. Irony is an effective specific for the disease of intellectual rigidity; a modern scholar has said, with more than a little justice, "It is in the mock encomium that irony of inversion reaches its greatest concentration and brilliance."[45] Not everything in the long tradition of the paradoxical encomium is pure gold, by any means, but the form at its best provides a happy wedding of rhetorical ingenuity and ironic vision.

5

Erasmus had said that "literary jests may have serious implications, and . . . a reader with a keen nose may get more from a skillful trifle than from a solemn and stately argument."[46] Within the framework of his mock encomium, Fielding could deftly satirize a number of the social and intellectual abuses that were of most serious and profound concern to him in his ceaseless war to proclaim valid ideals for the good society. Ridicule might not be the test of truth, but it could assuredly help, along with the other reductive devices inherent in his theme, to place in a truer light the arrogant nonsense of many contemporary authors, historians, and antiquaries, the absurdity of philosophical hair-splitting, the folly of a self-destructive ambition or avarice, and—most particularly—the truly subversive (to any legitimate social ideal) effect of a contemptible cringing before mere empty titles.

Fielding's satire in this last regard must not be misconstrued. He always insisted upon the necessity of paying the respect due to others and of recognizing the precedence and the honor owed to titles; but at the same time he stood firmly for the dignity of the individual, and he found

[45] David Worcester, *The Art of Satire* (Cambridge, Mass., 1940), p. 81.
[46] *The Praise of Folly*, transl. Leonard F. Dean (Chicago, 1946), p. 38.

the fawning servility so often exhibited before titles eminently distasteful. He had explained this, it will be remembered, in the *Essay on Conversation*: "Not that I would withdraw from [Titular Excellence] that Deference which the Policy of Government hath assigned it. On the contrary, I have laid down the most exact Compliance with this Respect, as a Fundamental in Good-Breeding; nay, I insist only that we may be admitted to pay it; and not treated with a Disdain even beyond what the Eastern Monarchs shew to their Slaves" (*Misc.*, I, 156-57). Within this general acquiescence in the right of title to its traditional respect, however, Fielding made discriminations; and it was his fundamental complaint that many of his contemporaries failed to do so, or did not do so intelligently. The satire in the *Essay on Nothing* is of a piece with his whole attack on false greatness and his sustained effort to educate society in valid estimates of social and moral worth. The vilest qualities, he had observed contemptuously in the preface to the *Miscellanies*, when "glossed over with Wealth and a Title, have been treated with the highest Respect and Veneration . . ." (*Misc.*, I, xxi). He had little patience with that "set of wretches who, while they are a disgrace to their ancestors . . . have the insolence to treat those with disregard who are at least equal to the founders of their own splendor" (*JA*, III, i; Henley, I, 216-17); and the second issue of the *Champion*, which contained a leading article on the indiscriminate honor paid to mere hereditary titles, offered "to my honourable and right-honourable Readers," the following cautions: "first, that they would endeavour to imitate their noble Ancestors in those Actions from whence their Honours were derived; and secondly, that they would not be too apt to scorn and despise such as resemble those very Ancestors, in all Things but their Riches."[47] His mockery

---

[47] *The Champion*, 17 November 1739 (coll. ed. [2v., 1741], I, 9). This issue, not in Henley, is by Fielding (cf. J. E. Wells, "The 'Champion'

and his indignation were never directed at titles per se, but at those who worshipped them without any measure of discrimination, and at those owners of titles who themselves failed to live up to their high responsibilities as the natural leaders of society and the nation. As Fielding syllogistically summed up the matter in the *Essay on Nothing* (*Misc.*, I, 245):

"The Respect paid to Men on account of their Titles, is paid at least to the Supposal of their superior Virtues and Abilities, or it is paid to *Nothing*.

"But when a Man is a notorious Knave or Fool, it is impossible there should be any such Supposal.

"The Conclusion is apparent."

In part, then, Fielding might have said of his paradoxical encomium, as Nashe did of his own praise of red herring "This is a light friskin of my witte . . . wherin I follow the trace of the famousest schollers of all ages, whom a wantonizing humour once in their life time hath possest to play with strawes, and turne mole-hils into mountaines."[48] But he could also claim, with Erasmus, to have turned his "wantonizing humour" to the service of a valid satire on the follies and vanities of his time. The highly traditional structure and devices of the *Essay on Nothing* would have provided, for an age that did not pant after "novelty" in its literature, a significant framework within which to display the fullest inventive ingenuity; and Fielding's ingenuity in amplifying and exploiting the theme of "Nothing" does not flag. The ironic inversions are amusing in themselves, they are pithy and to the point in satirical purpose, and they are structurally an

---

and Some Unclaimed Essays by Henry Fielding," *Englische Studien*, XLVI [1913], 355-66). The phrasing in this paper, "a right honourable Rogue (if ever such a Creature were) is the most contemptible, as well as ridiculous Object in the Universe" (I, 10), is echoed in the *Essay on Nothing's* "an infamous worthless Nobleman (if any such be) . . ." (*Misc.*, I, 244).

[48] *Works*, ed. McKerrow, III, 151.

organic part of the whole mock demonstration. In a word, the *Essay on Nothing*, though certainly an opuscule, is nonetheless certainly a little satiric gem.

2. "SOME PAPERS PROPER to be Read before the R———L SOCIETY"

Fielding's satire on the Royal Society was one of several items in the *Miscellanies* that had seen previous publication. It appeared in a six-penny pamphlet, 16 February 1743,[49] two months before its republication in the larger work. The version found in the *Miscellanies* is simply a reprint of the pamphlet with the addition of a brief "POSTSCRIPT."

The *terminus a quo* for its composition can be easily established, for the piece is an obvious satire of, and quotes from, a paper describing experiments by the great Swiss naturalist Abraham Trembley, which had been published in the *Philosophical Transactions* of the Royal Society "For *Thursday, January* 13. and *Thursday, January* 21. 1742-3." The issue of the *Transactions* so dated (No. 467) was apparently not published until 28 January;[50] hence Fielding could not have devoted overmuch time to the piecing together of his parody, if it were to be printed and advertised by 16 February. The work is short enough, however, not to have required extensive planning; and in view of the obvious rapidity with which Fielding composed the essays and satires that appear in his various periodicals, there is no reason to characterize this as an unusually hasty production.

[49] Publication was noted in the *Daily Advertiser* and the *Daily Post* of that date; see also Cross, III, 308.
[50] Publication was noted in the *Daily Advertiser* of that date. Cross (I, 391) erroneously supposed that Fielding's satire "had its origin in a paper contributed in November, 1742, to the 'Philosophical Transactions of the Royal Society' by Abraham Trembley." Dudden repeats this date (*Henry Fielding*, I, 404); but although there are two letters on the polypus in the *Philosophical Transactions* "For Part of *November*, and the Month of *December*, 1742" (No. 466), neither is by Trembley. There is nothing at all on the polypus in the journal (No. 465) that covered the early part of November.

2

In 1742 and 1743 a series of papers had been published in the *Philosophical Transactions* describing experiments made by several European naturalists upon the newly-discovered fresh-water polyp (*Chlorohydra viridissima*). The most indefatigable of these experimenters was Trembley (1710-1784);[51] and his description was published by the Secretary of the Royal Society as the culmination of their reports.

M. Trembley went into great detail in describing the "Polypus" and its habits, even to a rather nauseating word-picture of its capturing and swallowing a worm. But his most concentrated interest lay in the series of cutting operations that he had performed upon the creatures. He sliced them transversely, lengthwise, and in every intermediate fashion that he could conceive, always with the same result: each part grew into a new and whole polyp.

"If a *Polypus* is cut transversly [he reported], at the same Moment, into three or four Parts, they all equally become so many complete ones.

"The Animal is too small to be cut at the same time into a great Number of Parts; I therefore did it successively. I first cut a *Polypus* into four Parts, and let them grow; next, I cut those Quarters again; and at this rate I proceeded, till I had made 50 out of one single one: And here I stopp'd, for there would have been no End of the Experiment."[52]

Trembley concluded his paper with a description of

---

[51] See John R. Baker, *Abraham Trembley of Geneva: Scientist and Philosopher 1710-1784* (1952). Trembley's studies won him the Royal Society's gold medal in 1743. The polyps had been first discovered by Leeuwenhoek, who gave some account of the "plants," as he classified them, in the *Philosophical Transactions* for 1703 (No. 283), but their amazing power of regeneration had remained unknown until Trembley's experiments. The extensive implications of his discovery are dealt with in an interesting article by Aram Vartanian, "Trembley's Polyp, La Mettrie, and Eighteenth-Century French Materialism," *JHI*, xi (1950), 259-86.

[52] *Philosophical Transactions*, No. 467, p. viii.

turning polyps inside out ("their Inside is become their Outside, and their Outside their Inside: They eat, they grow, and they multiply, as if they had never been turned")[53] and with a paragraph explaining where the "Insects" were to be looked for.

These reports aroused fervid interest at the Royal Academy of Sciences in Paris, where Trembley's experiments were repeated and improved upon. Bonnet, Réaumur, and other men of curiosity "went about France cutting up all manner of worms and sea-animals to see if they would multiply like polyps."[54] And in England no less a virtuoso than Martin Folkes, the new president of the Royal Society, seized upon M. Trembley's lead and subjected the interesting little creatures to sustained experimentation. Something of the epidemic excitement that was generated, even in polite society, is reflected in Charles Hanbury Williams' poem, *Isabella; or, The Morning*, which must have been written about the same time. In this satire on the trifling conversations of the *beau monde*, Isabella, Duchess of Manchester, is represented as being visited by Charles Stanhope. She asks him the news in town, to which he replies:

> "Madam, I know of none; but I'm just come
> From seeing a curiosity at home:
> 'Twas sent to Martin Folkes, as being rare,
> And he and Desaguliers brought it there:
> It's called a *Polypus*."—"What's that?"—["]A creature,
> The wonderful'st of all the works of nature:
> Hither it came from Holland, where 'twas caught
> (I should not say it came, for it was brought);
> To-morrow we're to have it at Crane-court,
> And 'tis a reptile of so strange a sort,
> That if 'tis cut in two, it is not dead;

[53] *Ibid.*, p. x.   [54] Vartanian, pp. 259-63.

SATIRES

Its head shoots out a tail, its tail a head;
Take out its middle, and observe its ends,
Here a head rises, there a tail descends;
Or cut off any part that you desire,
That part extends, and makes itself entire:
But what it feeds on still remains a doubt,
Or how it generates, is not found out:
But at our Board, to-morrow, 'twill appear,
And then 'twill be consider'd and made clear,
For all the learned body will be there."

"Lord, I must see it, or I'm undone,"
The Duchess cry'd, "pray can't you get me one?
I never heard of such a thing before,
I long to cut it and make fifty more...."[55]

It is not difficult to imagine the amusement with which these apparently trivial studies of the polyp would be greeted by a humanist like Fielding. Merely to reproduce the reports from the *Philosophical Transactions*, with the addition of a few sly comments, would have been sufficient to provoke laughter at the expense of the much-satirized Royal Society. But Fielding's inventive genius and natural sense of the absurd suggested something even better: a happy parallel and a double-edged shaft of ridicule. By turning the polypus into the "Chrysipus" or English guinea, and M. Trembley into the learned Petrus Gualterus (an obvious *prosonomasia* for Fielding's old enemy, the notorious usurer, Peter Walter),[56] he converted his joke on the

[55] *The Works of the Right Honourable Sir Chas. Hanbury Williams* (3v., 1822), I, 82-84. Goldsmith had not forgotten, apparently, the excitement aroused by Trembley's discovery, when some sixteen years later he included among his "little great men," "the puny pedant, who finds one undiscovered property in the polype . . ." (*The Bee*, No. vi, 10 November 1759, in *The Works of Oliver Goldsmith*, ed. J. W. M. Gibbs [5v., 1884-1886], II, 416).
[56] On Fielding and Peter Walter see Dudden, I, 160-62, and the little epigram in the *Miscellanies* "On one who invited many Gentlemen to a small Dinner" (I, 52).

SATIRES

Royal Society into a sharply satiric attack, at the same time, upon avarice and misers.

3

Thoroughly delighted with its new discovery, the Royal Society had prefaced Trembley's report with a title page and frontmatter that placed at least three names (and a set of initials) of English Fellows before the public. The title page read as follows:

> SOME PAPERS Lately Read before the ROYAL SOCIETY Concerning the Fresh-water POLYPUS; AN INSECT, which hath this surprising Property, That being cut into several Pieces, each Piece becomes a perfect Animal, as complete as that of which it was originally only a Part. Collected and Published by CROMWELL MORTIMER, M. D. &c. *Secretary of the* ROYAL SOCIETY.

The next page identified the publication as the "PHILOSOPHICAL TRANSACTIONS. For *Thursday, January* 13. and *Thursday, January* 21. 1742-3" and gave the contents. This was followed by an "*Abstract of Part of a Letter from the Honourable* William Bentinck, *Esq;* F. R. S. *to* Martin Folkes, *Esq;* Pr. R. S. *communicating the following Paper from Mons.* Trembley, *of the* Hague." And the report itself was prefaced by the title, "*Observations and Experiments upon the* Fresh-water POLYPUS, *by Monsieur* Trembley, *at the* Hague. *Translated from the* French *by* P[hilip] H[enry] Z[ollman]. *F. R. S.*"

Fielding followed all this to the letter. His own title page read:

> SOME PAPERS PROPER to be Read before the R——L SOCIETY, Concerning the Terrestrial CHRYSIPUS, GOLDEN-FOOT or GUINEA; AN INSECT, or VEGETABLE, resembling the POLYPUS, which hath this surprising Property, That being

cut into several Pieces, each Piece becomes a perfect Animal, or Vegetable, as complete as that of which it was originally only a Part. COLLECTED By PETRUS GUALTERUS, But not Published till after His Death.

(*Misc.*, 1, 253)

His next page identified the paper as "PHILOSOPHICAL TRANSACTIONS. For the YEAR, 1742-3," and gave the contents; and this was followed by an "Abstract of *Part* of a Letter from the *Heer Rottenscrach* in *Germany*, communicating Observations on the CHRYSIPUS." And his own preface to the report read: "*Observations and Experiments upon the* TERRESTIAL CHRYSIPUS, *or* GUINEA, *by* Mynheer Petrus Gualterus. *Translated from the* FRENCH *by* P. H. I. Z. C. G. S." (1, 259). And to add the final touch of "authenticity," Fielding copied the diagram that in Trembley's paper had pictured *"The Figure of the Fresh-water* Polypus, *sticking to a Twig,"* with a carefully labeled picture of his own: "*The Figure of the* TERRESTRIAL CHRYSIPUS *sticking to a Finger"* (1, 259).

Declaring that "THE Animal in question is a terrestrial Vegetable or Insect, of which mention is made in the *Philosophical Transactions* for several Years, as may be seen in N°. ooo. Art. oooo. and N°. oo. Art. oo2. and N°. - - - - - - Art. 18," Fielding (as the editor, Rottenscrach) proceeds with learned documentation, to explain his diagram—a picture, of course, of the English guinea (1, 259-62).[57] This equivalence of the polypus and the

[57] The guinea of Fielding's diagram is that coined under Anne, after the union of England and Scotland in 1707. The reverse side of the coin, which is pictured, represents four shields (those of Ireland, France, and of England and Scotland impaled, the latter pair twice represented) arranged cross-wise around the Star of the Garter at the center (not shown in Fielding's diagram), and four sceptres in saltire (see H. A. Grueber, *Handbook of the Coins of Great Britain and Ireland in the British Museum* [1899], p. 140 and Plate XXXIV, No. 788). Fielding seizes upon the figures of the sceptres as phallic symbols and exploits them for some learned bawdry.

coin presents Fielding with the opportunity to indulge in the kind of ingenious parallel that he, like Swift, took so much pleasure in exploiting. He ponders whether the "Chrysipus" be animal or vegetable (as the virtuosi had with the polypus), and the fact that finally dissuades him from pronouncing it the former is "that I could never observe any Symptoms of voluntary Motion"—although he adds: "But though it hath not, or seems not to have any progressive Motion of its own, yet is it very easy to communicate a Motion to it. Indeed some Persons have made them fly all over the Town with great Velocity" (1, 262-63).

Quoting verbatim Trembley's account of the polypus trapping its prey, Fielding observes that there is a fundamental difference here: "Instead of conveying an Insect twice as large as its own Mouth into it, in Imitation of the *Polypus*, the poor *Chrysipus* is itself conveyed into the *Loculus* or Pouch of an *Insect* a thousand times as large as itself. Notwithstanding which, this wretched Animal (for so I think we may be allowed to call it) is so eager after its Prey, that if the *Insect* (which seldom happens) makes any Resistance, it summons other *Chrysipi* to its Aid, which in the End hardly ever fail of subduing it, and getting into its Pouch" (1, 263-64). Again, Trembley made much of the fact that the polypus seemed to reproduce without copulation; so Fielding (now as Petrus Gualterus) announces that, despite the fact that "they have no distinguished Place by which they bring forth their Young," he has seen the Chrysipi multiply under his very eyes: "I have for Sixty Years had under my Eye Thousands of them; and though I have OBSERVED THEM CONSTANTLY, and with ATTENTION, so as to watch them Night and Day, I have never observed any thing like the common Animal-Copulation" (1, 265).

Focusing more directly upon Peter Walter's ill-famed usury, Fielding has Gualterus further declare that in his assiduous experiments he found that with only two Chrysipi or guineas, he was unable to produce another complete Chrysipus: "Upon this, I tried a Hundred of them together;

by whose marvelous Union (whether it be, that they mix Total, like those Heavenly Spirits mentioned by *Milton*, or by any other Process not yet revealed to human Wit) they were found in the Year's End to produce three, four, and sometimes five complete *Chrysipi*" (1, 265-66). Indeed, he says, he has sometimes made them produce ten or twenty; but the latter has been held, he admits, a dangerous experiment, not only for the parent Chrysipi but for the ears of the philosopher himself.[58] Likewise, after quoting verbatim and at length from Trembley's account of his experiments in cutting up the polypus, Fielding (now as Rottenscrach, the communicator of Gualterus' paper) contrasts the procedure with the Chrysipus:

"Now in the Division and Subdivision of our *Chrysipus*, we are forced to proceed in quite a different manner; namely, by the Metabolic or Mutative, not by the Schystic or Divisive. Some have indeed attempted this latter Method; but, like that great Philosopher the Elder *Pliny*, they have perished in their Disquisitions, as he did, by Suffocation. Indeed there is a Method called the *Kleptistic*, which hath been preferred to the Metabolic: But this too is dangerous; the ingenious *Gualterus* never carried it farther than the Metabolic, contenting himself sometimes to divide the original *Chrysipus* into twenty two Parts, and again to subdivide these into twenty-five; but this requires great Art"—(1, 273).[59]

[58] Fielding's remarks have reference to the statute of 12 Anne, c. 16 (1713), by which the allowable rate of usury was reduced to five per cent; but the punishment for violation of this law did not include loss of the offender's ears, as Fielding implies (see Sir James F. Stephen, *A History of the Criminal Law of England* [3v., 1883], III, 199, and Thomas Wood, *An Institute of the Laws of England* [4th ed., 1728], p. 432). Possibly Fielding had in the back of his mind the punishment for forgery of coins or of charters, wills, or deeds, in which an offender might well lose one or both of his ears (see Wood, pp. 414-15). This was a danger from which Peter Walter had narrowly escaped around 1737, according to Pope, in Dialogue II of the *Epilogue to the Satires* (*Imitations of Horace*, ed. John Butt [Twickenham ed., Vol. IV, 2nd ed., 1953], p. 315 and note).

[59] It is doubtless presumptuous to explain that Fielding is contrasting the greater safety of legal usury, which produces only a small "change"

SATIRES

He had previously explained that the normal division of the Chrysipus was into "one and twenty Substances" (that is, shillings), which could then again "be subdivided, each of them into twenty four" (half-pence). "These subdivided Parts are by some observed to lose in a great degree their adherescent Quality: Notwithstanding which, *Gualterus* writes, that, from the minutest Observations upon his own Experience, they all adhered with equal Tenacity to his own Fingers" (1, 267-68).

Having discussed the question of longevity and the best method of preserving the Chrysipi (which is "in Bags or Chests, in large Numbers; for they seldom live long when they are alone. The Great *Gualterus* says, he thought he could never put enough of them together"—1, 274), Fielding quotes from Trembley on the habitat of the polypus: "They are to be look'd for in such Ditches whose Water is stock'd with small Insects. Pieces of Wood, Leaves, acquatic Plants, in short, every thing is to be taken out of the Water, that is met with . . . [and] put into a Glass of clear Water, and these Insects, if there are any, will soon discover themselves . . ." (1, 274).[60] He in turn describes the habitat of the guinea:

"The *Chrysipus* is to be look'd for in Scrutores, and behind Wainscotes in old Houses. In searching for them, particular Regard is to be had to the Persons who inhabit, or have inhabited in the same Houses, by observing which Rule, you may often prevent throwing away your Labour. They love to be rather with old than young Persons, and

---

(μεταβολή) in the hoard of guineas, with the methods of clipping the coins ("schystic" from σχίζειν, to split) or of outright stealing ("kleptistic" from κλέπτης, a thief). Clipping or counterfeiting coins was an offense of high treason punishable by death (see Leon Radzinowicz, A History of English Criminal Law and Its Administration from 1750 [3v., 1948-1956], 1, 652-54; and Wood, pp. 649-50). It is pleasing to note that the N. E. D. has conscientiously recorded "kleptistic" ("related to or consisting in stealing") and cited as the single illustration Fielding's use of it here.

[60] From *Phil. Trans.*, No. 467, p. xi.

detest Finery so much, that they are seldom to be found in the Pockets of laced Cloaths, and hardly ever in gilded Palaces"—(I, 275).

Promising a treatise by Gualterus on "several sure Methods" of procuring the Chrysipi, Fielding leaves his direct satire of Peter Walter and his parody of M. Trembley, to offer some ironic conclusions of his own: "I come now, in the last Place, to speak of the Virtues of the *Chrysipus*: In these it exceeds not only the *Polypus*, of which not one single Virtue is recorded, but all other Animals and Vegetables whatever" (I, 275). And its virtues are: first, that it will make a man talk or stop talking, be blind or deaf or what you will, if applied in the proper quantities; second, it has "a most miraculous Quality of turning Black into White, or White into Black," or, like a prism, reflecting what color it pleases; third, "It is the strongest Love-Powder in the World"; and finally, to give an idea of its medicinal quality: "It is a Medicine which the Physicians are so fond of taking themselves, that few of them care to visit a Patient, without swallowing a Dose of it" (I, 276-77).

Fielding had echoed William Bentinck's emphatic declaration in his own prefatory letter from "Heer Rottenscrach" (*"I can answer for the Truth of the Facts contained in the Paper I send you, as there is not one of them but what I have seen repeated above twenty times"*—I, 257)[61] and now he has him conclude the report with a similar ringing declaration: *"Facts like these I have related, to be admitted,* require the most convincing Proofs. I ven-

[61] Bentinck had said, "Mr. Trembley, the Gentleman who has made the Observations on the Insects, has drawn this Extract from his Journal: And I can answer for the Truth of the Facts therein contained, as there is not one of them but what I have seen repeated above Twenty times" (*Phil. Trans.*, No. 467, p. ii). Of course Bentinck meant that he had seen the experiments themselves repeated twenty times, not the facts; but it seems likely that Fielding, in reproducing Bentinck's careless phrasing, meant to imply that mere verbal repetition of the "facts" constituted proof to the virtuosi.

ture to say, I am able to produce such Proofs. In the mean time, I refer my curious Reader to the Treatise I have abovementioned, which is not yet published, and perhaps never may" (1, 277).[62] The rhetorical combination of an *epiphonema* (the striking sentence) supported by the *antistrophe* of "Proofs . . . Proofs" is neatly flattened by the final anticlimax to produce that effect of bluster which Fielding took the whole "scientific" account to represent.

We may add, as Fielding did, a "POSTSCRIPT." In the original paper he had included several political observations which glanced at the flow of English money to George II's little Hanoverian electorate. The prefatory letter from Rottenscrach "in *Germany*" described Gualterus as one *"famous for nothing so much as for an extraordinary Collection which he had made of the* Chrysipi" and added *"of which I doubt not but there are* still some *to be found in* England: *However, if that should be difficult, it may be easy to send some over to you; as they are at present very plentiful in these Parts"* (1, 257). In the body of the paper, it was said of the Chrysipi that "in *England,* they are observed of late to be much rarer than formerly, especially in the Country [that is, the "Country" interest, as opposed to the "Court" interest], where at present there are very few of them to be found: but at the same time it is remarked, that in some Places of the Continent, particularly in a certain Part of *Germany,* they are much plentier; being to be found in great Numbers, where formerly there were scarce any to be met with" (1, 261).[63] In the *Miscellanies*

[62] The first two sentences are a direct quotation from Trembley (*Phil. Trans.*, p. x), who went on to appeal to his experiments and a number of witnesses and experimenters, although "All this would require a Discussion too long to be here related."

[63] The immediate allusion is probably to the proposals of Carteret and Sir William Yonge that George II's Hanoverian troops be employed in the War of the Austrian Succession, then raging on the continent. In a pamphlet of 1741, which may be Fielding's, *The Plain Truth: A Dialogue between Sir Courtly Jobber . . . and Tom Telltruth,* Tom replies to Sir Courtly's observation that Hanover is a very rich country: "As for its being a rich Country, I don't believe it; though I do believe it is a great

Fielding added to these political observations a more general comment upon the vicious power of the guinea in English politics: "POSTSCRIPT. Since I composed the above Treatise, I have been informed, that these Animals swarm in *England* all over the Country, like the Locusts, once in SEVEN Years [that is, at election time]; and like them too, they generally cause much Mischief, and greatly ruin the Country in which they have swarmed" (I, 277).

4

The Royal Society had from its inception been the target of numerous attacks, some solemnly phrased, like those by Dr. Henry Stubbe and Dr. South, who associated the organization with the earlier Puritan groups that had sought to turn the universities away from classical and humanistic studies; and others couched in satirical terms, like Butler's (unpublished) poems, Shadwell's *Virtuoso* (1676)—with its famous character, Sir Nicholas Gimcrack—or Mrs. Aphra Behn's *Emperor in the Moon*, a farce on the virtuosi produced in 1687.[64]

In the eighteenth century, despite the fact that it was now more firmly established—and given greater security and eminence by the accomplishments of Isaac Newton, its president from 1703 to 1727—the Society continued to

---

deal richer now than it was some Years ago" (p. 20). An anonymous pamphlet of 1744, called *An Attempt towards a Natural History of the Hanover Rat*, attacked the Hanoverian mercenaries, employing almost the same kind of device that Fielding had used in the satire on the Royal Society, though now burlesquing Henry Baker's *Attempt towards a Natural History of the Polype* (1743). Gerard E. Jensen has set forth a persuasive argument that this pamphlet on the "Hanoverian Rat" was, in fact, by Fielding ("A Fielding Discovery," *Yale University Library Gazette*, x [1935], 23-32).

[64] See R. F. Jones, *Ancients and Moderns* (St. Louis, 1936), pp. 255-59, and Dorothy Stimson, *Scientists and Amateurs: A History of the Royal Society* (N.Y., 1948), p. 77, *et passim*. C. S. Duncan, "The Scientist as a Comic Type," *MP*, XIV (1916), 281-91, traces the virtuoso as a figure in comic drama from Shadwell to the middle of the eighteenth century. See also Walter E. Houghton, Jr., "The English Virtuoso in the Seventeenth Century," *JHI*, III (1942), 51-73, 190-219.

SATIRES

draw the fire of satirists, although serious opposition gradually tapered off. These attacks have been copiously documented by modern scholarship.[65] Among the best known are such gibes as Swift's, particularly in Gulliver's voyage to Laputa and Balnibarbi; the several humorous disparagements in the *Tatler* and *Spectator* papers, most notably, Nicholas Gimcrack's will, in *Tatler* No. 216; William King's burlesque version of the *Philosophical Transactions* in 1709; the *Scriblerus Papers*, which contain numerous satirical thrusts at the "scientific" attitude; and, of course, Book IV of the *Dunciad*, a withering satire of the virtuosi and pedants in general. The minor literature of the period is full of references—usually derogatory—to the Society and to the virtuosi who were almost invariably associated with it. The tone for most of these comments had been set from the beginning by Shadwell's hero, who protested, "'Tis below a *Virtuoso*, to trouble himself with Men and Manners. I study Insects"; and who, when seen "swimming" upon a table in the manner of a frog that he had under observation, carefully explained: "I content my self with the Speculative part of Swimming, I care not for the Practick. I seldom bring any thing to use, 'tis not my way."[66] The conventional criticism of the Society and it members, whether humorous or serious, tended to follow this same pattern. In one of the dialogues of *The Conversation of*

---

[65] Among many other articles on the subject are the important studies by Marjorie Nicolson and Nora Mohler in *Annals of Science*, II (1937), 299-334 and 405-30; and George R. Potter, "Swift and Natural Science," *PQ*, xx (1941), 97-118. See also Charles Kerby-Miller, ed., *Memoirs of Martinus Scriblerus* (New Haven, 1950), and Miriam K. Starkman, *Swift's Satire on Learning in A Tale of a Tub* (Princeton, 1950), pp. 64-86.

[66] *The Virtuoso* (1676), Act III, p. 44, and Act II, p. 27. It has been frequently overlooked that Shadwell (p. 25) makes a point of the fact that Sir Nicholas Gimcrack has been *refused* membership in the Royal Society. Potter has pointed out that much of the eighteenth-century satire of pedantic and trifling experiments would have been "highly acceptable to most members of the Royal Society," who themselves were contemptuous of the extreme virtuosi (p. 110). The fact remains, however, that in the popular mind, the Society was intimately associated with the "Gimcrack" type of scientist and that this popular connection was frequently exploited by satirists.

327

SATIRES

Gentlemen Considered (1738), a character, Eudoxus, says:

"I often wonder, with Concern, at the great Change in that young Gentleman, who was very rational, and agreeable, till he got acquainted with two or three of the *Royal Society*. Ever since, he has made me afraid of every one, that has the Name of a *Virtuoso*. For, tho' I am very sensible, that many of them are far from being so ridiculously absurd, yet many of them are little better, than this Gentleman, when once they grow fond of that Title. You can now scarce have any thing from him, but *petrified Snails, spontaneous Insects, exotick Plants, magnetical Emanations, hermetical Occlusions,* and the like."[67]

Natural philosophy, as such, was often granted to be a useful and even ennobling study; but to many literate men of the time it seemed that the Society, rather than engaging in rational and enlarging discourse, or even producing anything of real use to humanity, was all too often concentrating upon trifles and mere curiosities. As Steele declared: "They seem to be in a confederacy against men of polite genius, noble thought, and diffusive learning."[68]

Hence, despite the fact that by the 1740's the Society was solidly established and could, as its distinguished recent chronicler has observed, "look back with considerable satisfaction on what had been accomplished in the past forty years,"[69] those of a humanistic bias still regarded it with a cold eye. The Society's indefatigable curiosity about any and all natural wonders seemed to literary men such as Fielding not only indiscriminate but meaningless. What had they to do with such a conglomeration as mysterious electrical experiments, horrific medical cases reported in gruesome detail ("an extraordinary Stone voided by the

[67] *The Conversation of Gentlemen Considered* [attributed to John Constable] (1738), p. 169.
[68] *The Tatler*, No. 236; ed. G. A. Aitken (4v., 1898-1899) IV, 209-10.
[69] Sir Henry Lyons, *The Royal Society, 1660-1940* (Cambridge, 1944), p. 155.

SATIRES

Anus," "A Case wherein Part of the Lungs were coughed up," "An Account of a monstrous Fœtus, resembling a hooded Monkey"), astronomical phenomena (including comets, meteors, and "Remarkable Red Lights seen in the Air"), Leeuwenhoek's improved microscopes, and archaeological accounts of the recently discovered ruins of Herculaneum?[70] One need not be entirely surprised that Fielding should have found the Society's latest enthusiasm, for polyps, to be a subject worthy of his satire.

Fielding had, in fact, maintained an almost consistently satirical attitude toward the Royal Society and the virtuosi. The spirits "imported for the Goddess of Nonsense" in one of his early plays, *The Author's Farce* of 1730, include: "One hundred poets, players, doctors, and apothecaries, fellows of the colleges, and members of the Royal Society" (Henley, VIII, 231); and in *Pasquin* (1736), after Queen Ignorance has conquered Common-Sense, an envoy from Crane Court (the home of the Society at this time) arrives to congratulate her and offer a hamper full of "certain curiosities"—including a horse's tail, possessed of an hundred hairs more than usual, and the tooth of an elephant (Henley, XI, 225-26). Passing allusions in *The Mock Doctor* (Henley, X, 171) and in his periodical papers (for example, the *Champion*, 29 April 1740; Henley, XV, 293) are of the same tone as that displayed in the *Journey from This World to the Next*, where Fielding says that the bookseller showed his curious manuscript to the Royal Society, "but they shook their Heads, saying, there was nothing in it wonderful enough for them" (*Misc.*, II, 3). In *An Attempt towards a Natural History of the Hanover Rat* (1744), which I take to be Fielding's, he declared with mock solemnity: "As for my own Part, I cannot help paying a Respect to all those who make Discoveries in Nature, or Improvements in Art.—I have a just Regard for the Mem-

---

[70] These examples are all drawn from the *Philosophical Transactions* for the years 1740 and 1741.

ory of that ingenious *German* Artist, who spent twenty Years in making a Chain to bind a *Flea*; nor do I feel a less Veneration for that learned Member of the Royal Society, who hath spent fifty Years in making a Collection of *Butterflies* and *Cockle-shells*" (p. 20). The natural association that prevailed in the public mind between the Society and whatever sort of oddities, afforded Fielding any number of opportunities for jest: such as, for example, his long discourse in *Tom Jones* (xvi, iii; Henley, v, 210) upon the strange fowl that Black George delivers to Sophia when she is locked in her room. This bird, Fielding announces, would have delighted the Royal Society because, marvelous to relate, it carried a letter in its belly (smuggled in from Jones, of course).

Occasionally, however, Fielding's tone becomes more strongly condemnatory. In the *Journey from This World to the Next*, once again, he pictures a virtuoso appearing before Minos to be judged after his life:

"THE next Spirit that came up, declared, he had done neither Good nor Evil in the World: for that since his Arrival at Man's Estate, he had spent his whole Time in search of Curiosities; and particularly in the Study of Butterflies, of which he had collected an immense Number. Minos made him no Answer, but with great Scorn pushed him back"—(Chap. vii; *Misc.*, II, 54-55).

If sometimes Fielding classed the virtuosi with Dante's Trimmers who had contributed nothing either of good or ill to their world, at other times he felt that they had constituted a very definite influence—and that a bad one. The attention which their prodigies and monsters drew from the general public was evidence enough to a man of humanistic principles that the virtuosi were contributing to a wholesale corruption of the national taste. He made precisely this charge in one of the letters that he wrote for his sister Sarah's *Familiar Letters between the Principal*

SATIRES

Characters in David Simple in 1747;[71] and a late essay in the *Covent-Garden Journal* of 1752 shows that he had not seen cause to change his mind about the virtuosi and their pursuits. His satirical attack in that essay (No. 70; Jensen, II, 130-36) upon William Gould's *Account of English Ants* (1747) bears some resemblance to the ridicule of Trembley's studies of the polyp, though the satire on Gould is cast in the form of a dream-vision, and Fielding jests at "Natural Philosophy" in general, rather than concentrating his fire upon Gould. An earlier paper had examined the psychology of the virtuoso as arising from an inborn "vain Curiosity and Diligence in Trifles" (*CGJ* No. 24; Jensen, I, 274-78).

Clearly, at any rate, the satire on the Royal Society in the pamphlet of 1743 did not represent an isolated phenomenon in his work. The paper on Trembley was simply the most complete and most ingeniously contrived example of the great number of attacks he made upon the scientific spirit and the society which was the symbol of that spirit to the eighteenth century. The humanistic bias that underlies these attacks was one of the most consistent elements in Fielding's character and thought, one ruling attitude which in his long career never changed from its first expression to its last.

[71] Letter XL declares: "The first great corrupters of our taste are the Virtuoso's, a sort of people with which we abound to so prodigious a degree that their dexterities engross almost our whole conversation" (Henley, XVI, 29). Fielding sometimes implies, by attacking its opposite, that there may be a *true* natural philosophy which will search out the beauties of nature; for example, he continues in this letter: "These are a kind of burlesque natural philosophers, whose endeavours are not to discover the beauties, but the oddities and frolicks of nature. They are indeed a sort of natural jugglers, whose business it is to elevate and surprize, not to satisfy, inform, or entertain" (Henley, XVI, 29). In *Tom Jones*, he says that one of the amusements of young gentlemen of the age is "natural philosophy, or rather *unnatural*, which deals in the wonderful, and knows nothing of Nature, except her monsters and imperfections" (III, v; Henley, V, 49).

5

Normally, a satirist of the Royal Society would have been content to make his point about its (assumed) frivolities and let the matter rest at that. A Swift or a Fielding, however, was seldom satisfied with anything less than a commentary upon the vices and follies of humanity at large—and Fielding's satire upon the Royal Society is no exception. By spreading his net for Peter Walter, at the same time that he mimicked the reports of Trembley, Fielding extended the implications of his paper well beyond the single-minded limits that parody usually achieves.

Avarice, the secondary object of ridicule in this double-edged satire, is so well known to have been one of Fielding's major antipathies that documentation is almost presumptuous. His joyful adaptation of Molière's *L'Avare*, his relentless chase after Peter Walter, and the repeated and emphatic denunciations of miserliness in his plays, poems, and novels, are explicit and inescapable.[72] It is worth remarking, however, that for all of his continued castigation of avarice, Fielding showed no slightest interest in the psychology of the question. He *was* interested, as we have seen in discussing the *Essay on the Knowledge of the Characters of Men*, in the hidden motives and psychological nature of many other vices and unsocial attitudes. But he had no concern to understand the workings of a miser's mind; to Fielding such a creature was a kind of *lusus naturae*, outside the pale of humankind, afflicted (by his own choosing) with an incurable and peculiarly loathsome disease, and therefore to be mocked and scorned with all the revulsion that the normal and healthy instinctively feels for the freak.

Even more important was the certain fact that avarice, miserliness, was a serious crime against society. Fielding's

[72] Dr. Dudden presents a convenient "picture-gallery of misers" in Fielding's works (*Henry Fielding*, I, 121, n. 4, and I, 279, n. 1).

sense of economics was elementary: he could only conceive that when some men hoarded up and chuckled over their piles of gold and other men starved for want of a bread crust, society itself was affronted. And, characteristically, he did not look for an explanation in abstract laws or theories. He found it (and dramatized it) in a human figure: the miser. In one of his poems Fielding pictures the world

> Swelt'ring with Wealth, where Men unmov'd can hear
> The Orphans sigh, and see the Widow's Tear:
> Where griping Av'rice slights the Debtor's Pray'r,
> And Wretches wanting Bread deprives of Air.
> . . . .
> These wou'd not want, if those did never hoard;
> Enough for *Irus* falls from *Dives*' Board.
> And dost thou, common Son of Nature, dare
> From thy own Brother to with-hold his Share?[73]

The conventionality of this does not obscure the honest sense of indignation behind it: avarice was the utter negation of those virtues of good-nature, sympathetic identification with others' ills, and social consciousness which to Fielding represented the cornerstones of human society. "The last and greatest Stages of this Distemper," says Job Vinegar of avarice (in the *Champion*, 26 August 1740), "render a Man so dangerous a Member of Society, that

---

[73] *Of Good-Nature, Misc.*, I, 17-18. Cf. the *Covent-Garden Journal*, No. 39: "The Person who is void of all Liberality, is not worthy the Name of a Man; but is to be considered as an unnatural Monster, below the Dignity of Humanity." In the same issue Fielding cites (in addition to Scripture) Locke, Cumberland, Grotius, Pufendorf, and Barbeyrac as authorities on the Law of Nature who declare that "no Man hath any Right or Title to withhold from his Neighbour that Bread which he himself doth not want, and which his Neighbour absolutely doth want" (Jensen, I, 354-58).

wise Men have not scrupled to assert, he should be shut up, as well as any other Madman. . . ."[74]

Fielding's concern, then, was not at all to "understand" avarice and its psychological origins, but to condemn it out-of-hand as a threat to the happiness, indeed to the very existence, of others. The portrait that he drew of Julian in his incarnation as a miser in the *Journey from This World to the Next* (chap. xi) was as close as Fielding ever came (including Lovegold in *The Miser*) to a consideration of the miser qua human being. And here he has Julian explain that between scheming to procure money and worrying about preserving it, "I never had one Moment of Ease while awake, nor of Quiet when in my Sleep. In all the Characters through which I have passed, I have never undergone half the Misery I suffered in this . . ."; and indeed, Minos at the bar of judgment decides not to send him to Hell, "for that no body was to be d - - n'd in more Worlds than one" (*Misc.*, II, 89-95).[75]

Fielding was, of course, laboring in a traditional vineyard when he condemned avarice. Not only had the ancients freely satirized covetousness and made the miser a standard figure in the pantheon of fools and villains, but the whole weight of Christian moral disapproval had been continuously levied against that vice which represented the direct negation of the foremost Christian virtue, charity. In the *Covent-Garden Journal,* Fielding quoted the great latitudinarian, Isaac Barrow, on avarice:

"Other vicious Inclinations [Barrow says] combat Reason, and often baffle it; but seldom so vanquish it, as that a Man doth approve or applaud himself in his Miscarriage:

[74] *The Voyages of Mr. Job Vinegar, from The Champion* (1740), ed. S. J. Sackett (Augustan Reprint Society, No. 67; Los Angeles, Calif., 1958), p. 28.

[75] Cf. the *Champion,* 27 December 1739, which declares of avarice: "If there be any vice, which carries with it a more especial mark of madness than all the rest, it is this. The devil may be said to deal with the covetous man, as Dr. South tells us he does with the swearer, to cheat him of his soul without giving him any thing for it" (Henley, xv, 121-22).

but the covetous Humour seizeth on our Reason itself, and seateth itself therein; inducing it to favour and countenance what is done amiss. The voluptuous Man is swayed by the Violence of his Appetite, but the Covetous is seduced by the Dictates of his Judgment: he therefore scrapes and hoards and lets go nothing, because he esteems Wealth the best thing in the World, and then judges himself *most Wise* when he is most base"—(*CGJ*, No. 69; Jensen, II, 128).[76]

It was in part this belief that avarice was a sin of the head and not of the heart which incensed Fielding against it, for this made it seem to him a *deliberate* wickedness— as the theologian would say, a sin to which the reason had given its consent, a mortal sin. And though Fielding could be lenient toward sins of inadvertence, extravagance, or of the flesh, he was implacable against sins of meanness, malice, hypocrisy, or selfishness. The latter vices, he could feel, represented cases in which men deliberately and maliciously *willed* to be evil. In a chapter of *Amelia* (XI, v) that he entitled "CONTAINING MORE WORMWOOD AND OTHER INGREDIENTS," he spoke his own mind through Booth on the case of a thieving little servant girl:

"I do not think the girl in any light an object of mercy. She is not only guilty of dishonesty but of cruelty; for she must know our situation, and the very little we had left. She is besides guilty of ingratitude to you, who have treated her with so much kindness that you have rather acted the part of a mother than of a mistress. And, so far from thinking her youth an excuse, I think it rather an aggravation. It is true, indeed, there are faults which the youth of the party very strongly recommend to our pardon. Such are all those which proceed from carelessness and want of thought; but crimes of this black dye, which are committed with deliberation, and imply a bad mind, deserve a more severe punishment in a young person than in one of riper

[76] Cf. Barrow, *Theological Works*, ed. Napier, I, 45.

SATIRES

years; for what must the mind be in old age which hath acquired such a degree of perfection in villany so very early? Such persons as these it is really a charity to the public to put out of society; and, indeed, a religious man would put them out of the world for the sake of themselves; for whoever understands any thing of human nature must know that such people, the longer they live, the more they will accumulate vice and wickedness"—(Henley, VII, 270-71).

To Fielding, the ingrate and the hypocrite and the miser were alike "rogues by choice" (cf. *Amelia*, XI, ii; Henley, VII, 252). They deserved neither sympathy nor mercy for they had placed themselves not only outside human society but outside human nature. It was such a feeling, at any rate, that provoked him, in the *Essay on the Knowledge of the Characters of Men*, to the strongest and most bitter denunciations of such a "conscious" vice as hypocritical censoriousness; and it was such a feeling that led him to those relentless and incessant attacks upon avarice which reached a satiric peak in his paper on the Royal Society and Petrus Gualterus.

CHAPTER V. TRANSLATION

> SCARECROW. But I am afraid I am not qualified for a translator, for I understand no language but my own.
> BOOKWEIGHT. What, and translate Virgil?
> SCARECROW. Alas! I translated him out of Dryden.
> —*Author's Farce*, II, v.

MY epigraph is not (necessarily) intended as a slur upon Fielding's own practice in translating, but rather as an indication of the low estate into which that art had fallen in his time. The demands of a large, new, and ignorant reading public made hackwork translation a profitable game for the minor booksellers (if not for the poor translators), and many of them were not overscrupulous. As Bookweight replies to Scarecrow's admission: "Lay by your hat, sir, lay by your hat, and take your seat immediately. Not qualified! thou art as well versed in thy trade, as if thou hadst laboured in my garret these ten years. Let me tell you, friend, you will have more occasion for invention than learning here" (Henley, VIII, 222).

Fielding's own translations were largely hackwork, and I do not propose to treat them at length. He had made a spirited use of his knowledge of French in adapting Molière's *Le Médecin malgré lui* and *L'Avare* for the English stage; but whether or not he had any connection with the translation of Molière published in 1732 (which now seems doubtful),[1] the contrast between this uninspired collection and his own bright adaptations is instructive. That Fielding could read French with competence is indicated by numerous other borrowings from that lan-

---
[1] See L. P. Goggin, "Fielding and the *Select Comedies of Mr. De Moliere*," PQ, XXXI (1952), 344-50; and Joseph E. Tucker, "The Eighteenth-Century English Translations of Moliere," MLQ, III (1942), 83-103, esp. pp. 89-90.

guage;[2] and several of his hack translations draw upon this skill. Whatever part he may be supposed to have taken in translating Gustaf Adlerfeld's *Military History of Charles XII* (3v., 1740), he obviously worked from the French version of that text.[3] Again, some vague connection has been supposed between Fielding and the translation from the French of the Abbé Banier's *Mythology and Fables of the Ancients, Explain'd from History* (1739).[4]

Fielding's other translations include that curious production, *Ovid's Art of Love* [*Book I*] *Paraphrased and Adapted to the Present Time* (1747)[5] and his joint labor with William Young on Aristophanes' *Plutus*. The announced intention to continue with the rest of Aristophanes' plays came to nothing, presumably through a lack of interest on the part of the buying public; and Fielding's later plans with Young to translate Lucian also proved abortive. The latter, at least, we may consider a real loss.

[2] See G.-E. Parfitt, *L'influence française dans les œuvres de Fielding et dans le théâtre anglais contemporain de ses comédies* (Paris, 1928); Sidney E. Glenn, *Some French Influences on Henry Fielding* (Urbana, Ill., 1932: abstract of a doctoral diss.); Arthur L. Cooke, "Henry Fielding and the Writers of Heroic Romance," *PMLA*, LXII (1947), 984-94; Heinrich Schönzeler, *Fieldings Verhältnis zu LeSage und zu anderen Quellen* (Weimar, 1915); and Felix Lindner, *Henry Fieldings dramatische Werke* (Leipzig & Dresden, 1895). Some of Fielding's indebtedness to Jean-François Regnard (whose *Le retour imprévu* gave Fielding the idea for *The Intriguing Chambermaid*) has been noted; and doubtless in good time we will have an investigation of his debt to the *Théâtre italien de* [*Evaristo*] *Gherardi* (Paris, 1694; 6v., London, 1714; the edition in Fielding's library was that of Paris, 1717, in six volumes).

[3] See J. E. Wells, "Henry Fielding and the History of Charles XII," *JEGP*, XI (1912), 603-13; and Cross, I, 284-87.

[4] Cross, citing Fielding's appreciative references to the work in the *Jacobite's Journal* and *Tom Jones*, says, "Apparently Fielding had a personal interest in the work; he may have supervised the translation or a revision" (III, 336). Surely we need more evidence than this!

[5] Copies of the original London edition unknown to Cross (II, 52-54 and III, 313) have been incidentally described by Rupert C. Jarvis, "Fielding and the 'Forty-five," *N&Q*, CCII (1957), 20-21. The translation was reprinted in London and Dublin in 1759 (and perhaps earlier) as *The Lover's Assistant, or, New Year's Gift . . . Translated from the Latin, with Notes, by the Late Ingenious Henry Fielding of Facetious Memory*.

TRANSLATION

2

If there is no question concerning Fielding's competence in French and in Latin, there have always been doubts as to his mastery of Greek, and we may devote a few moments to a scrutiny of this vexed question, inasmuch as the translation we are to consider is from Demosthenes. Fielding would have received some instruction in Greek at Eton; indeed, if he had reached the sixth form, he would have had no inconsiderable exercise in reading and writing the language.[6] Cross (I, 43) does not believe that he went so far as the sixth form; but he infers this from Fielding's "lack of facility with Greek," a process of reasoning all too likely to involve us in a vicious circle. Arthur Murphy declared that Fielding, upon leaving Eton, "was said to be uncommonly versed in the Greek authors, and an early master of the Latin classics."[7] Murphy's observations seldom inspire great confidence; but this contemporary evidence is at least worth more than the dubious guess of even so eminent an authority as Cross. Moreover, it would seem likely that Fielding continued his classical studies (presumably including Greek) at the University of Leyden, where he was entered as "litterarum studiosus."

Dr. Dudden[8] took the description of Mr. Wilson's education in *Joseph Andrews* to be probably autobiographical on Fielding's part: "My education was liberal, and at a public school, in which I proceeded so far as to become master of the Latin, and to be tolerably versed in the

---

[6] See H. C. Maxwell Lyte, *A History of Eton College, 1440-1875* (rev. ed., 1877), pp. 314-19. The reading was largely in Homer, Lucian, the Greek Testament, and the anthology *Poetae Graeci*. See also M. L. Clarke, *Greek Studies in England, 1700-1830* (Cambridge, 1945), pp. 10-24, which places Lyte's evidence in a broader context.

[7] "An Essay on the Life and Genius of Henry Fielding, Esq;" in his edition of the *Works* (4v., 1762), I, 8. Christopher Smart, who knew Fielding, called him "THE Master of the GREEK and ROMAN page, / The lively scorner of a venal age" ("Epitaph on Henry Fielding, Esq.," in *Collected Poems*, ed. Norman Callan [2v., Cambridge, Mass., 1949], I, 35).

[8] *Henry Fielding*, I, 15, n. 3.

339

Greek, language" (*JA*, III, iii; Henley, I, 228-29). He might have added, with equal color, the comment upon Booth's education in *Amelia*: "Booth, as the reader may be pleased to remember, was a pretty good master of the classics; for his father, though he designed his son for the army, did not think it necessary to breed him up a blockhead. He did not, perhaps, imagine that a competent share of Latin or Greek would make his son either a pedant or a coward" (VIII, v; Henley, VII, 83). However this may be, Fielding in the jesting poem to Walpole of 1730 (see above, p. 127) had said: "*Tuscan* and *French* are in my Head; / *Latin* I write, and *Greek* I—read" (*Misc.*, I, 43). Now, it is surely true that his Latin was far superior to his Greek. This was true of nearly all educated gentlemen of the century ("The Greek, you will allow, is a hard language," says the little author in the sponging-house to Booth; "and there are few gentlemen that write who can read it without a good lexicon"—*Amelia*, VIII, v; Henley, VII, 85). But if Fielding had more Latin than Greek, it is still not unreasonable to suppose that as the years passed he further developed whatever formal acquaintance with Greek he had received in his schooling. The copy of Benjamin Hederich's *Lexicon manuale Graecum* in his personal library was said to be "cum notis. MSS Henr. Fielding"[9] (one would give a good deal to know how great a number)—and these might suggest a continued application to his studies in the language.

The numerous works of Greek authors in his library surely testify to an interest in the language (for most of them were available in other tongues); but they do not testify so clearly to Fielding's ability to read Greek. Vir-

---

[9] See the convenient reprinting of the sale-catalogue of Fielding's library in Ethel M. Thornbury, *Henry Fielding's Theory of the Comic Prose Epic* (Madison, Wisc., 1931), p. 177; and cf. the suggestion of Cross (III, 80-82) that Fielding probably assisted Young in compiling a new edition of Hedericus—which is plausible enough, thought we cannot prove it.

tually all the editions he possessed were bilingual, Greek and Latin (a normal publishing practice of the day), and would have enabled Fielding, like Mrs. Atkinson, "to read a little of Homer, at least with the help of looking now and then into the Latin" (*Amelia*, x, iv; Henley, VII, 205). In the eighteenth century, when Greek was taught by way of Latin, such a practice would scarcely have been unusual; and I think it can be shown that in translating Demosthenes, at any rate, Fielding himself had an eye on the Latin.

He obviously considered Greek to be the necessary accomplishment of a learned man—and this, one might venture, is in itself good evidence that he would have continued to prosecute his studies in the language. He was fond of displaying an apparent knowledge of fine points in Greek; and this sometimes led him into a kind of self-conscious pedantry that he did not so often display with Latin. Thus he was pleased to point out, in citing a parallel from the *Odyssey*, that "the English reader will not find this in the poem; for the sentiment is entirely left out in the translation" (*TJ*, IV, xiii; Henley, III, 197, n.), or again, through Booth, to criticize (dubiously) Pope's translation of the *Iliad* for failing in one line to give a causal force to the particle δέ (*Amelia*, VIII, v; Henley, VII, 85-86). When he cited (from Diogenes Laertius), in the fragmentary *Comment on Lord Bolingbroke's Essays*, a pair of Thales' apophthegms on the existence of God as an uncreated being and on the beauty of the universe as God's workmanship, he added a somewhat ostentatious footnote: "I submit to the learned reader the construction he will observe I have given to the different import of those terms, ἀγέννητον and ποίημα;[10] the first of which may be considered as a qualified, the latter as an

[10] Nonsensically misprinted as πόιημα in Henley (to indulge in a little pedantry myself).

341

absolute cause" (Henley, xvi, 320, n.).[11] He ventured upon several occasions to correct scriptural readings, citing the (supposed) authority of the Greek text;[12] and, of course, his clergymen heroes, Adams and Dr. Harrison, like his clergyman friend, Dr. Young, handled the language with familiarity. Thus Dr. Harrison subverts the incipient bluestocking, Mrs. Atkinson (again), by quoting Homer to her: "I have no Greek ears, sir," she admits; "I believe I could understand it in the Delphin Homer" (*Amelia*, xii, viii; Henley, vii, 335).[13] And when Fielding employed Parson Adams to pen a letter for his *True Patriot*, he concluded with a quotation in the original from Aristotle, which, he said, "for the sake of women, and those few gentlemen who do not understand Greek, I have rendered somewhat paraphrastically in the vernacular" (No. 13; Henley, xiv, 50). The tone of every one of these citations is that of a man who has an ability that he shares with the learned, recommends to all gentlemen, or ridicules pretenders for not actually possessing;[14] it is the tone that he

[11] Fielding's rendition (Diog. Laert., I. 35) is: "That God was the oldest of all beings, for he existed *without a previous cause* EVEN IN THE WAY OF GENERATION [ἀγέννητον γάρ]; that the world was the most beautiful of all things; for *it was* CREATED [ποίημα] BY God, &c." (Henley, xvi, 320). The reader might also have observed that this distinction is implicit in the Latin version printed with the Greek in the text that Fielding owned: "Antiquissimum eorum omnium quæ sunt, deus; ingenitus enim. Pulcherrimum, mundus; à deo enim factus est . . ." (Diogenes Laertius, *De Vitis, Dogmatibus et Apophthegmatibus Clarorum Philosophorum. Libri X*, ed. Marcus Meibom [2v., Amsterdam, 1692], I, 21).
[12] For example, *Joseph Andrews*, iii, viii (Henley, i, 286), and *Essay on the Knowledge of the Characters of Men* (*Misc.*, i, 208).
[13] The jest presumably lies in the nonexistence of a Delphin Homer; but Mrs. Atkinson may have had in mind the fact that the Delphin editions (largely of the *Latin* classics) customarily assisted the reader through difficult passages with an interpretation in simpler Latin at the foot of the page.
[14] The most ludicrous illustration is the parish priest in *Joseph Andrews* (ii, xi), who seizes Parson Adams' Aeschylus: "Æschylus! ho! ho! ho! I see now what it is—a manuscript of one of the fathers. I know a nobleman who would give a great deal of money for such a piece of antiquity. Aye, aye, question and answer, The beginning is the catechism in Greek. Aye, aye, *Pollaki toi*: What's your name?" (Henley, i, 171).

TRANSLATION

displays in the third *Covent-Garden Journal* when his pronouncement as Censor is that "no Author is to be admitted into the Order of Critics, until he hath read over, and understood, Aristotle, Horace, and Longinus, in their original Language . . ." (Jensen, I, 150).

None of this is certain evidence, of course. One can always uncharitably suppose that Fielding is pretending to a knowledge superior to that he actually possessed. His translation with Dr. Young of Aristophanes is dubious evidence also; for Fielding's task in that venture was most likely, as Cross argues (I, 364-65), to give a literary gloss to his scholarly partner's translation. On the other hand, when he and Young projected their version of Lucian, Fielding, though deferring to Young's greater mastery of the language, seemed to claim an equal role in the duties of translation: "As to the Abilities of one of the Gentlemen who propose this Translation I shall be silent; I will only venture to say, that no Man seems so likely to translate an Author well, as he who hath formed his Stile upon that very Author" (*CGJ*, No. 52; Jensen, II, 50). Even if this is an advertising "puff," the implication surely is that Fielding was well read in his great exemplar's original tongue.

Here perhaps we may leave the matter—unresolved but not, I hope, entirely unillumined. It would be my guess that Fielding did receive some early schooling in Greek at Eton and at Leyden, and that he continued all his life to read in the language, though never with the ease and certainty that he obviously enjoyed in reading Latin. The translation of Demosthenes, for reasons that will become clear, cannot be said in itself unequivocally to establish the degree of Fielding's competence in Greek; but it does at least show that he was able to follow a Greek text with comprehension. Beyond this, all conjecture depends upon the value we are willing to give to Fielding's own implication (in the citations noted) that he possessed a more

TRANSLATION

than adequate share of the language. I am inclined to believe him.

"THE FIRST OLYNTHIAC OF DEMOSTHENES."

The three *Olynthiac* orations of Demosthenes[15] were occasioned, like the *Philippics*, by the increasing power of Philip of Macedon and the consequent threat to Athens' security. Philip's neighbor, the city-state of Olynthus, had for a time allied itself with him against Athens; but about 352 B.C., disturbed at his growing strength, Olynthus began to make overtures to the Athenians. Within the next few years Philip invaded the territory of Olynthus and threatened the city itself. In 349 an Olynthian embassy was dispatched to Athens to ask their aid in repelling the invader. Little real opposition to the alliance was expressed in the Athenian assembly, and Demosthenes' lucid and forceful statement of the case for succoring Olynthus is more significant for its scope and insight than for its triumph over a peace-party. He demanded, as he had in the *First Philippic*, immediate action on two fronts as the only adequate answer to Philip's threat. The Athenians apparently responded with economical half-measures and, as Demosthenes had foreseen, thereby prepared the way for the death of Athens as an independent political entity.[16]

Wilbur Cross has argued that Fielding was moved to translate the *First Olynthiac* by the political situation existent in England around 1738-1739, when the War of Jenkins' Ear was in the offing.[17] England had—in Philip

---

[15] Classical scholars are not agreed upon the exact order of delivery, since all three orations are couched in fairly general terms and are not specifically datable; but the present numbering is the traditional one. If the ordering of Dionysius of Halicarnassus is followed (as it was, for example, in Thomas Leland's translation of Demosthenes in 1756-1770), the first *Olynthiac* becomes the third. Others have made it the second.

[16] Cf. Werner Jaeger, *Demosthenes: The Origin and Growth of His Policy* (Berkeley, Calif., 1938), chap. vi, "The Struggle for Olynthus," pp. 125-49.

[17] Cross (I, 386) actually says, "Somewhere in 1739 or 1740"; but since the whole point of the analogy between Athens and England is

TRANSLATION

V of Spain—its own Philip to contend with (even if Elizabeth Farnese was the real force and Spain's Philip nothing like his namesake). In the English as well as the Athenian situation the danger lay—or so the leaders of the Opposition to Walpole convinced themselves—as much in the inertia of the people and of those politicians who favored temporizing measures over direct action as it did in the actual threat of a conqueror. And the English people, like the Athenians, were being called upon to supply immediate substantial armies and monies for a common war upon a common enemy.[18] Cross adds, "Demosthenes was the Patriot of the Athenians. Let Pitt stand for Demosthenes, and the analogy becomes complete" (I, 386-87).

We cannot prove that Fielding's translation was specifically intended to exploit this analogy; but it is a likely supposition. I have only one reservation, and that I shall hold until I come to discuss the style of the work. Such a parallel had obviously occurred to others, as we can see by the translations of several orations from Demosthenes, which appeared as leading articles in the periodical of the war-party, *Common Sense*, in 1737 and early 1738.[19] These very loose "translations" were really more concerned with interpolating innuendoes that could be applied to the Walpole administration than they were with pointing out the

---

that action should *be* taken, it would surely seem to be applicable only before October 1739, when the war actually commenced. Cross also says, "It is probable that Fielding made *and published* this translation . . ." (*ibid.*; italics mine), but he gives no evidence of such early publication, and I know of none.

[18] See H. W. V. Temperley, "The Causes of the War of Jenkins' Ear, 1739," *Transactions of the Royal Historical Society*, 3rd Ser., III (1909), 197-236. The *Craftsman* and *Common Sense*, the leading anti-Walpole journals, had been urging war with Spain from early in 1737.

[19] The orations drawn upon seem to have been the *Third Olynthiac*, the *Third Philippic*, and the *Fourth Philippic* (*Common Sense*, Nos. 43 [26 November 1737], 47 [24 December 1737], and 53 [4 February 1738], respectively). Actually, the translations are so free and full of interpolations that it is difficult to ascertain from which originals they are drawn. Excerpts from each were published in the *London Magazine*.

threat posed by Philip of Spain; but the identification of the latter with Philip of Macedon was implicit and, indeed, obvious. That the translations stung the administration, at any rate, is indicated by a reply in Walpole's government organ, the *Daily Gazetteer*, in February 1738: "*Of Applying the Orations of* Demosthenes." This argued with lofty superiority that although translations of Demosthenes in other periods of English history had often been "well timed and well applied," those appearing in *Common Sense* did not have reason on their side. In the present days of crisis, said the *Gazetteer*, "the Spirit of our People resembles rather that of the *Lacedemonians* than that of the *Athenians*," and requires cooling rather than pricking.[20]

The "well timed and well applied" translations in which Demosthenes had been made to speak for British patriotism included the rendering by Thomas Wilson, in the reign of Elizabeth (1570), of the *Philippics* and the *Olynthiacs* to underline the danger offered by an earlier Philip of Spain. This work, "most nedefull to be redde in these daungerous dayes, of all them that loue their Countries libertie," had been paralleled by a translation of the same orations "by several Hands" in the first decade of the eighteenth century. Here the enemy identified with Philip of Macedon was, of course, Louis XIV of France.[21] It was natural enough, then, that in a new day of war fever, crisis, and impassioned speeches about liberty, Demosthenes should once again be called upon, that his orations might "With patriot zeal inspirit ev'ry breast, / And fire each *British* heart with *British* wrongs"; and it was not surpris-

[20] *Daily Gazetteer*, No. 823 (22 February 1738), repr. in the *London Magazine* (February 1738), pp. 87-89.
[21] *Several Orations of Demosthenes, to Encourage the Athenians to Oppose the Exorbitant Power of Philip of Macedon. English'd from the Greek by Several Hands* (1702). The "several hands" included George Granville (later Lord Lansdowne) and Dr. Garth; and the *First Olynthiac* was translated by the Earl of Peterborough. A new, revised edition of this translation appeared in 1744.

TRANSLATION

ing that Mark Akenside, who wrote these lines, should call his poem, "A BRITISH PHILIPPIC."[22]

2

Demosthenes' first Olynthiac oration may be quickly summarized:[23] After a brief *exordium*, urging that all counsels should be heard at this crisis, the statement of the case (the *narratio*) is presented. Here, Demosthenes gives his opinion that aid to the Olynthians should be immediately voted, and playing skillfully upon the Athenians' fears and hopes, sets forth Philip's strength and advantages *and* his present vulnerability because of the discontent of his vassal-allies. The *confirmatio*, as I take it, follows, including occasional refutations or anticipations as they are needed. This, the main body of the oration, falls into three parts: first, a section arguing the necessity of seizing the present opportunity (*kairos*) with vigor and personal resolution, thereby atoning for previous failures to combine against Philip. In the next section, Demosthenes presents succinctly his formal recommendation: a two-fold attack upon Philip's army in Olynthus and upon his home ground of Macedonia. To this end, either a special war tax (*eisphora*) must be levied or (he hints) the theoric fund, by tradition and by law reserved to the citizens for their public games, must be drawn upon. The third and final section of the *confirmatio* examines once again the present disadvantageous posture of Philip's affairs, encouraging the Athenians with the opportunity offered to them and

[22] "A BRITISH PHILIPPIC: *Occasion'd by the Insults of the* Spaniards, *and the present Preparations for* War," *Gentleman's Magazine* (August 1738), pp. 427-28. The poem was also published in two separate editions in 1738.
[23] I have ventured to apply the conventional divisions to this oration. Demosthenes' later and more complex works are less easily analyzed in these terms. Marcel Delaunois has argued that all of the orations after the early ones against his guardians are better approached in terms of a psychological plan of repetitions and variations of ideas than in terms of a logical (that is, rhetorical) plan ("Du plan logique au plan psychologique chez Démosthène," *Les Études classiques*, XIX [1951], 177-89).

frightening them with the fearful and inevitable consequence that must follow if they do not act decisively. The *peroratio* then sums up his belief that to carry the war directly to the enemy must appear to all—the wealthy, the young fighting men, the orators and advisors, alike— the most expedient choice. And the oration is concluded in a low key, with the quietly fervent prayer, "May the conclusion on every ground be favorable."

3

Fielding's translation of the *First Olynthiac* is, for the most part, literal to the point of stiffness.[24] The first question that arises concerning it, however (as I have already hinted), is: how much use did he make of the Latin text that accompanied the Greek? The edition that he employed was presumably the one in his personal library, *Demosthenis et Æschinis principum græciæ oratorvm opera* (Frankfurt, 1604), in which the Greek text was paralleled by the Latin translation of Hieronymus Wolfius. A com-

[24] Mindful of the sponging-house author's comment, "The Greek, you will allow, is a hard language," and not counting myself among the "few gentlemen that write who can read it without a good lexicon," I have sought a degree of authority for my conclusions in the following editions of the *Olynthiacs: Demosthenis et Æschinis principum græciæ oratorvm opera* (Frankfurt, 1604; Fielding's edition, with the Latin translation of Hieronymus Wolfius); *The Olynthiac Speeches of Demosthenes*, ed. J. M. MacGregor (Cambridge, 1915); *The First Philippic and the Olynthiacs of Demosthenes*, ed. J. E. Sandys (1910); and *Demosthenes: Olynthiacs, Philippics, Minor Public Speeches, Speech against Leptines*, with an English translation by J. H. Vince (Loeb Classical Library, 1954).

I have not been able to consult all the Latin translations to which Fielding might have had access, and the possibility remains that he looked at others than that of Wolfius or, indeed, at a different Greek text. But I have satisfied myself that he did not follow the Latin version accompanying the edition of Demosthenes published by Nicolaus Bryling (Basel, 1549) or the Latin translation by Nicolaus Carrus (1571) or by J. V. Lucchesinius (Rome, 1712). As Fielding read French with obvious fluency, I thought it prudent to compare his version with the most influential French translation of the period, Jacques de Tourreil's *Philippiques de Demosthene avec des remarques* (Paris, 1701; no accents in the original), which included the *Olynthiacs*. The results in this instance were also negative.

TRANSLATION

parison of Wolfius' Latin with Fielding's English translation reveals, first, that Fielding's phrasing and word-order often follow quite closely that of the Latin, and, second, that a number of Fielding's individual words echo the Latin terms of Wolfius. The first point would require excessive space to demonstrate in full; I shall let one illustration serve: "For my greatest Apprehension is, that the artful *Philip*, who well knows to improve every Opportunity, by Concessions, where they are most convenient, and by Threats, which we may believe him capable of fulfilling, at the same time objecting our Absence to our Allies, may draw from the whole some considerable Advantage to himself" (1, 283; *1st Ol.*, 3). The order of the Latin is: "Nam hoc maximè timendum est, ne Philippus (vt est homo callidus, & in rebus gerendis acer) partim concedendo, vbi res ita tulerit, partim minitando (qua quidem in parte non immeritò illi fides habebitur) partim nos & absentiam nostram criminando, de summa rerum interuertat aliquid, & ad sese transferat" (*Demosthenis*, sig. A₁).[25] Besides the resemblance in word-order, one may note that both Wolfius and Fielding have missed the reductive effect of Demosthenes' ἄνθρωπος ("the man") by introducing the actual name, Philip.[26]

Again, to move to my second point, the words that Fielding chooses echo, from time to time, the Latin of Wolfius. For example:

"your *Fortune*" (1, 282) (vestræ *fortunæ*: ὑμετέρας τύχης) (A₁);

"the *Benevolence* of the Gods" (1, 286) (diuinæ *beneuolentiæ*: ἐκείνων εὐνοίας—i.e., from the Gods) (A₁ᵛ);

[25] The Greek text, of course, presents an order that could not possibly be preserved in English with any regard for idiom.
[26] At a later point in the text when Wolfius correctly rendered καὶ ἄνθρωπος ὑβριστής (*1st Ol.*, 23) as "& *homo* importunus est" (A₂ᵛ), Fielding did likewise: "and *the Man* is . . . prone to Insolence" (1, 291-92; italics mine).

349

"but if he insensibly *consumes* it ... is *consumed* at the same Time" (1, 286) (Sin imprudens consumpserit vnà consumpsit: ἂν δ'ἀναλώσας λάθῃ, συνανάλωσε [sic]) (A₁ᵛ);

"Why therefore do you *commemorate* these Things to us now?" (1, 287) (Quid ergo ... ista nobis *commemoras* nunc?: τί οὖν ... ταῦτα λέγεις ἡμῖν νῦν) (A₂);

"and *sensibly* perceive" (1, 287) (& *sentiatis*: καὶ αἴσθησθε) (A₂);

"the reckless Disposition of Philip to undertake, and his *Alacrity* to execute" (1, 288) (perpetuam in rebus gerendis *alacritatem*, qua erga omnes Philippus vtitur: τὴν φιλοπραγμοσύνην, ᾗ πρὸς ἅπαντας [sic] χρῆται, καὶ συζῇ Φίλιππος) (A₂);

"turned out of their original *Patrimony*" (1, 288) (*patrimonijs* euertuntur: καὶ τῶν ἀρχαίων ἀπέστησαν) (A₂);

"the Part of a *Counsellor*" (1, 288) (id esse *consiliarij*: συμβούλου) (A₂).

Moreover, when Fielding has to render such an expression as "μὰ Δί', οὐκ ἔγωγε" [By Zeus! not I, certainly] he omits the Greek exclamation and follows the literal sense of the Latin "Ego *verò* nequaquam" (A₂ᵛ): "Not I *truly*" (1, 290).

Now, admitting that τύχη would very likely be translated "fortune" in any case (as, in other instances, λέγοντας could suggest "orators" without the hint of the Latin "oratores," and στρατιωτικά be applied to a fund "for military uses," without the Latin "militaris"), one still seems to have reasonably clear evidence that Fielding's version was influenced by the Latin. Coincidence can only go so far. This, then, is my ground for suggesting earlier that Fielding as he read Greek could, like Mrs. Atkinson, also find reassurance in peeking into the accompanying (and happily familiar) Latin text from time to time. Nevertheless, I believe that it was *only* "from time to time." For though some of the parallels cited above may seem particularly damning, they are still not very large in number—and I have cited almost all that I could find. The number is, I continue to believe, too large for coincidence; but it is a long way from being large enough to suggest that Fielding simply translated Demosthenes out of the Latin! Moreover, there are further considerations that militate against any such uncharitable conclusion. In the first place, since Greek was taught by way of Latin and since the Greek lexicons (like that of Hedericus) gave only Latin equivalents for their Greek words, Fielding's procedure in translating would necessarily have involved a Latin cast of thought. One of our parallels cited above could be explained, for instance, by recalling that Hedericus defined εὐνοίας ("goodness," etc.) as "beneuolentia." The most conclusive evidence, however, that Fielding did not translate Demosthenes out of the Latin of Wolfius lies in the very certainty that he *could* have translated the Latin precisely and without flaw—and he did not. His translation is sprinkled with palpable errors and omissions: and in almost every single instance the Latin version has a correct rendering that Fielding could easily have followed. To give just one example of an inaccurate translation: Fielding has "how pernicious it is to neglect the least Article of what ought to be done" (1, 287; 1st Ol., 14) where Wolfius offers the quite different (and quite adequate) "proijcere singulatim semper aliquid rerum, quàm non expediat" (τὸ προίεσθαι καθέκαστον [*sic*] αἰεί τι τῶν πραγμάτων, ὡς ἀλυσιτελές) (A₂). The same relative accuracy of the Latin could be shown for at least a half dozen other erroneous or questionable renderings in Field-

TRANSLATION

ing's text.[27] And his most notable omissions are also plainly set forth in the Latin: he could not have failed to see Wolfius' "& arcana & aperta" (A₁) in the description of Philip's councils (καὶ ῥητῶν καὶ ἀπορρήτων), but he nevertheless omitted "both public and private" from his own translation (1, 283).[28]

What are we to conclude, then, from this somewhat labored survey? My own conclusion would be that Fielding read the Greek of Demosthenes with one eye on Wolfius —but *only* one eye; for he sought to present an independent reading in the vast majority of his phrases. His independence, indeed, led him into a few departures from his text. His reading: "that the *Thessalians* would no longer open their Ports to him, nor suffer his Fleets to be victualled in their Markets" (1, 291; 1st Ol., 22) really leaves one curious—where did Fielding find "Fleets to be victualled" in ὡς οὐδὲ τοὺς λιμένας, καὶ τὰς ἀγορὰς ἔτι δώσοιεν αὐτῷ

[27] For example (1) "Let an Embassy be dispatched, not only to declare these our Intentions, but *to see them executed*" (1, 283; 1st Ol., 2-3; all italics mine). The Greek text has merely "to be present" or "overlook" our interests; Wolfius: "& rebus intersint."
(2) "That those who do their Duty to the Public, should receive their Reward from it [the theoric fund]" (1, 290; 1st Ol., 20). Demosthenes had actually been careful to say only that there should be *one uniform regulation* both for receiving payment and for doing one's duty; in Wolfius, "& vnam esse rationem, eandem & faciendi & accipiendi quæ oporteat" (A₂ᵛ).
(3) "The Phocians? they are not able to save themselves, unless you, or some one else, will assist them" (1, 293; 1st Ol., 26). Although Sandys, *ed cit*., p. 152n., argues for this reading of the phrase ἢ ἄλλος τις, Fielding's Greek text was otherwise pointed, and Wolfius had followed it in making the penultimate phrase in Fielding's version a question: "An Phocenses? Qui ne sua quidem sine vestris auxilijs tueri possunt. *Aut alius quispiam?*" (A₃). Fielding's striking departure here from both texts might suggest that he made use of another edition: but such departures are too infrequent to be conclusive.

[28] So also, when Demosthenes urges the Athenians to be willing and prepared to attend to the war, now or never (φημὶ δεῖν ἐθελῆσαι, καὶ παροξυνθῆναι, καὶ τῷ πολέμῳ προσέχειν, εἴπερ ποτε [sic], καὶ νῦν; Wolfius has "vt velitis & excitemini, bellóque si vnquam, nunc certè maximè incumbatis") (A₁ᵛ), Fielding gives only "your Resolutions must be for War, and to prosecute it with as much Vigour as you have formerly shewn on any Occasion" (1, 284; 1st Ol., 6).

352

καρποῦσθαι [in literal schoolboy fashion: "that neither of their ports and markets will they any more permit him to enjoy the revenue"]? One cannot tell; but it is certainly not in Wolfius' "non cõcessuros ei Thessalos posthac portoriorum & vectigalium vsumfructum" (A_2^r). All things considered, then, I shall in the remainder of my discussion assume that Fielding wrestled with the Greek text and I shall cite Wolfius only when he seems relevant.

4

Of all Demosthenes' public orations, this offers perhaps the fewest traps for the unwary translator, the fewest effects impossible to reproduce from the Greek. It is the least colorful and most purely abstract of them all, eschewing not only metaphor but the devices of *anaphora* and *anadiplosis* which together are almost the hallmark of Demosthenes' style. There are fewer parentheses and fewer rhetorical questions than were customary in his speeches. What Demosthenes was obviously seeking here was not so much the arousal of passions as a cold and firm clarity of understanding. Gilberte Ronnet has very accurately summed up the style of the *First Olynthiac* in saying that it displays "une langue sérieuse et abstraite, riche en noms de sentiments et de qualités, et en infinitifs substantivés, peu d'images, très peu de mouvement; la phrase aussi est simple, sans périodes qui frappent; l'orateur semble avoir cherché à convaincre la raison de ses auditeurs par une distinction et une réserve qui répudient presque toute éloquence."[29]

The rhetorical effects that Demosthenes did permit himself to employ in this sober oration have for the most part been successfully caught in Fielding's translation, though he did not attempt (nor did the Latin version) to repro-

[29] Ronnet, *Étude sur le style de Démosthène dans les discours politiques* (Paris, 1951), p. 183. I have drawn heavily upon this useful analysis.

duce an occasional difficult hyperbaton or periphrasis in the original. The effective *antitheses* arising from the very situation itself are properly emphasized; thus after describing Philip's advantages: "This indeed will contribute greatly to his Successes in the Field, but will have a contrary Effect, with Regard to that Truce which he is so desirous to make..." (*Misc.*, 1, 283; *1st Ol.*, 4-5). Or this, near the conclusion: "If the *Olynthians*, by your Assistance, are preserved, the Kingdom of *Philip* will be by your Forces invaded, and you may then retain your own Dominions, your own City in Safety; but should *Philip* once Master the *Olynthians*, who would oppose his March hither?" (1, 292; *1st Ol.*, 25). Almost the only other devices for arousing emotion that Demosthenes made use of were accumulation (*congeries*) and an occasional repetition. Fielding reproduces the effect of the first quite accurately through *asyndeton* and rapid succession of clauses, as in the description of Philip's frightening rise to power:

"He first became Master of *Amphipolis*, secondly of *Pydna*, next of *Potidea*, and then of *Methone*. After these Conquests, he turned his Arms towards *Thessaly*, where having reduced *Phera*, *Pagasæ*, *Magnesia*, he marched on to *Thrace*"—(1, 287; *1st Ol.*, 12-13).

The most notable use of *repetition* in the oration comes when Demosthenes is approaching the ticklish question of the theoric fund. He did not yet dare to propose outright that this fund for the public games be applied to the purposes of the campaign against Philip; but he wanted to emphasize the existence of the available resources. The passage is purposely oblique, and I do not think that Fielding has got quite the proper sense of it;[30] but the

[30] On the *theorica* see Werner Jaeger, pp. 140-42 and pp. 243-44, notes 35 and 38; also Sandys, pp. 144-46 and references. The confusion is compounded by a passage that is usually excised in modern texts, but that is found in all the MSS. and appeared in Fielding's text: καὶ ταῦτ' εἶναι στρατιωτικά [and that too should become a military fund] (A₂ᵛ). He translated, "That this Fund should be applied to it [the Army]" (1,

354

TRANSLATION

effect of Demosthenes' own emphatic repetition, at least, is adequately reproduced: "As for the Supply of Money to be raised; you have a Treasury, O *Athenians*, you have a Treasury fuller of Money, set apart for Military Uses, than any other City of Greece . . . if the Army be supplied this Way, you will want no Tax: If not, you will hardly find any Tax sufficient" (1, 289-90; *1st Ol.*, 19-20).

As for other devices, there is a use of *praeteritio* or "passing over" (rare in Demosthenes): "His Expeditions against the *Illyrians*, the *Pæonians* [,] against *Arymba*, and who can recount all the other Nations, I omit" (1, 287; *1st Ol.*, 13). There is the characteristic use of homely terms and comparisons, adequately enough rendered by Fielding: "If we settle a just Account with the Gods" (1, 286; *1st Ol.*, 10), or the extension of this economic image: "But it happens as in the Affair of Riches, of which, I think, it is proverbially said, that if a Man preserves the Wealth he attains, he is greatly thankful to Fortune; but if he insensibly consumes it, his Gratitude to Fortune is consumed at the same Time. So in public Affairs . . ." (1, 286; *1st Ol.*, 11). Finally, there is the characteristic *litotes* in Demosthenes, which Fielding (strangely enough) does not reproduce with any great skill: for example, the comment on Philip: "The Man is, as they say, prone to Insolence; which is indeed very credible . . ." (1, 291-92), a weak rendering of καὶ ἄνθρωπος ὑβριστής, ὥς φασι· καὶ μὰ δί' οὐδὲν ἄπιστον ἴσως (A₂ᵛ) [literally "and the man is overbearing (or oppressive, etc.), as they say, and, by Zeus, this is not perhaps beyond belief"] (*1st Ol.*, 23). Another example: "Add to this, the Insults of the Enemy, and that which to generous Minds is not inferior to any Loss, the Disgrace of such an Incident" (1, 293; *1st Ol.*, 27).

290; *1st Ol.*, 20). Clearly this would be a direct contradiction of Demosthenes' assertion that he did *not* intend to make such a direct proposal. That Fielding should have had difficulty with this section is not, then, surprising (cf. the second example in n. 27).

Fielding sometimes misses or obscures Demosthenes' mild examples of *prosopopoeia*. For example, early in the oration, where Demosthenes says that the present crisis (καιρός) calls upon the Athenians almost with an audible voice, the image is obscured in Fielding's phrasing: "The present Occasion wants only a Tongue to declare . . ." (I, 282; *1st Ol.*, 2). Again, as we have already observed, Fielding now and then omits or misses a phrase or a word that is clearly in the Greek text. The most interesting examples of such omission are those which present one with the naughty pleasure of psychologizing; as in Fielding's rendering of Demosthenes' exemplum, "I fear, O *Athenians*, that we shall imitate those who borrow Money [*thoughtlessly*] at great Usury, who for a short Affluence of present Wealth, are afterwards turned out of their original Patrimony" (I, 288; *1st Ol.*, 15). Fielding's omission of "thoughtlessly" (ῥᾳδίως: "temerè" in Wolfius) would afford the Freudian critic matter for conjecture. So also would the following, in Demosthenes' closing appeal to all classes: "The Rich, that for the many Things they [*happily*, or *deservedly*] possess, parting with a little, they may secure the quiet Possession of the rest" (I, 293-94; *1st Ol.*, 28). The Greek text has: ὧν, καλῶς ποιοῦντες, ἔχουσι; Wolfius reads: "quæ Deûm benignitate possident" (A₃). Is it that Fielding could not bring himself to say that these possessions were rightly or fortunately owned? It is amusing to think so.

Another omission, or rather neglect of emphasis, is curious: for it would have provided Fielding and the Opposition, one would think, with a point of propaganda against two of their major aversions: the standing army and the use of mercenaries. This emphasis in the original lies in Demosthenes' insistence, throughout the *First Olynthiac*, that the Athenians must *themselves* go into the field, constitute an army. The stress is constantly upon the pronominal αὐτός (self); mercenaries will not serve

TRANSLATION

the purpose—you, yourselves, he tells the Athenians, must go. The intensive pronoun (though it is also in Wolfius) is seldom reproduced in Fielding's translation; he says: "the Posture of these Affairs requires your immediate Application" (1, 282; *1st Ol.*, 2), not "take into your own hands the control" or "you must yourselves [αὐτοῖς] take these affairs in hand"; or again, says: "had we then assisted only one of these" (1, 285; *1st Ol.*, 9), rather than "had we in person [αὐτοί]"; or still again: "not only to dispatch the necessary Embassies, but to follow them with an Army" (1, 292; *1st Ol.*, 24), rather than "take the field yourselves in person [αὐτοὺς]." And so on. One can think of no ulterior motive in this failure to reproduce Demosthenes' emphasis, unless it is simply that the realities of warfare in Fielding's time made such an appeal irrelevant. Responsible citizens were seldom asked to go out and fight for their liberty in eighteenth-century London. Nevertheless, the English translation of 1702 had rendered the pronominal emphasis much more clearly.

To what is perhaps the fundamental emphasis in the *First Olynthiac*—the almost mesmeric reiteration of καιρός, opportunity—Fielding does ample justice. Werner Jaeger has commented brilliantly upon this motif of the opportune moment, the moment of destiny, that Demosthenes poses to the Athenians:

"This is what gives rise to Demosthenes' almost surprisingly extensive observations on the gods and the part they play in the present situation. . . . We have already encountered this religious motif in the *First Philippic*; but now it is developed at greater length and is peculiarly interwoven with the idea of the *Kairos,*—the favorable opportunity,—which plays such a large rôle in the politics of the time. In general, the *Kairos* meant to the Greeks nothing else than our present-day concept of opportunity. . . . But on deeper consideration, opportunity was seen to be an especially visible form of providential dispensation—

the *Tyche*; and just as *Tyche* was the greatest power in the contemporary religious thought and came at last, in the Hellenistic period, to push all the Olympian deities from their thrones, in the same way the *Kairos* was also made a god and represented as such by the artists. For Demosthenes 'the gods' and '*Tyche*' are almost synonymous. The *Kairos* too is a religious reality. It is preeminently an expression of the sway of a higher power. . . . Even if the Greeks had no philosophy of history in our sense, perhaps we may say that this very idea of *Tyche* took its place in the pre-Christian world. For Demosthenes, at any rate, it is an important factor in political willing and doing, and it deserves our full attention. Thus, for example, closer examination shows us that the entire *First Olynthiac* is built up on the motif of *Kairos*. The first part of the speech develops this idea at length, and uses the opportunity offered by *Tyche* herself as an occasion for sharply criticizing the inactivity and remissness of the Athenians. Demosthenes' practical proposals are then dispatched very briefly. . . . In the third part, which, like the first, is worked out in much greater detail, comes the contrasting section of the *akairia*—the unfavorableness —of the moment for Philip. . . ."[31]

Now obviously Fielding did not see all this in Demosthenes' use of *kairos*; but he was highly conscious of its ceaseless iteration and its importance, and this he sought to convey by repeating the word "Opportunity" even more frequently than Demosthenes had actually used *kairos*. Thus: "For we may be assured of this, that had *Philip* the same Opportunity [καιρὸν] and the War was near our Borders, he would be abundantly ready to invade us. Are you not then ashamed through Fear to omit bringing that on him, when you have an Opportunity [καιρὸν], which he, had he that Opportunity, would surely bring on you?" (I, 292; *1st Ol.*, 24). The last antithesis in the Greek did

[31] Jaeger, pp. 130-33.

not involve a further repetition of *kairos*; but Fielding, in the full spirit of the total oration, himself supplied it. Perhaps he felt the inadequacy of "Opportunity" in rendering the overtones of the Greek word, and hoped by a more frequent repetition of it to convey at least something of the sense of emphasis and urgency that Demosthenes imparted to *kairos*. With *tyche* less could be done. If he had rendered it as "Providence," he might have caught more of the overtones of the original; but the word was normally given as "Fortune" and Fielding so translated it throughout. He did, however, double it pleonastically (with no warrant from the text) at its first appearance ("I consider it as peculiar to your Fortune and good Genius"—I, 282; *1st Ol.*, 1), which may indicate that he felt the need to extend its implications.

5

Reference to the pleonastic pair, which we have earlier pointed out as a typical feature of Fielding's elevated style, may lead us into a comment upon the style he displays in this translation. Unhappily for any hope of identifying his part in other unassigned translations through distinctive marks of his style, it must be said that had not Fielding himself included this work in the *Miscellanies*, no one would have been likely to assign it to him (despite the occasional "hath-doth" constructions). The pleonastic pair mentioned is one of the very few in the whole translation; and of the rest, most are indeed suggested by the original. The same may be said of the normally dense parenthetical elements and the extension of final members that we have also noted as distinctive marks of Fielding's style. The prevailing hypotaxis in sentence structure is in Fielding's normal mode; but there is little or nothing in particular constructions to identify the sentences as his. Even when the opportunity arises, for instance, to employ his favorite correlative construction, "as . . . so . . . ," he does not use it. Consider the previously quoted sentence on borrowing money; it could, with perfect fidelity to the text, have been rendered: "I fear, Athenians, that *as* men who borrow Money thoughtlessly &c. . . . *so* we may find . . ."; but Fielding did not phrase it this way. It is true that in the earlier illustration, "But it happens *as* in the Affair of Riches . . . *So* in public Affairs . . ." (I, 286), we have something approaching Fielding's construction; but the subordinate location of "as" is atypical—and this is the only such example in the entire piece. Neither does the "though . . . yet . . ." construction appear, nor any of Fielding's favorite locutions such as "to say truth." Indeed, almost the only points at which the oration has any ring of Henry Fielding are those in which he is most closely indebted to the Latin (which might in itself provide food for thought!), for example, the aforementioned reference to "the Benevolence of the Gods" (I, 286; *1st Ol.*, 10-11) or his little dialogues rendering Demosthenes' use of *hypophora* (the technique of anticipating and answering an objection): "What? says some one, Do you move to have this Fund applied to the Army? Not I truly; I only suggest that an Army should be levied . . ." (I, 290; *1st Ol.*, 19-20); or again: "But should any Man say, Why therefore do you commemorate these Things to us now? my Answer is, That you may know, O *Athenians*, and sensibly perceive these two Things . . ." (I, 287; *1st Ol.*, 14). The latter formula (usually phrased, "To which I answer . . .") appears quite frequently in Fielding's essays—as I have previously suggested, he may have picked it up from Dr. South. Then there are a few typical words or phrases, such as Fielding's "to generous Minds" (I, 293) for the σώφροσιν (sound mind, prudent, discreet) of the original (*1st Ol.*, 27); but for the most part these are locutions that any writer might have used. So also with a sentence like this: "As to the Difference, whether the War be here or there, there is, I think no need of Argument: for if it was necessary for you to be

TRANSLATION

thirty Days in the Field within your own Territories, and to sustain your Army with your own Product, supposing no Enemy there at the same Time; I say, the Losses of your Husbandmen, who supply those Provisions, would be greater than the whole Expence of the preceding War" (I, 293; *1st Ol.*, 27). It is not a good sentence, but it sounds like Fielding. I should not, however, wish to assign an unclaimed essay to him on the grounds that it had a like sentence in it!

Otherwise, nothing. The translation might just as well be anonymous. And it is in this fact that my reservation, mentioned earlier, concerning Cross' assignment of this work to the late-1730's arises. For Fielding, one would think, could surely by that date have placed his personal stamp upon this translation without difficulty. Literal translation, or "metaphrase" as Dryden called it,[32] was not the usual aim of the age; to convey the *sense* in a vigorous manner was the important thing. As Fielding himself said in the preface to his and Young's version of Aristophanes' *Plutus*: "If the Original conveys clear and adequate Ideas to me, I must be capable of delivering them to others in that Language which I am myself a perfect Master of."[33] The *First Olynthiac*, however, represents "metaphrase": it is the almost literal rendering, one feels, of a student, not the mature translation of a man in his full powers. The mechanically correct rendering of the vocative "O Athenians" [ὦ ἄνδρες Ἀθηναῖοι], which could have been phrased in half a dozen different ways, smacks of the schoolboy: "But consider, O Athenians, and see ..."; "To me, O Athenians, it appears ..."; "It is our Parts then, O Athenians, to take Advantage ..." and so on. This shows small imagination (though it must be admitted that Wil-

[32] *Essays of John Dryden*, ed. W. P. Ker (2v., Oxford, 1900), I, 237, and II, 227.
[33] *Plutus, the God of Riches. A Comedy. Translated from the Original Greek of Aristophanes* (1742), p. viii.

361

son's rather lively translation in 1570 had done the same thing). Or consider the literalness, again, of such a sentence as this: "As to the rest, I think, all should contribute, largely if much wanted, less if little" (1, 290; *1st Ol.*, 20)—here we have simply a direct and unidiomatic transcription of the Greek (and, in this case, the Latin "si multis opus erit, multum: sin paucis, parum") ἂν πολλῶν δέῃ, πολλά· ἂν ὀλίγων, ὀλίγα (A_2^v). One could go on to cite numerous infelicities of phrasing, from "the Posture of these Affairs requires your immediate Application" (1, 282) to the redundancy of the conclusion, "May this *Success* be *happy*, for the Sake of every one" (1, 294; my italics); but I have perhaps spent in this essay sufficient time belaboring the obvious.

There are, nevertheless, enough good sentences and forceful expressions in the translation to make for a final inference that Fielding at some time subsequent to the original composition reworked the whole. Unless one is to suppose that he revised with greater skill and knowledge an earlier academic exercise, the curious mingling of competence and naiveté in his reproduction of the Greek text seems almost inexplicable. Perhaps the best solution is to imagine that he did just this, revising for its application to the events of the Spanish crisis a translation that he had made some years earlier in the course of his Greek studies. There is no certain evidence, however, and so far as I know Fielding did not publish the text until it appeared in the hodge-podge of the *Miscellanies*.

6

Demosthenes was often taken in the eighteenth century as the very type of the ardent patriot. Steele's essay on Love of Country in the *Tatler* (No. 183) employed Demosthenes as its chief exemplar; and the *Craftsman*, justifying its early attacks on Walpole, declared in 1730:

TRANSLATION

"A Person, who makes it his Business to excite the People to their Duty, or even to inflame and blow up their Passions against *bad Measures* and *wicked Ministers*, may be called an *Incendiary*; but whatever He is called, He is a valuable Member of the Commonwealth. . . . The two great Orators of *Greece* and *Rome*, who endeavour'd to stir up the Resentments of the People against *Philip* and *Mark Anthony*, were *Incendiaries* of this Sort; and though They both perished in the Attempt, under the Weight of Power; yet their Names and their Works are transmitted with Honour to the latest Posterity."[34]

It was natural that the elder Pitt, at this time a "Boy Patriot" in the Opposition, should be often associated with Demosthenes (Fielding himself made the association in *Tom Jones*, XIV, i), and we are told that it was in part upon the works of the great Greek orator that Pitt modeled his own forensic style.[35]

Fielding himself, however, seems to have admired Demosthenes considerably less than he did his honored Cicero. He cited the Greek orator only occasionally (for example, in the *Charge to the Grand Jury* of 1749, where he repeated "a most beautiful passage in the great orator Demosthenes" against "libels"—Henley, XIII, 216); and he seemed to take a deeper pleasure in relating stories that showed Demosthenes in a very bad light. For example, the ancient account of Demosthenes surrendering to a bribe was quoted in the notes to *Plutus* and called "a true and pleasant [story]";[36] and it was also quoted in the notes to Fielding's mock-pedantic *Vernoniad* of 1741 (Henley, XV, 50-51). Probably this was done in both cases with an eye upon Walpole

---

[34] The *Craftsman*, No. 221, 26 September 1730 (coll. ed. [14v., 1731-1737], VII, 40-41).

[35] See Basil Williams, *The Life of William Pitt, Earl of Chatham* (2v., 1913), I, 213; and cf. I, 66, 70, and 199.

[36] *Plutus*, p. 38n. The story is found in Plutarch's *Life of Demosthenes*, XXV (Loeb Library, VII, 60-63), and another version is related by Aulus Gellius, *Noctes Atticae*, XI. ix (Loeb Library, II, 318-21).

(supreme master of the bribe); and it is difficult to tell how seriously the tale entered into Fielding's actual estimate of Demosthenes. An earlier paper in the *Champion* (28 February 1740; a letter from "NICODEMUS BUNGLE," probably by Fielding), described an ancient "*antipudorific Lotion*" which washed away any sense of shame, and pictured Demosthenes seeking out the seller—since oratory is "a Profession which stands in great Need of this Wash." And further on, reference was made in curiously contemptuous tones to "so pretty a Gentleman as *Demosthenes*, who we are told was the greatest Beau, as well as the greatest Orator of his Age."[37] The contemporary associations that must lie behind this allusion escape me, and I find it difficult to reconcile the attitude displayed in these references of the early 1740's with the apparent identification of Demosthenes and the Opposition cause in the 1730's. I suppose one must add these mysteries to the others connected with that mysterious little exercise in translation, the *First Olynthiac* of Demosthenes, rendered by Henry Fielding almost without any mark of Henry Fielding to be found in it. If it is the least distinguished piece in the *Miscellanies* it has the dubious virtue, at any rate, of being one of the most puzzling.

[37] *The Champion*, coll. ed. (2v., 1741), I, 318.

CHAPTER VI. LUCIANIC SKETCHES

In a Word, I conclude, that all who have a true Taste of Humour must read Lucian with the most exquisite Pleasure, and those who have not, will find no other Means so proper to acquire that taste.—*Covent-Garden Journal*, 52

LUCIAN of Samosata, the second-century Syrian rhetorician who became the greatest of the Greek satirists after Aristophanes, enters English literary history in the sixteenth century. After being translated into Latin by Erasmus and Sir Thomas More, his works gradually "filtered through into the vernacular"; and numerous English translations and imitations in the seventeenth century attest his popularity in that period.[1] The cooperative translation (1710-1711) that included Dryden's life of Lucian —a translation that Fielding later criticized severely—provided the eighteenth-century reading public with very nearly the whole known corpus in a convenient and racy (if not correct) version.[2] The influence of Lucian upon Prior, Dryden, Swift, Lyttelton, and many minor authors of the time has been often noted.[3] The great debt that

[1] See Craig R. Thompson, *The Translations of Lucian by Erasmus and St. Thomas More* (Ithaca, N.Y., 1940) and Francis G. Allinson, *Lucian, Satirist and Artist* (Boston, 1926).

[2] See Hardin Craig, "Dryden's Lucian," *Classical Philology*, xvi (1921), 141-63, and F. M. K. Foster, *English Translations from the Greek* (N.Y., 1918), pp. 80-81. Booth speaks for Fielding in *Amelia* when he tells the hack-writer in the sponging house: "A good translation of him [Lucian] would be a valuable book. I have seen a wretched one published by Mr. Dryden, but translated by others, who in many places have misunderstood Lucian's meaning, and have nowhere preserved the spirit of the original" (VIII, v; Henley, VII, 85). It should be remembered, of course, that Fielding was at this very time projecting a translation of Lucian with William Young—and he was very well aware of the value of advertising!

[3] See Allinson, pp. 163-75, and various individual studies on the writers concerned. Aside from Swift and Fielding, Lucian's influence in England can perhaps best be studied in such minor writers as Charles Cotton and Tom Brown. Benjamin Boyce has copiously documented the influence

Henry Fielding owed to Lucian has also been frequently remarked but seldom analyzed. I shall accordingly devote the whole of this essay to the question.

Fielding paid tribute to Lucian many times: in *Tom Jones*, for instance, where he invoked the genius of the great comic writers of past ages (XIII, i; Henley, v, 33); in *Amelia*, where he pronounced Lucian "the greatest in the humorous way that ever the world produced" (VIII, v; Henley, VII, 84); and in the *Covent-Garden Journal*, where, speaking of his own proposal to translate Lucian (with William Young), he presented an eloquent panegyric upon "the Father of true Humour," and closed by acknowledging that he had formed his own style upon that of Lucian (No. 52; Jensen, II, 47-50). However true this may be in particular detail (and I think it is only partly true), his mind had surely become strongly impregnated with the Lucianic ether.

A specific indebtedness in forms, first of all, is not difficult to point out:[4] there are the "dialogues of the dead"

---

of a particular Lucianic genre (to which Fielding's *Journey from This World to the Next* belongs) in his "News from Hell: Satiric Communications with the Nether World in English Writing of the Seventeenth and Eighteenth Centuries," *PMLA*, LVIII (1943), 402-37. Fielding himself considered Swift the English Lucian and, indeed, in the panegyric he wrote upon Swift at the latter's death, ranked him above the Syrian satirist (*True Patriot*, No. 1, 5 November 1745). Though he later came to feel that even Swift could only follow Lucian "at a distance" (*Amelia*, VIII, v; Henley VII, 84), he nevertheless declared, "To say Truth, I can find no better Way of giving the English Reader an Idea of the Greek Author, than by telling him, that to translate Lucian well into English, is to give us another Swift in our own Language" (*CGJ*, No. 52; Jensen, II, 48). Dissenting opinions on the greatness of Lucian were frequent, particularly among the English clergy, who could not bear his gibes at the early Christians. As Edward Young phrased it, "Some Satyrical Wits, and Humorists, like their Father *Lucian*, laugh at every thing indiscriminately; which betrays such a poverty of wit, as cannot afford to part with any thing; and such a want of virtue, as to postpone it to a jest" (Preface to *Love of Fame* [2nd ed., 1728], sig. a verso).

[4] Levi R. Lind's note, "Lucian and Fielding," *Classical Weekly*, XXIX (1936), 84-86, cites brief parallels with Fielding's *Journey* and the two works under consideration here. H. K. Banerji has argued that in the auction scene of the *Historical Register*, Fielding may have had Lucian's

included in *The Author's Farce, Eurydice,* and the *Journey from This World to the Next;* the Lucianic vision in the *Champion* of 24 May 1740 (inspired by the tenth of the *Dialogi mortuorum*); the "dialogues of the gods," followed in the *Interlude between Jupiter, Juno, Apollo, and Mercury;* the *Dialogue between Alexander the Great and Diogenes the Cynic,* and indeed most of the set dialogues found in the journals—and some in the novels—which are Lucianic in form and tone.[5] Mrs. Heartfree's fantastic voyages in the original edition of *Jonathan Wild* and the voyage of Job Vinegar in the *Champion* find their ultimate exemplar in Lucian's *Vera historia.*

2

More difficult to assess, however, are correspondences in subject matter and attitude. Perhaps it is the better part of wisdom here to say only that Fielding and Lucian shared to the full many of the same antipathies and upheld many of the same ideals. No precise influence can be argued, but Fielding would have found in Lucian a relentless hammering at the same follies and vices that he himself was most concerned to attack: hypocrisy and malice, envy and slander (Lucian devotes a whole essay to the subject *Calumniae non temere credendum*), vanity and greed. As Lucian persistently exposes the various pretenders to philosophy or the art of rhetoric, and ridicules the ascetic and the fanatic, so Fielding rips the mask from narrow

---

Vitarum auctio in mind (*Henry Fielding: Playwright, Journalist, and Master of the Art of Fiction* [Oxford, 1929], p. 147).

[5] See for example, the *Covent-Garden Journal,* Nos. 30 and 54. Fielding calls the former a dialogue "After the Manner of PLATO"; but this is surely in jest. *Jonathan Wild* explicitly labels some of its scenes as pure dialogues: "A *Dialogue matrimonial, which passed between* JONATHAN WILD, *Esquire, and* LÆTITIA *his Wife*" (*Misc.,* III, 235), and "A *Dialogue between the* Ordinary of Newgate *and Mr.* Jonathan Wild the Great" (*Misc.,* III, 386). The set discourse between the Player and the Poet in *Joseph Andrews* (III, x), is also in the tradition of the dialogue, as are many less formal debates such as those in which Thwackum and Square become involved.

or "enthusiastic" piety and philosophy and displays in all its naked absurdity the affectation and hypocrisy of the perverse human animal. Both, however, were concerned to protest that they honored the *true* practitioner, in whatever profession, and that their satire was constructive in that it aimed to uphold and preserve the authentic ideals that the pretenders ignored—and, indeed, corrupted. Fielding could have stood with Lucian (as Parrhesiades or "Plain Speaker") before the bar of philosophy and truth, and declared: "I am a bluff-hater, cheat-hater, liar-hater, vanity-hater, and hate all that sort of scoundrels. . . . I am a truth-lover, a beauty-lover, a simplicity-lover, and a lover of all else that is kindred to love. . . . I am so constituted as to hate rascals and to commend and love honest men."[6]

Fielding did not share Lucian's thoroughgoing skepticism; and his love of the good showed itself more clearly and more often than did that of the Syrian—for whom praise was as likely to be a rhetorical exercise as an admiration for the worthy. Again, Lucian's merciless, savagely intellectual, and diamond-brilliant irony is more clearly reproduced in Swift than in Fielding. The broad compassion and generosity of spirit that counterbalance Fielding's hatred of evil (as well as his sense of the ridiculous) are not often felt in Lucian: the latter's keen perception of the gulf between human ideals and human practice is seldom complicated by any sympathy for the fallible mortal creature. Nevertheless, Fielding could find very much of himself in Lucian. Both were primarily interested in the common-sense ethical and moral aspects

[6] *Piscator* 20; *Lucian*, transl. A. M. Harmon (5v. to date, Loeb Library, 1913-36), III, 31-33. I have throughout used the Latin titles of Lucian's works, since anarchy prevails in the English titles. The translation of Lucian by H. W. and F. G. Fowler (4v., Oxford, 1905) is perhaps more engaging than Harmon's, but I have used it only for works not yet translated in the Loeb edition, since it has the defect for my purposes of obscuring Lucian's own tricks of style and phrase with well-known tags from English literature and whimsical inventions of the Fowlers themselves; and it is unforgivably bowdlerized.

of philosophy rather than in fine points of speculation or dogma. Both were keen observers of human nature and loved the revelatory detail that gave a key to character. Fielding's strong infusion of the milk of human kindness aside, both displayed the detachment that comes from a thorough schooling in rhetoric, the ability to argue (if not always to feel) both sides of a question and the maturity to see the possibilities of humor in even their own fondest convictions. And to both, the psychology of the abnormal —the freak, the fanatic, the ascetic, the mystic—was a closed book, or, better, a book that they had small concern to open. Lucian's mockery and detestation, for example, of the fanatic Peregrinus is matched by Fielding's uncompromising rejection from human society of the miser and the religious hypocrite and enthusiast. Lucian and Fielding were celebrants of the normal and the human and (to use an unfashionable word) the manly.

Both also shared (with almost every great comic writer who has ever lived) a masculine predilection for earthy and honest bawdry. Fielding disliked intensely the sniggering kind of play with sexuality that was later to become fashionable in the decent Victorian era and that too often continues to accompany moral immaturity in the modern English-speaking world; but he delighted, like all satirists, in jolting man's pride by reminding him of his inescapable biological tie to the animals. Moreover, his conception of "decency" was not that of an effeminate society, but that of a man. The same is largely true of Lucian. Even Lucian's preoccupation with the characteristic perversion of his age, as of Juvenal's—namely, the love of boys—belongs to the mores of a different world and need neither shock nor frighten us; but most of his open bawdry may be said to include that dimension of human conduct without which no satire can be said truly to have considered man-as-he-is. To emasculate his writings, as virtually all modern translations have done, in the name of "decency" is a crime not only against literature but against any true morality. As that wise old connoisseur of sin, and official in his Satanic Majesty's Lowerarchy, Screwtape, patiently explained to his nephew, the junior devil Wormwood, there is a distinction to be made in trying to seize the souls of those who talk "indecently": for one class of men "joke about sex because it gives rise to many incongruities; the second cultivate incongruities because they afford a pretext for talking about sex."[7] Fielding and Lucian assuredly belong to the first group; and to mistake their work for pornography is to be guilty of a viler—and more ludicrous—perversion of the moral spirit than anything to be found in the pages of the world's great comic artists.

3

The extent of Fielding's absorption in Lucian's writings is suggested by the fact that he had in his library no fewer than nine different editions of his works—in Greek, Latin, French, and English.[8] The copying of particular forms that I have commented on is further evidence. But the best evidence of all is very difficult to analyze: it lies in the pervasive Lucianic *tone* that one finds in all of Fielding's work, the characteristic mingling of irony and seriousness and high spirits. This is true as well, it may be said, of Aristophanes, Rabelais, Cervantes, Butler, and Swift, among Fielding's other favorite comic artists. I am not concerned to deny this: there is no certain way of separating their influence upon Fielding from that of Lucian. Thus, although I shall be dealing here only with the latter, it must be understood that at no point am I claiming for him Field-

[7] C. S. Lewis, *The Screwtape Letters* (1942), pp. 58-59.
[8] See the reprinting of the sale-catalogue of his library in Ethel M. Thornbury, *Henry Fielding's Theory of the Comic Prose Epic* (Madison, Wisc., 1931), and comments, pp. 10-11. Fielding may well have accumulated some of these extra editions for use in the projected translation with Young.

ing's sole inspiration. Lucian remains, however, after Aristophanes, the great *fons et origo* of western irony; all the later satirists I have mentioned drew upon him, and Fielding consistently gave him the place of honor in his own pantheon of humor. An analysis, therefore, of stylistic approaches and devices that the two men had in common, devices that reflect a like cast of mind, seems not altogether futile, though I would repeat that I do not argue specific indebtedness in any of the likenesses that follow. The ultimate relationship in style between these two masters of the comic mode is, as Maurice Croiset has said of Lucian's "esprit" itself, "fort aisé à sentir et à goûter, mais bien difficile à définir."[9]

Both men were able to call upon a wide variety of particular styles for particular occasions; but through all the changes the very individual voice of each can be plainly heard and recognized. Each had his favorite genres: Lucian's, of course, was dialogue and Fielding's the sustained narrative that Lucian, preferring a series of piquant episodes or details, never seriously sought to master. But they share a common pleasure in the concrete and the pictorial. Aside from their masterful *enargeia* or skill in bringing a picture to the mind's eye, both are very fond of citing pictorial analogies to reinforce their own portraits of character or scene. Fielding constantly calls upon Hogarth, as Lucian does upon Zeuxis or Apelles. The cynic Alcidamas, in Lucian's *Convivium*, insists upon taking up a position on the floor, "with his elbow squared under him and the bowl in his right hand, just as Heracles in the cave of Pholus is represented by the painters" (*Convivium* or *Symposium* 14; Loeb, I, 427). They are both realists to the core, but theirs is a comic realism and it inevitably has something of the exaggerated in it, of "fantaisie," as Croiset says. We

---

[9] Maurice Croiset, *Essai sur la vie et les œuvres de Lucien* (Paris, 1882), p. 297. It scarcely needs to be said that, like all modern students of Lucian, I am greatly in debt to M. Croiset.

371

LUCIANIC SKETCHES

are in another world, and yet one to which we feel the tie:[10] everything is drawn greater than life and yet nothing is false to human experience. The characters of Lucian's dialogues or of Fielding's novels are individualized and unique beings; but they are also so true to the essential and typical in human nature that we can still recognize them after two hundred years or after almost two thousand years.

Both authors delighted in allowing their fools and villains to expose themselves, through conduct or dialogue —or even in a letter, as Fielding does with Thwackum ("I am sorry you have given away the living of Westerton so hastily. I should have applied on that occasion earlier, had I thought you would not have acquainted me previous to the disposition. Your objection to pluralities is being righteous over-much. If there were any crime in the practice, so many godly men would not agree to it"—*TJ*, xviii, iv; Henley, v, 309), and as Lucian does with Hetoemocles the greedy philosopher, who has not been invited to Aristaenetus' banquet ("How I feel about dining out, my whole past life can testify; for although every day I am pestered by many men much richer than you are, nevertheless I am never forward about accepting, as I am familiar with the disturbances and riotous doings at dinner-parties. But in your case and yours only I think I have reason to be angry, because you, to whom I have so long ministered indefatigably, did not think fit to number me among your friends . . ."—*Convivium* 22; Loeb, I, 435-37). Finally, in terms of basic approaches, both Fielding and Lucian consistently employed the diversiform techniques of irony and rhetoric to shape and control their portraits, dialogues, and narratives. Lucian had been a rhetorician by trade; Fielding became one through the sheer love of it. And like all masters of the art, they delighted in em-

[10] Herman Melville's phrase: cf. *The Confidence Man*, chap. xxxiii (Chiltern Library, 1948), p. 219.

broidering a theme with the plausible facts and actions that gave it color and verisimilitude.

To choose from a number of more specific resemblances in technique, we may perhaps begin with the controls that they used to maintain an ironic tie between the worlds of historic truth and of fantasy. Such imaginative masterpieces as Lucian's *Vera historia* or his *Cataplus* (a voyage to Hades) abound in tricks and devices that Fielding likewise enjoyed using: for example, the straight-faced and solemn detail that lends comic credence to a fantastic narrative—as when Lucian describes the fish in the river of wine: "On catching and eating some of them, we became drunk, and when we cut into them we found them full of lees, of course" (*Vera historia* I. 7; Loeb, I, 257); or as when Menippus, having constructed a flying apparatus from the wing of an eagle and of a vulture, nears Heaven: "But when I had left the clouds far below and had got close to the moon, I felt myself getting tired, especially in the left wing, the vulture's" (*Icaromenippus* 11; Loeb, II, 285-87). In the same spirit, when Fielding's traveller, in the *Journey from This World to the Next*, boards a coach made of "immaterial Substance" for his voyage (a coach which normally held only six), he says: "We immediately began our Journey, being seven in Number; for as the Women wore no Hoops, three of them were but equal to two Men" (*Misc.*, II, 11). Allied to this device is the meticulous and scholarly caution with which very dubious materials—or bald lies—are presented, the reader being assured that his author offers no more than what he can be certain of as fact: "It was said [in the battle between the forces of the Sun and the Moon], too, that the stars over Cappadocia would send seventy thousand Sparrowcorns and five thousand Crane Dragoons. I did not get a look at them, as they did not come, so I have not ventured to write about their characteristics . . ." (*Vera historia* I. 13; Loeb, I, 265). So Fielding: "Reader, I am not superstitious, nor any great believer of modern miracles. I do not, therefore, deliver the following as a certain truth, for, indeed, I can scarce credit it myself: but the fidelity of an historian obliges me to relate what hath been confidently asserted. The horse, then, on which the guide rode, is reported to have been so charmed by Sophia's voice that he made a full stop, and expressed an unwillingness to proceed any farther" (*TJ*, x, ix; Henley, IV, 235).

Both Fielding and Lucian were enormously well read; and carrying this load of erudition with lightness, naturalness, and ease, they delighted in employing a pedantry or jargon of their own to mock that of others—as Lucian did in *Lexiphanes* and *Pseudosophista* and in the *Vera historia*, where he satirized the very form that he himself was using; and as Fielding did in the parody of academic or professional jargon throughout his novels, and in the scholarly footnotes of *The Tragedy of Tragedies* and the *Vernoniad*. This fondness for pedantic scoffing at pedantry appears also in the mock-etymologies and such tricks, which both were pleased to indulge in.[11] Both of them also drew up ironic "handbooks" of instruction for those who would succeed in the world-as-it-is, recommending in place of any solid accomplishment the mastery of a jargon and the cultivation of skillful hypocrisy and brazen effrontery.[12]

[11] In the *Vera historia*, for instance, Homer tells Lucian in the Isles of the Blest that he was in life actually a Babylonian named Tigranes, but "later on, when I was a hostage (*homeros*) among the Greeks, I changed my name" (II, 20; Loeb, I, 323). From numerous examples in Fielding, one may choose the ironic derivation in *Jonathan Wild* (IV, xvi; *Misc.*, III, 409) of *honesty*, "which is a Corruption of *Honosty*, a Word derived from what the *Greeks* call an *Ass*," i.e. ὄνος. Lucian also liked to pun on the Greek word for ass: cf. the *Dialogi meretricii* XIV: "It is a treat to hear him when he sings and tries to make himself agreeable; what is it they tell me about an ass [ὄνος] that would learn the lyre? Well, I wish you joy [ὄναιο] of him; you deserve no better luck; and may the child be like his father!" (*Works of Lucian of Samosata*, transl. H. W. and F. G. Fowler, IV, 77).

[12] See, for example, Lucian's *Rhetorum praeceptor*, a *vade-mecum* for success in the profession of rhetoric, and Fielding's essay in the *Champion* (29 January 1740; Henley, xv, 172-77), containing "some instructions

Again, Lucian and Fielding enjoyed the pose of mock ignorance or naiveté in their narrators. Menippus, plagued by doubts and questions, explains: "Being in that state of mind, I thought it best to learn about all these points from the philosophers, for I supposed that they surely would be able to tell the whole truth. So I picked out the best of them, so far as I could judge from their dourness of visage, paleness of complexion, and length of beard . . ." (*Icaromenippus* 5; Loeb, II, 275-77). Fielding also, as narrator, is forever taking things at their face value—as when he informs us that eight months after the marriage of Captain Blifil and Miss Allworthy, the latter was "by reason of a fright, delivered of a fine boy. The child was indeed to all appearances perfect; but the midwife discovered it was born a month before its full time" (*TJ*, II, ii; Henley, III, 66). This naive mask for a highly sophisticated mind also appears, of course, in the paradoxical encomium, where Lucian "proves" the superior virtues of a fly or parasite, as Fielding does of Nothing—or appears again, in his "proof" that the doctors called to attend Captain Blifil and his lady demonstrate the fact that "physicians are misrepresented as friends to death"; for when they find the former dead and the latter living, "So little then did our doctors delight in death, that they discharged the corpse after a single fee; but they were not so disgusted with their living patient; concerning whose case they immediately agreed, and fell to prescribing with great diligence" (*TJ*, II, ix; Henley, III, 103).

Fielding and Lucian are both inveterate quoters, and their citations are often used in a trifling or humorous way. They both like to pretend also that they are not quite sure of the exact source of their allusion (perhaps, indeed, they sometimes were not!). Again, anecdotes and exempla

---

whereby a man may arrive at that pitch of grandeur and honour in the world, which [Captain Vinegar] so falsely suggested to be attainable in the roads of virtue." *Jonathan Wild* is, in parts, an elaborate handbook on the Art of Thriving.

and similitudes are scattered through their works.[13] If Lucian can tell a fable about the King of Egypt's trained apes (who formed a very competent masked ballet until a spectator tossed some nuts on the floor and brought chaos) (*Piscator* 36; Loeb, III, 55), Fielding can make the same point—that "if we shut Nature out at the door, she will come in at the window,"—with a like account: "Thus fable reports that the fair Grimalkin, whom Venus, at the desire of a passionate lover, converted from a cat into a fine woman, no sooner perceived a mouse than, mindful of her former sport, and still retaining her pristine nature, she leaped from the bed of her husband to pursue the little animal" (*TJ*, XII, ii; Henley, IV, 305). Lucian can say of the pretender to philosophy, Peregrine, when he employs a salve to sharpen his vision before death (because Aeacus will not receive those with weak eyes), "It is as if a man about to go up to the cross should nurse the bruise on his finger" (*Peregrinus* 45; Loeb, v, 51); and Fielding can gain the like illumination from a homely comparison, declaring that to dissuade a young girl from a match with someone for whom she has a violent inclination is "an endeavor of the same kind as it would be very heartily and earnestly to entreat a moth not to fly into a candle" (*TJ*, XIII, iii; Henley, v, 41). And both can make equally good use of the inverted parallel: Lucian's Tychiades describes an amorous lady who is very fond of money—"The woman is very susceptible to that spell, and her case is the opposite to that of ghosts; if they hear a chink of bronze or iron, they take

---

[13] Lucian's *Demonax*, a collection of anecdotes about that philosopher, offers the following pleasant story, which perhaps bears repetition: "When the Sidonian sophist was once showing his powers at Athens, and was voicing his own praise to the effect that he was acquainted with all philosophy—but I may as well cite his very words: 'If Aristotle calls me to the Lyceum, I shall go with him; if Plato calls me to the Academy, I shall come; if Zeno calls, I shall spend my time in the Stoa; if Pythagoras calls, I shall hold my tongue.' Well, Demonax arose in the midst of the audience and said: 'Ho!' (addressing him by name), 'Pythagoras is calling you!'" (*Demonax* 14; Loeb, I, 153).

flight, so you say, but as for her, if silver chinks anywhere she goes toward the sound" (*Philopseudes* 15; Loeb, III, 343). So Fielding describes Jonathan Wild, as the day of his trial approaches: "for which, as *Socrates* did, he prepared himself; but not weakly and foolishly, like that Philosopher, with Patience and Resignation; but with a good Number of false Witnesses" (IV, xiii; *Misc.*, III, 382).

I trust it remains clear in my reader's memory that these citations are not set forth as "sources" or "influences"; nor have I sought to make the likenesses exact, for I am illustrating similar techniques, not parallel passages. Most of the "exact" parallels between Fielding and Lucian draw from a thematic stock that all satirists have treated: the shifts of the hypocrite, the pretension of the *soi-disant* sage, or the accursed thirst for gold that makes (nearly) the whole world kin. The power of gold, incidentally, will serve as the theme of another technique that Fielding and Lucian employ, which we may call the irony of "imputative merit." Lucian has Micyllus in *Somnium* (*Gallus*) demand, "Then what is the use of my telling you the rest of it—how many uses gold has, and how, when people have it, it renders them handsome and wise and strong, lending them honour and esteem, and not infrequently it makes inconspicuous and contemptible people admired and renowned in a short time?" And he describes a newly-rich friend, once a mere dirty fellow: "The women are actually in love with him now, and he flirts with them and slights them, and when he receives some and is gracious to them the others threaten to hang themselves on account of his neglect. You see, don't you, what blessings gold is able to bestow, when it transforms ugly people and renders them lovely, like the girdle [of Aphrodite] in poetry?" (*Somnium* [*Gallus*] 14; Loeb, II, 199, 201). Among many other like passages (including that at the conclusion of his account of the Chrysipus), Fielding has this, spoken by Apollo, in the *Interlude between Jupiter, Juno, Apollo, and Mercury*: "the God of Riches has more Interest there [on earth], than all the other Gods put together: Nay, he has supplanted us in all our Provinces; he gives Wit to Men I never heard of, and Beauty to Women *Venus* never saw —Nay, he ventures to make free with *Mars* himself; and sometimes, they tell me, puts Men at the Head of Military Affairs, who never saw an Enemy, nor of whom an Enemy ever could see any other than the Back" (*Misc.*, I, 348).

4

But enough, perhaps, of devices. This small sampling may serve to suggest that Fielding and Lucian made use of many of the same techniques in their ironic rendering of the human comedy. Let us now turn to a relationship even more difficult to define (and one that cannot truly be separated from "devices"): namely, style. When Fielding asserted that he had formed his own style upon that of Lucian, he was surely overlooking Addison, Tillotson, Swift, South, Cervantes, and a host of other influences. What did he think of as peculiarly Lucianic in his own style?[14] Part of the answer, if we may judge from the qualities the two writers most conspicuously share, would seem to be a particular sort of balance, a habit of parenthesis and afterthought, a pervasive litotes, and a self-conscious attention to levels of style.

The balancing of sentence elements that Fielding could find in Lucian is not that which we have analyzed in dis-

---

[14] The qualities that Fielding particularly praised in Lucian's style were his "Attic Elegance of Diction . . . the exquisite Pleasantry of his Humour . . . the Neatness of his Wit, and . . . the Poignancy of his Satire" (*CGJ*, No. 52; Jensen, II, 47). The question naturally arises: did Fielding draw his conception of Lucian's style directly from the Greek or indirectly through the accompanying Latin translation in most texts? I find it impossible to answer this, since Fielding gave us no direct translations of Lucian that might offer clues (on the order of those in his translation of Demosthenes considered above). In discussing likenesses of style, therefore, I have confined my attention to the stylistic traits in Lucian that would appear equally in the Latin or the Greek (or the English) version.

cussing the Tillotson-Addison *copia*. To be sure, Lucian is notorious for pleonasm; but his is not the use of superfluous words to achieve a rhythmic rise and fall—it is, rather, an exuberant and quite un-Ciceronian pouring out of words and phrases to expand upon and dramatize an idea. Zeus frets over his infinite labors, for example: "For if I drowse off, even for an instant, Epicurus is instantly confirmed in his assertion that we exercise no providence over what happens on earth. And we cannot make light of the danger if men are going to take his word for this: our temples will have no wreaths, our wayside shrines no savoury steam, our wine-bowls no drink-offerings, our altars will be cold, and in short there will be general dearth of sacrifices and oblations, and famine will be rife" (*Bis accusatus* 2; Loeb, III, 89). All of these phrases mean much the same thing; but they give a comic force to the picture, they blow it up until it reaches—what Lucian looked for—the level of burlesque.

This copiousness (which Fielding also reproduced upon occasion) does not, however, contribute very largely to the characteristic *balance* of Lucian's prose. That arises from the setting off of one idea against another and from the parenthetical elements that we shall shortly examine. B. E. Perry has called attention to a particular feature of the contraposition of ideas: "balancing of what is μέτριον [that is, reasonable, within measure, suitable] against what is not, by way of calling attention to something that deserves special emphasis, is a characteristic feature of Lucianic style."[15] For example, Lucian, after describing some of the humiliations a dependent scholar must undergo in a rich man's house, says, "All this is not

---

[15] "On the Authenticity of *Lucius sive Asinus*," *Classical Philology*, XXI (1926), 225-34. I have drawn very heavily upon Professor Perry's comprehensive discussion of the Lucianic idiom. See also, for a rather technical discussion of Lucian's use of the optative (revived during the Second Sophistic) for elevated style and the subjunctive for the familiar, B. J. Sims, "Final Clauses in Lucian," *Classical Quarterly*, XLVI (1952), 63-73.

so bad, perhaps [Ταῦτα μὲν οὖν ἴσως μέτρια]. But if Dives himself has a turn for writing poetry or prose and recites his own compositions at dinner, then you must certainly split yourself applauding . . ." (*De mercede conductis* 35; Loeb, III, 471). Among many like examples in Fielding, one thinks of poor Partridge before the bar for "striking" his shrewish wife: "Mr. Partridge bore all this patiently; but when his wife appealed to the blood on her face, as an evidence of his barbarity, he could not help laying claim to his own blood, for so it really was . . ." (*TJ*, II, iv; Henley, III, 78).

An even more characteristic feature of Lucian's style, however—perhaps the single *most* characteristic feature—is his habitual use of parenthetical and qualifying elements. To call upon Professor Perry again: "According to Guttentag [*De subdito qui inter Lucianeos legi solet dialogo Toxaride*, Berlin, 1860], parenthetical clauses . . . are more frequent in Lucian than in any other ancient author; and my own observation leads me to believe that this statement is not much exaggerated."[16] Almost any page of Lucian will yield examples of the parenthesis—for example, "He poured enough ambrosial speech over me to put out of date the famous Sirens (if there ever were any) and the nightingales and the lotus of Homer" (*Nigrinus* 3; Loeb, I, 103). Equally common are such related elements as the qualifying phrase, the adversative phrase, the afterthought, and so on—all of which contribute to the same effect of spontaneity and overflowing ideas at the same time that they suggest a mind in firm control, adding, qualifying, doubting, negating. When Lucian, wearing his mask of naiveté, tells of the myth that poplars along the Eridanus shed tears of amber in grief over Phaethon, he adds: "As a matter of fact, I did visit those parts not long ago (on another errand, to be sure); and as I had to go up the Eridanus, I kept a sharp lookout, but neither poplars nor

[16] Perry, p. 229.

amber were to be seen. Indeed, the very name of Phaethon was unknown to the natives" (*De electro* 2; Loeb, I, 75). Lucian's favorite phrase is perhaps the expression, μᾶλλον δέ, which may be translated as "rather" or "nay, more"; it appears everywhere in his writings, serious as well as humorous. One more passage may suffice to illustrate several of these elements: the lament of Timon:

"After raising so many Athenians to high station and making them rich when they were wretchedly poor before and helping all who were in want, nay more [μᾶλλον δέ], pouring out my wealth in floods to benefit my friends, now that I have become poor thereby I am no longer recognized or even looked at by the men who formerly cringed and kowtowed and hung upon my nod. On the contrary, if I chance to meet any of them in the road, they treat me as they would the gravestone of a man long dead which time has overturned, passing by without even a curious glance. Indeed, some of them, on catching sight of me in the distance, turn off in another direction, thinking that the man who not long ago showed himself their saviour and benefactor will be an unpleasant and repulsive spectacle"—(*Timon* 5; Loeb, II, 331).

I have perhaps sufficiently argued, in discussing Fielding's essays, that the parenthesis and the afterthought or extension and the qualifying phrase are highly typical of his serious style and the source as well of some of his most delectable humor. "Jones suspecting what had happened [namely, that his guide had lost the way], acquainted the guide with his apprehensions; but he insisted on it that they were in the right road, and added it would be very strange if he should not know the road to Bristol; though, in reality, it would have been much stranger if he had known it, having never passed through it in his life before" (*TJ*, VII, x; Henley, IV, 20). Fielding's prose style resembles Lucian in nothing so much as in these qualities of interruption and extension. Even the characteristic ὅλως that Lucian habitually uses in summing up a series or a set of oppositions is precisely paralleled by Fielding's equally characteristic, "in short. . . ." Another parenthetical phrase, ὡς ἀληθῶς, often translated as "truly" or "in truth," serves Lucian in the same manner that Fielding's "to say truth" serves him, that is, in conveying an air of sincerity and of honest thought about a question. Thus Hermes says of Timon: "Well, you might say that he was ruined by kind-heartedness and philanthropy and compassion on all those who were in want; but in reality [ὡς δὲ ἀληθεῖ λόγῳ] it was senselessness and folly and lack of discrimination in regard to his friends" (*Timon* 8; Loeb, II, 335).[17]

As these elements contribute to the characteristic prose-rhythm of both writers, so also do they serve in part to define the lightly ironic tone, the easy, casual litotes that sometimes rescues Lucian from shrewishness and that adds to Fielding's *suavitas* and dignity. We have already illustrated some of the devices of understatement and meticulous caution and apparent naiveté that both men employed; and these too play their role in creating the typical air of plausibility and control.[18] Further illustration would doubtless be gratuitous; but I should like to call attention to one other device that (although not strictly a matter of style) seems to me to pose a counterweight to enthusiasm, to keep the stylistic level at precisely that even keel we have described. If we were to take a page from Puttenham's book, we might call it "the Undercutter," for it consists in following a very moral or highly impassioned speech with a flat or commonplace response. Thus, when Philosophy in the *Fugitivi*, weeping over the wrongs against her, declares to Zeus, "When you observed that the life of man

[17] Perry (p. 232, n. 3) has a useful list of thirty Greek phrases which (though not found in Lucian's narrative *Vera historia*) are characteristic of his dialogue and essay style. Most of them, significantly enough, are parenthetical, adversative, or extensional elements.
[18] This commentary on *litotes* has little application, of course, to Lucian's diatribes, such as *Alexander*, *Adversus indoctum*, and *Peregrinus*.

was full of wrongdoing and transgression because stupidity and high-handedness were ingrained in it, and disturbed it, you pitied humanity, harried as it was by ignorance, and therefore sent me down, enjoining me to see to it that they should stop wronging each other, doing violence, and living like beasts . . ." (*Fugitivi* 5; Loeb, v, 61; with more of the like), the heightened effect is reduced to zero level once again, when Zeus simply grunts, "I know I said a great deal at the time, including all this." Fielding, in like manner, often "undercuts" a highly moral speech through the reaction of the audience. Allworthy's wise pontifications to Dr. Blifil upon love, the married state, beauty, fortune, and prudence, are all seriously enough intended (as, doubtless, Philosophy's speech was by Lucian), but Fielding had the instincts of the moralist who is also a humorist, and he knew how to make his solemn moral observations palatable: "Here Allworthy concluded his sermon, to which Blifil had listened with the profoundest attention, though it cost him some pains to prevent now and then a small discomposure of his muscles. He now praised every period of what he had heard with the warmth of a young divine who hath the honor to dine with a bishop the same day in which his lordship hath mounted the pulpit" (*TJ*, i, xii; Henley, iii, 60). Dr. Blifil's hypocrisy is disclosed; but the passage does not exist for that. It provides the reader with a chuckle and with a resting place on earth (not in the moral skies) where he may digest the truly good advice he has been presented. And the return to the normal level of style has been achieved.

Finally, in this commentary upon style, we are to observe another characteristic that Lucian and Fielding shared and delighted in (but which, once again, many other comic artists had employed, particularly in the eighteenth century): the mock-heroic elevation of diction. Lucian, like Fielding was fond of preparing the reader to appreciate his effects, of calling attention to the departure from his usual level of style. Thus Zeus objects to Hermes' proclamation assembling the gods: "How do I want you to do it? Ennoble your proclamation, I tell you, with metre and high-sounding, poetical words, so that they may be more eager to assemble" (*Iupiter tragoedus* 6; Loeb, II, 99); and so Hermes does. Likewise, in the *De sacrificiis*, as Lucian goes soaring in imagination up to Heaven, he observes, "and after that, the houses of the gods and the palace of Zeus, all very handsomely built by Hephaestus. 'The gods, assembled in the house of Zeus'—it is in order, I take it, to elevate one's diction when one is on high . . ." (*De sacrificiis* 8-9; Loeb, III, 163-65). The use of this pleasant device in Fielding is presumably too well known to require citation. I would only add that the disparity in diction is heightened in Lucian's narrative prose (for example, *Lucius sive Asinus*) where a popular and less finished style is the norm and poetic elevation takes on a correspondingly more incongruous air. The same effect, as Professor Perry has observed, is to be found in Apuleius and Petronius:[19] and obviously it is true of Fielding's narrative prose.

It is a temptation to continue with such "likenesses" in style as the absolute precision of diction, the unfailing tact in choice of words, that both Lucian and Fielding display—particularly since this very quality is a major factor in Fielding's greatness as a comic artist—but this would take us into complex terrain. I shall conclude, rather, by observing that the literary "personalities" of Lucian and Fielding are very much of a piece; and this I shall not attempt formally to demonstrate. One may simply note that both men, learned as they were, owed a very great debt to earlier tradition; and yet that no writers were ever more truly original, creative, and individual. M. Croiset's comment upon Lucian's absorption of the greatest Greek liter-

[19] Perry, p. 225.

ature, making it a living part of his own genius, is peculiarly applicable to Fielding also: "L'antiquité classique, pourrait-on dire, est derrière lui, semblable à une série de foyers lumineux qui l'éclairent; toutes ces lumières se concentrent dans son esprit comme dans un cristal transparent qui les réunit, et le rayon qui en sort les mêle si intimement, que le regard est désormais incapable de les discerner."[20]

Neither Lucian nor Fielding, as narrator, was of the reticent or withdrawn breed, trembling lest his presence on the scene be detected. Lucian is constantly making himself a figure (directly or implicitly) in his dialogues; and even in other genres the author's personality can seldom be separated from his narrative. The same is obviously and gloriously true of Fielding. And to conclude: for all their fundamental seriousness of purpose, both of these classic authors display an irrepressible vein of playfulness and sheer good spirits (for, once again—and ever again—*"may not a man speak truth with a smiling countenance"*). They will even descend from their awesome eminence, in that ultimate gesture of the truly assured and truly mature mind, to make ironic fun of themselves. So Lucian, at the conclusion of *De electro*, declares ruefully:

"But as for my talk, you already see how simple and matter-of-fact it is, and that there is no music to it. So look out that you do not set your hopes of me too high, and thereby have an experience like people who see things under water. They expect them to be as large as they looked through the water, from above, when the image was magnified under the light; and when they fish them up, they are annoyed to find them a great deal smaller"—(*De electro* 6; Loeb, I, 79).

And Fielding, concluding one of his introductory essays in *Tom Jones*, says:

"I am convinced I never make my reader laugh heartily but where I have laughed before him; unless it should

---

[20] Croiset, p. 294.

happen at any time that instead of laughing with me he should be inclined to laugh at me. Perhaps this may have been the case at some passages in this chapter, from which apprehension I will here put an end to it"—(IX, i; Henley, IV, 160).

1. "A DIALOGUE BETWEEN ALEXANDER THE GREAT AND DIOGENES THE CYNIC"

Nothing in this work can be said to contribute a definite clue to the date of its composition. The theme that Fielding exploits here was handled in similar terms in the poem *Of True Greatness* (see above), published in January 1741, though clearly written somewhat earlier:

> Scorn and Disdain the little *Cynick* hurl'd
> At the exulting Victor of the World.
> Greater than this what Soul can be descry'd?
> His who contemns the *Cynick*'s snarling Pride.
> Well might the haughty Son of *Philip* see
> Ambition's second Lot devolve on thee;
> Whose Breast Pride fires with scarce inferior Joy,
> And bids thee hate and shun Men, him destroy.
>   (*Misc.*, I, 5)

Fielding's interest in the contrast between Diogenes and Alexander appears in the fact that about sixty lines of his poem are dedicated to a commentary upon them. One cannot say with certainty whether the poem or the dialogue was the earlier. Nor, indeed, can one say that they were necessarily written about the same time, despite the fact that they have a number of sentiments in common. Mere parallels are notoriously unreliable as dating evidence.

2

Fielding's *Dialogue between Alexander the Great and Diogenes the Cynic* is a dramatized representation of the supposedly historical meeting between the tub philosopher and the great conqueror, which took place at Corinth while Alexander was confederating the Peloponnesian states.[21] As Fielding notes, however, he has anachronistically set the meeting after Alexander's Asiatic expedition, in order to present the opposition between the two characters more completely (*Misc.*, I, 326, n.). Beginning with Diogenes' refusal to pay homage to Alexander, and his famous request to "stand from between me and the Sun" (*Misc.*, I, 327), the dialogue leads into a debate on greatness. The debate is not, however, presented in the simple terms of protagonist and antagonist in which most contemporary dialogues were couched. Fielding erects instead an ingenious dual opposition: on the one hand, Alexander seeks to justify himself as worthy of the title of greatness—a claim which Diogenes scornfully refutes. On the other hand, Diogenes asserts the superiority of his own philosophical abnegation of the world, and his claim is in turn exposed by Alexander for what it truly represents.

Thus, to Alexander's declaration that his mighty exploits entitle him to be considered a true son of Jupiter, Diogenes returns:

". . . How vainly dost thou endeavour to raise thyself on the Monuments of thy Disgrace! I acknowledge, indeed, all the Exploits thou hast recounted, and the Millions thou hast to thy eternal Shame destroyed. But is it hence thou wouldst claim *Jupiter* for thy Father? Hath not then every Plague or pestilential Vapour the same Title?"—(*Misc.*, I, 329).

When Alexander objects that by professing this disregard for his glory, Diogenes is "undermining the Foundation of all that Honour, which is the Encouragement to, and Reward of, every thing truly great and noble," the Cynic replies that clearly Alexander has no idea of true Honor, which is of a different nature: "It results from the

[21] See Farrand Sayre, *Diogenes of Sinope: A Study of Greek Cynicism* (Baltimore, 1938), pp. 82-87.

secret Satisfaction of our own Minds, and is decreed us by Wise Men and the Gods; it is the Shadow of Wisdom and Virtue, and is inseparable from them . . ." (1, 331).

Diogenes' arguments proclaim his own impeccable virtue; but the initiative now shifts to Alexander, as he demands to know in what the "Wisdom and Virtue" of Diogenes really consist.

"DIOGENES. Not in ravaging Countries, burning Cities, plundering and massacring Mankind.

"ALEXANDER. No, rather in biting and snarling at them"— (1, 332).

And when Diogenes insists that he snarls at them for their vice and folly, Alexander replies: "If thou wouldst confess the Truth, Envy is the true Source of all thy Bitterness; it is that which begets thy Hatred, and from Hatred comes thy Railing. . . ." In an ironical passage, he continues: "Come, come, thou art not the poor-spirited Fellow thou wouldst appear. There is more Greatness of Soul in thee than at present shines forth. . . . Pride will not suffer thee to confess Passions which Fortune hath not put it in thy Power to gratify. It is therefore that thou deniest Ambition . . ." (1, 334). Diogenes strikes back eloquently, declaring that Alexander must be the most miserable of men, for "Thy Desire consists in nothing certain, and therefore with nothing certain can be gratified . . ." (1, 337). Alexander professes to accept this with good humor. Although his claims to "true greatness" have been demolished by the dialectical skill of the Cynic, he now shows himself, in turn, to be no mean practitioner of that art. Declaring that he likes the Cynic well, he suggests that as a manifestation of his friendship he will burn Athens to the ground, in revenge for its contemning of Diogenes' philosophy and its suspicion of his morals. Diogenes falls neatly into the trap and begins gleefully to contemplate his revenge upon Corinth and Lacedaemon as well. Alexander leads him on to further self-exposure by slyly suggesting that it might be better to preserve the physical cities, especially the wealth of Corinth, and only massacre the inhabitants. Diogenes professes to despise their wealth; but when Alexander then suggests that it be given to the soldiers, the Cynic interposes:

"Then you may give some of it to the Soldiers: but as the Dogs have formerly insulted me with their Riches, I will, if you please, retain a little—perhaps a Moiety, or not much more, to my own Use. It will give me at least an Opportunity of shewing the World, I can despise Riches when I possess them, as much as I did before in my Poverty"—(I, 339).

At this, his tempter bursts forth: "Art not thou a true Dog? Is this thy Contempt of Wealth? This thy Abhorrence of the Vices of Mankind? To sacrifice three of the noblest Cities of the World to thy Wrath and Revenge!" And he demands to know if Diogenes will impudently continue now to dispute the superiority which lies in the power of an Alexander. To which the wily Cynic replies: "I have still the same Superiority over thee, which thou dost challenge over thy Soldiers. I would have made thee the Tool of my Purpose" (I, 340). Alexander's soldiers threaten to fall upon the old man, but the conqueror restrains them ("Let him alone. I admire his Obstinacy; nay, I almost envy it"), and the dialogue ends with his legendary assertion: "Farewell, old Cynic; and if it will flatter thy Pride, be assured, I esteem thee so much, that *was I not* Alexander, *I could desire to be* Diogenes"; to which Fielding has the snarling Cynic retort: "Go to the Gibbet, and take with thee as a Mortification; that *was I not* Diogenes *I could almost content myself with being* Alexander" (I, 340).

3

Fielding's dialogue does not find any precise warrant in Lucian, who preferred to deal with mythological characters or shades in the lower regions or personified abstractions in his dialogues, rather than to re-enact "historical" scenes. The primary justification for calling it a Lucianic sketch (and I shall not quarrel if someone wishes to call it something else) is that Lucian fathered this order of lively dramatic dialogue and that Fielding could have found a number of hints in Lucian for his own piece. The protagonists, for instance, are favorite characters in Lucian's dialogues: Alexander appears in three of the *Dialogi mortuorum* (*Dialogues of the Dead*) and Diogenes is a character or is mentioned in at least six. Indeed, as a representative of the Cynic philosophy, Diogenes makes an appearance in a number of Lucianic works, including the *Vera historia*, the *Vitarum auctio* (*Sale of Philosophies*), *Quomodo historia conscribenda sit* (*The Way to Write History*), *Piscator*, and *Menippus*. Further, Lucian actually presented a dialogue between Alexander and Diogenes in Hades (*Dialogi mortuorum* xiii), which took a very anti-heroic tone toward the Macedonian conqueror. In it Diogenes professes to be astonished: "Dear me, Alexander, *you* dead like the rest of us?" And he taunts him for the lies about his godhood, concluding (as both Diogenes and Menippus usually did in Lucian's *Dialogues of the Dead*): "How do you like thinking over all the earthly bliss you left to come here . . . does the thought of them *hurt?*" Alexander weeps.[22]

In Lucian's somewhat ambivalent attitude toward Diogenes one finds a kind of literary authority for Fielding's own dramatization of him as both the exposer and the exposed, the critic and the criticized. Lucian normally presents him as a Menippus-like figure, laughing at the follies and vanities of men; but when he comes to consider the Cynic as the representative of a school of philosophy, his treatment is quite different. In the *Vitarum auctio*, for

[22] *Works*, transl. F. G. and H. W. Fowler, I, 129-30.

instance, Diogenes[23] instructs the buyer how to be a Cynic: "You should be impudent and bold, and should abuse all and each, both kings and commoners, for thus they will admire you and think you manly. Let your language be barbarous, your voice discordant and just like the barking of a dog.... In a word, let everything about you be bestial and savage. Put off modesty, decency and moderation, and wipe away blushes from your face completely."[24] This picture of the hypocritical reviler of mankind corresponds with the side of the Cynic exposed in the latter part of Fielding's dialogue, as the other Lucianic picture of Diogenes as an honest censurer of the follies of men corresponds to the exposer of Alexander's claims to true greatness.

Fielding need not have gone to Lucian to learn how the action of a dialogue should be handled. There were many contemporary models (which I shall shortly discuss), and Fielding's own dramatic training had prepared him to deal with such matters as exposition and identification of characters—though one might well turn this around and argue that a familiarity with Lucian's dialogues would be of no small assistance to a budding dramatist. It is perhaps enough to say that Lucian offered a famous model, and that Fielding handles with considerable acumen in this dialogue the techniques that Lucian had established. The sketch is apparently written to be read aloud (as Lucian's dialogues would seem to have been),[25] for, despite the name-tags present in the printed text, the two characters are care-

[23] Professor Harmon argues that the usual editorial practice of assigning specific names to the representatives of the various philosophies put on sale in the *Vitarum auctio*, though it is supported by some of the MSS., is probably a mistake, for "Lucian makes it perfectly plain that he is not selling specific philosophers" (Loeb, II, 449). Hence the speaker here would be "The Cynic," rather than "Diogenes." I have ventured to retain the personal name, because I am considering Lucian's influence upon Fielding; and Fielding's texts would have printed "Diogenes."
[24] *Vitarum auctio* 10; Loeb ed., transl. Harmon, II, 469.
[25] See Alfred R. Bellinger, "Lucian's Dramatic Technique," *Yale Classical Studies*, I (1928), 3-40. On this point and in the following discussion of Lucian's practice in his dialogues I am indebted to Mr. Bellinger's account.

fully made to identify themselves very early in the action—a practice that Lucian also was normally scrupulous to observe. The place is not identified in the speeches, either because the auditors, being familiar with the legend, would be presumed to recall it, or because to Fielding the confrontation itself is the significant thing and the place of no consequence. Lucian, too, seldom troubled to identify place, unless the understanding of something in his dialogue depended upon it. But what Fielding does do (and what Lucian did not always do) is to create an image of the characters in the auditor's mind through their opening words, and, with commendable dramatic economy, provide at the same time a sense of the scene and of the imminent conflict:

"ALEXANDER. WHAT Fellow art thou, who darest thus to lie at thy Ease in our Presence, when all others, as thou seest, rise to do us Homage? Dost thou not know us?

"DIOGENES. I cannot say I do: But by the Number of thy Attendants, by the Splendor of thy Habit; but, above all, by the Vanity of thy Appearance, and the Arrogance of thy Speech, I conceive thou mayst be *Alexander* the Son of *Philip*.

"ALEXANDER. And who can more justly challenge thy Respect, than *Alexander*, at the Head of that victorious Army, who hath performed such wonderful Exploits, and under his Conduct hath subdued the World?

"DIOGENES. Who? why the Taylor who made me this old Cloak.

"ALEXANDER. Thou art an odd Fellow, and I have a Curiosity to know thy Name.

"DIOGENES. I am not ashamed of it: I am called *Diogenes*; a Name composed of as many and as well sounding Syllables as *Alexander*"—(*Misc.*, I, 325-26).

Wherever Fielding may be thought to have derived his technique, he had clearly learned the lesson well. This is neatly done. Moreover, the dramatic contrast established between Alexander's lofty but affable tone and the defiant insolence of Diogenes is effectively maintained until the time arrives for Alexander, in his turn, to become crafty and insinuating. One is never in doubt as to the speaker (a matter of some importance, if the dialogue was intended to be read aloud): not only the matter but the manner, the tone, immediately identify each protagonist. And further to mark the transition from one speaker to another, Fielding frequently employs the device (used in almost all good dialogues, Platonic, Ciceronian, or Lucianic) of ending a speech with a question—the response, of course, indicating a new speaker. All in all, the skill displayed in this brief sketch is a striking earnest of the skill in conveying character, gesture, and tone through dialogue that he would manifest in his greater narratives. Only near the conclusion, when the soldiers become participants in the action, does Fielding find it necessary to fall back on written stage-directions: *"Here some of the Army would have fallen upon him, but Alexander interposed"* (*Misc.*, I, 340). This seems scarcely necessary; instead of "Let him alone," Alexander's next speech could easily have been "Nay, let him alone, soldiers," thus conveying the action of the stage-direction. But let us not rewrite Fielding—even minor Fielding. This seems to me the only real technical flaw in an adroit and convincing dramatic sketch.

4

The dialogue as a mode of literature enjoyed a striking vogue in the seventeenth and eighteenth centuries. A student of its history has said that between 1660 and 1725, "Few other literary forms had such wide, varied, and constant usage." It comprehended a great variety of productions: "The word was used to designate publications which ranged from completely undramatic half sheets of questions and answers to elaborate conversations in which characters were fully developed, action was clearly indicated, and background was carefully drawn."[26] Such diverse works as Walton's *Compleat Angler*, Dryden's *Of Dramatick Poesie*, Dennis's *Impartial Critick*, and Shaftesbury's *Moralists* were presented in dialogue form. Addison conveyed information about medals through the same device, Spence won Pope's friendship with his dialogues on the poet's *Odyssey*, and Bishop Berkeley attacked Shaftesbury's philosophy—among other things—in the vigorous dialogues of his *Alciphron*. Even a multitude of political journals were conducted in dialogue. And if Tom Brown and Ned Ward could use the dialogue for low-comedy purposes, Henry More could pen his lofty *Divine Dialogues* to discuss the questions of God's attributes and providence.

Obviously it is difficult to delimit so protean a form as this, and perhaps even more difficult to relate Fielding's work to the general tradition. For to speak of a "norm" in the use of dialogue is inevitably to falsify a highly complex picture, the keynote of which is variety. But one may at least venture to say that most of these dialogues, high and low, are singularly undramatic: their peculiar concern is the dialectical development of an idea, not the unfolding of character. Although most critics of the dialogue argued that it should resemble natural, or slightly heightened, conversation,[27] and dramatic qualities were often

---

[26] Both citations are from Eugene R. Purpus, "The 'Plain, Easy, and Familiar Way': The Dialogue in English Literature, 1660-1725," *ELH*, XVII (1950), 47-58; see pp. 58 and 52. See also Bartholow V. Crawford, "The Prose Dialogue of the Commonwealth and the Restoration," *PMLA*, XXXIV (1919), 601-09. Elizabeth Merrill has traced the larger pattern of *The Dialogue in English Literature* (N.Y., 1911), indicating something of the influence of the Platonic, Ciceronian, and Lucianic dialogues in England, and describing the various purposes which the dialogue subserved, particularly polemic, exposition, and philosophy. The standard discussion of the form at large is Rudolf Hirzel, *Der Dialog: ein literarhistorischer Versuch* (2v., Leipzig, 1895), but this work has little on the eighteenth century and after.

[27] Compare, for example, one popular and one sophisticated view: "I think, the best Criticks have observed, That *Dialogue* requires a peculiar Stile, different from all other Kinds of Writing. . . . It should resemble a natural Conversation, tho' it may be a little better than what the

LUCIANIC SKETCHES

praised, the dialogue in practice tended to become merely an essay divided among speakers. There was little real differentiation between the characters involved. When Richard Hurd came to comment upon the form, shortly after mid-century, he flatly announced the purpose of the dialogue to be philosophic, not dramatic;[28] and this may be regarded as simply a matter of criticism catching up with practice. Fielding, however, although he was in part concerned to examine an idea—"true greatness"—in his own dialogue, could not deny his dramatic instincts. What emerges in the *Dialogue between Alexander and Diogenes* is less a sense of idea argued than of character displayed.

Fielding's contemporaries would most likely have associated his dialogue with the particular species called "dialogues of the dead." Deriving ultimately from Lucian's *Dialogi mortuorum*, the dialogue of the dead was revived for the late seventeenth century by Fontenelle, and won considerable popularity in the century following as a vehicle for satiric and philosophic observation—in part, one would suppose, because of the (illegitimate, to be sure) air of authority and detachment that it gave to the most common pronouncement by placing it in the mouth of an eminent historical personage.[29] With the possible excep-

---

Generality of People are supposed to speak *extempore*, as a Picture may be like, tho' handsomer than the Original. Another Rule to be observed is, that every Person must speak in Character . . ." (*Common Sense*, 4 November 1738; coll. ed. [2v., 1738-1739], I, 228). William Melmoth, speaking of the popularity of the dialogue among the ancients, observed, with like emphasis: "Plato and Tully, it should seem, thought truth could never be examined with more advantage, than amidst the amicable opposition of well-regulated converse" (*Letters of Sir Thomas Fitzosborne* [7th ed., 1769], p. 367).

[28] Preface, *Moral and Political Dialogues* (3rd ed., 3v., 1765), I, i-lx, esp. pp. xxxi-xxxiii. The ponderous Hurd could not stomach Lucian.

[29] The genre has been treated in some detail by Johan S. Egilsrud, *Le "dialogue des morts" dans les littératures française, allemande et anglaise (1644-1789)* (Paris, 1934) and by Johannes Rentsch, "Das Totengespräch in der Litteratur," in his *Lucianstudien* (Plauen, 1895), pp. 15-40. Egilsrud discusses the pre-Lucianic elements of the genre (notably Book XI of the *Odyssey*, Book VI of the *Aeneid*, Aristophanes'

tion of William King's dialogues on the Phalaris controversy, the dialogue of the dead, as a genre, did not find expression in any significant literature in England until Lyttelton's *Dialogues of the Dead* in 1760; but there was a host of lively minor pieces representing conversations in the shades between contemporary or historical figures.[30]

Technically, Fielding's is not really a dialogue of the dead (that is, a conversation between shades in the afterworld). It is the re-enactment of a (supposedly) historical scene. Not to become engaged in a quibble over the meaning of "dead" in "dialogues of the dead," there is obviously a difference between characters who, as souls in the afterworld, can look back with detachment or with fuller knowledge upon their past lives, and characters of history caught in mid-career, unblessed with the vision that comes only to the dead. In a rhetorical sense, one might argue that the difference lies in the extended use of two forms of

---

Frogs and the writings of Menippus); but he agrees with Rentsch in stressing the central importance of Lucian to the later tradition. Benjamin Boyce has considered the conflation of the Dialogue of the Dead with the tradition of the visit to the nether world in his "News from Hell," cited previously. The most immediately influential models in the genre for the eighteenth century were Fontenelle (*Nouveaux dialogues des morts*, Paris, 1683) and Fénelon (*Dialogues des morts*, Paris, 1712). The latter work, incidentally, included a meeting between Alexander and Diogenes, and a portrayal of Alexander in quite unheroic terms. On Fontenelle and the background of his dialogues, see John W. Cosentini, *Fontenelle's Art of Dialogue* (N.Y., 1952); Mr. Cosentini minimizes Fontenelle's debt to Lucian and stresses the affinity of his work with the dialogues of Plato. His argument may serve as a useful corrective, provided one does not forget that when Fontenelle published the *Nouveaux dialogues* in 1683, it was with the dedication, "A LUCIEN. AUX CHAMPS ELISIENS" (cited here from the Amsterdam ed. of 1701, sig. *2).

[30] Egilsrud (pp. 13, 150) considers the genre as really beginning in England only with Lyttelton's *Dialogues of the Dead*; although it is true that the appearance of this work in 1760 inspired a new vogue, the form had been popular in England long before this and Egilsrud's bibliography for the earlier years needs considerable amplification. Even so early as the Restoration, the anonymous author of *A Dialogue betwixt H. B.'s Ghost, and His Dear Author R. L. S.* [1681?] commented upon the popularity of the genre: "We have had so many arise from the Dead of late, that they are grown familiar, and almost contemptible" (cf. Purpus, p. 54, n. 30). See also Boyce, "News from Hell," *passim*.

prosopopoeia: Fielding's dialogue between deceased personages represented as alive is an example of *prosopopoeia* proper; the dialogue of the dead may be said (without, I think, stretching the term) to make use of the variety of that device known as *eidolopoeia,* or finding words for the dead to speak. Again, so far as the literary tradition is concerned, Fénelon, among others, had actually employed living persons and even fictional characters in his *Dialogues des morts* (1712), a usage that Lyttelton called attention to when he himself wished to depict a "dialogue of the dead" between Ulysses and Circe.[31] This offshoot, legitimate or no, from the proper dialogue of shades leads into the historical dialogues of Richard Hurd and the epistles of John Langhorne later in the century, and thence to Landor's *Imaginary Conversations,* at which point the offshoot may surely be said to gain equal status with its parent. Hence one may be pleased to call Fielding's dialogue retrospectively an "imaginary conversation"; but at the time its affinity would clearly have appeared to be with the dialogues of the dead.

Fielding had used the more conventional dialogue for conventional purposes in (if the work is really his) *The Plain Truth: A Dialogue between Sir Courtly Jobber . . . and Tom Telltruth* (1741); and he employed it later in two other political pieces, *A Dialogue between the Devil, the Pope, and the Pretender* (1745) and *A Dialogue between a Gentleman of London . . . and an Honest Alderman of the Country Party* (1747). The dialogue in the *Miscellanies,* however, has a more literary purpose: Fielding is not seeking (as most contemporary exploiters of the form were) to comment on the current political, religious,

---

[31] *Dialogues of the Dead* (1760), Dialogue v. Lyttelton says in a note: "This cannot be properly called a Dialogue of the Dead; but we have one of the same kind among Cambray's Dialogues, between Ulysses and his companion Grillus, when turned to a boar by the enchantments of Circe; and two or three others, that are supposed to have past between living persons" (*Works* [1774], p. 356).

or social scene; he is not conveying technical information, writing a polemic against a particular person or group, or presenting a philosophical system. He is aiming simply to present Alexander and Diogenes in the exact light in which he viewed them, both as historical characters and, more importantly, as symbols. As historical characters, both the Macedonian conqueror and the snarling Cynic were objects of his most profound contempt; as symbols, they represented two of his abiding aversions: the figure of worldly "greatness" and the figure of the ill-natured, ascetic censurer of human happiness. And this will require further comment.

5

We have discussed Fielding's hatred of what he considered false greatness (see above, *Of True Greatness*) as well as his detestation of the hypocritical censurer (above, *Essay on the Knowledge of the Characters of Men*). That he should have come to dramatize these views in a conflict between Alexander and Diogenes seems really almost inevitable, for these two were commonly taken in the eighteenth century as standard symbols of the vices of overweening ambition and churlish raillery, respectively.

Modern scholarship has documented at some length the expression in eighteenth-century letters of that ancient commonplace, the criminality of the great conqueror.[32] The menace of Louis XIV (who was pleased to identify himself with Alexander) and of Charles XII;[33] the rising

[32] See Aurélien Digeon, *Les romans de Fielding* (Paris, 1923), p. 128; W. R. Irwin, *The Making of Jonathan Wild* (N.Y., 1941), pp. 48-49, *et passim*; and, among various other comments, David Worcester, *The Art of Satire* (Cambridge, Mass., 1940), pp. 82-88. Cf. above, p. 53.

[33] J. E. Wells, commenting on Fielding's part in the translation of Adlerfeld's *Military History of Charles XII* (1740), notes that he frequently classed Charles with Alexander as a butcher of mankind in later works, and thinks "perhaps Fielding got some of his antipathy to such 'Heroes' from his labors on this very book" ("Henry Fielding and the History of Charles XII," *JEGP*, xi [1912], 606). One may at least suppose that Adlerfeld's uncritical admiration for the Swedish conqueror did not sit well with his translator.

LUCIANIC SKETCHES

benevolist school of moral thought; the generally antiheroic bias of the newly influential middle class; the attack upon "greatness" by the opposition to Walpole—such various currents and attitudes combined to sponsor a popular image of the great conqueror as the epitome of ruthless and overriding personal ambition. Alexander, of course, as among the foremost heroes of antiquity, was with fair consistency[34] portrayed as one of "the principal *Directors* and *Disturbers* of the Affairs of Mankind."[35] To Pope he was "Macedonia's madman," to Thomson, "The Macedonian vulture"; and the author of "*Mrs.* MIDNIGHT's *Letter to the Ghost of* ALEXANDER *the Great*" in Smart's *Midwife* burst out: "Was I not certified by the Writings of *Quintus Curtius* and others, I shou'd have concluded, that you was begot by an *Hottentot*, born of a Tygress, and educated by a Butcher. . . . I believe you to be the greatest Scoundrel that ever existed."[36] The *Craftsman*

[34] Although the prevailing attitude toward Alexander was undoubtedly one of disapproval, the heroic conception did not by any means entirely die out, and many writers continued to speak of his magnanimity and "sublimity." Fielding was well enough aware of this current, and a comment in *Jonathan Wild* presents his estimate of it: "In the Histories of Alexander and *Cæsar*, we are frequently [1754 ed. adds: "and indeed impertinently"] reminded of their Benevolence and Generosity. When the former had with Fire and Sword overrun a whole Empire, and destroyed the Lives of Millions of innocent People, we are told as an Example of his Benevolence, that he did not cut the Throat of an old Woman, and ravish her Daughters whom he had before undone" (I, i; *Misc.*, III, 5).

[35] Thomas Gordon, *The Humourist* (2v., 1720-1725), II, 23; Caesar and Alexander are included under this head.

[36] Pope, *Essay on Man*, Epist. IV, l. 220; Thomson, *Liberty*, Part II, l. 479; Smart (ed.) *The Midwife: or the Old Woman's Magazine* (3v., 1751?-1753), II, 30. One of the most virulent attacks upon the heroic conception of Alexander was that of Edward Young:

> The *Grecian* chief, th' Enthusiast of his pride,
> With Rage and Terror stalking by his side,
> Raves round the globe; he soars into a God!
> . . . .
> With orphans tears his impious bowl o'erflows,
> And cries of kingdoms lull him to repose.
> And cannot thrice ten hundred years unpraise
> The boyst'rous boy, and blast his guilty bays?
> ("Satire the Last [VII]," *Love of Fame*
> [2nd ed., 1728], pp. 163-64)

399

(with one eye on Walpole) expressed this prevalent animus in its most anti-heroic terms: "*Alexander, Cæsar,* and most of the great Conquerors of old, were no better than *Imperial Cut-throats,* or *Banditti,* who robb'd and murther'd in Gangs, too strong to be opposed, and escaped the Gallows, which they deserved, by being above Law."[37] So also, in Gay's *Polly,* the noble Indian chief takes Morano (Macheath) to task for his ambition and his crimes, and receives the reply: "*Alexander* the great was more successful. That's all."[38] The difference between brigandry or villainy and worldly glory, many writers were concerned to insist, was merely a question of degree.

This theme was pointed up by another contrast which, as we have observed, was frequently made: that between greatness and goodness. Thus Isaac Barrow in the late seventeenth century had said:

"The fame of such a person [the good man] is, in the best judgments, far more precious and truly glorious, than is the fame of those who have excelled in any other deeds or qualities. For what sober man doth not in his thoughts afford a more high and hearty respect to those poor fishermen, who by their heroical activity and patience did honour God in the propagation of his heavenly truth, than to all those Hectors in chivalry, those conquerors and achievers of mighty exploits, (those Alexanders and Cæsars) who have been renowned for doing things which seemed great, rather than for performing what was truly good?"[39]

[37] *The Craftsman,* No. 320, 19 August 1732; coll. ed. (14v., 1731-1737), IX, 216. The same comparison had been made in 1723: "Besides what was *Alexander* but a Publick Robber? Did he not Plunder the whole World and yet who had more Honour paid him than *Alexander?* . . . Then why shou'd any Plunderers of the Publick Repine?" (Anon., *An Essay in Praise of Knavery* [1723], p. 19).

[38] Act III, sc. xi; Poetical Works, ed. G. C. Faber (1926), p. 584. Fielding makes precisely the same point in the *Champion,* 4 March 1740: "Reputation is ever the companion of success. . . . Had Alexander been entirely defeated in his first battle in Asia, he would have been called only a robber by posterity" (Henley, xv, 229).

[39] Sermon, "The Reward of Honouring God," *Theological Works,* ed. Napier (9v., Cambridge, 1859), I, 267.

So also Timothy Hooker in 1741: "To them [the protective guardian spirits] the *Man of Ross* appears in a fairer Light in the *Book of Remembrance,* and will make a much more illustrious Figure at the last Great Day than *Alexander* or *Cæsar,* or *William the Conqueror,* tho' a *Christian.* For my own Part, when I consider the Bulk of Military Heroes, the Conquerors of Nations who stand foremost in the Lists of Fame, I esteem them no better than so many *glorious Robbers,* and *illustrious Plunderers,* born to be the Scourges and Plagues of Mankind...."[40]

Between these two clerics, a host of others had said the same.

Fielding's own censures of Alexander the Great are frequent and caustic. As early as *The Temple Beau,* his second published play, the following exchange occurs:

"LADY LUCY PEDANT. ... Your wit and beauty, Bellaria, were intended to enslave mankind. Your eyes should first conquer the world, and then weep, like Alexander's, for more worlds to conquer.

"BELLARIA. I rather think he should have wept for those he had conquered. He had no more title to sacrifice the lives of men to his ambition than a woman has their ease" —(Act II, sc. vii; Henley, VIII, 124).

This was the tone maintained through the *Champion* and Fielding's later journals, where there are various passing strictures upon Alexander.[41] In the *Journey from This World to the Next,* he portrayed the Macedonian as a favorite at the court of the Emperor of Death (*Misc.,* II,

[40] *An Essay on Honour* (1741), p. 14.
[41] See, for example, the *Champion,* Henley, xv, 78, the *True Patriot,* No. 8 (24 December 1745), and the *Covent-Garden Journal,* No. 19 (Jensen, I, 251). Fielding was fond of applying to Alexander (see the *Champion,* Henley, xv, 79, and the *True Patriot, loc.cit.*) a general observation that Sir William Temple had made: "I know not, whether of all the numbers of mankind that live within the compass of a thousand years, for one man that is born capable of making such a poet as Homer or Virgil, there may not be a thousand born capable of making as great generals of armies, or ministers of state, as any the most renowned in story" ("Of Poetry," *Works* [4v., 1814], III, 416-17).

37); and the villainous Jonathan Wild, we are told, "was a passionate Admirer of Heroes, particularly *Alexander* the Great, between whom and the late King of *Sweden* [Charles XII] he would frequently draw Parallels . . ." (I, iii; *Misc.*, III, 18; see also pp. 90-91, 210, 314, 383, and 416).

In Fielding's later works, there are fewer mentions of Alexander himself (though the *Covent-Garden Journal* ironically cites his burning of the city of Persepolis as "a Performance of most exquisite Humour"—No. 19; Jensen, I, 251); but Fielding firmly maintained his anti-heroical bias. In *Amelia*, for instance, he said of his heroine and her children, grieving over Booth's arrest:

"These are, indeed, to a well-disposed mind, the most tragical sights that human nature can furnish, and afford a juster motive to grief and tears in the beholder than it would be to see all the heroes who had ever infested the earth hanged all together in a string"—(IX, i; Henley, VII, 125).

In his *Dialogue*, then, Fielding reflected not only the reigning contemporary opinion of Alexander the Great, but his own consistent attitude toward the historic figure and the evil kind of "heroism" he represented. We have remarked, in discussing the poem *Of True Greatness*, that Fielding considered the crux of the problem to lie in the *aura popularis* that maintained false greatness in power. In the *Dialogue*, Alexander himself is made to ask: "For in what doth all Honour, Glory, and Fame consist, but in the Breath of that Multitude, whose Estimation with such ill-grounded Scorn thou [Diogenes] dost affect to despise" (*Misc.*, I, 330). Fielding's consistent end was to educate that multitude to a nobler and more humane conception of true greatness than that found in the image of an Alexander.

Diogenes was, of course, a less striking figure, and a figure toward whom there existed some variance of opinion. On the one hand, the fable of his searching for an honest man persisted,[42] and his raillery was praised as cutting through the shams of pretenders.[43] This had been, according to a recent study, the predominant view of Diogenes in the Renaissance, the literature of which most frequently presented him as "a corrector of manners and morals, a kind of Greek Cato." On the other hand, a minority estimate in the Renaissance saw him as "a brute, a dirty, ill-tempered, snarling cur."[44] And by the late seventeenth and early eighteenth century, this had become the majority view: for most of the writers of this period he is the "snarling Philosopher,"[45] the "CYNICK Churl, ... proud of causeless Snarl,"[46] whose motivations were envy and pure ill-nature. The Earl of Rochester cited him, further, as an example of the false reason that cut men off from the practical world;[47] and Samuel Parker the Younger insisted that (although Antisthenes was normally called the "Father of the *Cynicks*"), "It does not appear that *Antisthenes* brought *Cynicism* to its Perfection of *Scurrility*

---

[42] See, for instance, the *Spectator*, No. 354 (Everyman ed., III, 109).

[43] *The Guardian* No. 94 (29 June 1713) praised "a fine Answer of *Diogenes*"; and a writer in the *Universal Spectator*, No. 529, declared: "A few *Diogenes's* among us might be of excellent Use to cure a great Number of our Youths of that little *Womanish* Vanity in their Tempers, which they are so studious of indulging . . ." (quoted in the *Gentleman's Magazine* [November 1738], p. 591). Chesterfield cited Diogenes with approval to his son (*Letters*, ed. Charles Strachey and Annette Calthrop [2v., 1901], I, 37), but made the following reservation, when speaking of the foolish ceremonies and customs of social life: "Diogenes the Cynic was a wise man for despising them; but a fool for showing it. Be wiser than other people, if you can; but do not tell them so" (I, 140).

[44] John L. Lievsay, "Some Renaissance Views of Diogenes the Cynic," in *Joseph Quincy Adams: Memorial Studies*, ed. James G. McManaway, et al. (Washington, 1948), pp. 447-55. Most of the stories about Diogenes preserved in classical texts "present him in a favorable light and probably came from Cynic or Stoic sources" (Farrand Sayre, *Diogenes of Sinope*, p. 103).

[45] Bonnell Thornton, *Have at You All: or, The Drury-Lane Journal* (coll. ed., 1752), p. 93.

[46] Samuel Wesley, "The DOG. A MILTONICK FRAGMENT," *Poems on Several Occasions* (1736), p. 150. See also p. 168.

[47] "A Satyr against Mankind," *Poems*, ed. V. de Sola Pinto (1953), pp. 120-21.

and *Brutishness*. . . . No, 'twas a Work to which *Diogenes* was design'd, the fetching up of the Rigidity of his Sect to an exquisite Inhumanity, the starting of the *Levelling Principle* among the *Greeks*, the making it an Heroical Exercise of Wit to affront Princes, and droll upon the sacred Character of *Monarchs*."[48]

The sentiment is what one would expect from the son of the high-flying Bishop of Oxford: but to make Diogenes the whipping-boy for the Puritan rebellion is indeed droll. Whipping-boy was, however, to be the Cynic's part in many eighteenth-century moral works, and he often stood as the symbol of false and surly pride. Buckingham, writing "ON VANITY," cautioned himself: "YET while I thus blame others, it occurs to my memory what PLATO so wittily reply'd to DIOGENES, trampling with his dirty feet on one of his embroider'd couches, and crying out, *Thus I trample on the pride of* PLATO; who only shook his head, saying, *But with more pride thou do'st it, good* DIOGENES."[49] Another version of this anecdote was told by Prior;[50] and the *Athenian Oracle* in response to the query, "*Was it Humility or Pride that made* Diogenes *the* Cynick *chuse to live in a Tub?*" replied: "The proud Ill-natur'd Dog chose it, because he would be troubled with no bad Inmates"—except his own fleas!"[51]

The prevailing tone is clearly not friendly. Fielding himself, aside from the poem *Of True Greatness* and the *Dialogue*, seldom mentioned the Cynic philosopher;[52] but in

[48] Samuel Parker, "AN INTRODUCTION TO THE HISTORY OF THE Anarchical and Levelling OPINIONS," *Sylva. Familiar Letters upon Occasional Subjects* (1701), p. 114.
[49] "ON VANITY," *The Works of John Sheffield . . . Duke of Buckingham* (2nd ed., 2v., 1729), II, 236.
[50] "A Dialogue between Mr: John Lock and Seigneur de Montaigne," *Literary Works of Matthew Prior*, ed. H. B. Wright and M. K. Spears [2v., Oxford, 1959], I, 616. The ultimate source of the anecdote would seem to be Diogenes Laertius, VI. 26.
[51] *The Athenian Oracle* (3rd ed., 4v., 1728), II, 294.
[52] However, it may be noted that in the *Champion* of 26 January 1740,

drawing the portrait of Diogenes as an envious and hypocritical censurer, he was embodying a widely current contemporary attitude and probably presenting his own conception of the historic Diogenes. For if Alexander represented a positive threat to society, Diogenes represented to Fielding the negation of man's deepest instincts. As he said (citing Harris) in the *Essay on Conversation*, man is a social animal, and those who savagely shun the company of others "live in a constant Opposition to their own Nature, and are no less Monsters than the most wanton Abortions or extravagant Births" (*Misc.*, 1, 122). So, when Diogenes in the *Dialogue* asserts that his snarling is the effect of his love "in order, by my Invectives against Vice, to frighten Men from it, and drive them into the Road of Virtue," Alexander responds with what to Fielding (and most of his contemporaries) would have appeared an absolutely crushing rejoinder: "For which Purpose thou hast forsworn Society, and art retired to preach to Trees and Stones" (*Misc.*, 1, 333). Authentic virtue could bloom only in human society.

6

The confrontation of these two figures—Alexander, symbol of worldly greatness, and Diogenes, symbol of utter contempt for that grandeur (a contempt arising from philosophy, asceticism, pride, or envy, according to the view of the delineator)—had seized the imaginations of men

---

a "correspondent," speaking of Bacon's argument for wearing only the mask of virtue says: "This is such philosophical diet as a man may grow fat by feeding on. No chimerical system, which hath starved all its professors, which savours of the romantic tub of Diogenes, and would soon reduce us to be glad of a tub to live in" (Henley, xv, 170). If we straighten out the inverted values of the ironic context, then, we find that here Fielding is apparently associating Diogenes with a laudable kind of philosophic ideal that wicked men call "romantic." However, in the letter describing Nicodemus Bungle's wash against blushing (*Champion*, 28 February 1740; coll. ed. [2v., 1741], 1, 314-19), that lotion is given as the explanation for Diogenes' "Assurance."

from earliest times. From its relation by Cicero,[53] through its expansion by Plutarch and Arrian and later writers, the anecdote of the meeting between conqueror and Cynic had been employed to point a moral or adorn a tale. In the seventeenth century, for example, it could be used for such disparate purposes as that of framing a collection of antifeminist stories (surely a long stretch!) or, holding more closely to the legend, that of emphasizing moral fearlessness in the face of aristocratic vice:[54]

> He spake as free to *Alexanders* face,
> As if the meanest Plow-man were in place.
> Twas not mens persons that he did respect;
> Nor any calling: Vice he durst detect.[55]

This attitude was frequently taken in later years, even into the eighteenth century. Diogenes might be considered a churl and a hypocrite, but when placed opposite the haughty Alexander he took on a sympathetic coloring—he became a symbolic agent whereby the pride of the mighty was humbled. The contrast between them was, moreover, useful in underscoring a moral point:

"I dare be bold to say [observes Timothy Nourse in 1686], that he who Frames his desires to the Circumstances of his Life, and to the Objects which lie before him, is really as happy as one that is in a warm Pursuit of all those things, which lie within the Immense Prospect of

---

[53] *Tusc. Disp.* v. xxxii. 92, which, according to Farrand Sayre (p. 110), is the oldest extant account.

[54] William Goddard, *A Satirycall Dialogve or a Sharplye-Invectiue Conference, betweene Allexander the Great, and That Truelye Woman-Hater Diogynes* (1615); Anthony Stafford, *Staffords Heauenly Dogge* (1615); Samuel Rowlands, *Diogines Lanthorne* (1607).

[55] *Ibid.*, sig. A₂ (cited from *The Complete Works of Samuel Rowlands* [3v., Glasgow, 1880], Vol. 1 [individual pagination for each work], p. 3). William Davenant used Diogenes as the representative of the ascetic Puritan, in staging a debate between him and Aristophanes on the merits of public entertainment (*The First Days Entertainment at Rutland House*, in *The Dramatic Works of Sir William D'Avenant* [5v., Edinburgh & London, 1872-1874], III, 193-230).

Mans Imagination. We have an Eminent Instance of this Truth in that famous Interview, betwixt *Alexander* and *Diogenes*, of whom the latter certainly better deserv'd the Name of Conquerour in the Dominion he gain'd over his own Desires and Appetite, and did enjoy more within the narrow Circumscription of his Tub, than the other could ever meet with in the vast Circles of the Universe."[56]

The same moral was facetiously expressed in verse by Joseph Mitchell in 1729;[57] and Anthony Collins, in his *Discourse concerning Ridicule and Irony in Writing* (1729), though reflecting the conception of Diogenes as boor, gave him the victory:

". . . Even the rude *Diogenes*, the *Cynick*, has given us a most incomparable Example [of an impressive witty saying], in his occasional Conference with *Alexander the Great*, who was put into such Temper by the mere Freedom and Raillery of the Philosopher, as to take every thing in good part he said to him, and consequently be dispos'd to reflect upon it, and to act with Discretion."[58]

Fielding's use of Diogenes, then, as the critic of Alexander's greatness was part of a common moral tradition. His inversion of this opposition, however, to present Alexander as the critic of Diogenes' hypocrisy, was rather a novel

[56] *A Discourse upon the Nature and Faculties of Man* (1686), p. 383.
[57] "THE CHARMS of INDOLENCE," *Poems on Several Occasions* (2v., 1729), I, 62:
>Thou to high-fated ALEXANDER's Face
>Maintaind'st, that Ease was nobler far than Place.
>Th' insulted World before him bow'd the Knee:
>Thou sat'st unmov'd, more Conqueror than He.

[58] P. 17. The *London Magazine* in October 1751 (pp. 455-56) printed a letter, "Diogenes *the Cynick, to* Alexander *the Great, reproaching his ambitious Proceedings*," which also placed Diogenes in a morally superior position. Against such voices a few still insisted upon condemning Diogenes, even when set against Alexander: thus Ned Ward's poem on *The Tipling Philosophers* (1710) characterizes the Cynic as "DIOGENES, Surly and Proud, / Who Snarl'd at the *Macedon* Youth" (p. 17), and adds in a note: "DIOGENES, a *Sinopese* by Birth, who fled his Country into *Athens* for Coining false Money, was so cynically Proud, that he bid *Alexander* the Great stand out of his Sunshine . . ." (p. 18).

turn—although it made use of an equally common set of assumptions about the philosopher. The joining of these ambiguous, if not contradictory, traditions in the dialogue provides it with the ironic tension that good paradox normally offers. There is, of course, nothing inherently inconsistent (psychologically) in the fact that Diogenes, although a hypocrite, can see through Alexander's claims to greatness as clearly as any philosopher, nor in the fact that Alexander, who is mad enough to consider himself the son of a god, can with equal shrewdness penetrate the ascetic pose of the Cynic. The reversal of roles as the dialogue unfolds piques the imagination and provides that fine surprise which, according to most eighteenth-century critics, was of the essence of effective writing.

Thus Fielding has, in the *Dialogue between Alexander and Diogenes* at least, improved upon Lucian; for whereas Lucian was normally content to create a mentor character, a *persona*, who would express his own skepticism of human motives and human rationalizations, Fielding has set up two figures, each of whom in turn plays the exposer and the exposed. The counterpoint of this ingenious fugue on human hypocrisy and affectation is conducted with no little skill. And in the use of the dialogue as an instrument to present his views, in the shrewd delineation of character through conversation, and in the emphasis upon contrast—both between particular characters and between an individual's avowed philosophy and his actual behavior—Fielding was working with techniques that he exploited habitually and with high artistry in his novels. The *Dialogue* offers another insight into the sources of Fielding's narrative skill, and its affinities with the Lucianic dialogue make it of particular interest as a further suggestion of that great satirist's significance for him. Finally, it is still another illustration of that amazing fertility of invention which enabled Henry Fielding to set forth the ruling con-

LUCIANIC SKETCHES

cepts of his deeply traditional moral philosophy in such a happy variety of dramatic forms and guises.

2. "AN INTERLUDE BETWEEN *Jupiter, Juno, Apollo,* and *Mercury*"

The title page of the *Interlude*, in the *Miscellanies*, says that it was "originally intended as an INTRODUCTION to a COMEDY, CALLED, JUPITER's *Descent on Earth*" (*Misc.*, I, [341]). This comedy, if any of it was actually penned, has not survived; and one can only speculate as to its probable date. Cross (I, 386) supposed that "probably the failure of 'Eurydice' had discouraged [Fielding] from proceeding with 'Jupiter's Descent on Earth.'" This is purely a guess, of course, and one might as easily imagine that the Licensing Act, which ended Fielding's dramatic career in 1737, had also nipped in the bud his comedy on Jupiter.

As a matter of fact, there is no positive evidence that the comedy was even Fielding's. It could equally well have been written by someone else, the *Interlude* alone (as a kind of prologue) being his. If this were the case, the years 1736-1737, when Fielding was managing the Little Theatre in the Haymarket, would still seem the most likely date for such a theatrical introduction.[59] One might add that the burlesque treatment of mythological characters featured in the *Interlude* was also employed in *Tumble-Down Dick* in 1736 and in *Eurydice* in 1737. On the other hand, burlesque and travesty were characteristic Fielding techniques throughout his career. Moreover, the *Interlude* is, generically, not so much a dramatic work as it is a dialogue in the manner of Lucian's *Dialogues of the Gods*—and the

[59] After 1737, Fielding had little occasion to write original drama. Of the three dramatic works by Fielding published after that date, two —*The Wedding Day* and *The Good-Natured Man*, published as *The Fathers*—had been written much earlier in his career (see the preface to the *Miscellanies*, I, xi-xiv), and the third, *Miss Lucy in Town*, acted in 1742, was a piece in which Fielding claimed to have had only "a very small Share" (*Misc.*, I [xxxvii], misnumbered xxvii).

Lucianic influence cannot be confined to any single period of Fielding's life.

A recent study has pointed out that the Juno-Jupiter pattern of the termagant and the henpecked husband repeats that of Proserpine and Pluto in *Eurydice*; and the speculation is offered that their relationship, like the Apshinken household in the *Grub-Street Opera*, represents a slanting allusion to the matrimonial difficulties of the royal household.[60] This is quite possible: such political overtones are to be looked for in Fielding. But it is necessary to remark that the husband-wife opposition exploited here is to be found throughout the whole course of his work;[61] and the allusion—however probable—cannot be accepted as dating evidence.

Cross (I, 386) made the further suggestion that the scenes which Fielding had written as the introduction

---

[60] William Peterson, "Satire in Fielding's *An Interlude between Jupiter, Juno, Apollo, and Mercury*," MLN, LXV (1950), 200-02.

[61] One may, for example, take Juno's indignant phrase, "I desire you will treat me with Good-Manners at least" (*Misc.*, I, 344), and observe its repetition by three other aggrieved Fielding matrons: Mrs. Boncour in *The Fathers*: "I desire you will treat me with good manners at least; that I think I may expect" (Henley, XII, 158); Laetitia in *Jonathan Wild*: "I flattered myself that I should at least have been used with good Manners" (*Misc.*, III, 240-41); and Mrs. James in *Amelia*: "Though you have married a tall, awkward monster, Mr. James, I think she hath a right to be treated, as your wife, with respect at least: indeed, I shall never require any more . . ." (Henley, VII, 239). Clearly, Fielding is presenting the Jupiter-Juno quarrel in the same terms he used for many of his matrimonial debates; and to imagine that he had George II and Caroline in mind every time he represented a husband and wife quarreling would be more, I am sure, than Mr. Peterson would wish to imply. I do not, incidentally, believe that his further attempts to find allusions to the royal pair in Fielding's *Interlude* are truly convincing. For example, when Juno declares that her votaries—women of strict virtue—continually rail against men, Jupiter replies that he can hear "at this Instant several grave black Gentlemen railing at Riches, and enjoying them, or at least coveting them, at the same Time" (*Misc.*, I, 345). Fielding was fond at this period of equating gravity and hypocrisy, and the assertion that those (including clergymen) who attack a vice are often those who covet or practise it was common with him. But Peterson suggests that "the 'grave black Gentlemen' may be Caroline's favorite prelates, with whom she was fond of arguing theology" (p. 201). I do not see any evidence for such a specific interpretation.

LUCIANIC SKETCHES

to a projected comedy on Jupiter were molded into an interlude "while his translation of 'Plutus' was fresh in memory." It is true that the allusions to Plutus in scene ii of the *Interlude* bear some resemblance to the attitude taken toward the god of wealth in Aristophanes' comedy, which Fielding and Young had translated, and published in May 1742. Once again, however, no clear and definite link exists: the restoration of Plutus' sight, which is the crux of the play, is not mentioned in the *Interlude*, nor is the dethronement of Jupiter in favor of Plutus more than vaguely hinted at. The allusions in the *Interlude* are, in fact, quite general enough to have been made long before Fielding ever thought of translating Aristophanes.

2

The *Interlude* consists of four "scenes" or dialogues on Olympus, leading up to Jupiter's preparation to visit the earth. In the opening scene we see "Mr. *Jupiter*" in the role of henpecked husband to the aggressively virtuous Juno:

"JUNO. . . . I desire you will treat me with Good-Manners at least. I should have had that, if I had married a Mortal, tho' he had spent my Fortune, and lain with my Chamber-Maids, as you suffer Men to do with Impunity, highly to your Honour be it spoken.

"JUP. Faith! Madam, I know but one Way to prevent them, which is, by annihilating Mankind . . ."—(*Misc.*, I, 344).

The dialogue continues in this vein till at last Juno threatens that if Jupiter will not make men better, she will go down to Earth and make women worse: "That every House may be too hot for a Husband, as I will shortly make Heaven for you." Jupiter returns that if she makes women worse he will then take Hymen and hang him: "For I will take some Care of my Votaries, as well as you of yours" (I, 346).

Scene ii finds Jupiter and Apollo in conversation. Jupiter demands, "What dost thou think the foolishest Thing a Man can do?" Apollo replies glumly, "Turn Poet"; but Jupiter insists that it is to marry (1, 346). Their conversation then turns to books, and Jupiter announces that he is extremely pleased with the dedications he has recently read. These have proved to him that there are men —those to whom the effusive dedications are addressed— of really transcendent virtue. This (along with his wife's tongue) has made him decide to visit earth "and spend some Time in such God-like Company" (1, 347).[62] He invites Apollo to accompany him, but that god replies that he has been unable to gain admission to these people; their favorite is Plutus—"The God of Riches has more Interest there, than all the other Gods put together . . ." (1, 348). Jupiter nevertheless reasserts his intention to visit the Earth and see the estimable men described "in those little Histories called Dedications" (1, 348).

The next scene presents a dialogue between Mercury, Jupiter, and Apollo. The first explains that he has been passing the time "at Blind-man's buff with the Nine Muses," and incidentally in watching a Poet on earth invoking "Miss *Thally*": "Such a Scene of Courtship or Invocation as you call it. *Say, O Thalia,* cries the Bard; and then he scratches his Head: And then, *Say, O Thalia,* again; and repeated it an hundred times over; but the devil a Word would she say" (1, 349).[63] Jupiter tells Mercury of his proposed visit, and declares that should he find "the prodigious Virtue of Mankind" as great as represented in the dedications, "I believe I shall leave Madam *Juno* for Good-and-all, and live entirely amongst Men." Mercury replies somewhat

[62] A Lucianic vision by some other hand than Fielding's appeared in the *Champion,* 19 January 1740, and pictured Jupiter coming down to earth to hear mankind's wishes (coll. ed. [2v., 1741], 1, 199-203).
[63] Cf. *Tom Jones* (VIII, i): "Lord Shaftesbury observes that nothing is more cold than the invocation of a muse by a modern; he might have added that nothing can be more absurd" (Henley, IV, 60).

skeptically: "I shall be glad to be introduced by you into the Company of these virtuous Men; for I am quite weary of the little Rogues you put me at the Head of"; and he concludes: "And I must tell you, Sir, I will be God of Rogues no longer, if you suffer it to be an establish'd Maxim, that no Rich Man can be a Rogue" (1, 350-51).

The final scene represents a discussion between Mercury and Apollo, which opens with Mercury scoffing at Jupiter's avowed purpose in visiting Earth. It is not, the winged god says, the great virtue of mankind which draws him, but the "little Virtue of Womankind rather—Do you know him no better, than to think he would budge a Step after human Virtue: Besides, Where the devil should he find it, if he would?" Apollo explains, "You have not read the late Dedications of my Votaries"; to which Mercury retorts, "Of my Votaries you mean: I hope you will not dispute my Title to the Dedications, as the God of Thieves. You make no Distinction, I hope, between robbing with a Pistol and with a Pen" (1, 351). And he insists that they are his for the same reason that Lawyers are—for their venality.

After some further discussion along this line, Mercury declares his intention of disabusing Jupiter about the virtue of earthlings: "For Men are such Hypocrites, that the greatest Part deceive even themselves, and are much worse than they think themselves to be." Apollo agrees, and adds that Jupiter, though the greatest, is far from the wisest of the Gods. True, Mercury says: "His own Honesty makes him the less suspicious of others; for, except in regard to Women, he is as honest a Fellow as any Deity in all the *Elysian Fields* . . ." (1, 354). An exchange of parting compliments then brings the scene and the *Interlude* to a close. Presumably, the play to follow would have exploited in a terrestrial setting the themes and relationships established in the introduction on Olympus.

3

The *Interlude*, as I have pointed out, is in its origins not a dramatic work, but a group of Lucianic dialogues. The dialogue is ever just a step away from drama, however, and their interrelationship in English literature has always been close.[64] Thus the manner of handling the "dramatic" problems of entrances and exits and identification of characters in the *Interlude* can profitably be compared with the practice of Lucian in his dialogues. As Bellinger has shown, Lucian included "off-stage" characters in his "action," introduced new arrivals in the midst of dialogues (anticipating them with the stock dramatic formula, "Here comes Hermes!" and the like), and made clear when any of the speakers had left the "stage." But if Fielding's dramatic devices in the *Interlude* are comparable with Lucian's, they are equally like those of his own stage plays. The four scenes of the *Interlude* could, almost without change, be placed in a typical eighteenth-century comedy and no difference in technique felt. The first scene, for example, opens in a bustle, with Jupiter crying: "PRAY be pacified":

"JUNO. It is intolerable, insufferable, and I never will submit to it.

"JUP. But, my Dear.

"JUNO. Good Mr. *Jupiter*, leave off that odious Word: You know I detest it. Use it to the Trollop V*enus*, and the rest of your Sluts. It sounds most agreeable to their Ears, but it is nauseous to a Goddess of strict Virtue"— (*Misc.*, I, 343).

Juno's exit at the end of Scene i is not marked; but Scene ii begins with *"Enter* APOLLO," and he is immediately identified by Jupiter—"*Apollo*, how dost thou?" (I, 346). At the end of Scene ii, Jupiter says: "I am eager to be with

[64] See, for instance, Elizabeth Merrill, *The Dialogue in English Literature* (N.Y., 1911), pp. 25, 32, 34, *et passim*.

him [Man], that I may make another Promotion to the Stars; and here comes my Son of Fortune to accompany us" (1, 348-49). This anticipation of Mercury introduces Scene iii, which begins with the stage-direction "MERCURY *kneels*." The three figures then on stage converse like any well-bred group in an eighteenth-century comedy:

"MERC. Pray, Father *Jupiter*, be pleased to bless me.

"JUP. I do, my Boy. What Part of Heaven, pray, have you been spending your Time in?

"MERC. With some Ladies of your Acquaintance, *Apollo* . . ."—(*Misc.*, 1, 349).

Scene iii closes with a line that clearly ushers Jupiter off stage ("JUP. We'll talk of that hereafter. I'll now go put on my travelling Cloaths, order my Charge, and be ready for you in half an Hour"—1, 351); and Apollo and Mercury are left to conduct Scene iv. The *Interlude* concludes with the social amenities, once again, of any comedy of the time:

"MERC. . . . But I shall make him [Jupiter] wait for me —Dear Mr. *Apollo*, I am your humble Servant.

"APOL. My dear *Mercury*, a good Journey to you; at your Return, I shall be glad to drink a Bottle of Nectar with you.

"MERC. I shall be proud to kiss your Hands"—(1, 354).

As the title page tells us, this group of scenes was specifically intended for the stage, as an introduction to a comedy (or, more likely, farce). But Fielding's own farces display a technique very much like that of the *Interlude*, interspersing discussion and commentary upon ideas with the mere "business" of getting characters in position to talk; and the very close resemblance to the Lucianic dialogues suggests that the latter might have played a significant part in leading Fielding away from the more sophisticated dramatic structures toward the kind of farcical "dramatic satire" that satisfied his true moral-artistic ends in the theatre. However speculative this may be, there is no doubt that the dialogue, usually with two or three "interlocutors," remained a basic structural element with Fielding even in his novels; and it is partly his skill in this form—which by its very nature demands that action, setting, and character be conveyed through the words of the speakers—that makes the conversations of the novels so lively, dramatic, and revealing of character.

4

The contemporary popularity of the dialogue as a literary form—and of the dialogues of the dead in particular—has been previously discussed (see above, *Dialogue between Alexander and Diogenes*). The Lucianic *Dialogi deorum* (*Dialogues of the Gods*), to which the *Interlude* is obviously allied, did not exert anything approaching the influence of his *Dialogi mortuorum* upon seventeenth- and eighteenth-century authors. Charles Cotton put them into comic verse in 1675 in his *Burlesque upon Burlesque: or, The Scoffer Scoft*, which was repeated in the several eighteenth-century editions of Cotton's *Works*; and it is difficult to say how much the contemporary burlesque treatments of Greek and Roman deities owe to Lucian, how much to Cotton, and how much to the general popularity of travesty and burlesque in the vein of Scarron and Butler.[65] Moreover, the French "théâtre de la foire" (and even some legitimate French drama) had frequently vulgarized or burlesqued the pagan divinities,[66] and this, too, might well have influenced the English tradition. When Addison wished, however, to illustrate by example that type of

[65] See Sturgis E. Leavitt, "Paul Scarron and English Travesty," *SP*, xvi (1919), 108-20. Lucian was a favorite subject for travesty in the Restoration period.
[66] See H. Carrington Lancaster, *Sunset: A History of Parisian Drama in the Last Years of Louis XIV, 1701-1715* (Baltimore, 1945), pp. 320-29, *et passim*. Lancaster also mentions (p. 221 and n.) that J. F. Regnard's *Les Ménechmes ou les Jumeaux* (Paris, 1706), adapted from Plautus, featured a prologue-dialogue between Apollo and Mercury, in which the poor state of comedy since the death of Molière was discussed. Fielding had in his library, incidentally, a ten-volume collection of plays from the *Théâtre de la foire*.

LUCIANIC SKETCHES

burlesque which represented "great Persons acting and speaking, like the basest among the People," his first thought was "*Lucian's Gods.*"[67] Regardless of source, it is certain that a tradition (given further impetus by the travesties of Ovid) had grown up, in which Jupiter was represented as the henpecked husband and Juno as the scolding wife. An epigram in 1727 says: "THAT speech surpasses force, is no new whim: / Jove caus'd the heav'ns to tremble; *Juno* him."[68] And the ballad-opera version in 1729 of Louis Fuzelier's *Momus fabuliste* (Paris, 1719) portrayed the pair in like terms.[69] This marital discord was furthered, of course, in the legend, by Jupiter's frequent earthly visitations. As Gay put it: "Like mortal man, great *Jove* (grown fond of change) / Of old was wont this nether world to range / To seek amours. . . ."[70] This "ranging" was often depicted on the English

[67] *Spectator* No. 249, Everyman ed., II, 239.
[68] "Lingua potentior armis," Epigram No. LXXV in [William Oldys?], *A Collection of Epigrams* (1727). Fielding's song in the *Grub-Street Opera* declares:

> Would he have curst mankind
> (If Juno's drawn to life)
> When Jupiter Pandora sent,
> He should have sent his wife. . . .
> (Henley, IX, 258)

[69] *Momus Turn'd Fabulist: or, Vulcan's Wedding. An Opera: After the Manner of the Beggar's Opera* (1729).
[70] *Trivia*, Book II, lines 107-09; *Poetical Works*, ed. G. C. Faber (1926), p. 67. In Fielding's *Tumble-Down Dick*, Jupiter is represented as a gentleman lecher, and Neptune as his procurer (Henley, XII, 29); in the *Tragedy of Tragedies* (II, 4), King Arthur compares Tom Thumb with Jupiter:

> Now in his turn to kiss, and now to fight;
> And now to kiss again. So, mighty Jove,
> When with excessive thundering tired above,
> Comes down to earth, and takes a bit—and then
> Flies to his trade of thundering back again.
> (Henley, IX, 41)

And a song in the *Grub-Street Opera* bluntly refers to him as "that whore-master Jove" (Henley, IX, 215). The ultimate source of the tradition is referred to in Nicholas Amhurst's lines on "JUPITER and CLOE" in *Poems on Several Occasions* (1720), pp. 62-63:

> Young CLOE, frolicksome and gay,
> Was reading, once upon a day,

417

stage: for example, in Crowne's court masque, *Calisto* (1675), Dryden's *Amphitryon* (1690), the anonymous *Jupiter and Io* (1735), and *The Descent of the Heathen Gods*. With *the Loves of Jupiter and Alcmena* performed at Bartholomew Fair in 1749;[71] and in many eighteenth-century treatments of the theme, Juno responded like any mortal wife, by making heaven, in Fielding's phrase, "too hot for a Husband"!

There was, besides Lucian's example, obvious classical warrant for such representations. Fielding, in the *Champion*, mentions Arbuthnot's humorous pamphlet on the subject: "A certain ingenious and learned gentleman, some years since, published a very elaborate treatise on The Art of Altercation or Scolding, wherein he proved, much to its honour, that the gods, goddesses, and heroes of the ancients, were great proficients therein, and produced several passages from Homer and others, where Juno, Venus, Pallas, &c., fight (to express myself in a proper language on this occasion) very handsome bouts thereat" (5 February 1740; Henley, xv, 183).[72] Swift had said parenthetically in *Cadenus and Vanessa*: "For Gods, we are by *Homer* told, / Can in Celestial Language scold"; and Mrs. Lennox, in 1759, was "amazed to find in Homer a scolding Juno, a brawling Thersites, a blustering Ajax, and an

---

How JOVE, as OVID's lines record
(And Ladies will take OVID's word)
Us'd to descend in borrow'd shapes,
And sport in Cuckoldoms and Rapes. . . .

[71] Cf. Allardyce Nicoll, *History of English Drama, 1660-1900* (6v., Cambridge, 1952-1959), II, 376 and 451. R. H. Griffith cites a poem called "The Progress of Deformity" in *Cythereia: or New Poems of Love and Intrigue* (published by Curll in 1723), which pictures Juno establishing a cabal of gods to punish Jupiter's earthly philandering ("The Progress Pieces of the Eighteenth Century," *Texas Review*, v [1920], 220).

[72] The work referred to was called *A Brief Account of Mr. John Ginglicutt's Treatise concerning the Altercation or Scolding of the Ancients*; published anonymously in 1731, it was reprinted in *The Miscellaneous Works of the Late Dr. Arbuthnot* (2nd ed., 2v., Glasgow, 1751), I, 40-52.

abusive Agamemnon."[73] In Fielding's own *Tumble-Down Dick*, the author, Machine, explains to Sneerwell that the first scene of his play "is in the true altercative, or scolding style of the ancients" (Henley, XII, 14). This vulgarization of classic myth, exploited also in Fielding's *Eurydice*, was something that an age steeped in the classics found inexpressibly amusing. It is, I think, less appealing today, perhaps because our approach to the classics is at once more serious and less intimate: the result is commonly a solemnity of regard that the eighteenth century displayed only in a Richard Bentley or a Zachary Pearce.

The dialogues of the *Interlude* borrow few of Lucian's major themes, which are usually drawn from the traditional myths; but they do follow the Lucianic tone and attitude toward the mythological personages—a tone which, as we have seen, was one the age could find congenial. Lucian's *Dialogues of the Gods* were normally separate and relatively independent pieces, whereas Fielding has linked the four dialogues of his *Interlude* together, though tenuously, by the theme of Jupiter's projected visit to earth. Aside from this, the material is drawn from the stock of major themes that drew his satirical attention many times elsewhere, in the plays, journals, and novels: marital difficulties, effusive dedications, the power of wealth, and the diversiform hypocrisies of men. But if there is little novelty in the *Interlude*, it is a satisfactory "curtain-raiser." The satirical strokes are lively and the characters display in their brief appearances a dramatic validity and individuality that make them engaging. If the play that the *Interlude* was planned to introduce actually was a project of Fielding's, one rather regrets the circumstances, whatever they were, that led him to lay aside his pen.

[73] *The Poems of Jonathan Swift*, ed. Harold Williams (2nd ed., 3v., Oxford, 1958), II, 695; Charlotte Lennox (transl.), *The Greek Theatre of Father Brumoy* (3v., 1759), I, vii. An entertainment at Bartholomew Fair in 1741 had the suggestive title of *The Wrangling Deities, or Venus upon Earth* (Allardyce Nicoll, *History of English Drama, 1660-1900*, II, 387).

CHAPTER VII
SOME CONCLUDING OBSERVATIONS

> Je me suis aperçu, à chaque page de ce livre, combien il est difficile de bien parler d'un auteur qui a touché à tant de choses.—Maurice Croiset, *Essai sur la vie et les œuvres de Lucien*

EACH of Henry Fielding's writings shows us, in a manner, a different person: at first thought, one has difficulty in believing that *Tom Thumb* and *The Modern Husband*, the *Essay on Conversation* and the *Essay on Nothing*, *Jonathan Wild* and *Tom Jones* could all be the products of a single author's pen. And yet Wilbur Cross (III, 274-75) is quite right in declaring that "his works, though they unroll in different patterns, were really all of a piece. No writer was ever more uniformly himself." For despite his mastery of many literary styles and his ability to adapt his ruling tone almost unerringly to the material at hand and the end desired, Fielding in his proper person remains the same. His major convictions mature and deepen and ramify, rather than truly change, as he grows older. And his own character, formed from the first upon those ideals of reasoned good-nature, virile integrity, and practical Christianity to which he consistently subscribed, shines through all of his works—whether expressed in honest indignation, jesting ridicule, or dignified and urbane criticism of life.

John Jay Chapman has spoken of Lucian in terms that in some respects seem peculiarly applicable to Fielding:

"Behind the cutting irony and savage invective of the dialogues there is a benevolent person whose philosophy of life is sunny. This may seem to be too simple a summary of a man who wrote under so many dazzling disguises; but when you have read one of Lucian's dialogues, you have

SOME CONCLUDING OBSERVATIONS

the key to all of them. In truth, he expresses the whole of himself in each one of them. His ideas are few: the variety of the symbols by which he expresses them is all but miraculous."[1]

I have argued that Fielding's ironic vision and his concern to give equal weight to many antipodal values make for a highly complex texture in his fiction: but his ruling moral conceptions, like Lucian's, were few and relatively uncomplicated. Fielding possessed that "freedom of wise simplicity," which has been called "the last gift that the reluctant muse yields to her servants."[2] But if his personal philosophy and world vision can be summed up without undue recourse to the jargon of the schools, it is not less true that "the variety of the symbols by which he expresses them is all but miraculous." To appreciate fully the enormous power of invention that Fielding displayed in giving life and form to his ruling ideas, one must know his works as a whole: the novels, though transcendently his greatest achievement, do not present all the surfaces of his genius.

The *Miscellanies* offer, in this regard, a rich sampling of his efforts in a number of genres. Some are frankly experiments, some are purely bagatelles, but all the various items we have surveyed from Volume One, even the youthful verses, testify to the wide range of his interests and powers and to the imaginative boldness with which he approached the central problem of incorporating his ideas and convictions in useful and delightful literary forms. *Utile et dulce* was not a dead phrase to Fielding: it was the central conception about which all of his writing revolved. And he experimented endlessly until he found in the "comic prose epic" the particular medium ideally suited to his own unique qualities of imagination.

[1] *Lucian, Plato, and Greek Morals* (Boston & N.Y., 1931), pp. 14-15.
[2] David Worcester, *The Art of Satire* (Cambridge, Mass., 1940), p. 60. Worcester is here speaking of Rabelais.

SOME CONCLUDING OBSERVATIONS

I have not sought in these essays to impose upon the first volume of the *Miscellanies* a unity of thought or purpose that Fielding himself disavowed; but clearly enough certain themes bulk large—and others I have thought proper to emphasize in countering a tendency to read eighteenth-century works too exclusively with twentieth-century eyes.

Fielding's vital concern with manners (implying not only "the unbought grace of life" but the crucial interdependence of the social and the moral) is attested in almost every piece. One cannot be surprised, of course, to find that the celebration of that complex of values summed up for Fielding in "good-nature" and the infinitely varied critical anatomy of "greatness" are both carried on throughout this volume, and not only in the poems dedicated particularly to them. The search for an ideal selflessness and a valid social conscience may sound, to a generation nurtured on fragmented complexities and abstruse symbols, rather puerile: but the literary embodiment of this search (that in fact continues to occupy the talents of our own best writers) is no puerile thing. Even the finest poesy of the pure aesthete must ultimately in some measure confront the relation of man and his society—and to do so in loathing and despair is not necessarily a more mature or profound approach to the problem, than to do so in openness and love.

I have already set down my belief that the realization of the *civitas bona* offered a guiding inspiration to Fielding, an inspiration that shaped and gave focus to his aims as a comic moralist, as it also accorded with his temperamental aversion for the "unsocial" vices and approbation of those virtues that make for an harmonious society. But, as I have argued before, he was not altogether sanguine concerning the establishment of this heavenly city on man's corrupted earth. For Fielding, man was not *animal bonus*, but only *bonus capax*; and perfectibility was not the automatic result of a benevolent historical process. If he looked

SOME CONCLUDING OBSERVATIONS

with tolerance and laughter upon the inevitable frailties (though not the capacity for egoism or malice) of humankind, he also shrewdly assessed the social failure that such frailties betokened. Nevertheless his faith in principles remained. He did not despair (not even in his most nearly despairing work, *Amelia*); but neither did he regard with complacency the hard facts of the human situation. Only the most naive conception of comedy will suppose that it was necessary for him to do so.

Indeed, as I have particularly argued in connection with the essay, *Of the Remedy of Affliction*, Fielding's pleasure in the ludicrous aspects of man's pilgrimage was tempered and given depth by his consciousness of the shadows that also marked that journey. The measure of his comedy is that it could embrace these sadder truths with full comprehension and yet remain a yea-saying acceptance of life and of the fascinating, pathetic, amusing, and damnable nature of man. Optimistic, in any simple sense, his work is not: the road is too hard and human nature too refractory for simple or automatic guarantees of bliss. But hopeful it is: for the great end of comedy is spiritual reassurance and the assertion of the essential community of man. The fictional worlds that Henry Fielding created are worlds in which "happy endings" occur, because this is the *mythos* of comedy. The successful resolution of difficulties is the very essence of the comic mode, and it is neither more nor less *true* as a prospect of reality than the merely unhappy conclusion or the "open" ending in vogue today. But I have tried to show that, though the comic mode of the novels demands happy endings and though Fielding's constitutional hopefulness made such resolutions pleasant to him, they do not represent the totality of his vision. "All's well that ends well" does not sum up his comic world any more than it does that of Shakespeare.

Fielding's work, like that of most great comic writers, remains very close to the norm of human nature, constantly

SOME CONCLUDING OBSERVATIONS

reminding us how little that basic nature has changed, despite varying mores and fashions—and the varying fashions of the literature that describes them. In great comedy we are always very close to the abiding center of human personality and human experience. In the hands of a master, comedy becomes a profound analysis of the human condition that denies the hopelessness of that condition. Perhaps Fielding was, for the modern world, somewhat too optimistic in supposing that a decent regard for others and a reasonably balanced mental life for oneself were within every uncorrupted (nonpsychopathic) man's attaining. On the other hand, though this belief lay at the heart of his conception of good-nature and, indeed, of his adjurations as a moralist, it was not altogether unqualified. True greatness, the "true sublime," for instance, was not within every person's grasp. Nevertheless, everyone was responsible for honoring it and for recognizing and denying the pretensions of the false. Even a consistent "good-nature" Fielding believed (or so I have argued) was not possible to everyone; but everyone was, once again, responsible for his conduct toward his fellows and for honoring the ideal of a true human community. If there was, as I have suggested, an element of determinism in Fielding's conception of human character, it was largely confined to those psychopathic, antisocial beings who were insensible to moral or humane urging. Fielding's primary emphasis was—despite the truth of Cross' remark (III, 276) that "he threw the emphasis on the unheroic side of human nature"—always upon the moral *responsibility* of the normal individual. Sometimes, inconsistently enough perhaps, he insisted upon that of the *lusus naturae* himself: for comedy has this "limitation," that it must consider moral evil as responsible villainy.

The examination of Fielding's congruent views on such seemingly unrelated subjects as liberty and good-breeding and hypocrisy has shown, I think, the essential integrity

SOME CONCLUDING OBSERVATIONS

of his social-moral-political *Weltansicht*. He was a profound conservative in an era of turbulent and disturbing innovation; and his attitudes were shaped by a high conception of the need for responsible conduct in human life. Contemporary democratic sentiment will surely boggle at Fielding's social and political estimate of the lower classes: but this bias clearly did not prevent him from admiring honest worth and humanity in whatever guise they appeared. Again, the moral formalist today as in Fielding's own time will quarrel with his ethics: but the vast human warmth and the tolerance of mortal frailty that light up his work will, we may hope, always hold their ground against the ascetic and the censorial mentality that represented to Fielding all that was most warped and twisted in the human soul.

As some of my essays have for purposes of analysis tended to emphasize the "dualities" or "polarities" of Fielding's thought, I am the more concerned in these concluding remarks to insist upon the essential integrity of his views. Bishop Hoadly is supposed to have said of Dr. Sherlock that he had not only a tendency, but even a "gravitation" to inconsistency:[3] the undisguised exposition of the *Miscellanies* may at first lead one to believe that Fielding was subject to no less a gravitation. I do not believe for a moment that he escaped inconsistency (few thinking men have); but the contradictions in his thought do not represent mere confusion. Indeed, I have been moved to argue that many of the "inconsistencies" in Fielding's view of man and of what was needful for him proved intellectually and dramatically fruitful in his fiction. He was a man of very strong convictions: but he was rescued from any danger of bigotry as he was rescued from the literary danger of mere didacticism by the *felt pull* of contrary

[3] Cf. *The Conversation of Gentlemen Considered* [by John Constable?] (1738), p. 241.

SOME CONCLUDING OBSERVATIONS

positions that both his essential fair-mindedness and his self-critical native irony urged him to weigh and consider—and inevitably to dramatize. As I have argued, this play of opposed ideas in Fielding's prose fiction makes no small contribution to its complex fabric. And it provokes, not the bitterness that attends mere perverse logomachies, but the exhilaration that arises from engagement in an honest moral struggle.

The poems and essays and humorous sketches of the first volume of the *Miscellanies* reinforce in many details our consciousness of Fielding's moral construct, informed by a very personal reading of latitudinarian Christianity, an intimate regard for the wisdom of Aristotelian and Stoic moral principles, and a wide-ranging direct experience of man and society at every level. One need not, of course, entirely accept a great writer's world view (Homer or Dante being obvious cases in point) to appreciate his literary merit. But the reflective reader, in addition to pleasing his learned taste for intricacies of style or structure, properly seeks in literature a link with humanity, a thoughtful rendering of a deeply felt experience of life. One need not share all of Fielding's opinions to share his concern with and his delight in the drama of human nature. To be sure, a number of his individual prejudices and convictions (particularly as they are seen in the starker nonfictional modes of the *Miscellanies*) would be labeled not only unfashionable but unforgivable today. It does not seem to me merely a paradox to suggest that they have for precisely that reason the greater value in teasing us into thought. To echo (with proper pontificality) Johnson on friendship—one's values should be kept in constant repair. No sharper tool can be found to this end than the honest entertainment of ideas and attitudes that challenge reigning assumptions and that foster an ironic, a healthily skeptical, habit of mind under the imperious tyranny of the currently *fashionable*—whether it flourish in morals or in literature.

SOME CONCLUDING OBSERVATIONS

These essays have (of necessity) been somewhat less extensively concerned with the conscious artistry of Fielding's novels. But the detailed analyses of his formal satires and the examination of his formal style may have suggested something of the care with which his minor pieces were constructed and of the attention to technique that marked them. The implications for his larger and greater works are surely obvious. Fielding deserves all the praise that has been bestowed upon his extraordinary plotting in *Tom Jones*; but it is perhaps time to examine in more detail the contribution that finer strokes of the brush have made to the novels' enduring comic power (normally a most perishable commodity) and to their continuing acuity and freshness.

Fielding opened the preface to the *Miscellanies* with the modest observation:

"THE Volumes I now present the Public, consist, as their Title indicates, of various Matter; treating of Subjects which bear not the least Relation to each other; and perhaps, what *Martial* says of his Epigrams, may be applicable to these several Productions.

Sunt bona, sunt quædam mediocria,
sunt mala PLURA.

At least, if the *Bona* be denied me, I shall, I apprehend, be allowed the other Two"—(*Misc.*, I, i-ii).

Measured against the supreme achievement of the novels, most of the pieces we have surveyed are as literature undeniably *mediocria* (that is, of a middle flight). Taken on their own terms, however, they represent more than merely competent exercises in a variety of genres, and I have tried to demonstrate that they are frequently informed by that same combination of high seriousness and comic sense of the incongruous which Fielding brought to his novels. In the essays, the serious tone is dominant and properly so; but the satires and the Lucianic pieces are delightful minor effusions and display to the full that vast ingenuity of invention which is the hallmark of Fielding the formal satirist. And the variety of forms and genres which he attempted in the *Miscellanies* is testimony to the experimental temper and literary boldness that made it possible for Henry Fielding to be "the founder of a new province of writing"—a province for which he would dare to make what laws he pleased.

INDEX

An asterisk indicates that the person was a subscriber to the *Miscellanies*. Works cited, except anonymous or periodical publications, will be found under the author's name. The following abbreviations and short titles are employed: *Dialogue* (*A Dialogue between Alexander the Great and Diogenes the Cynic*); F (Fielding); *Misc.* (*Miscellanies by Henry Fielding, Esq.*); *Of the Characters of Men* (*An Essay on the Knowledge of the Characters of Men*); *Some Papers* (*Some Papers Proper to Be Read before the Royal Society*).

A

A., D., *Whole Art of Converse*, 168n, 178.
*Abney, William, of the Inner Temple, 16.
abnormal (*lusus naturae*), F not concerned with, 332-36; Lucian and F on, 367-68, 369; morally responsible, 424.
accumulation (*congeries*), in *Essay on Nothing*, 283-84; in F's Demosthenes, 354. See also rhetoric.
Adams, Joseph Quincy, 403n.
*Adamson, Mr. [Thomas?], of Lincoln's Inn, 16.
Addison, Joseph, 24, 57n, 79, 108n, 179, 185, 378, 379; good-nature, moral virtue and natural, 68-69n; liberty, 91-92, 130; on Lucian, 416-17; on physiognomy, 193n; *Cato*, 20, 103, 255; *Dialogues upon the Usefulness of Ancient Medals*, 394; "Letter from Italy," 91-92; *Spectator*, 68-69n, 193n, 248, 248n, 416-17; *Whig Examiner*, 307, 309. See also *Spectator*, *Tatler*.
Style of, cadences, 152, 161n; "copiousness," 152, 157-58; development of "Senecan amble," 155-56; F's greater fervor than, 151; F's less "modern" than, 159; John Mason on, 156; Johnson on, 150; paratactic, for "characters," 159n; Tillotson's influence on, 156.
Adlerfeld, Gustaf, *Military History of Charles XII*, translated by F, 6, 338, 398n.

Admonitions from the Dead, in Epistles to the Living, scolds F, 78-79.
Aeschines, 348.
Aeschylus, Parson Adams and, 342n; *Prometheus Bound*, 276n.
affectation, 193-94; preface to *JA* on, 175n, 200n. See also hypocrisy, vanity.
Agincourt, 90.
Aitken, George A., 328n.
Akenside, Mark, "A British Philippic," 346-47 and n.
Alcidamas, 303.
Alcmena, 123.
Alexander the Great, 297; confrontation with Diogenes, 405-07; contrasted by Rooke with George II, 54; criminal conqueror, 398-401; in Fénelon, 396n; F's censures of, 401-02; in F's *Dialogue*, 386-409; in F's *Of True Greatness*, 386; heroic conception of, 399n; in Lucian, 390; Nathaniel Lee's portrait of, 88n.
allegory, F's satiric, in drama, 274, in poetry, 273. See also poetry, satire.
Allen, Ralph, 5n; Pope and *Misc.*, 25, 27.
Allestree, Richard (attrib.), *Art of Patience*, 239n, 244, 246 and n.
Allinson, Francis G., 365n.
alliteration, in F's poetry and prose, 38, prose, 158. See also style.
ambiguity, in satire, 288-89. See also duality, rhetoric.
ambition, 52, 64, 282-83, 284; in Alexander, 386, 388, 398; in false greatness, 49, 51; satirized,

INDEX

297, 312; in women, 106. *See also* greatness.
Ambrose, Saint, 240, 242.
America, 19, 24.
Amhurst, Nicholas, *Poems on Several Occasions*, 417-18n.
Amphitheatrum sapientiae socraticae joco-seriae, see Dornavius, Caspar.
amplification (*auxesis, amplificatio*), Aristotle and Quintilian on, 281; in epideictic oratory, 281; in *Essay on Nothing*, 282-84. See also rhetoric.
anacoluthon, frequent in F, 159. See also style.
anadiplosis (form of repetition), in Demosthenes, 353. See also rhetoric.
analogy, see comparison.
anaphora (initial repetition), 154; in Demosthenes, 353; in F's poetry, 37. See also rhetoric.
Anaxagoras, subject of *exemplum*, 231n.
Andrew, Sarah, Cross connects with F's version of Juvenal, 138; F's affair with, 138 and n.
Anne, Queen, 320n, 322n.
Annual Register, anecdote in 1762 about F, 26n.
Antal, Friedrich, 111-12n, 193n.
anticlimax, in F's poetry, 37; in *Some Papers*, 325. See also rhetoric.
antifeminism, see women.
antimetabole (transposed repetition), in Senecan prose and heroic couplet, 38-39. See also rhetoric.
antiquary, satire of, in *Essay on Nothing*, 293, 312.
Antisthenes, 403.
antistrophe (end repetition), in *Some Papers*, 325. See also rhetoric.
antithesis (*antitheton*), in F's Demosthenes, 354; in F's poetry, 36-37; in Senecan prose and heroic couplet, 38-39; in *Some Papers*, 280. See also rhetoric.
Apelles, 371.
Apollo, 409ff, 416n.
Apollonius, see Plutarch.

Apuleius, Lucius, 384.
Arbuthnot, Dr. John, subscribed to Mitchell's poems, 25; *Brief Account of Mr. John Ginglicutt's Treatise*, 418 and n; *Miscellaneous Works*, 311n, 418n.
Argumentorum ludicrorum, 299n.
*Argyll, John Campbell, 2nd Duke of, 17; bravery complimented, 173; true greatness in, 46.
Aristophanes, 311, 365, 370, 371, 406n; censured for ridiculing Socrates, 73n; paradoxical encomia in, 303; *The Frogs*, 395-96n; *Plutus*, translated by F and Young, 8, 17, 138, 140, 338, 343, 361, 363, 411.
Aristotle, 67, 70, 177n, 205, 254, 426; cited by F, 84-85, in Greek, 342; decorum, 221; *genera* and ends of orations, 156; man a social animal, 167; modes of proof, 284-88; philosophy as habit of virtue, 265n; on physiognomy, 192; on prudence, 227-28n; to be read in Greek, 343; source of ideal greatness, 48n; *Nicomachean Ethics*, 69n, 76, 219n, 220n, 227-28n; *Politics*, 84-85, 167; *Rhetoric*, 146n, 147, 263, 281, 284-88.
army, jest on, in F's Juvenal, 140; mercenaries, 356-57; satire of generals, 378; soldiers, 93n; standing, 356-57; subscribers to *Misc.* from, 24.
Arnot, Hugo, *Essay on Nothing*, 301.
Arrian (Flavius Arrianus), *Anabasis*, 406; translated by John Rooke, 54.
arrogance, see contempt.
ars moriendi, tradition of, 248 and n. See also death.
art, disguises nature, 116; nature and, complementary, 223.
Art of Complaisance or the Means to Oblige in Conversation, The, see C., S.
Art of Conversation, The, reworking of Guazzo (q.v.), 174 and n.
Art of Patience under All Afflictions, The, see Allestree, Richard.

430

INDEX

Art of Thriving, The, 191.
ascetic, Diogenes as, 386ff; F's antipathy toward, 425.
asyndeton (omission of conjunctions), in F's Demosthenes, 354; in F's poetry, 37. See also rhetoric.
atheism, *see* religion.
Athenian Oracle, The, 301n, 404.
Athens, 344ff, 388.
Ault, Norman, 300n.
aura popularis, *see* society.
Aurelius Antoninus, Marcus, 256, 303; difference from Old Stoa, 258; F's admiration for, 257.
Autarchy: or, The Art of Self-Government, see B., G.
authors, satirized, 295, 312.
auxesis, *see* amplification.
avarice, 49, 169, 284, 297, 312; crime against society, 332-36; epigrams on miser, 131-32; F's hatred of, 332; Lucian and F on, 367; misery of, 334; satirized in *Some Papers*, 321ff, 333ff; sin of the reason, 335-36; traditional censure of, 334-35.
Avery, Emmett L., 134n.
"Axylus" (pseudonym of F), letter of, to *CGJ*, 69n, 212.

B

B., G. (George Burghope?), *Autarchy*, 51-52n, 77n.
Babbitt, Frank C., 229n.
Bacon, Sir Francis, 405n.
Baker, Henry, *Natural History of the Polype*, 326n.
Baker, John R., 316n.
Baker, Sheridan, 36n.
balance, in F and Lucian, 378-80. See *also* parallelism, style.
Balguy, John, *Foundation of Moral Goodness*, 68n.
"Ballad on Nothing, A," in *London Magazine*, 301.
Banerji, Hiran K., 366n.
Banier, Antoine, Abbé, *Mythology and Fables of the Ancients*, 338 and n.
Barber, John, monument to Butler, 133.

Barbeyrac, Jean, on law of nature, 333n.
*Barker, Dr. John, 19n.
Barnard, Sir John, praised by F, 44.
*Barrington, William Wildman (Barrington-Shute), 2nd Viscount, 17, 18.
Barrow, Isaac, 69n, 86, 245n, 334-35, 400; funeral sermons, 245; on great men, 53-54n; latitudinarian, 67; on natural goodness, 208; reason in grief, 243-44; style no model for prose, 156n; tolerance of hypocrite, 202-03n.
Bartholomew Fair, 418, 419n.
Basore, John W., 229n.
Batchelor's Estimate of the Expences of a Married Life, The, 109.
Bateson, Frederick W., 114n.
Bath, 25, 30, 136-37, 137n, 140, 165.
*Bath, William Pulteney, Earl of, 17; possibly glanced at in poem to Hayes, 116n.
Bathurst, Allen Bathurst, 1st Baron (later 1st Earl), 20.
*Bathurst, Henry (later 2nd Earl Bathurst), 20.
*Bathurst, Peter, 17, 19n.
Battestin, Martin C., 7, 20, 66n, 191n.
*Bayntun-Rolt, Edward, 18, 19n.
beau, claim to greatness, 45; Demosthenes a, 364; metaphor of critic, 36; ridiculed, 172, 186; satiric poems on, 130-31.
*Beaufort, Henry Somerset Scudamore, 3rd Duke of, 20.
beauty, wives chosen for, 103ff.
Beccuti, Francesco (Il Coppetta), 299n.
*Bedford, Gertrude Russell, Duchess of, 22n.
*Bedford, John Russell, 4th Duke of, 17.
beggars, 168-69 and n; F's censure of, 85n; insight into human nature, 200-01; life of, superior to ambition, 52.
Behn, Aphra, *Emperor in the Moon*, 326.
Bellegarde, Jean Baptiste Morvan

INDEX

de, on complaisance, 178-79; a favorite with F, 177; on flattery, 201n; on politeness, 186; Reflexions upon Ridicule, 177n, 178-79, 186, 196n, 201n.
Bellinger, Alfred R., 391n, 414.
benevolence, 198, 225, 360; Balguy's case against, 68n; example of, in *Essay on Conversation*, 170; Hawkins' attack on, 69, 79-80; natural to man, 66, 73-74; preached by nonlatitudinarians, 67. *See also* benevolism, charity, good-nature, goodness, human nature, virtue.
benevolism, 206; against conquerors, 398-99; against Stoics, 254n, 255-56, 258; sentimental, avoided by F, 76.
Bentinck, William, 319, 324 and n.
Bentley, Richard, 125, 419.
Berenger, Moses, 19.
Berenger, Penelope (Temple), wife of Moses, 19.
*Berenger, Richard, 19, 25.
Berkeley, George, Bishop of Cloyne, *Alciphron*, 394.
*Berkeley, George, Master of St. Katherine's by the Tower, 26n.
*Berkeley, Norborne, 18.
*Bertie, Norreys, 18.
Bible, *see* Scripture.
Billingsley, Nicholas, *Cosmobrephia*, 300.
Birch, Thomas, his *Lives* published by subscription, 25n.
Blackmore, Sir Richard, 309, 310n.
Blackwall, Anthony, *Introduction to the Classics*, 174n.
Blanchard, Frederic T., 26n, 27n, 28n, 78n.
Blanchard, Rae, 43n, 209n, 255n.
*Blandford, Maria Godolphin, Marchioness of, 21-22.
Blandy, Mary, 22.
Blenheim, 90.
Bloom, Edward A., 103n.
Boethius, Anicius Manlius Severinus, *De consolatione philosophiae*, 242.
Boheme, Anthony, actor, 125n, 126.
Bolingbroke, Henry St. John, Viscount, 20, 156n, 274; essays, 146. *See also* F's *A Fragment of a Comment on Lord Bolingbroke's Essays*.
Bond, Richmond P., 310n.
Bonnet, Charles, Swiss naturalist, 317.
booksellers, unscrupulous, 337.
Booth, Barton, 20, 125n, 126.
*Bootle, Thomas, Chancellor to the Prince of Wales, 17.
Bowmont, Robert Ker, styled Marquess of, *see* Roxburghe.
Bowyer, William, the younger, printed third volume of *Misc.*, 13.
Boyce, Benjamin, 240n, 365-66n, 396n.
Boyer, Abel, *see* English Theophrastus.
Boyle lecturers, 294n.
Boyse, Samuel, *The Deity*, quoted by F, 32.
Brauer, George C., 176n, 185n.
*Brereton, Owen Salusbury, 23.
*Brewster, Dr. Thomas, 137, 165-66; alluded to in *TJ*, 23; allusion to his translation of Persius, 165 and n; question of death of, 165-66 and n.
Bristol, 25, 26n.
British Apollo, The, 301n.
Brown, Ralph S., Jr., 18n.
Brown, Thomas (Tom), 36, 394; influenced by Lucian, 365n; mock encomia, 306 and n; translation of Lucian, 159n; translations of Sulpicius and Cicero, 247n; "A Consolatory Letter," 247n.
Browne, James P., 28
Brumoy, Pierre, *Greek Theatre*, transl. Charlotte Lennox, 419n.
Brutus, Marcus Junius, 261.
Bryant, Donald C., 148n.
Bryling, Nicolaus, 348n.
Buckingham, John Sheffield, Duke of, "On Vanity," 404.
Bullitt, John M., 308n.
Bunyan, John, 51n.
Buresch, Carolus [Charles], 240n.
Burgess, Theodore C., 240n, 303n.
Burghope, George, *see* B., G.
Burke, Edmund, 99n.

432

INDEX

Burkitt, William, *Expository Notes on the New Testament*, 196.
burlesque, criticism, 274; F's early bent for, 120, 142, 276; in F's plays, 274, 276, satires, 276n, 277, verse, 31, 137-42; history, 274; of Juvenal, 137ff; in Lucian, 379; of mythological characters, 409, 416-19; in Restoration, 308; of Virgil, 135-36. See also drama, poetry, satire.
*Burlington, Richard Boyle, 3rd Earl of, 17.
Burnet, Gilbert, Bishop of Salisbury, latitudinarian, 67.
Burns, Robert, 301-02.
Burroughs, Thomas, *Soveraign Remedy*, 244, 245 and n.
Bury, John B., 28n.
Butler, Harold E., 146-47n, 280n.
Butler, Samuel, 370, 416; attacks on Royal Society, 326; F's epitaph on, 133; F's indebtedness to, in burlesque of Juvenal, 138, 139n; legend of his death, 133 and n; poetic model for F, 31-32; *Hudibras*, 138, 139n, 196; Hudibrastic tradition, 126.
Butt, John, 300n, 322n.

C

C., S., *The Art of Complaisance*, 178, 179n.
cadence, 152, 279. See also cursus, style, velox.
Caesar, Gaius Julius, 297; linked with Alexander, 399n, 400, 401.
Callan, Norman, 339n.
Calthrop, Annette, 403n.
Cambridge, 114n, 306.
*Cardigan, George Brudenell, 4th Earl of, 20.
Carey, Henry, 109n; *A Dissertation on Dumpling*, 310, 311n; *Namby-Pamby*, 309, 310n; "Sally in our Alley," 25.
*Carey, Mr. [Henry?], subscriber to *Misc.*, 25.
Caroline, Queen, 410 and n.
Carrus, Nicolaus (Nicolas Carr), Latin translation of Demosthenes, 348n.

Carter, Elizabeth, 78.
Carteret, John Carteret, Baron (later Earl Granville), tribute to, 46; probable allusion to, 325n.
Castiglione, Baldassare, 177.
Cato, Marcus Porcius, Uticensis, 255.
Caxton, William, 248.
*Cay, John, *Abridgement of Publick Statutes*, 22.
"Celia," poems to, 122-27, not all addressed to Charlotte Cradock, 122-23.
censorial court, in F's journals, 274. See also satire.
censoriousness, attacked, 195-97, 198-99, 202-03, in F's novels and plays, 202-05, in *Of Good-Nature*, 58-59; deliberate vice, 336; in Diogenes, 386ff, 398, 405; theme in *Misc.*, 425.
ceremony, courtesy-books on, 175 and n; distinguished from "civility," 176; essential to good breeding, 169, 176, 187-88; F's balanced view on, 176; form not substance, 169; maintains structure of society, 102; satirized in *Amelia*, 182.
Cervantes Saavedra, Miguel de, 370, 378; dignity and humor in, 163; influence on F's style, 157; "Sancho" in F's poem, 123; *Don Quixote*, 233n.
Chaigneau, William (attrib. author), *History of Jack Connor*, epigraph from *Misc.* in, 27.
Chaloner, Thomas, 304.
Chamberlayne, John, *Magnae Britanniae Notitia*, 21n.
Chapman, John Jay, 420-21.
Chapone, Hester (Mulso), censures F's morality, 78.
characters, delineation of, by dialogue, 408, 416; in *Essay on Conversation*, 169ff, 181-82, expanded in novels, 182-84; F's objections to perfect, in fiction, 223 and n, 270n; use of, in courtesy-books, 169.
character-writers, see Theophrastus.
charity, 87; active and rational nature of, 64; Allworthy on, 210;

433

INDEX

avarice negation of, 334; commanded by Law of Nature, 333n; identified with good-nature, 58, 63-65; proportioned to merit, 60 and n. See also benevolence, good-nature.
Charles II, 283, 298.
Charles XII, of Sweden, 398 and n, 402. See also Adlerfeld, Gustaf.
Chedworth, John Howe, 4th Baron, allusion to Misc., 28.
*Chesterfield, Philip Dormer Stanhope, 4th Earl of, 17, 20n, 179, 291, 403n; complimented in *Of Good-Nature*, 60; linked with F and Swift, on politeness, 27n; praised by raillery, 173; true greatness in, 46.
Chew, Audrey, 256n.
chiasmus, in F's poetry, 36-37. See also rhetoric.
*Cholmondeley, George Cholmondeley, 3rd Earl, 20.
Choyce Drollery, 307.
Churchill, Anna Maria (Walpole), 20.
Churchill, General Charles, brother of Marlborough, 24.
*Churchill, General Charles, natural son of former, 20-21, 24.
"Chrysipus" (the English guinea), in *Some Papers*, 278, 318ff; virtues of, 324.
Cibber, Colley, 125n.
Cicero, Marcus Tullius, 85n, 177n, 223, 240, 240n, 247n, 254, 257, 258n, 259, 379; analogue to essay, 146 and n; authority on conversation, 174n; *beneficentia* and good-nature, 60n; cited by F, 238, in *Amelia*, 244n, in *TJ* by Square, 262n; cited in sermons, 244; on consolation, 229, 230n, 231-32, 233n, 234n, 235n, 236n, 237n, 238n, 240, 242, 243, 246n; *copia verborum* of, 152ff; cumulative effect of suspended period in, 155; death not an evil, 238; dialogue, 393, 394n, 395n; F's admiration for, 257, 261, 363; *humanitas* and good-nature, 67; levels of style, 161n; source of ideal greatness, 48n; status of a case, 292; variation in divisions of oration, 149; on wisdom, 258; *Ad Atticum*, 249; *De consolatione* (spurious), 250-51 and n; *De inventione*, 65; *De officiis*, 60n, 257, 258n; *De oratore*, 146n, 152, 292; *De partitione oratoria*, 146n, 149; *De senectute*, 237, 244n, 246n; *Epistulae ad familiares*, 229n, 230n, 232n, 236n, 238n, 240, 246n; *Orator*, 292; *Tusculan Disputations*, 208n, 219n, 229, 230n, 231n, 231-32n, 233n, 234n, 235n, 237n, 239n, 240, 242, 243, 244n, 262n, 406.
city versus country, theme in F, 127.
civility, distinguished from ceremony, 176.
civitas bona, see society.
Clarendon, Edward Hyde, Earl of, essays, 146.
Clark(e), Elizabeth, see Harris, Elizabeth (Clark).
*Clark(e), John, 18-19.
*Clark(e), John, Jr., 18-19.
Clarke, Martin L., 339n.
Clarke, Samuel, 203n, 294n; affliction is providential, 245n; distinction between benevolism of, and F's, 68-69; funeral sermons, 245; rationalist, 67; *Sermons on Several Subjects*, 194, 245n.
class, behavior to superiors, equals, and inferiors, 170 and n; F's conservative views on, 425; F's sympathy for every, 100-01; good breeding not a matter of, 173, 186; hierarchy of, must be respected, 99-101, 168-69, 170, 176-77, 312-14; liberty different for each, 98-100; mercantile world ill-bred, 198; natural not political equality, 100-01; titles, gloss over vice, 49, respect for, necessary, 168-69, 170, 312-14, satire of empty, 283, 296, 312-14.
lower, F urges condescension to, 171-72; F's increasing sternness toward, 96-98, 101n; F's

434

INDEX

political distrust of, 96, 101n, 302; worthy and unworthy, 101n. *upper*, company of, essential for social grace, 97, 186-88; F attacked, for failing responsibility, 102, insolence, 177, marriages, 103ff, 105n, 112; F nearer to values of, 188; "mob" includes, 101; vices of, moral but not political evil, 102n. *See also* good breeding, liberty, society.

classics, 270; on abstinence from revenge, 72n; attack on avarice in, 334; *consolatio* (*see* consolation); F's ethical debt to, 67; F's intimate approach to, 419; liberty and republicanism of, 90; not for general conversation, 181-82; oration as structure for essay, 146; paradoxical encomium, 302ff; translation, 337-44. *See also* Greek, Latin.

Claudius Caesar, 245n.
Clayton, Sir Robert, 247n.
Cleanthes of Assos, Stoic philosopher, Cicero's criticism of, 230.
clergy, priests attacked in *Liberty*, 89; satirized, 410n; subscribers to *Misc.* among, 23. *See also* religion.
Clifford, James L., 93n.
*Clive, Catherine (Kitty), 24; allusion to in F's Juvenal, 141.
*Cobham, Anne Temple, Viscountess, 19.
*Cobham, Richard Temple, 1st Viscount, 17, 113-17; the "Cobham cousinhood," 19.
cola (sing. *colon*, integral member of a period), analysis in terms of, 153-54. *See also* rhetoric.
Coley, William B., 48n, 163n.
Collection of Epigrams, A, see Oldys, William.
Collection of Miscellany Letters, A, 241n.
Collection of Poems in Six Volumes, A, see Dodsley, Robert.
*Collier, Arthur, LL.D., 19n.
Collier, Jane, 19n.
Collier, Jeremy, *Essays*, 67.
Collier, John Payne, 300n.
Collier, Margaret, 19n.

Collins, Anthony, 294n; *Discourse concerning Ridicule*, 407.
Collins, William, *Persian Eclogues*, 13-14n.
comedy, abstract pattern of, 271; bawdry in, 369-70; close to norm of human nature, 423-24; ends of, 423; evil impotent in, 76; of humours, 275; Lucian and, 366ff; of manners, 274; moral evil in, 424; providential order in, 275; reassurance of, 270; reconciles to human situation, 275; satire and, 274-75. *See also* drama, satire.
 Fielding's, commentary in, 275; complex nature of, 144-45; darker element gives depth to, 9, 144-45, 206, 250, 271, 275, 423; ends of, serious, 263-64, 427; goodness often foolish in, 264-66; human dualism in, 115, 269.
commentary, in F and Lucian, 385; F's, achieves comic control, 275, combines conjunction and disjunction, 289-90, in farces and dialogues, 415, personal relationship of, 278, rehearsal plays and, 278, in satire, 288.
Common Sense, on dialogue, 394-95n; praise of silence in, 310n; translations of Demosthenes in, 345-46, 345n; war-party in, 345 and n.
comparison (analogy, parallel), in F's Demosthenes, 355, *Essay on Nothing*, 283, 295, *Some Papers*, 321ff; in F and Lucian, inverted, 376-77, pictorial, 371, 376. *See also* rhetoric.
complaint, F's amorous, 118-19, burlesque, 119-20. *See also* poetry, satire.
complaisance, *see* good breeding.
congeries, see accumulation.
Congreve, William, subscribed to Mitchell's poems, 25; "Of Pleasing," quoted by F in *JA*, 175n.
conqueror, claim to greatness satirized, 43; moral attacks on, 53-54, 398-99ff, 406-07. *See also* greatness.
conservative, F a, in moral, political, social views, 424-25. *See*

435

INDEX

also class, liberty, moral, politics, society.

consolation, broad tradition of, 239n; Christian topics of, emphasized by F, 145, 252, 270, some not used by F, 244-46, 251-53; classic *consolatione*, parallels with, 230ff; comedy and, 275; for death, tradition of, 239-40; in F's novels, 250-51, 264-66; mood of, basic to F, 144-45, 270-71; philosophic, 230-38, 241-44; religious, 238-39, 241, 244-47, 251-53; *solacia* and *praecepta*, 247n; Solon's refusal of, cited, 266; traditional topics of, 230ff, 242-43; traditions related to, 247-48; value of, in affliction, 164, 249-50. See also death, grief, religion.

Constable, John (attrib. author), *The Conversation of Gentlemen Considered*, 178 and n, 327-28, 328n, 425.

contempt, F's censure of, 168 and n, 170-71, 177, 181; in novels, 182-83.

contrast, as technique, 408. See also rhetoric.

controversiae, 263.

conversation, ceremony and civility in, 176-77; courtesy-book tradition of 174ff; dialogue should resemble, 394-95; F's moral earnestness concerning, 179, non-utilitarian motives, 179-80, rules simpler than Italianate tradition, 174-76; importance of, 180-81; in plays, 415; rules for, in sermons and tracts, 174n; "social criminals" in F's novels, 182-84; theme of *Essay on Conversation*, 164-89; trifling, in beau monde, 317-18; virtuosi and, 328, 331n. See also good breeding, raillery, society.

 as social intercourse, 166-72: natural to man, 167; art of pleasing, 167, 169-70; good-breeding and, 167-68, 173, 184-89; general precepts of, avoid contempt, 168, 170-71, show respect, 168-69; rules for, in visiting, 169-70; complaisance, first rule of, 169-70; behavior to superiors, equals, and inferiors, 170-72; lesser faults in, 171-72.

 as social talk, 172-73: adapted to company, 172, 181-82; sins against good breeding in, 172, 181-82; topics to be avoided in, 172; danger of raillery in, 172-73; end of, happiness, 172.

Conversation of Gentlemen Considered, The, see Constable, John.

Cooke, Arthur L., 338n.

*Cooke, Thomas, 25.

Coolidge, John S., 221n.

Cooper, Thomas, bookseller, 111, 301.

"copiousness" (*copia verborum,* clausal parallelism, pleonasm, duplication of predicates, &c.), 152, 157-58, 279, 359-60, 379. See also rhetoric, style.

Coquelet, Louis, *Eloge de rien,* 301.

Corinth, 387-89.

*Cornwallis, Charles Cornwallis, 5th Baron (later 1st Earl), 20.

Cornwallis, Sir William, 307; "Prayse of Nothing," 300.

Corruption Bill, 121n.

Cosentini, John W., 396n.

Cotton, Charles, 138; influenced by Lucian, 365n; translation of Montaigne, 159n; travesty of Virgil, 136; *Burlesque upon Burlesque,* 416; *Scarronides,* 136.

*Cotton, Sir John Hynde, Bart., 20.

courage, false, in *JA*, 264; not in fierce aspect, 193.

court favorite, claim to greatness satirized, 43.

courtesy-book, 169, 186, 199; *Essay on Conversation* a, 143, 166-67; ideal gentleman in, 184-85; tradition of, 174 and n, 175ff.

Courtin, Antoine de, 177.

Coventry, Francis, *Pompey the Little,* 301 and n.

Cowley, Abraham, 32.

Cowper, William, 310n.

Cradock, Catherine, sister of Charlotte, 121, 131.

436

INDEX

Cradock, Charlotte, see Fielding, Charlotte (Cradock).
Craftsman, The, 93; on the criminal conqueror, 399-400; on incendiaries, 362-63; war-party in, 345n.
Craig, Hardin, 365n.
Crane Court, 317, 329.
Crane, Ronald S., 66n, 255n, 275n.
*Craven, Fulwar Craven, 4th Baron, 20.
Crawford, Bartholow V., 394.
Crécy, 90.
Creech, William, allusion to F, 27.
criminal, F on highwaymen, 85n.
critic, character of a, 36; claim to greatness satirized, 43-44; criticism, burlesque, in F's journals, 274. See also satire.
Croesus, king of Lydia, 238n.
Croiset, Maurice, 371 and n, 384-85, 420.
Croll, Morris W., 39, 152n.
Cross, Wilbur L., 4n, 5n, 7, 14, 17, 22, 23, 26n, 31n, 43n, 116n, 120n, 128n, 131, 137n, 180n, 229n, 272, 338n, 340n, 343, 344, 344-45n, 345, 409, 410-11, 420, 424; dubious point in, 103, 138, 338n, 339, 344-45n, 361-62; error in, 17n, 23, 119n, 315n.
Crowne, John, Calisto, 418.
Cudworth, Ralph, 68n.
Cumberland, Richard, the elder, on Law of Nature, 333n.
Cumberland, Richard, the younger, anecdote of JW, 26.
Cupid, 123-24.
Cupid and Hymen, 109n.
Curll, Edmund, 418n.
cursus (cadenced end-pattern), in Addison and F, 152. See also rhetoric, style.
Cutler, Sir John, 309.
Cynics, in Lucian's Vitarum auctio, 390-91; Stoics confused with, 258, Seneca's distinction, 258. See also Antisthenes, Diogenes, Stilpo.
Cythereia: or New Poems of Love and Intrigue, 418n.

D

Daily Advertiser, 11n, 14, 301n, 315n.
Daily Gazetteer, answer to war party, 346; F denies writing for, 6.
Daily Post, 3-4, 11-12, 14n, 315n.
Dante Alighieri, 271, 330, 426.
Dartmouth, William Legge, 1st Earl of, 22.
*Dashwood, Sir Francis, Bart., 17, 21.
*Dashwood, Sir James, Bart., 17.
Daunce, Edward, Prayse of Nothing, 299.
Davenant, William, 406n.
Davie, Donald, 39n.
Davis, Herbert, 166n, 174n, 180, 225n, 307n.
*Dawkins, James, 23.
Day, Angel, 240n.
Dean, Leonard F., 312n.
death, common to all, 230-31, 242; of friends (see consolation, grief); not real evil, 236-38, 242; numberless avenues to, 234; tradition against fear of, 247-48; tradition of ars moriendi, 248.
De Castro, J. Paul, 12n, 19n, 119n, 137n, 138n, 165 and n, 291n.
deceit, see hypocrisy.
decorum, tradition of human nature, 221.
dedications, satire of, 412-13, 419.
*Deerhurst, Thomas Henry Coventry, styled Viscount, 20.
Defoe, Daniel, Hymn to the Pillory, 309; Use and Abuse of the Marriage Bed, 111n.
Deism, 71n; attack on, in Champion, 72n. See also religion.
Delaunois, Marcel, 347n.
*De La Warr, John West, 7th Baron (later 1st Earl), 21, 24n.
Della Casa, Giovanni, Galateo, 175n, 177.
Della rime piacevoli del Berni et d'altri auttori, 304n.
"Delphin classics," 342 and n.
Demosthenes, called on by Akenside, 346-47; comment on, in Daily Gazetteer, 346; F's am-

437

INDEX

biguous attitude toward, 363-64; F's translation of, 344-64; translation by Thomas Wilson, 346, 361-62, by "several hands," 346 and n, 357; translations in *Common Sense*, 345-46; type of the patriot, 362-63, 364; *Demosthenis et Æschinis Opera*, in F's library, 348 and n, cited, 349ff; *Olynthiacs*, 344 and n, 345n, 346; *Philippics*, 344, 345n, 346; *Several Orations, by Several Hands*, 346 and n, 357. See also Fielding, *First Olynthiac*.

Denbigh, Isabella Feilding, Countess of, 22.

*Denbigh, William Feilding, 5th Earl of, kinsman of F, 21.

Denham, Sir John, 32.

Dennis, John, 125 and n; *Impartial Critick*, 394.

depravity, Anglican church and, 208; conviction of, dangerous, 210-11; definition of, 207-08n; F's use of term, 207ff. See also human nature, religion, vice.

deprecation, formulas of, feature of irony, 151n, in *JA*, 162n. See also rhetoric.

DeQuincey, Thomas, 311.

Derrick, Samuel, 5n.

Desaguliers, John Theophilus, 317.

Descartes, René, 205.

Descent of the Heathen Gods, The, 418.

descriptio (*diatyposis, hypotyposis*), 227n. See also rhetoric.

determinism, in F's view of human nature, 219-23, 424.

detraction, *see* censoriousness.

*Devonshire, William Cavendish, 3rd Duke of, 20.

dialogue, closeness to drama, 414-16; in contemporary literature, 393-98; F's, between Alexander and Diogenes, 386-409, between the gods, 409-19, satirical, in journals, 274, 367, in novels, 367, 393, 408, 416, in poetry, 30 and n, other, 397-98; F's skill in, 408, technique in, 391-93, training for, 391; Lucianic, 389-93; should resemble conversation, 394-95. See also poetry, satire.

Dialogue betwixt H. B.'s Ghost, and R. L. S., A, 396n.

dialogues of the dead, 395-97; in F, 366. See also Lucian.

dialogues of the gods, 367, 416-17. See also Lucian.

diatribe, F's poetic, 125-26; satiric, in F's journals, 274. See also poetry, satire.

diatyposis, see descriptio.

Dickens, Charles, 289.

diction, levels of: plain (*subtilis, tenuis*), middle (*medius*), elegant middle, grand (*gravis, vehemens*), 151, 161n; in F and Lucian, 378, 383-84; precision of, in F, 35-36, 384. See also rhetoric, style.

Digeon, Aurélien, 10, 398n.

Diogenes Laertius, *De vitis clarorum philosophorum*, 266n, 341-42n, 404n.

Diogenes of Sinope, 307, 341-42n; ambivalent attitude toward in Lucian and F, 390-91; confrontation with Alexander, 405-07; contemporary attitude toward, 402-05; in Fénelon, 396n; in F's *Dialogue*, 386-409; in F's *Of True Greatness*, 386; F's view of, 404-05.

Dion Chrysostom (Dio of Prusa), 303.

Dionysius of Halicarnassus, 344n.

distortion, in satire, 288. See also satire.

Dobrée, Bonamy, 92n.

Doctor Anthony's Poem in Praise of the Pox, 310.

Doddridge, Philip, 247; funeral sermons, 245; God's providence not questioned, 245n.

*Dodington, George Bubb, 17, 26; defended by F, 43n; extravagant compliments to, 46n; *Of True Greatness* dedicated to, 6, 8, 42.

*Dodsley, Robert, 26n; *Collection of Poems*, 27, F's "Plain Truth" in, 30, F's poem to Walpole reprinted in, 127n.

Dodwell, Henry, 294n.

438

INDEX

*Doneraile, Arthur Mohun St. Leger, 3rd Viscount, 17.
Donne, John, 32.
Dornavius, Caspar, *Amphitheatrum*, 304.
drama, allusions to, in F's Juvenal, 141; corrective end of F's, 42, 144; dialogue and, 391, 414-16; "false greatness" in F's, 47; F's career in, 409, training in, 290, 391; marriage as theme in F's, 112; rhetoric in F's, 284; satire in F's, 182n, 274, 288-89, 419; songs for, 134-35. See also burlesque, comedy, farce, satire, theatre.
Draper, John W., 248n.
"Drawcansir, Sir Alexander," F's pseudonym in *CGJ*, 29.
dream-vision, in *CGJ*, 331; *The Opposition*, 274; satiric, in F's journals, 274. See also satire.
Drelincourt, Charles, *The Christian's Defence*, 248 and n.
drunkenness, differences in F's judgment of, 84-85n.
Drury-Lane Journal, see Thornton, Bonnell.
Drury Lane Theatre, 24, 125n; Footmen's Riot at, 102n.
Dryden, John, 34, 34n, 44, 118; essays, 146; influenced by Lucian, 365; on Juvenal, 107; life of Lucian, 365 and n; "loose" Senecan style, 155; on translation, 361; translation of Juvenal, 107, 138, 138-39n; translation of Virgil, 15, 337; *Amphitryon*, 418; *Of Dramatick Poesie*, 394; *Mac-Flecknoe*, 308.
duality, creates complex texture in F's work, 144-45, 264, 266-69, 421, 425-26; in F's ironic vision, 421, 425-26; forms of, 267; in human nature, 115, 269; not mere inconsistency, 425-26; rescues F from bigotry or didacticism, 425-26; in satirical method, 289-90n. See also polarities.
  in F's attitude toward: class, 100-01 et passim; ceremony, 176; consolation, value of, 251, 266; education, 218-20; good-nature, 63-64, 84-87, 267, prevalence of, 73-76; goodness, 73-76, 209ff; gravity, 85n; greatness, 267; moral judgment, 84-85n; passions, 269; prudence, 227 and n; reason, 61, 266; religion, 76-83, 164, 251-54, 262-65, 269-70; self-interest, 64-65, 191-92; Stoicism, 257-58.
Du Bois, Arthur E., 19n.
*Ducarel, Andrew, LL.B., 21
*Ducarel, James Coltee, 21.
Dudden, F. Homes, 5, 5n, 31n, 318n, 339; error in, 315n; on misers in F, 332n.
Duncan, Carson S., 326n.
Dunton, John, 248n; *Athenian Sport*, 300, 309n.
Du Refuge, Eustache, *Traité de la cour*, 178.
Du Vair, Guillaume, *Moral Philosophie of the Stoicks*, 256.

E

Eastbury, Dodington's estate, 26.
Ebsworth, Joseph Woodfall, 300n, 307n.
education, 198, 208; of corrupt minds difficult, 220-21, 224-25; criticism of women's, 105-06; effect of wrong, 191, 223; F's ambivalence on, 218-20; of goodness against hypocrisy, 227-28; intensifies innate propensities, 215; modifies original evil, 214; necessary to good breeding, 188, on power of, 218; skepticism concerning, 216; will and, 217. See also human nature.
Edward III, 90.
Edwards, Jonathan, 207n.
Egilsrud, Johan S., 395-96n.
*Egmont, John Perceval, 1st Earl of, 17.
egoism, blinds even good men, 197; fictional dissection of, 42; F implacable toward, 335-36, 423; self-interest compatible with good-nature, 64-65, self-interest evil, 191-92.
Ehrenpreis, Irvin, 99n.
eidolopoeia (making dead speak),

439

INDEX

in dialogues of the dead, 397. See also rhetoric.
elections, corrupt, satirized, 121, 326.
elegy, related to *meditatio mortis*, 248; elegiac quality gives depth to F's comedy, 9, 144-45, 164, 206, 250, 271, 275, 423.
Elizabeth I, 346.
*Elton, Abraham, 26n.
*Elton, Isaac, 26n.
Emlyn, Thomas, *Funeral Consolations*, 244 and n, 247.
Empson, William, 269n.
enargeia, creation of emotional identification by, 57 and n, 224, 226-27, 227n; Lucian and F's mastery of, 371. See also rhetoric.
encomium, 286; rhetoric of, 292, 302-03, 305-06.
  mock: 272 and n; *Essay on Nothing*, 281-88, 292-312; in F and Lucian, 375; and *JW*, 277; in journals, 274; in prose, 274; tradition of, 302-12. See also satire.
England, encomium upon, 121.
English Theophrastus, The (attrib. to Abel Boyer), 107n, 175, 179, 192n.
enthusiasm, see religion.
enthymeme, in *Essay on Nothing*, 285-88, 297; fallacious, 286-88; in forensic oratory, 281. See also rhetoric.
envy, in Diogenes, 388-89, 405; Lucian and F on, 367.
epic, comic prose, 421.
Epictetus, 256; different from Old Stoa, 258; translation by George Stanhope, 174n.
Epicurus, 205, 233n.
epigram, F's, 31, 123, 124, 125, 130, 130-31, 131, 131, 131-32, 132; satiric, 273. See also poetry, satire.
epiphonema (striking sentence), in F's poetry, 37; in Senecan prose and heroic couplet, 38-39; in *Some Papers*, 325. See also rhetoric.
epistle, poetic (*see* verse-epistle);

satiric, in F's journals, 274. See also satire.
epitaph, congenial exercise to Augustans, 132; F's poetic, 132-33, others, 132n; mock, 31, 133, 273. See also poetry, satire.
epitaphios (battle oration), 240.
Erasmus, Desiderius, 235n, 240n, 273n, 311; translated Lucian, 365; *Encomium moriae*, 304, 307, 312, 314.
erotesis, see rhetorical question.
Esprit, Jacques, *La fausseté des vertus humaines*, 86-87, 87n.
essay, concept of "imperfect offer," 146; F's best examples in periodicals and novels, 145; history of English, 145n; not a classical genre, 146; poetic (*see* verse-essay); satiric, in F's journals, 274; serious tone dominant in, 427. See also rhetoric, style, satire.
  F's in *Misc*.: discussion of, 143-64: aim to instruct and reform, 143; introductory comment on *Essay on Conversation*, 143-44, on *Essay on the Knowledge of the Characters of Men*, 144, on *Of the Remedy of Affliction*, 144-45; structural models for, 146-50, in classic oration, 146-49, in sermons, 149-50; style of, 150-64; influence of in F's work, 164.
Essay on Gibing, 310.
Essay on Living in a Garret, An, 310, 311n.
Essay on Polite Behaviour, An, 178.
Essay in Praise of Knavery, An, 309, 400n.
Essex, Elizabeth Percy, Countess of, 247n.
Essex, John, *Young Ladies Conduct*, 108.
esteem, for others (*see* good breeding); professor of, warning against, 195.
ethics, see moral.
ethos, appeal of, in rhetoric, 158, inverted, 293. See also rhetoric.
Eton, 135; F's study of classics, 146, 339 and n, 343; numerous graduates of, subscribers to *Misc.*, 21.
Euripides, cited by Plutarch, 234n.

440

INDEX

evil, harder than goodness, 51; impotent in comedy, 76; instructed goodness a match for, 191 and n, 227; overbalances happiness in life, 237-38; punishment of, not inconsistent with good-nature, 62; rooted, cannot be corrected, 220-21, 224-25; youthful, should be cut off, 335-36. *See also* greatness, human nature, moral, sin, vice.

example (*exemplum*), of Anaxagoras, 231n; of Croesus and Solon, 238n; in deliberative oratory, 281; in *Essay on Nothing*, 285-86, 295, 297; in F and Lucian, 375-76; in F's Demosthenes, 356; F's faith in, over precept, 181 and n, 225; in satire, 288-89. *See also* rhetoric.

experience, in F's moral construct, 228, 426; necessary to judge human nature, 76, 194.

extension, 160-61; in F and Lucian, 380-83; in F's Demosthenes, 359; in *JA*, 162n. *See also* style.

F

Faber, Geoffrey C., 400n, 417n.
fable, poetic, 123-24. *See also* poetry, satire.
*Fairfax, Major Robert, 24.
*Fairfax, Thomas Fairfax, 6th Baron, in America, 24.
family, behavior to, index of character, 197 and n.
farce, F's, 274; Lucianic dialogue and, 415-16; technique of F's, 415-16. *See also* drama, satire.
Farnese, Elizabeth, 345.
Favez, Charles, 240, 242n, 246n, 247n.
Fénelon, François de Salignac de la Mothe, *Dialogues des morts*, 396n, 397.
Fern, Sister Mary Edmond, 240n.
Fiddes, Richard, funeral sermons, 245; *Fifty Two Practical Discourses*, 176.
Fielding, Charlotte (Cradock), 104, 107, 118, 228-29, 237-38; as Amelia, 19, 113; as "Celia," 122-27; death of, 249, 252; illness of, 8-9; poems written to, 121ff.
Fielding, Charlotte, daughter of Henry, 249, 252-53; death of, 9, 228-29, 237-38.
Fielding, Edmund, father of Henry, army associates, 20-21; death of, 9.

FIELDING, HENRY: Works:

I. Miscellanies

Circumstances of publication, 3-28: proposals for, 3, 8; projected before 1742, 3, 166n; difficulties during composition, 5-10; early and newly written material in, 10, 190; postponements of publication, 10-12; printers of, 12-13; "second edition," 14, 27; Dublin reprint, 14, 27; financial success of subscription, 15-16; subscribers, 16-26; mild reception of, 26-28.

Preface to Miscellanies, 6, 16, 313, 427; apology for poems, 29; on burlesque of Juvenal, 137-38; difficulties in writing *Misc.*, 8-10, 15; on *Essay on Conversation*, 184; on goodness, greatness, and sham greatness, 42ff, 51-54; *JW* not general human nature, 211; on *Of the Characters of Men*, 205; on plays, 409n; on women, 106, 137-38.

Volume I:

General comment on, 420-28.
Poetry, discussion of, 29-41. *See also* poetry.
Verse-essays, 42-118, significance of, 42.

Of True Greatness, 34n, 386, 404; discussion of, 42-54: summary of, 43-46; published separately, 6, 43n; theme of greatness, 46-54, 398, 402. *See also* greatness.

Of Good-Nature, 17n, 21, 27, 214n, 333; discussion of, 54-88: summary of, 55-60; lines from *Champion* in, 30n, 55n, 59; dating of, 55n; theme of good-

441

INDEX

nature, 60-88; contemporary context, 66-81. See also good-nature.

Liberty, 29, 103n; discussion of, 88-103: summary of, 88-93; dating of, 88; contemporary context, 91-93; theme of liberty and democracy, 94-103. See also class, liberty.

To a Friend on the Choice of a Wife, discussion of, 103-13: dating of, 103, summary of, 103-07; tradition of, 107-09; theme of marriage, contemporary views, 108-11, F's views, 111-13. See also marriage, women.

To John Hayes, Esq., discussion of, 113-18: summary of, 113-16; theme of complex human nature, 113-18, 222, 224 and n; other sources, 116-17. See also human nature.

Light verse, 118-42: pleasant features of, 118; experimentation in, 118; mostly composed 1728-1733, 118.

"To Euthalia," amorous complaint, 118-19.

"A Description of U[pton] G[rey]," burlesque complaint, 119-20; early bent for burlesque, 276.

"Written Extempore, on a Half-Penny," delicate touch in, 120; earlier version of, 120n.

"To the Master of the Salisbury Assembly," animated triplet, 120-21.

[Untitled] "The Queen of Beauty, t'other Day . . . ," allusive poem, 121; F's note to, 121-22.

"Advice to the Nymphs of New S[aru]m . . . ," praise of Charlotte Cradock, 122.

"The Question," Charlotte Cradock may not always be "Celia," 122-23.

"An Epigram ['When Jove with fair Alcmena lay']," 123; echoes Prior, 123n.

"To Celia . . . Cupid Call'd to Account," 30; charming fable, 123-24.

"To the Same. On Her Wishing to Have a Lilliputian, to Play With," 123, 124.

"Similes. To the Same," 124.

"The Price. To the Same," epigram, 124.

"Her Christian Name. To the Same. A Rebus," 124.

"To the Same: Having Blamed Mr. Gay for His Severity on Her Sex," 125.

"To Celia ['I hate the Town, and all its ways']," diatribe, 125-26; affinity with "satires on the town," 126-27; F's prejudice against the city, 126-27.

"To the Right Honourable Sir Robert Walpole," 340; another version of, 27; mock epistle, 127-28.

"To the Same. Anno 1731," epistle on Walpole's levees, 128-29.

"J[oh]n W[at]ts at a Play," theatrical poem, 129-30.

"On a Lady, Coquetting with a Very Silly Fellow," epigram, 130.

"On the Same," epigram echoing Prior, 130-31.

"An Epigram ['That Kate weds a fool']," epigram on marriage, 131.

"Another [Epigram: 'Miss Molly lays down as a positive rule']," on marriage, 131.

"The Cat and Fiddle," epigram on a miser, 131-32.

"Epigram on One Who Invited Many Gentlemen to a Small Dinner," on Peter Walter, 132, 318n.

"Epitaph on Butler's Monument," 133.

"Another [Epitaph]. On a Wicked Fellow," 133.

"The Beggar. A Song," Petrarcan theme, 134.

"A Sailor's Song," rollicking piece, 134-35.

"A Simile, from Silius Italicus," brief translation, 135.

"A Parody, from the First

442

INDEX

ited to, 28n; "optimistic" atmosphere of, 74; "social criminals" in, 182-83; Sophia as wifely ideal, 110-11; styles in, 161-62; "sublime" style in, 161n; Thwackum and Square and *Champion*, 262-63; views of human nature in, 212n.

Fielding, John, letter to, by F, 180.
Fielding, Sarah, *Familiar Letters*, 330-31, F's letter in, 331n.
Fielding, Timothy, possible author of "A Dialogue," 30.
figure, 163n, 288-89; for emphasis, not embellishment, in formal essays, 151. *See also* metaphor, rhetoric, satire, simile, style, trope.
Fink, Zera S., 91n.
*Firebrace, Sir Cordell, Bart., 17.
Fitzosborne, Sir Thomas (pseud.), *see* Melmoth, William.
*Fitzwilliam, William Fitzwilliam, 3rd Earl, 21.
Flanders, 140.
Flanders, Henry, 26n.
flattery, in F's novels, 200-01; warning against, 195.
*Fleetwood, Charles, allusion in F's *Juvenal*, 141; manager of Drury Lane, 24.
Fleetwood, William, Bishop of Ely, 307.
Folkes, Martin, president of the Royal Society, 317, 319.
Fontenelle, Bernard le Bovier, Sieur de, *Nouveaux dialogues des morts*, 395-96 and n.
footmen, F no love for, 101-02n.
Fordhook, Middlesex, 268.
Forrester, Col. James, *Polite Philosopher*, 178.
Fortescue, Lucy, *see* Littleton, Lucy (Fortescue).
fortune, wise man not subject to, 231. *See also* tyche.
Foster, Finley M. K., 365n.
Fowler, Francis G., 368n, 374n, 390.
Fowler, Henry W., 368n, 374n, 390.
*Fox, Henry (later 1st Baron Holland), 21.

France, 141, 320n; good breeding in, 188. *See also* French.
Fraser, Alexander C., 194n.
*Frederick, Prince of Wales, 17, 23, 24, 25n.
Frederick the Great, 23.
freedom, *see* liberty.
Freese, John H., 146n, 263n, 281n.
French, F's knowledge of, 337-38, 340; translations of Lucian in F's library, 370.
Freud, Sigmund, 67; Freudian critic, 356.
friendship, 56, 195n; grief for death of friends (*see* grief); must be based on feeling, 62.
Fronto, Marcus Cornelius, 303.
Frye, Northrop, 271n.
Fulwood, William, *Enemie of Idlenesse*, 146 and n.
*Furnese, Henry, 17.
Fussell, Paul, Jr., 33n.
Fuzelier, Louis, *Momus fabuliste*, 417

G

*Gage, Thomas Gage, 1st Viscount, 17, 24n.
*Garrard, Thomas, 22.
*Garrick, David, 24; *Good-Natured Man* and *Wedding Day* written for, 8.
Garth, Sir Samuel, translation of Demosthenes, 346n.
Gay, John, poetic model for F, 32; publication by subscription, 15; "town eclogues," 126; *Beggar's Opera*, F's song on, 30, probable allusion to, 125; *Panegyrical Epistle*, 309, 310n; *Polly*, 400; *Trivia*, 417, imitators of, 126.
Geddes, James, 152.
Gellius, Aulus, *Noctes Atticae*, on Demosthenes, 363n.
General Evening Post, 12, 14.
Geneva: A Poem, 310.
gentleman, *see* good breeding, honor.
Gentleman's Library, The, 178.
Gentleman's Magazine, The, 114n, 124, 125n, 133n, 301n, 347n, 403n; epistle to Walpole first printed in, 127n; on *TJ*, 78.

447

INDEX

George II, 24, 26n, 54, 116n, 309, 310n, 325 and n, 410 and n.
George III, 24.
georgics, in eighteenth century, 309.
Germany, 141, 330; ironic comment on Hanover, 325, 325-26n.
Gherardi, Evaristo, *Théâtre italien de Gherardi*, F's debt to, 338n.
Gibbon, Edward, *Decline and Fall of the Roman Empire*, allusion to *Misc.* in, 27-28, 28n.
Gibbs, J. W. M., 27n, 101n, 318n.
Gilbert, Thomas, "A View of the Town," 127n.
"Gimcrack, Sir Nicholas," see Shadwell, *The Virtuoso*.
Glenn, Sidney E., 338n.
Glover, Arnold, 212n.
Goddard, William, *A Satirycall Dialogue*, 406n.
Godden, Gertrude M., 6n, 7, 7n.
Goggin, Leo P., 31n, 192n, 337n.
Goldsmith, Oliver, allusion to *Misc.*, 27; on liberty, 91; *The Bee*, 318n; *Citizen of the World*, 91; *The Traveller*, 101; *Vicar of Wakefield*, 241n.
*Goldwyre, Edward, 19.
good breeding, in actions and words, 167ff; adapts to company, 172; art of pleasing, 184; ceremony essential to, 176; complaisance, mark of, 169-70, 176, 178-79, 185-87; contemporary moralists on, 185-86; in conversation, 165-89; *Essay on Conversation* an enchiridion of, 143; F called good writer on, 27; F on, 184-89, 424-25; good company essential to, 186-88; good-nature essential to, 167-68, 185, 187-88; goodness, not rank, shows, 173; importance of, 189; lacking in lower classes, 97; makes social intercourse rewarding, 176; in polite world, 185-86; Shaftesbury's emphasis upon, 73; shows respect to rank, 313; word corrupted, 167. *See also* class, conversation, honor, society.
good humor, mistaken for good-nature, 56; smile of, fraudulent, 193.

good-nature, appearance of, 194; avarice denies, 333; Barrow on, 208; censoriousness and envy antitypes of, 59; in *Champion*, 60ff; charity identified with, 58, 63-65; classical conception of, 67-68; complex term for F, 54-55; continuum of values, 61; conversation and, 176; difference in F's definition of, and exhortation to, 64; does not make invidious comparisons, 59-60; dualities in, 267; easily feigned, 56; essential to good breeding, 167-68; false greatness lacks, 49; feeling necessary to, 61; F interested in conflict of, with false greatness, 54; F's characters must learn more than, 47; F's conception of, in benevolist tradition, 66-68, distinguished from benevolism of: Clarke and physico-theologians, 68-69, Hutcheson, 69, Shaftesbury, 69-73, Latitudinarian clergy, 76-83; F's tolerance of vices accompanied by, 81-83; good in itself and useful, 65; good breeding is polished, 185, 187-88; good of the whole and, 62, 64 (*see also* Stoicism); judgment emphasized in, 60-61; Jupiter's, makes him vulnerable, 413; laughter not a sign of, 76; moral complement to religion, 71-72, 87; moral, social, and religious virtue, 65-66; natural prey of hypocrisy, 63, 144, 191-92 and n, 225, 227, 413, inadequacy of this theme, 63; need for ethical imperative transcending, 84-87; not abstract contemplation of virtue, 70; not contemptuous, 171; not inconsistent with: revenge, 62, 72n, satire, 62, self-interest, 64-65; not passive sentiment, 61-62; not possible for all, 73-76, 222, 424; other passions mistaken for, 56; outgoing force, 63; prevalence of, confidence and skepticism on, 73-76; religion goes beyond, 72 and n, 86 and n; root ideal, 87-88; skepticism about, in *Amelia*, 84-87; in social context, 189; sometimes misses mark, 168;

448

INDEX

sometimes thoughtless, 226-27; a strength, conflicts with view of vulnerability, 62; sympathetic identification in, 57, 60; theme of *Misc.*, 42, 422; theme of poem *Of Good-Nature*, 54-88; true nature of, 56-57; vice cannot exist with, 55-56, 65; virtue equated with, 55-63. See also benevolence, charity, goodness, sympathy, virtue.

goodness, easier than villainy, 51; F more interested in average, 48; good-and-great, 47-49, 87; good breeding and, 173; greatness and, 46, 400-01; ideal of, 263; instructed, a match for evil, 191 and n, 227; lower in scale than true greatness, 61; man only *bonus capax*, 422; mere, not enough, 47; not attainable by all, 222-23; theme of *Misc.*, 422; victim of hypocrisy, 50, 62, 144. See also benevolence, good-nature, human nature, virtue.

good of the whole, argued in JW, 95; good-nature concerned with, 62, 64; Stoicism associated with, 192, 257, 259-60. See also Stoicism.

Gordon, Thomas, 126; on conversation, 182; *The Humourist*, 91, 182, 310-11, 399n.

Gorgias, 303.

Gough, John W., 91n.

Gould, Henry, the elder, F's maternal uncle, 22.

*Gould, Henry, the younger, cousin of F, 22.

Gould, William, *Account of English Ants*, ridiculed by F, 331.

government, advantages of limited monarchy, 95-96.

Gower, Lady Evelyn (Pierrepont), 22n.

*Gower, John Leveson-Gower, 2nd Baron (later 1st Earl), 20, 22n.

grace, see religion.

Granville, George (Lord Lansdowne), translation of Demosthenes, 346n.

graveyard poetry, related to *meditatio mortis*, 248.

gravity, austerity and, mark of hypocrite, 197, 203, 410n, not of wisdom, 193; different associations for F, 85n.

Gray, Thomas, 248n, 310n.

greatness, 144, 185; debate on, in *A Dialogue*, 387ff, 395, 398; dualities in, 267; false claimants to, 43-45, 50; goodness and, 400-01; ideal of, 263; mock demonstration of F's, over Walpole's, 127; "modern" conception of, in Steele, 43n; moral triad of goodness and two kinds of, 46-51; Rochester on, 298n; theme in *Misc.*, 42, 422; theme in poem, *Of True Greatness*, 42-54; vulgar image of, answered by goodness, 87; Wild's maxims for, 194n.

false: in Alexander, 386ff; attack on, in *Essay on Nothing*, 313; character of, 49-50; delineated, 43-45, 50; F interested in contrast between good-nature and, 54; honored by society, 14, 43, 402; in JW, 42, 191n, 194n, 200; misery and perversity of, 51-53; preys on goodness, 50-51; tragic comedy of, 53; Walpole specific target of attacks on, 53, and larger moral frame, 53-54.

true: beyond moral censure, 54; good-and-great, 47-49; ideal in continuum of values, 61; image of, 45-46; moral inspiration, 48-49; source of, in Aristotle and Cicero, 48n. See also goodness.

Greek, F and Lucian, 366-86, 378n, *et passim*; F's knowledge of, 339-44: Latin better than, 340, 343; respect for, 341-43; self-conscious use of, 341-42; study of, 339; translation of Aristophanes, 338, of Demosthenes, 348-64; in *Some Papers*, 280; works in F's library, 340-41, bilingual, 341, 342n, 348.

Greene, George W., 92n, 307n.

*Grenville, George, 19, 21.

Grenville, Hester (Temple), wife of Richard, the elder, 19.

449

INDEX

Grenville, Hester, *see* Pitt, Hester (Grenville).
*Grenville, James, 19n.
Grenville, Richard, the elder, 19.
*Grenville, Richard, the younger, subscriber (?) to *Misc.*, 19 and n.
grief, for death of friends, 228-48: F's personal experience of, 228-29, 249; afflicts best men, 230; eased by forethought, 230-31, 242; tempered by reason, 232-33, 242, 243, 247, 253n, and time, 233, 243; exorbitant, selfish, 233-34, 235-36, 242; recollection of, folly, 233, 243, not classic topic, 233, 242; diversions ineffectual, 233; unjust to God, 234, 242; death not true calamity, 236-38, 242; no consolation for, in hope, 249. *See also* consolation, death.
Griffith, Reginald H., 418n, *Alexander Pope: A Bibliography*, 189n.
Grotius, Hugo (de Groot), on law of nature, 333n.
Grubbs, Henry A., 236n.
Grub-Street Journal, 125 and n, 310n.
Grueber, Herbert A., 320n.
"Gualterus, Petrus," *see* Walter, Peter.
Guardian, The, on Diogenes, 403n.
Guazzo, Stefano, *La civil conversatione*, 174 and n, 177.
Gummere, Richard M., 146n, 229n.
Guthkelch, Adolph C., 299n, 308n.
Guttentag, Isidor, 380.

H

habit, shapes character, 219 and n. *See also* education, human nature.
*Halifax, George Montagu Dunk, 2nd Earl of, 18, 21.
Halifax, George Savile, Marquis of, essays, 146; "loose" Senecan style, 155, 159; *Advice to a Daughter*, 108.
Hall, Clayton M, 256n.
Hall, Joseph, 256n.

Hamilton, Gavin, 302.
Hammond, James, *Love Elegies*, 291 and n.
Hampshire, 119.
Hanover, *see* Germany.
happiness, avarice a threat to, of others, 334; every man's desire, 50n, interest, 65; hypocrite censures, 203; men not always capable of judging own, 167; more evil than, in life, 237-38; not the end of avarice, 297; served by conversation, 172, 180; well-bred contribute to, of others, 170, 184; wise man's, not subject to fortune, 231. *See also* pleasure, virtue.
Harborough, Philip Sherrard, 2nd Earl of, 22.
Harmon, Austin M., 368n, 391n.
*Harrington, Dr. Edward, 137n; alluded to in *TJ*, 23, 165.
*Harrington, William Stanhope, 1st Earl of, 20n, 21.
Harris, Catharine (Knatchbull), 18.
*Harris, Lady Elizabeth (Ashley Cooper), 18; died before *Misc.* published, 166n.
Harris, Elizabeth (Clark), wife of James, 19.
*Harris, James, 18-19, 166n, 405; "Concerning Happiness, A Dialogue," alluded to, 164-65; *Hermes*, 18.
*Harris, Thomas, brother of James, 18.
Harris, Thomas, London bookseller, 18n.
Hartcliffe, John, *Treatise of Moral and Intellectual Virtues*, 77n, 174n.
Hatchett, William, *Chinese Orphan*, printed by Woodfall, 13-14n.
Hauffen, Adolf, 299n, 304n.
Hawkins, George, bookseller, 291.
Hawkins, Sir John, *Life of Johnson*, attack on F, 69, 79-80.
Hayes, John (of Dublin), 113-14n.
*Hayes, John (of Wolverhampton), of Middle Temple, 113-14n; poem addressed to, 113-18, 222, 224 and n.

450

INDEX

Hayward, John, 110n.
Hazlitt, William, 212.
Hazlitt, William Carew, 207n.
head, *see* reason.
heart, *see* passions.
Heathcote [George, Sir Gilbert, or Sir John?], praised by F, 44.
Hederich (Hedericus), Benjamin, *Lexicon*, in F's library, 340 and n; gave Latin equivalents for Greek, 351.
Heinrich, Joachim, 108n.
Heinsius, Daniel, 304.
Helen of Troy, 130.
Hell-Fire Club, 17.
Hemlow, Joyce, 174n.
Henderson, Thomas F., 302n.
Henley, Anthony, Queen Anne wit, 18.
*Henley, Anthony, son of above, 18.
Henley, Jane (Husband), 165; F's poetic compliment to, 136-37; identification not positive, 137n; marriage to Robert Henley, 137.
*Henley, Robert (later, Earl of Northington), 18, 22, 137.
Henley, William Ernest, ed. Burns, 302n; "Henley" edition of F's works cited *passim*.
Henry V, 90.
Herculaneum, 329.
hermit, claim to greatness satirized, 43.
Herrick, Marvin T., 221n.
Herring, Thomas, Archbishop of Canterbury, on natural benevolence, 70n.
Hill, Aaron, ordered *Misc.* through Richardson, 25; subscribed to Mitchell's poems, 25.
Hill, George Birkbeck, 98n, 150n, 299n.
*Hippisley, Robert, 24.
Hirzel, Rudolf, 394n.
history, burlesque, in F's journals, 274 (*see also* satire); historian, 284, satire of, in *Essay on Nothing*, 293, 312.
History of Jack Connor, The, *see* Chaigneau, William.
History of Martin, The, abstract of, in *Tale of a Tub*, 308n.

Hoadly, Benjamin, Bishop of Winchester, 46, 71n, 78, 425; latitudinarian, 67; sons subscribers to *Misc.*, 23.
*Hoadly, Dr. Benjamin, 25; in F's *Juvenal*, 23.
*Hoadly, John, Chaplain to the Prince of Wales and Chancellor of the diocese of Winchester, 23, 25.
Hobbes, Thomas, 71n, 294n, 305; essays, 146; F ambiguous toward, 209n; reaction against, 208-09; weapons against, in Shaftesbury, 72.
Hock Norton, Oxfordshire, 119n.
Hoddington House (Upton Grey), 119n.
Hogarth, William, 260n; F cites, 371; planned cycle on "Happy Marriage," 111n; "Characters and Caricaturas," 193n.
Holdsworth, Sir William, 121n.
Holland, 141, 152, 317. *See also* Leyden.
Homer, 223n, 342, 374n, 418, 426; in bilingual edition, 341; F on Greek version of, 341; read at Eton, 339n; *Iliad*, Pope's translation of, 341; *Odyssey*, 341, 395n, Pope's translation of, 394.
homonymy (equivocation), in *Essay on Nothing*, 287-88. *See also* rhetoric.
honor, not central quality of gentleman, 184-85; true and false, 387-88.
Hooker, Timothy, *Essay on Honour*, 401.
Horace (Quintus Horatius Flaccus), 32, 119, 126, 273-74, 285; authority on conversation, 174n; decorum, 221; to be read in Latin, 343; *Carmina*, 97n, 113; *Epistulae*, 117 and n, 177n; *Sermones*, 143, 261.
Hornbeak, Katherine G., 108n, 146n.
Houghton, Walter E., Jr., 326n.
Howell, Wilbur S., 147n.
Hughes, Helen S., 30n.
human nature, actions as index to, 194-97, 335-36; amiable weak-

451

INDEX

nesses of, 232, 262-63, 267-70; cannot be a science, 228; comedy of, 423-24; comedy reconciles man to his, 274-75; contradictions in, theme of poem *To John Hayes*, 113-18; conversation natural to, 167, noblest privilege of, 180; education and, 214-20; experience necessary to judge, 76, 194; F not concerned with abnormal, 332-36, 367-69; F's latitudinarian problem concerning, 209-10; F's use of term "depravity," 207ff; F's wish to believe well of, 212-13; free will, 215-19, and determinism, 219-23, 424; good-nature core of attitude toward, 55; goodness of, F's ambiguity on, 73-76, 209ff; greatness in moral view of, 54; innate propensities in, 215-17, to evil, 191, 212-14, 216; insight into, of beggars, 200-01; man only *bonus capax*, 422; man a social animal, 73-74, 144, 166, 185, 405; "masculine" qualities in, 269, "feminine," 269; mixed character of, 73, 223, 269-70; men do not know own interests, 50, 144, 167; men use art to hide, 116; physiognomy as index to, 192-94, 222; reform unlikely in corrupted, 220-21, 224-25, 335-36; requires polish to purge natural malevolence, 97, 213; "seed" used of basic, 218-19; static view of, in rhetoric, 221; Stoicism elevates, 257; theme of *Misc.*, 42; Thwackum and Square on, 212n, 262; two views of, 211-12; understanding of, necessary, 117-18, 144, 191-92 and n, 227; valuable, even when flawed, 265; vanity and self-love in, 197; variety in, 207, 215. *See also* abnormal, depravity, determinism, evil, experience, good-nature, goodness, habit, humours, hypocrisy, imagination, moral, motives, nature, passions, physiognomy, reason, sin, sympathy, vice, virtue, will.

humanist, outlook central to F, 331.
Hume, David, *Enquiry concerning Human Understanding*, 225-26.
humor, *see* burlesque, comedy, farce, irony, mock-heroic, parody, satire, travesty.
humours, used in bad sense in *CGJ*, 214.
Humphreys, Arthur R., 68n, 108n.
Hunt, John, 294n.
Hurd, Richard, Bishop of Worcester, *Moral and Political Dialogues*, 395 and n, 397.
Husband, Jane, *see* Henley, Jane (Husband).
Hutcheson, Francis, 67, 206; distinction between benevolism of, and F's, 69.
Hutten, Ulrich von, 299n.
hyperbaton (transposition of words), in Demosthenes, 354. *See also* rhetoric.
hyperbole, in *Some Papers*, 280; in *Essay on Nothing*, 284. *See also* rhetoric.
hypocrisy, 413, 419; actions expose, 194-97; bane of all virtue, 205; "character" of, 159; deceit and, 192ff, 200; in Diogenes, 386ff, 405; escapes discernment, 194; examples of, in F's novels, 200-05; F and Lucian on, 367, 369ff; F implacable toward, 335; F satirizes broadly, 204-05; good men victims of, 47, 144, hope of schooling against, 227-28; gravity associated with, 85n, 197, 203, 410n; mock epitaph on, 133; *Of Characters of Men* a handbook on, 191ff; physiognomy as penetrator of, 192-94; in public life, 197-98; self-interest in, 192; in *Shamela*, 294n; theme in *Misc.*, 424-25; tradition of attack on, 199; two basic types of, 200; value of guards against, 164; vanity and, equated with ridiculous, 42; warning against various kinds of, 195-97. *See also* affectation, ascetic, censoriousness, egoism, esteem, flattery, greatness, human nature, inquisitive-

452

INDEX

ness, masquerade, motives, patriotism, promiser, prude, prudence, religion, saint, sin, slander, vanity, vice.
hypophora (anticipating and answering objection), in F's translation of Demosthenes, 360; mannerism of South, 150n, 360. See also rhetoric.
hypotaxis, see period: hypotactic.
hypotyposis, see descriptio.

I

ill-nature, 193; in contempt, 168, 171; ill breeding equated with, 173.
image, see figure.
imagination, importance to F's moral ends, 57; seized by pictures, 57 and n, 225-27. See also enargeia, invention.
imitation, devices of, in satire, 289. See also satire.
immortality, 239, 241, 246 and n, 247; in classical literature, 246n; F's emphasis upon, 270, faith in, 252-53. See also religion.
incongruity, in satire, 288-89. See also satire.
incrementum (climax), in Essay on Nothing, 282, 284, 295, 297. See also rhetoric.
indecency, in conversation, censured, 172, 178; example of, in JA, 182.
ingénu, in F's journals, 274. See also satire.
ingratitude, F implacable towards, 335-36; shown to good-nature, 62-63.
Inns of Court, 16, 178; large role in Misc. subscriptions, 16, 22-23; Gray's Inn, 16n, 25; Inner Temple, 16, 16n; Lincoln's Inn, 16; Middle Temple, 5, 113-14n.
innuendo, satirical device, 162n. See also satire.
inquisitiveness, example of, in Partridge, 202; warning against, 195.
insolence, see contempt.
invention, F's fertility of, 273, 276-77, 290, 314, 318, 321, 372-73, 408-09, 421, 428. See also rhetoric.
inversion, in Essay on Nothing, 282, 293, 314; in F's poetry, 36-37, and prose, 38; in satire, 288-89; stylistic, in F, 159. See also rhetoric.
invocation, satire of, 412 and n.
Ireland, 320n.
irony, 151n; double vision of, 421, 425-26, lacking in poetry, 40-41; dropped for direct statement, 204; in Essay on Nothing, 282, 296, 314; in F and Lucian, 368, 370, 371ff; in F and Swift, 279; of "imputative merit," 377-78; in mock encomium, 311-12; in satire, 288-89; in Some Papers, 280. See also rhetoric, satire.
Irving, William H., 126n.
Irwin, William R., 51n, 53-54, 398n.
Iser, Wolfgang, 254n.
Isocrates, 303, 304; Encomium on Helen, 304-05.
Italian, F claimed to read, 340; Italy, 141.

J

Jacob, Hildebrand, "The Patriot," 48n.
Jacobites, 20, 22.
Jaeger, Werner, 344n, 354n, 357-58.
James, Thomas, translated DuVair, 256n.
jargon, in conversation, 172, example of Adams, 183; parody of, in F and Lucian, 374.
Jarvis, Rupert C., 338n.
Jensen, Gerard E., 326n. See Covent-Garden Journal, passim.
Jerome, Saint, 240, 242, 256.
Joesten, Maria, 254n.
Johnson, Samuel, 156, 426; on Addison's style, 150; on liberty, 98, 103; on Rochester, 298; "An Essay on Epitaphs," 132-33; Lives, 98, 150, 298; The Rambler, 311n.
Johnson, Samuel, of Cheshire,

INDEX

Vision of Heaven printed by Woodfall, 13n.
Jones, Benjamin Maelor, 5n, 26n.
Jones, Richard Foster, 174n, 326.
Jonson, Ben, 38, 274.
journals, dialogues in F's, 367 and n; F's best essays in, 145; F's training in, 290; satire in F's, 274, 419.
judgment, difficulty of moral, a favorite theme of F, 115, 224; essential in charity, 64; good-nature requires, 60-61, emphasized to counter charge of weakness, 61-62. See also reason.
Julian the Apostate, 307.
Juno, 409ff; tradition of scolding, 417-19.
Jupiter (Jove), 120, 121, 123, 139, 387, 409ff; tradition of amours, 417-18.
Jupiter and Io, 418.
Jupiter's Descent on Earth, 409.
Juvenal (Decimus Junius Juvenalis), 32, 107n, 369; F's burlesque of, 118, 136, 137-42; imitations of, 126; a model for *On the Choice of a Wife*, 106-07; *The Satires Translated by Mr. Dryden, and Several Other Eminent Hands*, 139n; *Third Satire*, 126; *Sixth Satire*, 106-07, 118, 137-42.
juxtaposition, in satire, 288-89; in *Some Papers*, 280. See also rhetoric.

K

kairos (opportunity), repetition of, in Demosthenes, 347, 356, 357-59.
*Keate, Sir Henry Hoo, Bart., 26n.
Keckermann, Batholomew, *Rhetoricae Ecclesiasticae*, 149.
Kelso, Ruth, 108n.
Ker, William P., 361n.
Kerby-Miller, Charles, 193n, 294n, 327n.
*Ketelbey, Robert, 23.
king, divine right of, attacked, 89; a good, the slave of his people, 89n.

King, John E., 208, 229n.
King, Joseph, 7; sues F, 5.
King, William, *Dialogues of the Dead*, 396; *Useful Transactions in Philosophy*, 327.
*Kingston, Evelyn Pierrepont, 2nd Duke of, 22n; F's cousin, 21.
Kinsley, James, 34n, 107n.
Kirk, Rudolf, 256n.
Klaeber, Frederick, 39n, 152n.
Kliger, Samuel, 91n.
Knatchbull, Alice (Wyndham), 18.
*Knatchbull, Edward, 18.
Knatchbull, Sir Edward, Bart., 18.

L

Lacedaemon, 388.
*Lacy, Mr. [James?], subscriber to *Misc.*, 24.
Lady's Advocate, The, 108.
Lancaster, H. Carrington, 416n.
Landa, Louis A., 93n, 101n.
Landor, Walter Savage, *Imaginary Conversations*, 397.
Langhorne, John, 397.
Lannering, Jan, 152 and n, 155-56 and n, 159n.
La Rochefoucauld, François de, *Maximes*, 117, 236.
Latin, F's Demosthenes close to, 349ff, 360; F's Juvenal adds notes in, 139; F's mastery of, 338-41; F's translation of Juvenal, 137-42, Ovid, 338, Silius Italicus, 135, Virgil, 135-36; Greek editions bi-lingual, 341, 342n, 348, 370, 378n; poetry in, preferred to English, 32. See also burlesque, classics, Greek, translation, travesty.
latitudinarian, F a, 66, 76-83; view of man's goodness, 208-09, 426. See also benevolism, religion.
Lauderdale, Charles Maitland, 6th Earl of, 48n.
laughter, F attacks empty, 193n; not a sign of good-nature, 76.
law, conflict of equity and, 263; F's training in, 290; freedom necessarily restricted by, 99-100; of Nature, against avarice, 333n; on usury and forgery, 322n, 322-

INDEX

23n; lawyers, attacked in *Liberty*, 89, satire of, 413. See also Inns of Court.
Lawrence, Frederick, 79.
*Leake, James, Bath bookseller, brother-in-law to Richardson, 25.
Learned Dissertation on Dumpling, A, see Carey, Henry.
Leavitt, Sturgis E., 136n, 416n.
Lee, Nathaniel, *The Rival Queens*, 88n.
Lee, Sir William, Lord Chief Justice, true greatness in, 46.
*Leeds, Thomas Osborne, 4th Duke of, 24n.
Leeuwenhoek, Anton van, 316n, 329.
*Legge, Heneage, 22.
Lehmann, Paul, 299n.
*Leigh, Thomas Leigh, 4th Baron, 20.
Leland, Thomas, translation of Demosthenes, 344n.
Lennox, Charlotte, transl. *Greek Theatre of Father Brumoy*, 419.
letter, as a written oration, 146; use of, by F and Lucian, 372.
levee, poem on Walpole's, 128-29; portrayals in F's works, 129.
Leveridge, Richard, 31n.
Lewis, Clive S., 370.
Lewis, Wilmarth S., 18n.
Leyden, 135; University of, 118, 119, F's study of classics at, 339, 343, tradition of rhetorical disputation at, 306.
liberty, apostrophe to, 90; association of, with classical republicanism, 90, with Gothic north, 90; background of F's and Thomson's poems on, 91-93; Britain natural home of, 90; concept of, defined, 99; F's antidemocratic views on, 94-103, 94n; historical rise of, 88-89; natural not political equality, 100-01; not absolute, 98-99; not same for all classes, 98-100; obligations of, 103; social compact, 88n, 89; theme in *Misc.*, 42, 424-25; theme of poem, *Liberty*, 88-103; theme of war-party, 346; under law, 99. See also class.

Licensing Act, 274, 409.
Lievsay, John L., 174n, 403n.
Lily, William, allusion to Latin grammar of, 131.
Limbrey, John, 119n.
Lind, Levi R., 366n.
Lindner, Felix, 338n.
Lipsius, Justus, 256n, 304.
literature, F's *Misc.* not thought of as, 24; subscribers meager in field of, 24-25.
litotes, in F and Lucian, 378, 382; in F's Demosthenes, 355; in *Some Papers*, 280. See also rhetoric.
Little Theatre in the Haymarket, 134n, 409.
Lives and Characters of Illustrious Persons of Great Britain, see Birch, Thomas.
Locke, John, 57n, 88, 118, 179, 205, 219; association of ideas, 226; on charity, 333n; essays, 146; on good breeding, 185; on habit, 219n; on social grace, 187, 188; *Essay concerning Human Understanding*, 194n; *Some Thoughts concerning Education*, 167n, 185, 187, 188.
Locke, Louis G., 156n.
Loewenberg, R. D., 193n.
London, 118, 141-42; poems on, 125-27.
London Daily Post and General Advertiser, 12n.
London Magazine, 291, 301n, 345n, 346n, 407n.
*Long, Sir Robert, Bart., 17, 19n.
Longinus, 227n; to be read in Greek, 343.
Louis XIV, of France, 346, 398.
love, and wealth, 324; necessary in marriage, 104, 111-13. See also benevolence, good-nature, marriage, virtue, women.
Lowde, James, *Discourse*, 209.
Lucchesinius, Joannes V. (Giovanni V. Lucchesini), Latin translation of Demosthenes, 348n.
Lucian of Samosata, 75, 272 and n, 274, 288, 304, 311, 412n, 420-21, 427-28; "Dryden" translation of, criticized, 365 and n;

455

INDEX

influence in English literature, 365; read at Eton, 339n; translation by Tom Brown, 159n.

dialogues: 389-96; F improves upon, in *Dialogue between Alexander and Diogenes*, 408; in F's farces, 416; in F's *Interlude*, 409, 414-16, 419; influence of *Dialogi deorum*, 409, 412n; influence of *Dialogi mortuorum*, 395 and n, 395-96n; subjects of, 389; techniques of, 389-93, 394n, 414-15; travestied, 416n.

F's relationship to, 366-86: correspondences in attitude, 367-70; devices in common, 371-78; editions in F's library, 370; F's specific indebtedness to, 366-67; F's tributes to, 366; literary personalities of F and, 384-86; style, 157, 343, 366, 378-86; translation projected by F, 338, 365n, 366, 370n, puff in *CGJ*, 343.

works: *Adversus indoctum* (*The Ignorant Book-Collector*), 382n; *Alexander*, 382n; *Bis accusatus* (*The Double Indictment*), 379; *Calumniae non temere credendum* (*Slander, a Warning*), 367; *Cataplus* (*The Voyage Downward*), 373; *Convivium* or *Symposium* (*The Banquet*), 371, 372; *De electro* (*Amber; or the Swans*), 380-81, 385; *De mercede conductis* (*The Hired Companions*), 379-80; *De sacrificiis*, 384; *Demonax*, 376n; *Dialogi deorum* (*Dialogues of the Gods*), influence of, 409, 412n, 416-17, 419; *Dialogi Meretricii* (*Dialogues of the Courtesans*), 374n; *Dialogi mortuorum* (*Dialogues of the Dead*), 367, 390, 416, influence of, 395 and n, 395-96n; *Fugitivi* (*The Fugitives*), 382-83; *Icaromenippus*, 373, 375; *Iupiter tragoedus*, 384; *Laus muscae, see Muscae encomium; Lexiphanes*, 374; *Lucius sive Asinus* (*Lucius, or The Ass*), 384; *Menippus*, 390; *Muscae encomium* (*Praise of the Fly*), 272n, 303, 375; *Nigrinus*, 380;

Parasitus (*The Parasite*), 272n, 375; *Peregrinus*, 369, 376, 382n; *Philopseudes* (*The Lover of Lies*), 376-77; *Piscator* (*The Fisher*), 368n, 376, 390; *Pseudosophista* (*The Purist*), 374; *Quomodo historia conscribenda sit* (*How to Write History*), 390; *Rhetorum praeceptor* (*The Professor of Rhetoric*), 374n; *Somnium* (*Gallus*) (*The Dream; or The Cock*), 377; *Timon*, 381, 382; (attrib.) *Tragopodagra* (*The Gout-Tragedy*), 303 and n; *Vera historia* (*The True History*), 367, 373, 374 and n, 382n, 390; *Vitarum auctio* (*The Sale of Philosophies*), 367n, 390, 390-91 and n. *See also* dialogue, style.

Lucretia, 130.

Lucretius, Carus Titus, *De rerum natura*, 52n, 305n; rise of society portrayed in, 88.

lusus naturae, see abnormal.

luxury, F's version of Juvenal's attack on, 141.

Lyme Regis, Dorsetshire, 119n, 138.

*Lymington, John Wallop, 1st Viscount (later 1st Earl of Portsmouth), 21, 24.

Lyon, Sir Henry, 328n.

Lysias, 303.

Lyte, H. C. Maxwell, 339n.

Lyttelton, Lady Christian (Temple), wife of Sir Thomas, 19.

*Lyttelton, George (later 1st Baron Lyttelton), 17, 25, 93, 98n; of "Cobham cousinhood," 19; complimented, 173; F's *To a Friend* not addressed to, 103 and n; F's *Liberty* dedicated to, 88; influenced by Lucian, 365; satirically portrayed by Hanbury Williams, 88n; true greatness in, 46; *Advice to a Lady*, 108, 111; *Dialogues of the Dead*, 396 and n, 397 and n; *Letters from a Persian in England*, 88 and n.

Lyttelton, Lucy (Fortescue), marriage to George, 103n.

Lyttelton, Sir Thomas, Bart., father of George, 19.

456

INDEX

M

Macedonia, 347ff.
MacGregor, John Marshall, 348n.
Mack, Maynard, 114-15n, 255n.
magistrate, F's moral and social views influenced by position as, 84-85 and n, 101n, 212.
Malebranche, Nicolas, 205.
malice, fictional dissection of, 42; F implacable toward sins of, 335-36, 423; Lucian and F on, 367.
*Mallett, David, 25 and n.
Malmesbury, James Harris, 1st Earl of, 164-65.
Malone, Kemp, 39n.
Manchester, Isabella Churchill, Duchess of, 317-18.
Mandeville, Bernard, 71n, 206, 209; F ambiguous toward, 209n; F uses similar arguments to justify luxury, 102n; weapons against, in Shaftesbury, 72; *Fable of the Bees*, 102n, 309.
Man Superior to Woman, 111.
manners, foreign, F's version of Juvenal's attack on, 141; social, *see* conversation, good breeding, society.
Marcia, *see* Seneca.
Marcilius, Theodore, 299n.
Marcus Aurelius, *see* Aurelius.
*Marlborough, Charles Spencer, 3rd Duke of, 21, 26n.
Marlborough, John Churchill, 1st Duke of, 20, 24; F's personal hero, 90; true greatness in, 46.
Marlborough, Sarah Churchill, Duchess of, 6, 21; not patroness of F, 7, 7n.
marriage, epigrams on, 131; false education in ideals, of, 105-06; favorite theme with F, 103; F's seriousness concerning, 110; love necessary in, 104, 111-13; modern profanation of, 103-04ff; ridicule of, in Restoration drama, 109-10; satire on, 410 and n, 419, in F's *Interlude*, 410ff; theme in *Misc.*, 42; theme of poem *On the Choice of a Wife*, 103-13; tradition of advice to women on, 107-09; wifely ideal in, 104, 105-07, in novels, 110-13. *See also* women.
Mars, 139, 378.
Martha [Benjamin] Constant, 240n.
Martial (Marcus Valerius Martialis), 190n; *Epigrammaton*, 427.
*Martyn, Benjamin, 25; letter cited, 25n.
Marvell, Andrew, *Rehearsal Transprosed*, 274.
Mason, John, *Essay on Prosaic Numbers*, 152, on Addison, 156.
Mason, John E., 166n, 174n.
masquerade, 192n, 222. *See also* Fielding: *The Masquerade*.
Masson, David, 311n.
maxim, 281; in *Essay on Nothing*, 285, 295, 297. *See also* rhetoric.
Mayer, C. A., 303n, 304n.
McKerrow, Ronald B., 303n, 305n, 314n.
McKillop, Alan D., 25n, 91n, 92-93.
McManaway, James G., 403n.
mechanism, in satire, 289. *See also* satire.
meditatio mortis, literature of, 247-48n.
Meibom, Marcus, 342n.
Melanchthon, Philipp, 304.
Melmoth, William, *Letters of Fitzosborne*, 210, 212-13n, 395.
Melville, Herman, 372n.
Memoirs of Martinus Scriblerus, 294n; satire of physiognomy, 193n; satire of science, 327.
Menippus of Gadara, 272, 396n; in Lucian, 390.
merchant, *see* trade.
Mercury, 409ff, 416n.
Merrill, Elizabeth, 394, 414n.
Merry Drollery, "A Song of Nothing," 300.
metaphor, used in "grand style," 161n. *See also* style.
Midwife, The, 310, 311n, 399. *See also* Smart, Christopher.
*Millar, Andrew, 14; distributor of *Misc.*, 4, 11-12, 12n.
Milton, John, 15, 32; on liberty, 99; *Paradise Lost*, 322.
"Misargurus," letter in *CGJ*, 58n.
miser, *see* avarice.

457

INDEX

*Mitchell, Andrew, 23.
Mitchell, Joseph, distinguished subscribers to his *Poems*, 25; on true greatness, 48n; *Poems on Several Occasions*, 25, 48n, 311 and n, 407 and n; *The Shoe-Heel*, 309n.
Mitchell, W. Fraser, 149 and n, 156n.
mock-heroic, in eighteenth century, 309, Restoration, 308; in F and Lucian, 383-84, F's drama, 274. See also satire.
moderation, F and Seneca on, 260-61n.
Mohler, Nora, 327n.
Molière, Jean Baptiste Poquelin de, 416n; *L'Avare*, adapted by F, 332, 337; *Le médecin malgré lui*, adapted by F, 337; *The Select Comedies of Mr. De Moliere*, 337 and n; *Tartuffe*, 199.
Momus turn'd Fabulist: An Opera, 417 and n.
Montagu, George, 18n.
Montagu, Lady Mary Wortley, 21, 189n; compliment to, 121; duplication of lines in F, 135n; on Lyttelton's *Advice*, 111; "town eclogues," 126.
Montaigne, Michel de, 117, 207n, 238 and n; essays, 146; rambling hypotactic structure of late style, 159; translation by Cotton, 159n.
Montesquieu, Charles de Secondat, Baron de la Brède et de, *Lettres Persanes* continued by Lyttelton, 88n.
*Montfort, Henry Bromley, 1st Baron, praised in *Of Good-Nature*, 21, 55n, 59.
Moore, Cecil A., 92n, 247-48n.
Moore, Edward, *The Foundling* praised by F, 227n.
Moore, John Robert, 43n.
moral, attitudes, modification of F's, 84-85 and n, 101n, 212, 214, 420; debt to classics, 67; ideals, value of, even flawed, 265, 269-70; judgment, difficulty of, 115, 224, F's sterner in later works, 84-85 and n; nature equated with social nature, 42, 143-44, 422ff; philosophy, 426; responsibility, 424; rigorism, 68-69; tolerance, 81-83, 425; values and man's fallibility, 263. See also duality, imagination, pleasure, religion, vice, virtue.
moralist, exhortation of, to act from good passions, 225; F as comic, 383, 422ff; F dismissed corrupt from concern of, 224-25; F not a conventional, 264; F's dilemma as a, 222-23ff, ends as a, 263-64, function as a, 262; Hume's two types of, 225-26; must believe in possible change, 215.
Moran, Sister Mary Evaristus, 240n.
More, Henry, *Divine Dialogues*, 394.
More, Sir Thomas, translated Lucian, 365.
"Morpheus," of the Inner Temple, contributed to the *Champion*, 16n.
Mortimer, Cromwell, secretary of the Royal Society, 316, 319.
motives, F's attempts to expose, 144; for human actions not single, 115. See also human nature.
Motte, Benjamin, publisher of Pope-Swift *Miscellanies*, 108.
Mulso, Hester, see Chapone.
Murch, Jerom, 137n.
Murphy, Arthur, "An Essay on Fielding," account of F's difficulties, 5, 249, 250-51, on F's Greek and Latin, 339.
music, soothes or inflames passions, 233.

N

naiveté, mock, in F and Lucian, 375, 382. See also satire.
Namier, Sir Lewis, 16.
Napier, Alexander, 53n, 203n, 208n, 244n, 245n, 335n, 400n.
Nashe, Thomas, 303n; *Praise of Red Herring*, 305, 314.
nature, 376; art and, complementary, 223; avarice condemned by

458

INDEX

law of, 333n; in man: is disguised, 116, opposes rational consolation, 269, overcomes philosophy, 268; state of: democracy and barbarism, 96; man free in, 88-89, offers bounty to all, 58; virtuosi know nothing of, 331n.
navy, subscribers to *Misc.* from, 24.
Needler, Henry, 241n.
Newgate Prison, 50n, 52, 95, 96.
*Newcastle, Thomas Pelham-Holles, 1st Duke of, 17.
New Sarum, *see* Salisbury.
Newton, Isaac, 118, 326.
Nichols, Charles W., 182n, 277.
Nichols, John, 129n.
Nicoll, Allardyce, 418n, 419n.
Nicolson, Marjorie, 327n.
None but Fools Marry; or a Vindication of the Batchelor's Estimate, 109.
Nonpareil, The, 311.
Norfolk, Thomas Howard, 8th Duke of, allusion to, 125.
Norlin, George, 305n.
Norris, John, of Bemerton, *A Collection of Miscellanies*, consolatory letter in, 247n.
Northington, Robert Henley, 1st Earl of, *see* Henley.
Nothing, F's essay on, 291-315; tradition of celebrating, 298-302.
Nourse, Timothy, *Discourse upon Man*, 174n, 175n, 406-07.
novels, comedy and high seriousness in, 427; comic mode of, 423; *consolatione* in, 250; corrective end of F's, 144; dialogue in, 367 and n, 393, 408, 416; do not present all F's genius, 421; ironic vision in, 40-41, 421, 425-26; moral complexity of, 425-26 (*see also* duality); rhetoric in, 284, 378-86 (*see also* rhetoric); satire in, 288-90, 419 (*see also* satire); "social criminals" in, 182-84; style in, 34-41, 161-62, 162-63n, 275, 427 (*see also* commentary, style); techniques in, 393, 408; visits and conversations in, 176.
Noyes, Gertrude E., 174n.

O

O'Connor, Sister Mary C., 248n.
*Odiarn, Wentworth, Sergeant-at-Arms to the House of Commons, 22.
Old England, periodical, allusions to F's projected law-book, 26n; attacks on F, 26.
Oldys, William (attrib. editor) *A Collection of Epigrams*, 417n.
Olynthus, 344ff.
onomatopoeia, F's use of, 163. See *also* style.
Opposition, *see* Walpole, opposition to.
optimism, F's not sentimental, 75, or uncritical, 145; in F's comedy, 270-71, 423-24.
oration, structure of, model for essay, 146-49. See *also* rhetoric, sermon.
  divisions of: *exordium*, 147, 158, 230n, 292, 347; *narratio*, 148, 293, 347; *divisio*, 148, 168 and n, 170n, 234, 241n, 295; *confirmatio*, 148, 292, 293ff, 347; *refutatio*, 148; *peroratio*, 148, 158, 298, 348; variations of, 149.
  genera of: deliberative, 147, 281; forensic (judicial), 147, 281; epideictic (demonstrative), 147, 240 and n, 281, 292, 302, 303n, 305-06.
Orford, Robert Walpole, 1st Earl of, *see* Walpole, Sir Robert.
Orpheus, 132.
*Orrery, John Boyle, 5th Earl of, 17.
Ortigue, Pierre d', Sieur de Vaumorière, *Art de plaire dans la conversation*, 175, 177.
Overbury, Sir Thomas, *A Wife*, 109n.
Ovid (Publius Ovidius Naso), 417-18n; cited by Montaigne and F, 238n; travesty of, 417; *Amores*, echo of, 124; *Ars Amatoria*, first book translated by F, 338 and n; *Metamorphoses*, 265.
Oxford, 306.
Ozell, John, *Art of Pleasing in Con-*

INDEX

versation, transl. of Ortigue, 175 and n, 177n.

P

P., P. T., article on Woodfall in N&Q, 3n, 13n.
Page, William, 119n.
panegyric, see encomium.
Panegyric on a Court, A, 310n.
Panegyrick Epistle to S[ir] R[ichard] B[lackmore], A, 309, 310n.
paradox, in *Dialogue*, 408; in F's poetry, 37; in seventeenth century, 308. See also satire.
paradoxical encomium, see encomium (mock).
parallel, see comparison.
parallelism, in F's poetry, 36-37; in prose, 152, 157-58, 279, 359-60, 379. See also balance, "copiousness," style.
parataxis, see period: paratactic.
parenthesis, in F and Lucian, 378, 379, 380-81; in F's Demosthenes, 353, 359; in F's essays, 160; in *JA*, 162n; variety of, in F, 40. See also rhetoric, style.
Parfitt, George-Edgar, 338n.
parison (balance of equal members), in heroic couplet, 38-39. See also rhetoric.
Parker, Samuel, the elder, Bishop of Oxford, 404.
Parker, Samuel, the younger, on Diogenes, 403-04; praises good-nature, 56n; *Sylva*, 56n, 182n, 403-04.
parody, 273, 274; in F, 31, 135-36; F's satires, 276-77, 290; in *JA*, 102n; of jargon and pedantry in F and Lucian, 374; restricted range of, 277, 332; in satire, 288-89; in *Some Papers*, 272, 277ff, 315ff. See also satire.
Pascal, Blaise, 117.
Passerati, Joannes (Jean Passerat), *Nihil*, 298-99, 300.
passions, Adams an enemy to, 265n; contradictory mixture of, in man, 113ff; danger and virtue of, 269; harmony of, desirable, 218, 225; man a complex of, 224n; necessity of acting from good, 225; overcome philosophy in *Voyage*, 268; positive value of, 66; the springs of human action, 225. See also human nature, reason, will.
heart: good, with good head, 47; badness of, 171, 207; Booth on, vs. head, 266; sins of, inadvertent, 335-36.
ruling passions: in *Amelia*, 61, 266; as handle to man's nature, 117; mark countenance, 192-93.
pathos, appeal of, in rhetoric, 158. See also rhetoric.
Patrick, Simon, *A Consolatory Discourse*, 230n, 231n, 232n, 234n, 235n, 236n, 237n, 243, 244, 245n, 246n, 247n.
patriot, Demosthenes as type of, 362-63; false, 94, 116 and n; in Opposition (see Walpole, opposition to); patriotism: liberty and theme of, 92n, not a native passion, 198, 218. See also politics.
Paul, Saint, 256.
Paulinus, Saint, Bishop of Nola, 240, 242.
Pearce, Zachary, 419.
Pease, Arthur S., 303n.
pedantry, claim to greatness of, satirized, 43; F and Lucian on, 374; mock: in burlesque of Juvenal, 139-40, in F's journals, 274, in F and Lucian, 374. See also satire.
Pelagian, 77n, 81, 206. See also benevolism, latitudinarian, religion.
Pelham, Henry, 161n.
*Pembroke, Henry Herbert, 9th Earl of, 19n, 20, 24.
Perceval, John Perceval, 1st Viscount, see Egmont.
Peri Bathous, see Pope.
periergia (excessive care) *Some Papers*, 280-81. See also rhetoric.
period, *hypotactic* (heavy dependence upon subordinating conjunctions), norm in F's formal style, 153ff, 162n, 359; rambling form of, 159-60; *paratactic* (clauses

460

INDEX

linked by coordination that omits connectives), typical of "curt" Senecanism, 158; F's use in Theophrastan characters, 159; in *JA*, 162n; *suspended* ("periodic sentence") rare in F's formal style, 153, 155. See also style.
periodicals, see journals.
periphrasis, in Demosthenes, 354. See also rhetoric.
Perry, Ben Edwin, 379 and n, 380, 382n, 384.
Persepolis, 402.
Persius Flaccus, Aulus, *Saturae*, allusion to Brewster's translation of, 165 and n.
persona, 408; in *Essay on Nothing*, 282; F seeks to become, 279; in F's journals, 274; in *Some Papers*, 278-79; Swift and, 279. See also satire.
Peterborough, Charles Mordaunt, 3rd Earl of, translation of Demosthenes, 346n.
Peterson, William, 410n.
Petrarca, Francesco, 134.
Petronius Arbiter, Gaius, 384.
Pettie, George, translation of Guazzo, 174n.
Phalaris, controversy, 396.
Philemon, Greek dramatist, cited by Plutarch, 235n.
Philip of Macedon, 344ff.
Philip II, of Spain, 346.
Philip V, of Spain, 344-45, 346.
*Philipps, Sir Erasmus, Bart., 17.
Philips, Ambrose, 309-10; *Distrest Mother*, travestied by F, 276 and n.
Philips, John, *Splendid Shilling*, 309n.
"Philogamus" (pseudonym), *The Present State of Matrimony*, 109.
philosopher, experimental, 295 (*see also* science, virtuoso); satire of, in *Essay on Nothing*, 293, 312.
Philosophical Transactions, see Royal Society.
philosophy, classics and (*see* classics); ethical heroism of, inspiring, 253-54, 261; fallibility of, 230, 262, 264-65, 268-70; ideally beyond calamity, 232, 265-66n;

natural (*see* science); passions overcome, 268; pretenders to, satirized, 367, 375-76; religion complements, 234, 241, surpasses, 238-39, 253 and n, 259; shows folly of immoderate grief, 235, 241; Stoicism and F, 254-63 (*see also* Stoicism). See also duality, human nature, moral, nature, religion, society.
physicians, needed for the mind, 229-30, 262; satirized, 324, in *TJ*, 375; subscribers to *Misc.*, 23-24; surgeon in *TJ*, 295n.
physico-theologians, distinction between benevolism of, and F's, 68-69.
physiognomy, F's interest in, 192-94, 195n, 198, 222; contemporary status of, 193n.
pictures, see imagination.
Pierrepont, Lady Evelyn, see Gower, Lady Evelyn (Pierrepont).
Pinto, Vivian de Sola, 207n, 298, 299n, 403n.
Pitt, Hester (Grenville), wife of William, 19.
*Pitt, William (later 1st Earl of Chatham), 17, 19, 21; compared to Demosthenes, 345, 363.
Pittacus of Mitylene, law of, on drunkenness, 84-85n.
Plato, 43, 70, 205, 254, 367n, 404; death not an evil, 238; dialogue, 393, 394n, 395n, 396n; the just society, 42; *Laws*, 219n.
Plautus, Titus Maccus, 416n; Dryden's *Amphitryon*, 418.
plays, see drama, theatre.
pleasure, F and Seneca on, 260-61n.
pleonasm (redundancy), 152, 279, 359-60; instrument of ironic exaggeration in Cervantes, 157, in Lucian, 379; non-rhythmic use, 159; rhythmic and distributive function of, 156. See also "copiousness," style.
Pliny the Elder (Gaius Plinius Secundus), 322.
Plutarch, 177n, 240n, 254; analogue to essay, 146 and n; authority on conversation, 174n; cited in sermons, 244; on De-

461

INDEX

mosthenes, 363n; the just society, 42; *Consolatio ad Apollonium,* 231n, 232n, 234n, 235n, 236n, 237n, 238n, 245n; *Lives,* 363n, 406; *Moralia,* 207n, 229n.
Pluto, 410.
Plutus, in F's *Interlude,* 411ff. See also Aristophanes.
poet, claim to true greatness, 44-45; foolish to become a, 412.
Poetae Graeci, anthology read at Eton, 339n.
poetry, couplet as discipline, 35-36; F modest about, 29; F's freer than Pope's, 39; F's, other than *Misc.*, 30-31, theatrical, 31; F's training in, 31ff, 290; satiric forms in F's, 273; "strength" in, 39.
F's, in Misc.: discussion of, 29-41: interest in content, 32-33; lacks ironic vision, 40-41, parenthetical element, 40; light verse best of, 41; models for, 31-32, Pope, 33-34, 114; range of types in, 31; relation to prose of, 34-41; rhetorical devices in, 36-39; themes explicit in, 30; value of, 41, 421.
forms of: see allegory, burlesque, complaint, dialogue, diatribe, epigram, epitaph, fable, progress poem, rebus, simile, verse-epistle, verse-essay.
polarities, F gives weight to opposed, 267-69, 421, 425. See also duality.
politics, allusions to, in F, 410; bribery of voters, 121, 326; F's conservatism in, 94-103; need for adequate ideals, 50n; satire on, in *Some Papers,* 325-26; writers on, ridiculed, 292; politicians: blockheads, 94; minister, 298; should study beggars, 201. See also elections, government, king, liberty, patriotism, statesman, Walpole.
Polybius, see Seneca.
Polycrates, 303.
polyptoton (repetition in different form), in F's poetry, 37. See also rhetoric.
Polypus (polyp), "Chrysipus" substituted for by F, 278, 315ff.

Pope, Alexander, 3n, 36, 38, 39, 121, 273; echoes of, 34n, in F's lines on beau, 45; F's poetic debt to, 29, 31, 33-34, 114; letter to Allen on *Misc.*, 27; ordered set of *Misc.*, 25; on Peter Walter, 132 and n; psychological skepticism in, 113-17; publication by subscription, 15, satire on the virtuosi, 327; subscribed to Mitchell's poems, 25; "town eclogues," 126; translation of *Iliad* criticized by F, 341; translation of *Odyssey*, 394; *Dunciad,* 308, 327; *Epilogue to the Satires,* 34n, 322n; *Epistle to Arbuthnot,* 34n; *Epistle to Cobham,* 113-17; *Essay on Man,* 113-17, 255, 399; *Horace, Satire II. i. Imitated,* 132 and n, 309, 310n; *Letters,* 189 and n; *Of the Characters of Women,* 108; "On Silence," 300; *Peri Bathous,* 29.
Porritt, Edward, 121n.
Posidonius, Stoic philosopher, cited by Cicero, 240.
Potter, George R., 327n.
Powney, Henry, 32.
praecepta (abstract precepts), of consolation, 247n.
praeteritio (passing over), in F's translation of Demosthenes, 355. See also rhetoric.
"Praise of Nothing, The," ballad, 299-300.
predicate, duplication of, see "copiousness."
Present State of Matrimony, The, see "Philogamus."
pride, 193; "character" of, in *Essay on Conversation,* 159; in contempt, 168n, 171; in Diogenes, 386, 388-89, 398, 404; Diogenes as humbler of, 406-07; Lucian and F on, 367. See also vanity.
primitivism, in *Of Good-Nature,* 58; used as political weapon by Lyttelton and F, 88n.
Prior, Matthew, 248n, 404; influenced by Lucian, 365; poetic model for F, 31-32, 123 and n, 130-31 and n; publication by subscription, 15.

462

INDEX

progress poem, *Liberty* an example of, 88. See also poetry.
prolepsis, see *hypophora, rejectio.*
promiser, examples in F's novels, 201-02; warning against, 195.
proof, 375; Aristotle on modes of, 281, 284-88; "artificial" (examples and enthymemes) in *Essay on Nothing*, 285-88; "inartificial," in *Essay on Nothing*, 284. See also rhetoric.
prose fiction, see novels.
Proserpine, 410.
prosonomasia (jesting nickname), 318. See also rhetoric.
prosopopoeia (personification) in dialogues of the dead, 396-97 (*see also eidolopoeia*); in F's translation of Demosthenes, 356; Swift and F, use of, 279. See also rhetoric.
prude, hypocritical, 204; Juno as, 411ff; mistake to marry a, 104.
prudence, F's ambivalence toward, 227 and n; Jones must acquire, 86.
Pufendorf, Samuel, on Law of Nature, 333n.
"puff," satiric, in F's journals, 274. See also satire.
Pulteney, William, see Bath, Earl of.
Puritans, 326, 404, 406n; reaction against, 208. See also religion.
Purpus, Eugene R., 394n, 396n.
Puttenham, George (attrib. author), *Arte of English Poesie*, 281n, 382; "figures sententious" in, 38.

Q

qualification, 160; in F and Lucian, 380-83. See also style.
*Queensberry, Charles Douglas, 3rd Duke of, 17.
Quintilian (Marcus Fabius Quintilianus), *Institutio oratoria*, 146-47n, 295; on amplification, 281-84; on *enargeia*, 227n; on *periergia*, 280-81; on perspicuity, 163n; status of a case, 292.

R

Rabelais, François, 273n, 311, 370, 421n; mock encomia in, 303, 304n.
Racine, Jean, *Andromaque*, 276n.
Rackham, Harris, 69n, 146n, 220n.
*Radnor, John Robartes, 4th Earl of, 21, 24n.
Radzinowicz, Leon, 323n.
raillery, danger of, 172-73, 178; in Diogenes, 398, 403; permissible kind of, 173; Swift and Steele on, 179. See also conversation.
Ralph, James, 32; parallels in style with F, 163n; portrayed in *The Opposition*, 7.
Ramsland, Clement, 92n.
Ramus (Pierre de la Ramée), rhetorical reforms, 149.
*Ranby, John, sergeant-surgeon to the king, alluded to in *TJ* and *Amelia*, 23.
ratiocinatio (augmentation by inference), in *Essay on Nothing*, 283. See also rhetoric.
realism, comic, in F and Lucian, 371-72.
reason, 226; Adams on, to conquer passions, 265n; Booth on, versus heart, 266; essential but not dependable in moral conduct, 61; harmonizes passions, 225; masculine quality of, 268; office of, under affliction, 230, 232-33, 242, 243, 247, 253n; pride from a depraved, 207; required for true greatness, 47; sins of, deliberate, 335-36; will and, 218. See also human nature, passions, will.
Réaumur, René Antoine Ferchault de, 317.
rebus, F's, 31, 124. See also poetry.
Reed, Amy L., 248n.
Reed, Isaac, reprints *Essay on Nothing* in his *Repository*, 28.
Regnard, Jean-François, F indebted to, 338n; *Les ménechmes*, 416n; *Le retour imprévu*, 338n.
rehearsal play, 274; fascination of, for F, 278; technique of, like *Some Papers*, 278. See also satire.

463

INDEX

rejectio (anticipating and dismissing objection), in *Essay on Nothing*, 294. See also rhetoric.

religion, blasphemy and irreverence censured, 172, 178, 183 and n; Christian condemnation of avarice, 334-35; Christian humanism central to F, 42, 145, 420; Christian topics of consolation: emphasized by F, 145, 252, 270, in *JA*, 251, not all used by F in *Remedy*, 244-46, 251-53; comedy reflects providential order of, 275; contemporaries on lack of, in F's novels, 78-79; Deists attacked, 71n, 72n; depravity: as concept in, 207-08, and goodness, 72, conviction of, leads to atheism or enthusiasm, 210; F emphasizes social and psychological in, 81; F latitudinarian in, 66, 76, distinguished from latitudinarian clergy, 76-83; F preferred hope to submission in, 164, 251-52, 253-54; fallibility in remedies of, 262-65, 269-70; good-nature: a virtue of, 65-66, complementary to, 71-72, 87, transcended morally by, 72 and n, in *Amelia*, 86 and n; goodness in Christian, 47; hate not mark of Christian, 196; grace, Adams on, 265n, not emphasized in F, 77-81; hypocrisy and, 195-97, in Lucian and F, 367-68, 369; immortality, 72, 164, 239, 241, 246-47, 252; insolence impious, 177; moral rigorism in Christian, 79-80; philosophy complemented by, 234, 241, surpassed by, 238-39, 253 and n, 259; rewards and punishments necessary in, 71; speculation detrimental to, 294n; theological elements of, scanted by F, 77-81, 77n; Thwackum's devotion to, 83; ultimate basis of moral behavior, 71 and n, 72, 87; view of greatness in, 52-53, 53n; works stressed over doctrine, 66; writers on, ridiculed, 292. See also ascetic, benevolism, censoriousness, clergy, Deism, depravity, immortality, latitudinarian, Pelagian, philosophy, physico-theologians, Puritans, saint, Scripture, sermon, sin, vice, virtue.

Rentsch, Johannes, 395-96n.

repetition, in F's poetry, 36-37, and prose, 38; in F's translation of Demosthenes, 354-55; of phrases or allusions in F, 190n. See also *anadiplosis*, *anaphora*, *antimetabole*, *antistrophe*, *polyptoton*, rhetoric.

Repository, The, see Reed, Isaac.

Restoration, comedy, 274; F quotes playwrights of, 32; satire, 308; stage, 109.

revenge, 64; Christianity and wisdom oppose, 72n; Diogenes' thirst for, 389; good-nature not incompatible with, 62, 72n.

rhetoric, "colors" of, 280; decline of, in nineteenth century, 304, 311; education in, in eighteenth century, 306; in *Essay on Nothing*, 281-88, 302ff; in F and Lucian, 369, 372-73ff, F and Swift, 279, F's translation of Demosthenes, 353-59, 360ff; figure of, elaborated, 280, 287-88; humor and, 284; offices of: *inventio*, 290 (*see also* invention), *dispositio*, 290 (*see also* oration), *elocutio*, 290 (*see also* style); in poetry, 36-38, 42-142 *passim*, in prose, 38-39, 150-64, 284, 378-86; pretenders to, in Lucian, 367, 374 and n; satire and, 288-90 (*see also* satire); in *Some Papers*, 280-81; static view of human nature in, 221; topics of panegyric, 273, 305-06; varieties of, for particular occasions, 146-47: deliberative, epideictic, judicial, 147, appropriate devices for, 281.

terms of, see accumulation, ambiguity, amplification, *anadiplosis*, *anaphora*, anticlimax, *antimetabole*, *antistrophe*, antithesis, *asyndeton*, *chiasmus*, *cola*, comparison, contrast, "copiousness," *cursus*, deprecation, *descriptio*, *eidolopoeia*, *enargeia*, enthy-

464

INDEX

meme, *epiphonema, ethos,* example, *homonymy, hyperbaton,* hyperbole, *hypophora, incrementum,* inversion, irony, juxtaposition, litotes, maxim, parenthesis, *parison, pathos, periergia,* periphrasis, *polyptoton, praeteritio,* proof, *prosonomasia, prosopopoeia, ratiocinatio, rejectio,* repetition, rhetorical question, satire, *sententia,* status, style, *synchoresis,* topics.
Rhetorica ad Herennium, 149; divisions of oration, 147.
rhetorical question (*erotesis*), 160; in Demosthenes, 353; in F's poetry and prose, 38.
Ricciardi, Giovanni Battista, 299n.
Richardson, Samuel, 108n; allusion in F's Juvenal, 138; attacked in *Shamela,* 6; brother-in-law (Leake) a subscriber to *Misc.,* 25; on consolation, 247n; on conversation, 174n; printer's devices, 13; procured set of *Misc.* for Aaron Hill, 25; subscribed to Mitchell's poems, 25; *Letters on the Most Important Occasions,* 174n, 247n; *Pamela,* 102n, 138.
Richmond, Charles Lennox, 2nd Duke of, F's *Miser* dedicated to, 57n; F's *Of Good-Nature* dedicated to, 17n, 54; not subscriber to *Misc.,* 17n, 57n; praised, 57-58.
*Richmond, Sarah Lennox, Duchess of, complimented in *Of Good-Nature,* 17n, 59.
ridicule, 312; attack on Aristophanes for, 73n; F on Shaftesbury's use of, 72, 72-73n; ridiculous, preface to *JA* on, 275.
"roasting," attacked in *Champion,* 227, in *JA,* 182.
Robertson, Durant W., Jr., 13n.
Robin-Hood Society, satirized in *CGJ,* 101n, 302. *See also* class.
Robin's Panegyrick; or, The Norfolk Miscellany, 310n.
Rochester, John Wilmot, Earl of, 190n; attributed couplet on marriage, 109-10; on Diogenes, 403; *Satyr against Mankind,* 207

and n; *Upon Nothing,* 298 and n, 299n, 300, 301 and n, 302, 307.
*Rockingham, Lewis Watson, 2nd Earl of, 21.
Rogers, the Rev. Samuel, F's poem to Miss Husband reprinted by, 137n; circle of, at Bath, 137n.
Rogers, Winfield H., 277.
rogue-biography, and *JW,* 277.
Rome, 283.
*Romney, Robert Marsham, 2nd Baron, 21.
Ronnet, Gilberte, 353 and n.
Rooke, John, translator of Arrian, on greatness, 54.
Rosa, Salvator, 299n.
Rowe, Nicholas, publication by subscription, 15.
Rowlands, Samuel, *Diogines Lanthorne,* 406n.
*Roxburghe, Robert Ker, 2nd Duke of, 17.
Royal Academy of Sciences, Paris, 317.
Royal Society, 132; contemporary attacks on, 326-29; fellows of, subscribers to *Misc.,* 24n; F's attacks on, 329-31; *Philosophical Transactions* of, 328-29, Trembley's paper in, 316-17ff, parodied by F, 277-81, 315-36; the virtuosi in, 280, 324n, 326n, F on, 330-31, not all members of, 327 and n, 328. *See also* science.
*Rutland, John Manners, 3rd Duke of, 21.
Ruud, Martin B., 39n.

S

S., H. K. St. J., contributor to *N&Q,* 137n.
S., S, "In the praise of Nothing," 300.
Sackett, Samuel J., 106n, 184n, 334n.
Sackton, Alexander H., 303n.
Sailor's Opera, The, ballad-opera, 134n.
saint, dissection of hypocritical, 195-97, 198-99, 202-03. *See also* religion.

465

INDEX

*St. Albans, Charles Beauclerk, 2nd Duke of, 20.
St. Évremond, Charles Marguetel de Saint-Denis, Seigneur de, 233n; essays, 146.
St. James's Evening Post, 12.
Sale, William M., 13.
Salisbury, 19n, 118, 120-21, 122, 123, 164.
*Salkeld, Robert, 22.
Salkeld, William, the elder, *Reports of Cases in the King's Bench*, 22.
*Salkeld, William, the younger, 22.
Salmon, Thomas, *Critical Essay concerning Marriage*, 109.
Sams, Henry W., 255n.
Sandys, Sir John Edwin, 348n, 352n, 354n.
satire, 427-28; of abuses more effective than ideal portraits, 181; attention to technique in F's, 427; conjunction and disjunction in, 288-90; devices, F's range in, 275, 288-89; dichotomies in method of, 289-90n; double implications of F's, 332; F's and Lucian's, constructive, 368, parallels in, 368ff; F's dramatic, and Lucianic dialogue, 415-16; F's ingenuity of invention in, 428; F's use of mock encomium for, 312ff; good-nature not inconsistent with, 62; ironic praise in, 308; just society and, 42; Juvenal's, on women, modernized by F, 137ff; in Lucianic sketches (*see* Lucian); in Restoration, 308; parody in F's, 276-77, 288; rhetoric in F's, 272ff, 288-90 (*see also* rhetoric); themes of F's, 419; variations upon a theme in F's, 276.
F's in Misc., discussion of, 272-91: formal, 272; *Essay on Nothing*, a mock encomium, 272; *Some Papers*, a parody, 272; F's mastery of, 273-77; range of forms in, 273-74; comedy and, 274-75; parody and burlesque in F's, 275-77; devices in *Some Papers*, 277-81; devices in *Essay on Nothing*, 281-88; significance of F's formal, 288-91.
devices of, *see* distortion, imitation, incongruity, innuendo, irony, mechanism, naiveté (mock), paradox, *persona*, trope, undercutting. *See also* rhetoric, terms of.
forms of, see allegory, censorial court, complaint, criticism (burlesque), dialogue, diatribe, dream-vision, encomium (mock), epigram, epistle, epitaph (mock), essay, fable, history (burlesque), *ingénu*, pedantry (mock), "puff," rehearsal play, verse-epistle, verse-essay.
See also burlesque, comedy, farce, irony, mock heroic, parody, travesty.
Saunders, Jason L., 256n.
*Savage, Richard (the poet?), subscriber to *Misc.*, 24-25.
Sayre, Farrand, 387n, 403n, 406n.
Scarron, Paul, 416; Cotton's *Scarronides*, 136; *Virgile travesty en vers burlesques*, 135-36.
Schönzeler, Heinrich, 338n.
scholasticism, 205.
Schotel, Gilles D. J., 306n.
science, 290-91; existence of a true, 331n; experimental philosophers, 295; F and Swift on, 279-80; F's attitude toward, 328-31; humanist attitude toward, 328. *See also* Royal Society.
Sclater family, 119n.
Scotland, 320n.
Scriblerus Papers, see Memoirs of Martinus Scriblerus.
Scripture, 65, 190n, 194, 195n, 196, 199, 237, 246n, 333n; Golden Rule, qualified by degree, 176-77, sum of good breeding, 167 and n; Greek testament cited by F, 342, read at Eton, 339n; texts on subjection of wives, 108 and n.
Seagrim, Randolph, sued by F, 5n.
Seasonable Admonition to a Great Man, A, 92n.
Secker, Thomas, Archbishop of Canterbury, funeral sermons, 245.
Sedgewick, O., *Universal Masquerade*, 174n.
Selby-Bigge, Sir Lewis A., 226n.
selfishness, *see* egoism.

466

INDEX

Seneca, Lucius Annaeus, 240n, 254, 256, 265-66n; analogue to essay, 146 and n; cited in sermons, 244, 247n; on consolation, 229n, 231n, 232n, 233n, 240, *et passim*; difference from Old Stoa, 258; distinction between Stoic and Cynic, 258; F's admiration for, 257-58, 261; on sympathy, 260; *TJ* and, 260-61n; *Ad Helviam matrem*, 240; *De clementia*, 258; *De consolatione ad Marciam*, 231n, 234n, 235n, 236n, 237n, 238n, 240, 242, 246n; *De consolatione ad Polybium*, 231n, 232n, 236n, 240, 245n, 246n; *De vita beata*, 101n, 260-61n; *Epistulae morales*, 228, 229n, 231n, 232n, 233n, 240, 258, 260.
    Senecan prose style, 38-40; "curt" form, 155, parataxis in, 158-59, used by character writers, 159, 162n; "Senecan amble," 155-56. *See also* style.
sententia, in F's poetry, 37; in Senecan prose and heroic couplet, 38-39. *See also* rhetoric.
sentimentalism, distinguished from good-nature, 60-61.
sequence, 160, in *JA*, 162n. *See also* style.
sermon, changes in structure after Ramistic reforms, 149; divisions in, 150; *explicatio verborum* in, 149; F's debt to, in essays, 149-50; structural model for essay in, 146, 149-50. *See also* oration, rhetoric.
Shadwell, Thomas, 274; *The Virtuoso*, 326 and n, 327 and n.
Shaftesbury, Anthony Ashley Cooper, 3rd Earl of, 67, 155, 185, 206, 217, 394, 412n; balance of passions, 218; brother of Lady Elizabeth Harris, 18; cited on God in *Champion*, 66 and n; cited by Square in *TJ*, 262n; on complaisance, 179 and n; essays, 146; on gravity, 85n; importance of image in, 57n; mixed nature of man, 223; on raillery, 179 and n; relationship between moral philosophy of, and F's, 69-73; *Characteristicks*, 66 and n, 168-69 and n, 179 and n; *Letter concerning Enthusiasm*, 66 and n, 85n, 169n, 196n; *Moralists*, 394; *Sensus Communis*, 179n.
*Shaftesbury, Anthony Cooper, 4th Earl of, subscribes to Birch's *Lives* through Martyn, 25n.
*Shaftesbury, Susannah Cooper, Countess of, 25n; complimented by F in *Of Good-Nature*, 17n, 59.
Shakespeare, William, 32, 423; Malvolio, 199.
Shepperson, Archibald B., 94n.
Sherbo, Arthur, 190n.
Sherburn, George, 27n, 93n, 94n, 127, 189n.
Sheridan, Richard Brinsley, *Ode to the Genius of Scandal*, 310; *Ridotto of Bath*, 310.
Sherlock, Thomas, Bishop of London, 425.
Sherlock, William, Dean of St. Paul's *Practical Discourse concerning Death*, 239 and n, 247, 248 and n.
Shero, Lucius R., 132n.
*Sherrard, John, 22.
Sidney, Algernon, 88.
Silius Italicus, Tiberius Catius Asconius, *Punica*, epigraph from, in *CGJ*, 97n, F's translation from, 135.
simile, admiration of Augustans for, 124; F's poetic, 124, 135; translation of a, from Silius Italicus, 135. *See also* poetry, style.
Simonides of Ceos, epigraph to F's *Amelia*, 113n.
Simplicius of Cilicia, 174n.
Sims, B. J., 379n.
sin, of head, F implacable toward, 335-36; of heart, F lenient toward, 335; term used by hypocrites, 203. *See also* religion, vice.
Skelton, John, 141.
*Skinner, Matthew, His Majesty's Prime Sergeant-at-Law, 22.
slander, attacks on, 172, 178, 183, 195, 202, 224-25; censoriousness

INDEX

a form of, 197; F and Lucian on, 367.
Smart, Christopher, 311n; "Epitaph on Fielding," 339n; *The Midwife,* 310, 311n, 399.
Smith, Adam, *Theory of Moral Sentiments* anticipated, 57 and n.
Smith, David Nichol, 299n, 308n.
Smith, J., bookseller, published Pope's *Letters,* 189n.
Smith, John, bookseller, published Dublin edition of *Misc.,* 15.
Smithers, Peter, 156n.
Smollett, Tobias, 26n.
Snow, Thomas, 309, 310n.
society, amenities of, in drama, 415; *aura popularis* supports false greatness in, 43, 402; avarice a crime against, 332-36; the *civitas bona,* 43, 422, 424-25; ceremony important to, 102; conversation essential to, 166-67, advances happiness of, 172; evil youth should be put out of, 335-36; F not an iconoclast concerning, 176; F's pamphlets on evils in, 84; good breeding contributes to, 176; hierarchical concept of, 99-101; importance of relationships in, 164, 180; man naturally formed for, 73-74, 144, 166, 185, 405; order the desideratum of, 99-100; rise of, portrayed in *Liberty,* 88-89; satire on, in *Essay on Nothing,* 296-97, 312ff; values of: education required in, 47, 50, 312-14, explicit in *Essay on Conversation,* 189, interdependent with moral values, 42, 143-44, 422ff, writer must define, 50-51; virtue authentic only in, 405.
Socrates, 261, 283, 377; example of good breeding, 186; F censures Aristophanes for ridiculing, 73n; on life as an evil, 237.
solacia, letters to particular mourners, 247n.
Solon, 238n; rebuttal of consolation, 266.
"Somnus," of Gray's Inn, contributor to *Champion,* 16n.

*Sone, Philip, chaplain to the Prince of Wales, 23.
"Song of Nothing, A," in *Merry Drollery,* 300.
songs, F's, in *Misc.,* 134-35; F's, not in *Misc.,* 30-31; F's rhythmic sense in, 134-35; "The Dusky Night Rides down the Sky," 31; "The Roast Beef of Old England," 31 and n.
Sophists, 304-05.
South, Robert, 77-78, 203n, 326, 334n, 378; on credulity of good-nature, 63n; on detraction, 190n; on the fear of death, 248; on flattery, 201; influence on F's style, 157; on revenge, 190n; on submission, 77n; use of *hypophora,* 150n, 360.
Spain, appeal for war with, 92, 344-47.
Spartans, 181.
Spears, Monroe K., 123n, 131n, 404n.
Spectator, The, 68n, 146, 233n, 248, 248n, 307, 416-17; allusion to Rochester, 300; attacks on Royal Society, 327; on consolation, 249-50; on Diogenes, 403n. *See also* Addison, Steele.
Spence, Joseph, *Essay on Pope's Odyssey,* 394.
*Spencer, John, brother of Charles, Duke of Marlborough, 26n.
Spenser, Edmund, no imitation of, in F, 32.
Spingarn, Joel E., 175n.
squire, claim to greatness of, satirized, 45.
Stafford, Anthony, *Staffords Heavenly Dogge,* 406n.
Stamp Act, 19.
Stanhope, Charles, 317-18.
Stanhope, George, translator of Epictetus, 174n; *Christianity the Only True Comfort,* 244-45.
*Stanhope, John, 20n.
*Stanhope, Philip Stanhope, 2nd Earl, 20n, 24n.
*Stanhope, Sir William, 20n.
Starkman, Miriam K., 327n.
statesman, moral attacks on great, 53; qualities of a good, 48n.

468

INDEX

Statesman's Progress, The, 51n.
status, in rhetoric, 292. *See also* rhetoric.
Steele, Sir Richard, 24, 108n, 185; on Demosthenes, 362; influence on F's style, 157; letter on false greatness, 43n; on raillery, 179; subscribed to Mitchell's poems, 25; *Christian Hero,* 209n, 255 and n; *Ladies Library,* published by, 108; *Spectator,* 179; *Tatler,* 328, 362. *See also Guardian, Spectator, Tatler.*
Sterne, Laurence, 175n, 301, 310n.
Stephen, Sir James F., 322n.
Stillingfleet, Benjamin, poetic *Essay on Conversation* confused with F's, 166n.
Stilpo, Cynic philosopher, 207, 258; F's censure of, 231n.
Stimson, Dorothy, 326n.
Stoicism, 205, 224, 243, 265n, 403n, 426; *ataraxia* of, qualified, 232n; concept of the general good in, 192, 257, 259-60; contemporary criticism of, 254-56, 258; Cynics, Old Stoa, and, 258; fallacy of detachment in, 229-30; F and Shaftesbury share debt to, 70; F's attitude toward 145, 254-63ff: virtues of, 254n, 257, 259-60, 268, defects of, 255-56, 262, parallels with, 258-60; masculine quality of, 268; paradox of virtue over vice in, 56; Parson Adams and Christian, 264-65 and n; relation of, to Christianity, 256, 270, complements, 259, shares flaws, 262-63; Square's fallible, 262n.
Strachey, Charles, 403n.
Strafford, Thomas Wentworth, Earl of, alluded to by F, 125.
Strahan, William, printer of first volume of *Misc.,* 12, 13n.
*Strode, William, 18.
Stubbe, Henry, 326.
Sturgess, Herbert A. C., 113n.
style, attention to technique in F's, 427; commentary and F's (*see* commentary); F's mastery of, controls comic vision, 275; in F's translation of Demosthenes, 359-62; humor and dignity in F's, 40, 142, 382; relation of F's poetry to prose, 34-41; rhetorical devices in (*see* rhetoric); satiric (*see* satire); Senecan prose and F's, 38-40, 155ff, 158-59, 162n; variety of, in F, 279, 420.

devices of, *see* alliteration, anacoluthon, balance, cadence, "copiousness," *cursus,* diction, extension, figure, metaphor, onomatopoeia, parallelism, parenthesis, period, pleonasm, qualification, sequence, simile. *See also* rhetoric, terms of; satire, devices of.

in F and Lucian, 378-86: qualities praised by F, 378n; balance of sentence elements, 378-80; burlesque "copiousness," 379; parenthesis, 380-81; qualification and extension, 380-83; litotes, 382; undercutting, 382-83; levels of diction, 383-84; commentary, 385.

of F's formal essays, 150-64: equable base, 150-51; simple diction, 151; images, 151, 161n; formulae of deprecation, 151n, 162n; "copiousness," 152, 155, 157-58, 279, 379; cadence, 152, 279; sentence-structure, 153ff; hypotactic period, 153ff, 159-60, 162n, 359; committed syntax, 155; "Senecan amble," 155; debt to Tillotson and Addison, 155-58; pleonastic word-pairs, 156-57, 159, 279, 359-60, 379; paratactic period, 158-59, 162n; anacoluthon, 159; sense of old-fashioned, 159; "hath-doth" usage, 159n, 359; sequences, 160, 162n; coordinate constructions, 160, 163n, 359-60; parenthesis, 40, 160, 162n, 359, 378-81; extension and qualification, 160-61, 162n, 359, 380-83; grammatical solecisms avoided, 161n; basis of narrative style, 161-62, 162-63n; levels of diction, 161n, 383-84; clarity, 163; tropes and figures, 163n.

469

INDEX

See also diction, rhetoric, satire, sermon.
subscription, publication by, 15.
substance, "immaterial," controversy over, 293-94 and n, 373.
Suckling, Sir John, 32.
Suffolk, Henrietta Howard, Countess of, 26n.
Sulpicius Rufus, Servius, consolation to Cicero, 238n, translated by Tom Brown, 247n.
Summers, Montague, 309n.
Sutton, Edward W., 146n.
Swift, Jonathan, 17, 75, 99n, 103, 132, 180, 185, 210, 289, 311, 321, 370, 378; attacks on Royal Society, 327 and n; on complaisance, 179; F on the Lilliputians, 124 and n; F on Lucian and, 366n; influence on F's style, 157; influenced by Lucian, 365, 368; linked with F and Chesterfield on politeness, 27n; mock encomium, 308 and n; *persona* of F and, 279; poetic model for F, 32; on raillery, 179; as satirist, 332; science and, 279-80; subscribed to Mitchell's poems, 25; *Cadenus and Vanessa*, 418; *Compleat Collection of Genteel Conversation*, 182n; *Gulliver's Travels*, 124 and n, 308, 327 and n; "Hints toward an Essay on Conversation," 166, 179; *Letter of Thanks*, 307; *Letter to a Very Young Lady*, 108; *Modest Proposal*, 279; "On Good-Manners and Good-Breeding," 166-67n, 170n; *Tale of a Tub*, 273, 299n, 302, 308; "Thoughts on Various Subjects," 225n.
syllogism, 293, 314; enthymeme and, 285.
sympathy, aroused by pictorial imagination, 57 and n, 224, 226-27, 227n: denied by avarice, 333; fundamental in good-nature, 57; imaginative, impossible to false greatness, 49-50.
synchoresis (concession), 151. *See also* rhetoric.
Synesius of Cyrene, 303.

T

Talbot, Eugène, 303n.
*Talbot, William Talbot, 2nd Baron (later 1st Earl), 17, 21; *Plutus* dedicated to, 17.
taste, most men lack, 222-23; in Shaftesbury, 73.
Tatler, The, 146, 362; attacks on Royal Society, 327. *See also* Addison, Steele.
Tave, Stuart M., 66n.
Taylor, John, the Water Poet, 15; *Ale Ale-Vated into the Ale-titude*, 307.
Temperley, Harold W. V., 345n.
Temple, Christian, *see* Lyttelton, Lady Christian (Temple).
Temple, Hester, *see* Grenville, Hester (Temple).
Temple, Penelope, *see* Berenger, Penelope (Temple).
Temple, Richard, Viscount Cobham, *see* Cobham.
Temple, Sir William, 179, 180n; on consolation, 247n; essays, 146; on good breeding, 185; Senecan and Ciceronian elements in style of, 155, 159; *Essay upon the Ancient and Modern Learning*, 155-56n; "Heads Designed for an Essay on Conversation," 167n, 180n, 185; *Of Poetry*, 401n; "To the Countess of Essex," 247n.
Thales of Miletus, 341; on life as an evil, 237.
Thalia, 412.
theatre, allusions to, 125-26; F's career in, ended by Licensing Act, 5; F's poem on Watts at, 129-30; friends from, subscribe to *Misc.*, 24; metaphor for human actions, 116; in Restoration, 109. *See also* drama.
Théâtre de la foire, 416 and n.
Theophrastus, 159, 177n; emphasized vices rather than virtues, 181n; Theophrastan character, 199, in poetry, 36, uses paratactic style, 159.
theory, and practice in F, 264-66, 270 and n.
*Thomas, Sir Edmund, Bart., 17.

470

INDEX

Thomas, W. Moy, 111n, 135n.
Thompson, Craig R., 303n, 365n.
Thomson, James, *Liberty*, 93n, 399, background of, 91-93; *Works*, printed by Woodfall, 13n.
Thornbury, Ethel M., 34on, 37on.
Thornton, Bonnell, *Drury-Lane Journal*, 302, 403n.
Tibullus, Albius, translation of in *CGJ*, 29.
Tillotson, Geoffrey, 36.
Tillotson, John, Archbishop of Canterbury, 8on, 203n, 253, 378, 379; on conversation, 174n; "copiousness" in style of, 157-58; funeral sermons, 245; latitudinarian, 67; sermons against the fear of death, 248; stylistic influence on Addison, 156 and n, on F, 156ff.
time, best remedy for grief, 230, 233, 243.
Tinker, Chauncey Brewster, 66n.
Titian (Tiziano Vecellio), 115.
Titius, *see* Cicero.
Toland, John, *Miscellaneous Works*, consolatory letter in, 247n.
Tonson, Jacob, the elder, 15.
topics (*topoi*, places), 292, 301n, 302; of encomium, 292, 302-03, 305-06, mock encomium, 309-11; in *Essay on Nothing*, 292, 295, 296. *See also* rhetoric.
Tories, anti-Walpole subscribers to *Misc.*, 20.
Tourreil, Jacques de, French translation of Demosthenes, 348n.
Towers, Augustus Robert, 68n, 110n.
trade, 177; improved stature of merchant, 44; gentry of, ill-bred, 186, 188; "Paul Traffick" in *CGJ*, 100n.
tragedy, F not fond of, 10.
translation, contemporary hackwork, 337; F's in *Misc.*, discussion of, 337-44; F's largely hackwork, 337, F's knowledge of French, 337, Latin, 337, Greek, 339-44; F's verse, 31, 135; literal, not aim of age, 361; of Lucian criticized by F, 365 and n. *See also* classics, Latin, Greek.

travel-literature, and *JW*, 277.
travesty, 409; F's dramatic, 274; in F's verse, 135-36, 273. *See also* satire.
Trembley, Abraham, 315ff, 331.
Tripler, T., *Elogy of Nothing*, 301 and n.
trope, 163n; in satire, 288-89. *See also* figure, satire.
Tucker, Joseph E., 337n.
Tullia, daughter of Cicero, 238n.
Tunbridge Wells, 140.
Turnbull, John M., 175n.
Tuveson, Ernest, 57n, 81.
*Tweeddale, John Hay, 4th Marquis of, 23.
tyche (fortune), repetition of, in Demosthenes, 349-50, 357-59.
*Tyers, Jonathan, alluded to in *Amelia*, 26n.

U

undercutting, in F and Lucian, 382-83; of sententiousness, 40; in *Some Papers*, 280. *See also* satire.
Universal Spectator, The, on Diogenes, 403n.
Upton Grey, Hampshire, 119 and n, 276.
Ustick, W. Lee, 185n, 231n, 255n.
usury, 322-23n, 356; attacked in *Some Papers*, 321ff; law concerning, 322n.

V

values, F's moral (*see* moral); philosophical (*see* philosophy); religious (*see* religion); social (*see* society); complexity of F's (*see* duality); simplicity of F's ruling, 421.
Vanbrugh, Sir John, F on a couplet of, 41.
*Vandeput, George, 18.
Vane, Frances Anne, Viscountess, 26n.
*Vane, William Holles Vane, 2nd Viscount, 26n.
Van Hook, Larue, 305n.
vanity, blinds good men, 197; ill bred, 173; mock encomium of, in *JA*, 310; the ridiculous and,

471

INDEX

42; unsocial, 168, 171, 181; women educated in, 106. *See also* pride.
Vartanian, Aram, 316n, 317n.
Vauxhall, 26n.
velox (long cadence), characteristic of Addison's style, 152.
Venn, John, 114n.
Venn, John Archibald, 114n.
Venus, 30, 121, 123-24, 135, 376, 377.
verisimilitude, comic, in F and Lucian, 373ff.
*Vernon, Admiral Edward, celebrated in *Vernoniad*, 24.
Versailles, 120.
verse-epistle, F's, 31, 127-28, 128-29, satiric, 273. *See also* poetry, satire.
verse-essay, F's, 31, 42-118, satiric, 273. *See also* poetry, satire.
vice, cannot exist with good-nature, 55-56, 65; F's antipathy to unsocial, 422; of head and heart, 335-36; pictured to imagination, 226-27; political, different from moral, 102n. *See also* affectation, ambition, ascetic, avarice, censoriousness, contempt, depravity, egoism, envy, evil, flattery, greatness, human nature, hypocrisy, ill-nature, indecency, ingratitude, luxury, malice, pride, revenge, "roasting," sin, usury, vanity.
Vince, James H., 348n.
Vincent, Howard P., 30n.
Virgil (Publius Vergilius Maro), 32; Dryden's translation of, 337, published by subscription, 15; quoted in *Some Papers*, 280; *Aeneid*, 280, 395n, F's travesty of lines from, 135-36, 138.
virtue, approbation of social, 422; beauty of naked, 71n, 190n; brings no worldly reward, 71n, 298; defined as outgoing force, 63; Diogenes on, 388; exhortation to, must be continual, 199; F not a moral rigorist in defining, 68-69; F's approval of Esprit on Christian, 86-87; good breeding a social, 185; good-nature: equated with, 55-63, a moral, social, and religious, 65-66, required for, 82-83; habit of, superior to affliction, 266n; hypocrisy: the bane of, 205, feigns, 203, ostentatious in, 197; moral inefficacy of abstract, 71n; philosophy a habit of, 261; pictured to imagination, 226-27; self-interest not inconsistent with, 64-65; skepticism of human, 413; society only field of, 405; Stoic conception of, praised, 257 (*see also* Stoic); vices mixed with, in human nature, 115. *See also* benevolence, charity, civility, complaisance, friendship, good breeding, good-nature, goodness, human nature, love, moderation, philosophy, sympathy, wisdom.
virtuoso, *see* Royal Society.

W

Wales, Prince of, *see* Frederick.
Walker, Alice, 281n.
Walker, Obadiah, *Of Education*, 175 and n.
Waller, Alfred R., 212n.
Waller, Edmund, 32.
Walpole, Horace, anecdote concerning F, 17-18.
*Walpole, Sir Robert (Earl of Orford), 7, 48n, 57n, 88, 94ff, 113n, 116n, 198, 340, 345-46, 400; apologists for, 92n; associates of, subscribers to *Misc.*, 20-21; attacked for undermining liberty, 92-93; Dodington defended against writers of, 43n; fall of, preceded JW, 26; F on bribery, 363-64; F's epistles to, 127-29; mock encomia of, 310 and n; possible allusion to, 298; symbol of evil greatness, 54n; target of specific attacks on greatness, 53, 399. *See also* greatness, liberty, politics.
opposition to: 198, 291; against standing army and mercenaries, 356-57; attack upon greatness, 399; *Craftsman* justifies, 362-63; Demosthenes and, 362-64; F's disillusionment with, 7, 116n,

INDEX

191n; *Liberty* a contribution to, 88, 91-93; slogan of, in *Pasquin*, 96; subscribers to *Misc.*, 16-17, 19-21; war-party, 345-47. *See also* liberty, politics, patriotism.
Walter, Peter, 291; allusion to, in *Essay on Conversation*, 169; F's satiric epigram on, 132; other attacks upon, 132; satirized in *Some Papers*, 278, 318 and n, 320ff, 322n, 332ff.
Walton, Izaak, 99n; *Compleat Angler*, 394.
Wann, Louis, 145n.
War of the Austrian Succession, 325n.
War of Jenkins' Ear, 344-47.
Ward, Edward (Ned), 394; on Diogenes, 407n; *London Spy*, 126; *Tipling Philosophers*, 407n.
*Wasey, Dr. William, 23.
Washington, George, 24.
Waterland, Daniel, on education, 219n; on hierarchy, 177n.
Watt, Ian, 108n.
Watts, John, printer, F's poem on, 129-30; *Musical Miscellany*, dialogue possibly by F in, 30.
wealth, 313; desirable, 260-61n; Diogenes' hypocrisy concerning, 389; F and Lucian on, 376-78; ironic comment on, 323-24, 325-26; primitivist attack on, 58 and n; satire on, 412, 413; thoughtless borrowing of, 356; in trading society, 100n; wives chosen for, 103ff.
Wedel, Theodore O., 255n.
Weekly Miscellany, 301n.
Wells, John E., 6n, 12n, 14n, 55n, 128n, 313n, 338n, 398n.
Wendt, Allan, 47n, 190n.
Wesley, Samuel, the younger, *Poems*, 133n, 403n.
*Westmorland, John Fane, 7th Earl of, 21, 24.
Wharncliffe, James Archibald Stuart-Wortley-Mackenzie, 1st Baron, 111n, 135n.
Whichcote, Benjamin, *Select Sermons*, praises good-nature, 56n.
Whig, anti-Walpole groups, subscribers to *Misc.*, 16-17, 19-20; tradition, from Glorious Revolution, 91-92.
Whig Examiner, The, see Addison, Joseph.
Whitehead, Paul, *State Dunces*, 310n.
*Whitehead, William, of Gray's Inn, 25.
Whitehead, William, poet, 25.
Whole Art of Converse, The, see A., D.
Wichelns, Herbert A., 148n.
will, conquest of self by, 218, 262; determinism opposed to free, 219-23, 424; F's conception of, 217-19; harmonizes passions, 225; importance of, in reform, 217-18; should overcome grief, 243. *See also* human nature, reason, passions.
Willcock, Gladys D., 281n.
William of Poitiers, poem on Nothing, 299.
Williams, Basil, 363n.
*William, Sir Charles Hanbury, 21, 25, 132; satirizes Lyttelton and "patriots," 88n; "Isabella; or, The Morning," 317-18.
Williams, Harold, 419n.
Williams, W. Glynn, 229n.
Williamson, George, 38-39, 152n, 155.
*Williams-Wynn, Sir Watkin, Bart., 20.
Willis, Mr., of Oxford, 306.
*Willoughby, Richard, alluded to in *TJ*, 22.
*Wilmot, Dr. Edward (later Sir Edward), physician-in-ordinary to the king, 23.
Wilson, James Southall, 94n.
Wilson, Thomas, translation of Demosthenes, 346, 361-62.
Wiltshire, numerous subscribers to *Misc.* from, 19n.
Wimsatt, William K., 152n.
*Windsor, Herbert Windsor, 2nd Viscount, 19n.
*Winnington, Thomas, later defended by F, 26n.
wisdom, austerity not an index of, 193; concerns of, 298; Diogenes

on, 388; F and Stoics on, 258-60; foresees contingencies, 231.
*Woffington, Margaret (Peg), 24; allusion to, in F's Juvenal, 141.
Wolfius, Hieronymus (Jerome Wolf), Latin translation of Demosthenes, 348 and n, comparison of F's translation with, 349-53, 356ff.
Woman's Advocate, The, 108.
women, advice to, literary tradition, 107-09; antifeminism, tradition of, 107, 406 and n; charm in dancing, 170; complaisance to beaus of, 130; faulty education of, 105-06; F disclaims understanding of, 193n; F's gallantry toward, 106, 121-22, 137-38; F's paragon, 104, 106-07; F's version of Juvenal's satire on, 137ff; "fine lady" ridiculed, 172, 186; little virtue of, 413. See also beauty, love, marriage, prude.
Wood, Frederick T., 109n, 311n.
Wood, Thomas, *Institute of the Laws*, 322n, 323n.
Woodfall, Henry, the elder, printer of JA, 3 and n; probable printer of second volume of *Misc.*, 13, 13-14n; proposals for *Misc.*, 3.
Woodfall, Henry, the younger, 3n.
Woods, Charles B., 277.
Worcester, David, 273n, 276n, 312n, 398n, 421n.
Wordsworth, Christopher, 306n.
Work, James A., 66n.
Wrangling Deities, The, 419n.

Wright, H. Bunker, 123n, 131n, 404n.
*Wright, William, 22.
Wycherley, William, mock encomia, 309.
*Wyndham, Thomas Wyndham, 1st Baron, of Finglass, 18, 19n.
*Wynne, William, 22-23.

Y

Yonge, Sir William, 325n.
Yorick's Meditations, 301.
Young, Edward, 121; against Lucian, 366n; on Alexander, 399; on good breeding, 186; poetic model for F, 31; on women, 108; *Love of Fame*, 108, 186, 192n, 366n, 399; *Night Thoughts*, 246n.
*Young, Edward (same as above?), subscriber to *Misc.*, 24-25.
Young, William, 342; edition of Hedericus, 340n; projected translation of Lucian with F, 365n, 366, 370n; translation of Aristophanes' *Plutus* with F, 8, 17, 138, 140, 338, 343, 361, 363, 411.
youth, and crime, 335-36.

Z

Zeno of Citium, Old Stoa and later Stoics, 258.
Zeuxis, 371.
Zollman, Philip Henry, 319.